浙江省经济信息中心
ZHEJIANG ECONOMIC & INFORMATION CENTRE
·省新型重点专业智库·

BLUE BOOK FOR ZHEJIANG PROVINCE'S ACTIONS ON RESPONDING TO CLIMATE CHANGE AND LOW-CARBON DEVELOPMENT（2022）

浙江省应对气候变化和低碳发展蓝皮书（2022）

黄 炜 蒋 明 王 诚 魏丹青 肖相泽 著

中国环境出版集团·北京

图书在版编目（CIP）数据

浙江省应对气候变化和低碳发展蓝皮书.2022：汉、英 / 黄炜等著 . —北京：中国环境出版集团，2023.5
ISBN 978-7-5111-5529-0

Ⅰ.①浙…　Ⅱ.①黄…　Ⅲ.①气候变化—关系—低碳经济—区域经济发展—研究报告—浙江—2022—汉、英 Ⅳ.①P467 ②F127.55

中国国家版本馆 CIP 数据核字（2023）第 095052 号

出 版 人　武德凯
责任编辑　刘梦晗
封面设计　光大印艺

出版发行　中国环境出版集团
　　　　　（100062　北京市东城区广渠门内大街 16 号）
　　　　　网　　　址：http：//www.cesp.com.cn
　　　　　电子邮箱：bjgl@cesp.com.cn
　　　　　联系电话：010-67112765（编辑管理部）
　　　　　　　　　　010-67175507（第六分社）
　　　　　发行热线：010-67125803，010-67113405（传真）
印　　刷　玖龙（天津）印刷有限公司
经　　销　各地新华书店
版　　次　2023 年 5 月第 1 版
印　　次　2023 年 5 月第 1 次印刷
开　　本　787×1092　1/16
印　　张　47.25
字　　数　856 千字
定　　价　398.00 元

中国环境出版集团郑重承诺：
中国环境出版集团合作的印刷单位、材料单位均具有中国环境标志产品认证。

著作组

浙江省经济信息中心著作组

黄 炜[1]	蒋 明	王 诚	魏丹青	肖相泽
张天佑	杨首权	邬梦晓俊	俞明东	吴海泽
郦依洒	王希莉	林 朗	王逸伦	杜伟杰
王 一	吕 希	叶津宏	杨元一	张 伟

参与著作人员（按姓氏拼音字母排序）

白鸿宇　浙江省交通运输科学研究院交通发展研究中心副主任（主持）

柴麒敏　国家应对气候变化战略研究和国际合作中心战略规划部主任

陈建芳　自然资源部第二海洋研究所研究员

戴建飞　杭州市乡村振兴服务中心科长

丁　德　浙江大学建筑设计研究院有限公司技术总监

顾　蕾　浙江农林大学教授

顾兴国　浙江省农业科学院副研究员

郭　豪　清华大学气候变化与可持续发展研究院助理研究员

韩大庆　浙江省杭州市桐庐县富春江镇综合办主任

胡　畅　浙江省湖州市发展和改革委员会副主任

黄虹飞　浙江浙能碳资产管理有限责任公司市场运营部主任

蒋建平　浙江省标准化研究院副院长

金海燕　自然资源部第二海洋研究所研究员

李　翀　浙江农林大学副教授

刘诚刚　自然资源部第二海洋研究所副研究员

1　浙江省经济信息中心能源环境首席专家

刘红飞　浙江省衢州市发展改革委环资处处长

陆巧玲　浙江省湖州市发展和改革委员会干部

马海华　浙江省永康市发展和改革局局长

马　明　浙江省嘉兴市发展规划研究院能源低碳领域负责人

泉江东　浙江省湖州市德清县下渚湖街道党工委书记、下渚湖湿地
　　　　风景区管委会主任

阮阗怡　杭州市环境保护科学研究设计有限公司工程师

孙　可　国网浙江省电力有限公司经济技术研究院智库首席专家

孙轶恺　国网浙江省电力有限公司经济技术研究院智库秘书

唐　玮　北京大成（上海）律师事务所顾问

宛图南　北京大成（上海）律师事务所律师助理

王鹤霖　浙江省嘉兴市发展规划研究院能源低碳领域研究人员

王曦冉　国网浙江省电力有限公司经济技术研究院工程师

王雪晴　浙江省杭州市桐庐县富春江镇人民政府副镇长

吴佳艳　浙江大学建筑设计研究院有限公司副主任工程师

吴良欢　浙江大学环境与资源学院资源科学系教授

辛　升　国家节能中心推广处处长、高级工程师

徐　靓　吉利控股数科板块双碳业务负责人

杨姗姗　清华－力拓资源能源与可持续发展联合研究中心高级工程师

杨　秀　清华大学气候变化与可持续发展研究院副研究员

于培松　自然资源部第二海洋研究所副研究员

曾江宁　自然资源部第二海洋研究所研究员

张　伟　吉利控股集团碳中和负责人

张玺玲　浙江省农业农村厅挂职干部

周国模　浙江农林大学教授

周立颖　浙江浙能碳资产管理有限公司碳市场开发部专职

周　云　浙江省杭州市桐庐县富春江镇环旅办一级科员

周之林　浙江省农业农村厅主任科员

朱东锋　浙江省标准化研究院标准化工程师

Zhejiang Economic Information Center Writing Group

Huang Wei [1]	Jiang Ming	Wang Cheng	Wei Danqing
Xiao Xiangze	Zhang Tianyou	Yang Shouquan	Wu Mengxiaojun
Yu Mingdong	Wu Haize	Li Yisa	Wang Xili
Lin Lang	Wang Yilun	Du Weijie	Wang Yi
Lyu Xi	Ye Jinhong	Yang Yuanyi	Zhang Wei

Participating Authors(Sort by surname in alphabetical order)

Bai Hongyu Deputy Director of Traffic Development Research Center of Zhejiang Academy of Communications and Transport Science (in charge of the work)

Chai Qimin Director of the Strategic Planning Department of the National Strategy Research and International Cooperation Center for Climate Change

Chen Jianfang Researcher at the Second Institute of Oceanography of the Ministry of Natural Resources

Dai Jianfei Section Chief of the Rural Revitalization Service Center in Hangzhou

Ding De Technical Director of The Architectural Design & Research Institute of Zhejiang University Co., Ltd.

Gu Lei Associate Professor at Zhejiang Agriculture and Forestry University

Gu Xingguo Deputy Researcher at the Zhejiang Academy of Agricultural Sciences, specializes in ecological agriculture

---

1 Chief Expert in Energy and Environment of Zhejiang Economic and Information Centre

Guo Hao	Assistanter Research at the Institute of Climate Change and Sustainable Development, Tsinghua University
Han Daqing	Director of Comprehensive Office of Fuchunjiang Town, Tonglu County, Hangzhou, Zhejiang Province
Hu Chang	Deputy Director of the Development and Reform Commission in Huzhou
Huang Hongfei	Director of Market Operation Department of Zhejiang Energy Carbon Asset Management Co., Ltd.
Jiang Jianping	Deputy Director of Zhejiang Standardization Research Institute
Jin Haiyan	Researcher of the Second Institute of Oceanography, Ministry of Natural Resources
Li Chong	Associate Professor at Zhejiang Agriculture and Forestry University
Liu Chenggang	Associate Researcher at the Second Institute of Oceanography, Ministry of Natural Resources
Liu Hongfei	Division Director of the Environment and Resources Department of the Development and Reform Commission in Quzhou, Zhejiang Province
Lu Qiaoling	Clerk of the Development and Reform Commission in Huzhou, Zhejiang Province
Ma Haihua	Director-General of the Development and Reform Bureau of Yongkang, Zhejiang Province
Ma Ming	Director of Energy and Low-carbon Field in Jiaxing Development Planning Research Institute
Quan Jiangdong	Secretary of the Party Working Committee of Xiazhu Lake Street in Deqing County, Huzhou, Zhejiang Province, and Director of the Management Committee of Xiazhu Lake Wetland Scenic Area Management Committee
Ruan Tianyi	Engineer at Hangzhou Environment Protection Science Research and Design Co., Ltd.
Sun Ke	Chief Expert of the Think Tank of the Economic and Technological Research Institute of State Grid Zhejiang Electric Power Co., Ltd.

Sun Yikai	Secretary of the Think Tank of the Economic and Technological Research Institute of State Grid Zhejiang Electric Power Co., Ltd.
Tang Wei	Advisor at Dentons Shanghai
Wan Tunan	Paralegal at Dentons Shanghai
Wang Helin	Researcher in the Energy and Low-carbon Field of the Jiaxing Development Planning Research Institute
Wang Xiran	Engineer of the Economic and Technological Research Institute of State Grid Zhejiang Electric Power Co., Ltd.
Wang Xueqing	Deputy Township Mayor of Fuchunjiang Town People's Government
Wu Jiayan	Deputy Chief Engineer of The Architectural Design & Research Institute of Zhejiang University Co., Ltd.
Wu Lianghuan	Professor in the Department of Resource Science at the School of Environment and Resource Sciences of Zhejiang University
Xin Sheng	Director of the Promotion Department of the National Energy Conservation Center, Senior Engineer
Xu Liang	Director of Dual Carbon Business Manager in the Digital Technology Sector of Geely Holding Group
Yang Shanshan	Senior Engineer at Tsinghua-Lituo Resources Energy and Sustainability Joint Research Center
Yang Xiu	Associate Researcher at the Institute of Change Climate and Sustainable Development, Tsinghua University
Yu Peisong	Associate Researcher at the Second Institute of Oceanography, Ministry of Natural Resources
Zeng Jiangning	Researcher at the Second Institute of Oceanography, Ministry Natural of Resources
Zhang Wei	Geely Holdings' Carbon Neutrality Manager
Zhang Xiling	In-service Cadres in the Agriculture and Rural Affairs Department of Zhejiang Province
Zhou Guomo	Professor of Zhejiang Agriculture and Forestry University
Zhou Liying	Project Dirctor of Carbon Market Development Department of Zhejiang Provincial Energe Group Carbon

Assets Management Co., Ltd.

Zhou Yun   First-level Clerk of the Environmental and Tourism Office in Fuchunjiang Town, Tonglu County, Hangzhou, Zhejiang Province

Zhou Zhilin   Principal Staff Member of the Agriculture and Rural Affairs Department of Zhejiang Province

Zhu Dongfeng   Standardization Engineer of Zhejiang Standardization Research Institute

气候变化是全球性挑战，自 1992 年《联合国气候变化框架公约》确立以来，不管国际形势如何变化，应对气候变化一直是国际事务的一项重要议题。作为世界上最大的发展中国家，我国也愿意承担与发展水平相称的国际责任，为全球气候治理贡献力量。特别是党的十八大以来，以习近平同志为核心的党中央对应对气候变化工作高度重视，实施积极应对气候变化国家战略，以前所未有的决心和力度，开展了一系列根本性、开创性、长远性工作。2020 年 9 月 22 日，习近平主席在第七十五届联合国大会一般性辩论上向全世界郑重宣布，我国二氧化碳排放力争于 2030 年前达到峰值，努力争取 2060 年前实现碳中和。这进一步提高了我国国家自主贡献目标，也标志着我国生态文明建设进入以降碳为重点战略方向的新阶段。

实现碳达峰碳中和是一场广泛而深刻的经济社会系统性变革，既需要坚持全国统筹，强化顶层设计，发挥制度优势，也需要根据各地实际分类施策，鼓励主动作为、率先达峰。浙江是习近平总书记曾经工作过的地方，是习近平生态文明思想的重要萌发地和率先实践地。"生态兴则文明兴"的生态文明观和"绿水青山就是金山银山"的科学论断等已成为习近平生态文明思想的重要内容，也在高起点上为浙江应对气候变化和低碳发展奠定了坚实的思想、理论和实践基础。

多年来，浙江立足经济大省和资源小省的现实基础条件，始终坚持走生态优先、绿色低碳发展道路，全面深化产业、能源结构调整和绿色低碳发展，以占全国 1% 的土地、4% 的人口、4% 的二氧化碳排放量，创造了全国 6.26% 的国内生产总值，绿色低碳发展综合水平保持全国领先。浙江坚持以改革创新意识为引领，在协同推进各领域应对气候变化行动的同时，在全国最早建立省、市、县三级全覆盖的温室气体清单报告机制，建成省级气候变化研究交流平台，多项工作走在全国前列。

本书集合了浙江应对气候变化和低碳发展的生动实践，也是在省级层面上率先发布的兼顾实践与理论的应对气候变化综合性成果。全书具有国际视野，创新体例框架，精选丰富内容，注重历史与未来、整体与重点、政策与研究的有机统一，既有对浙江应对气候变化的长期观察、系统提炼，也有对重点领域、重点区域、重点问题的现实观照、学理探究、案例剖析，纵向和横向结合，实践与学术并重，是对浙江应对气候变化和低碳发展的全面客观记录、创新探索思考，可为全国其他地区提供有益参考。

著作单位浙江省经济信息中心是应对气候变化和低碳发展领域的长期耕耘者、专业研究者和实践参与推动者，在全国率先成立应对气候变化省级研究机构——浙江省应对气候变化和低碳发展合作中心，培养了一批高学历、高素质的专业技术人才，建成全国首个"双碳"智治平台，为浙江高质量推进应对气候变化和低碳发展提供了基础性、全局性支撑，放眼全国都具有一定的领先性、启示性。

当前，随着百年未有之大变局深入演进，国际环境更加复杂多变，全球气候治理体系正在经历系统性变革。习近平总书记强调，实现"双碳"目标，不是别人让我们做，而是我们自己必须要做。面对新形势新要求，我们要始终保持战略定力，坚定不移走好绿色低碳高质量发展道路。期望作为经济发达地区的浙江能够勇担使命，切实发挥好示范先行作用，在加快制造业绿色低碳转型、能源生产和消费结构重塑、碳排放"双控"制度创新、绿色科技创新体系构建等关键方面积极探索探路、创新创造，努力打造更多原创性、突破性成果，以浙江的"低碳之窗"展现我国的"气候之治"。

徐华清

国家应对气候变化战略研究和国际合作中心主任

2023 年 5 月于北京

习近平总书记在浙江工作期间，对应对气候变化工作高度重视，将进一步发挥浙江的生态优势，创建生态省，打造"绿色浙江"纳入了"八八战略"。浙江省坚定不移沿着"八八战略"指引的方向抓好应对气候变化工作，较早成立了浙江省应对气候变化领导小组，并设立浙江省应对气候变化和低碳发展合作中心为专门的省级研究机构，开启了应对气候变化工作省域新实践，为浙江高质量推进应对气候变化奠定扎实基础。

2012 年，党的十八大将生态文明建设纳入了中国特色社会主义事业"五位一体"总体布局，应对气候变化工作提升到了新的高度。浙江沿着习近平总书记指引的方向，"干在实处、走在前列、勇立潮头"，积极作为、主动创新，探索建立设区市碳强度降低目标考核机制，推动形成多层级低碳试点体系建设。特别是按照国家决策部署，结合浙江实际，成为全国首个全面推行省—市—县三级温室气体清单编制常态化的省份，得到了国家发展改革委的充分肯定。

2020 年 9 月，习近平总书记向全世界宣布我国碳达峰、碳中和"30·60"目标。国家有部署，浙江见行动！浙江迅速成立由省委、省政府主要领导挂帅的工作领导小组，率先制定实施全省"双碳"实施意见、碳达峰实施方案和"6+1"领域、11 个设区市实施方案，构建起完善的目标体系、工作体系、政策体系、评价体系。同时，充分发挥数字化改革优势，率先建成"双碳"智治平台。浙江省在应对气候变化方面进行了大量卓有成效的探索和实践，获得国家和兄弟省市的高度肯定，为我国应对气候变化大局贡献了"浙江力量"。

浙江省经济信息中心是浙江省发展和改革委员会直属事业单位，是浙江省应对气候变化和低碳发展合作中心的依托单位，多年来积极发挥重要智力支撑作用，不仅在省级相关政策文件制定中发挥重要作用，更是"双碳"智治平台的谋划设计者、建设运营方，同时多次参加联合国气候大会和国内高层次会议，宣传交流浙江经验做法，有力支撑全省发展改革系统应对气候变化工作。我有幸在

2010 年至 2018 年担任浙江省发展和改革委员会副主任期间分管应对气候变化工作，同时分管浙江省经济信息中心，浙江省经济信息中心气候团队勤恳务实、能打硬仗的作风和能力给我留下了深刻印象。

本书立足浙江省经济信息中心在应对气候变化领域的长期积累、专业沉淀，全面系统展现浙江在应对气候变化和低碳发展上开展的实践、取得的成效，是了解浙江省近年来应对气候变化探索与实践的窗口。本书具有三个特征：一是综合性，既有对全省面上情况的概括，又有对于六大领域、各个区域行动实践的提炼评价，点线面全覆盖。二是专业性，在总结提炼各领域、各地区经验时，特别注意避免面面俱到，而是以其中的关键创新点为核心，重新构建内容体系，扎实论证观点。三是前瞻性，本书最后两部分对"双碳"领域的关键热点和前沿问题进行了关注，充分体现出作者支撑当下、谋划长远的担当，其中关于能耗双控转碳排放双控、碳足迹、碳标签等内容，正在逐步达成共识。

今年 3 月，联合国政府间气候变化专门委员会（IPCC）发布的第六次评估报告指出，当前全球气温已比工业化前高出 1.1℃，气候变暖已是不争事实，应对气候变化的紧迫性、严峻性毋庸置疑。希望本书能够为各界人士开展应对气候变化工作提供有益启示和参考借鉴，同时希望本书能吸引更多人关注、支持、参与到应对气候变化的工作中，为这项全人类共同的事业贡献力量。

浙江省人民代表大会财政经济委员会副主任委员

2023 年 5 月于杭州

PREFACE 1

Climate change is a global challenge, and no matter how the global landscape shifts, responding to climate change has been a major issue in international affairs since the establishment of the United Nations Framework Convention on Climate Change (UNFCCC) in 1992. As the world's largest developing country, China is ready to assume international responsibilities commensurate with its level of development and contribute to global climate governance. Especially since the 18th CPC National Congress in 2012, the Party Central Committee, with Comrade Xi Jinping at its core, has attached great importance to tackling climate change, implemented national strategies to actively tackle climate change, and conducted a series of fundamental, groundbreaking and long-term work with unprecedented determination and efforts. At the General Debate of the 75th Session of The United Nations General Assembly on September 22, 2020, Chinese President Xi Jinping solemnly announced to the world that China "aims to have CO_2 emissions peak before 2030 and achieve carbon neutrality before 2060". This has updated China's nationally determined contributions (NDCs) targets, marking a new stage in China's ecological civilization construction with carbon reduction as the key strategic direction.

To achieve carbon peaking and carbon neutrality is an extensive and profound socioeconomic institutional change. This requires not only adhering to the nationwide coordination, strengthening the top-level design, giving full play to the institutional advantages, but also implementing policies according to local conditions, and encouraging taking the initiative and pioneering to reach carbon peaking. Zhejiang is the province where General Secretary Xi Jinping used to work, as well as the key place where Xi Jinping Thought on Ecological Civilization sprang up and was first practiced. The thought on ecological civilization that "A civilization may thrive if its natural surroundings thrive" and the scientific assertion that "lucid waters and lush mountains are invaluable assets" have become key elements of Xi Jinping Thought on Ecological Civilization, and have laid a solid ideological, theoretical and practical foundation for Zhejiang's response to climate change and its low-carbon development on high ground.

Based on the real conditions of its good economic strength yet inadequate resource endowment, Zhejiang always follows a path of prioritizing ecological conservation and pursuing green development for many years, deepens the industrial restructuring in a comprehensive manner, and accelerates energy mix readjustment for a green and low-carbon development. With 1% of the country's land, 4% of the national population, and 4% of CO_2 emissions, Zhejiang generates 6.26% of GDP and maintains a domestically leading position in terms of its comprehensive level of green and low-carbon development. Particularly, while collaboratively promoting actions to tackle climate change in various sectors, Zhejiang was the first in China to establish a greenhouse gas inventory reporting mechanism with full coverage at the county, municipal and provincial levels, and it has built a provincial climate change research and exchange platform. In addition, Zhejiang, with a strong sense of reform and innovation, is also at the forefront of many efforts in the country.

This Blue Book is an integrated work on Zhejiang's vivid practice in responding to climate change and promoting its low-carbon development, and the first integrated outcome on climate change at the provincial level that combines practice with theory. With an international perspective, innovative stylistic framework and rich content, this Blue Book stresses the organic integration of history and future, wholeness and focus, policy and research. It includes long-term observation and systematic refinement of Zhejiang's response to climate change, as well as realistic observation, theoretical investigation and case analysis of major areas, regions and issues. Through the combination of vertical and horizontal views, practice and academic research, the Blue Book forms an overall objective record, an innovative exploration and a creative idea of Zhejiang's response to climate change and its implementation of low-carbon development, which expect to provide useful references for other regions in China.

Zhejiang Economic and Information Center, the editorial unit of this Blue Book, is a persistent cultivator, professional researcher and practical enabler in addressing climate change and promoting low-carbon development. The Center is the first unit in China to establish a provincial research institution to tackle climate change-Zhejiang Center for Climate Change and Low-carbon Development Cooperation. Besides, the Center has also cultivated a group of highly educated and qualified technical professionals, built the first platform for dual carbon smart governance in China, and provided holistic support for Zhejiang to tackle climate change and promote low-carbon development with high quality. Looking at the whole country, Zhejiang practice is of pioneering and enlightening significance.

With the deep evolution of unprecedented changes, the international situation tends to be more complex and volatile, and the global climate governance system is undergoing systemic transformations. General Secretary Xi Jinping reiterated that achieving the "dual carbon" goals is not something we are forced to do, but something we must do. Facing new situations and new requirements, we need to maintain our strategic determination and unswervingly stick to the path of green, low-carbon, and high-quality development. Zhejiang, as a major economically developed province, is expected to shoulder its mission, give full play to its pioneering and exemplary role, and actively explore and innovate such key areas as accelerating the green and low-carbon transformation of the manufacturing industry, reshaping the energy production and consumption structure, innovating to control both the amount and intensity of carbon emissions and building a green technology innovation system. In this way, Zhejiang is committed to making more original and breakthrough achievements, showcasing China's "climate governance" with its "low-carbon window".

Director of National Center for Climate Change Strategy and
International Cooperation (NCSC)
May, 2023, Beijing

During his work in Zhejiang, General Secretary Xi Jinping paid high attention to responding to climate change and incorporated further leveraging ecological advantages of Zhejiang, building an ecological province, and forming a "green Zhejiang" into the "Double Eight Strategy". Under the guidance of the "Double Eight Strategy", Zhejiang Province adheres to tackling climate change through great efforts, establishes a provincial leading group on climate change response at an early stage nationwide, and pioneers in setting up the Zhejiang Center for Climate Change and Low-carbon Development Cooperation as a specialized provincial research institution. In this way, Zhejiang has created a new provincial practice of responding to climate change and laid a solid foundation for Zhejiang to promote a high-quality response to climate change.

At the 18th National Congress of the Communist Party of China in 2012, ecological advancement was included in the "five-sphere integrated plan" for the cause of socialism with Chinese characteristics, and response to climate change was raised to a new height. In accordance with General Secretary Xi Jinping's requirements of "doing solid work, walking in the forefront, and braving the tide", Zhejiang actively takes actions and innovates to explore an assessment mechanism for carbon intensity reduction targets in cities, and promotes the construction of a multi-level low-carbon pilot system. In particular, according to the relevant national decisions and arrangements and combined with the actual local conditions, Zhejiang has carried out the first national greenhouse gas inventory in an innovative manner at the level of county, city and province, which has been fully affirmed by the National Development and Reform Commission.

In September 2020, General Secretary Xi Jinping announced the "30·60" Decarbonization Goal to the world. Since the state has made deployment,

Zhejiang will surely act. Zhejiang has quickly established a leadership group led by the main cadres of the provincial party committee and government, taken the lead in formulating and carrying out the provincial implementation opinions on "carbon peaking and carbon neutrality", carbon peaking implementation plans, and implementation plans for the "6+1" sectors and 11 districted cities, and built a comprehensive target system, work system, policy system, and evaluation system. At the same time, Zhejiang fully leverages the digital reform and pioneers to build an intelligence governance system for carbon peaking and carbon neutrality. Zhejiang has made a lot of fruitful explorations and practice in response to climate change and won high recognition from other provinces, cities and the country, thus contributing "Zhejiang strength" to China's overall response to climate change.

Zhejiang Economic and Information Center is a directly affiliated institution of the Zhejiang Provincial Development and Reform Commission and a supporting unit of Zhejiang Center for Climate Change and Low-carbon Development Cooperation. Over the years, it has actively played an important intellectual support role, not only in the formulation of relevant provincial policy documents but also as the designer and operator of the intelligence governance platform for carbon peaking and carbon neutrality. Meanwhile, it has promoted and exchanged experiences and practices in Zhejiang at multiple United Nations climate conferences and high-level domestic conferences, effectively supporting the development and reform system of the province in addressing climate change. I was fortunate to be in charge of climate change during my tenure as Deputy Director of Zhejiang Provincial Development and Reform Commission from 2010 to 2018, and in charge of Zhejiang Economic and Information Center. I was deeply impressed by the diligent pragmatic working style and strong ability of the Zhejiang Economic and Information Center's climate team.

Based on the long-term accumulation and professional precipitation of Zhejiang Economic and Information Center in the field of climate change, this book comprehensively and systematically presents the practices and achievements of Zhejiang in responding to climate change and promoting low-carbon development. It is a window to understand Zhejiang's recent exploration and practice in responding to climate change. This book highlights three features. The first feature is its comprehensiveness, in that it not only summarizes the general situation of the province, but also refines and evaluates the action practices in six major sectors and various regions, covering all points, lines, and areas. The second feature is its professionalism, in that it pays special attention to avoiding comprehensive summary and refinement of various fields and regions, but takes the key innovation as the core to rebuild the framework and solidly prove the viewpoint. The third feature is its forefront. In this book, the last two parts focus on the key hot spots and cutting-edge issues in the field of "carbon peaking and carbon neutrality", which fully reflects the authors' responsibility to be pragmatic and far-sighted. Among them, the consensus is gradually formed on the transition from dual control of total energy consumption and intensity to dual control of total carbon emissions and carbon emission intensity, carbon footprint and carbon labeling, etc.

According to the United Nations Intergovernmental Panel on Climate Change (IPCC) Sixth Assessment Report Climate Change 2023 released in March this year, the current global temperatures have already risen to 1.1°C above pre-industrial levels, so global warming is an undeniable fact. The urgency and severity of responding to climate change are beyond doubt. I hope this book may provide useful inspiration and reference for people from all walks of life in their work on response to climate change. Meanwhile, I hope to attract more people to pay attention to, support and participate in response to climate change, and contribute to the common cause of mankind.

Vice Chairman of the Finance and Economic Committee of
the Zhejiang People's Congress
May, 2023, Hangzhou

目录
CATALOGUE

第一部分
综合评价

浙江省应对气候变化和低碳发展战略与实践——十五年回顾与展望　// 3

"四个维度"平衡视角下浙江省应对气候变化和低碳发展进展评估　// 34

第二部分
领域行动

新型电力系统助力浙江省能源清洁低碳转型的改革实践　// 63

浙江省工业碳效码的设计与实践　// 70

践行绿色低碳使命　共绘低碳建筑未来　// 81

浙江交通推进高质量绿色低碳发展的改革与创新探索简述　// 89

农业碳达峰的"浙江经验"与工作展望　// 97

浙江碳普惠引领居民生活领域碳达峰　// 107

第三部分
区域典型

衢州市基于碳账户改革的"双碳"实践与探索　// 121

湖州市以碳效改革推动全域绿色低碳转型　// 129

循环经济助力降碳的"永康模式"　// 137

从竹小汇到先行区——嘉善聚力打造长三角绿色生态一体化示范区绿色低碳最佳实践案例　//　145

富春江镇深耕绿色发展　雕绘低碳高质共富新局　//　154

下渚湖湿地全力做好生态修复　在全省率先推出湿地碳汇生态补偿模式　//　163

低碳湖滨　时尚未来　//　170

吉利全产业链碳中和实践　//　180

第四部分
专项创新

地方立法推进发展方式绿色转型的思考与建议　//　193

加快节能降碳先进技术研发和推广应用，促进绿色高质量发展　//　201

标准化助力浙江省碳达峰碳中和行动　//　209

浅谈企业碳资产管理　//　216

构建数智治理体系　助推"双碳"目标实现　//　223

"双碳"背景下，浙江省绿色金融发展新使命　//　229

第五部分
研究专论

全球碳中和进程下碳足迹碳标签制度发展动向　//　237

建立碳排放"双控"制度的思考与展望　//　243

"双碳"背景下浙江蓝碳领域的机遇和挑战　//　255

探索林业碳汇生态产品市场补偿机制的浙江实践路径　//　266

PART ONE		
COMPREHENSIVE EVALUATION		

Strategy and Practice of Responding to Climate Change and Low-carbon Development in Zhejiang Province—Fifteen-Year History Review and Future Prospects   // 279

Assessment of Zhejiang's Progress in Climate Change and Low-carbon Development from the Perspective of "Four Dimensions" Balance   // 335

PART TWO		
SECTOR ACTIONS		

Reform Practice of the New Power System Promoting the Transformation toward Clean and Low-carbon Development in Zhejiang Province   // 377

Design and Practice of Industrial Carbon Efficiency Code in Zhejiang Province   // 389

Pursing the Development of Green and Low-carbon, and Jointly Creating the Future of Low-carbon Buildings   // 408

A Review on the Reform and Innovative Explorations of Zhejiang Province on Promoting High-quality, Green and Low-carbon Development in Transportation   // 422

"Zhejiang Experience" and Prospect of Carbon Peaking in the Agriculture Sector   // 437

Zhejiang's Carbon Inclusiveness Leading Carbon Peaking in Residents' Lives   // 453

PART THREE
REGIONAL TYPICAL CASES

Quzhou's Practice and Exploration of "Carbon Peaking and Carbon Neutrality" based on the Carbon Account Reform   // 477

Global Green and Low Carbon Transformation Efforts through Carbon Efficiency Reform in Huzhou City   // 491

"Yongkang Model" of Circular Economy to Assist in Carbon Reduction   // 505

Zhuxiaohui Village as Trailblazer Exemplifying Jiashan County's Effort to Build Eco-green Integrated Development Demonstration Zone in the Yangtze River Delta   // 519

Fuchunjiang Town is Deeply Committed to Green Development, Striving for New Progress on the Low-Carbon, High-Quality Path to Common Prosperity   // 534

Ecological Restoration of Xiazhu Lake Wetland: Province-first Ecological Compensation Mechanism for Wetland Carbon Sinks   // 547

Low-carbon and Fashionable Hubin Subdistrict   // 558

Carbon Neutrality Practice of Geely Holding's Whole Industry Chain   // 573

PART FOUR
SPECIAL INNOVATIONS

Reflection and Suggestions on Local Legislation to Promote the Green Transformation of Development Methods   // 591

Accelerating the R&D, Promotion, and Application of Advanced Energy-Saving and Carbon Emission Reduction Technologies to Promote Green and High-quality Development   // 605

Standardization Facilitates Carbon Peaking and Carbon Neutrality Actions in Zhejiang Province   // 619

A Brief Introduction to Corporate Carbon Asset Management   // 630

Construction of a Digital Intelligence Governance System to Promote the Realization of the "Dual Carbon" Goals   // 641

New Mission of Green Finance Development in the Context of Carbon Peaking and Carbon Neutrality in Zhejiang Province   // 652

| PART FIVE |
| RESEARCH MONOGRAPHS |

Trend of Carbon Footprint and Carbon Labelling System Development in the Global Transition towards Carbon Neutrality   // 667

Reflections and Prospects on the System of "Controlling both the Amount and Intensity of Carbon Emissions"   // 676

Opportunities and Challenges of the Blue Carbon Sink Sector in Zhejiang Province under the Context of Dual Carbon Goals   // 694

Exploring the Zhejiang Practice Path to Establish a Market Compensation Mechanism for Forestry Carbon Sink Ecological Products   // 710

第一部分　综合评价

浙江省应对气候变化和低碳发展战略与实践
——十五年回顾与展望

近年来，浙江始终坚持走绿色低碳发展之路，积极实施应对气候变化战略，相关工作走在全国前列，成为全球气候治理进程重要的推动者和践行者。本章全面分析了浙江绿色低碳发展基础，回顾了自 2007 年以来浙江省应对气候变化历史沿革，并从减缓与适应"两条主线"总结了浙江的实践做法与工作成效。同时，结合"双碳"背景下应对气候变化发展新形势新要求，研究提出了浙江实现绿色、低碳、循环的高质量可持续发展的若干建议。

气候变化是全球性挑战，任何一国都无法置身事外。各国受经济复苏压力增大影响，绿色贸易壁垒兴起，全球性挑战叠加，给应对气候变化增加了不确定性和巨大挑战，如何变"危"为"机"，需要国际社会携手应对气候变化挑战，推动构建人与自然生命共同体。党的二十大报告提出"积极稳妥推进碳达峰碳中和"，为持续推动绿色低碳转型提供了新的遵循，需进一步统筹处理好发展与减排关系，以实现减污降碳协同增效。当前，浙江正处于深入实施"八八战略"，强力推进创新深化、改革攻坚、开放提升的关键期，必须完整、准确、全面贯彻新发展理念，积极抢占低碳零碳产业发展和技术创新制高点，全力推动经济社会绿色转型。认真回望过去、方能面向未来，在新形势、新背景下，有必要对浙江省应对气候变化工作开展总结，明晰发展思路，坚定发展信念，切实履行减排承诺与绿色发展义务，为浙江省在高质量发展中实现"两个先行"贡献力量。

一、发展基础

浙江地处中国东南沿海长江三角洲南翼，东临东海，南接福建，西与江西、安徽相连，北与上海、江苏接壤。全省陆域面积为 10.55 万 km²，下辖 11 个设区市，90 个县（市、区），常住人口 6 577 万人。

浙江地处亚热带中部，属季风性湿润气候，气温适中，四季分明，光照充足，雨量丰沛。近 50 年，全省平均气温明显上升，增温速率为 0.47 ℃ /10 a，高于全国同期增温速率（0.36 ℃ /10 a），全年平均气温为 15～18 ℃。因受海洋和东南亚季风影响，浙江冬夏盛行风向有显著变化，降水亦有明显季节变化，全年日照时数为 1 100～2 200 h，年均降水量为 1 100～2 000 mm，5 月、6 月为集中降雨期。同时，受西风带和东风带天气系统的双重影响，气象灾害繁多，浙江是我国受台风、暴雨、干旱、寒潮、大风、冰雹、冻害等灾害影响较为严重的地区之一。

（二）资源禀赋

浙江作为华东地区重要的生态屏障，森林资源相对丰富，截至 2022 年年底，全省现有森林面积 9 113 万亩[1]，森林蓄积 3.46 亿 m³，61.15% 的森林覆盖率居全国前列。但同时，浙江也是个"七山二水一分田"的资源小省，人多地少，在能源、耕地、金属矿产等资源禀赋上并不突出，基本上依赖省外和国外市场。其中，煤、油、气等一次能源匮乏，化石能源供应对外依赖度高，2022 年全省外来电占全社会用电比例近 36%。光伏、海上风电等可再生能源资源储量相对丰富，但随着用地、用海、涉林等政策趋严，可再生能源开发制约因素不断增加。

（三）产业基础

2022 年，浙江生产总值达 77 715 亿元，稳居全国第四位；人均 GDP 突破 11 万元，达到高收入经济体水平；三次产业结构调整优化为 3.0：42.7：54.3，现代经济体系基本形成。制造业结构趋向高端化，战略性新兴产业和高新技术产业增加值占规模以上工业增加值比重分别为 33.5% 和 65.3%，"415X"先进制造业集群初具规模。第三产业对经济贡献度持续提高，数字经济发展稳居全国第一梯队，数字经济核心产业增加值占 GDP 比重为 11.6%，绿色发展走在全国前列。

---

1 1 亩 ≈666.67 m²。

4 个世界级产业集群。依托浙江省数字经济和产业特色优势,着力打造绿色石化、数字安防、汽车、现代纺织等世界级产业集群。

15 个优势产业集群。结合传统制造业改造提升,在消费品制造、原材料制造、机械装备制造等传统优势领域,培育现代五金、泵阀、橡胶塑料、有色金属、文体用品、电机、光纤电缆、绿色家居、绿色电池等特色优势产业集群。聚焦数字经济、生物经济等新经济领域,重点培育软件与信息技术服务、生命健康、智能制造装备、智能电气、智能家电、光伏设备等新兴制造业集群。

X 个 "新星" 产业群。聚焦数字经济、生命健康、新材料等战略性新兴产业、未来产业和产业链补短补缺领域,以龙头企业带动产业链围绕产业细分领域分工协作、链接互动、创新融通、共生发展,培育形成 50 个以上具有技术领先和国际竞争力的百亿级 "新星" 产业群。

(四)生态环境

2005 年 8 月 15 日,在浙江余村,时任浙江省委书记的习近平同志提出 "绿水青山就是金山银山" 的重要论断。近年来,浙江省深入践行 "绿水青山就是金山银山" 理念,持续推进 "五水共治"、"清新空气示范区"、全域 "无废城市" 建设,强化塑料污染全链条治理,建成全国首个生态省,"千村示范、万村整治" 工程获联合国地球卫士奖,绿水青山俨然已成为浙江最亮丽的一张金名片。2022 年,全省地表水国控断面优良水质比例达 99.4%,跃居全国第一;省控断面优良水质比例达 97.6%,同比提升 3.4 个百分点;设区城市 $PM_{2.5}$ 平均浓度为 24 μg/m³,空气质量优良天数比率为 89.3%,持续领跑长三角。

二、总体战略沿革

早在 2007 年,浙江即成立了浙江省应对气候变化领导小组,是全国最早开展应对气候变化工作的省份之一。回望过去 16 年应对气候变化工作,大致可分为 4 个阶段:

(一)第一阶段(2007—2012 年)是夯基垒台的起步阶段

"十一五" 末、"十二五" 初是浙江经济快速发展的阶段,2012 年,浙江地区生产总值为 3.46 万亿元,能源消费总量约 1.81 亿 t 标准煤,万元 GDP 能耗为 0.55 t 标准煤,在 31 个省(区、市)中排名仅次于北京和广东,居全国第三。此阶段应对气候变化工作重点是搭建应对气候变化的工作架构、政策体系，加强基础能力建设，因地制宜推动低碳试点创新，积极参与国际合作交流等。

1. 建立健全工作机制

2007年，由省长挂帅、31个省级部门为成员的浙江省应对气候变化及节能减排工作领导小组成立，负责统筹协调全省应对气候变化工作。领导小组办公室设在省发展和改革委员会，承担领导小组日常事务。参照省级要求，各设区市、部分县（市、区）也陆续成立应对气候变化议事协调机构。到2008年，浙江就已建立省领导小组牵头抓总、省市县三级联动的工作格局。此外，浙江在全国率先成立应对气候变化省级研究机构——浙江省应对气候变化和低碳发展合作中心，为政府决策提供智力支持。

2. 制定出台政策文件

根据国家统一部署，2010年10月《浙江省人民政府关于印发浙江省应对气候变化方案的通知》（浙政发〔2010〕50号，图1-1）明确了至2012年全省应对气候变化工作的总体目标、重点领域及任务举措等。同时，陆续出台转变经济发展方式、促进节能减排、加快新能源推广利用、推进生态文明建设、发展循环经济等一揽子应对气候变化相关政策文件，形成了以省级应对气候变化方案为核心的"1+N"政策体系。

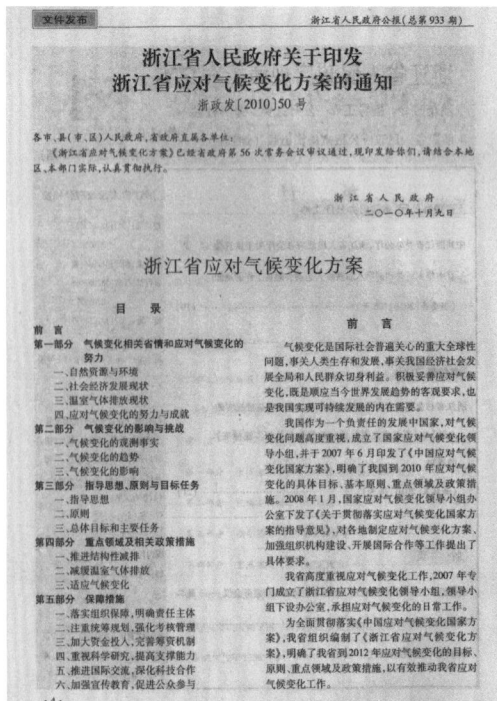

图1-1 《浙江省应对气候变化方案》（节选）

3. 积极推动试点探索

在温室气体清单编制上，作为全国 7 个省级试点之一，浙江于 2011 年印发实施《浙江省温室气体清单编制工作方案》，推动组建了跨部门、跨领域的清单编制工作机制。同步开发温室气体清单数据库，为后续常态化清单报告编制奠定坚实基础。在地方创新实践上，2010 年 7 月，杭州市成功入选全国首批低碳城市试点，按照低碳经济、低碳建筑、低碳交通、低碳生活、低碳环境、低碳社会"六位一体"思路，全面推进试点建设；2012 年 11 月，国家发展改革委同意宁波市、温州市开展第二批低碳城市试点建设。

4. 务实开展合作交流

浙江是国内较早参与清洁发展机制（CDM）的省份之一，实施项目呈现类型多样、特色明显、减排量大、地域分布广等特征。截至 2012 年年底，全省共开发 CDM 项目 199 个，所涉领域包括天然气、风力、生物质能、余热余压发电等，其中成功注册项目 55 个，获得签发项目 24 个，签发减排量约为 1.395 亿 t 二氧化碳当量，占同期全国累计签发量的 20.1%，项目数与签发量均居全国首位，获取国际资金近 100 亿元。同时，在政府层面，浙江省聚焦低碳技术、低碳建筑、低碳交通、低碳园区及低碳融资五大领域深入开展国际合作，如宁波市与世界银行、亚洲开发银行等多个国际机构合作，完成了"城镇生活废弃物收集循环利用示范""低碳城市综合能效示范""建筑能耗预警体系建设和低碳城市规划"等多个重大项目。

（二）第二阶段（2013—2017 年）是积厚成势的探索阶段

"十二五"期间，浙江省大力发展数字经济"一号工程"，持续推进产业结构低碳化，2015 年，全省单位 GDP 碳排放降至 1.0 t/ 万元，碳强度较 2010 年累计下降 24.68%，超额完成国家下达的下降 19% 的任务。此阶段应对气候变化工作重点是探索建立碳强度降低目标考核机制，积极推动多层级试点体系建设，全面推开省、市、县三级温室气体清单编制等。

1. 探索建立低碳目标引领机制

在全国率先印发实施《浙江省低碳发展"十三五"规划》，明确"十三五"期间全省低碳发展的总体思路、主要目标及工作举措等。建立健全碳排放考核机制，分解下达全省碳排放强度控制目标，完成设区市"十二五"碳强度降低目标考核。不断完善碳排放统计体系，统一能源、农业、废弃物处理等领域数据统计口径，制定形成包括 25 张表、248 个指标的应对气候变化基础统计报表制度。

> **专栏2 "十三五"控制温室气体排放目标责任评价考核办法**
>
> 2017年10月，经浙江省政府同意，浙江省发展和改革委员会印发了《浙江省"十三五"设区市人民政府控制温室气体排放目标责任考核试行办法》（浙发改资环〔2017〕854号），正式启动对设区市人民政府控制温室气体排放目标责任的考核。
>
> 考核主要从碳强度目标完成情况、能源节约与结构优化、低碳产业体系建设、城镇化低碳发展、区域低碳发展、碳市场建设和运行、低碳科技创新、基础能力支撑、相关保障措施9个方面考核各设区市人民政府年度控温目标完成情况及政策措施落实情况。
>
> 其中，碳强度目标完成情况考核工作包括两部分：一是单位地区生产总值二氧化碳排放年度降低目标，作为年度考核的否决性指标；二是单位地区生产总值二氧化碳排放累计进度目标，作为五年规划期末考核的否决性指标。

2. 加快探索多层级低碳试点体系

深化拓展国家级试点建设，总体呈现量质齐升，已批复的3个试点城市不断取得成效，如杭州市在G20期间向世界展示了"六位一体"打造低碳城市试点的成效；宁波市以峰值目标倒逼港口城市低碳转型；温州市依托金融改革探索低碳发展道路。2017年2月和7月，丽水市成功入选国家气候适应型城市建设试点，嘉兴市、衢州市和金华市成为第三批国家低碳城市试点。

初步建立省级低碳试点体系，印发《浙江省发展和改革委员会关于开展省级低碳试点工作的通知》（浙发改资环〔2016〕18号），启动首批次8个低碳县（市、区）试点建设，重点在碳排放总量控制制度、温室气体排放统计核算制度等方面创新实践。

> **专栏3 浙江省首批次低碳县（市、区）试点制度创新重点**
>
> 北仑区、瑞安市：以打造沿海工业强市低碳转型先行区为目标，探索建立企业碳生产力评价制度、重点行业碳排放总量控制制度等。
>
> 文成县：以打造低碳扶贫示范区为目标，探索低碳惠民机制和县（市、区）低碳发展考核评价制度等。
>
> 庆元县：聚焦生态工业转型，探索建立以低碳发展为核心的资源要素节约制度、县（市、区）低碳发展考核评价制度等。
>
> 景宁县：以打造山区经济绿色转型示范区、浙南山地重点生态功能区为目标，探索低碳惠民机制（光伏小康工程）和县（市、区）低碳发展考核评价制度等。

> 龙泉市：以打造县域低碳发展制度创新区、低碳经济示范区、低碳文化宣传区、碳汇能力建设实验区为目标，建立碳汇惠民机制，大力推进光伏"精准扶贫"等工作。
>
> 武义县：以打造浙中地区"传统产业低碳转型、新兴产业低碳发展"的新模式为目标，探索建立园区项目碳排放准入标准制度，出台扶持新能源发展等相关政策。
>
> 开化县：以打造低碳扶贫示范区为目标，启动碳汇专项基金计划，开发碳汇林等项目，探索建立低碳惠民机制。

3. 全面推开省、市、县三级温室气体清单编制

作为全国最早推行三级清单编制常态化的省份之一，2014 年浙江省在全国率先印发清单编制的地方性指南，2017 年又制定出台省级清单管理办法，并以此为基础完成了省级 2005—2017 年度温室气体清单、11 个设区市、90 个县（市、区）2010—2017 年度温室气体清单。同步迭代升级浙江省气候变化研究交流平台，建成了覆盖省、市、县三级全流程的在线采集、审核、管理、分析、研判系统，有效掌握了省、市、县、企业四类主体、五大领域、六大类温室气体排放情况。

4. 扎实推动重点领域绿色低碳转型

在低碳经济方面，传统工业深化转型升级，初步形成低能耗、低污染、低碳排放的产业格局。在能源结构方面，不断加快推进光伏、天然气和省外清洁电力等低碳能源利用，煤炭消费总量持续下降，2017 年全省非化石能源占一次能源消费总量比重提高至 16.7%。在低碳建筑方面，颁布实施《浙江省绿色建筑条例》，制定《绿色建筑设计标准》（DB 33/1092—2021），建筑领域节能降碳制度建设不断完善。在低碳交通方面，全省积极创建绿色交通运输示范省，着力完善低碳交通运输体系，单位运输周转量和客运量能耗持续下降。在碳汇方面，巩固森林碳汇能力，加强湿地保护管理，推进"蓝色碳汇"行动。

5. 积极参与全国碳交易市场建设

自 2014 年起，浙江省每年组织近 450 家碳交易纳入企业和近 1 300 家非碳交易纳入企业开展碳报告报送工作，委托 10 余家第三方核（复）查机构分批开展核（复）查工作。建立核复查人员业务能力考评、核查机构绩效评价通报和现场复查等多项机制，启动《浙江省重点企（事）业单位温室气体排放报告暂行管理办法》研究，健全完善全省监测、报告和核查（MRV）体系。

6. 深入开展对外合作交流

成功举办"浙江省应对气候变化南南合作经验分享与技术研讨会"等系列活

动（图 1-2、图 1-3）。积极推进浙江省—美国加利福尼亚州低碳新能源合作前期工作，促成与加利福尼亚州低碳新能源合作事宜。2017 年，在联合国开发计划署（UNDP）指导下，浙江省应对气候变化和低碳发展合作中心完成《发展绿色物流，浙江在行动》报告。

图 1-2　2017 年 3 月，联合国气候大会分享会在杭州顺利举办

图 1-3　2017 年 11 月，成功举办浙江省气候变化南南合作培训班

（三）第三阶段（2018—2020 年）是新旧整合的过渡阶段

2018 年应对气候变化职能完成转隶，具体事务由生态环境相关部门负责。此阶段浙江应对气候变化工作重点是加快推动机构重组整合，全面加强业务能力建设，持续完善 MRV 体系，积极参与全国碳交易市场建设，创新探索新型试点示范等。

1. 加强业务能力建设

2019 年 9 月 26—27 日，由浙江省生态环境厅主办的"浙江省应对气候变化工作能力建设培训会"在宁波召开（图 1-4），这是应对气候变化工作职能转隶后，浙江省生态环境系统首次组织的大规模、全方位的业务培训。会议要求开展碳排放强度形势分析和评估，强化碳排放动态预测预警。

图 1-4　2019 年"浙江省应对气候变化工作能力建设培训会"在宁波召开

2. 全面参与碳交易市场建设

深入实施应对气候变化低碳大数据示范工程，持续推动浙江省气候变化研究交流平台优化升级，2019—2020 年组织完成 1 200 余家企业数据报送，以及290 家企业核查和 145 家企业复查工作。组织做好发电企业参与碳市场前期工作，核实确定 143 家纳入碳市场的发电企业名单，为浙江企业参与全国碳市场交易打牢基础。

3. 创新探索新型试点示范

以强化"零碳"技术的研发与应用、深化碳排放管理为重点，探索打造"近零市""近零县""近零城镇""近零村（社区）""近零企业"等多层级的近零碳排放试验区，构建面向深度减排的试点体系。积极探索协同减排，组织开展温室气体和大气污染物协同减排前期研究，探索开展协同减排试点示范。全面总结城市、县（市）、园区、社区、企业等各级各类试点的创建成效，凝练低碳发展路径和做法。

（四）第四阶段（2020 年 9 月至今）是协同高效的发展阶段

2020 年 9 月 22 日，习近平主席在第 75 届联合国大会一般性辩论上向国际社会作出碳达峰碳中和的郑重承诺，中国二氧化碳排放力争于 2030 年前达到峰值，努力争取 2060 年前实现碳中和。本阶段浙江应对气候变化工作重点是以碳达峰碳中和为核心，推动建立"1+N+X"政策体系，系统谋划"4+6+1"实现路径，全面推进经济社会绿色低碳转型。

1. 构建高位推动的工作格局

一方面，抓好顶层制度设计。自 2020 年 9 月起，浙江省启动谋划"双碳"工作，成立由省委、省政府主要领导挂帅的工作领导小组，制定实施全省碳达峰实施方案和"6+1"领域、11 个设区市实施方案，配套出台财政、金融、计量、考核等系列政策，启动绿色低碳转型促进条例起草工作，进一步构建起"双碳"目标体系、工作体系、政策体系、评价体系。另一方面，抓好社会全面动员。省级实施意见和方案印发后，省市联动围绕"双碳"顶层设计深入开展宣传报道，积极组织专家学者在省媒党报推出理论阐释文章，举办领导干部能力培训班，同时，开发上线碳普惠应用（图 1-5），积极推动广大居民践行绿色低碳生活，累计用户超过 130 万人，低碳行为突破 2 413 万次，"双碳"工作获得社会广泛关注。

图 1-5　浙江碳普惠应用界面

2. 谋划"4+6+1"碳达峰碳中和路径

2021 年 5 月 21 日，时任浙江省委书记的袁家军在全省碳达峰碳中和工作推进会上强调要以数字化改革为引领，以科技创新和制度创新为动力，以结构调整为关键，统筹经济发展、能源安全、碳排放、居民生活，率先实现经济社会发展全面绿色低碳转型。总体思路和路径是"4+6+1"（图 1-6）。

"4"是指瞄准 4 个核心指标。系统分析能源消耗总量、碳排放总量、能耗强度和碳排放强度 4 个指标，科学制定碳达峰实施方案。重点压减碳排放强度和能耗强度，以强度下降带动总量下降，实现科学达峰。

"6"是指系统推进六大领域的绿色低碳变革。统筹做好增量和存量文章，抓实抓好能源、工业、建筑、交通、农业和居民生活六个重点领域的绿色低碳转型，实行梯次达峰。

"1"是指用好科技创新这一关键变量。制定碳达峰碳中和的技术路线图，率先构建绿色低碳技术创新体系，依靠技术变量抢抓制高点，高质量支撑实现碳达峰碳中和。

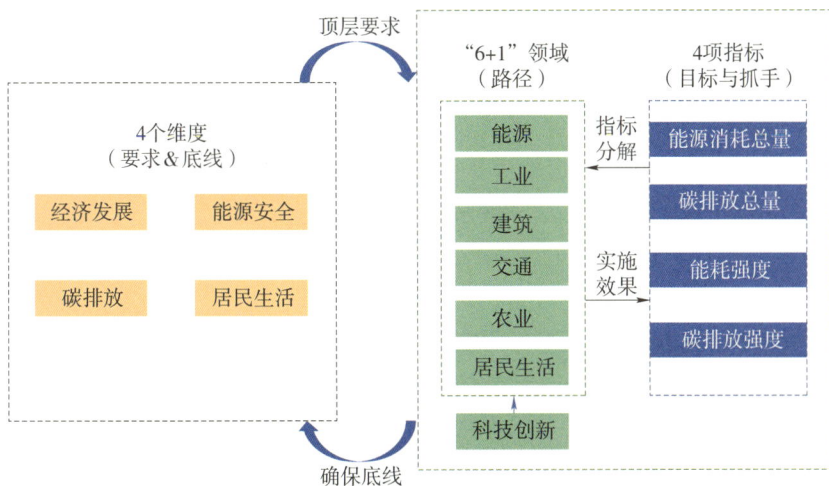

图 1-6 浙江省碳达峰碳中和 "4+6+1" 总体思路与路径

3. 率先建成 "双碳" 智治平台

充分发挥浙江数字发展优势,推动数字化赋能低碳发展,建成全省统一的碳排放数据库、全国最早的碳账户应用之一,初步实现六大领域、11 个设区市以及 4.7 万余家企业碳排放动态监测研判。围绕政府、企业、个人三方需求,打造 "改革 + 应用" 的重大成果,平台已上线碳排放统计核算及预测预警、节能降碳 e 本账、碳试点、碳普惠等 10 余个重大场景。浙江省在全国率先建成 "双碳" 综合管理平台的经验做法 (图 1–7),获国家 《双碳简报》 刊登并推广。

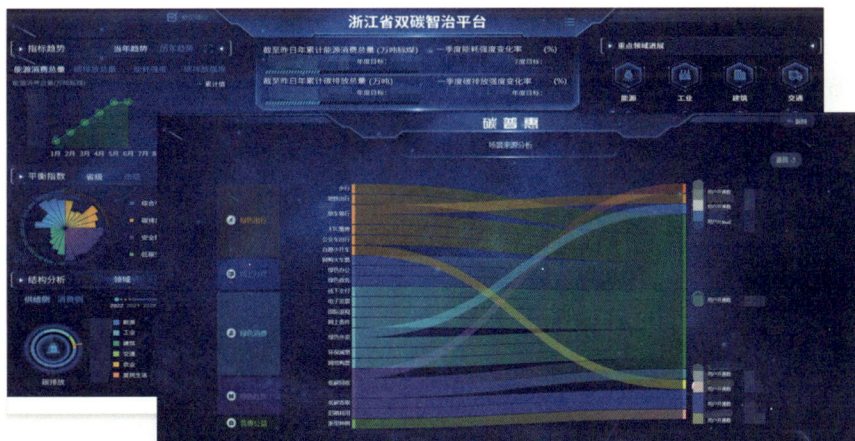

图 1-7 浙江省 "双碳" 智治平台驾驶舱

4. 打造低 (零) 碳试点体系

2021 年 8 月,浙江省印发 《浙江省关于开展低 (零) 碳试点建设的指导意见》 (浙双碳办 〔2021〕5 号),提出按照 "点上突破、线上推进、面上展开"

13

思路，建设包含低碳试点县、乡镇、村、工业园区、工厂等多领域、多层级、多样化的低（零）碳试点示范体系。截至 2022 年年底，全省共建成低碳试点县 23 个、低（零）碳乡镇（街道）80 个、低（零）碳村（社区）632 个、减污降碳协同试点 18 个、林业增汇试点县 4 个、新型储能示范项目 34 个、绿色低碳工厂 279 家和绿色低碳园区 20 个、低碳生态农场创建单位 279 家，遴选形成全省首批 40 个绿色低碳转型典型案例（图 1–8）。

图 1-8　部分省级绿色低碳转型典型案例简介

5. 推进减污降碳协同增效

2022 年 9 月，生态环境部复函支持浙江省建设全国首个减污降碳协同创新区。12 月，浙江省生态环境厅牵头印发《浙江省减污降碳协同创新区建设实施方案》，提出创新区建设目标，梳理源头防控、模式创新、提升协同能力等 8 方面 29 项具体工作任务。同时，推进 26 个减污降碳协同标杆项目建设，打造首批余杭区数字赋能减污降碳协同、上虞经开区减污降碳协同数字智治等 5 个典型案例。

三、减缓战略与主要做法

减缓是一种减少温室气体排放源或增加汇的人为干预手段。近年来，浙江始终坚持"绿水青山就是金山银山"理念，陆续实施"生态省""美丽浙江""大花园"等重大战略，推动形成绿色低碳的生产生活方式，以自身的绿色低碳发展，全力减缓气候变化影响。回望过去，浙江省重点围绕能源、工业、建筑、交通、居民生活以及碳汇等领域发力，减缓工作取得积极成效。

（一）能源发展方式低碳转型

1. 推动可再生能源实现跨越式发展

对浙江而言，发展可再生能源是破解能源约束、实现能源结构转型的关键之举。一直以来，浙江省高度重视可再生能源发展，积极推进风、光、水等可再生能源规模化发展。特别是在光伏发展方面，从支持工商业分布式光伏发展、实施百万家庭屋顶光伏行动计划，再到实施"风光倍增工程"，全省光伏装机规模迅速增长，且开发应用形式多，基本涵盖了屋顶光伏、农光互补、渔光互补、水面漂浮式光伏等各种类型。同时，浙江利用海洋资源优势不断加快海上风电发展步伐。截至 2022 年年底，全社会风电及光伏装机容量突破 3 000 万 kW，占全省电源总装机比重超 1/4。此外，浙江还加快布局抽水蓄能项目建设，已建和在建抽水蓄能电站总装机规模领跑全国。值得一提的是，浙江始终坚持安全、有序地推进核电发展，2020 年全国首个民营资本参股投资民用核电项目——三澳核电一期工程正式开工，截至 2022 年，浙江核电装机容量 913 万 kW，发电量累计730.5 亿 kW·h，皆居全国第三。

2. 全力调整优化能源结构

2014 年，浙江率先开展国家清洁能源示范省创建，通过控制能源消费总量和强度，有效提升清洁能源消费比重，天然气消费量从 2010 年的 31.8 亿 m^3 大幅提升至 2022 年的 180 亿 m^3，非化石能源占能源消费总量比重为 19.0%，比2010 年的 9.8% 提高 9.2 个百分点。同时，浙江统筹能源安全和低碳发展，严格控制煤炭消费总量，通过实施"煤改气""煤改电"工程，有序压减生产生活用煤，煤炭消费量占能源消费比重从 2010 年的 61.3% 下降至 2022 年的 41.7%，远低于全国平均水平。通过开展煤电机组超低排放改造等措施，全省煤炭清洁高效利用水平有效提升，煤电平均供电标准煤耗从 2010 年的 312 g/（kW·h）下降至 2022 年的 294 g/（kW·h）。此外，浙江不断加大省外清洁电力入浙项目建设力度，相继投运溪洛渡—浙江高压直流输电、白鹤滩输浙特高压直流等重大工程，能源结构低碳化水平进一步提升。

3. 持续推进能效水平提升

浙江不仅在能源供应结构优化上发力，也高度重视在消费侧能效水平提升上提档加速。"十二五"以来，浙江以"能耗双控"制度为抓手，全面推进能源消费方式变革，重点推动高耗能重污染行业整治，倒逼能效水平落后的产能有序退出、加快企业节能改造步伐，并实施"万吨千家"企业节能、严把能评准入关等系列举措，单位产出能耗稳步下降。同时，浙江积极推进能源要素配置改革，成功列入全国首批用能权有偿使用和交易试点省，通过完善用能权交易制度体系，建成全省统一的用能权交易平台，用能权交易完成项目数、交易规模领跑全国。浙江还组织制定并定期修订《浙江省产业能效指南》，对能源消耗超过单位产品能耗限额标准的企业严格执行阶梯电价政策。此外，浙江大力推动公共机构节能降碳管理数字化转型，构建了全省公共机构节能在线监测"一张网"，公共机构节能取得明显成效。"十一五"以来连续 3 个五年计划均顺利完成国家下达的约束性目标，2021 年万元 GDP 能耗 0.38 t 标准煤（2020 年价），比 2012 年累计下降 20.3%，其中，规模以上工业单位增加值能耗累计下降 23.8%，千吨以上和重点监测用能企业单位增加值能耗分别下降 26.9% 和 26.5%，工作成效较为显著。

（二）工业碳生产力有效提升

1. 加快传统产业低碳转型升级

早在 21 世纪初，浙江省为破解资源环境约束与经济粗放发展之间的矛盾，提出实施"腾笼换鸟、凤凰涅槃"行动，加快传统产业转型升级，推动产业结构高度化发展。在推进机制上，浙江专门成立省工业转型升级领导小组，每年召开全省工作推进会议部署推动，特别是 2010 年以来，浙江打出"退二进三""四换三名"等转型升级系列组合拳，淘汰整治高耗低效企业、有效遏制"两高一低"项目盲目发展，仅"十三五"时期全省累计淘汰落后和过剩产能涉及企业 8 250 家，累计腾出用能空间 600 万 t 标准煤以上。近年来，浙江以"亩均论英雄"、新一轮制造业"腾笼换鸟、凤凰涅槃"攻坚行动为具体抓手，加快推动发展方式转变、经济结构优化、增长动力转换，2021 年，工信部正式同意支持浙江建设国家传统制造业改造升级示范区。同时，浙江持续强化体制机制创新，制定实施"区域能评、环评 + 区块能耗、环境标准"改革指导意见，新批工业用地基本实现"标准地"出让，确保产业增量的绿色高效。

2. 推进新兴产业高质量发展

加快新旧动能转化、促进经济结构优化升级是减缓气候变化的重要应对举措，而持续优化经济结构、稳步提升发展质量，离不开战略性新兴产业的引领和支撑作用。2020 年，浙江省提出全力打造"互联网 +"、生命健康和新材料三大科创高地，加速科技资源汇聚。在三大科创高地建设的牵引下，通过实施数字经济"一号工程"，浙江省新产业、新业态、新模式的"三新"产业经济发展迅速，从 2022 年的统计数据来看，"三新"经济增加值占 GDP 的 28.1%，数字经济核心产业增加值达 8 977 亿元，比上年增长 6.3%，特别是以高新技术产业为代表的新动能持续引领增长，2010 年高新技术产业增加值为 2 396 亿元，仅为 2022 年的 16.7%，发展成效较为显著。

3. 注重工业低碳发展试点示范

围绕工业领域绿色低碳转型发展，浙江省通过试点引领、示范带动，重点聚焦企业、园区等工业发展主体和平台，开展了系列试点示范，形成一批可复制、可推广的先进经验，以点带面推动工业低碳转型发展。企业层面，浙江省连续实施 3 轮循环经济"991"行动计划，每年遴选一批具有示范意义、资源社会效益的企业重点项目开展省级专项资金支持。同时，全面推进绿色制造体系建设，开展绿色低碳工厂创建，制定绿色低碳工厂建设评价导则，明确能源与资源投入、产品、环境排放等综合要求，打造绿色供应链管理示范企业、绿色设计示范企业。截至 2023 年 5 月，已公布两批次共 200 家省级绿色低碳工厂。园区层面，浙江主要以园区循环化改造为抓手，推动块状经济绿色低碳转型，自 2014 年起，累计组织开展 5 批省级园区循环化改造示范试点，推动 70 个省级以上园区实施循环化改造，助推园区经济在资源环境压力下抢占绿色发展先机。同时，制定绿色低碳工业园区建设评价导则，对绿色低碳工业园区的认定进行详细规定，加快推动工业发展绿色低碳转型，截至 2022 年年底，全省已建成省级绿色低碳工业园区 20 个。

（三）绿色低碳交通体系稳步构建

1. 持续优化交通运输结构

从浙江全省的碳排放占比看，交通领域碳排放占全社会排放总量的 9%，是控制碳排放的重点领域之一。近年来，在高水平建设交通强省背景下，浙江通过发展多式联运、构筑"四港"联动格局等路径，不断优化运输结构调整，绿色低碳交通建设成效显著，成为全国首批绿色交通省创建试点。从具体路径来看，浙江以示范线路、示范项目为抓手，大力发展多式联运，积极推进大宗货物运输"公转铁""公转水"，据统计，2021 年浙江完成江海联运量 55.1 万标准箱、海河联运量 53.1 万标准箱、海铁联运量 120.4 万标准箱，均呈上涨态势。同时，浙江积极构筑"四港"联动发展格局，在 2019 年印发《加快推进海港陆港空港信息港发展建设方案》，加快海、陆、空运输方式之间相互衔接，发挥组合效益，实现综合交通体系优化、运输增效、物流降费。

2. 大力推进交通运输装备低碳化

浙江通过大力推广新能源车辆、推进老旧营运车辆淘汰、加快船舶能源替代等措施，有效推动交通运输装备清洁化、低碳化。特别是在公共交通领域，通过全力推进城市公共交通清洁能源化，杭州、湖州已实现清洁能源公交全覆盖，宁波、湖州、绍兴已实现清洁能源出租车全覆盖。同时，浙江在这两年相继制定印发交通运输新型基础设施建设、公路沿线充电基础设施建设等相关实施方案，布局建设充换电基础设施和加氢站，进一步完善交通运输新能源基础设施。老旧运营车辆淘汰方面，2019年浙江省交通运输厅等六部门联合印发《关于印发加快推进老旧运营车辆淘汰实施意见的函》（浙交函〔2019〕35号），大力推进国Ⅲ及以下排放标准营运柴油货车提前淘汰更新，截至2022年年底，全省共淘汰国Ⅲ及以下老旧营运柴油货车近7万辆。此外，在"十三五"期间，浙江大力推广LNG动力运输船舶和环保型客船应用，全省水路营运船舶单位运输周转量能耗下降率为22.7%。

3. 不断完善公共交通体系

一直以来，浙江省始终抓牢"公共交通优先发展"这一"牛鼻子"，通过不断提升公共交通基础设施建设和完善公共交通服务品质，使公共交通的吸引力和竞争力得到有力提升，绿色低碳出行得到大力倡导，从已有数据来看，全省公共交通机动化出行分担率由2010年的18.4%上升至2020年的36.7%。基础设施建设方面，浙江着力打造"轨道＋公交＋慢行"三网融合的绿色出行体系，"十二五"以来，杭州、宁波地铁，温州、绍兴、嘉兴城市轨道交通均实现"从0到1"的突破；织密公交车线网密度，全省常规公交运营线路近6 000条，公交专用道里程达840 km；城市绿道网等慢行系统建设更加完善。同时，浙江大力提升公共交通服务品质，推行城市公交"最后一公里"多样化服务，特别是通过微信公众号等多种途径，推出"浙里畅行"网上一站式服务。因地制宜地开通高峰通勤巴士、地铁接驳公交、定制公交、水上巴士等灵活多样的公交服务，以杭州小红车为代表的公共自行车体系更加完善，为公众采用公共交通工具出行提供了极大的便利。

（四）绿色建筑发展全面推进

1. 建立完善绿色建筑发展工作体系

浙江省围绕城乡建设进程中建筑领域能耗以及碳排放量持续增长这一现状，始终将建筑节能和绿色建筑工作作为应对气候变化和低碳发展的重要一招，不断建立完善推动绿色建筑发展的工作体系，在全国率先建立覆盖规划、设计、施工、竣工验收、运营等全过程完整的绿色建筑发展制度。具体来看，早在2011年，浙江就以省政府名义印发《关于积极推进绿色建筑发展的若干意见》，全方位推进建筑绿色化发展。持续推进绿色建筑专项规划编制工作，明确要求各地加快编制实施绿色建筑专项规划，统筹推进绿色建筑发展。同时，浙江不断健全法规、标准等制度体系，2015 年出台《浙江省绿色建筑条例》，以立法的方式强制推行绿色建筑；制定《既有民用建筑加装太阳能光伏系统设计导则》等一系列地方标准，强化绿色建筑发展技术支撑。此外，浙江还建立了覆盖所有设区市的公共建筑能耗监管信息平台，并与省级监管平台实现数据共享，对全省公共建筑能耗实施动态监测。

2. 有效提升新建建筑低碳发展水平

标准体系方面，2021 年浙江省制定发布了《浙江省公共建筑节能设计标准》《绿色建筑设计标准》《居住建筑节能设计标准》等系列标准导则，明确要求全省居住建筑设计节能率达到 75%。新建建筑方面，浙江大力推广装配式等新型建造方式，截至 2022 年年底，全省累计完成装配式建筑超 4 亿 m^2，占新建建筑比例连续 3 年超过 30%，4 个城市、23 家企业被列为国家装配式建筑示范城市和产业基地。此外，浙江大力推进可再生能源应用，推动可再生能源应用与建筑一体化设计、施工和安装，截至 2022 年，完成可再生能源建筑应用面积 2 500 万 m^2，累计完成太阳能等可再生能源建筑应用面积 1.4 亿 m^2，城镇绿色建筑占新建建筑比重超过 98%。

3. 稳步推进既有建筑节能改造

浙江省高度重视城乡建设各环节的绿色低碳发展，特别是对提升既有建筑能效水平尤为重视，采取了系列举措稳步开展节能改造。"十二五"以来，浙江省结合老旧小区改造、城市有机更新、海绵城市建设、"未来社区"建设工程等重点工作，通过采用建筑外墙外保温、活动外遮阳、隔热屋面、太阳能、地源热泵等较为成熟的节能技术，推广应用绿色建材，既有建筑节能改造取得了显著成效，截至 2022 年，全省累计完成既有公共建筑节能改造 1 200 万 m^2。同时，浙江制定发布了《既有国家机关办公建筑节能改造技术规程》，为指导公共建筑节能改造提供了重要参考。

（五）生态系统碳汇能力巩固提升

1. 全力推进林业碳汇发展

近年来，浙江将林业碳汇发展纳入全省应对气候变化工作总体布局，部署开展高质量"森林浙江"建设，实现了"质"和"量"的双提升。提质方面，浙江省相继开展珍贵彩色森林建设工程、千万亩森林质量精准提升工程等重点举措，有效优化林分结构，森林质量持续提升；增量方面，浙江扎实推进"一村万树"

行动、新增百万亩国土绿化行动等系列举措，森林质量持续提升，截至 2022 年年底，全省森林覆盖率达到 61.24%（含灌木林），森林蓄积量达到 4.2 亿 m^3，乔木林单位面积蓄积量年增率持续位居全国前列。同时，不断完善林业碳汇管理机制，丽水市、安吉县先后成立全国首个市级、县级森林碳汇管理局，淳安县在全国率先设立乡镇森林碳汇服务中心，理顺地方林业管理体制机制，森林生态系统的整体保护和管理得到有效强化。

2. 有力提升湿地、海洋碳汇能力

除林业碳汇外，浙江还拥有大量湿地、海洋碳汇资源，湿地海洋碳汇也是发展重点之一。在湿地碳汇方面，相继出台《浙江省湿地保护条例》《关于加强湿地保护修复工作的实施意见》等政策文件，全面加强湿地保护修复，碳库水平持续提升。截至 2022 年年底，全省拥有湿地面积约 124 万 hm^2，拥有国际重要湿地 2 处，国家重要湿地 2 处，省级重要湿地 87 处，湿地类自然保护地 79 个。同时稳步推进海洋碳汇发展，印发实施《浙江省"蓝碳"科技创新专项行动方案》《浙江省自然资源领域蓝碳工作方案》，强化海洋碳汇发展科技支撑，开展全省蓝碳家底调查。值得一提的是，2023 年浙江印发省级层面海洋碳汇领域方案——《浙江省海洋碳汇能力提升指导意见》，全面部署海洋碳汇生态系统固碳增汇相关工作。地市层面，部分沿海地区也积极推进海洋碳汇保护提升，如温州市有序开展红树林恢复、种植，在乐清湾、瓯江口等区域已种植红树林 200 多 hm^2；舟山市率先印发《舟山市蓝碳经济发展行动方案（2021—2025）》，加快构建以蓝碳能力提升为核心的经济体系。

3. 探索推进碳汇市场化机制创新

早在 2010 年，浙江省就成立了经国家林业局批准的华东林业产权交易所，主要从事林权交易、林业碳汇交易等服务，成为当时全国唯一林业碳汇交易试点平台。在浙科研院所也积极推进林业碳汇相关方法学研究，如浙江农林大学牵头开展了《竹林经营碳汇项目方法学》《竹子造林碳汇项目方法学》等标准研究并获得了国家发展改革委备案，成功纳入中国核证减排量（CCER）方法学体系，这让全国的竹林碳汇交易项目有了"浙江标准"。此外，浙江部分地市积极开展森林碳汇项目方法学和交易机制研究，拥有多个"全国首个"的亮眼成果，如2013 年温州市研究制定了全国首个森林经营碳汇项目技术规程、2014 年杭州临安发布全国首个农户森林经营碳汇交易体系等。浙江也围绕地方碳汇资源特色禀赋，开展碳汇交易示范试点建设，力求试点先行、早出经验，丽水市、安吉县被列为全省森林碳汇、竹林碳汇交易试点，特别是丽水市，在 2020 年制定了《浙江省丽水市森林经营碳普惠方法学》和《浙江省丽水市林业碳汇开发及交易管理暂行办法》，开展了交易探索。同时，浙江还印发了《浙江省用于大型活动（会议）碳中和的碳普惠减排量管理办法（试行）》，明确林业碳汇开发、管理、委托核证、登记备案等流程，碳汇发展的市场化机制得到不断完善。

（六）绿色低碳生活方式成为新风尚

1. 大力倡导绿色低碳消费

应对气候变化和低碳发展不仅需要供给侧的绿色低碳转型，更需要在消费侧加快形成绿色低碳的消费方式。近年来，浙江省制定出台了系列政策措施，积极引导全社会形成绿色低碳的消费理念。在供给端，2019年浙江多部门联合印发全国首个省级层面出台的绿色产品认证文件——《关于加快推进绿色产品认证工作的意见》，有力推动了绿色产品的有效供给。在需求端，2019年，浙江省生活垃圾分类工作领导小组办公室等十部门联合印发了《关于限制一次性消费用品的通知》，在全省范围掀起一波限制一次性消费用品使用的高潮。同时，浙江借力数字经济发展优势，电子发票、线上生活缴费、二手回收等绿色消费应用场景得到有效应用。此外，通过定期举办"全国节能宣传周""全国低碳日"等主题宣传活动，"光盘"行动、"菜篮子""布袋子"等低碳生活模式更加深入人心，绿色低碳的消费方式正在成为越来越多消费者的自觉行动。

2. 全面推行城乡生活垃圾分类

强化生活垃圾分类管理，推动前端减量化，后端资源化、无害化，有助于减缓气候变化的脚步。近年来，特别是2018年习近平总书记提出"垃圾分类工作就是新时尚"的理念以来，浙江省不断加大城乡生活垃圾分类力度，在推进体系、制度政策方面有效发力，取得了显著成效。2018年成立浙江省生活垃圾分类工作领导小组，推动形成部门协同、省市县一体推进的工作体系。随后相继印发了《浙江省城镇生活垃圾分类管理办法》《浙江省生活垃圾管理条例》等规范性文件，并在2019年发布了全国第一部城镇生活垃圾分类省级标准——《城镇生活垃圾分类标准》，生活垃圾分类制度规范和标准体系基本建立。此外，在推进"垃圾革命"的进程中，浙江省也涌现了"虎哥回收""两次四分法"等一批可复制、可推广的典型经验，垃圾分类成效走在全国前列，截至2022年年底，全省城乡生活垃圾分类处理覆盖面已达100%。

3. 探索创新碳普惠机制

为鼓励和引导全社会积极参与到应对气候变化和低碳发展中来，进而形成人人参与、共建共享的绿色低碳生活新风尚，浙江在碳普惠机制上不断探索创新，从省级到地方，都开创了一批典型做法。省级层面，借力数字化改革优势，省发展改革委牵头开发了"浙江碳普惠"应用，并于 2022 年在"浙里办"App 正式上线，该应用覆盖了绿色出行、绿色消费、在线办理等五大场景，全省居民在衣、食、住、行各个领域的"低碳生活"都可以累积碳积分，兑换各类权益。截至 2023 年 5 月，"浙江碳普惠"应用用户已突破百万，已成为场景全面、权益丰富的省级碳普惠平台。地方上，湖州市创新构建碳积分体系，金融机构通过大数据建模，将居民绿色行为转化为碳积分，并配套开发绿色信贷产品、给予利率优惠支持。仙居县提出"绿色货币"理念，鼓励游客通过践行绿色生活方式兑换绿色货币，践行"碳补偿""碳抵消"的消费理念。衢州市以生活垃圾回收资源化利用为切口上线"零废生活"数字化应用场景，通过参与绿色环保行为为个人"碳账户"累计积分，积分还能够兑换商品，形成了一种有效的低碳行为激励模式。

四、适应战略与主要做法

适应是自然或人类系统在实际或预期的气候变化刺激下进行的一种调整反应。近年来，浙江不断完善气候变化工作体制，重点围绕基础设施、森林生态、海洋环境、水资源、应急防灾等方面，积极推动适应气候变化全面融入社会经济发展大局，发布了首份全省适应气候变化评估报告，落地了国家级适应型城市建设试点，相关工作取得积极成效。

（一）强化经济社会系统适应气候变化能力

1. 强化基础设施适应气候变化能力

长期以来，浙江始终坚持致力于推动基础设施气候韧性建设，有效规避气候风险损失。在交通设施气候韧性方面，浙江以交通强省建设为牵引，聚力建设现代化综合交通运输体系，增强系统韧性，构建自然灾害交通防治体系，特别是印发实施了《浙江省公路应急保障基地建设管理办法》，布局建设一批应急保障基地，已建成 5 个省级公路应急保障基地，全面保障公路部门有效应对台风、洪涝、雨雪冰冻等极端天气和自然灾害。同时，加强能源设施气候韧性建设，浙江应用"防台抗灾电网"体系评价平台，在诊断全省供电网格的基础上差异化改造电网，提升电网防汛防台风能力。通过开展长周期人工智能负荷预测，灵活调整高峰时段电网运行方式，全力保障极端高温下的电力供应。加强能源项目适应性技术应用，如舟山普陀 6 号海上风电项目通过"海上升压站百分之百抗台型大孤岛"技术，有效保障在极端气候条件下风电场的安全性。此外，在加强水利设施气候韧性方面，2013 年浙江省作出"五水共治"决策部署，全面推进防洪水、排涝水等密切适应气候变化的重点工作，相继实施了百项千亿防洪排涝工程、海塘安澜千亿工程等重大标志性工程，水利基础设施适应气候变化能力得到大幅提升，截至 2023 年 5 月，浙江全省主要流域防洪排涝体系已基本形成，干堤达标率提高至 90%。

2. 强化城市领域适应气候变化能力

浙江位处长三角城市群，城镇化水平高，对气候变化的敏感度较高，长期以来也一直注重城市领域适应气候变化的能力建设。从工作路径来看，浙江重点以海绵城市建设为牵引，加强城市排水防涝治理，增强城市适应性能力。2016 年，出台《浙江省人民政府办公厅关于推进全省海绵城市建设的实施意见》，以试点示范的形式在全省推广海绵城市建设，重点通过建设屋顶绿化、雨水花园、储水池塘、生物滞留设置等城市海绵体的方式，加快构建气候友好型城市生态系统。其中嘉兴市、宁波市、杭州市、金华市相继入选国家海绵城市建设试点城市（图1-9），获中央财政资金大力支持，在管网提升、河道综保工程、管廊和地下空间开发等方面取得一批试点实效。在省级试点方面，绍兴、衢州、兰溪、温岭4 个城市聚焦平原河网、山地丘陵、沿海滩涂等不同地理条件，加强海绵城市建设模式创新，为全省其他县市提供经验示范。从建设成效来看，截至"十三五"末，浙江设区市建成区 25%、县（市、区）建成区 20% 以上面积达到了海绵城市建设目标要求，建设工作初显成效。此外，浙江印发了《浙江省城市内涝治理实施方案》《关于进一步加强城市排水防涝工作的意见》《关于提升城市配电设施防涝能力的若干意见》等系列文件，对城市内涝治理进行了系统性的部署，重点实施"固河堤、疏河道、新开河、畅管网、除涝点、强设施"六大工程，使城市内涝灾害防治能力大幅提升。截至"十三五"末，全省综合整治城市河道 876 条，建设雨水管网 6 861.8 km，进一步提升城市排水防涝能力以适应气候变化。

图 1-9　金华市海绵城市建设典型项目——燕尾洲公园

3. 强化人体健康领域适应气候变化能力

浙江省始终将"人民至上、生命至上"放在所有工作的首位，通过开展"健康浙江"行动，走出一条富有浙江特色的健康建设和发展之路，特别是在强化人体健康领域适应气候变化能力方面，浙江注重提升政府适应气候变化的公共服务能力和管理水平。针对极端天气特征，推进建立健康监测、调查和风险评估制度及标准体系，积极做好高温天气医疗卫生服务工作。同时，加强与气候变化密切相关的疾病防控、疫情动态变化监测和影响因素研究，制定了与气候变化密切相关的公共卫生应急预案和救援机制。值得一提的是，浙江积极完善气候变化对人体健康影响的监测预警系统，加强极端事件健康预警和流行性疾病预警，在各市部署开展了公共场所健康危害因素监测试点，建立高温热浪与健康风险早期预警系统。此外，浙江科研院校也进一步加强适应气候变化人群健康领域研究，组织开展适应气候变化保护人类健康项目，增强公众应对高温热浪等极端天气的能力。

（二）提升重点领域气候适应水平

1. 提升农业领域适应气候变化能力

浙江地处东南沿海，具有优良的光、热、水、土等农业发展禀赋，是农、林、牧、渔全面发展的综合性农业区域，素有"鱼米之乡""丝茶之府"之称。因此加强农业领域气候韧性也一直是浙江推进农业农村现代化建设的主要着力点，从顶层设计到工作推进，农业领域适应气候变化能力得到有效提升。顶层设计方面，浙江省制定印发现代农业发展五年规划以及相关行动计划等政策文件，全面打造全国现代生态循环农业试点省和国家农产品质量安全示范省，积极应对由气候变化诱发的地区旱涝不均、病虫害突发、极端气候事件对农业生产的不利影响。具体工作推进上，特别是在推广农业适应性节水技术方面，2015年，浙江专门出台《关于加快推进高效节水灌溉工程建设的意见》，大力推广高效节水灌溉技术，开展高效节水灌溉"四个百万工程"建设，全省农田水利设施加快提升改善，大中型灌区现代化改造深入开展，农田灌溉、防洪排涝能力持续增强，至2022年年底，浙江有万亩以上灌区122处，骨干设施完好率达85%以上。同时，浙江加大适应气候变化的作物品种选育和推广力度，积极引进和推广抗旱节水稻，取得了一定成效，2021年全省抗旱节水稻种植面积6万亩左右。此外，浙江还结合数字化改革优势，打造智慧农业云平台，通过汇聚各级农业业务应用及数据，形成"大农业"数据中心，能够实现现代农业综合管理、应急指挥和灾变预警等功能，有力提升农业生产适应气候变化的能力。

2. 提升林业领域适应气候变化能力

拥有61.24%森林覆盖率的浙江，也一直将提升林业领域适应气候变化能力作为增强浙江整体适应水平的重要抓手，努力维护生态安全、气候安全。大力加强森林气候韧性，围绕国家《林业适应气候变化行动方案（2016—2020年）》工作要求，浙江有序增加耐火、耐旱（湿）、抗病虫、抗极温等树种的造林比例，推广适应气候变化的森林培育经营模式，加大对森林及天然林资源保护力度，并通过加强火灾、有害生物入侵等森林灾害的监测防控力度，增强森林生态系统对气候变化的适应性和韧性。另外，浙江不断强化林地保护，在全国首创路林共建新模式，推进防火巡护道与农村公路共同建设，同时强化信息化建设在森林防灾方面的应用，构建了一套"防、控、救"融合的森林火灾专题应用系统，有效预警森林火灾风险，"十三五"以来全省发生森林火灾同比减少45%。此外，浙江印发《关于建立自然保护地体系的实施意见》大力推动自然保护区体系建设，扩大自然保护区规模，推进自然保护区规范化、标准化和能力建设。深入开展钱江源国家公园体制试点，积极探索国家级自然保护区省政府垂直管理模式，提高了自然保护区的保护管理能力与水平。

3. 提升水资源领域适应气候变化能力

浙江虽然河湖密布、通江达海，单位面积产水量位居全国前列，但人均水资源量远低于全国平均水平，水资源保障仍面临较大压力，特别是在气候变化等因素叠加影响下，加强水资源领域适应性建设显得尤为重要。总体来看，浙江主要以"五水共治"决策部署为牵引，从优化水资源配置、加强水污染防治、推进节水型社会建设等方面来进一步提升水资源的气候韧性。在水资源优化配置方面，以重点水源和骨干引调水工程建设为主体，优化水资源配置网络，相继建成浙东引水工程、千岛湖配水工程等重点项目，截至2021年年底，全省共有大小水库总库容量达449亿m³。水污染治理方面，浙江以治水为突破口加快推进产业转型升级，联动推动水环境质量显著改善，特别是创新开展"河长制"，有效推进水资源保护、水污染防治、水环境治理等重要任务落地实施，到2022年年底，已全面消灭劣V类水，全省地表水国控和省控断面优良水质比例分别达99.4%、97.6%，再创历史新高。同时，浙江强化水资源分析评价与预测预报体系建设，建立水资源承载力预警机制，有效强化水资源承载力的刚性约束。在节水型社会建设方面，浙江印发实施《浙江省节水行动实施方案》，重点以县域为单元、政府为主体，分批次推进节水型社会建设，打造了一批国家级、省级节水型城市。此外，浙江在2022年印发实施《浙江水网建设规划》，重点以八大水系为基本脉络，以新安江等重要湖库为枢纽节点，新建浙东、浙中、浙北等一批水资源配置通道和洪涝水分泄通道，使自然水系、水利设施交互成网，构建"三纵八横十枢"的总体格局，有效提升水资源适应气候变化的弹性。

（三）加强重点区域适应气候变化

1. 提升浙西南山区适应气候变化能力

浙江省地形以山地为主，有"七山一水二分田"之称，特别是浙西南山区，"多山"的地理环境较为显著，也是全省地势最高的区域，生态系统类型非常丰富，是华东地区重要的生态屏障。在全球气候变暖的背景下，浙西南山区等敏感性区域面临着降水模式变化和自然灾害加剧等发展挑战。丽水市是典型的"九山半水半分田"的浙西南山区城市，也是灾害性天气多发区。为缓解气候影响，降低气候灾害，丽水市在适应气候变化工作方面积极先行探索，取得显著成效。2017年，丽水市入选首批国家气候适应型城市建设试点，建立气候适应型城市建设领导机制，同时明确开展适应气候变化的工作思路，重点识别气候变化条件下的突出问题和关键事项，主要开展了地质灾害易发区适应气候变化研究、生态用水体系研究等重点工作。特别是丽水积极提升山区城市适应气候变化能力，打造地下地上、山内山外相结合的城市空间利用模式，提升城市气候环境舒适度，增强城市在高温、暴雨等极端天气应急和防灾减灾等方面的能力。同时，加快完善引调水工程等水利基础设施，强化建筑节能改造，提高建筑适应气候变化能力，并立足全省生态旅游核心区的实际，建立旅游安全预警系统、应急预案和应急体系，有效提升丽水旅游业的舒适度和安全系数。

除丽水地区外，同样位于浙西南山区的衢州市也不断提升适应气候变化能力。具体来看，作为浙江母亲河钱塘江的发源地，衢州开化县以钱江源国家公园试点建设为抓手，积极推进钱塘江源头水源地生态保护和修复，提升森林生态系统对气候变化的响应和适应。在流域尺度上，衢州实行流域总量控制和强度控制，制定跨区域主要流域水量分配方案，明确水资源利用上限和生态流量底线，有效提升水资源适应气候变化能力。在制度创新上，衢州构建市、县两级区域用水总量、强度控制指标体系，明确节水主体责任。城乡建设上，充分考虑气候变化影响，新城选址、城区扩建、乡镇建设要进行气候变化风险评估。防灾减灾上，衢州在全国率先推进建立了"网格＋气象"工作模式，形成部门信息共享共通、高效快速的协同处置机制。值得一提的是，衢州创新开展面向涉农部门和种植大户的"直通式"气象服务，建立茶叶、油茶等政策性保险气象指数，"气象指数保险智能速办应用"入选全省数字化改革"一地创新、全省共享"一本账。

2. 提升浙北平原区域适应气候变化能力

浙北平原区域包括杭嘉湖平原和宁绍平原，是全省人口集聚度及城镇化水平最高的地区，交通、能源、水利等网络型基础设施建设较为完备，是全省经济最为发达的区域，加强防洪排涝基础设施建设是平原地区适应气候变化的工作重点。为此，浙江省实施了太嘉河工程、苕溪清水入湖河道整治工程、杭嘉湖地区环湖河道整治工程、扩大杭嘉湖南排工程、西险大塘达标加固工程等一系列重大水利工程，有效提升浙北平原地区适应气候变化能力，将洪涝灾害所带来的损失降到最低，基本形成"洪水北排长江、东出黄浦江、南入杭州湾"的防洪格局。从时间维度上看，2011—2012 年浙江出台《浙江省杭嘉湖圩区整治项目管理办法》《杭嘉湖圩区整治技术导则（试行）》等政策文件，全面指导推进杭嘉湖地区的圩区建设，提升圩区防洪减灾能力和生态环境保护水平；2013 年，浙江作出"五水共治"的重大决策部署，将防洪水、排涝水作为治水重点全面推进，一批防洪排涝骨干工程应运而生；2016 年，浙江省召开百项千亿防洪排涝工作动员大会，提出加快实施百项千亿防洪排涝工程，将全省所有平原排涝能力达到 20 年一遇标准，全面补齐了防洪排涝短板，八大流域干堤达标率由不到 50% 提高至 90%。

同时，为解决浙北平原地区水资源的时空分布不均问题，进一步提升水资源适应气候变化能力，浙江不断优化水资源配置。2021 年，历时 18 年建设的浙东引水工程全线贯通，这是浙江省跨流域跨区域最多、引调水线路最长、受益面最广的水资源战略配置工程，实现了浙东水网重构，在水资源保障、水灾害防御等方面取得了巨大的社会效益和经济效益。

3. 提升浙东沿海地区适应气候变化能力

作为拥有 26 万 km^2 海域面积、海岸线总长度 6 400 多 km 的海洋大省，浙江通过科学实施涉海开发活动、强化海洋生态系统保护修复、加强海洋灾害防御能力建设等路径，不断提升沿海地区和海岸带适应气候变化的韧性。2011 年，国务院批复建设浙江海洋经济发展示范区，这是国家赋予浙江的首个涉海国家战略，掀起了科学实施涉海开发活动的新高潮，沿海各地纷纷编制示范区规划实施方案和重要海域海岛等海洋资源的开发利用与保护方案，统筹推进示范区建设，在这一过程中，适应气候变化和可持续的海洋经济发展格局基本建立。

在海洋生态环境保护提升方面，浙江创新性地开展了近岸海域浮标实时监测，建成国控、省控和市控三级为主的海洋环境监测站网，"陆海"联动污染治理体系基本建立。特别是"十三五"以来，浙江相继开展"蓝色海湾"综合整治行动、生态海岸带建设等系列工作，杭州湾、三门湾、台州湾等湾区生态环境综合治理，以及钱塘江、瓯江、椒江等主要入海河流污染治理和生态工程建设成效更加显著，"十三五"末全省优良海水比例均值达到42.7%。同时，浙江不断完善海洋生态环境保护制度，制定实施海洋主体功能区、海岸线保护利用、无居民海岛保护等规划，有效控制海洋开发强度，建立了海洋生态保护红线制度，划定海洋生态保护红线1.4万 km²。海洋蓝色生态屏障也更加坚实，累计获批国家级海洋生态文明建设示范区4个，建成国家级、省级各类海洋保护地18个，总面积逾4 000 km²。

通过保护提升海洋生态环境来增强海洋及海岸带适应气候的韧性之外，浙江还十分重视海洋灾害防御能力建设。"十二五"期间，浙江省围绕"以防为主、综合减灾"工作理念，实施了海洋灾害综合观测网、预警网、信息服务网、应急指挥体系、风险评估与区划五大工程，初步建成全省海洋灾害应急管理业务体系，在国内率先开展了海洋灾害重点防御区划定、海洋灾害隐患排查、海洋气象观测网建设、海洋灾害风险评估等工作。特别是近年来浙江省加快推进海塘安澜千亿工程，印发实施《浙江省海塘安澜千亿工程建设规划》，加快解决沿海岸线塘身沉降、结构破损等问题，推动海塘安全提标，进一步提高了沿海地区防台防潮能力。

（四）完善气候防灾减灾体系建设

1. 有效完善防灾救灾机制

近年来，受全球气候变暖影响，气候风险持续增加，暴雨洪涝、超强台风、高温热浪等极端天气事件频发，浙江省通过开展气候灾害评估、构建灾害预案体系、完善应急管理制度等措施，不断建立健全防灾救灾机制，有效强化适应气候变化能力。围绕开展气候灾害评估，制定实施浙江省气象灾害调查与风险评估实施细则，完成5个试点县市（3个国家试点县）的气象灾害普查工作。同时，浙江还构建全省人口、经济和水稻等精细化承灾体数据，为气象灾害风险评估区划提供有力支撑。在灾害预案体系建设方面，浙江早在2009年就率先颁发了政府级海洋灾害应急预案——《浙江省海洋灾害应急预案》，对浙江省范围内风暴潮、海啸和赤潮等海洋灾害的预防和应急处置进行了明确的规定。同时浙江还创新数字化智慧防灾应用建设，开发了浙江省静止卫星林火监测系统及 App，提供10分钟频次、85%以上准确性的全省覆盖林火实时监测体系。值得一提的是，浙江省注重开展灾害风险应急管理的制度建设，有效强化灾害风险管理的法制化建设，并构建省、市、县、乡一体的自然灾害应急救助预案体系，同时开发浙江省自然灾害风险防控和应急救援平台，创新建立自然灾害防控"五色图"机制，为各地防灾减灾提供决策支撑。

2. 不断提升灾前预警能力

浙江省一直努力实现从注重灾后救助向注重灾前预防转变，注重加强灾害综合风险监测预警体系建设，特别是结合浙江数字化改革优势，建立了极端天气事件信息管理系统和预警预报发布平台，实现与 18 个横向部门对接和业务化运行，并通过"浙政钉"政务平台向基层干部覆盖，有效提升灾害预警的服务水平。预警预报发布平台的统计显示，浙江在 2021 年出现重大天气过程 31 次，启动应急响应 15 次共 1 514 h，其中一级响应 111.5 h，发布地质灾害、山洪、城市内涝等灾害风险预警 1 395 条，预警服务满意度 95.4 分，居全国第二。此外，浙江还基于预警平台开展强化风险形势研判，组织实施灾害风险调查和重点隐患排查工程，加强自然灾害防治重点工程的统筹协调，同时开展极端天气与气候事件的科学研究，以及高温热浪、暴雨、台风、森林火灾等灾害的防灾减灾措施的研究，以制定新的防御综合灾害的长期规划。

3. 建立健全灾后保障制度

长期以来，浙江省积极提升灾害风险防范水平和灾后救助能力，逐步形成多元化灾害风险分担机制和民生保障体系，重大灾害风险治理水平得到大幅提升。在制度建设方面，浙江省于 2021 年印发实施《关于推进防灾减灾救灾体制机制改革的实施意见》，提出健全灾后恢复重建工作制度，特别是明确要求建立完善灾后保障的组织体系、规划体系、政策体系、实施体系和监管体系。同时，浙江创新性地引入金融保险机制，通过实施农业气象保险机制、创新气象指数保险产品、深化气象保险服务等举措，有效保障农户在极端气候事件中的财产安全。具体来看，农业气象保险方面，出台了《浙江省人民政府办公厅关于加快农业保险高质量发展的实施意见》《浙江省人民政府办公厅进一步加快推动农业保险高质量发展行动方案》等政策文件，强化工作指导，仅在 2021 年，种植险为全省农户提供 342 亿元风险保障，支付赔款 8.0 亿元。同时创新开发低温 / 高温气象指数保险、降雨气象指数保险、干旱指数保险等气象指数类新型险种，为农户应对极端气象变化灾害提供有力风险保障，2021 年，气象指数类保险共为 4.6 万户农户提供 11 亿元的风险保障。此外，浙江还开展了省级层面巨灾保险试点，重点利用大数据等技术实现农户理赔"零次跑""零资料提交"，简化理赔流程，开通绿色理赔通道。

五、结语与展望

浙江作为全国第四大经济省份，也是民营经济大省，温室气体排放规模大，节能降碳任务较重，受气候变化影响显著，绿色低碳转型需求迫切。10 多年来，浙江深入践行"绿水青山就是金山银山"理念，始终保持应对气候变化的战略定力，举全省之力推进"生态省""绿色浙江""生态浙江""美丽浙江""大花园"建设等工作载体迭代升级，应对气候变化工作从认识、理念到实践都发生了历史性、转折性的变化，已基本构建起"双碳"目标体系、工作体系、政策体系、评价体系。

2020 年，习近平总书记考察浙江时，明确要求浙江"生态文明建设要先行示范"。浙江省第十五次党代会报告指出，要高水平推进人与自然和谐共生的现代化，打造生态文明高地。当前，浙江正处于应对气候变化、减少灾害风险和实现可持续发展目标的"决定性十年"，气候治理仍任重道远，必须完整准确全面贯彻新发展理念，坚持"高质量发展是硬任务，能源安全是硬底线，碳排放是硬约束，百姓品质生活是硬需求"原则，将应对气候变化纳入经济社会发展整体布局，重点围绕能耗双控转碳排放"双控"、数智控碳、绿色金融、市场标准准入及绿色技术引领"5 大战略"，聚焦能源结构降碳、产业结构减碳、建筑交通控碳、科技数智低碳、生态系统固碳"5 大路径"，构建具有浙江特色的"5+5"应对气候变化和低碳发展工作体系，加快推动减污降碳协同增效，实现绿色、低碳、循环的高质量可持续发展。

（一）在战略上，突出制度创新，打造绿色低碳循环发展的全国示范样本

一是打造双控制度转型先行区。能耗双控转向碳排放双控已成为未来一段时期内的政策导向，浙江作为美丽中国先行示范区，未来应以此为核心，率先构建系统完备的碳排放政策制度体系。逐步建立碳排放预算管理制度，充分发挥市场化的资源配置和交易机制作用，更灵活、更高效地促进产业和能源结构低碳化、高端化的转型升级。建立起固定资产投资项目碳排放评价制度，研究制定重点行业碳排放评价标准和方法学，从源头上促进投资项目降低能源消耗和减少碳排放。形成较为成熟的碳减排目标分解与监督制度和碳排放统计监测制度，为科学决策提供基础数据支撑。

二是打造"双碳"数智先导区。浙江省"双碳"数字化改革起步早、进展快，未来应在此基础上，迭代升级基础应用和综合应用场景，搭建碳排放智能监测和动态核算体系，加快打造数智控碳体系，形成"目标制定—任务分解—跟踪预警—服务管控—评估整改"闭环管理模式，全面实现政府治碳"一站通"，企业减碳"一网清"，个人低碳"一键惠"。同时，通过平台引导和约束浙江省内各

地按照碳承载力谋划经济产业发展，强化碳生产力布局，实现数智控碳。

三是打造绿色金融转型样板区。高碳行业的低碳转型对于浙江省顺利实现碳中和目标至关重要，转型金融则是助力高碳行业转型的新命题。浙江省作为绿色金融改革创新试验区，未来需实现绿色金融与转型金融的有序有效衔接，加快构建转型金融与绿色金融高效协同体系。构建气候变化投融资体系，创新多元化气候投融资模式，提升气候投融资服务质效和数智化水平，积极创新和应用碳金融产品，发挥投融资对减缓和适应气候变化的支撑作用。创新推出转型相关债券，引导更多的社会资金支持高碳经济活动，包括企业、项目和金融资产向低碳与零碳目标转型，促进实体经济的减排和业务转型，加速全社会实现碳达峰与碳中和目标的进程。

四是打造"双碳"标准集聚区。加快健全"双碳"标准体系，是完善重点领域绿色发展标准化保障，实现标准化生态效益的具体任务。当前，浙江已印发碳达峰碳中和工作标准体系实施方案，未来需实现标准在重点领域全面覆盖。聚焦工业、能源、建筑、交通、农业、居民生活六大领域，从强度、总量、空间、业态、技术等多方面、多维度确定准入标准的管控方向，对标国际国内先进水平，分类分层分批次确定碳排放相关标准，规范碳排放活动，全面构建与浙江省生态文明先行示范相适应的"一总六分"碳达峰碳中和标准体系。

五是打造绿色技术推广示范区。绿色技术创新在应对气候变化和实现碳减排方面，正发挥着关键作用。浙江省科技创新综合实力位列全国第一方阵，未来需借助"315"科技创新体系建设工程，进一步强化绿色技术创新引导。全面构建面向碳中和的浙江省绿色低碳技术创新体系，重点基于 AI、大数据、物联网等数字技术，推动可再生能源、储能、氢能、碳捕集利用与封存（CCUS）、生态碳汇等关键核心技术达到国际先进水平，协同推进能源、工业、交通、建筑等重点领域深度脱碳。积极发挥国家绿色技术交易中心作用，推动跨地区绿色技术成果转化交易，做好绿色发展与创新的大文章。

（二）在路径上，把握工作节奏，有力有序推进碳达峰碳中和

一是推动能源结构深度"降碳"。以能源绿色低碳发展和保供稳价工程为主抓手，围绕清洁能源项目攻坚、外来能源资源提质、能效创新引领、绿色消费促进、市场改革深化"五大核心"，全力推动能源结构转型。重点是优先发展新能源，接续实施"风光倍增"工程，安全有序发展核电，科学发展抽水蓄能，合理布局清洁高效火电，积极争取清洁外来电，加快打造高标准能源设施网。加强煤炭清洁高效利用，推动煤电机组"三改联动"。发挥能效标准引领作用，严守

新上项目 0.52 t 标准煤 / 万元的能效准入标准。分批、分行业对七大行业 4 000 家左右企业开展能效诊断，实行"区域能评 + 产业能效技术标准"准入机制。积极推动绿色电力交易，加大绿色电力证书推广应用。完善"省－市－县－企业"四级用能预算管理机制。深化用能权交易改革，探索建立用能权交易现货市场。推广使用电能替代燃煤、燃油等传统消费方式。

二是推动产业结构持续"减碳"。将产业结构调整作为重要抓手，着力构建绿色低碳循环发展的现代产业体系，推动产业规模和产业结构"凤凰涅槃"，在落实"双碳"目标中锻造新的产业竞争优势。重点是加快培育新兴产业，全力打造 4 个万亿级世界级先进产业群，大力培育 15 个千亿级省级特色产业集群和一批百亿级"新星"产业群，发展光伏、风电、氢能、储能等新能源产业。持续推进国家传统制造业改造升级示范区建设，实施七大重点用能行业碳达峰专项行动，推动重点行业绿色低碳转型。健全完善绿色制造分级培育机制，深入推进流程系统节能改造，打造绿色制造标准体系。以数字化引领工业节能降碳，大力发展"产业大脑 + 未来工厂"新范式，推进工业企业、细分行业、产业集群数字化转型。

三是推动建筑交通全面"控碳"。建筑方面，聚焦减少建筑能耗和优化建筑用能结构"两个关键"。重点是加快推进绿色低碳建筑迭代升级，制修订《超低能耗居住建筑节能设计标准》《绿色生态城区评价标准》等。加快推行新型建筑工业化，推广绿色建材应用及绿色施工。加大新能源新建建筑的可再生能源应用力度，重点推进太阳能光伏发电、空气源热泵、太阳能光热等在新建建筑中的应用。交通运输方面，迭代升级运输结构、交通装备、组织效率等"交通全链条"，重点是以"四港"联动发展为核心，加强"铁公水""江海河"等联运枢纽建设，重点推进义甬舟开放大通道建设，着力打造宁波—金华国家综合货运枢纽补链强链城市（群）、中欧班列华东集结中心、衢州四省边际联运枢纽、嘉兴海河联运枢纽等重大平台。通过综合性政策引导，加快推动公共交通高频运输车辆更新和老旧营运车船淘汰。推动城市交通综合治理，大力发展慢行交通及共享单车等共享交通模式。

四是推动科技数智助力"低碳"。一方面，要抢占绿色低碳科技创新制高点，重点是深入实施"双尖双顶"计划，围绕零碳电力、零碳非电能源、零碳流程重塑，零碳系统耦合、碳普及利用与封存及碳汇等方向，创新科研攻关机制，采用揭榜挂帅、赛马制、择优委托等方式，抓紧部署低碳前沿技术研究。加快建设能源领域省实验室，加强能源清洁利用、含氟温室气体替代及控制处理等国家重点实验室建设，打造国内领先的低碳技术创新集聚区。深化国家绿色技术交易中心建设，推动碳达峰碳中和技术转化利用。落实国家绿色技术创新"十百千"行动，强化技术产业协同发展。另外，要发挥浙江数字化改革优势，深化"双碳"智治平台建设。探索建设产品碳足迹数据库，推动统计、电力、用能等数据入仓，指导衢州推动碳账户体系提质扩面，强化区域及重点领域碳排放动态监测和预测预警功能，完善服务端功能，助力企业降碳、个人低碳。

五是推动生态系统有效"固碳"。浙江省拥有丰富的森林、海洋、湿地等自然生态资源，具有巨大的"固碳"潜力。要发挥好绿色生态优势，严守生态保护红线，强化国土空间规划和用途管控，构建有利于碳达峰碳中和的国土空间开发保护格局。要持续深入开展蓝天、碧水、净土攻坚行动，坚持源头治污、精准治污、科学治污、依法治污，集中力量解决突出环境问题，切实筑牢生态安全屏障。要加强山水林田湖草沙生命共同体建设，抓紧实施重要生态系统保护和修复重大工程，扎实开展国土绿化、森林质量提升、生物多样性保护等重大行动，构建以国家公园为主体的自然保护地体系，充分发挥森林、海洋、湿地、湖泊、土壤等固碳作用，全面提升生态系统的碳汇增量。

作者：浙江省经济信息中心著作组

"四个维度"平衡视角下浙江省应对气候变化和低碳发展进展评估

碳达峰碳中和国家战略对区域的低碳发展评估提出了新要求。本章围绕经济发展、能源安全、碳排放、居民生活 4 个维度，构建涵盖碳减排、经济社会发展，尤其是公正转型在内的多维度的应对气候变化和低碳发展评估体系，并开展省级对标、市级对比的实证分析。发现浙江应对气候变化和低碳发展实现平稳提升，与广东相似，除能源安全和碳汇增汇两个受资源禀赋影响较大的维度外，其余维度均不断提升。浙江省 11 个设区市低碳高质量发展程度呈不断提高趋势，杭州、温州、丽水排名靠前。后续可从拓展和完善评价指标、扩大评估范围、改进评估方法等方面改进完善。

一、引言

开展区域的低碳发展评价是较为常见的学术研究议题，不论在评价指标选取上，还是方法选择上，都已有较为成熟的范式。而本研究的开展，即"四个维度"平衡视角下浙江省应对气候变化和低碳发展进展评估，仍存在 3 个不同点。一是浙江作为"绿水青山就是金山银山"理念发源地，绿色低碳发展历来为其重视，而以浙江省为对象的低碳发展评价仍较为少见，尤其是将省与省比较、市与市比较并行开展的尚未能见到。但毫无疑问的是，作这一比较本身是有必要的，也是有意义的。二是本章所作评估被冠以"四个维度"，即浙江省在推进碳达峰碳中和工作中持续强调必须做好经济发展、能源安全、碳排放、居民生活 4 个维度的综合平衡。也是因此，本章所作的评价也就不再是拘泥于降碳减碳的评价，而是更多关注其与社会经济发展的相互影响，比如就业、可支配收入等涉及公正转型的内容。三是在碳达峰碳中和工作推进已有两年有余之际，对于碳排放、碳减排的认识亦有进步，如按浙江做法，则有必要将碳排放对应分解至能源、工业、建筑、交通、农业、居民生活 6 个领域，并分别考察其总量、效率、质量等维度的特征，这些共同构成为区域碳排放的主要特征，而这些特征是开展低碳发展评价的起步点。

考察近来有关低碳发展评价相关之文献，主要可分为两个方向。一是在指标选取上，主要可分为三类。第一类评价了经济社会情况，同时还评价了其中公正转型相关指标，比如参考文献 [1]；第二类仅评价碳排放情况，不涉及经济社会发展，比如参考文献 [2]、[3]、[8]、[9]；第三类在评价碳排放情况基础上，纳入了经济社会评价指标，但不涉及公正转型相关指标，比如参考文献 [4]、[5]、[6]、[7]、[10]。由此，将公正转型相关指标与碳排放绩效联合考虑评价的研究仍较为鲜见。本章的指标选取将结合前述研究，将评价指标以碳排放为基础，打开为各领域特征，同时增加经济社会发展相关评价指标，尤其是与公正转型密切相关的评价指标。二是在评价方法上，主要可概括为两类，一类采用了 TOPSIS 及其改进的相关方法 [3]、[4]、[7]、[8]、[9]；另外一类采用了其他方法，而这些方法相对略显分化，主要有耦合协调度模型 [1]，Dagum 基尼系数及其分解、Kernel 密度估计、二次指派程序相结合的方法 [2]，模糊评价方法 [5]，简单加权方法 [6]，动态综合测度模型与区域差异法相结合的方法 [10]。由此可见，TOPSIS 仍是较为主流的方法。值得注意的是，TOPSIS 方法涉及指标的权重确定问题，相关研究较多采用了熵权法及其改进方法 [3]、[4]、[7]、[8]、[9]，这更多是由于该方法确定权重具有客观性。而作为对实际情况更为熟悉的背景，本章将直接采用主观权重。

本章主要围绕经济发展、能源安全、碳排放、居民生活 4 个维度，打开碳排放领域特征，引入公正转型相关指标，构建低碳发展评价指标体系。同时，创新构建两级的 TOPSIS 评价方法体系。后续内容安排如下：第二部分介绍评估指标、评估方法，第三部分介绍浙江与江苏、山东、福建、广东的评价结果及其比较，第四部分介绍浙江省内 11 个设区市的评价结果及其比较，第五部分做出结论，给出下一步展望。

二、评估指标体系与方法

（一）评估指标

参照相关研究，结合浙江省实际情况，设立维度 – 指标的两级评估指标体系。其中，维度共有 10 个，第 1 个维度是经济发展，第 2 个维度是能源安全，第 3～9 个维度是碳排放下各领域，第 10 个维度是百姓生活。下面分别论述。

1. 经济发展维度

经济发展维度主要包括 3 个指标。

碳排放脱钩指数，即碳排放增速相对 GDP 增速的比值，测度经济发展对碳排放的依赖程度。在经济发展、GDP 增速为正的情况下，该指标越小越好。当大于 1 时，说明碳排放增速大于 GDP 增速，经济处于高碳化进程；当位于 0 和 1 区间时，说明碳排放增速小于 GDP 增速，经济处于低碳转型中；当等于 0 时，代表碳排放量不再增长；当小于 0 时，代表碳排放量出现下降。

R&D 经费投入强度，即 R&D 经费与 GDP 的比值。科技创新是推动实现碳达峰碳中和的关键变量，而要确保科技创新的产出，就需要有力的科技创新投入。

企业法人数量增长率，即企业法人数量的同比增长率，测度在推进碳达峰碳中和进程中，对营商环境造成的影响。若带来不利影响，则可能导致企业法人数量减少。

2. 能源安全维度

能源安全维度主要包括 2 个指标。

可再生能源利用率，采用非水可再生能源发电量 / 非水可再生能源装机量测度，主要体现能源系统的低碳化程度。由于全国都在建设可再生能源的高潮期，对其利用水平予以评价，以避免相关资产搁浅。

电力自给率，采用外调入电力 / 电力消费总量测度，主要体现区域内电力可以自我保供的程度。

3. 能源领域碳减排

能源领域碳减排主要包含 3 个指标。各领域碳减排指标一般都是 3 个，分别代表碳排放的效率、碳排放的结构，以及对该部门就业的影响。后者是公正转型的一个具象刻画。

单位能源碳排放，采用地区的碳排放量 / 能源消费量测度，主要体现能源系统的低碳化程度。

煤炭消费占比，采用地区的终端煤炭消费碳排放 / 碳排放量测度，主要体现碳排放的能源结构。为避免大型电源项目的影响，只考虑终端消费用煤的占比。

能源领域就业增长，采用能源领域就业增速 / 常住人口增速，主要体现碳减排对能源部门就业的影响。要保持全社会就业比例不下降，则就业人口增速须不低于常住人口增速，若就业人口增速低于常住人口增速，则表明该部门就业将拉低全体常住人口的就业率。

4. 工业领域碳减排

工业领域碳减排主要包含 3 个指标。

单位工业增加值碳排放，采用地区的工业领域碳排放／工业增加值测度，主要体现为单位增加值的产出需要依赖多少量的碳排放。

战略性新兴产业增加值增速，主要体现工业结构的低碳化程度。战略性新兴产业相较于其他工业行业具有更高的碳生产力，规模的扩大将带动工业部门单位增加值碳排放下降。

工业领域就业增长，同能源领域对应指标。

5. 建筑领域碳减排

建筑领域碳减排主要包含 3 个指标。

建筑领域单位增加值碳排放，采用地区的建筑领域碳排放／工业增加值测度，主要体现为 1 单位增加值的产出需要依赖多少量的碳排放。由于建筑领域包括建筑业、公共建筑两个部门，碳排放、增加值也是两个部门之和。

建筑领域电力碳排放占比，主要体现建筑用能结构的低碳化程度。相较于其他能源，电力具有相对较低的碳排放因子，且仍处于持续下降进程中。扩大电力使用占比，将可在不降低能耗的情况下降低碳排放。

建筑领域就业增长，同能源领域对应指标。

6. 交通领域碳减排

交通领域碳减排主要包含 3 个指标。

单位运输周转量碳排放，采用地区的交通运输业碳排放／货物运输周转量测度，主要体现为 1 单位货物运输周转量的产出需要依赖多少量的碳排放。交通领域包括营运交通、非营运交通，这里只考虑营运交通部分。

交通领域电力碳排放占比，主要体现交通用能结构的低碳化程度。

交通领域就业增长，同能源领域对应指标。

7. 农业领域碳减排

农业领域碳减排主要包含 2 个指标。农业领域排放量较小，不再考虑结构指标。

单位农业增加值碳排放，采用地区的农业碳排放／农业增加值，主要体现为 1 单位农业增加值的产出需要依赖多少量的碳排放。

农业领域就业增长，同能源领域对应指标。

8. 居民生活领域碳减排

居民生活领域碳减排主要包含 3 个指标。

人均生活用电量，采用地区的居民生活用电量／常住人口，主要体现居民的生活质量。在居民生活非移动源用能几乎全部为电的情况下，生活电力用量一定程度上可代表生活质量水平。

常住人口城镇化率，主要体现常住人口结构的低碳化程度。按已有研究，由于更为集聚，城镇居民通常具有更低的人均生活碳排放。在一定的总常住人口下，城镇化率提升有助于降低碳排放。

居民总体就业增长，采用就业人口增速/常住人口增速测度，意义同能源等领域，主要测度推行碳减排对全体居民的就业影响。

9. 碳汇领域增汇

碳汇领域增汇主要包含 2 个指标。

人均森林面积，主要测度人均森林资源。

森林覆盖率，主要测度森林资源。

10. 百姓生活维度

百姓生活维度主要包含 3 个指标。

人均可支配收入，主要体现碳减排对收入值的影响。

经济发展成果共享程度，采用人均可支配收入占人均 GDP 比重，主要体现碳减排对经济发展成果共享的影响。碳减排通常具有规模效应和资本密集的特点，很有可能随着碳减排的推进，工资性收入在 GDP 中的比重出现降低，这与公正转型是背道而驰的。

$PM_{2.5}$，主要体现碳减排对生态环境的影响。

以上合计 10 个维度、27 个指标见表 2-1。

表 2-1 "四个维度"平衡视角下应对气候变化和低碳发展进展评估指标体系

维度	指标	测度含义	计算方法	备注
经济发展	碳排放脱钩指数	经济发展对碳排放的依赖程度	碳排放增速相对经济增速的比值	—
	R&D 经费投入强度	科技创新对碳减排的支撑	—	—
	企业法人数量增长率	碳减排对营商环境的影响	企业法人数的同比增长率	—
能源安全	可再生能源利用率	能源低碳化	非水可再生能源发电量/非水可再生能源装机量	不适用于设区市
	电力自给率	能源安全保供	外调入电力/电力消费总量	不适用于设区市
能源领域碳减排	单位能源碳排放	能源低碳发展质量	碳排放量/能源消费量	—
	煤炭消费占比	用能结构的低碳化	终端煤炭消费碳排放/碳排放量	—
	能源领域就业增长	碳减排对能源部门就业的影响	能源领域就业增速/常住人口增速	—

维度	指标	测度含义	计算方法	备注
工业领域碳减排	单位工业增加值碳排放	工业低碳发展质量	—	—
	战略性新兴产业增加值增速	工业结构低碳化	—	—
	工业领域就业增长	碳减排对工业部门就业的影响	工业领域就业增速/常住人口增速	—
建筑领域碳减排	建筑领域单位增加值碳排放	建筑低碳发展质量	—	—
	建筑领域电力碳排放占比	建筑用能结构低碳化	—	—
	建筑领域就业增长	碳减排对建筑部门就业的影响	建筑领域就业增速/常住人口增速	—
交通领域碳减排	单位运输周转量碳排放	交通低碳发展质量	—	—
	交通领域电力碳排放占比	交通用能结构低碳化	—	—
	交通领域就业增长	碳减排对交通部门就业的影响	交通领域就业增速/常住人口增速	—
农业领域碳减排	单位农业增加值碳排放	农村低碳发展质量	—	—
	农业领域就业增长	碳减排对农业部门就业的影响	农业领域就业增速/常住人口增速	—
居民生活领域碳减排	人均生活用电量	居民生活质量	—	—
	常住人口城镇化率	居民结构低碳化	—	—
	居民总体就业增长	碳减排对整体就业的影响	就业人口增速/常住人口增速	—
碳汇领域增汇	人均森林面积	人均森林资源	—	—
	森林覆盖率	森林资源	—	—
百姓生活	人均可支配收入	碳减排对收入的影响	—	—
	经济发展成果共享程度	碳减排对经济发展成果共享的影响	人均可支配收入占人均GDP比重	—
	$PM_{2.5}$	碳减排对生态环境的影响,与大气污染物的协同减排	—	—

(二)评估方法

采用两级 TOPSIS 方法。

1. 第一级计算

对于各维度分别进行计算其相对接近度。此时，理想解、负理想解采用各评价单元的最大值或最小值的组合。用 i 表示指标序号，用 j 表示评价单元序号，主要步骤如下：

（1）标准化

对于正向指标，

$$x_{ij} = \frac{X_{ij} - \min\limits_{j}(X_{ij})}{\max\limits_{j}(X_{ij}) - \min\limits_{j}(X_{ij})} \qquad (2-1)$$

对于负向指标，

$$x_{ij} = \frac{\max\limits_{j}(X_{ij}) - X_{ij}}{\max\limits_{j}(X_{ij}) - \min\limits_{j}(X_{ij})} \qquad (2-2)$$

（2）选取理想解、负理想解

理想解

$$Z^+ = (x_1^+, \cdots, x_n^+), \qquad (2-3)$$

其中

$$x_i^+ = \max_{j}(x_{ij}) \qquad (2-4)$$

负理想解

$$Z^- = (x_1^-, \cdots, x_n^-), \qquad (2-5)$$

其中

$$x_i^- = \min_{j}(x_{ij}) \qquad (2-6)$$

（3）计算各单元到理想解、负理想解的距离

到理想解的距离为

$$d_j^+ = \sqrt{\sum_i w_i (x_{ij} - x_i^+)^2} \qquad (2-7)$$

到负理想解的距离为

$$d_j^- = \sqrt{\sum_i w_i (x_{ij} - x_i^-)^2} \qquad (2-8)$$

（4）计算各评价单元的相对接近度

各评价单元的相对接近度为

$$s_j = \frac{d_j^-}{d_j^- + d_j^+}\text{。} \qquad (2-9)$$

注意到

$$d_j^+ \text{、} d_j^- > 0, \forall j$$

因此有

$$\frac{0}{d_j^- + d_j^+} \leqslant s_j = \frac{d_j^-}{d_j^- + d_j^+} \leqslant \frac{d_j^-}{d_j^- + 0}, \qquad (2-10)$$

即有 $0 \leqslant s_j \leqslant 1$。当取 0 时，评价单元与负理想解重合，即其在所有维度均为最差值；当取 1 时，评价单元与理想解重合，即其在所有维度均为最优值。

2. 第二级计算

主要步骤同第一级计算。由于相对接近度理论上区间为 [0，1]，因而将理

想解固定为各分项均为 1，同理负理想解各分项固定为 0，再次计算集成各维度的相对接近度，作为各省市和设区市应对气候变化和低碳发展的综合评价结果。

三、省级评估及比较

（一）总体评估结果及其演变

选取与浙江省经济体量接近、发展进程相似的 4 个沿海省份——江苏、山东、福建、广东作为评估对象，开展省级低碳发展进展评价。

从整体趋势看，可以将 5 个省份分为 3 种类型，即稳定型、平稳提升型和波动增长型（图 2-1）。福建省属于稳定型，其低碳发展相对接近度稳定维持在 0.6～0.62，在 5 个省份中始终保持先进水平。平稳提升型包括浙江省和广东省，2016—2020 年，其相对接近度始终保持增长，并且两省整体相对接近度接近，浙江省在 2020 年相对接近度排名第一，超过了过去 4 年一直排名第一的福建省，广东省排名第三。波动增长型包括江苏省和山东省，两省在 2018 年相对接近度最低，之后在 2020 年又明显提升，排名在 5 个省份中未发生变动。

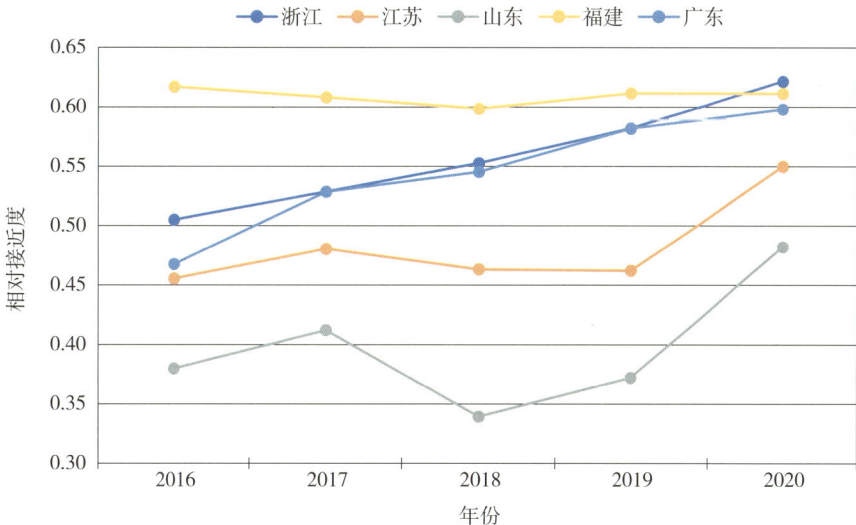

图 2-1　五省份相对接近度变化趋势

出现不同相对接近度波动可能与各省份选择的发展方式不同有关（图 2-2～图 2-6）。福建选择了保守型发展模式，在领域碳减排中保持平稳发展，且分维度的相对接近度波动较小，始终保持平稳向上趋势。平稳提升型省份在大多数领域均实现了相对接近度的不断增加，从而稳步推进整体的低碳发展。浙江省除能源安全和碳汇增汇领域外，其他领域均不断向绿色低碳发展。而广东省除工业领域碳减排外，均能实现低碳发展的稳步推进。碳减排波动增长型则选择先激进发展后治理的模式，尤其在 2020 年整体低碳发展水平明显提高。

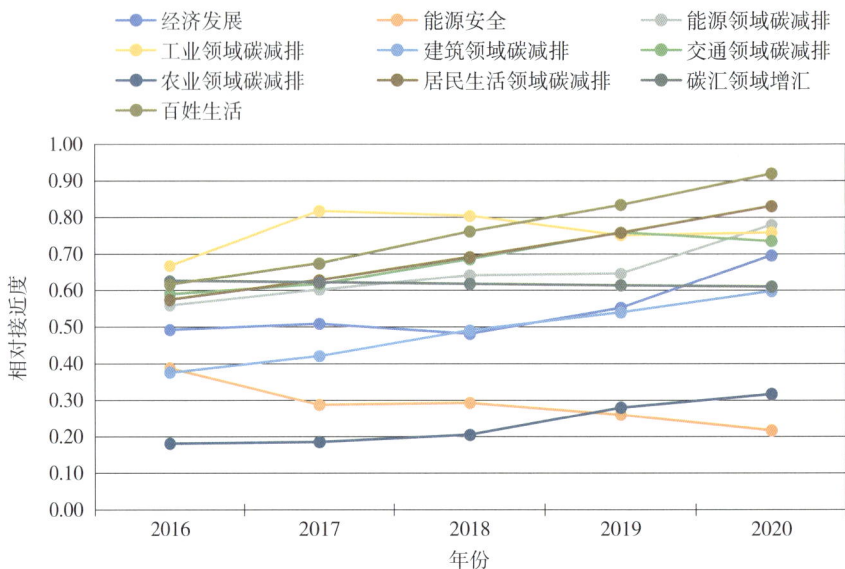

图 2-2　浙江省分维度相对接近度趋势

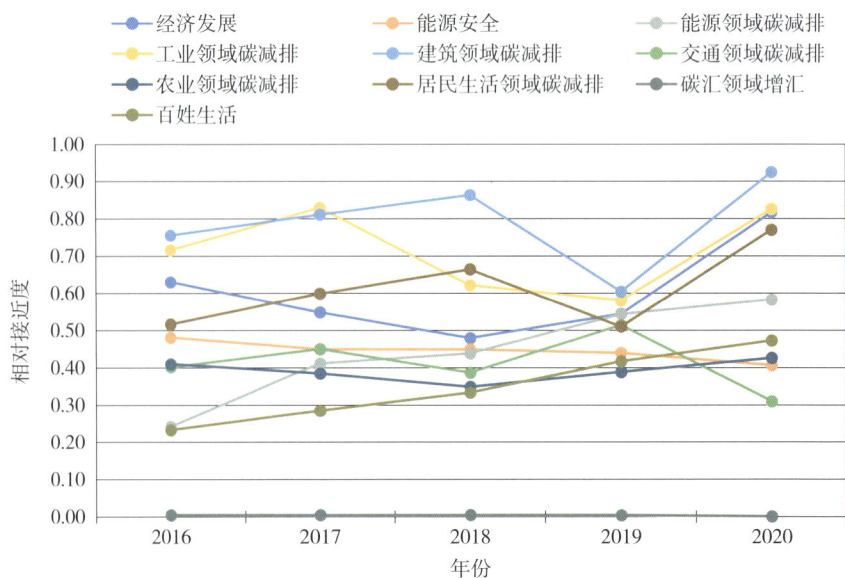

图 2-3　江苏省分维度相对接近度趋势

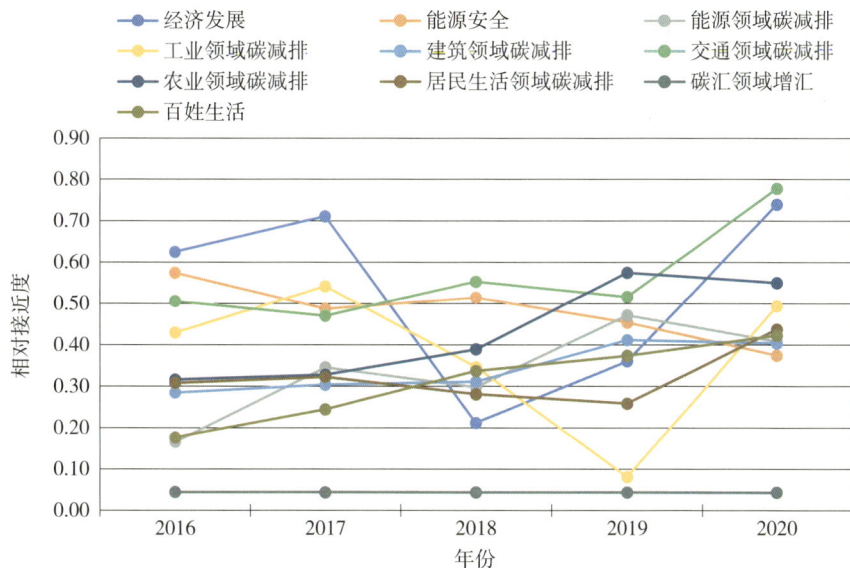

图 2-4　山东省分维度相对接近度趋势

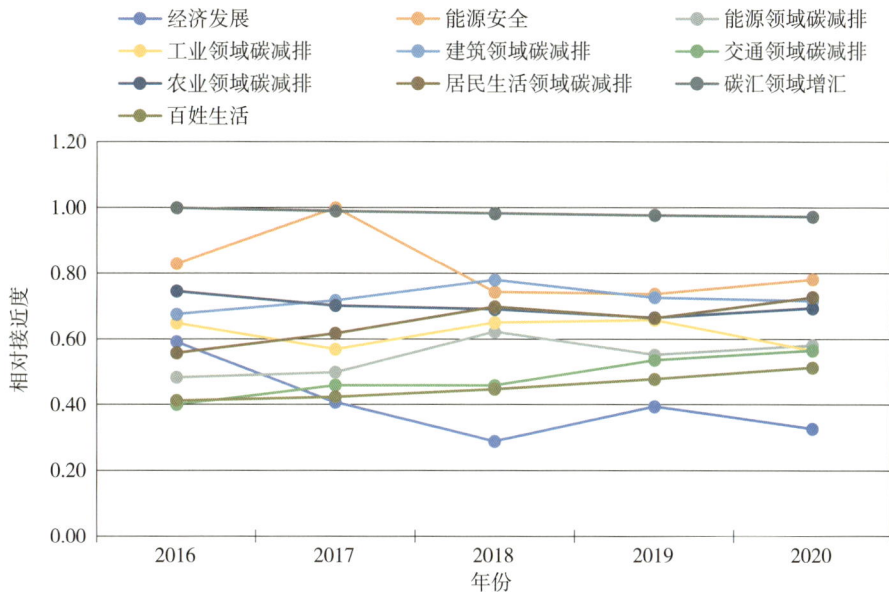

图 2-5　福建省分维度相对接近度趋势

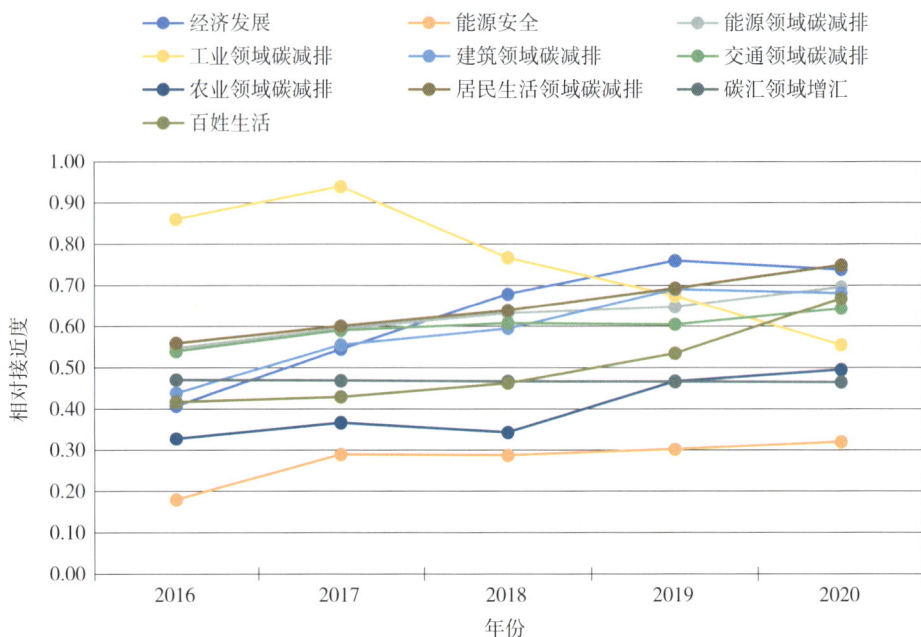

图 2-6　广东省分维度相对接近度趋势

（二）分维度评估结果及其演变

从经济发展看（图 2-7），五省份间变化波动较大。浙江和江苏两省呈现相似的发展情况，"十三五"期间呈现"U"形发展，即 2016—2018 年相对接近度不断下降，之后不断增长，整体形势较 2016 年趋向更好发展，这与两省碳排放脱钩指数呈现弱脱钩，甚至强脱钩有关。而广东则呈现倒"U"形，经济发展相对接近度在 2019 年前不断增长，在 2020 年有轻微下降，但整体增长幅度最大，与其优化营商环境和科研投入，吸引更多先进企业在广东发展密切相关。山东省呈现增长—下降—再增长的趋势，尽管波动较大，但经济绿色发展水平仍然在"十三五"期间有所提升，这也与山东省整体低碳发展趋势接近。而与其他省份不同，福建省在"十三五"期间经济绿色发展水平波动下降，排名从 2016 年第三位跌至 2020 年的最后一位，这与其经济发展与碳排放之间的脱钩程度不足相关，尤其是在 2020 年，受到新冠肺炎疫情影响，其碳排放增速超过经济增速，导致整体相对接近度偏低。

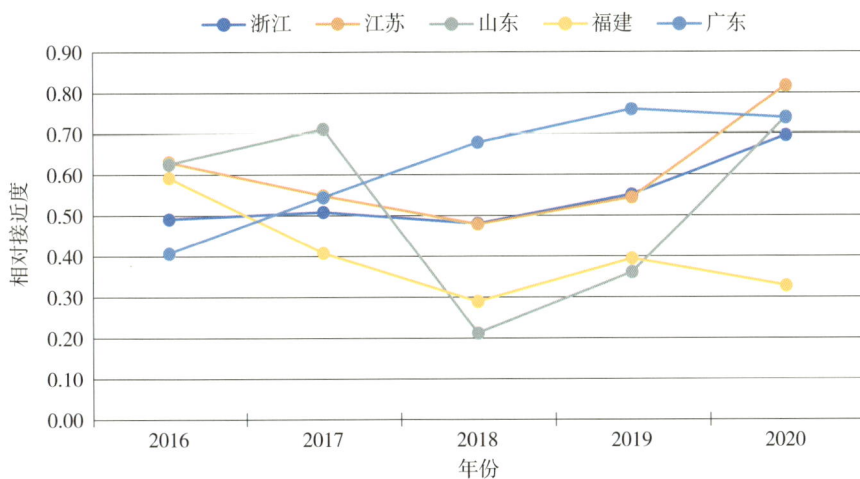

图 2-7 经济发展相对接近度趋势

从能源安全看（图 2-8），除广东外，其他地区能源安全发展均有下行趋势。能源安全发展主要考虑可再生能源发展及电力自给程度，评价省份中仅有福建省因核电等建设实现了电力自给自足，其他省市仍然部分依赖于外来电力，能源安全维度福建省排名始终保持第一。对于浙江、江苏和山东三省，尽管整体上可再生能源发电 / 装机量不断提升，但是受到煤炭消费控制目标约束，火电供给存在不足，为保障民生和产业发展安全，导致必须引入大量的外来电力，2016—2020 年外来电消费占比持续增长，对外依赖程度不断加深，电力供给风险增加。广东省大力发展可再生能源，从而减少对外调电力的依赖，外来电占比从 2016 年的 33% 下降到 2020 年的 22%，能源安全得到较好保障。

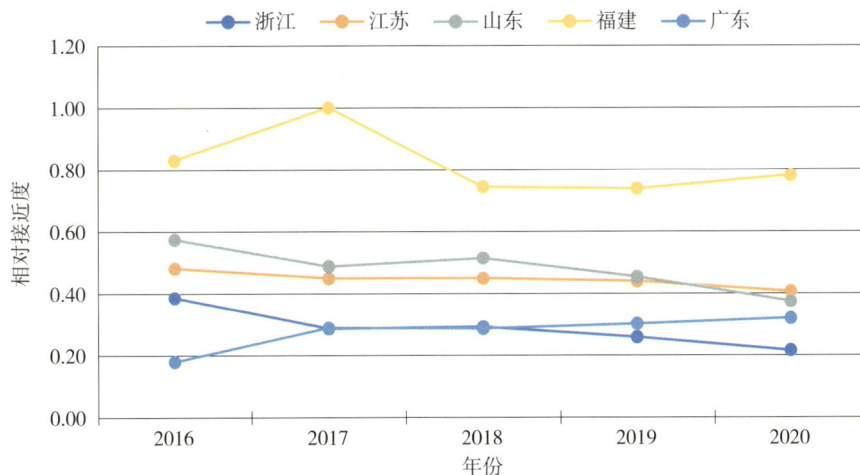

图 2-8 能源安全相对接近度趋势

从能源领域碳减排看（图 2-9），全部省份能源领域碳减排实现整体优化。能源结构优化是实现能源领域碳减排的关键，伴随能耗双控、煤炭消费控制等政策的深入开展和优化，全部省份的煤炭消费占比都实现持续下降，高碳能源消费减少，大部分区域的单位能源碳排放量均持续降低。浙江省煤炭消费占比在 2020 年下降到 6.38%，是占比最低的省份，单位能源碳排放也不断减少，在能源碳减排评价中排名第一。推动能源领域碳减排有序进行的同时也需考虑其对产业发展的影响，以行业就业变动与常住人口变动的比例作为衡量指标，发现在部分年份能源行业就业人员减少。

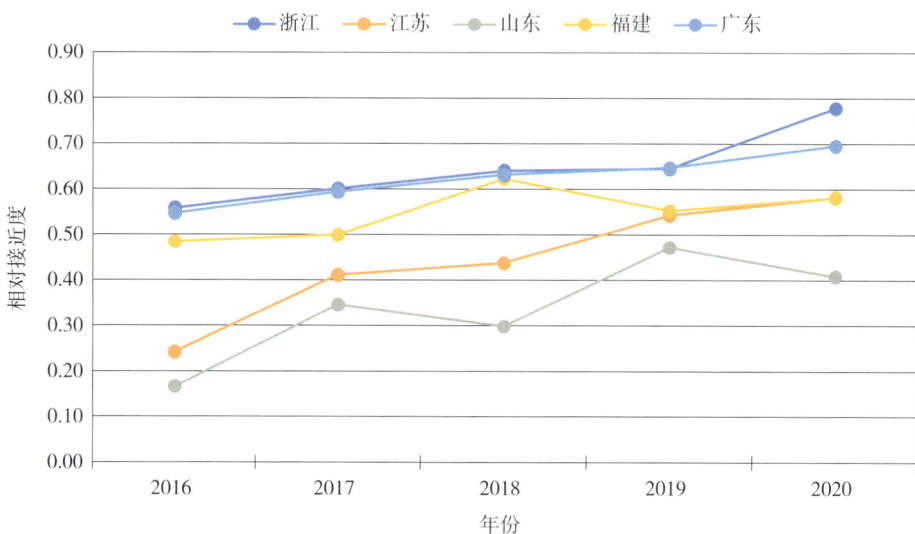

图 2-9　能源领域碳减排相对接近度趋势

从工业领域碳减排看（图 2-10），因产业结构和发展方向产生差异。从工业碳排放强度角度，浙江、江苏、福建和广东都实现整体下降，碳效水平得到明显提升，有利于工业领域碳减排，而山东省工业能耗强度 2016—2019 年明显增长，在 2020 年有所回落，但整体有所增长，与山东省产业结构整体偏重有关，也因此山东省工业领域碳减排排名处于末位。广东省工业领域碳减排评价自 2017 年后持续下降，与战略性新兴产业增加值增速自 2017 年后持续下降有关。战略性新兴产业一般为低碳高效产业，有利于工业产业结构的整体优化，产业增长放缓对拉动产业低碳化发展的力度可能存在不足。同时，伴随整体产业结构的优化调整和技术升级，在工业领域的就业人数持续减少，随着碳减排要求的提高，吸纳就业的能力可能降低。

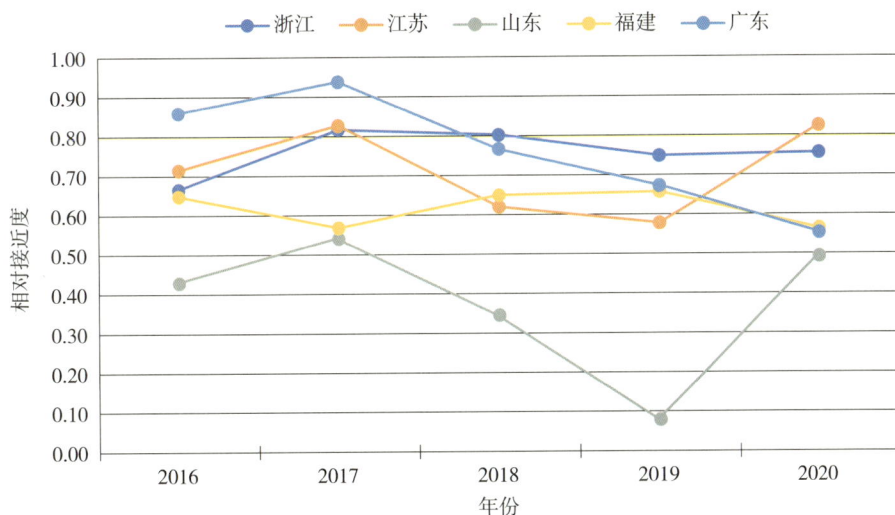

图 2-10　工业领域碳减排相对接近度趋势

从建筑领域碳减排看（图 2-11），随着电气化程度和碳效提升，所有省份在建筑领域的碳减排工作不断优化。从建筑领域单位增加值碳排放看，所有省份均不断降低，意味着建筑领域碳效水平不断提升，但省份之间因电气化程度基础差异较大，导致相对接近度差异较大。江苏省建筑领域电力碳排放占比在五省之间最高，超过了 90%，而平均水平最低的山东省最高也仅达到 58.1%（2019 年）。同时，从相对接近度变化看，广东省是提升最大的省份，一方面广东省建筑领域电力碳排放占比 2020 年较 2016 年增长约 9.2 个百分点，增长幅度明显，另一方面，在建筑领域不断推动减排的过程中，广东省建筑领域就业人员增速也超过常住人口增速，意味着领域发展有所扩张，实现了减排与发展协同。

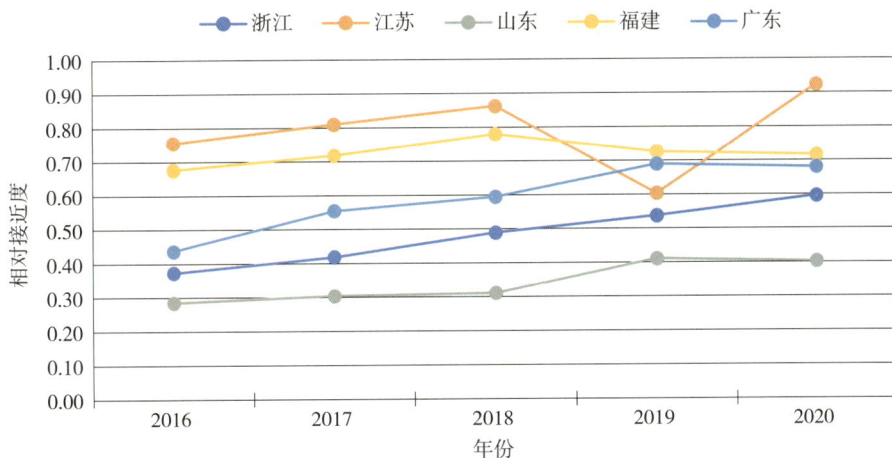

图 2-11　建筑领域碳减排相对接近度趋势

从交通领域碳减排看（图 2-12），除江苏外，其他省份相对接近度均有提升。交通领域碳减排主要考虑单位运输周转量碳排放及交通领域电力碳排放占比。浙江省交通领域碳减排相对接近度明显增加，并在 2020 年前始终保持领先优势，主要由于整体交通运输周转量碳排放较低，并且交通业电气化率不断上升，2020 年电力碳排放占比达到 10.3%。与浙江省状况相似的还有同为快递大省的广东，其相对接近度不断提高，但整体低于浙江，主要差别在于交通领域电气化水平提升速度低于浙江，导致排名也始终低于浙江。山东省的相对接近度波动最大，同时增量也最高，尤其在 2020 年，山东省单位运输周转量碳排放较 2019 年增长 23%，运输清洁化水平明显提高，使得其碳减排取得有效成果。而江苏省尽管单位周转量碳排放和电气水平均不断提升，但在 2020 年，运输业受疫情影响严重，导致大量就业人员流失，行业明显萎缩，造成 2020 年相对接近度下降。

图 2-12 交通领域碳减排相对接近度趋势

从农业领域碳减排看（图 2-13），伴随农机更新换代和高标准农田建设，农业领域碳减排初步取得成效。从相对接近度排名看，福建省始终排名第一，主要由于福建农业有较好的资源禀赋，名优产品较多，农产品附加值高，因此其单位农业增加值碳排放远低于其他省份。但是，近年来从事农业生产的人员不断减少，导致农业安全保障不足，使得其相对接近度有所减少。相对接近度增长多的是山东省，其单位农业增加值碳排放下降约 25.9%，也是下降最多的省份。而浙江省农业领域碳减排相对接近度排名最低，单位农业增加值碳排放最高，这与浙江省农田少、地形复杂、机械作业需求高相关，同时也需要持续加强农机迭代，提高农业碳效水平。

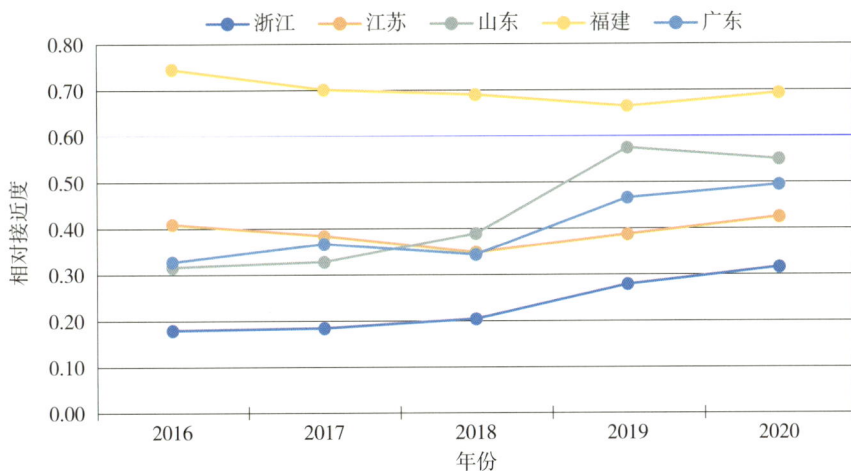

图 2-13　农业领域碳减排相对接近度趋势

从居民生活领域碳减排看（图 2-14），除山东省外，其他四省相对接近度较为接近。5 个省份的居民生活领域碳减排的相对接近度均整体提升，到 2020 年，除山东省外，其他省份的相对接近度均超过 0.7。山东省相对接近度偏低主要由于两方面原因，一是城镇化率可以促进生活和产业聚集，带来能效水平提升，而山东省城镇化率在各省中偏低；二是山东省就业形势较差，对居民生活产生影响。浙江居民生活领域碳减排的相对接近度增长最多，并且在 2020 年排名第一，这与浙江省城镇化率较高，且居民生活电气水平较高有关。

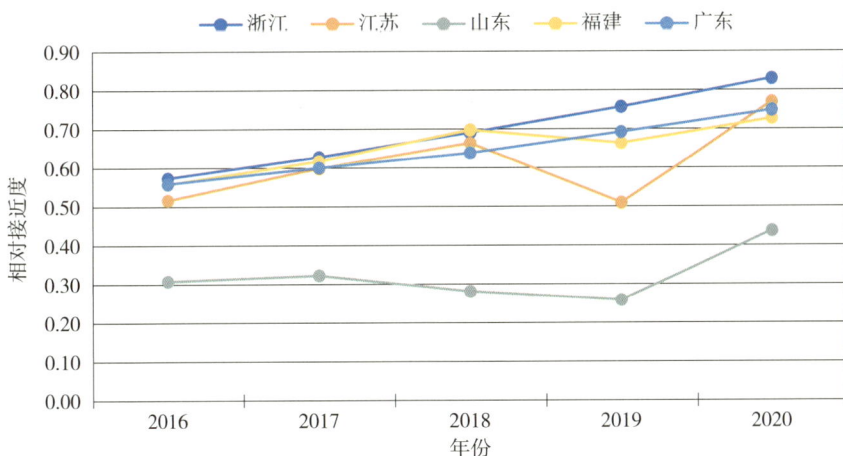

图 2-14　居民生活领域碳减排相对接近度趋势

从碳汇领域看（图 2-15），区域资源禀赋基本决定了碳汇增汇情况。福建省人均森林面积达到 0.2 hm^2，比浙江省多出近 1 倍，比人均森林面积最少的江苏省多出近 9 倍，并且森林覆盖率高达 66.8%，因此福建碳汇增汇相对接近度最高。浙江省作为人均森林面积和森林覆盖率均排名第二，相对接近度排名第二。福建和浙江两省伴随城市建设用地的情况，导致人均森林面积有所减少，相对接近度有所减少。其他地区碳汇领域增汇相对接近度排名也与森林面积和覆盖率排名一致，且由于森林面积增长缓慢，相对接近度变化较小。

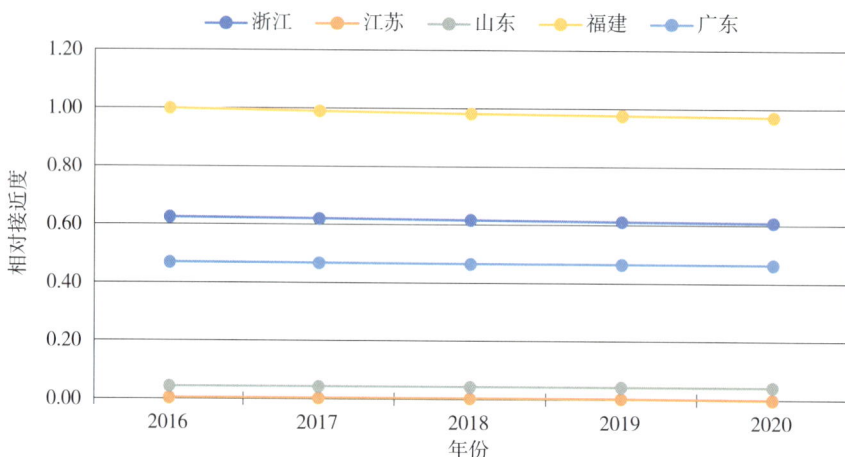

图 2-15 碳汇领域增汇相对接近度趋势

从百姓生活看（图2-16），经济发展和生态环境改善带来百姓生活水平不断提高。浙江省百姓生活相对接近度排名第一，并且相对接近度增长最为明显，作为共同富裕示范区，坚持"藏富于民"的原则，居民人均可支配收入在2020年达到5.4万元，占人均GDP比重超过50%。其他省份的百姓生活相对接近度排名依次为广东、福建、江苏和山东，其中江苏是人均可支配收入排名第二的省份，但是由于占人均GDP比重偏低并且空气质量在各省中排名偏后，造成了江苏百姓生活排名靠后。

图 2-16 百姓生活相对接近度趋势

四、设区市评估及比较

（一）总体评估结果及其演变

对浙江省 11 个设区市 2016—2021 年年度评估结果进行分析（图 2-17），整体来看，全省各设区市在过去 6 年间，虽然在新冠疫情期间，受经济发展变化影响，有一个较为明显的波动，但低碳高质量发展程度仍然在不断提高。

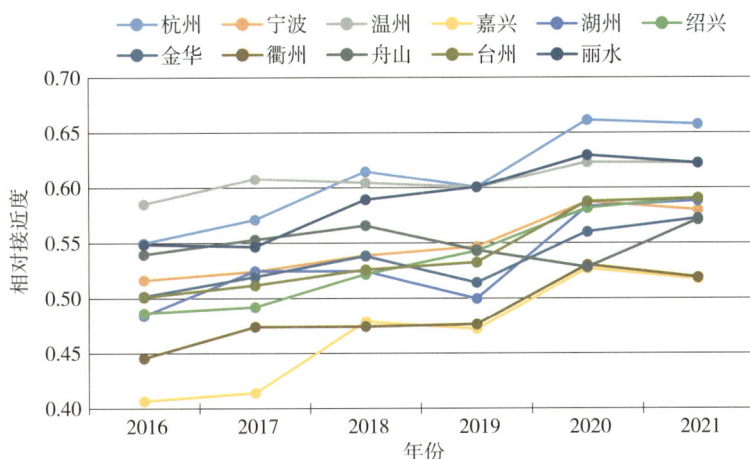

图 2-17　设区市 2016—2021 年低碳高质量发展评估变化

从总体评估结果来看，当前杭州、温州、丽水整体低碳高质量发展程度排名靠前，衢州、嘉兴处在较靠后的位置。杭州作为省会城市，经济发展与居民生活质量较好，能源、工业、建筑、交通等重要领域的用能结构与碳生产力相对较好；温州整体在经济发展上有较好的基础，能源领域碳排放结构逐步优化，煤炭消费在能源领域的比重逐年下降。丽水在碳汇领域和能源结构上有较为突出的优势，同时工业领域的碳生产力与工业领域的就业率情况都在低碳高质量发展上有较好的表现。嘉兴虽然在经济发展和服务业就业情况上有较大优势，但全市煤炭消费占比较大，百姓生活质量一定程度上受环境污染等影响，并在节能意识上有待提高，建筑、交通等领域的电气化水平与其他市仍有差距，同时，工业和能源领域的就业吸纳程度有待加强。衢州则在能源、工业、居民生活领域的碳减排上有待提升。

从低碳高质量发展变化来看，杭州、湖州、嘉兴的低碳高质量发展在全省各设区市中的提高程度位居前三。杭州主要在建筑领域减排、百姓生活质量提高和农业领域减排取得显著成效，过去 6 年，杭州人均可支配收入显著提高，环境污染治理成效显著，服务业发展迅猛，城市用能结构不断优化。湖州在百姓生活质量提高、交通领域减排有明显成效，交通领域新能源推广成效显著，居民经济收入有较大改善，环境治理也取得了显著成效。嘉兴在居民生活质量提高、建筑领域减排和居民生活领域减排成效显著，与杭州相似，服务业在带来经济发展的同时，用能结构也在不断改善，在城镇化率逐年上升的同时，居民节能意识同步提高，居民生活环境和经济水平向好。其他设区市普遍在居民生活质量和服务业电气化程度上有较大提升。

（二）分维度评估结果及其演变

通过对 11 个设区市在经济发展、能源领域减排、工业领域减排、建筑领域减排、交通领域减排、农业领域减排、居民生活领域减排、碳汇领域增汇、百姓生活质量等不同维度评分结果及近 6 年评分变化趋势分析，11 个设区市在不同维度上的低碳高质量发展大部分有所提高。

从经济发展维度来看（图 2-18），杭州、嘉兴、湖州对企业的吸引程度较高，在科技发展上的投入也位居全省前列，嘉兴、温州、衢州的碳排放与经济发展脱钩程度较好，宁波、舟山的碳排放脱钩程度有待提高，全省大部分设区市的经济发展维度在近 6 年有所提高，相对而言，温州、舟山由于 R&D 投入相对较低、企业增长整体偏缓，在经济发展维度上有更多的改善空间。

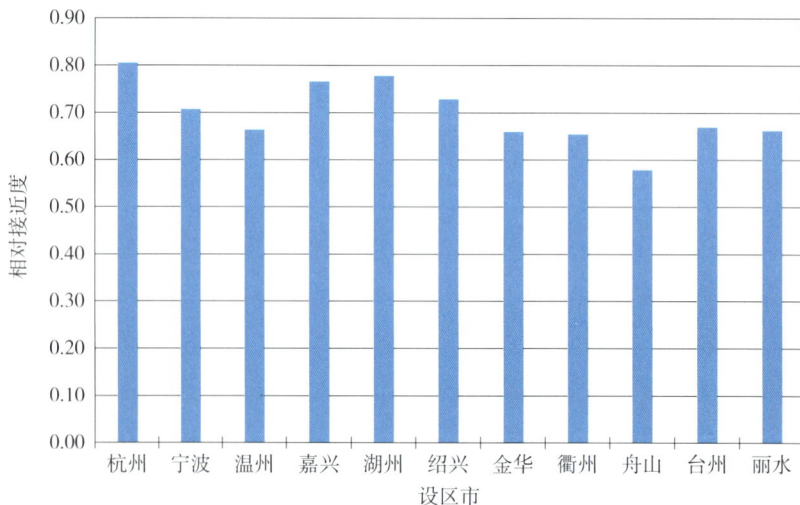

图 2-18　设区市经济发展维度

从能源领域碳减排维度来看（图 2-19），温州、杭州以良好的能源消费结构、能源领域对人才就业的高吸纳程度位居全省前列。衢州、宁波等地由于煤炭消费在能源结构中占比偏高，能源碳排放结构有待完善，在全省排名靠后。宁波、温州、台州、丽水等能源碳排放结构近 6 年在全省的排名有所下降。

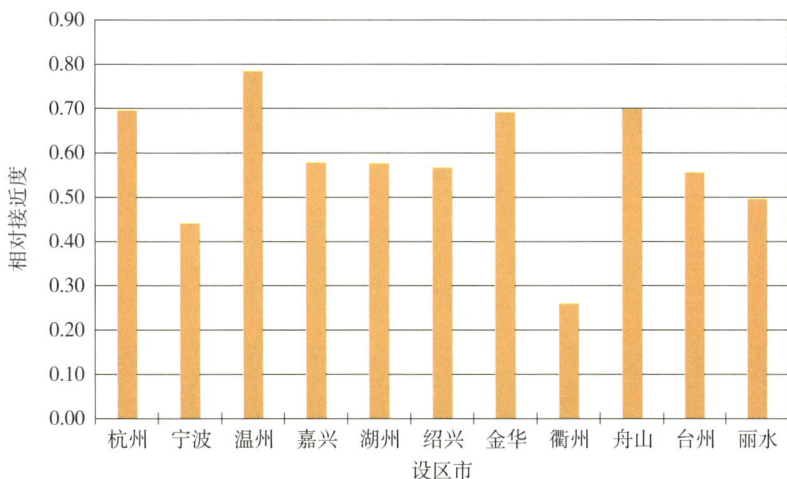

图 2-19　设区市能源领域减排维度

从工业领域碳减排维度来看（图 2-20），金华、丽水、杭州大力发展高新技术产业、降低单位工业增加值碳排放，工业领域人才吸纳速度加快，工业领域减排成效显著。舟山由于浙石化等高耗能行业的投产、衢州由于工业能源碳排结构不够低碳化，工业领域碳减排评估结果有待提高。同时，湖州、杭州、丽水等地单位工业增加值碳排放较低，绍兴、嘉兴等地高新技术产业增长较快，综合考量下处在全省居中的位置。近 6 年，台州受工业领域就业人口占比萎缩影响和相对不高的高新技术产业增加值增速，和舟山一样，在工业领域碳减排排名有所下降。

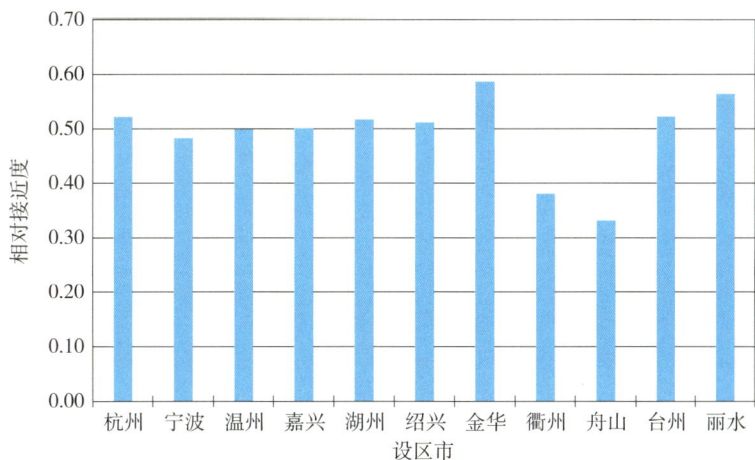

图 2-20　设区市工业领域减排维度

从建筑领域碳减排维度来看（图 2-21），杭州和宁波由于建筑领域电气化程度高，服务业和建筑业有着较高的增加值和碳生产力，在全省位列第一梯队。台州、舟山同样各方发展较为均衡，位列第二梯队。嘉兴虽然三产就业人口增速较高，但单位增加值碳排放和电气化水平较低，温州则是由于服务业偏低的电气化水平和行业就业人口萎缩，两市在全省排名靠后。近 6 年，温州、金华、丽水建筑领域减排的排名有所下滑。

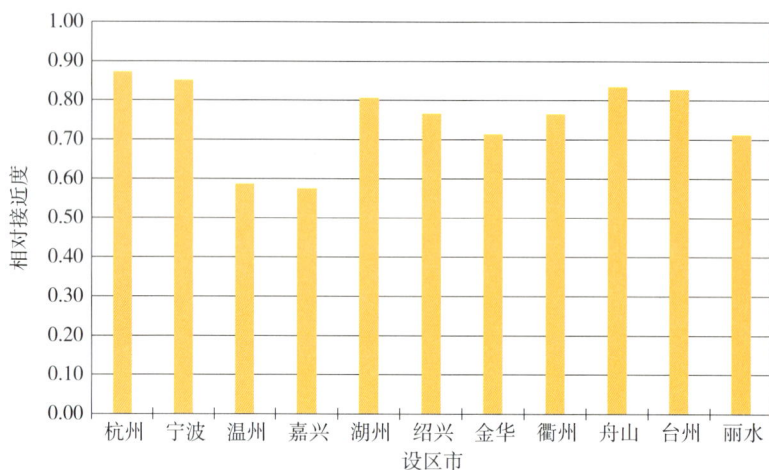

图 2-21　设区市建筑领域减排维度

从交通领域碳减排维度来看（图 2-22），湖州、杭州、衢州的交通领域电力碳排放占比较高，同时单位运输周转量碳排放处在全省相对较好的位置，交通领域就业形势较好，位于全省第一梯队。宁波、台州虽然单位运输周转量碳排放较低，但交通领域新能源使用占比偏低，舟山、嘉兴情况与宁波、台州类似，但交通领域就业形势向好。丽水、金华受较高的单位运输周转量碳排放影响，金华交通新能源占比偏低，丽水交通领域就业形势较差，因此排名靠后。近 6 年，宁波、金华、丽水在交通领域的排名有所下滑。

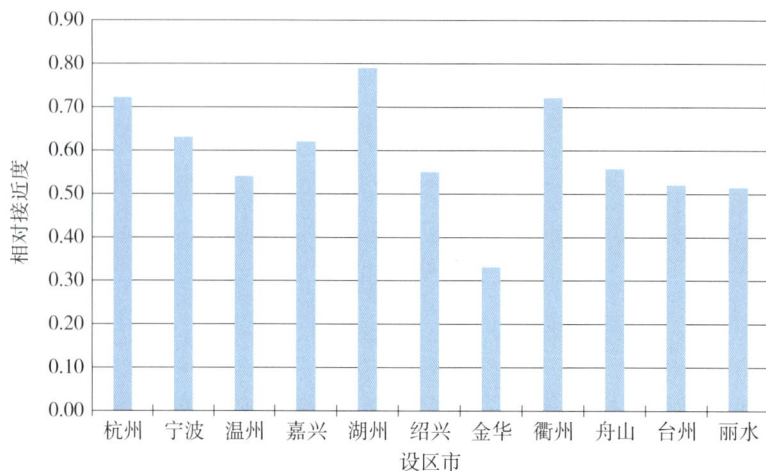

图 2-22　设区市交通领域减排维度

从农业领域碳减排维度来看（图2-23），舟山、丽水、温州、绍兴、杭州都有较好的表现，农业就业形势和农业碳生产力都有所提高。嘉兴、衢州农业领域碳排放减缓有待提升，农业就业人口流失较大，因此排名靠后。但近6年，各市在农业领域碳减排上均取得了较好成效，整体碳减排水平提升。

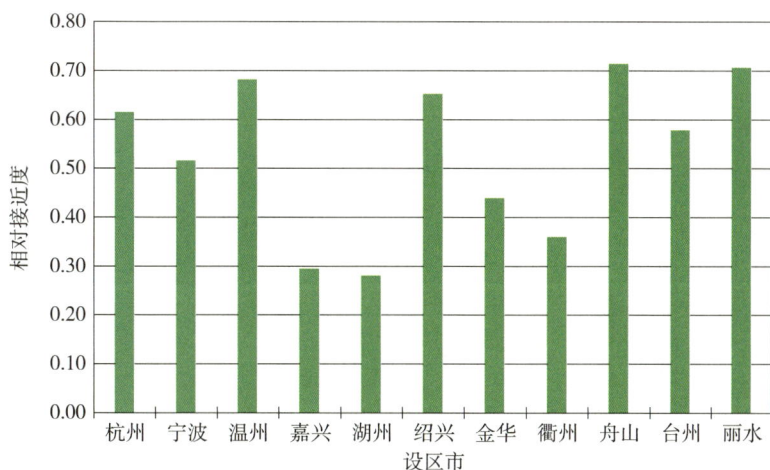

图 2-23　设区市农业领域减排维度

从居民生活领域碳减排维度来看（图2-24），杭州、宁波、温州很好地保障了居民用电需求，城镇化率逐年攀升，居民生活领域得到保障，处在第一梯队。衢州在城镇化水平和就业率上相对有待提高，因此影响了整体排名。近6年，11个设区市在居民生活领域减排都取得了良好成效。

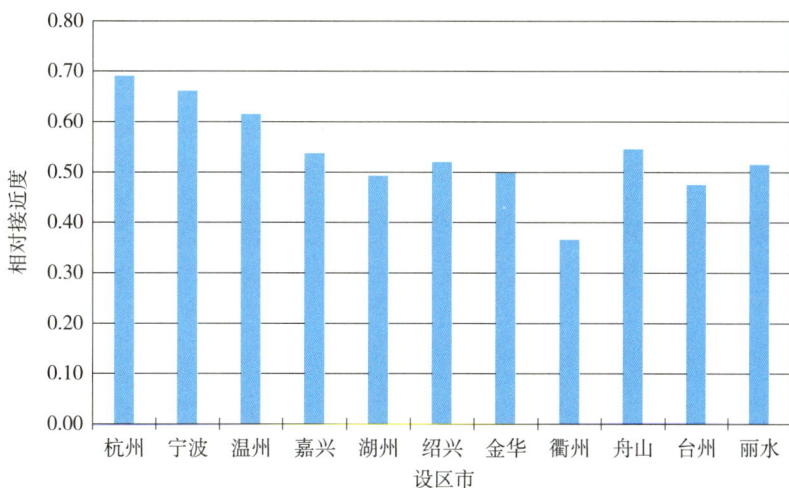

图 2-24　设区市居民生活领域减排维度

从碳汇领域增汇维度来看（图 2-25），丽水、衢州拥有较好的资源禀赋，开展生态环境保护工作，以及较高的人均森林面积，在碳汇领域拥有优势，位居全省前列。其余设区市因人口增长、资源禀赋限制，以及近 6 年对碳汇资源的保护情况依序得到评分。

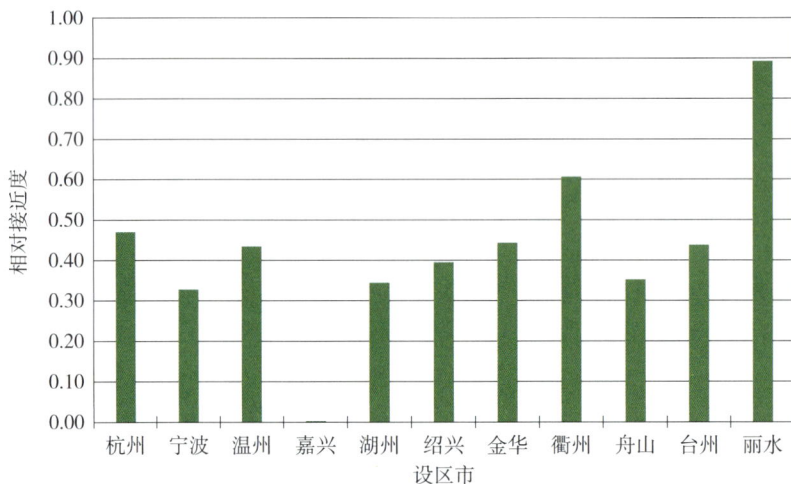

图 2-25　设区市碳汇增汇维度

从百姓生活质量维度来看（图 2-26），温州、金华、台州、湖州由于较好的环境污染控制、较为平衡的人均可支配收入与 GDP 之间的占比，位居全省前列。杭州虽然有较高的人均可支配收入，但受较高的 $PM_{2.5}$ 等环境污染的影响，在百姓生活质量上排名靠后，衢州则由于居民收入相对偏低排名靠后。但整体而言，全省各设区市的居民生活质量在过去 6 年均得到了提升。

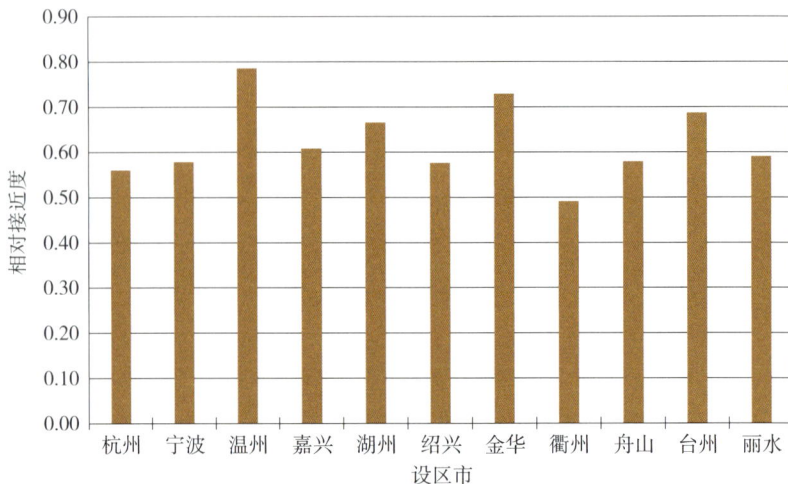

图 2-26　设区市百姓生活维度

（三）设区市聚类演变情况

作为一个最简单的探索，首先对各设区市 2021 年度综合的相对接近度进行聚类，其结果如图 2-27 所示。从图 2-27 中可以看出，11 个设区市较为清晰地分为了三类，按照相对接近度从高到低看，分别是杭州、温州、丽水为第一类，其低碳发展程度最好，嘉兴、衢州为第三类，其低碳发展程度相对不高，其余 6 个设区市处于中间一类。

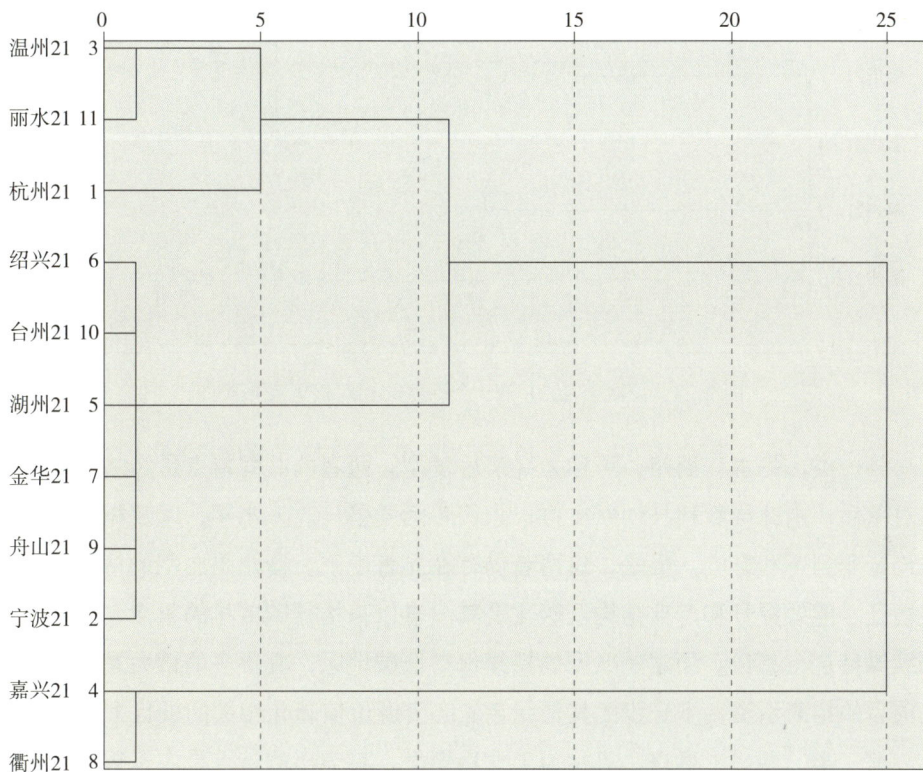

图 2-27　设区市 2021 年综合的相对接近度聚类图

综合的相对接近度虽然可以对设区市进行分类，但仅能表征其低碳发展水平的高低，难以概括得出类别关键特征。为此，进行第二轮聚类分析，以各维度作为对象，对其相对接近度进行聚类分析。结果如图 2-28 所示。从图中可以看出，11 个设区市较为清晰地分为了四类，分别是第一类：丽水、衢州。第二类：湖州、嘉兴。第三类：绍兴、台州、宁波、舟山、杭州。第四类：温州、金华。

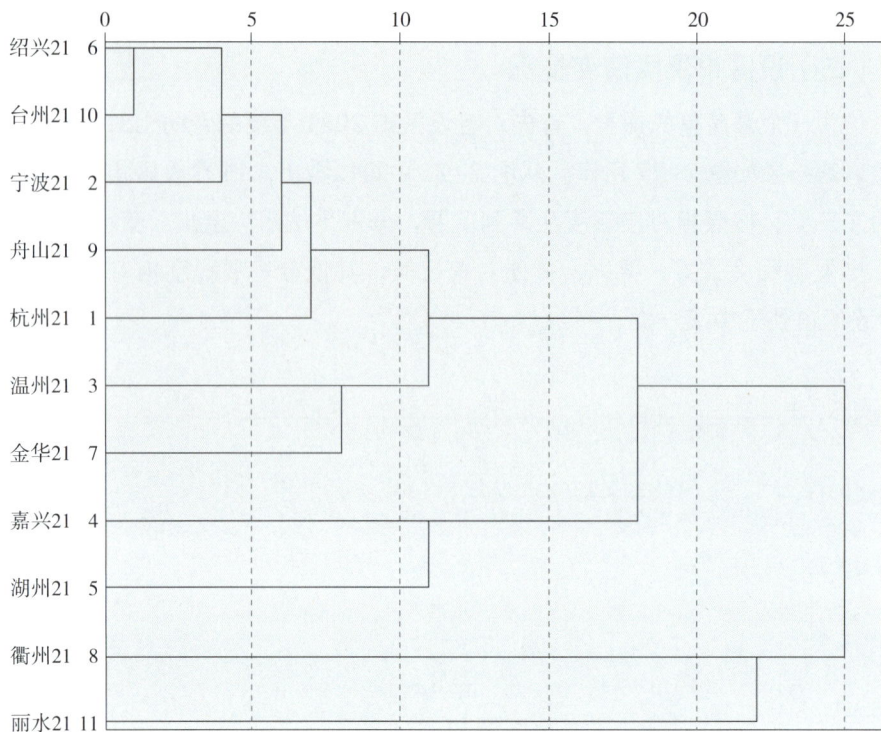

图 2-28　设区市 2021 年 9 个维度的相对接近度聚类图

第一类，丽水、衢州，可称为经济后发型。两者的共同特点是经济发展程度相对落后，由此导致科技创新支撑、人民生活质量与收入水平，以及相关的产业结构皆受到不利影响。但是，这两者仍存在显著差别。衢州是典型的从高碳到低碳地区，能效提升和产业结构低碳化是其一直以来推行碳减排的重点，后续也将继续维持这一趋势。丽水是典型的持续保持低碳地区，其更多的精力是花费在产业项目的招商引资，下一步尤其是绿色生态资源价值转化相关的项目上。

第二类，湖州、嘉兴，可称为工业集聚型，其突出的特点是由于天然的平原优势，工业企业、工业项目高度密集布局，由此导致当地在能源资源消耗、生态资源本底保持上面临较大压力，但也因为大量的工业项目，居民生活质量和收入水平得以维持在较高水平。对于这两地而言，产业的转型升级是重中之重，如何将传统生产力逐步替代为新兴的低碳生产力，是其下一步的降碳重点。

第三类，温州、金华，可称为工业分散型。这一类和第二类可做鲜明比较。由于浙中南地区山地较多，工业项目难以连片布局，取而代之的是块状经济。而与之相对的就是，块状经济再向外就很少有工业项目。也是因此，虽然依托工业项目可保障较好的收入水平，但其同时也可保有相对较好的生态资源本底。对于这两地而言，关键的因素是土地利用效率的提升，从而降低单位建设用地面积的碳排放。

第四类，绍兴、台州、宁波、舟山、杭州，可称为综合型。这一类的情况较为复杂，其更多是由于多个维度相互抵消而被归拢为一类的。

五、主要结论及展望

本研究围绕经济发展、能源安全、碳排放、百姓生活 4 个维度，构建了涵盖碳减排、经济社会发展，尤其是公正转型维度在内的应对气候变化和低碳发展评估体系，并从省级对标、市级对比的角度做了实证分析，主要结论如下：

在省级对标中，浙江的应对气候变化和低碳发展实现平稳提升，与广东省处于相似类型。此外，福建处于稳定的高水平，山东、江苏呈现出波动的特征。2020 年，浙江省的表现在五省份中达到历史最好的第一位。分维度看，除能源安全和碳汇增汇两个受资源禀赋影响较大维度外，其余 8 个维度浙江均表现出不断提升特征。

在市级对比中，总体而言 11 个设区市低碳高质量发展程度表现出不断提高趋势。从绝对值看，杭州、温州、丽水整体低碳高质量发展程度排名靠前，衢州、嘉兴则较为靠后。

从对设区市的分类分析看，主要可分为四类。丽水、衢州，可称为经济后发型，前者建议以能效提升和产业结构低碳化为降碳重点，后者重点关注绿色生态资源价值转化。湖州、嘉兴，可称为工业集聚型，如何将传统生产力逐步替代为新兴的低碳生产力，是其下一步的降碳重点。温州、金华，可称为工业分散型，关键是要提升土地利用效率，降低单位建设用地面积的碳排放。绍兴、台州、宁波、舟山、杭州，可称为综合型，应考虑从 6 个领域全面推进经济社会的绿色低碳转型。

虽在评价指标与方法上有所创新，然而经济社会的绿色低碳转型发展是一个极为综合、复杂的巨系统，本研究也只是一个初步的尝试。后续，可以考虑从拓展和完善评价指标，尤其是公正转型、共同富裕等战略与绿色低碳发展转型结合紧密的角度上选择提炼；扩大评估的范围，包括从空间和时间尺度上增加评估的对象；改进评估的方法，包括对于权重确定的操作，以及个别异常值的处理等。

作者：浙江省经济信息中心著作组

第一部分　综合评价

参考文献

[1] 潘庆婕，赵守国.中国绿色创新与经济发展耦合协调性测度与评价 [J].科技管理研究，2023，43（3）：215-222.

[2] 李旭辉，陶贻涛."双碳"目标下中国绿色低碳创新发展测度、区域差异及成因识别 [J].中国人口·资源与环境，2023，33（1）：124-136.

[3] 李铜山，王艳蕊.基于熵权 TOPSIS 模型的区域农业碳中和能力评价研究 [J].区域经济评论，2022，57（3）：92-98.

[4] 孙奇，吴巧生，李思瑶，等.中国城市低碳发展绩效指数测算 [J].统计与决策，2021，37（17）：75-79.

[5] 陈静.基于对象—过程—主体分析方法的区域低碳交通评价研究 [J].生态经济，2021，37（3）：38-42.

[6] 付琳，曹颖，郭豪，等."十二五"以来中国低碳发展进展及政策评估 [J].中国环境管理，2021，13（1）：16-24.

[7] 唐德才，张燕，王路霞.长江经济带碳减排能力综合评价研究 [J].生态经济，2021，37（6）：44-50.

[8] 王晶晶，李琦芬，杨涌文.基于变权理论的近零碳排放园区综合评价研究 [J].科学技术与工程，2021，21（1）：334-340.

[9] 李春花，孙振清.碳达峰目标下区域绿色设计能力评价研究 [J].科技管理研究，2021，41（19）：177-183.

[10] 梁刚.中国绿色低碳循环发展经济体系建设水平测度 [J].统计与决策，2021，37（15）：47-51.

第二部分　领域行动

新型电力系统助力
浙江省能源清洁低碳转型的改革实践

浙江作为能源资源匮乏的受端地区，如何平衡安全、低碳和经济的三重发展目标，如何在经济指标高涨、能耗指标受限、民企稳价诉求强烈的大背景下探索区域低碳转型的发展道路一直是能源电力行业的从业者长期努力的方向，本文综述了浙江省能源低碳转型面临的机遇和挑战，提炼出建设新型电力系统推动能源低碳转型的发展路径，列举了相关实践案例，为浙江建设省域现代化先行示范提供思路和经验。

一、浙江省能源清洁低碳转型面临的机遇和挑战

浙江是经济大省、工业强省、资源小省，煤、油、气等化石能源资源储量几乎为零，完全依靠外部调入。电力方面，依靠大力开发建设的本地常规电源以及新能源，对外依赖程度较低，但也超过1/3。当前，在走出疫情恢复生产需要增加供能、国际能源供应形势复杂多变、局部极端气象灾害频发的背景下，"能源饭碗不完全掌握在自己手中"的问题日益凸显。如何处理好能源安全和能源自给之间的平衡关系是亟须解决的难题。浙江清洁能源发展不具有优势，水资源已开发殆尽，风光资源质量和空间条件有限，光照属于三类资源地区，处于全国中下游水平，风电受土地资源、地理条件制约，不具备大规模集中开发的经济性优势。因此，寻找适合浙江的低碳转型道路和发展模式成为建设清洁能源示范省的必答题。

2021年3月15日，习近平总书记在中央财经委第九次会议上提出构建新型电力系统。这是自2014年6月中央财经领导小组第六次会议上提出"四个革命、一个合作"能源安全新战略以来，再次对能源电力发展作出的系统阐述，明

确了新型电力系统在实现"双碳"目标中的基础地位，为能源电力发展指明了科学方向、提供了根本遵循。

二、建设新型电力系统是资源匮乏的受端地区清洁低碳转型的必由之路

电能是风能、太阳能、核能、水能等清洁能源开发利用的主要形式，电网连接着全省水、核、风、光、生物质等 13 类能源，贯通了能源的产、供、储、消全环节，满足着消费侧冷、热、电、氢等多种用能需求，覆盖了全省 2 000 多万大工业、工商业和居民用户。因此，电力系统天然成为浙江能源体系的核心载体。

新型电力系统是尚未形成统一公认的概念，但能满足电力大范围优化配置、能便捷接入各种用能供能主体、能适应多种能源高效转换、能保障在事故及灾害下的韧性是其显著的特征。总体来说，新型电力系统是传统电力系统的跨越升级，是清洁低碳、安全高效能源体系的重要组成部分，承载着能源转型的历史使命。

构建新型电力系统，对于国家和浙江而言，有 4 个方面的重要意义。一是加快生态文明建设。2021 年，国家发展改革委提出，我国的生态文明建设迈入以降碳为重点战略方向的新阶段。浙江大力发展风电、太阳能发电等非化石能源，是能源领域降碳的主要途径。二是保障国家能源安全。能源安全关系区域经济发展和国家安全，实现以清洁低碳转型，将大幅降低浙江油气对外依存度，显著提高区域能源安全保障能力。三是构建新发展格局。终端用能电气化将推动能源利用节能提效，增强绿色发展内生动力，为浙江建设中国特色社会主义先行省，提供基础支撑和持续动能。四是推动能源产业链转型升级。通过自主创新，集中突破能源电力领域核心和颠覆性技术，摆脱关键技术装备对外依赖，推动能源电力产业全链条自主可控和转型升级。因此，对浙江而言，构建新型电力系统是浙江实现电力保供"去依附"的必由之路，是推动全省能源清洁低碳转型的关键之举。

三、浙江构建新型电力系统的改革实践

2021 年以来，浙江以先行者的姿态，积极打造能源领域清洁低碳转型的示范窗口，在发展目标、体系构建和跨界融合方面开展了系列改革实践。

（一）制定浙江"五年一台阶、十五年一跨越"的新型电力系统发展目标

构建新型电力系统能够为浙江探索出一条资源匮乏型受端地区能源低碳转型的发展道路，实现安全可靠、清洁低碳、经济高效的统筹兼顾。从目标来看，浙江新型电力系统的发展目标，可以概括为"五年一台阶、十五年一跨越"。

2021—2035年实现量变到质变，浙江新型电力系统省级示范区全面建成。到2025年，新能源装机占比27%，需求侧响应能力达到最高负荷8%，构建以"特高压交流环网为主心骨、特高压直流为受电主动脉"的大受端电网格局。到2030年，新能源装机占比34%，需求侧响应能力达到最高负荷10%，形成"一环四直"的大受端电网格局，省级示范区基本建成，引领浙江高质量碳达峰。到2035年，新能源成为出力主体，形成"强交强直"的大受端电网格局，全域实现大电网与分布式电源、微电网融合发展，省级示范区全面建成，支撑浙江奋力推进共同富裕示范先行。

2036—2050年实现质变到跃变，浙江新型电力系统在安全可靠、绿色低碳、清洁高效等方面达到国际先进水平。源网荷储全面协调、可持续发展，新能源成为电力供应主体，持续争取外来电资源，大受端电网交直流互备、多供区互济，配电网实现电力流、数据流和价值流的高阶融合，成为能源互补、能效提升的低碳能源网络和资源共享、多方共赢的价值创造中枢，支撑浙江全力推进社会主义现代化先行。

（二）打造新型能源体系的产供储运的"四个载体"

浙江以新型电力系统为核心载体，贯彻党的二十大关于构建新型能源体系的重要指示精神，积极打造能源体系产供储运的"四个载体"。

一是自主能源供应载体。从能源体系中化石能源下游转化二次能源，向加大清洁能源利用逐步增加能源供给占比转变，从10年前不到1%，到当前20%左右，未来将超过50%。

二是能源运输与布局协同提效载体。增量油气资源的海洋运输特性巩固了浙江沿海大电源密集布局的基础，电力互联覆盖特征优势为降低化石储运成本、减少堵塞提供了高效通道。

三是多边能量存储载体。从依赖电煤5～10 d库存、天然气5%左右储备能力进行电源调节，转向抽蓄、新型储能、虚拟电厂的运行过程存储调节，形成多边存储能力。

四是市场联动载体。化石能源在量价两方面与电力紧密耦合，构建电力量价波动反馈机制，联动电力市场与化石能源市场进行综合治理，系统性保障能源安全。加快售电公司价格成本透明化和信息公开化，促进行业市场有序竞争。

四、促进消费侧领域的"六个融合"

一是促进能源领域的互补竞争融合。宜电则电、宜气则气、宜煤则煤，通过稳定化石能源供应、增加一次电力供应充分激活能源市场，增强能源互补能力，促进能源技术相互促进迭代，最终清洁能源在市场价格与技术进步上实现对化石能源替代，安全、清洁、经济三位一体成为可能。

二是促进工业领域的交互发展融合。化石能源消费向原料利用进行集聚，工业能源完善梯级利用模式，绿电交易与碳市场并轨协调，促进工业企业通过市场方式灵活调节排放并满足用能发展需求。促进工业生产高效化，完善两部制电价，根据供应充裕度进行煤电、气电容量电价引导，提升能源系统效率。促进交互式用能，新增工业企业形成固定比例可控负荷，完善梯级响应能力。

三是促进农业领域的生态经济融合。加快电动农机普及，农村新能源、即插即用接口与农机配套关联，扭转农业部门油品占能源消费比例超 90% 的现状。促进农业部门运行成本下降与终端用能清洁度提升。

四是促进交通领域的智慧低碳融合。提前筹备电动汽车比例提升后有序充电模式和排序入网模式，加快车网、路网、充电网融合，构建汽车电池家用返供机制与技术配套。

五是促进建筑领域的节能减碳融合。加大短流程炼钢占比，加大电磁炉等高效低运行成本设备替代应用，强化余热回收、CCUS 等技术在水泥生产中提前应用。研发适应工程建设临时变压器、配套设备与应急支撑设备，促进工程机械电气化施工。

六是促进民生领域的便捷智能融合。通过储能、生物质灵活应用提升居民用电安全保障，助力共富创建。加快空调覆盖，形成规模化无感调节能力。挖掘灵活热源需求，传导上游余热余能分布式利用。

五、推进区域清洁低碳转型的案例与成效

国网浙江电力作为新型电力系统的主要建设单位，从 2021 年起积极推进新型电力系统示范区建设，2 年多来形成了强交流强直流的骨干网架建设、能源大

数据中心的全景监测、高比例分布式新能源的就地消纳等多个方面的实践经验。

（一）案例 1：建设"一环四直"特高压骨干网架，承载内外清洁能源供应

在"十四五"期间，浙江将建成由吴江、宁绍、台温 3 座 1 000 kV 交流特高压变电站构成的特高压通道，与已有的浙西通道一起，共同构成了省内特高压交流环网。为浙东南大量沿海电源接入提前创造条件，极大地促进了长三角区域电力的互联互通，推动了华东四省一市的一体化发展。在此基础上，结合已建的宾金、灵绍、白鹤滩 3 条 ±800 kV 特高压直流，以及待建的甘肃—浙江第四直流，将形成"一环四直"的骨干网架结构。为浙江外来清洁能源的可靠馈入和本地清洁能源的开发消纳构建强有力的支撑载体，满足 35% 以上高比例外来电受入，满足 50% 以上高比例非化石电源装机安全消纳，满足浙江省负荷中高速增长并在中长期"翻番"的需求。

（二）案例 2：浙江省能源大数据中心动态监测浙江能源运行全景

为有效指导和规范能源全景数据业务，推动能源行业全过程数据集聚融合、共享交换、准实时监测、分析应用、辅助决策和规划支持，国网浙江电力公司联合浙江省政府共同建设多能耦合、数据融合、服务共享、价值共创、合作共赢的省级能源大数据中心，实现数字化助推节能降碳，服务"双碳"目标。

能源大数据中心汇集全省煤、油、气、电等全品种能源数据，开展全环节能流碳流分析，打造连接政府单位、社会民众、能源行业、用能企业的能源信息互联平台。截至 2022 年年底，中心已覆盖 10 余个省级部门 342 项指标数据；聚合全省 46 770 家规上企业、2 168 个省级重点项目、43 万个个人的碳账户信息，培育数字化应用超过百余项。

（三）案例 3：嘉兴海宁源网荷储一体化项目实现地区高比例分布式新能源就地消纳

海宁尖山地区本地清洁能源占一次能源比例为 50.2%，清洁电量占全社会用电量比例为 57.0%，电能在终端消费占比达到 57.48%，是浙江省分布式新能源最为密集的区域。大量的间歇性新能源所带来的不稳定，与嘉兴海宁当地众多的精密制造企业用电要求矛盾，国网浙江电力通过交直流混联的新型配电网建设和碳化硅能量路由器等新技术、新装备的应用，构建形成满足高比例分布式新能源就地消纳的新型电力系统雏形。在"十四五"期间经济增长和能源消费 9%

的高增长预期下，实现了清洁能源消费占比超过 59%，分布式光伏就地消纳 98%，供电可靠性提高到 99.995% 以上的显著成效。

（四）案例 4：空调负荷互动响应提升系统弹性

浙江电网转变传统"源随荷动"的调节模式，充分发挥市场灵活、用户敏感、敢于变革的有利因素，周密调研全省空调负荷结构和体量，测算得出夏季居民最大空调负荷占比为 40%，总量超过两个三峡的发电装机。基于这个庞大的基数，浙江电力联合浙江政府系统性推进空调柔性负荷管理。一是构建"数字牵引、分类施策"应用体系。根据空调种类、应用场景、响应效果梳理形成四大类、十四小类末端感知技术方案。二是建立"政企联动、行业主管"管控机制。协助省发展和改革委员会发布《关于进一步加强空调负荷柔性调控、促进全社会节能提效的指导意见》，与省机关事务管理局达成公共机构空调负荷管控意向，7 个地市、45 个区（县）政府同步出台支持政策。三是实行"试点突破、由点及面"推广路径。瞄准公共机构、商业楼宇、家电云平台，制定空调负荷管理三年行动方案，2022 年已完成现场普查 3 万余户，改造接入 3 000 余户，其中家电云平台贯通接入 643 户。一年下来，建立了 910 万 kW 负荷构成的调节资源池，具备最大 380 万 kW 调节能力。

（五）案例 5：平湖精细用电提升系统能效

浙江在"高增长、高能耗、高成本"的粗放模式之中寻求改变，探索一条通过提升系统能效，在不降低企业生产能力的前提下，通过精细用电，既降低了企业的用能，又节省了生产成本，同时满足了生产需求、用电限制和节能降耗三大诉求。2022 年，国网浙江电力与嘉兴平湖政府合作，于 3 月印发《关于修订 2022 年全市有序用电方案的通知》，明确开展能效提升的试点，在迎峰度夏期间，浙江电网经过对 1 174 家工业企业用能需求的逐一分析，深入工艺流程内部环节，采用标准化核算方法，为地区提出企业精细用电模式，仅 7—8 月，每天能节约当地企业用能 100 t 标准煤以上，提高全社会产值近 300 万元，年减少二氧化碳排放 3.95 万 t。

（六）案例 6：绿电交易促成绿色亚运

2022 年浙江电力稳步推广绿电交易市场，常态化开展绿电交易，全年累计达成交易电量 25.76 亿 kW·h，较 2021 年增长 600% 以上。根据国家发展改革委等部门《促进绿色消费实施方案》《关于完善能源绿色低碳转型体制机制和政策措施的意见》指示，浙江电力配合政府加快通过"年度＋月度＋月内"组合形式，规范、定期组织绿电交易，实现省内绿电交易常态化连续开市。引导浙江省内用户购买、消费绿电，累计服务零售用户超 600 家。加快 29 家聚合商代理浙江省内近 2 000 家分布式电源，达成绿电交易 2.39 亿 kW·h。多渠道促成绿色交易，依托北京电力交易中心绿证交易平台，促成省内 2 家售电公司达成绿证交易 21 000 张。实现了亚运所有场馆 100% 的绿电供应。

当前，新型电力系统的建设进入从试点示范到深入推广的发展阶段，通过 2 年多的建设，浙江新型电力系统平均每年消纳清洁电 1 900 亿 kW·h，减排二氧化碳超 1.4 亿 t，相当于为 1 亿户普通家庭提供了一整年的清洁无污染能源。全省清洁电力占比已达 2/3 以上。在实现转型的同时经受住了黑格比、灿都等多个超强台风的考验，渡过了全国煤价上涨导致的结构性缺电难关，总体保持了浙江电价的平稳有序。未来，随着新型能源体系的构建，浙江的新型电力系统势必将更全面地展现其引领性和示范性，必将为浙江的省域现代化先行示范作出新的电力贡献。

作者：孙轶恺[1]，王曦冉[2]，孙可[3]

1 孙轶恺，高级工程师，国网浙江省电力有限公司经济技术研究院智库秘书，长期从事电网规划领域的研究工作。
2 王曦冉，工程师，从事电网输变电工程设计、省级电网规划、能源经济与"双碳"目标等领域的研究工作。
3 孙可，教授级高级工程师，国网浙江省电力有限公司经济技术研究院智库首席专家，长期从事电网规划、能源经济、低碳转型等领域的研究工作，被授予浙江省 151 人才、国家电网优秀专家人才等多项荣誉称号。

浙江省工业碳效码的设计与实践

在当前碳达峰碳中和工作中，深度调整产业结构是一项重要任务，为此，需要及时、准确地了解工业领域中重点碳排放产业的碳生产力情况，将碳效作为衡量产业低碳发展的重要标尺，引导产业绿色低碳高质量发展。浙江省率先在工业领域的绿色低碳发展中作出积极探索，在全国首创提出"碳效码"，为全国工业领域碳达峰碳中和工作的推进，提供了可复制、可推广的"浙江经验"。

一、碳效码助力准确识别减碳工作突破口

（一）浙江省工业低碳发展背景

实现碳达峰碳中和是党中央作出的重大战略决策，是我们对国际社会的庄严承诺，也是推动高质量发展的内在要求。工业领域是能源消耗的最大部门，同时也是碳排放的最大来源，其占比约为浙江省全省碳排放总量的60%，工业领域碳排放控制的成效将在很大程度上影响碳达峰目标能否顺利实现。

浙江省工业结构高碳化较为明显（图4-1），2015年至2021年，各行业碳排放占比结构不断发生变化，但纺织、化学品等七大高碳行业的碳排放占比始终远高于其增加值占比。同时，碳生产力水平亟须提升，构建高质量的低碳工业体系迫在眉睫。

（二）识别工业领域减碳突破口

2021年，浙江省在全国首创推出了"工业碳效码"。所谓"碳效"，即碳排放强度，是指企业每单位经济产出所排放的二氧化碳量。作为一个综合性指标，"碳效"既可以反映企业的生产效率高低，还可以反映出能源结构的低碳化水平。将企业进行碳效对标并分级分档，再赋予相应的标志，也就是所谓的"碳效码"。

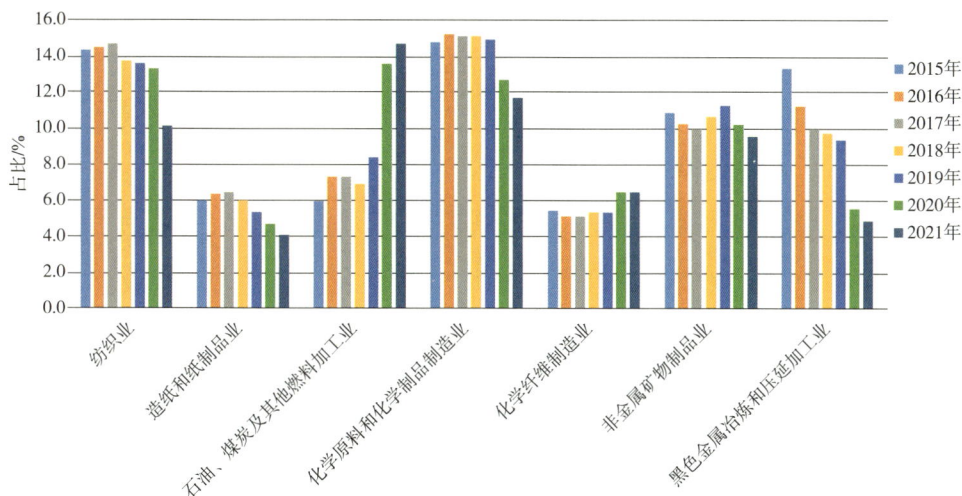

图 4-1 2015—2021 年七大高碳行业碳排放占规模以上工业碳排放比例

碳效码可为浙江省工业领域碳达峰精准施策提供重要基础。浙江省明确提出要大力发展低碳高效行业、改造提升高碳高效行业[1]。基于碳效码，工业主管部门可以采用统一的评价方法和标准，来识别需要减碳的重点行业、重点企业，并根据不同的分类结果精准施策，找准低碳高效、高碳高效行业等关键突破口，加快推进工业结构低碳转型。

碳效码可为工业企业开展节能减碳行动提供有效的对标对表信息。企业在制定能源消费和碳排放控制目标时缺少依据，将影响企业开展节能减碳行动的效果和积极性。碳效码作为全省统一且权威的碳效对标信息，可助力企业自主采取低碳行动。金融机构可以较为准确地评估企业碳效水平和减碳潜力，持续跟踪企业的减碳表现；同时，可研发基于碳效的绿色金融产品来支持企业低碳转型或绿色发展。

碳效码可为主管部门优化要素配置和采取差别化政策提供支撑。未来，碳效将有可能成为一个重要的评价指标。能源、资金、土地等要素都将有可能优先倾斜给低碳高效的行业和企业。绿色金融服务、节能技改服务、碳交易、用能权交易等服务与市场化机制，都将作用于不同碳效水平的行业和企业。相关主管部门可有针对性地出台相关政策制度，推动资源要素的优化配置，助力推动高碳企业低碳转型、低碳高效企业绿色发展。

第二部分 领域行动

---

1 2021 年，浙江省委、省政府，《关于完整准确全面贯彻新发展理念 做好碳达峰碳中和工作的实施意见》。

二、统一精准的碳效评价模式设计

（一）方法学总体考虑

如何构建一套可操作、可推广且准确度高的碳效评价方法，考虑需要规范的数据来源、精准的碳效评价方法和智能的碳效应用。

1. 规范的数据来源

企业作为温室气体基本排放源，其碳排放相关数据的获取一直以来都存在数据来源口径多元、数据准确性存疑、数据更新频率滞后等问题。为了解决这些问题，需明确一个稳定且可靠的数据来源，确保准确、及时地获取企业碳排放相关数据。

工业碳效码数据来源于浙江省规模以上工业企业，归集的指标包括煤、电、油、气等主要能源品种终端消费、加工转换消费、用于原材料消费和回收能等数据。在数据的权威性方面，浙江省工业碳效码的数据归集和核算主要由浙江省统计局牵头，对连续两年以上工业在库并正常生产经营的规模以上工业企业开展碳效核算和评价。在数据的准确性方面，在进行碳效评价前，统计部门会对基础数据进行审核、核实和确认，比如依托统计平台，可以对各能源消费品种涉及的30余个指标进行表内和表间审核。在数据的时效性方面，碳效码数据在每年年中进行碳效综合测算，并对标形成碳效等级评价结果。未来，随着数据基础的进一步夯实，各项指标有可能做到月度更新，可探索实现更高的时效性。

2. 精准的碳效评价

浙江省工业行业众多，不同行业之间差异性较大。需要建立一套统一的工业企业碳效评价标准与模式，既能反映行业之间的差异，也能反映同一行业内部不同碳效水平的企业情况。整体来看，碳效评价应分为两个步骤，首先需要明确碳效水平的核算方法，其次需明确碳效水平的分级方法和划分标准。

（1）碳效水平计算

$$C = \frac{CE}{EVA} \qquad\qquad （4-1）$$

式中：C——企业碳强度，即企业单位增加值碳排放量；

　　　CE——企业碳排放量；

　　　EVA——企业增加值。

单位增加值碳排放量越大，碳效水平越低，反之则碳效水平越高。

（2）碳效水平分级

结合浙江实际，工业碳效码从工业维度和行业维度分别对企业碳效情况进行分档。碳效码中工业维度的分档设置与浙江省工业领域碳达峰目标相衔接，工业碳效码工业、行业维度的分档标准为碳强度 0.6 t/万元、2.0 t/万元，它们分别是浙江省低碳产业、高碳行业划分的参考标准。工业维度上，根据规模以上工业企业碳效水平在规模以上工业中的分布情况，可分为三档。行业维度上，通过企业碳效和其所属行业的平均碳效比较，确定企业在行业中的碳效水平，将企业划分为五档。为了更精准反映企业在所属行业中碳效水平，碳效码在行业维度将浙江省工业领域的七大高碳行业和非高碳重点行业细分至小类行业（4 位行业码），使这些重点行业企业能够更加细化精准地开展减碳工作。具体碳效智能对标分档情况见表 4-1。

表 4-1　浙江省工业碳效码碳效智能对标分档

行业碳效智能对标		工业碳效智能对标		
		一档	二档	三档
		$C\leq0.6$	$0.6<C\leq2.0$	$C>2.0$
一档	$C\leq0.5K_i$			
二档	$0.5K_i<C\leq1K_i$			
三档	$1K_i<C\leq1.5K_i$			
四档	$1.5K_i<C\leq2K_i$			
五档	$C>2K_i$ 或 $C<0$			

注：K_i 表示企业所属行业 i 的平均碳强度。绿色部分表示企业属于工业一档行业一、二档，作为低碳高效企业；蓝色部分表示除低碳高效企业外的所有工业碳效为一、二档的企业，作为低碳低效企业和一般碳效水平的企业；黄色部分表示工业三档中行业一至四档的企业，作为高碳高效企业；红色部分表示工业三档中行业五档的企业，作为高碳低效企业。

在考虑碳效水平分级时，主要是有两类参数影响碳效评级结果，一类是工业维度的分档参数，在全省规模以上工业整体碳效水平上进行对标，可以作为整个产业结构优化转型的参考；另一类是行业维度的分档，这个会随着行业差异性而各有不同，帮助企业在行业内对标对表提升碳效。

3. 智能的碳效应用

浙江省的数字化改革走在全国前列，通过与数字化平台相结合，可以进一步扩大碳效评价的适用范围，加快工业碳效码推广与应用。基于浙江省碳达峰碳中和智治平台，可以高效获取碳排放相关数据、快速对全省规模以上工业企业进行统一赋码，金融机构也可参考工业碳效码赋码情况，为企业提供不同类型的绿色金融或转型金融产品，主管部门可通过企业碳效码跟踪重点企业节能技改、碳效提升等低碳发展情况。

政策领域应用。工业主管部门通过浙江省碳达峰碳中和智治平台企业碳账户等重点应用，提高"亩均论英雄"、绿色低碳工厂等评价体系中碳效指标的比重，把碳效对标评价指标和碳效指数评价指标作为企业和区域评价的基础性指标，推动碳效评价结果应用覆盖差别化用地、用能、用水等领域。

金融机构应用。工业碳效码作为评价企业主体绿色低碳发展程度与未来减碳潜力的重要指标，金融机构可设计基于碳效评价结果的金融产品，以差异化的信贷、融资支持绿色低碳企业发展。中国人民银行、银保监局等部门对接工业碳效码进行金融领域融合应用，开展碳账户金融工作，以线上线下相结合的形式，推出浙里碳效贷、节能减碳技改贷、工业碳惠贷等多种基于碳效的绿色金融服务。

技改提效应用。工业主管部门在梳理筛选各行业高碳低效企业清单时，通过将碳技改与工业碳效码赋码情况相结合，在面向企业的"碳诊断""碳技改"等移动端开展节能诊断线上服务，并重点关注到碳效偏低的企业，针对性地提供技术支持。尤其对处于"工业三档、行业五档"的高碳企业重点开展"碳效 + 能效"节能减排诊断服务，帮助企业科学制定和实施绿色技改项目，提高企业节能降碳管理水平。

（二）工作机制建立

为了切实推动工业碳效码的落地和推广，需要建立多部门协同的工作机制、统一规范碳效评价技术标准，以及高效协同的应用推广机制。

1. 建立多部门协同的工作机制

浙江省在《关于完整准确全面贯彻新发展理念做好碳达峰碳中和工作的实施意见》《加快建立健全绿色低碳循环发展经济体系的实施意见》等顶层文件中，对"碳效"相关工作作出了明确的要求。在此背景下，省发展和改革委员会、省统计局、省经信厅等部门按照各自职责分工，协同推进碳效码相关工作。

统计部门。省统计局牵头全省碳效评价的核算和评级工作，通过浙江统计数字平台和一套表联网直报平台，归集企业煤炭、油品、天然气、电力、热力等主要能源品种消费和加工转换消费等数据，以及企业增加值等生产数据，作为碳效水平核算的基础。协同省发展和改革委员会、省经信厅等部门，明确碳效水平分级原则和相关参数，合理对全省规上企业进行工业维度、行业维度的分级分档，并将评价结果推送至相关部门，助力开展绿色金融、节能技改、绿色制造体系建设等。

经信部门。省经信厅作为全省工业领域"双碳"工作的牵头单位，梳理企业所属行业、行业平均碳效水平、行业对标和强度对标等级等相关内容，联合省统计局等部门进一步明确碳效评价标准；研究制定工业碳效码管理办法、工业碳效码相关平台操作细则等，进一步完善碳效评价的应用；在绿色工业园区、工厂、节能减碳技改项目申报等工作中，加大推广碳效码的应用场景。

发展和改革部门。省发展和改革委员会作为全省"双碳"工作的牵头单位，协同统计、经信、金融等部门共同开展工业碳效码相关建设与应用推广工作。与统计部门等平台贯通，将碳效码整合进全省"双碳"智治平台的企业碳账户中，实现同步更新、多端访问。同时，通过湖州、衢州等地的碳账户金融相关试点工作，丰富工业碳效码的多元化应用场景。

2. 规范碳效评价的技术标准

碳效评价方法是碳效码的核心，其科学性、准确性、合理性将会决定碳效码的应用推广范围（图4-2）。为了进一步提升工业碳效评价的权威性、规范性，由浙江省统计局作为归口管理部门，浙江省经济信息中心牵头起草了浙江省省级标准《工业企业碳效综合评估与分级赋码规范》（以下简称《规范》），将碳效评价和分级方法以标准的形式正式确定下来。《规范》统一了全省工业企业二氧化碳排放核算方法、碳效水平评估、碳效水平分级与赋码等内容，已通过专家评审会。

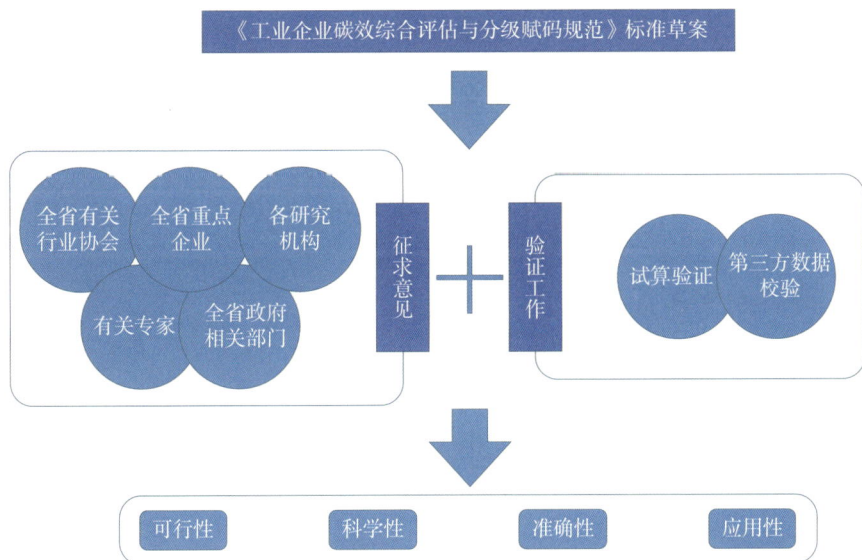

图4-2 《工业企业碳效综合评估与分级赋码规范》研究制定过程

在研究起草《规范》的过程中，为了确保标准的可行性，我们经过充分的企业调研并向全省有关行业协会、重点企业征求意见。为了确保标准的科学性和准确性，在广泛征求各研究机构和有关专家意见之外，开展标准验证工作，包括试算验证和第三方数据校验，2021年规模以上工业企业的试算结果成功对企业进行快速分类，识别出 5 000 余家浙江省需要重点控碳的企业，同时对比浙江省"十四五"规划纲要，试算为一档的低碳行业与浙江省重点支持的低碳行业领域一致。为了确保标准的应用性，我们也广泛征求了政府相关部门的意见，后续重点关注碳效码在"碳监测""碳对标"等方向的应用。

3. 建立高效协同的应用推广机制

工业碳效码作为一种工业企业碳效水平的评价工具，其最终目标是助力推动工业领域的绿色低碳发展。因此，在碳效码的设计与应用推广时，都需要与全省碳达峰碳中和相关工作相协同。通过碳效码的多场景应用来助推资源高效配置，有效衔接了浙江省推进工业结构低碳化目标，助力各地各相关部门将土地、能耗、排污、金融等资源要素向低碳新兴产业倾斜的"双碳"工作要求。

经信部门将碳效码联动"双碳"目标下的绿色制造体系建设，修改完善绿色低碳工业园区和绿色低碳工厂的评价体系，将碳效评价结果作为基础条件，倒逼工业园区和企业绿色低碳转型，在全省范围达成绿色低碳发展的广泛共识。碳效码推动节能减碳技改项目实施，政府通过碳效码对企业实施"碳效 + 能效服务"，组织专业机构更有针对性地开展节能诊断，推动高碳低效企业实施节能减碳技改。碳效码深化绿色金融、转型金融助力企业碳达峰碳中和工作，通过碳效码识别企业碳效发展现状与潜力，对低碳企业扩大产能和高碳企业节能技改给予贷款额度、利率等差别化待遇，引导并助力企业绿色低碳发展。

三、碳效码助推经济社会低碳发展应用实践

工业碳效码应用于不同场景，多点发力推动经济社会低碳发展。在浙江省工业碳效码应用推广过程中，碳效对标智能赋码为政府识别重点行业、企业碳效并精准施策提供了有力抓手，企业主体则通过碳效码了解自身碳效水平、制定低碳发展策略，同时，工业碳效码为引导社会资源要素以碳效为重点合理分配提供高效准确的支持。

（一）助力政府精准治碳

对于"双碳"工作的主管部门而言，可以精准识别减碳工作的重点行业和主体，有针对性地出台政策。

识别重点行业碳效。工业碳效码实现智能赋码后，浙江省规模以上工业行业碳效得到清晰地聚类与划分，碳效码数据有效地帮助政府明确了行业现状，并提供了未来的攻坚方向。浙江省规模以上工业 38 个大类行业中，处于工业一档

的行业为汽车制造、医药制造等 14 个行业，作为浙江省重点支持的低碳工业行业，大力发展这些行业有助于浙江省"十四五"碳强度目标的顺利达成。同时，通过全省工业碳效码赋码的行业分析，浙江省存在碳排放行业集中度高、高碳强度和高能耗强度行业明显重合的行业碳效特征，精准识别不同区域需要进行针对性碳效提升的重点行业。

精准对标企业碳效。工业碳效码的精准对标，实现对行业、企业的快速分类，在工业维度上，针对各工业行业的生产特征与差异，可以快速识别出高碳行业、低碳行业；在行业维度上，可以快速甄别出某个行业内的高效企业、低效企业。实现企业综合维度的精准对标，根据企业的碳效情况和生产水平，将工业对标和行业对标结合起来，多维度地精准定位企业碳效情况，可将企业进一步在工业碳效智能对标、行业碳效智能对标两个维度上，细分为高碳低效、高碳高效、低碳高效、低碳低效四大类。政府能够更加精准地识别处在不同行业先进碳效水平的企业，避免由于行业限制，对企业施策"一刀切"，有针对性地对低碳低效、高碳高效企业开展碳效提升专项行动，开展合规检查，制定整治提升方案，根据赋码情况实施"一企一策"对标提升。

（二）推动企业低碳发展

浙江省级已有 4 万多家规模以上工业企业信息同步接入。对企业而言，在低碳有红利、高碳有压力的环境下，通过碳效码可以提升自身的低碳意识、了解绿色发展水平和未来改进的方向。

浙江省民营企业数量多、行业分布广泛，纺织、化纤、非金属矿物等高碳排放行业占比较高，同时，企业存在对所处的行业排放情况认知不足、对自身碳效发展水平了解不清等问题，工业碳效码在典型城市开展试点，进一步推广至全省工业领域，为企业低碳发展提供了有力推动。

> **江山市某公司**
>
> 企业属于传统化工行业，主要生产原料双氧水，在这一过程中不可避免地将产生大量二氧化碳。根据碳效码赋码等碳效评估，化工行业属于省内节能降碳的重点行业，该企业提出明确低碳转型目标，希望引入转化设备将产生的二氧化碳再利用，预计设备成型后每年可减少 7.5 万 t 二氧化碳。农业银行衢州市分行根据企业碳效变化的实际情况和该企业的减碳目标书，发放优惠利率的贷款来帮助企业上马减碳设备，并将在贷后持续跟踪企业的减碳目标完成情况。

长兴某科技股份有限公司

该企业是一家以从事非金属矿物制品为主的企业，最初赋码时的工业碳效码行业碳效智能对标显示为四档，单位增加值碳排放为行业平均值的 1.5 倍。工业碳效码的赋码情况为企业碳效情况拉响了警钟，随后企业开展低碳技术改造。最终促成企业实施碳效提升技改项目，将配电房换上新款变压器、对服役超龄的磨粉机及配套设备进行节能绿色改造。预计改造完成后，每年可增加产值 600 万元，减少碳排放 184 t。

（三）引导资源要素倾斜

对金融机构等第三方机构而言，工业碳效码提供了碳金融所需的精准、权威的企业碳效评价。根据企业在工业和行业维度上的智能对标赋码情况，银行等金融机构可结合工业碳效码的碳效评价结果，针对性地对申请企业给予金融要素支持，助力企业低碳发展。一方面，助力金融机构等识别可提供金融等要素支持的企业主体；另一方面，可在要素支持后，对企业碳效提升成效进行长期跟踪。

湖州市的某钢集团

该企业主要从事特殊钢深加工产品，而钢铁行业正是浙江省七大节能降碳的重点行业之一，在工业碳效智能对标上属于高碳行业。在行业碳效智能对标上初次赋码时为五档，在同行业中处于中下水平。工业碳效码的赋码情况警示并鞭策了企业要加大节能低碳改造的力度。企业引入墨烯电机、改造加热炉，减少能源消耗，同时与宝钢、华兴、永兴等头部企业合作，开发高附加值产品，通过提升单位增加值水平来实现产品的转型升级；企业通过成立再生物资回收子公司，实现废钢清洁化，高效化助力其转型发展为绿色钢企。完成一系列的减碳改造后，工业碳效码赋码情况及时更新，企业行业碳效智能对标提升至四档。

湖州市安吉某竹木公司

企业主要生产竹、藤等家具，属于家具制造业。根据工业维度上的碳效对标，浙江省竹藤家具制造行业属于低碳行业。同时，根据行业维度上的碳效对标，该公司的碳效达到了同行业的先进水平，生产产品为得到认证的绿色产品，绿色低碳发展水平较高。湖州银行根据企业的赋码等企业碳效评价情况，认定该企业为低碳高效企业，符合优惠扶持的条件，给予了面向绿色企业的低碳成长贷，用于企业日常资金的周转，银行同时将持续跟踪企业的碳效变化。

四、碳效码应用的启示

工业碳效码在浙江省数据获取、实际应用与推广过程中，也遇到了一些可能广泛存在于全国层面的共性问题。通过工业碳效码在浙江省实际应用，形成未来碳效码在全国推广的一些启示。

（一）统一规范的数据获取

浙江省民营企业众多，企业环境信息披露机制缺失，数据积累与记录不全面，存在难以快速获取统一口径、真实准确的企业碳排放相关数据等问题。

为了保障数据规范性和统一性，工业碳效码基础数据统一在国家统计局平台上进行相关数据的填报汇总，既有规模以上工业企业能源消耗数据、增加值数据可直接从统计部门获取，无需二次填报，电力能源消费由于数据采集频率高，可通过与电力部门协同直接获取。为确保数据的真实性和准确性，在碳效码评估之前，需要对基础数据进行审核、核实和确认，包括对省统计局统计联网直报平台上企业填报的能源相关报表进行数据校验，通过与第三方现场核查报告比对；并且明确碳效码基础数据在获取频率、区域、覆盖范围方面的要求，包括时间要求上，为最近一年内企业连续产生的数据；区域要求上，要从实际企业碳排放发生所在的区域收集数据；完整性要求上，所采集的数据应当涵盖核算范围内所有的数据。

（二）与绿色金融和转型金融相衔接

企业在低碳转型的过程中，亟需资金来支持技术改造或产品转型，但在传统绿色金融模式下，企业覆盖面十分有限，缺乏针对性的金融产品支持。金融机构亟需通过转型金融来支持这类高碳企业开展低碳转型，也需要准确评估企业的碳效水平和转型潜力，但常面临专业性强、服务成本高等问题。

精准识别有转型金融需求的企业。基于工业碳效码多维度赋码的结果，银行等金融机构能够根据多维度赋码的碳效码划分企业为高碳低效、低碳高效、高碳高效、低碳低效4种不同类型，精准识别具有低碳转型潜力的高碳高效、低碳低效企业。针对不同类型企业金融设计不同的金融产品，如对已是低碳高效的企业发放普惠性质的贷款，支持企业的日常生产经营；对高碳高效和低碳低效企业，引导企业基于碳效码设计未来的低碳化路径，提供转型类的金融支持，帮助企业进行技术改造或产品转型升级，并持续跟踪，监督企业的碳效码赋码变化情况。

（三）提升市场主体的低碳意识

部分企业对"双碳"工作中碳效提升的认识尚未深入，在工业低碳高质量发展要求下，存在"能耗不高不用改""投入太大不想改"的心态。同时，部分第三方机构由于对低碳相关的专业技术、相关政策规范缺乏了解和投资风险等原因，在对企业低碳转型的支持上有所顾虑。

政府部门应通过碳效相关政策制定，拓展企业碳效评估结果应用范围，引导企业重视碳效提升；通过完善计量评估体系，利用碳效码等有力工具，建立全流程碳效跟踪监管体系；同时，加大财政对企业低碳转型的支持力度。龙头企业率先发挥引领作用，要根据碳效码的赋码情况，制定企业低碳管理方案，促进生产方式绿色转型，主动披露碳效相关环境信息。第三方机构要不断创新绿色业务模式，将"碳效"作为识别绿色主体、计算和评估企业或项目环境效益的关键指标之一，创新以引导企业碳效提升为目标的转型金融服务产品和技改服务渠道。

作者：浙江省经济信息中心著作组

践行绿色低碳使命　共绘低碳建筑未来

为了更好适应碳达峰碳中和发展的新形势，绿色低碳建筑已经成为建筑行业高质量发展的必然趋势。本章基于浙江省建筑碳排放现状，建筑领域技术路径及建筑节能减碳的主要实践探索及成效，得出建筑节能必须遵循"被动优先，主动优化"原则；同时浙江省建立的建设全过程闭环管理机制，为实现建筑领域的节能减碳提供了重要支持与保障，是浙江省建设管理的重要经验。最后，对浙江省建筑领域的节能减碳的整体规划与布局提出进一步展望。

一、引言

2015 年 11 月，习近平主席在气候变化巴黎大会上，提出了发展绿色建筑的要求。2020 年 9 月，习近平总书记首次提出了中国二氧化碳排放力争于 2030 年前达到峰值，努力争取 2060 年前实现碳中和。2021 年 3 月，习近平总书记在中央财经委第九次会议上明确要求建筑领域要提升节能标准，强调要把碳达峰碳中和纳入生态文明建设整体布局。碳达峰已成为"十四五"规划的关键词，而建筑全生命周期的碳排放约占全社会碳排放的 40%。

建筑领域碳排放因叙述语境不同数据口径也不同，可分为大、中、小 3 个口径：大口径是指建筑全生命周期碳排放，包括隐含碳排放和运行碳排放，其中隐含碳排放包括建材生产、运输和施工建造的建筑物化碳排放，以及建筑改造和拆除碳排放；运行碳排放包括公共建筑居住建筑运行碳排放。中口径与大口径相比不包含建材生产与运输碳排放。小口径与中口径相比则将根据碳排放按领域划分，将居住建筑碳排放归入居民生活。

根据统计局的能源平衡表，2019 年浙江省建筑领域的建造业施工、公共建筑运行碳排放总量占浙江省碳排放总量的比例约为 11.4%。其中建筑业施工碳排放总量约占 2.1%，公共建筑运行碳排放总量约 9.3%。2010—2019 年，浙江省建筑领域能耗总量扩大 1.81 倍，碳排放总量扩大 1.43 倍，其中公共建筑年均增速最大为 4.2%。总体来看，碳排放的年均增速低于能耗增速，表明建筑领域的间接碳排放因子整体呈现逐年降低的态势，浙江省建筑领域对于高排放因子的化石能源使用比例在减少，对于低排放因子的能源使用比例在增加。

建筑领域直接碳排放总量呈先升后降的发展趋势。建筑业、公共建筑总体直接碳排放以 2014 年为转折点，之后直接碳排放总量和占比均呈现逐年下降的趋势，其中公共建筑领域直接碳排放变化最明显。说明煤、石油等化石能源在建筑领域的直接应用逐渐减少，消费端能源结构逐步向更高质量转型升级。2010 年建筑业电力消费量占比为 1/3，到 2019 年增加至近一半；公共建筑电力消费量到 2019 年接近 4/5。建筑领域终端消费电气化水平稳步提升，不断推进建筑领域的低碳发展水平。

从强度分析，浙江省 2019 年公共建筑人均碳排放强度 0.67 t 二氧化碳 / 人，居住建筑人均碳排放强度 0.7 t 二氧化碳 / 人，总计 1.37 t 二氧化碳 / 人。近 10 年来，建筑领域人均碳排放量与单位服务业 GDP 碳排放强度呈现显著上升的趋势。依据《2020 年浙江省统计年鉴》2010 年至 2019 年年末常住人口及城镇化率，可以发现公共建筑人均排放量增速较年均人口增速要快得多，即人数不变，单位人口的生活用能习惯导致的平均增速影响更大。如果按服务业 GDP 增速计算强度，考虑物价上涨因素，按 2015 可比价，可以发现近 10 年服务业 GDP 年均增速较单位服务业 GDP 的碳排放年均增速要快得多。

二、建筑领域低碳技术路径

建筑领域低碳技术可分为 3 个路径，分别是减碳、去碳和无碳技术。减碳技术包括建筑运行过程中对于高能耗、二氧化碳高排放环节的节能技术。去碳技术包括基于建筑的二氧化碳的捕获、埋存和利用技术，如植物、海洋的碳汇作用，以及材料对二氧化碳的吸收、捕集、固碳与储碳。但是，目前建筑领域的去碳技术，国内外行业内尚处于研究阶段，在建筑领域还未能实现大规模应用阶段。无碳技术包括核能、太阳能、风能、生物质能等清洁能源技术的建筑应用。

建筑领域的建筑节能、绿色性能、低碳技术互相交融重合又相互区别。建筑节能是低碳技术的最重要的减碳部分，建筑的可再生能源利用是低碳技术的无碳部分。建筑绿色性能包括安全耐久、健康舒适、生活便利、环境宜居、资源节约。建筑的安全耐久可以减少建筑建设的隐含碳排放；建筑的生活便利、环境宜居可以减少建筑使用者对于环境与交通工具的依赖，减少相应领域的碳排放；建筑的资源节约可以减少建筑运行碳排放与建筑建设与使用中的材料碳排放。

我国的建筑节能工作始于 20 世纪 80 年代，最早制定的建筑节能部署分三步走。第一步节能设计目标是在当地通用设计能耗水平（20 世纪 80 年代设计建筑）基础上普遍降低 30%。第二步节能设计目标要求在达到第一阶段要求的基础上节能 30%，相比原有 20 世纪 80 年代设计建筑节能率达到大约 50%。第三步节能设计目标是在第二步节能要求上再节能 30%，相比原有 20 世纪 80 年代设计建筑节能率达到大约 65%。

三步走阶段后，建筑节能设计目标迈向低能耗、超低能耗、近零能耗和零能耗。低能耗建筑主要是指建筑能耗水平应在第三阶段要求的基础上再节能 25%～30%，即设计建筑节能率达到约 75%。超低能耗建筑能耗水平应较第三阶段的国家和行业标准设计节能率基础上再降低 50% 以上，大约为 82.5%。近零能耗建筑能耗水平应较第三阶段的国家行业标准降低 60%～75%，设计节能率达到 90% 左右。零能耗建筑则要求在近零能耗基础上充分利用建筑本体和周边的可再生能源资源，使可再生能源年产能大于或等于建筑全年全部用能的建筑。

建筑中的无碳技术主要通过建筑可再生能源一体化建设与应用实现。浙江省可再生能源应用主要大力提倡太阳能光伏利用、太阳能光热利用；提倡空气源热泵热水系统；适宜地区提倡土壤源热泵、地表水水源热泵、太阳能光诱导系统；少量适宜地区可采用风能、生物质能、潮汐能等可再生能源。

其中，随着太阳能光伏系统的发展，太阳能光伏系统初投资大幅降低，年发电量显著增加，太阳能光伏系统已经在浙江省地区具有良好的经济效益。光伏建筑一体化，是将太阳能光伏发电方阵安装在建筑的围护结构外表面来提供电力[1]。光伏建筑一体化可分为两大类：一类是光伏方阵与建筑的结合，光伏板与建筑屋面的结合，是分布式光伏发电系统在城市中广泛应用的最佳安装方式；另一类是光伏方阵与建筑的集成[2]，如光电瓦屋顶、光电幕墙和光电采光顶等，光伏组件不仅要满足光伏发电的功能要求同时还要兼顾建筑的基本功能，如遮阳功能要求。

分布式光伏发电系统的理想应用方式为"光储直柔"应用。光是指充分利用建筑表面，发展光伏；储是指蓄电池储电，峰电并网，谷电储电；直是指内部直接直流配电，通过直流电压的变化传递对负载用电的需求[3]；柔是指在上述技术配置上，在应用策略方面，作为弹性负载，实现柔性用电。

建筑可再生能源一体化建设与应用过程中同时需要兼顾重视对城市生态的影响，城市风环境的影响，城市地貌的影响。例如，太阳能在城市建筑中的应用时必须考虑太阳能组件与构件的反光对城市风貌的影响，太阳能光伏发电系统并网应考虑对电网的影响。风能在城市建筑中的应用必须考虑风速场对城市通风廊道的影响，噪声对声环境的影响，风车叶轮对飞禽飞行的影响。地下水的水源热泵由于地下水的开采，对地质塌陷、地面沉降及地下水污染的风险与影响，一般情况下慎重使用或限制使用。

三、浙江省建筑节能减碳的主要实践探索及成效

浙江省建筑领域节能减碳的实践，注重制度建设与顶层设计。浙江省节能管理工作从 1998 年人民代表大会常务委员会通过《浙江省实施〈中华人民共和国节约能源法〉办法》开始，推进了 20 多年。2007 年，浙江省制定了《太阳能在建筑中利用实施的若干意见》；2011 年浙江省政府在全国率先出台了《关于积极推进绿色建筑发展的若干意见》；同年，浙江建设管理部门制定了《民用建筑项目节能评估和审查管理办法》等规范性文件，建立起绿色建筑监管制度体系，加大了对新建民用建筑执行强制性绿色建筑设计标准的监管力度。2012 年 5 月，浙江省第十一届人民代表大会通过《浙江省可再生能源开发利用促进条例》；2014 年发布《政府投资公益性建筑及大型公共建筑建设中全面推进绿色建筑行动的通知》；2015 年浙江省第十二届人民代表大会常务委员会第二十四次会议通过《浙江省绿色建筑条例》。

浙江省建筑领域的节能工作以技术标准的不断迭代提高为引领。2003 年浙江省发布设计节能率为 50% 的地方工程建设标准《居住建筑节能设计标准》（DB 33/1015—2003）；并在 2015 年修编，设计节能率提高至 65%；2021 年二次修编，进一步提高设计节能率至 75% 以上。对于公共建筑，2007 年浙江省发布设计节能率为 60% 的地方工程建设标准《公共建筑节能设计标准》（DB 33/1036）；2021 年修编，将设计节能率提高至 75% 以上。民用建筑的设计节能率稳步迭代提高，大大降低了建筑碳排放。

同时，结合绿色建筑技术，浙江省发布地方工程建设标准《绿色建筑设计标准》（DB 33/1092）。设计标准对照国家标准《绿色建筑评价标准》（GB/T 50378）梳理评价条款，结合浙江省的经济发展条件、气候与地域条件、技术完善程度，将原本需要大量模拟分析评价的条款在标准编制的时候做了预模拟分析，因地制宜变成设计师可操作的设计语言与设计技术条款。

此外，浙江省建筑领域还发布了《民用建筑可再生能源应用核算标准》（DBJ33/T 1105）、《绿色建筑专项规划编制导则》《民用建筑项目节能评估技术

规程》等一系列地方性工程建设标准、规程、导则，引领整个绿色节能减碳的建设过程。

截至 2020 年 11 月，浙江省累计按绿色建筑标准建设的新建建筑 9.9 亿 m²，累计已有 897 项建筑获得国家绿色建筑评价标识的自愿认证，总建筑面积约 1 亿 m²，其中公共建筑 465 项，居住建筑 426 项，工业建筑 6 项。二星级项目占比最大，高达 67%，而一星级、三星级项目占比较小，占比分别为 19% 及 14%。

四、经验启示

浙江省地处夏热冬冷地区，建筑节能必须遵循"被动优先"原则，即被动优先，主动优化原则。在浙江省的建筑节能实践中，充分适应本地区气候特点，在节能减碳的同时，重视建筑室内环境和健康性，强调以人为本的设计理念，注重自然资源转化应用，是浙江省的建筑节能减碳的技术经验。

被动节能是指以降低建筑的用能需求为目的的节能措施，以非机械电气设备干预手段实现；主动节能是当用能需求产生后，提高用能设备系统及效率来降低用能能耗。采用被动优先原则的原因在于：一是被动节能的建筑的寿命期远大于主动节能的设备系统的寿命期；二是主动节能对设备和技术的要求高，一次性投资大，在使用过程中还需要消耗能源。因此在建筑节能的技术路径上，首先尽量在不使用设备的情况下，采用被动式节能技术设计出环境品质相对优良的建筑。只有在环境恶劣、被动式方法达不到建筑使用要求的时候，才由设备工程师加以主动式设计的辅助和补充[4]。

浙江省的气候特征不同于其他气候带，其气候特点主要为春秋季节短，冬夏季节长，且夏季炎热、冬季湿冷的气候特征。随着人民对美好生活的向往，对室内环境要求的提高，建筑大多通过加装采暖空调设备调节室内温、湿度，来改善室内热环境。空调能耗在建筑环境维持能耗中占 30%～50%。通过研究围护结构各因素对空调能耗及节能率影响分析：浙江省建筑窗墙比对空调负荷及节能率影响显著；其他各因素影响排序为外窗传热系数＞屋面传热系数＞遮阳系数＞外墙传热系数。因此，对于浙江省建筑实施节能措施时，需在建筑设计阶段考虑选取合适的窗墙比，尤其规范大面积透光玻璃幕墙的使用，并充分考虑遮阳、采光、通风的相互影响，合理采用设计外窗。在设置围护结构保温时，要保证外窗及屋面热工性能以及充分考虑遮阳最优化，其次再考虑优化墙体保温[5]。

浙江省的建筑被动节能还要考虑对自然资源的免费利用。浙江省大部分建筑在使用过程中有自然通风需求，尤其春秋季或者夜间无人状态空调停用时，采用自然通风来消除室内积蓄热量实现"免费供冷"，从而减少空调耗能的同时也提高室内空气品质。根据清华大学在全国的一项调查，80%以上的人喜欢自然风。外窗能开启，可以满足人们亲近自然的心理，提高人们对室内环境品质的主观评价满意率。自然风与机械风在频谱、湍流度等物理特性上有很大差别。自然风的物理特性对人的生理和心理刺激所产生的舒适感无法替代。对自然资源的利用还包括对自然光资源的利用。建筑室内照明在建筑能耗中占20%～30%，在考虑节能措施时，可通过增加外窗面积，采用自然采光来减少照明能耗，但自然采光同时要兼顾采光窗墙面积比增加对空调能耗影响。

从主动节能技术角度，建筑节能减碳通过用能结构优化及用能设备与系统效率迭代更新实现。浙江省建筑中还存在高碳排放因子的化石燃料的能源使用。同样标准当量煤情况下，煤炭的碳排放因子最高，石油次之，天然气最低。电力的碳排放因子根据电力生产端发电类型不同而不同，在大力发展清洁发电的未来趋势下，电力能源的碳排放因子逐步下降，因此提高建筑用能电气化水平是浙江省建筑减碳的技术路径之一。以浙江省2019年的数据为例，若公共建筑的煤炭、石油改用电力能源；将城镇建筑的煤炭、石油改用电力能源；将乡村建筑的煤炭改用电力能源、石油改用天然气能源，对建筑领域用能结构优化，全年减碳量大约48.56万t。

用能设备与系统效率迭代更新包含两方面，一方面在于提升用能设备产品的效率水平，采用能效水平达到2级及以上的用能设备，尤其对于2000年之前早期建设的存量公共建筑普遍存在高能耗低舒适性的突出问题，对用能设备迭代更新，及时淘汰低效能设备，可推动既有建筑用能设备能效提升；另一方面需要在设计过程中不能仅仅孤立看待用能设备，还要综合平衡与考虑用能系统的效率提升，例如将建筑能源去中心化，通过能源总线技术进行能源互补，将不同空间分布的分散资源集成聚集到总线中共享，起到能源枢纽或电网聚集器的作用，通过分析不同能源需求，分质分品利用能源，对余能废能回收利用。

除建筑作为产品的节能特性外，建筑的建设也有节能与减碳的空间。建筑建设过程中推广装配式建造方式、推广绿色建材应用、推动建筑材料回收利用、可循环材料的利用。装配式建筑把传统建造方式中的大量现场作业工作改变在工厂中流水线机械化生产，在工厂加工制作好建筑用构件和配件（如楼板、墙板、楼梯、阳台等），运输到建筑施工现场，通过可靠的连接方式在现场装配安装而成的建筑，大大有利于减少建筑业的人工与低效高能耗。相比传统建造方式，装配式建筑节约能耗10%～30%。有研究对北京、上海、沈阳、深圳、合肥、济南等11个城市的装配式混凝土建筑工程对比分析，装配式混凝土建筑在建造阶段单位面积可减少碳排放 24.31 kg[6]。

除了技术层面，浙江省建筑领域的节能工作从政策机制上形成了完整的闭环工作体系。精细化的顶层设计为实现建筑节能与低碳提供了良好的保障。浙江省建筑节能架构了规划、设计、建设、运行的体系。在设计前端架构了节能评估、图审管理体系，在建设阶段架构了施工、能效测评、竣工验收管理体系，在运行阶段架构了能耗监测体系，从而建立了闭环管理，强化节能低碳建筑的建设监管。

在规划阶段，通过规划引领确定绿色减碳目标。绿色建筑专项规划明确绿色建筑发展目标，并确定各类新建民用建筑的绿色建筑等级、可再生能源应用要求、碳减排要求。城镇建设用地在使用权、拍卖或者挂牌公告中，依据绿色建筑专项规划明确该地块建筑建设目标要求。

在设计阶段，通过设计监管分解绿色减碳目标。设计阶段将绿色、低碳、节能等有关技术内容落实到具体项目，并进行专项节能评估和审查；施工图设计文件审查时，审核施工图设计文件是否符合绿色建筑强制性标准，是否落实节能审查意见，不符合绿色建筑强制性标准或者未落实节能审查意见的，不得出具施工图设计文件审查合格证书。

在建设阶段，通过施工监管实现绿色减碳目标。在建设过程中，施工单位按照施工图设计文件和绿色建筑强制性标准进行施工，在竣工之前依照规定对项目进行竣工能效测评，主要是对民用建筑围护结构保温隔热性能和用能系统效率等指标是否落实节能评估和审查的要求进行测评，确保绿色节能低碳指标在建设过程切实落到项目主体中。

在运行阶段，通过运行监管运行调适实现绿色减碳目标。省和设区的市城乡建设主管部门建立公共建筑运行能耗监管信息平台，实施公共建筑能耗动态监测和信息共享。新建国家机关办公建筑、建筑面积大于 10 000 m² 的公共建筑，应设置建筑用能分类计量及数据采集装置。通过运行过程中建筑用能监测，确保节能措施的有效性。

当前，全省节能低碳建筑的建设监管，基本已建立从规划到设计到施工到验收的全过程闭环管理机制。浙江省建筑建设全过程闭环管理机制的建立，对于实现浙江建筑领域的节能减碳提供了重要支持与保障，是浙江省建设管理的重要经验。

五、未来展望

随着浙江省建筑领域的节能减碳的整体规划与布局，建筑节能从旧三步走逐渐向新三步走的迭代升级，高星级绿色建筑、近零（零）能耗建筑、低碳建筑等各类示范项目建设，将会打造出一批具有浙江辨识度的硬核成果。同时，建筑节能减碳重点从建筑产品及建筑产品建设端向建筑产品使用运行管理转移，利用数字化手段与平台，实现建筑工程全过程管理、工作协同、数据分析以及信息共享。按照推进城乡建设一体化发展、转变城乡建设发展方式、提升绿色发展管理水平这 3 个维度，城乡建设必将引来新的绿色发展。

作者：丁德[1]，吴佳艳[2]

参考文献

[1] 金婷婷 . 可再生能源建筑应用技术集成系统的研究 [D]. 淮南：安徽理工大学，2015.

[2] 周舒灵 . 浙江省高速公路服务区改扩建建筑设计研究 [J]. 建筑与文化，2020（7）：4.

[3] 朱妍 . 让建筑成为新能源电力生产者（院士谈能源）[N]. 中国能源报，2021-04-05.

[4] 陈华晋，李宝骏，董志峰 . 浅谈建筑被动式节能设计 [J]. 建筑节能，2007，35（3）：3.

[5] 吴佳艳，沈恒根 . 夏热冬冷地区高大公用建筑空调能耗特性分析 [J]. 建筑热能通风空调，2012，31（3）：4.

[6] 王广明，文林峰，刘美霞，等 . 装配式混凝土建筑增量成本与节能减排效益分析及政策建议 [J]. 建设科技，2018（16）：6.

---

1 丁德，浙江大学建筑设计研究院有限公司技术总监，中国工程建设标准化协会绿建与生态城区分会理事，中国勘察设计协会标准化工作委员会委员，浙江省建筑领域碳达峰实施方案主要编制者，主要研究方向为建筑节能与碳排放，建筑绿色性能，建筑绿色低碳数字化等。

2 吴佳艳，浙江大学建筑设计研究院有限公司副主任工程师，主要研究方向为气候适应性建筑性能研究，绿色低碳建筑及数字化等，浙江省建筑领域碳达峰实施方案主要编制者。

浙江交通推进高质量绿色低碳发展的
改革与创新探索简述

围绕浙江省交通领域碳达峰的整体推进，从数据创新、管理创新、服务创新、技术创新和应用创新 5 个方面，系统性地总结了过去几年全省交通领域推进"双碳"工作的经验做法。对省级交通碳排放数据库、交通碳指数、企业碳效码、数字化平台、典型应用等创新成果的目的逻辑、核心内容做了简要介绍。聚焦三个"一号工程"在交通"双碳"领域的落地，进行了精准转化落地方面的展望。

一、引言

浙江交通是浙江省国民经济和社会发展的兴省之器、强国之基，也是应对气候变化、推动绿色发展的主战场[1]，交通领域碳排放占全省碳排放总量的 9%[2]。近年来，浙江省交通运输发展实现了历史性跨越，综合线网里程、运输规模、运输装备等方面均居全国前列。行业高度重视节能减排，始终以低碳发展作为交通运输体系构建底色。特别是党的十九大以来，在习近平新时代中国特色社会主义思想指引下，全省交通系统加快转变发展理念，积极调整运输结构，大力推进新能源和清洁能源应用，强化低碳治理能力建设，低碳交通体系建设取得显著成效，为应对气候变化和加强生态文明建设作出重要贡献，近年来围绕"数据创新、管理创新、服务创新、技术创新和应用创新"5 个方面，进行实践探索并形成了一定的改革做法，简述如下。

二、主要实践探索及成效

（一）创新交通领域碳排放数据采集核算方法

交通运输是一个复杂的巨系统，碳排放统计核算是制定政策、推动工作等的重要依据。目前全省交通行业碳排放主要采用 IPCC"自上而下"法进行碳排放测算[3]，优点是数据容易获取，计算便捷，局限性是数据范围、更新频次等无法实现交通领域碳排放细账。因此以问题导向，创新交通领域碳排放数据采集方法。

1. 根据"自上而下"等方法，明确全省交通领域碳排放的主要构成

经分析识别目前交通领域碳减排的关键为营运交通，其碳排放约占交通领域碳排放总量的 70%；公路运输碳排放占营运性交通碳排放的 70% 左右[4]，公路运输的单位周转量碳强度为铁路的 4 倍、水路的 10 倍，营运交通碳排放达峰关键变量在于公路运输。"居民生活"划分至交通运输领域的碳排放（主要是私人小汽车的碳排放）近 10 年呈不断上升趋势，占非营运性交通碳排放的比例超50%，非营运交通碳排放达峰关键变量在于私家车。

2. 围绕"重中之重"等领域，开展全省道路交通碳排放的数据采集

围绕交通领域碳排放重点，浙江省开展了全省道路运输领域碳排放专项调研。调查对象涉及全省 11 个地市道路货运、公路客运、公交客运、出租客运车辆所有营运性道路运输车辆。调查内容包括道路运输车辆的运输生产、行驶里程、能耗情况等数据。调查方法创新性地将设备监测调查、企业自有系统调查、车辆问卷调查 3 种方式互相补充、互相校正。调查结果是在全国范围内率先建立省级百公里单耗计算模型，形成不同车型、不同燃料类型、不同排放标准、不同车龄、不同工况的百公里单耗标准库和百公里油耗数据库。结果显示，浙江省中重型道路货运车辆实际百公里能耗重型车普遍低于标准限值，小微型货车实际百公里能耗重型车普遍高于标准限值，营运性客车和出租车实际百公里单耗与标准限值差异不大，城市公交车百公里能耗基本低于国家标准限值。

3. 聚焦"全面精准"等要求，开展全省交通领域碳排放的数据核算

基于省级百公里单耗标准库，贯通全省车辆审批系统属性、车辆运行轨迹、特殊工况下的运输信息，分别构建能源消耗测算模型，创建一套可实现实时动态高频监测的道路运输行业能耗测算规则。对全省及各市的分领域全年能耗进行核算，实现公路运输行业中不同细分领域（公路客运、道路货运、城市公交、出租车等）能耗细账核算，创建浙江省道路运输行业能源消耗一本账。通过数据库比对，2022年，全省营运性货车全年能耗610万t标准煤、出租车（网约车）近70万t标准煤、公交车53万t标准煤、营运性客车近30万t标准煤。

（二）创新交通领域碳减排战略目标管理模型

聚焦全省交通行业六大领域14项减排举措，省级层面率先开展交通低碳指数研究和评价工作，作为跟踪评估省市两级交通领域碳达峰工作总体效果的量化工具，在辅助决策等方面具有重要意义。

1. 以量化应用为导向，明确全省交通低碳指数的构建方法和原则

交通低碳指数在交通运输行业具备一定的经济水平和生产规模，发展的内外生需求均向绿色低碳转变，通过采取一系列节能降碳措施，最大程度提高行业能源效率。评价体系体现三个特色：一是定量评价。选取可量化的评价指标，减少定性指标在纵向比较中的短板，最终评价得分实现交通运输低碳发展水平的横向、纵向比较。二是逐级评价。能够实现省、市、县三级的交通运输低碳发展水平评价，不同层级评价中实现核心结论和核心指标的互相印证。三是评价弹性。适时对部分指标进行调整，定期更新指标权重，以反映不同阶段的工作重点。评价指标体系包括交通发展质量、交通能耗排放、交通低碳管理3个方面。

2. 以指标落地为目标，构建全省交通低碳指数对应的指标体系

围绕交通发展质量、交通能耗排放、交通低碳管理3个方面，构建交通运输低碳发展评价指标池。交通发展质量类指标13项[5]，交通能耗排放类指标8项[6]，交通低碳管理类指标36项。经过多轮迭代，最终选取13项指标用于指数测算。交通发展质量类指标反映地区交通经济与生产活动强度，交通能耗排放类指标反映地区交通运输行业节能降碳效果，交通低碳管理类指标反映地区交通碳达峰相关工作开展进程。地区碳指数的最终结果受交通活动强度、节能降碳效果以及低碳工作开展进程的共同影响。

3. 以指数提升为目的，构建分地市分领域交通碳达峰任务清单

以指数提升为目的，聚焦各地市推进交通领域碳达峰的重点难点任务落地，杭州应着重在公转水、岸电推广方面持续发力，争取成为全省交通领域低碳工作的样板城市。嘉兴、湖州、舟山、宁波等水运发达地区在交通节能减碳方面具有天然地理优势，碳排放强度本身较低，下一步应加大交通领域非化石能源使用，加快低碳装备升级和组织效率提升工作。丽水、金华、衢州等欠发达地区运输规模和装备数量较小，一定程度上降低运输装备升级和运输结构调整难度，可以优先推进运输装备升级等工作。

（三）创新交通领域服务企业低碳转型的工具

运输企业是运输服务的主要提供者，已成为影响交通领域碳达峰的关键变量。交通领域创新性地打造碳效码的应用工具，表征分行业分领域的运输企业碳排放强度，服务运输企业绿色转型发展。

1. 聚焦企业基础，制定赋码规则

省级行业主管部门于 2022 年 6 月出台《浙江省规上道路货物运输企业碳效码分类分级办法（试行）》，正式启动全省规模以上道路货运企业的碳效码赋码与推广工作。企业分类根据企业拥有车辆的经营范围，将全省规模以上道路货物运输企业分为普通货物运输企业、货物专用运输企业、危险货物运输企业以及综合运输企业 4 种类型分别进行赋码。关于企业分级赋码，碳效码由企业碳排放强度、企业低碳发展基础和附加分三部分组成，根据道路货物运输企业碳效码得分从高到低，每类企业碳效码等级分别赋予绿码、蓝码、红码 3 种状态，并按季度更新。

2. 助力企业发展，测算绿色基础

目前已对全省所有规模以上货运企业进行碳效码赋码，覆盖约 10 万辆营运性货车。从总体情况来看，企业平均得分由 2022 年第一季度的 70 分级提档至 80 分级；企业绿码率由第一季度的不足 50% 上升至第四季度的 60%；企业平均单位周转量碳排放强度明显下降，行业整体绿色低碳发展水平有所提升。细分四大类道路货运企业来看，综合运输企业最高，危险货物运输企业最低；企业绿码率综合运输企业最高，普通货物运输企业最低。浙江省道路货运行业的碳减排工作管理应重点聚焦普货物企业，引导企业规模化、专业化发展。平均单位周转量碳排放强度货物专用运输行业最低，主要原因分析为集装箱等专用运输车运输组织效率相对较高，危险货物运输行业最高，主要原因分析为危货车辆回场管理严格，一定程度上影响了其回程货的装载，降低了运输组织效率。

3. 服务企业转型，完善政策闭环

围绕碳效码发挥更大作用，助力地方开展碳效码与政策挂钩的闭环体系。绿色金融政策方面，2022 年 5 月，中国人民银行绍兴市中心支行、中国银保监会绍兴监管分局、绍兴市交通运输局 3 家单位联合印发《关于金融支持绿色交通促进低碳循环发展的指导意见》，绿码企业可申请更高额度贷款并享受更低利率。目前已依托"碳效码"累计为绿码企业授信 1 800 万元、低息贷款 784 万元。防疫补助促进政策。2022 年 7 月，绍兴市交通运输局、绍兴市财政局印发《绍兴市公路水路运输企业防疫补助政策实施细则》，对已申领交通碳效码且为绿码的规上道路货运企业额外给予 1 万元补助奖励，共计兑现绿码企业奖补资金 40 万元。

（四）创新交通领域低碳发展的数字化管理手段

针对交通碳排放源点多量大、流动性强、核算监管难度大等难点堵点问题，创新性地搭建了全国首个省级交通碳达峰数字化应用平台，面向政府、企业、公众三类重点用户，数字化实现"区域端碳指数、企业端碳效码、公众端碳积分"三大碳工具智控体系，实现交通领域碳减排任务在线管理，推进行业碳排放系统感知、量化核算和闭环监管。

1. 问题导向，明确平台定位

明确主要问题。一是国家层面暂未考虑应用建设，目前全国层面并无建设统一数字化应用的计划，浙江省先行谋划建应用、创示范。二是省级层面无实质性应用成果，省级层面碳排放相关的数字化应用建设可借鉴经验较少。三是交通领域碳达峰体系需重构，交通领域碳排放核算自身的数据统计体系和数据核算体系仍处于摸索阶段。

明确应用定位。交通碳达峰数字化应用平台是交通行业推动绿色低碳转型的抓总平台，是浙江省交通领域数字化改革的重点应用。针对碳达峰工作管理主体多、运输装备多、监管范围广、数据监测难等问题，围绕碳排放总量、能耗总量、碳排放强度和能耗强度"4个值"，服务管理部门、运输企业、社会公众三类对象，努力实现碳排放管理从"看不见"到"看得见"的转变；实现碳排放核算从"算大账"到"算细账"的转变；实现碳排放政策从"粗线条"到"精细化"的转变；实现企业和个人从"不关心"到"离不开"的转变。

2. 三张清单，明确平台重点

明确六项重大需求清单。一是重点解决碳排放粗感知，数据颗粒度不细。二是碳核算看不见、无标准，结果权威性不高。三是碳政策无体系，实施精准度不够。四是碳源头管理存在空白，职责覆盖面不全。五是碳监管有跨部门交叉，管理集中度不高。六是碳减排缺乏动力和吸引力，主体参与度不足。

聚焦三项多跨场景清单。一是面向政府侧的多跨场景。聚焦运输装备升级与运输结构调整是两大关键变量，需跨环保、公安、交通等部门协同。二是面向企业侧的多跨场景。主要解决企业碳积分核算、挂钩政府相关碳排放政策两方面问题，实现"政策制定 – 积分核算 – 政策评估"闭环。三是面向公众侧的多跨场景。主要解决个人碳足迹还原、碳积分交易两方面问题，实现"足迹监测 – 平台核算 – 积分兑换"闭环。

破题五项重大改革清单。一是改革现有数据统计模式，建立统一碳排放"一套表"统计体系。二是改革现有业务管理模式，构建碳达峰统一工作体系。三是改革现有政策激励体系，实现政策精准闭环发力。四是改革现有市场准入制度，构建减排导向的行业规范标准体系。五是改革现有主体监管模式，引导企业等参与交通碳减排。

3. "133X"，落地平台场景

碳达峰数字化应用总体业务架构为"133X"，即 1 个交通大脑、3 类用户、3 个工具、X 个应用场景。1 个交通大脑指交通领域碳达峰算法规则。3 类用户指碳达峰数字化应用重点面向管理部门（省、市、县三级）、运输企业、社会公众。3 个工具指碳指数、碳效码、碳积分。实现五大功能。

监测"一屏感知"：绘制碳达峰智治地图，展示全省各地区碳达峰工作的完成进度和状态，通过建立一套可更新、可复用、高时效的全数据收集、报送体系，推进省、市、县三级碳达峰数据一体化。

核算"一表清算"：打造全省碳达峰数据统一"一套表"，融合行业数据，形成标准化的数据集成体系及核算体系。分地市、分行业、分企业自动核算能源消耗总量、碳排放总量、能耗强度、碳排放强度。

预警"一图研判"：绘制交通领域碳排放"一张图"，实现能源消费总量、碳排放总量、能耗强度、碳排放强度"4 个值"的评估；跟踪行动方案中六大领域 14 项举措指标分区域，提供省级行业管理部门"指标下达－跟踪预警－指标评价"闭环管理系统支撑。

决策"一网覆盖"：探索建成碳达峰数字化应用"一张网"，根据各地市碳减排任务，对碳减排工作实施前后的减排效果分别进行预测和评价，指导未来减排政策制定与优化，实现"效果预测－成果评价－政策优化"的碳减排工作闭环管理。

信用"一码通达"：建立企业"碳效码"、社会公众"碳积分"，将其与政府补贴、企业经营（融资成本、经营许可等）、路权配置、车险费率、补贴奖励等挂钩，嵌入企业和个人生产生活环节。

（五）创新交通领域低碳政策应用场景闭环

交通运输领域围绕运输装备升级和运输结构调整等关键领域，以数字化为手段，结合各地实际，在衢州市和台州市等地开展数字化的应用场景闭环设计，取得阶段性成果。

1. 围绕交通领域运输结构调整，先行推进大宗货物"公转水"场景闭环

从运输结构来看，发达国家大宗货物中长距离运输以水路为主要方式，浙江省目前仍以公路运输为主要方式，运输结构有较大优化空间。从碳排放强度

来看，水路运输的单位周转量碳排放强度仅为公路的 1/10，具有较大的减排优势。其逻辑闭环为将大宗货物"公转水"的碳减排量折算为能源消耗量，并将其作为企业用能配额的增量，激发企业内生动力，引导货主企业主动选择水路运输方式。

从"公转水"的配套政策完善方面来看。一是"公转水"节能量与企业用能预算指标挂钩奖励政策，以碳减排量为纽带，建立"公转水"运量与能耗指标的关联关系，将"公转水"碳减排量作为能源双控指标中能源消费总量的激励因素，直接用于货主企业；二是"公转水"补助政策，对集装箱江海河联运、从事水路运输的内河航运企业、通联码头、船公司等主体进行补贴。

2. 围绕交通领域运输装备升级，探索推进城市绿色配送场景闭环

装备保有量方面，全省 173 万辆货车中，近 80% 为轻型及以下货车，其中大部分为城市配送车辆，且行业管理的权责相对模糊。碳排放方面，浙江省重载货运车辆碳排放占交通领域碳排放的 42%，是整个公路运输碳排放重点。其逻辑闭环为围绕重货企业的碳减排，以碳效码分级分类作为手段，配置差异化的引导政策，助力企业进行运输装备的新能源化升级，并引导企业提升运输效率。

从"绿色配送"的配套政策完善方面来看。一是实施资金补助政策，更新新能源车辆运营奖补办法，将补贴标准与企业碳效码分级挂钩，执行差异化补贴；二是实施路权管理政策，优化城配车辆城市限行区通行细则，初步考虑新能源城配车辆在限行区内继续不受限制，非新能源车辆根据企业碳效码等级予以分级路权管理；三是实施停车管理政策，优化既有车辆差异化停车管理办法，继续执行新能源城配车辆在政府经营公共停车位免费停车，非新能源车辆根据企业碳效码分别给予相应的优惠。

三、经验启示

一是推动交通领域碳达峰是一项系统工程，应顺应社会经济高质量发展大势而为，应顺应交通领域高兼容发展优势而为，应顺应运输市场高效率发展而为，应顺应绿色技术高标准发展而为。二是应积极构建适应浙江省实际的交通领域碳达峰目标管理的政策手段和发展方式，推进交通运输领域结构性和节奏型减排，提高政策与市场需求的匹配度，同时通过效果评价进行政策优化。三是应积极推进交通碳达峰数字化应用建设，创新数据采集方式，创建数据处理标准，创造数字化应用，助力交通领域碳达峰目标的实现。

四、展望

2023 年是全面贯彻党的二十大精神的开局之年，也是深化推进"双碳"工作落地见效的关键之年。交通领域将进一步用好改革和创新的工具箱，努力将交通"双碳"工作作为践行落实省委"三个一号工程"的重要融合点、发力点，坚定不移贯彻新发展理念，创新深化工作体系和发展模式，持续推动交通高质量发展取得新成效。同时坚定不移咬定"2030 年交通领域碳排放进入峰值平台期"的达峰目标，改革攻坚重点难点工作任务，多措并举务实推进，坚定不移推动变革重塑，开放提升"交通 + 能源"等产业经济，因地施策加快交通绿色治理一体化转型。全面推动"三个一号工程"在交通"双碳"领域精准转化落地。

作者：白鸿宇[1]

参考文献

[1] 谢守红，王丽霞，邵珠龙. 国内外碳排放研究综述 [J]. 干旱区地理，2014，（4）：720–730.

[2] 曹更永. 浙江省交通运输领域碳达峰研究报告 [R]. 杭州：浙江省交通运输科学研究院，2021：27–28.

[3] 唐炜祺. 中国及各省区能源碳排放达峰路径分析 [D]. 杭州：浙江大学，2020.

[4] 王本梅，冯冬焕，柳月玲. 碳达峰背景下浙江省货运结构调整对策 [J]. 综合运输，2021（43）：103–108.

[5] 欧阳斌，张跃军，郭杰. 低碳交通运输的综合评价指标及其应用 [J]. 北京理工大学学报（社会科学版），2014（16）：7–13.

[6] 张宇欢. 高质量发展背景下交通运输碳排放区域差异与影响因素研究 [D]. 西安：长安大学，2021.

---

1 白鸿宇，浙江省交通运输科学研究院交通发展研究中心副主任（主持）、交通经济运行监测中心负责人（兼），中国公路学会交通低碳工作委员会委员。主持"浙江省交通领域碳达峰研究报告"多项省市级课题，研究支撑并参与编写多项政策文件；主持国际合作交流课题"浙江省交通运输领域碳中和路径与对策研究""碳中和愿景下浙江省道路货运转型研究"；编制出台《道路运输企业碳账户碳排放核算与评价指南》（DB3308/T 099—2021）标准等。

农业碳达峰的"浙江经验"与工作展望

农业系统既是生产系统又是生态系统，既有碳排放又有碳固定。2005年，时任浙江省委书记的习近平就提出"大力发展高效生态农业"，之后浙江通过污染治理、产业转型、减排固碳等协同推进农业绿色可持续发展。本章分析了浙江农业领域率先碳达峰的主要路径，总结了减排固碳的"浙江经验"，预测了未来10年碳排放趋势，提出了下一步工作思路。

一、引言

农业减排固碳影响广泛且深远。农业生产涉及全球最广袤的土地面积，最广泛的人口，第三次全国国土调查结果显示，我国耕地面积达到19.18亿亩，以占全球耕地不到13%的耕地面积养活了18%的人口。农田作为占我国1/8的土地利用形式，农业领域减排固碳与人民日常生活息息相关，影响面最广泛而深远，既是碳达峰实现的重要手段，又在碳中和阶段有巨大潜力。随着中国农业生产方式的绿色转型，近5年农作物生产领域的碳排放已经开始下降，浙江省更是已经达到峰值，将发挥率先达峰的引领作用；着眼于碳中和目标，农业领域减排固碳需提前谋划，发挥其巨大潜力。

农业生产既是碳源又是碳汇。一方面，农业生产既是生产系统，又是生态系统的重要组成部分。农业生产的碳排放组成较复杂，不同农作制度、生产模式对生态环境的作用均有不同，农业生产活动中，能源消耗、畜禽养殖、农用物资投入、水稻种植、土壤等均可以排放温室气体，排放的温室气体主要包括二氧化碳、甲烷、氧化亚氮，是非 CO_2 温室气体的主要排放源。另一方面，农田土壤、海洋等作为支撑农业生产的物质基础，同时又是巨大的生态系统。农田土壤有机质水平的提高，可以增加农田土壤碳库，提升碳收集能力。在稳定粮食生产、保障农业可持续发展的同时，其资源循环、生态净化、固碳增汇作用，是十分重要且不可替代的。

农业减排固碳具有多元协同价值。农业领域的减排固碳，从内涵与系统路径上，与绿色发展、污染治理、产业增长均具有协同意义。在淘汰高耗能农机，推动可再生能源替代推动减排方面，协同推进农业产业结构调整，农业绿色发展；在浙江省减污降碳协同创新区建设中，从农业投入品减量、废弃物资源化利用等减排与治污协同性最强的方面发力，可以找准农业生态环境保护"最大公约数"，发挥防治面源污染与减少碳排放的双重效益；在推广减排技术与生态模式，发掘农业碳汇上出实招，对于在不牺牲生产力发展的前提下，统筹减排固碳与产业增长有协同价值。

二、主要实践探索及成效

回顾浙江省高效生态农业发展历程，我们可以发现近 20 年来，浙江省在兼顾农业高质量发展与农业生态的命题下，久久为功、创新深化。早在 2005 年，时任浙江省委书记的习近平就作出了"大力发展高效生态农业"的重大决策；2010 年，浙江成为全国唯一的现代生态循环农业试点省；2017 年，浙江省被原农业部确定为第一批首个整省制创建农业绿色发展试点先行区；2019 年，浙江省启动"肥药两制"改革，作为农业绿色发展的主要抓手；2021 年浙江省数字化改革以来，农业绿色发展迈入全面推进投入减量化、资源高效化、环境生态化、产品优质化的高效生态农业集成改革阶段，2023 年提出"建设高效生态农业强省"，将其作为"农业强国，浙江先行"的发力方向。多年实践中，浙江省从淘汰落后低效产能、推动可再生能源替代、提高农业生产效能、资源循环利用、探索农业碳汇上出实招，为推动农业领域率先达峰发挥了巨大作用。

（一）主要实践探索

1. 在淘汰落后低效产能上出实招

在淘汰老旧农机方面，随着浙江省农业机械化水平的提升，一批能耗高、污染重、安全性能低的老旧农机也逐渐累积起来，为此，浙江省加强购机政策引导，制修订农机报废补贴政策，鼓励和引导省内从事农业生产的组织和个人主动报废低效老旧农机。例如目前享受补贴政策的产品都符合国Ⅲ柴油发动机排放标准；开展变型拖拉机专项整治行动，2021 年 6 月，全省 5 万余台存量变型拖拉机全面清零，提前 1 年完成省级任务，提前 4 年半完成国家级任务。

减少捕捞渔船碳排放对于减少农业领域碳排放以及保护海洋生态环境均具有重要意义。2014 年开始，浙江省推行"一打三整治"专项执法行动，即严厉打击涉渔"三无"船舶、严厉整治"绝户网""船证不符"渔船和海洋环境污染，其间先后制定出台了一系列制度，规范渔船管控、伏休管理、环境治理等，如坚持和深化海洋渔船功率、数量的"双控"制度，通过海洋渔船减船转产补助为减船渔民兜底等。浙江沿海已累计取缔涉渔"三无渔船"1.9 万余艘，占全国取缔总数的近一半。

2. 在推动可再生能源替代上出实招

积极引导农业生产主体改善能源结构，推动设施农业电气化改造，合理开发使用生物质能、太阳能等清洁可再生能源。引导在大型规模养殖场及养殖密集区建设畜禽粪污沼气发电工程，鼓励有条件地区推进沼气集中供气，替代化石能源。将使用生物质颗粒为热源的粮食烘干装备纳入农机补贴。至 2021 年，浙江省 5 700 余台粮食烘干机中，利用清洁生物质的热风炉 2 502 台，约占43.63%。

引导推动"农光互补"，在不影响农业生产和农用地保护的前提下，合理利用农业设施棚顶、农副产品加工冷库、鱼塘水面等发展光伏农业。比如建德三都镇"渔光互补"项目自三都光伏电站建成以来，每年可向杭州建德地区输送清洁电量约 2 000 万 kW·h，大约相当于三都镇当地一年的用电量，折合每年节约标准煤 0.8 万 t、减排二氧化碳 1.7 万 t。

3. 在提高农业生产效能上出实招

农业投入品减量，减少不合理施用在农业领域非 CO_2 排放减量中发挥着最基础和关键的作用，在"肥药两制"总体布局下，通过源头减量、优化农资供给侧结构、农废回收等方面的举措，夯实了浙江省绿色低碳发展的基础，化肥、农药用量实现了"九连降"。例如 2021 年浙江启动供给端"配方肥替代平衡肥"行动，一改 10 多年来平衡肥占据农资市场主导地位的局面，2022 年配方肥已占化肥总销售量的 77.5%，加大有机肥施用，应用畜粪肥等各类有机肥 100 万 t以上。

土地集约化、经营规模化是节本增效、提高能源利用率的前提，在提高农事作业规模效率上，有序推动闲置耕地向家庭农场、合作社集中。浙江省积极推进搭建规模化、专业化、一站式的现代化农事服务中心，发挥全程机械化作业服务以及集中育苗、农技服务等的"1+X"的综合服务功能。至 2021 年年底，全省建成现代农业综合服务中心 311 家、产业农合联 313 家，庄稼医院 1 097 家，基本形成布局全省、覆盖乡镇的农业社会化服务网络。

在提升机械化水平上，将高效、节能、复式、智能农机具纳入农机购置补贴，推广符合国家排放标准的联合收割机、插秧机，积极推动飞防植保、山地轨道等减肥减药效果好、输运作业效率高的农机装备投入使用。自2018年开始，对植保无人机补贴，2020—2022年共补贴3 402台。全省农作物耕种收综合机械化率达到77.2%，建成数字农业工厂（基地）278家、未来农场20家。

在畜禽养殖规模化方面，提出以"六化"（标准化、绿色化、规模化、循环化、数字化、基地化）为引领建设高水平现代化养殖场，在大型规模养殖场配套建设或改造提升精准饲喂、节水和养殖污染治理畜禽粪污资源化利用设施，推广应用养殖臭气综合治理技术装备，推动畜禽养殖进一步朝着高标准、低排放、高效益的集约模式转型升级。至2022年年底，全省按照"六化"标准建成投产万头以上猪场124家。

在农业数字化方面，推动监管服务数字化，实施全周期、全过程服务管理和监测预警，打造"浙农优品""畜牧产业大脑""渔业产业大脑"等数字化应用，将数字化和智能化手段贯穿农业生产全过程；提升农业标准化水平，推进数字农业工厂建设和规模种养基地数字化改造；推动组织生产数字化，依托"浙农机"等数字化应用科学开展农机跨区调度和动态作业；慈溪等地试点推广共享冷库，避免冷库资源季节性空置，冷库综合利用率提高15%以上。

4. 在资源循环利用上出实招

农业废弃物资源化利用，尤其是农作物秸秆全量化、高值化综合利用是农业低碳技术创新最密集的领域，具有较大的减排固碳潜力，离田秸秆可以用来生产有机肥、生物炭、压制板材，还可以作为成型燃料提供能源，秸秆还田是农田土壤固碳的重要措施。浙江省围绕肥料化、饲料化等"五化"利用，大力推进秸秆多途径、高值化利用，优化秸秆利用结构，大力发展生物质成型燃料和气化清洁能源等技术模式，在德清、永康、天台三县（市、区）创建全国农作物秸秆全量化利用试点县，秸秆综合利用率达95%以上。

深化农牧对接等资源化利用方式，浙江省每年畜禽粪污除20%以截污纳管的形式在粪污产生高峰期和沼液消纳淡季兜底外，其余的80%通过沼液还田进行资源化利用。通过合理配套消纳田块，加强沼液配送链条、田间贮存设施建设，形成养殖户、服务组织和种植主体紧密衔接的现代生态循环模式，在畜禽主产区配套建设有机肥加工厂。例如龙游县循环利用沼液，根治养殖排泄物污染，并利用养殖场周边丘陵地貌特征，建立"沼气池—沼液池—管道—施肥"的循环利用系统。

示范"稻虾轮作""秸秆种菇"等生态种养技术模式，全省总结、推广立体种养、水旱轮作、旱地多熟和园地套种四大类 50 种理念先进、生态高效的新型农作制度。例如与水稻单作系统相比，稻鱼共生系统排放的温室气体更少，环境影响更小，生态和经济效益更高。青田县稻鱼共生生态循环模式入选 2022 年度绿色低碳转型典型案例。

5. 在探索农业固碳增汇上出实招

在挖掘农业固碳能力上，持续开展高标准农田建设。开展耕地质量提升行动，推广保护性耕作模式，通过有机肥施用、秸秆还田等技术应用推动土壤改良。构建以浅海贝藻养殖为载体的海洋碳汇，增强海洋渔业碳汇功能。例如在"三农九方"科技协同中列入新型秸秆炭基肥、二氧化碳气肥、生猪养殖场臭气收集处理、生物炭等科研项目，生物炭首先是移除大气中二氧化碳的方法之一，其次可以改良土质，有利于土壤中的微生物生长，最后由于生物炭的碱性比较强，还能够促进土壤酸碱平衡，减少对化肥的需求。

在开展农业碳监测、报告和核查体系研究上，联合浙江大学、中国农业大学、省农科院、同济大学、浙江农林大学等高等院校和科研机构，推进农业碳排放核算评价标准研究，推动农业碳账户数字化模型建设。2021 年年底，衢州市率先发布农业碳账户碳排放核算与评价地方标准，在水稻、生猪、有机肥、胡柚产业率先开展 1 000 余家主体碳排放核算。

（二）农业领域碳减排成效

由于碳达峰目标下，我国的"净零排放"侧重 CO_2，对浙江省农业领域碳排放情况进行的测算主要集中在 CO_2 排放，基于统计年鉴、能源平衡表、渔业船舶油耗情况等资料，汇总测算了浙江省农业领域二氧化碳排放量（图 7–1）。

从排放总量来看，2017 年，浙江省农业领域 CO_2 排放已率先达峰，达到峰值 657 万 t，之后得益于变型拖拉机清理和渔业"一打三整治"等行动，出现了明显的下降过程。从占比来看，农业领域消费端碳排放量占全社会碳排放量的 1.44%。

从能源消费结构来看，农机、渔船主要消耗汽油、柴油，规模化养殖场主要消耗电力，2018 年开始，得益于以燃煤为热源的粮食烘干机的整治淘汰，煤炭消费基本趋零。从排放领域来看，农机、渔船和规模养殖（含设施农业）为主要二氧化碳排放领域，排放量分别占总排放量的 27.42%、48.75% 和 23.83%。

图 7-1　全省 2005—2019 年农业领域碳排放总量趋势

三、经验启示

（一）传统生态方法与现代农业技术相结合

浙江省从生态循环农业到高效生态农业集成改革的一脉相承，究其源头可以追溯到浙江省丰富农业文化遗产中，在"天人合一"这一中华传统哲学体系下，千百年来农业生产方式不断传承延续，汇聚成生态、有机、循环的农业生产技术和农业知识理念。而今，浙江省一方面延续发展一批生态循环的传统农业技术进行低碳生产，例如用还田、深埋、集中处理等方式解决作物秸秆等问题；另一方面，积极推广各种低碳农业新技术，例如示范应用水肥一体化、侧深施肥、理化诱控、生物防治等技术。依托农业科技联盟等平台，通过"三农九方"科技协同项目，推动农业低碳技术创新研究。召开低碳农业论坛，邀请院士专家、科研院所开展技术交流，促进技术引领落地，助力节能减排。

（二）发挥低碳相关政策引导的关键作用

浙江省在低碳农业发展道路上，一直发挥着政策引导的关键作用，通过全国现代生态循环农业试点省、全国畜牧业绿色发展示范省、全国农业"机器换人"示范省、国家农业绿色发展试点先行区等一批"国字号"创建抓手，尤其是得益于变型拖拉机清理、渔业"一打三整治"和"肥药两制"改革，碳排放总量实现了率先达峰，绿色低碳，成为浙江农业鲜明的底色。在新政策制度创设中，积极融入碳中和发展要求，以低碳生态农场创建为抓手，提前布局、有的放矢地推动农业生产标准提升、推进二氧化碳与非二氧化碳温室气体协同控制。

（三）注重市场机制的引入与应用

自农业作为全省"6+1"领域开展"双碳"工作以来，浙江省积极鼓励地方先行先试，在引入市场机制上勇于探索，以激励主体转型升级，应用低碳生态技术，在低碳生态农场创建的基础上，形成低碳合作团，推动低碳生态农场产销对接等方面的价值实现。2022年，衢州市通过1 000家农业主体碳账户贴标情况，配套金融信贷，共发放贷款2亿元；温州市完成1万t海洋渔业碳汇交易，经核算，当地贝藻养殖3年碳汇量达到2.3万t；杭州、嘉兴两地通过对葡萄、红美人、沃柑、旱稻、草莓农产品全生命周期实地碳足迹调查，形成第一批符合国际标准的农产品碳标签，在实现农业低碳市场价值，推动低碳发展普惠农民上，作出多样探索。

（四）推动数字化技术的利用与支撑

农业碳排放具有特殊性，属于面源排放，精确定量检测难度大。在浙江省实现"双碳"目标过程中，农业数字化发挥重要作用，既有必然性也有可能性。从必然性来看，农业碳排放方法学特性决定了其可以形成智能模型，以数字化的方式提高核算效率，衢州、舟山在出台核算地方标准的基础上已经建立起农业碳账户核算模型；另一方面，浙江省农业"双碳"工作开展以来，"浙农"系统应用的数据积淀越来越多，高度贯通的应用发挥了数据价值，浙农应用中生产记录、产量等数据为农业碳账户模型以及农产品碳标签的核算提供了重要支撑。数字化对于降低农业碳排放核算成本，助力市场机制运用，完善"双碳"联农带农机制方面具有前瞻意义。

四、工作展望

（一）落实总量控制

在增强适应气候变化能力、保障粮食安全基础上，坚持降低排放强度和控制排放总量并举。保障"十四五"期间，全省农业领域能源活动碳排放触顶相对峰值650万t后平稳回落。将农业碳达峰工作列入全省高质量推进乡村全面振兴、农业农村现代化发展规划等重要文件内容。重点工作举措与生态文明建设、农业农村数字化改革、中央环保督察问题整改等中心工作紧密结合，建立碳达峰任务清单化、闭环化管理机制。

基于农业增产保供和产业发展、能源消费结构进一步优化、能源利用效率持续提高 3 个方面的分析和研判，对浙江省农业领域碳达峰情况进行了预测（图 7-2）。预计全省农业领域能源活动碳排放将保持缓慢增长，在 2025 年达到相对高峰值 650 万 t 后进入平台期，此后缓慢下降。

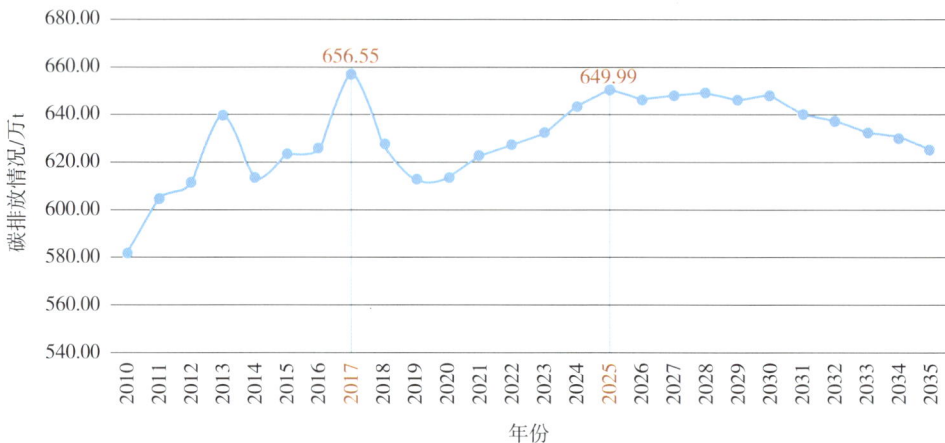

图 7-2　浙江省农业领域碳排放情况及预测

（二）创新工作抓手

以低碳生态农场建设、渔船减船转产、机械强农等行动为主要抓手，根据产业分布和能耗结构，在沿海地区抓好渔船减排，在平原地区抓好农机减排，在山地丘陵地区抓好低碳（零碳）农业试点等工作。以低碳生态农场创建为基础，建立"浙农优品生态低碳农场共富联合体"，以此项工作载体创新生产主体之间、生产主体与市场销售的交流合作机制。

（三）鼓励技术创新

充分发挥"三农九方"科技协同、农业技术联盟等政产学研一体化平台优势，引导科研院校、产业协会、农合联、龙头企业等多方力量参与，组织农业减排固碳联合攻关，推动建立农业碳汇监测、核算标准体系，在农业温室气体资源减排项目方法学上研究创新。实施低碳农业专业人才培养工程。

（四）深化数字赋能

核心业务流、执行流要在"浙农优品""浙农牧""浙农渔"等应用上形成数据流、决策流，通过业务融合、数据融合、技术融合，推动实现低碳生态农场创建工作高效化、业务监管精准化。

（五）加强能力建设

统筹中央和地方各类涉农资金，加大市县财政投入力度，支持农业减碳固碳项目建设。探索建立以主体绿色发展评价和碳账户核算为依据的农业生态补偿机制，推动落实农业生产用电价格等政策。

作者：张玺玲[1]，顾兴国[2]，吴良欢[3]，周之林[4]，戴建飞[5]

参考文献

[1] The World Statistics Pocketbook 2022 edition（Series V，No. 46）.

[2] 金书秦，林煜，牛坤玉. 以低碳带动农业绿色转型：中国农业碳排放特征及其减排路径 [J]. 改革，2021，5：29-37.

[3] 张卫建，严圣吉，张俊，等. 国家粮食安全与农业双碳目标的双赢策略 [J]. 中国农业科学，2021，54（18）：3892-3902.

[4] 谭秋成. 中国农业温室气体排放：现状及挑战 [J]. 中国人口·资源与环境，2011，21（10）：69-75.

[5] 李波，张俊飚，李海鹏. 中国农业碳排放时空特征及影响因素分解 [J]. 中国人口·资源与环境，2011，21（8）：80-86.

[6] IPCC. Climate change 2013：The physical science basis. Contribution of Working Group I to the fifth assessment report of the intergovernmental panel on climate change[R]. Cambridge：Cambridge University Press，2013.

1　张玺玲，浙江省农业农村厅挂职干部，主要研究方向为农业绿色发展、农业领域双碳。

2　顾兴国，浙江省农业科学院副研究员，主要研究方向为生态农业。

3　吴良欢，浙江大学环境与资源学院资源科学系教授，主要研究方向为植物应用环境生态学、有机农业与食品安全。

4　周之林，浙江省农业农村厅主任科员，主要负责农业绿色发展、农业领域双碳工作。

5　戴建飞，杭州市乡村振兴服务中心科长，工程师，主要从事乡村建设、乡村产业发展以及乡村治理等领域工作。

第二部分　领域行动

[7] 陈庆强，沈承德，易惟熙，等. 土壤碳循环研究进展 [J]. 地球科学进展，1998，6：46-54.

[8] 潘根兴，赵其国. 我国农田土壤碳库演变研究：全球变化和国家粮食安全 [J]. 地球科学进展，2005，4：384-393.

[9] 崔文超，焦雯珺，闵庆文，等. 基于碳足迹的传统农业系统环境影响评价——以青田稻鱼共生系统为例 [J]. 生态学报，2020，40（13）：4362-4370.

浙江碳普惠引领居民生活领域碳达峰

居民生活是碳排放的主要来源之一，且居民生活领域碳排放仍然保持刚性增长态势。在满足人民对美好生活向往的前提下，对居民生活领域用能既要充分保障，又要引导居民合理用能、积极践行低碳生活。本章主要介绍碳普惠对居民生活领域碳达峰的影响，提出浙江省推进碳普惠工作的思路，对浙江碳普惠应用建设的成效和存在的问题进行梳理。最后，根据浙江省实际和目前存在的问题，对下一步深化碳普惠工作提出几点建议。

随着经济快速发展，居民生活水平得到极大改善，消费水平明显提高，导致居民生活领域碳排放持续增加，成为带动碳排放增加的重要因素。在"双碳"背景下，浙江省推进碳达峰工作之初便提出要处理好碳排放与居民生活的关系，按照"既要满足人民对美好生活的向往，又要实现碳达峰"要求，浙江省积极开展碳普惠探索，推动形成绿色生产和生活方式。

一、引言

（一）居民生活领域碳排放现状及趋势分析

1. 浙江省居民生活领域碳排放特征

现阶段人均 GDP、人均可支配收入、人均消费支出与居民生活领域碳排放呈正相关。根据第七次全国人口普查情况，浙江省常住人口保持较快增长，目前常住人口数已突破 6 500 万人（图 8–1）。随着居民生活水平的提高，人均碳排放还将保持较高的水平，在人口基数持续增长的态势下，全省居民生活领域碳排放在一定时期内还将保持增长。"十三五"期间浙江省人均 GDP 年均增长8.12%，人均可支配收入增长 8.86%，人均消费支出增长 7.35%，消费倾向指数保持在 0.64，浙江省居民生活碳排放年均增长 4.70%。

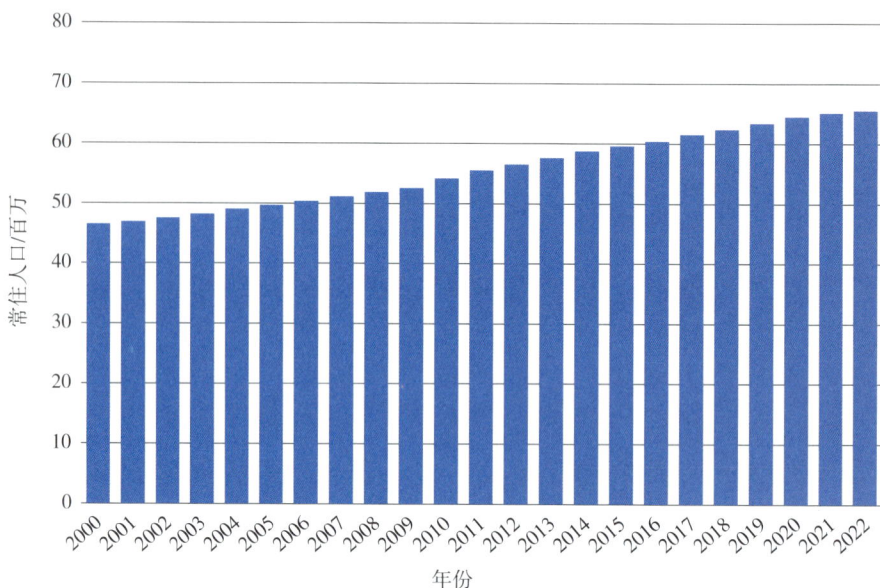

图 8-1　2000—2022 年浙江省人口数

　　从能源消费结构看，居民生活领域能源消费主要为电力、天然气、油品（液化石油气）及少量煤炭。根据历史趋势，居民生活领域煤炭消费逐年递减，天然气消费占比提升明显，"十三五"期间天然气消费量年均增速达到 13%，未来将成为居民生活领域主要的碳排放源。电力是居民生活领域最主要的能源品种，2019 年消费量较 2010 年翻了一番，"十三五"期间电力消费年均增速达到 7.8%，尤其在 2022 年，居民生活领域电力消费较 2021 年增速超过 22.46%。随着风电、光电、核电等清洁能源比例的增加，电力碳排放因子不断降低，电力消耗产生的碳排放总量最终会呈下降趋势。

2.浙江省居民生活领域碳排放趋势分析

　　居民生活领域未来碳排放的预测主要基于对浙江省未来发展趋势的研判，根据《浙江省国民经济和社会发展第十四个五年规划和二〇三五年远景目标纲要》的相关内容，"十四五"和"十五五"期间 GDP 年均增速设定为 5.6% 和 4.8%，对浙江省人口的研判主要设定为每年 0.8%（"十四五"时期）、0.5%（"十五五"时期）的自然增长率，城镇化水平初步设定为年均增长 1% 左右。

　　根据对碳排放历史趋势的分析和未来发展的研判，预计未来浙江省居民生活领域能源总量以及人均能耗仍将长期处于增长期。但随着居民生活方式的低碳转型，居民生活领域能源消费从煤炭、石油等高排放因子能源向天然气、电力等低排放因子能源转变，且电力排放因子随着可再生能源的发展保持降低的趋势，居民生活领域直接产生的碳排放将在短期内呈现持续增长的态势，随后，碳排放量预计在 2035 年后进入平台期。浙江省居民领域实现碳达峰时，人均用电量等关键指标预计达到的水平见表 8-1。

表 8-1 达峰年浙江省与国外居民生活领域能耗指标对照表

指标	浙江	韩国 2018	日本 2018	英国 2018	法国 2018	德国 2018	美国 2018
人均 GDP/ 万美元	2.9～3.1	3.12	4.02	4.30	4.16	4.78	6.30
用电量 /（kW·h/人）	1 600～1 700	1 305	2 077	1 581	2 361	1 546	4 474
用气量 /（kg 标准煤/人）	130～180	263	98	514	227	384	513
能耗 /（t 标准煤/人）	0.55～0.63	0.71	0.72	1.02	1.06	1.01	1.84

注：主要指标为估算数据。

（二）碳普惠对引领居民生活领域减碳的作用

居民生活领域是六大领域中的重要排放领域，在推进居民生活领域碳达峰碳工作中，对居民绿色出行、绿色消费等低碳行为主要依靠引导、鼓励等方式，居民低碳行为的培养缺少有力抓手。

1. 碳普惠机制介绍

碳普惠是通过核算公众低碳行为的减碳量，并将其转化为可用于兑换权益的碳积分。碳普惠是绿色低碳发展的机制，通过建立政策激励、商业激励等公众低碳正向引导机制，作为消费端和生产端的媒介，将个人绿色低碳行为凝聚为参与"双碳"目标的洪流，逐渐成为引导公众参与绿色生活的重要途径。

碳普惠的主要实现思路是利用移动互联网、大数据、区块链等技术，按照低碳行为碳减排量方法学或标准，对各类绿色低碳行为进行量化，形成个人的"碳账户"，并通过减排量交易、政策激励、市场化激励等措施，对减碳行为给予奖励。

2. 开展碳普惠探索的意义

碳普惠是推动形成绿色低碳生活方式的重要手段，促进全社会从微小处改变生产和生活习惯，对加快形成绿色生产和生活方式具有重要意义，有利于推动生态文明建设和生态环境治理现代化，进而助力"双碳"目标实现。

对政府而言，碳普惠机制可促进区域性居民生活领域实现碳达峰，还可以正向引导和激励居民的低碳生活行为，并建立长效机制，有利于实现社会精准化、精细化治理，是践行习近平生态文明思想的积极探索。碳普惠将全社会各类资源整合在一起，围绕消费端减碳，有利于形成合力，实现社会良性互动，不断巩固节能降碳的成果。

对企业而言，在碳普惠机制推广下，居民更倾向于购买具有绿色认证的产品，培养绿色消费的生活习惯，从而推动企业生产更多绿色低碳产品并促进供应链低碳转型，达到激励企业自愿减排的效用。

对公众而言，随着居民参与绿色生活、融入低碳发展的意愿不断增强，碳普惠机制涵盖了交通、居住、消费等各个领域，为公众参与实现"双碳"目标提供有效通道；同时，居民的低碳行为可以转换为碳积分并兑换相应权益，以数字化和市场化手段优化公共资源配置，将绿色低碳行为转化为进一步的绿色低碳权益，实现环境和经济的双重收益。

二、碳普惠实践

国际和国内其他省市针对碳普惠开展了大量实践，为浙江省开展碳普惠工作提供了可供参考的经验。

（一）国内外碳普惠实践

1. 国外碳普惠实践

国外对于公众参与碳减排的实践起步较早，虽然未提出明确的碳普惠概念，但开展了大量与碳普惠相似的机制探索。2011 年韩国环境部为鼓励社会大众践行绿色低碳行为、扩展绿色消费市场，建立了包括碳积分及绿卡积分在内的绿色信用卡体系。凡使用绿卡在特定商店购买具有绿色标识或碳标签的产品、选乘公共交通、在银行缴费时，即可获取相应绿卡积分、折扣及消费返还。此外，韩国光州实施了"碳银行制"，以家庭为单位，将日常生活中节约水电气的量转化为具有消费、折现等功能的"碳积分"，以此激励家庭的碳减排行为。

2009 年 5 月—2010 年 3 月，为促进节能环保家电的销售及使用，日本政府在全国实施"环保积分制度"。该制度是指居民购买"统一节能标签"四星及以上节能性能的空调、冰箱及电视即可根据具体规格获取相应环保积分。购买节能环保家电一般可获得相当于该产品价格 5%～20% 的环保积分。环保积分可用于兑换商品券、乘车卡、地方特产等 271 项节能产品或服务。2011 年起，日本又推出新的"环保积分"项目，将环保行为扩大至包括参与公害防治管理、3R 活动（如垃圾处理）和自然保护活动等行为，并扩大了环保积分的使用范围。

除韩国、日本开展类似机制外，2010—2013 年澳大利亚开展了诺福克岛个人碳交易计划，即个人拥有一定的碳配额用于购买汽油及能源使用，配额如有剩余，可用于兑换现金。2002—2005 年，荷兰鹿特丹港市实施了绿色回馈积分制，即购买节能计划商店的商品或购买其他指定环保产品，可得到用于乘坐公共交通、换取景区门票等的积分，但由于缺乏长期资金支持等原因，未能持续下去。

2. 国内碳普惠实践

（1）上海市碳普惠实践

2022 年，上海市公开征求《上海市碳普惠体系建设工作方案》意见，该方案提出 2022—2023 年上海市将形成碳普惠体系顶层设计，构建相关制度标准和方法学体系，搭建碳普惠平台，选取基础好、有代表性的区域及统计基础好、数据可获得性强的项目和场景先行开展试点示范，衔接上海碳市场，探索多层次消纳渠道，探索建立区域性个人碳账户，打造上海碳普惠"样板间"。2024—2025 年，逐步扩大碳普惠覆盖区域和项目类型，完善碳普惠平台建设，形成规范、有序的碳普惠运行体系，探索通过商业激励机制，逐步形成规则明确、场景丰富、发展可持续的碳普惠生态圈。

（2）广东省碳普惠实践

2015 年，广东省启动了碳普惠制试点工作，是我国首批推行碳普惠制的试点地区。2015 年 7 月，广东省发改委印发《广东省碳普惠制试点工作实施方案》和《广东省碳普惠制试点建设指南》，明确要建设全省统一的碳普惠制推广平台、碳普惠核证减排量交易机制和商业激励机制，开发相应的碳普惠方法学，并选取社区（小区）、公共交通、旅游景区、节能低碳产品作为碳普惠制试点领域。通过建立碳普惠网站和公众号、开发碳普惠 App 等向公众开放碳普惠平台，注册用户可通过节约用水、公交出行来获得碳币。2022 年 4 月，广东省生态环境厅印发《广东省碳普惠交易管理办法》（粤环发〔2022〕4 号），进一步深化完善自愿减排机制，明确了碳普惠管理、交易、监督等内容。

（3）其他地区碳普惠实践

2017 年 6 月，基于"碳币体系"创新研究，武汉市推出了倡导公众低碳出行的"碳宝包"App 和微信平台，市民步行、骑行和租新能源汽车出行等都能获得相应的碳积分，达到一定数量的碳积分可兑换电影票、餐饮券和其他商品等。目前，"碳宝包"正与资本对接，产品功能正逐渐完善。

2020 年 3 月，成都市人民政府印发了《关于构建"碳惠天府"机制的实施意见》，建立"碳惠天府"碳普惠机制。该机制涵盖两条路径：一是通过碳积分兑换的方式，对公众节能减碳以及相关环保行为予以奖励；二是根据相关方法学开发项目碳减排量（以下简称 CDCER），并通过碳中和的方式进行消纳，使碳减排项目产生的环境效益呈现经济价值，激励公众和小微企业的减排积极性。

2021年11月，深圳市人民政府办公厅印发《深圳碳普惠体系建设工作方案》，指出要推动碳普惠体系跨区域合作。深圳市生态环境局于2022年3月发布《深圳市碳普惠管理办法》，规范深圳碳普惠体系的建设运行和监督管理，进一步明确公众、小微企业节能减碳行为所产生减排量的管理流程和使用规则。

"碳普惠合作网络"成立

2022年6月15日全国低碳日，为凝聚社会合力，倡导公众践行绿色生活方式，推动消费端减污降碳，充分发挥数字化手段在"形成绿色生活方式"中的作用，生态环境部宣传教育中心联合中华环保联合会、中国互联网发展基金会、国家发展和改革委员会国际合作中心、中国生态文明研究与促进会共同发起创立"碳普惠合作网络"，网络由能源基金会支持。"碳普惠合作网络"致力于以创新碳普惠为路径，聚合社会各方力量，推动全民绿色低碳行动。

（二）浙江碳普惠推进思路

浙江省推进碳普惠工作选择以数字化应用为切入点，将个人作为主体，通过个人对低碳生活的广泛参与，推进社会低碳风尚的形成。

1. 总体流程

开展碳普惠工作，在流程上总体分为3个环节，即个人低碳行为践行、个人低碳行为减碳量化、个人低碳行为权益获取，并通过数字化工具进行实现。碳普惠机制运行流程见图8-2。

图8-2　碳普惠机制运行流程

（1）个人低碳行为践行

这是碳普惠机制的基础，居民"衣食住行用"过程中能够实现节能、减碳、保护生态环境、节约资源等行为均可以被界定为低碳行为。例如，在深圳和成都的碳普惠方案中，提出要打造出行、消费、生活、公益等各类型低碳场景，就是对低碳行为进行界定，鼓励公众践行的过程。

（2）个人低碳行为减碳量化

对践行的低碳行为的减碳量进行核算量化，明确行为对碳减排的贡献，并以此为依据明确公众的减碳贡献。目前，在各地的实践中，均采用将减碳量换算为碳积分的方式，量化公众减碳行为。

（3）个人低碳行为权益获取

这是将量化后的减碳量兑换为权益，实现碳"惠"过程，让公众在践行低碳行为中有获得感、成就感。广东地区即采用了商业激励的方式，打通碳积分与商品之间的渠道，实现实物和服务激励，促进更多人参与低碳行为。

2. 低碳场景设计思路

在推进低碳场景设计时，浙江碳普惠充分考虑本省实际情况，按照"先易后难、逐步扩大"的原则，以政企合作的模式系统搭建浙江碳普惠应用场景体系（图8-3）。在数据归集方式上，基于浙江移动互联网发达的基础条件，充分考虑已有数据基础，与蚂蚁森林、菜鸟、虎哥回收等已有低碳领域应用开展对接合作，将浙江碳普惠场景体系与已有绿色低碳工作有机结合，全方位整合个人低碳数据，尽可能降低数据归集成本。在数据采集维度上，从场景侧、支付侧等多维度收集个人低碳数据，提高数据收集的高效性、可得性，实现个人低碳数据的"无感收集"，不增加个人的负担。

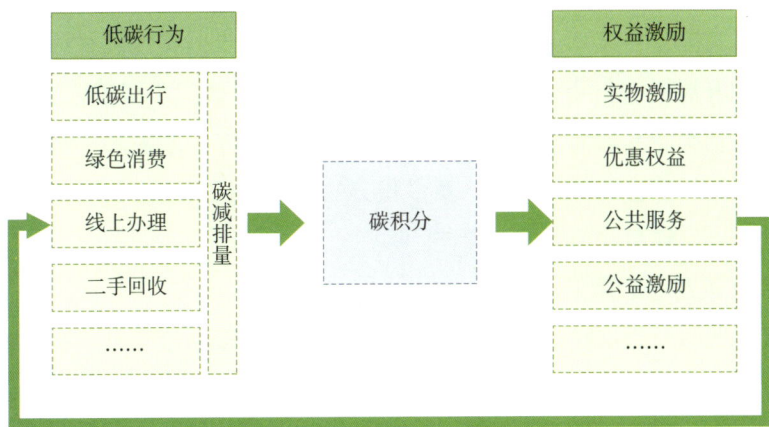

图 8-3 浙江碳普惠应用场景体系

3. 碳积分体系设计思路

碳普惠积分体系的构建主要考虑以下 3 个因素。

首先，考虑兑换权益的频次，从活跃用户的角度，积分的具体数值设定考虑了权益兑换的频次。其次，考虑碳减排贡献，对具体每个子场景产生的碳积分，主要考虑该场景带来的减排量贡献，减排量目前主要基于已有的方法学、其他省市相关的经验数据及相关文献，更准确的积分设定后续随着浙江碳普惠方法学的完善分步推进。最后，考虑政府引导方向，对量化减排量较困难的场景，主要考虑该行为产生的减排效应以及对全社会减碳氛围的带动，对鼓励类行为设定较高的积分。

4. 权益体系设计思路

权益体系的设计从权益本身主要考虑权益的"低碳"属性，一方面该权益可以本身属于低碳产品，如带有明显绿色标识（如碳标签等）的消费品；另一方面权益可进一步推动低碳行为的发生，如公交、地铁优惠券，使用权益的过程中本身属于低碳行为。在考虑权益设计时还要充分考虑公众对消纳方式的接受程度和激励的喜好。

（1）设计合理可行的碳积分消纳方式

公众参与碳普惠机制，以自身减碳量兑换碳积分，而碳积分兑换权益的过程中，单向的公众兑换权益的可持续性差，难以为商户带来更多利益，最终导致权益减少，活跃度降低。因此需要多渠道消纳公众碳积分，考虑碳积分在个人和商户中的流通，个人碳积分对应的减排量通过积分兑换可用于实现商户和商品的碳减排和碳中和，加大商家供给碳普惠产品和服务的积极性。

（2）拓展碳普惠激励方式

单一的碳普惠激励对大多数用户的吸引力可能不足，而不断扩展激励方式，从参与感、获得感和荣誉感等多方面强化激励效果，可以实现碳普惠机制的长效运营。例如开展低碳行为征集活动，鼓励用户开展低碳行为辨识，提高参与感；增加更多实物类商品激励，丰富产品品类，覆盖更多年龄段需求，满足各类人群的获得感；建立碳普惠等级认证，更多积分的个人、机构或企业可以得到相应的荣誉称号，以荣誉激励更多用户参与。

5. 浙江碳普惠应用设计思路

浙江碳普惠应用依托浙江政务服务网一体化平台移动端应用"浙里办"开发建设，按照全省统建的方式开发运行，应用向全体浙江省居民开放，通过"浙里办"App或者小程序（支付宝、微信等）都可使用浙江碳普惠应用。浙江碳普惠对各地区开发个性化专区保持开放，按照"分级管理"的原则，各地可基于本地特色需求谋划"地方专区"，开展应用场景谋划并推广到全省，上线本地特色权益或活动，构建个性化碳积分消纳体系。

三、浙江碳普惠应用建设成效和不足

（一）建设成效

1.总体成效

浙江省以"低碳行动、积分核算、权益兑换"为核心，将居民的减碳行为核算为减碳量，并根据减碳量赋予碳积分，积分可用于兑换商业权益等产品的兑换，通过激励方式推动全社会低碳行动，建成全国领先的政府引导、市场主导、全民参与下的绿色低碳社会建设新模式。在应用场景、权益兑换等方面充分体现浙江省特色，初步形成具有"浙江特色"的碳普惠体系（图8-4）。

图 8-4　浙江碳普惠应用首页及场景页

自2022年3月29日正式上线以来，用户量持续增加，2022年7月25日，浙江碳普惠用户突破50万，成为全国主流的碳普惠平台之一；10月18日，浙江碳普惠用户突破100万，成为全国首个突破百万用户的省级碳普惠平台。截至2023年4月底，浙江碳普惠应用用户已突破135万人，成为浙江引领居民低碳生活的"金名片"。

2.构建浙江特色的应用场景体系

在浙江碳普惠应用汇总已经开发建设五大类超过20小类低碳应用场景（表8-2），主要联合了蚂蚁森林、虎哥回收、菜鸟裹裹、浙里种树、浙商保险等企事业单位，不断拓展碳积分的来源，丰富应用场景。在层级设计上，应用场景体系包括绿色出行、线上办理、绿色消费、绿色社区和普惠公益五个一级场景，每一大类下细分二级子场景，如绿色出行包含步行、公交车出行、单车出行、地铁出行、自愿少开车、ETC 缴费等 6 个二级子场景。后续，浙江碳普惠应用还将与更多的企业主体合作，合作开发其他低碳场景。

表 8-2　浙江碳普惠应用场景列表

序号	大类场景	子场景
1	绿色出行	步行、公交车出行、单车骑行（含蚂蚁森林、潮城骑行 2 个数据源）、地铁出行、自愿少开车、ETC 缴费
2	线上办理	绿色办公、网购火车票、绿色政务
3	绿色消费	线上支付、电子发票、国际退税、网上寄件、绿色外卖、环保减塑、网络购票
4	绿色社区	低碳回收、旧箱利用、低碳寄取
5	普惠公益	浙里种树

3. 上下联动、政企合作的碳普惠合作模式

居民低碳行为数据分散在各个部门和多个平台，在保证数据安全的前提下，浙江省将浙江碳普惠定位为一个开放性平台，按照"政企合作"模式，与蚂蚁、银联、菜鸟等多个市场主体开展应用场景合作。在权益兑换上，省级部门与企业、社会组织等开展沟通合作，得到了全省"耀眼明珠"等多个景区以及省能源集团、银联浙江公司等多家企业的支持，让全省居民得到实实在在的优惠。

在碳普惠宣传中，采用"线上 + 线下"的形式创新碳普惠推广模式。在线上，与省林业局、支付宝、菜鸟等开展联合宣传，并对宣传内容深度合作，上线"我为亚运种棵树""出行盲盒"等公益活动推广浙江碳普惠，通过政企合作不断提高各类用户触达率。在线下，省级有关部门多次组织线下活动，在"节能宣传周""绿色出行宣传月"等系列宣传活动中鼓励用户使用浙江碳普惠，在线下活动中兑换景区门票、帆布袋等权益，采用多元激励方式拓展用户群体。

（二）存在的不足

1. 浙江碳普惠用户活跃度偏低，个人"碳资产"价值尚未充分体现

浙江碳普惠应用上线一年多以来，用户数虽然已经超过 135 万，但用户数从 0～50 万用了 4 个月，50 万增加到 100 万用了 3 个月，但后续随着热度的降低，尤其是在碳普惠宣传力度下降后，浙江碳普惠用户数增加缓慢。2022 年 9 月，月活人数超过 25 万人，且单月新增用户近 24 万人，但进入 2023 年后，月增用户数不足 2 万人，日均活跃人数仅 1 万人左右。用户普遍反映浙江碳普惠

权益吸引力不足，且目前数据贯通能力有欠缺，部分用户的低碳数据无法被收集。

深究用户活跃度低的原因，一方面是权益不够丰富和吸引人，另一方面在于个人"碳资产"的价值还未充分发挥出来，针对浙江碳普惠不同等级或碳积分的用户，未真正体现出可获得服务的差异性。目前，对于个人碳积分价值的多元转化路径或机制尚未建立，需要通过强化运营、资源衔接等多个渠道弥补。

2. 碳普惠的影响主要体现在居民消费侧，在生产侧触达层级较浅

省发改委牵头并联合多部门，与众多企业在场景开发、权益供给方面开展了广泛的合作，得到了蚂蚁森林、虎哥回收、菜鸟、饿了么等多个平台的支持，对个人低碳行为数据的收集作出了贡献。浙江碳普惠对居民低碳习惯的养成产生了一定的积极影响，但目前影响主要体现在消费侧。由于碳足迹、碳标签等体系建设尚不健全，对于诸多消费品的"低碳"属性难以准确，对于企业生产侧的影响尚未触达，有必要进一步强化绿色消费对低碳生产的带动作用。

3. 碳普惠标准体系尚不健全，碳减排量的核算尚不支持

目前国内其他省市在推进碳普惠工作中，在团体标准和方法学方面开展了一定的研究，近年来，在团体标准上发布了《通过新能源汽车替代出行实现温室气体减排量评估技术规范》《电动汽车出行碳减排核算方法》《私人小客车合乘出行项目温室气体减排量评估技术规范》等，为开展碳普惠相关的碳减排量核算提供了一定参考。但目前团体标准提供的更多是核算规范，浙江省除在出行方面开展地方标准的研究外，在绿色消费、低碳居住等方面的标准还缺失，对全省居民各个低碳行为的碳减排量还无法开展系统性计算，无法真实量化每个人对碳减排的贡献。

四、未来设想

（一）完善顶层设计，推动碳普惠标准体系建立

目前碳普惠机制运行出现的问题很多是由于制度设计的不合理或缺失，政府在制定制度文件时必须要充分考虑碳普惠实际操作中涉及的各个主体、环节，调动全社会的力量参与进来。目前，按照边实践、边总结的思路，浙江省已出台《浙江省大型活动（会议）碳中和碳普惠管理意见》，实现全省大型活动（会议）碳中和的碳普惠核证减排量的管理规范化。接下来，浙江省还要继续做好碳普惠制度体系建设，在促进消费端碳减排、支持碳普惠模式方面，尽快出台体系化指导意见，明确鼓励和引导的方向，指导各地开展创新实践。

碳普惠标准规范体系是一项庞大的工程，需要社会各界共同的努力。组织开发绿色出行、绿色消费、绿色社区等领域减排量核算方法学，加强方法学应用，推动

成熟方法学提升为减碳量核算地方标准。制定碳普惠场景评价体系，科学评估不同低碳行为减碳成效，建立碳普惠低碳场景评价规范。还需要建立碳普惠平台建设规范，明确平台建设架构、技术标准、接口规范等，建立统一的数据标准和场景接入规范，鼓励地方谋划地方特色应用，按照统一标准规范接入浙江碳普惠应用。

（二）创新碳普惠运营方式，拓展个人"碳资产"多元价值

基于"省级统筹、政企合作、共享共建、全民参与"原则，以碳普惠运营市场化助推形成绿色低碳生产生活方式，在省级主管部门的统筹和管理下，选取专业运营公司，给予第三方主体浙江碳普惠运营的主导权，在不损害用户利益的前提下，开展独立化的运营活动，不断提升碳普惠活跃度。

另外，还需要建立个人碳账户，在碳账户中全面覆盖个人碳排放数据采集、核算、碳评级和场景应用等功能，在未来自愿减排碳市场建立和成熟后，个人碳资产的价值将得到进一步强化。如目前在浙江碳普惠应用上，对碳积分位于不同范围的用户授予不同级别勋章奖励，并在头像上体现个人碳评级，并探索与个人信用、征信等体系打通，实现绿色表现与其他政策、商业资源的联动，切实提升个人碳资产的价值。

（三）集聚全社会力量，引领全社会低碳生产、绿色消费

对企业、社会组织来说，在碳普惠机制推进中需要进一步发挥作用，对企业来说，可以围绕自身业务特征，积极提供优惠的商品或服务作为低碳行为的奖励，并生产低碳产品，积极履行企业社会责任。对于国际组织、行业协会、社会团体等社会组织，要积极动员公众参与碳普惠活动，传播生活消费领域碳减排信息，讲好低碳生活的浙江故事，全方位提升公众的绿色消费的意识。

随着消费者意识的转变，通过绿色认证或具有碳标签的产品将在市场中更具吸引力，依托逐步构建的低碳产品供应链产业链体系，持续推动扩大绿色产品服务新供给，倒逼和引导企业生产方式绿色转型，最终实现公众获益、商家增收、全社会减排的良性循环模式。各方力量共同推动建立绿色产品标准、标识体系，逐步构建低碳产品供应体系，以绿色消费倒逼生产方式绿色转型，建立消费生产互促模式。

作者：浙江省经济信息中心著作组

第三部分　区域典型

衢州市基于碳账户改革的"双碳"实践与探索

　　碳达峰既是宏观的国家战略，也是每家企业、每个人身体力行做出来的。如何激发和调动企业、个人碳减排的积极性，实施个性化、精准性的减碳政策，成为一项热点和难点。衢州市首创建立 239.6 万个碳账户，覆盖工业、农业、能源、建筑、交通和居民生活六大领域，动态核算记录企业、个人的碳排放量和减排量，自动生成碳评价、精准绘出"碳画像"。以碳账户为基础，衢州市谋划落地扩投资促转型、企业减碳降本协同增效、碳普惠助力群众增收等应用场景，探索市场化推进机制，走出了发展与减排双赢的新赛道。

一、引言

　　衢州市位于浙江省西部、钱塘江源头，是全省乃至华东地区的生态屏障，全市森林覆盖率 69.66%，出境水水质保持 II 类以上。同时，依托当年全国八大化工基地之一的巨化，发展成为国家氟硅新材料产业基地、中国电子化学材料产业基地等，重化工业产值占比长期保持在 70% 以上，全市万元 GDP 能耗、工业增加值能耗分别是全省的 1.95 倍和 2.42 倍。衢州具有较好的绿色低碳工作基础，累计开展 9 个国家级循环经济试点建设，成为全国唯一的循环经济试点示范"大满贯"市。衢州把"双碳"作为解决发展内在深层次矛盾的重大契机，以碳账户改革撬动经济社会绿色低碳发展，形成碳账户智能监测和动态核算、碳账户金融撬动绿色低碳投资、企业减碳降本增效协同、碳普惠助力共同富裕等特色模式，实现降碳、减污、扩绿、增长"四位一体"良好发展态势，碳排放总量保持稳定，碳排放强度持续下降，生态环境质量优中更好。

二、主要做法

衢州市对接省"双碳"数智平台建设思路，以碳账户为数据治理工具，链式挖掘工业、农业（林业）、能源、建筑、交通和居民生活六大重点涉碳领域的碳轨迹，建立贯穿生产端到消费端的碳排放计量体系，形成反映行业水平、区域贡献、历史下降的多维碳评价，应用到碳金融、用能预算化管理、"双碳"科技等各个方面。

（一）分领域建设碳账户，开展碳评价

按照"数据精准、核算科学、评价公正"要求，运用新一代信息技术手段，建立了覆盖工业、农业、能源、建筑、交通、居民生活和林业碳汇七大领域的碳账户，共开设碳账户 239.6 万个，规模以上企业和居民个人覆盖率分别达 100%、93%。

1. 工业碳账户

依托能源大数据中心，接入规模以上工业企业 1 077 家和规模以下 1 695 家，高频采集归集电、煤、气、热等全品类能源数据，其中规模以上企业用能除煤外，均实现自动化采集归集。委托东北电力大学研究团队建立方法学，自动核算企业碳排放总量和碳排放强度。对标行业碳效基准值和全市税收碳强度、工业增加值碳强度平均值，对企业进行"红、黄、浅绿、深绿"四色贴标评价。

2. 能源碳账户

按照非零碳机组和零碳机组的分类，接入 98 家能源生产企业，委托东北电力大学研究团队建立方法学，采集核算能源企业供电量、供热量、脱硫剂使用量、燃料消耗量、碳排放量、碳排放强度等数据，制定评价标准，按照单位供电（热）量碳排放强度实行四色贴标管理。

3. 建筑碳账户

按照既有建筑和新建建筑的分类，接入 119 家既有建筑和 10 家新建建筑，依托浙江大学建筑设计院研究团队建立方法学，围绕新建建筑提升标准、可再生能源推广促进、既有建筑能效提升和绿色建筑转型升级，采集试点项目基本信息、围护结构保温系统信息、建筑用能系统信息等数据，根据碳排放量进行贴标评价。

4. 交通碳账户

以应用需求为导向，接入全市 73 家交通企业，按月采集城市公交、城乡公交、城际客运、巡游出租车、规模以上货运企业等主体的车辆数、行驶里程数、

货运完成量、周转量以及交通运输工具用能等数据，依托华北电力大学和浙江省交通规划设计院研究团队建立方法学，形成交通领域"碳账户"。

5. 农业碳账户

依托中国农大研究团队的农业碳中和率理论，建立农业碳账户，接入 1 000 家农业企业，以传统种养殖生产、畜牧业循环利用、肥料使用等环节作为减排关键点，确定农作物秸秆综合利用、土壤固碳机制、畜禽粪污资源化利用 3 条碳中和路径，折算碳中和值。

6. 林业碳账户

依托浙江省森林资源监测中心的碳汇量核算方法，建立林业碳账户，接入 2 135 个林业经营主体，从资源账户、碳汇工程和碳汇应用 3 个维度，统计分析衢州市林业资源、区域碳汇质量、碳汇工程和碳汇应用等数据信息。

7. 居民碳账户

依托浙江省金融学会等专业机构的理论支撑，从节电节水、绿色出行、绿色支付等方面折算个人减碳量，构建涵盖绿色支付、绿色生活、绿色出行三大核心领域，覆盖居民衣食住行等多方面的居民"碳账户"体系。

（二）多场景挖掘碳评价应用

聚焦群众高频需求、企业共性需求和"双碳"治理难点堵点，开发各领域多跨应用场景，集成到政府治碳"一站通"、企业减碳"一网清"、个人低碳"一键惠"。

1. 金融领域：碳账户金融

构建碳排放 e 账本、碳征信 e 报告、碳政策 e 发布、碳金融 e 超市、碳效益 e 评估的"5e"闭环系统，实现政府智能治碳、企业智能减碳、金融智能支持。全市 33 家金融机构上架 55 款碳金融产品，累计发放企业碳账户贷款 543.83 亿元、余额 409.57 亿元。

2. 能源领域：用能预算化管理

以数字化手段对全市 1 087 家规模以上工业企业用能实施全过程预算化管理，通过"能耗双控调节系数"及"能源优化配置系数"，合理分配企业年度用能预算，优化能源要素配置，推动能源要素向高效低耗和新兴产业倾斜。

3. 工业领域：产品碳足迹核算应用

核算产品生命周期所需能耗及碳排放情况，为出口型企业提供碳足迹核算报告，通过企业自比及同产品类比等方式，实现企业及产品的碳数据可视监控及产品碳排放水平评估，助力企业发掘自身减碳潜力，辅助政府监控行业碳排放趋势水平，精准发布减碳政策。

4.交通领域："公转水"在线

依托浙江省"四联"联动智慧物流云平台，打通物流全程运输的运输链、信息链、管理链、服务链，实时监测入库企业运行状态、物流运行效率、货物结构及流向等数据，并通过科学核算货主企业"公转水"增量碳减排量，与企业用能预算化指标闭环挂钩，将货主企业运输环节的碳减排效益转化为用能指标增量。

5.建筑领域：装配式建筑推广应用

依托浙江省建科院，与宝业集团等市场方开展合作，明确方法学论证、研究扶持装配式建筑推广政策、建立数字化平台印证理论体系与建设成效，建设装配式构件生产低碳示范基地，打造衢州市低碳科普馆，谋划低碳"百年宅"示范小区。

6.农业领域：低碳农场

对农场从播种至收获的生产过程进行生产数据收集、核算，通过对关键环节消耗化肥、农药等数据的采集分析，精准定位固碳、减排关键环节，制定分级评价标准，推广"节本增效、质量安全、绿色环保"的农业绿色生产技术模式。

7.林业领域：林汇共富在线

将原 CCER 林业碳汇项目开发七大环节优化为"计划管理、项目落图、项目监测、审核备案"4 个环节，将原先需要的 29 项文件整合为 9 项，实现全流程线上办理，并打通与浙江省"森林资源一张图"数据连接，实现自动地块审核、自动布设样地、自动碳汇计算、自动生成报告。

8.居民领域："零废生活"

通过"回收一键呼叫""数据一库采集""核算一套标准""激励一揽政策"等应用，解决碳积分"怎么来，怎么算，怎么用"问题，归集、量化、评价、激励居民参与生活垃圾资源化利用促进减污降碳，在全社会倡导绿色低碳的生活方式。

9.科技领域："双碳"科技

由碳成果推广、碳技术攻关、碳智库三大应用场景组成。"碳成果推广"汇聚了科技成果 1.7 万余项，一站征集企业技术需求并实现智能匹配。"碳技术攻关"场景，由企业填报攻关需求，系统智能产生"攻关尽调报告"。"碳智库"场景，汇聚了大型仪器 45 万余台、专家 1 000 余人、创新载体 640 多个。

三、主要成效和经验模式

衢州碳账户做法和经验写入国家发展改革委《关于印发高质量发展建设共同

富裕示范区第一批典型经验的通知》和生态环境部《中国应对气候变化的政策与行动 2022 年度报告》，在 2022 年联合国气候大会上作案例介绍。

（一）创新碳监测核算体系，摸清了"碳家底"。

1."自动采集 + 全量归集"，数据实时监测

探索建立各类主体涉碳数据自动化采集和全量化归集机制，实现现场直采企业用电、天然气、蒸汽等能源数据，采集频率达到 15 min/ 次的最短时限间隔，精准掌握辖区企业碳耗点和碳排周期。打破发改、经信、生态环境、农业农村、住建、统计、税务、金融、国网电力等单位数据壁垒，纵向贯通省、市、县、园区、企业等各个层级，统一归集分散于各系统的能耗用量、产品产量、增加值及税收等基础数据。

2."有规依规 + 无规建规"，核算系统集成

按照"有规依规、无规建规"，依托各高校研究团队，建立了农业碳中和率核算法、工业碳排数据连续监测法、能源碳排放数据连续监测法、建筑碳账户评价法、环境信息披露、碳征信制度 6 个填补国内空白的理论方法学，其中农业碳中和率核算法在国内首次提出；发布 7 个覆盖从生产端到消费端的碳账户核算与评价建设地方标准。

3."三维评价 + 四色贴标"，评价客观公正

从行业先进性、区域贡献度、历史下降法 3 个维度，对企业低碳减碳实行"深绿、浅绿、黄、红"四色贴标。具体以单位工业增加值碳排放强度、单位税收碳排放强度反映区域贡献度，以单位产品产量碳排放强度反映行业先进性，以指标每年的变化曲线反映企业低碳减碳努力程度。其中产品产量贴标评价办法为全国首创。

（二）创新"双碳"精准治理工具，提升了"碳效能"

1. 金融精准支持

将碳账户评价结果转化为企业碳征信报告，靶向配套金融优惠激励政策，对低碳企业和减碳项目在贷款额度、利率定价等方面给予支持。例如，江山市双氧水公司拟投资 1 500 万元实施二氧化碳储存设备技改。农业银行衢州分行基于企业碳评价"浅绿企业"，给予降低贷款利率 30 个 BP，发放贷款 500 万元。项目建成后企业月均捕捉碳排放 2 500 t，二氧化碳中和率从原来的 20.3% 提升至38.6%。13 家金融机构将碳征信报告导入核心系统，10 个地市全面复制碳账户金融模式。

2. 用能精准保障

通过两个系数对企业实施差异化用能预算分配，推动能源要素向单位能耗产出效益高的产业和项目倾斜。2022 年，衢州市从 184 家低效企业调整出 45.45 万 t 标准煤，用于支持 974 家企业。全市水泥行业的可比熟料综合能耗，达到领跑者行列；钢铁行业（元立）焦炭工艺、烧结工序、转炉工序等单位产品能耗，达到全国同行业先进水平。

3. 企业精准服务

根据碳账户企业能效（碳效）水平诊断报告，为企业提供碳管家"一站式"服务，并组建"双碳"研究中心，促成"双碳"技术交易 11 宗。基于碳账户对企业的客观评价，整治高碳低效企业 241 家，腾出 12 万 t 标准煤用能空间；推动 223 家企业对标国内外行业先进水平，投入 60 余亿元开展生产工艺改造升级；开展水泥、钢铁行业减量置换工作，淘汰化工企业 78 家。

（三）创新"双碳"市场化推进机制，实现了"碳增收"

1. 创新企业减碳降本协同增效模式

紧扣企业降本的刚性需求，全面梳理各个领域碳账户应用的切入点，创新减碳降本协同增效模式。在能源领域，应用碳账户实时精准监测功能，分析企业节能降碳、绿能减碳及储能套利的需求，探索"节能＋绿能＋储能＋碳资产"第三方投资方式。目前在 26 家企业开展试点建设，预计可实现节能减碳降本 1 亿元以上。在交通领域，开发上线大宗货物"公转水"在线应用，为 123 家企业提供"公转水"全程物流市场化解决方案，综合物流成本下降 15%，节约运输费用约 1 亿元，实现碳减排量 1.2 万 t。

2. 创新碳普惠助力共富模式

建立以个人碳积分为核心的居民低碳生活激励机制，开展"低碳农村""低碳停车""低碳公交"等碳普惠活动，累计发放个人碳积分贷款 89.68 亿元、余额 64.85 亿元。创新开展林业碳账户一二级账户联动开发模式，全市开立 6 个一级账户，600 余个二级账户，对全市约 3 万亩林地开展林业碳汇（碳普惠）项目开发，产生碳汇量 4.94 万 t。在浙江省首批浙林碳汇减排量开发集中交易会议上，以每吨 100 元价格交易 1 750 t。

3. 创新"双碳"产业发展模式

紧抓碳达峰前产业转型的"最后窗口期"，大力发展新能源、新材料、节能环保等"双碳"受益产业，力争通过 5 年努力，实现全市工业产值翻番、亩均效益倍增。重点推进锂电材料向储能电池和动力电池延链发展，光伏产业向风光储一体化发展，氟硅材料向循环经济发展。到 2025 年，打造形成总产值超 2 000 亿元的"双碳"产业基地。2022 年以来相继落地了时代锂电、吉利动力和储能电池等一大批重大项目，5 个抽蓄项目纳入国家能源局"抽水蓄能中长期发展规划"，其中 4 个为"十四五"重点实施类项目；打造全产业链全生命周期服务体系，引进落地 8 个投资超百亿元的绿色低碳产业项目。

四、展望

坚持以碳账户体系建设牵引和撬动全社会绿色低碳转型，紧扣扩大绿色投资、促进绿色消费、服务绿色出口，发展绿色产业主线，继续夯实碳账户建设基础，提升碳账户应用实效，打造碳账户硬核成果。

一是碳账户强基提质。力争与省发改委共同制定发布《浙江省碳账户建设规范》，争取"零废生活"核算评价标准、"公转水"碳减排核算标准上升为省标，争取银行个人碳账户标准上升为国家金标；推进个人碳账户与省碳普惠平台全面打通；与省林业局共同谋划将林业碳账户打造成省林业碳普惠交易的底座；推进碳账户数据管理条例立法；健全碳账户数据全量采集和自动归集机制，建立数据质量定期抽查复核机制，推进各领域各区块碳账户应用实战实用实效闭环。

二是绿色低碳投资"双百"示范。组织 100 家左右工业企业参加第三方投资的减碳降本增效示范工程，推行"节能＋绿能＋储能＋碳资产"EMC 模式，推广节能技术、低碳技术、储能技术、充换电技术；实施 100 个左右节能减碳、绿能降碳、低碳产业、循环经济、减污降碳、生态固碳等"双碳"重大项目，其中谋划建设新型储能、氢能、虚拟电厂等重大标志性项目 20 个以上。创新项目碳账户金融产品，争取纳入央行碳减排支持工具。

三是打造碳标签产业基地。依托工业品碳足迹核算服务绿色出口，由"双碳"公司与第三方开展合作，挂牌成立中国（衢州）碳标签产业基地，建立工业品碳足迹核算应用与第三方认证机构的互认机制，打造具有全国影响力的碳足迹碳标签实验室和数据中心、标准中心、评价中心、技术转化中心，推动碳账户与碳标签相结合，充实和完善碳足迹碳标签数据库，制定有利于国际贸易和产业竞争的碳足迹碳标签标准，探索碳账户碳标签赋能企业的市场化运作模式，打造碳标签供应链及产业化应用体系。

四是创建绿色低碳生活共同行动试点城市。依托个人碳账户推动绿色生活和绿色消费，协调市内主要商超、景区、影院、酒店等消费场所，成立绿色低碳生活共同行动联盟，发布绿色低碳生活共同行动倡议，建立以个人碳账户为媒介的绿色低碳生活（消费）引导和促进机制，打造全国首个绿色低碳生活共同行动试点城市。

五是争创各领域绿色低碳国家试点示范。创成国家绿色金融改革创新示范区，推进国家林业碳汇试点市、全国绿色低碳农业先行区、国家绿色出行创建城市等试点示范创建，争取国家首批碳达峰试点园区、国家气候投融资试点城市，争取浙江省能耗"双控"向碳排放"双控"转变国家试点率先在衢州落地，重点探索建立碳预算化管理和项目碳评价机制，力争实现各领域省级及以上试点示范全覆盖，着力打造绿色低碳领域国家级试点示范最多城市。

作者：刘红飞[1]

---

1 刘红飞，浙江省衢州市发展改革委环资处处长，在"两山"转化和"双碳"转型方面研究较深，谋划提出并推动多项全国首创机制在衢州落地实践。

湖州市以碳效改革推动全域绿色低碳转型

企业是经济社会发展的生命力所在，但同时也是能耗和碳排放的绝对主体。在碳达峰碳中和国家战略提出后，以分业管理为主的企业管理模式由于精准性不足，已难以满足政府需要，由此碳效改革应运而生。湖州是全国碳效改革的首倡地，工业碳效改革入选"中国改革地方全面深化改革典型案例"。除工业之外，湖州还在居民生活、公共建筑等领域持续探索碳效改革，不断拓展碳效评价应用场景，从治理和服务两方面推进各领域碳减排实效。

一、引言

在"双碳"目标下，一套系统的、行之有效的碳生产力水平评价体系是实现精准治理、高效服务的基础。近年来，湖州市坚持小切口大牵引，以工业领域为突破口，探索建立了以"碳效"作为企业碳生产力水平的评价应用体系，通过"研究碳排放方法论—制定碳效评价标准—归集数据建立平台—制定政策拓展应用"的模式，实现了碳效评价体系的"从 0 到 1"，获批全省唯一碳效码试点城市，工业碳效改革入选"中国改革地方全面深化改革典型案例"。在复制工业碳效体系建设模式的基础上，湖州市继续在其他领域开展探索创新。已建立覆盖企业、个人、公共机构（公共建筑责任主体）等碳排放行为主体的碳效评价体系，并在金融、节能改造、碳权益交易等多方面开展碳效应用实践，为全领域的低碳转型打下了坚实基础。

二、主要做法及成效

（一）"一码三标识"立体描绘工业企业"碳画像"

针对数据分散、缺乏协同、底数不清及企业碳效缺乏精准评价等问题，围绕碳排放"测、评、用、治"等关键环节，创新构建工业碳效评价体系，上线全国首个工业碳平台，首创工业"碳效码"（图 10-1），以"一码三标识"的形式从单位增加值碳排放、同行业碳排放对比、绿电使用情况三方面评价企业碳排放水平；同时出台 19 项相关制度规范，为碳效码的应用推广建立全套规范、标准、政策等理论制度体系。

图 10-1 "工业碳效码" 2.0

1. 紧盯行动目标，配强团队"建"体系

成立由市政府秘书长为牵头人的工业碳效改革专班，整合经信、电力、统计、生态环境等 8 个部门及区县多个专业力量，打造跨部门、跨层级、跨业务的快速反应链。邀请清华大学能源所、低碳实验室、中国石油大学等专家学者及本地企业对"碳效码"评价体系进行专家认证完善。评价模型得到了清华大学江亿院士等多位专家，以及工业和信息化部双碳研究中心、中国标准化研究院等专业机构认可。

2. 梳理核心业务，归集数据"搭"平台

通过 IRS 平台以接口方式归集统计、税务、电力等部门 14 类 2 300 余万条数据，形成工业碳效数据仓，对全市 33 个行业 381 个细分行业煤油气电热等五大类 39 种能源品消费情况进行大数据分析，上线全国首个"工业碳平台"，建设"碳监测""碳对标""碳中和""碳应用"核心模块，分区域、分行业绘制全市"碳地图"，实现数据匹配融合形成"碳效指数"，开发工业碳平台驾驶舱，为碳管理、碳考核打造一体化数字平台。2.0 版工业碳平台正式上线，成为省工业碳平台。

3. 优化评价模型，双码融合"绘"标识

围绕企业碳排放水平、碳利用效率、碳中和情况，开展三大指标智能"对

标"，形成集三个标识于一体的"碳效码"。创新"企业码 + 碳效码"双码融合，上线碳诊断、碳技改、碳金融、绿色工厂申报、绿电交易五大办事模块，实现"一键办理"。工业碳效码在全省全面推广，目前全省4.2万家规模以上工业企业全部赋码；还完成5 000余家规模以下企业的评价赋码，并可进行季度动态更新。

4. 加强制度规范，编制标准"管"长效

率先在全省制定出台《湖州市工业碳效对标（碳效码）管理办法（试行）》《湖州市碳效评价数据归集与结果发布机制》《湖州市推进工业领域碳效改革工作方案》等19项相关制度规范，建立了一整套规范、标准、法律等理论制度体系。发布湖州市地方标准《工业企业碳效评价规范》，为监碳、测碳、评碳提供"标尺"。将碳效码纳入《湖州市绿色金融促进条例》，首次以地方立法形式，建立碳排放信息披露机制。

（二）"碳积分 + 碳减排量"赋能个人碳减排价值实现

生活领域行为主体（个人）多且散、低碳行为数据难收集难定量。由此，该领域碳效评价体系侧重于正向激励引导，以自愿参与为原则，选取个人减碳行为中引领性强、发生频次高、数据可获得的行为作为评价指标。对于较容易核算减碳量的行为赋予"碳减排量"，对于方法学为暂时得不到认可、减碳量难以计算的行为赋予"碳积分"，以"碳积分 + 碳减排量"的形式衡量个人行为的减碳贡献度。通过打造"碳达人·惠湖州"数智平台、建立碳减排量交易机制、建立形式丰富的碳积分兑换体系，构建起"识别精准、参与便捷、场景丰富、普惠有力"的可持续运行机制，推动个人绿色行为碳减排价值实现。目前，平台已有用户数2万余人，累计产生碳积分58.16万余分、碳减排量4 136.33余t。

1. 建立制度标准体系，工作开展有依据

强化顶层设计。制定实施《湖州市建立"碳惠湖州"调节机制工作方案》，明确建设、交通、电力、宣传等部门职责，为数据归集、平台宣传等明确计划安排与职责分工。开展方法学研究。对绿色出行、绿色消费、循环利用、减纸减塑、高效节能等50余种发生频次高的绿色行为进行全面梳理，并逐一绘制行为图谱，为有效识别绿色行为提供有力支撑。制定标准政策。制定出台《碳普惠屋顶分布式光伏发电碳减排量核证规范》等系列标准，科学度量各类绿色行为的碳减排量。

2. 建立绿色场景体系，群众参与有途径

上线"碳达人·惠湖州"数智平台，通过搭建绿色消费、绿色出行、垃圾分类、户用光伏、零碳车主、智能空调等绿色行为场景及"领积分""兑积分""做公益""赚现金""个人碳中和""碳惠点滴""达人助手"等模块，打造集算碳、汇碳、卖碳、兑碳、论碳等功能于一体的综合性交互平台。同时，整合贯通蚂蚁森林、湖州公共出行平台、湖州垃圾分类、新能源云平台等绿色低碳行为数据资源，汇聚形成绿色生活"数据库"，实现对平台用户绿色行为数据的自动采集和实时共享。平台上线以来，已汇聚各类绿色生活行为数据 1651 万条。

3.建立市场交易体系，碳减排量消纳有闭环

通过打通碳减排量交易闭环，实现平台自我造血功能，推动整个体系可持续运行。对于户用光伏、新能源汽车出行等算法较精确、定量数据易采集的绿色行为率先制定碳普惠系列核证地方标准，并规范碳减排量核算、核证等流程，为碳减排量交易奠定基础。建立以平台用户为碳减排量供给主体，公共机构、企业、绿色示范主体为主要需求方，数字人民币和智能合约增值提效的线上一站式交易流程，实现碳减排量在市域范围内的流动转化。目前，已接入 2 万余家居民分布式光伏，预计每年平均可供给 12.6 万 t 光伏发电碳减排量；已累计完成 280 余 t 碳减排量交易。

4.建立普惠反哺体系，积分兑换有保障

建立物质激励与精神激励相结合的普惠模式，以丰富的碳积分兑换形式吸引公众践行绿色行为。组建绿色低碳商家联盟，推动碳积分兑换商业优惠与公共服务，累计征集景区门票、优惠券、公交券等碳积分兑换权益价值约 10 万元。设计碳积分排名、"绿色低碳达人"等荣誉机制，2022 年，评选出 5 名年度"碳达人"作为践行绿色低碳行为典型代表。成立长三角生态能源碳汇基金，倡导企业、公众以"购买碳汇"的低碳方式支持植树造林、湿地保护等碳汇公益项目，不断提升公众参与绿色行为的自我价值实现感。基金成立以来，已获得个人与企业捐赠 200 余笔，推动建设湖州梁希国家森林公园等 10 个合作基地，累计造林面积 23.5 亩。

（三）建筑碳效码精准掌控公共建筑碳排放

同一责任主体（如学校、医院等）往往包含多栋建筑，若拆分成单个建筑去评价其碳排放水平不具有应用价值，且能耗等数据更难获取。因此，建筑领域以同一单位构成的建筑组作为碳效评价的基本单元。通过明确公共建筑碳效码基础数据的采集方法、碳排放分级标准，并建立数字化综合平台，研究基于建筑"碳效码"的政策工具，搭建起了建筑领域碳效改革体系。2023 年 3 月湖州市公共建筑"碳效码"研究成果暨数智平台发布会召开（图 10-2），标志着湖州市在全国率先将"碳效码"延伸至建筑领域。

图 10-2　湖州市公共建筑"碳效码"研究成果暨数智平台发布会

1. 开展基础排摸，确保科学算"碳"

联合清华大学开展建筑"碳效码"评价和应用研究，调研湖州本地公共建筑发展概况、能耗数据采集与标准现状，结合国内典型城市（北京、上海、深圳、杭州等）公共建筑的碳排放数据采集方法与机制，研究符合湖州公共建筑能耗与碳排放管理工作特点的、适宜成本的规模化采集方法与机制；以覆盖三区三县的600余座公共建筑信息及能耗数据为样本，对湖州公共建筑碳排放进行核算分析，并通过核实建筑面积、历年耗能情况、建筑使用习惯等信息，校准建筑信息错误、绿电使用情况、"多户一表"等问题，进一步优化碳效计算模型。

2. 制定分类分级标准，推动合理评"碳"

对标国内现有的建筑运行能耗（限额）及碳排放数据分级方法和标准，围绕湖州建筑领域碳减排目标、重点碳减排对象等管理需求，制定分级标准。经研究论证与优化完善，将湖州公共建筑分为办公建筑、宾馆饭店、商业综合体、医疗建筑、教育建筑、文旅建筑、科研建筑、体育场馆 8 种常见类型，并按 A～E 五级进行碳效分级，分别对应优秀、较优秀、有减排潜力、减排潜力大、需减排改造五种节能减排管理思路。湖州建筑"碳效码"数据采集方法与标准、碳排放计算方法、分级管理方案得到了住房和城乡建设部、浙江大学、同济大学、重庆大学等单位节能降碳领域领导与专家的一致认可。

3. 搭建数字化平台，实现动态测"碳"

打造基于 GIS+ 大数据分析的数字化管理平台，赋予"全市域公建数据接入、全类型能源数据整合、全维度科学碳效评价、全生命周期运行管理、全过程智能诊断决策、全方位建碳资产管控"六大功能，通过快速采集数据、智能算法分析，自动形成碳效评价，实现建筑领域从看静态的"设计节能率"向看动态的"实际运行数据"的转变。目前，已打通住建、经信、电力、统计、发改、金融机构等数据，贯通"碳—能—电"数据链条，建立公共建筑全能耗数据库，累计接入1 173.75 万 m² 公共建筑，获取 30 万条数据，预计接入全市既有公共建筑 1.27 亿 m²。

4. 建立政策制度体系，促进高效管"碳"

制定《湖州市公共建筑碳效码认证与管理规范》，并建立基于"碳效码"的建筑能耗 / 碳排放相关数据与技术对标、披露与共享机制，确保落实表彰并给予奖励资金、表彰但无奖励资金、需加强运行管理、需开展能源审计、需强制开展节能降碳改造 5 种对应 A~E 5 个碳效等级的具体管理策略。据清华大学推算，若"十四五"期间湖州市全面推行建筑"碳效码"，全市公共建筑可节省电量约 3 亿 kW·h，相当于减少碳排放量约 14.8 万 t。

（四）"碳效 +"应用体系释放碳效改革强劲动能

碳效评价本身不是目的，而是用于对主体碳生产力水平的测度，反映出其进一步节能降碳的潜力。但更为重要的是，如何将这部分潜力变为现实，也就是如何将碳效评价实质性地运用起来。这方面湖州市也做了多元化的探索。

1."碳效 + 能效服务"，促进各类主体节能改造

对工业"碳效码"中评价为 4、5 两级和碳效水平处于高碳的企业开展节能诊断服务，推动实施绿色技改项目。已累计对 360 家企业开展节能诊断服务，推动实施节能降碳技术改造项目 380 个，预计节约标准煤 20 万 t。对建筑碳效码中 C、D、E 等级对应的公共建筑开展节能改造，预计仅对当前建筑"碳效码"覆盖的 600 余个样本建筑进行管理，已可超额完成湖州"十四五"期间的既有公共建筑节能改造任务。

2."碳效 + 绿色金融"，引导各领域绿色低碳升级

创新推出"碳效贷""碳惠贷"等金融产品，对低碳高效企业给予信贷支持和贷款利率优惠，已累计发放贷款 1 285 笔，共计 132 亿元。建筑领域以碳效码能耗数据为基础，通过"清单化"管理，为既有建筑绿色节能改造项目提供点对点金融支持，确保愿改能改、应改即改，已印发《金融支持建筑绿色节能改造重点项目（首批）清单》，节能改造面积达 185.89 万 m²，累计为清单内项目提供授信 4.11 亿元。

3."碳效 + 协同评价"，倒逼企业低碳转型

将工业企业的碳效评价结果纳入绿色工厂星级管理评价体系，已应用于3 466 家星级绿色工厂，推动了 126 家企业完成清洁生产审核，完成 450 家绿色工厂"提质升星"行动。在全省率先出台"亩均论英雄"3.0 版，将碳效评价结

果纳入"亩均论英雄"评价体系,权重15分,"绿色低碳"成为亩均评价中企业的重要得分点。根据测算,增设碳效指标后,评价结果发生变化的规模以上工业企业有337家,占比11.04%。

4."碳效+市场交易",推动跨领域协同减碳

将个人绿色行为产生的碳减排量交易于有减碳需求的企业、公共机构(公共建筑责任主体),既提升了企业、公共机构碳效等级,又促进了碳减排量交易的可持续运行。出台《湖州市碳权益交易结果应用于工业碳效评价实施细则》,将企业交易情况纳入碳效评价,鼓励企业积极购买碳减排量,目前已实现工业碳效码平台与"碳达人·惠湖州"平台贯通,并推动企业认购核证碳减排量4 000 t。制定大型活动(会议)碳中和规范,通过购买碳减排量,助力市"两会"、中国绿色低碳创新大会等会议实现碳中和。

三、主要启示

(一)碳效改革应有步骤、分阶段推进

碳效改革的两个重点是给出碳效评价结果,运用这个结果推动减碳,而这都是需要循序渐进的。在给出碳效评价结果上,需充分考虑数据可得性、方法成熟性。从湖州经验看,目前已建成的三类分别是依托于规模以上工业用能统计体系的工业碳效码、通过授权机制实现的个人碳积分、主要用电的公共建筑,数据基础相对较好,而除个人碳减排量尚未全量核算外,其他两个的碳排放核算方法也相对简单。与之相对,数据来源和核算方法更为复杂的交通、农业领域,可作为后续探索的方向。在碳效评价运用上,更多是结合能源、金融、经信等主管部门已在开展的相关工作,为其提供更为精准的主体级碳画像,以制定实施更具针对性的政策。若部门未开展这些工作,这些结合的应用场景也将难以落地。

(二)碳效改革对于企业应引导、倒逼并重

企业是经济社会发展的生命力所在,但同时也是能耗和碳排放的绝对主体。开展碳效改革,很重要的目标即是在以前粗放的分业管理基础上,进一步做到行业内部的分类管理,提升精准水平。但是,若仍将关注重点置于管理二字上,则并不能很好满足企业的实际需要。实际上,企业不仅需要减碳的目标,更需要相应能力的指导、服务的提供,以确保减碳的可行性,这才是碳效改革的目标。从湖州经验看,大量关于金融、技术等方面的应用场景,无不是为企业提供要素和能力的支撑,而这对于吸引企业参与、保障改革顺利推行是不可或缺的。

（三）碳效改革应通过数字化改革落地

碳效改革需要搞数字化平台，这已几乎是所有开展这一改革地方的共识，但是对于应该建设怎样的数字化平台，却仍然是存在一些分歧的。从湖州的经验看，主要是以创新改革为目标，汇聚多源数据建设碳账户，治理和服务功能同步推进，这些实质上都是浙江数字化改革范畴的内容。从这一点来说，数字化平台只是一个载体，它的输入/输出更为关键，也更多是数字化以外的内容。由此，若其他地方有意愿建设碳效相关数字化平台，仍应考虑按照数字化改革的完整流程、规范范式走下来，步步推进。

四、展望

碳效改革目前已在全国多地推广应用，这也是其生命力的有效验证。但这项改革本身还远未结束，面向未来，在碳效的评价、应用维度仍需继续强化探索。

在碳效评价上，一方面，可进一步优化碳排放、碳效相关计算方法，提升数据的准确性和权威性，加强方法的推广性；另一方面，可进一步拓宽碳效改革覆盖面，尤其是向交通、农业等领域延伸，向中小微企业延伸，向农村延伸。

在碳效应用上，主要是可拓展碳效评价在碳排放预算化管理、绿色金融、碳权益交易等方面应用，深化碳效码与绿色建筑、绿色工厂等评价体系的相互联通机制，不断增加碳效评价的使用范围和场景；同时，也可开展"碳效领跑者"等典型评选宣传，不断提升公众号召力和社会影响力。

作者：胡畅[1]，陆巧玲[2]

1 胡畅，湖州市发展和改革委员会副主任，长期从事资源环境领域工作，主要负责绿色低碳发展规划、碳达峰碳中和政策、生态产品价值实现机制等领域的研究与实践。
2 陆巧玲，硕士研究生，发表论文6篇，其中SCI期刊论文4篇，任职于湖州市发展和改革委员会，主要从事资源环境领域工作。

循环经济助力降碳的"永康模式"

永康五金手工业源远流长，历来就有"五金工匠走四方，府府县县不离康"的美名，"补锅补壶、打铜修锁"等技艺实现了最原始的资源循环利用。随着循环经济工作的不断推进，资源循环利用产业由粗放分拣向精密制造转型，形成了企业小循环、园区大循环的循环体系，率先走出一条工业化程度高、资源利用效率高、经济较为发达、环境容量小的地区循环经济发展新路子，为浙江乃至全国其他地区发展循环经济提供了"永康模式"。

一、引言

永康是全国闻名的五金之都，五金产业集群发达，但同时自然资源相对薄弱，是典型的工业强市、资源小市。为更好践行"绿水青山就是金山银山"理念，助力五金现代化嬗变谱写"世界五金之都"，永康以国家循环经济示范城市创建地区、全国唯一再生资源回收体系建设试点县、省级园区循环化改造示范试点等一批试点建设为契机，探索形成"再生金属—五金制品—废旧金属回收—再生金属"的循环产业链，构建了以废旧金属材料市场和再生物资回收利用中心为原材料供应基地，经济开发区和省级高新产业园区为生产基地，中国科技五金城和网上商城为产品集散销售中心的"回收体系—原料基地—生产利用—专业市场"的"永康模式"，在全国率先开展了县级循环经济发展指数研究，探索建立了全国首个县级资源产出率统计核算体系，走出了一条发展循环经济独特而成熟的"永康路径"，成为全省乃至全国典范。

二、主要做法与成效

（一）构建现代循环产业体系

1. 高质量发展循环型制造业

大力发展工业循环经济，通过创建绿色工厂推动绿色制造、以低效用地拆建小微企业园、"亩均论英雄"改革促进低效企业改造提升、差别化政策促企业转型升级等措施逐步形成了资源节约型、清洁生产型、环境友好型的循环型工业体系框架。规模以上企业清洁生产审核率近 40%；获评国家级绿色工厂 3 家、绿色设计产品 2 个，省级绿色工厂 2 家，省级节水型企业 33 家。

2. 提升发展循环型服务业

依托现有五金产业的高集聚度，推进五金产业总部中心建设，构建完善集聚金融保险、创意资讯、信息技术、会计法律、电子商务等各类服务及配套设施的生产性服务业体系。依托国家五金工具及门类产品质量监督检验中心（浙江）的建设，拉长五金产业服务产业链，进一步激发市场活力。依托永康五金产业集聚区，以五金文化为主题，结合现有的山水旅游资源，"山水 + 工业"的工业旅游发展新格局成型。

3. 积极发展现代生态循环农业

以全省首个现代农业装备高新技术产业园区建设作为永康现代农机装备"升级版"的切入点和突破口，推动现代农机装备向大型化、集成化、智能化方向专深发展。依据"减量化、循环化、再使用"的原则，对畜禽粪便、农作物秸秆等废弃物进行循环再利用，形成了"资源—废弃物—再生资源"循环型农业生态链。

（二）健全物资循环利用体系

1. 完善再生资源回收体系

以"无废城市"建设为抓手，加快各类循环经济项目建设，建成 1 个再生资源分拣中心、54 个再生资源回收网点为依托的再生资源回收利用体系，将金属相关加工制造业产生的金属边角料、碎屑、废纸、废塑料等再生资源重新回流到利废企业，促进再生资源的再回收、再利用，极大降低生产成本，节约大量能源资源，减少二氧化碳、甲烷、氮氧化物、烟气（粉尘）等主要污染物排放，大气、水、土壤环境质量明显改善。

2. 提升再生资源利用水平

培育组建全省首个无废产业联盟，基本形成工业固体废物、建筑垃圾、生活垃圾（餐厨垃圾）资源化利用和再生资源回收利用的固体废物处置产业集群。截至 2021 年，无废产业联盟通过良性运作，已累计处置一般工业固体废物 8.1 万 t，收运处置餐厨垃圾 6 万余 t，累计回收农药包装废弃物 250 余 t。推进实施生活垃圾焚烧扩容工程，深化农村生活垃圾"三化"处理中心、餐厨垃圾资源化综合利用和无害化处置中心建设，生活垃圾处置利用能力显著提升。截至 2021 年，实现废塑料、废橡胶回收率 78%，废纸回收率 84%，废农膜回收利用率 96%，农作物秸秆综合利用率 96.3%。通过改进自身工艺，充分利用建筑垃圾与垃圾焚烧场残渣进行生产，实现建筑材料的循环利用。同时提升各类固体废物资源化利用水平，实现主要再生有色金属回收率 96.5%，产生的固态燃料和肥料等，有效降低对自然资源的消耗，减少燃煤等化石能源消耗。

3. 促进生活垃圾分类工作提质增效

大力推进生活垃圾"两定四分"集中投放点建设，同时不断提高垃圾回收处理水平，探索出"垃圾源头分类、再生资源回收、餐厨垃圾资源化、不可回收垃圾就地减量化处理＋智慧化回收平台"的"4+1"智慧化处理方式，打造形成农村生活垃圾分类回收处置的"永康样板"。通过改造提升太阳能堆肥房，预计每天处理生活垃圾约 212 t，初步形成了垃圾分类的"永康模式"，运营至今共处理厨余垃圾 2 300 余 t，产出初级肥 690 余 t，回收各类低价值再生资源 700 余 t，无害化处置率达 100%。截至 2021 年，生活垃圾城区分类覆盖面达 100%，生活垃圾回收利用率超过 60%。

（三）推进资源节约集约利用

1. 深入开展园区循环化改造

积极开展开发区园区循环化改造，通过产业转型升级、低小散危企业整治，低效工业用地改造，实现园区企业集聚发展；通过企业技术升级、工艺改造、加强废物循环利用、提升循环经济技术与装备，扩充循环经济产业链，减少原料消耗、增加物质再利用和循环利用水平，大幅降低企业生产的原料成本和能源消耗，工业固体废物产生量持续下降、工业固体废物综合利用水平持续保持 100%，水资源产出率不断攀升、工业用水重复利用率达到 90%，大大减少污染物排放。到 2020 年，永康市工业固体废物产生强度年度增长率实现负增长。2021 年，园区单位生产总值能耗 0.38 t 标准煤／万元，园区固体废物实现零排放，工业废水排放量、化学需氧量、氨氮等环境指标均超额完成上级下达的减排指标。

2. 深入推进能源消费革命

推动开展区域能评改革，严格控制新增高耗能项目，加强重点领域和重点单位的节能管理，全面推进高污染燃料"五炉"整治工作，单位 GDP 能耗持续下降。逐步推行企业煤改气工作，已有 80 家企业实现了煤改气，开发区范围内燃煤锅炉基本淘汰。大力推广屋顶太阳能分布式发电，总装机容量达 20 MWp。出台《永康市电动汽车充电桩基础建设管理实施方案》，新建公（专）用充电桩730 个。永康市单位 GDP 能耗降至 0.35 t 煤 / 万元，优于全省平均水平，规模以上企业用煤量 0.04 万 t，较 2012 年减少 15.87 万 t，煤炭消耗量下降明显；全市清洁能源消费占比逐年提高。2021 年，全市能源产出率达到 2.86 万元 /t 标准煤，是 2012 年开展循环经济工作时的 1.5 倍。

3. 高标准实施节水行动

通过强化实施《永康市取水用户计划用水管理办法》，合理优化水资源配置与管理，加强对洗车行业、洗浴业、游泳池等行业的管理，并通过节水型单位建设、水平衡测试、超计划用水累计加价水费及节水器具改造等措施推动节水型社会建设，城市节水减排力度显著增强。创成省级节水型企业 33 家、节水型单位15 家。2021 年，水资源产出率达到 450 元 /t，较 2012 年增长 1.6 倍；单位工业增加值用水量为 0.000 7 t/ 元，较 2012 年下降近 80%。

4. 全面推进节约集约用地

建立工业领域"亩产论英雄"约束评判机制，通过细算"亩产账"，奖励"高效用地"，挤出"低效占地"，以"空间换土地"集约用地发展高附加值产业，实现工业企业亩产税收的整体大提升。出台《关于鼓励企业改造低效厂房提高土地集约水平的实施意见》，强化亩产效益的理念，减轻了标兵示范企业的发展压力，同时坚定实行《工业建设项目用地规划指导适建标准》，设置亩均投资底线，在集约用地的同时实现大批低效企业改造提升、转型升级。持续推进淘汰落后产能，加快"低散乱"小企业整治提升，2021 年整治"低散乱"企业（作坊）1 164 家，淘汰落后产能涉及企业 33 家。

（四）健全循环发展体制机制

1. 强化数字化改革的引领作用

搭建永康市无废城市管理平台，与餐厨垃圾信息化管理平台、餐厨垃圾台账制度同步建立，实现收运数据的管理、共享和监管，并由信息化管理平台进行统一监控、调度、指挥，处理过程实时监控，物料、废水、成品量实时录入，实现动态管理。搭建工业固体废物精密智控闭环监管协同应用，形成工业固体废物全过程数字化、可追溯、可预警、闭环式的智能集中处置体系，实现对工业固体废物产出、运输、处置的全方位、多层次、立体式、精细化、智能化闭环监控和管理。

2.完善循环经济政策体系

设立创建国家循环经济领导小组，建立健全循环经济建设的目标责任考核体系，出台了《永康市促进循环经济发展的实施意见》《关于加强节能降耗发展循环经济工作的实施意见》等规范性文件，先后出台再生资源回收、垃圾分类处置等13个政策意见，为再生资源循环利用提供制度保障。制定了制造水平升级、骨干企业培育、科技创新驱动、绿色清洁生产等一系列相关政策措施。构建循环经济发展指数评价体系，集评价功能、考核功能、预警功能于一体，科学评价全市循环经济发展水平。

3.完善绿色金融体系

大力支持不同经济成分与投资主体以多种形式参与循环经济发展。出台《关于设立永康市产业发展引导基金的实施意见》，提高"五大百亿"产业与循环经济在融资上的结合度，减少重点产业的融资难度，以子基金、直接投资、让利性股权投资、投资联动等模式运作资金，减少投资风险。同时，出台了《永康市促进循环经济发展的实施意见》《关于加大金融支持力度促进循环经济发展的指导意见》（永银发〔2014〕74号）等相关政策，从发挥信贷资金导向作用、提升循环经济金融服务水平、完善支持循环经济金融服务体系、构建循环经济信贷投放长效机制等四大方面，进一步改进、创新金融服务，扎实推进了循环经济"1445"行动计划。

三、经验启示

（一）强化夯实组织、政策、金融要素保障

建立工作领导小组等有效组织机构，建立发改、经信、环保、国土等各相关部门协调配合的工作机制，高效推进循环经济项目的建设和实施运营，同时加强产业转型升级、节能减排、低效用地改造等工作指导，推动实现多部门高效协作。强化政策保障，对政策的制定、项目的规划进行顶层设计，联动推进，并出台促进循环经济发展相关系列政策，为后续工作推进及项目的高效运营提供政策支持。推动完善支持循环经济发展的金融服务体系，提升循环经济金融服务水平、不断创新金融服务。

（二）建立健全园区、产业、企业循环链条

以废弃资源综合利用为核心工作，重点提升资源重复利用效率，着力延伸企业产品生产链条，打造循环经济信息服务平台，推动形成企业之间、企业内部的物质、能量的流动闭环，构建园区、产业、企业3个层次立体化的循环体系。生产制造过程中产生的废钢、废线缆、废零部件等，通过企业内部自我回收利用，或者由第三方资源综合利用企业进行统一资源化处理。鼓励企业投资资源循环利用产业，加强对消费领域不同类型的装备制造产品进行回收再利用。此外，鼓励企业进行技术创新、改进工艺和设备更新，提高钢材、塑料器件、金属铜线等利用效率，减少物料损耗，同时引导企业开发各类高效、环保、节能型产品。

（三）构建完善配套、生产、回收循环体系

完善基础设施配套体系，遵循开发建设基础设施先行先建原则，确保基本实现"五通一平"，道路、供电、供水等基础设施建设框架基本成型。规范清洁生产体系，积极在企业中推广清洁生产和绿色企业创建工作，培育示范典型，以循环化改造从源头减少污染物生产，以点带面推动循环经济发展。创新垃圾回收体系，采用"政府引导、企业付费、第三方服务"的方式，建立工业固体废物从"分类、回收、运输、终端处置"全过程数字化、可追溯、封闭式处理体系。

（四）推动实现智造、用能、产业效益升级

以推进传统产业智能化制造改造为切入点，实施"机器换人"专项行动，开展智能化无人工厂（车间）等建设，稳步推进传统制造业改造提升步伐，推动实现能耗下降、废弃物减排与降本增效。推动能源利用升级，推广分布式光伏发电项目，提高清洁能源使用率，通过地热能利用，推进生产中节能；推进企业以节能技术改造为主的清洁化生产技术改造，鼓励企业积极实施余热余压利用，提升经济与减排效益。推动循环产业升级。开展园区循环化改造，有效构建循环型产业链。

（五）统筹搭建科技、治理、服务支撑平台

建立政府引导、企业为主的科技创新平台，整合政府、科研院所、企业、行业协会、专业机构等各方的优势，构建信息化共享科技服务平台，以点带面全面提升行业现代化生产水平。搭建源头整治平台。建立"亩产论英雄"约束评判机制，以现代化的小微企业创业园和生态化园区作为治理"低小散危"企业平台，

持续深入推动"低小散危"整治企业，有效破解"僵尸企业"用地，处置"围墙圈地"与"低效用地"，消化批而未供土地，最大程度提高工业用地产出率。搭建公共服务平台，建立人才培训、信息服务、物流服务等多功能产业信息服务平台，并根据产业园实际和企业需求，及时发布行业内的市场、技术和人才信息，为企业提供信息查询服务。组建和完善政务服务中心，建立健全项目报批、企业报税等一站式服务窗口；吸收社会中介机构，组建专业咨询队伍，及时为企业提供科技、经济、人才、政策、法律等综合服务的能力。

四、展望

永康工业发展史就是循环经济发展的探索史，从传统五金技艺走南闯北的实践，跨越到大五金、大数据的今天，奠定了循环经济发展的深厚底蕴。下一步，永康将不断拓展和延伸发展循环经济的"永康模式"，为国家循环经济发展探索永康实践、永康素材和永康经验，加快打造先进制造业基地，实现从传统"小五金"到现代"大五金"蝶变转型、从"中国五金之都"到"世界五金之都"的迭代跃升。

（一）强化组织领导，完善考核体系建设

充分发挥循环经济示范县创建领导小组的作用，优化营商环境，为企业的健康和可持续发展提供良好保障。借助示范创建经验，做好向导工作，引导企业建设发展方向。完善循环经济考核评价体系，将循环经济发展工作目标作为基本内容，将经济转型升级、产业融合、生态发展等作为专项考核重点，形成多层次、立体化的考核评价体系。

（二）强化部门协同，创新激励监管机制

加强多部门合作，进一步对相关部门、权限、责任、内容提出明确要求，全面完善建立循环经济发展机制。出台相关政策扶持方案，优化循环经济专项发展基金扶持范围及力度。完善相应的监督性地方法规、政策，形成激励与监督并行的措施促进循环经济发展。推进"无废永康"信息监管平台建设，推动全品类固体废物治理体系和治理能力现代化，着力打造监管"一张网"。

（三）强化要素支撑，完善技术服务平台

进一步引导、鼓励企业加大对循环经济共性技术、关键支撑技术的开发研

究，积极引进吸收世界先进的循环经济技术，加强对循环经济先进技术的推广应用，对创新成果政府给予嘉奖。优化完善技术咨询服务平台、信息交换平台等，及时组织开展技术咨询、技术推广等，及时向社会发布有关循环经济的技术、管理、政策等信息。探索建立循环经济专家问诊制，定期组织专家对园区循环化改造进行指导。加快固废处置终端建设，推进生活垃圾焚烧扩容工程，补齐生活垃圾处置能力缺口；提高现有易腐垃圾终端（城区餐厨垃圾处置中心和农村"三化"中心）的处置率、利用率，减轻末端焚烧处置压力；实施标准化生活垃圾分拣中心改造提升项目。

（四）强化宣传教育，培育推广典型模式

总结循环经济发展的典型经验，通过新闻出版、广播影视等途径和社会团体，推广各个部门、企业循环经济创建工作中比较成熟的模式，通过典型示范引领循环经济发展，进一步将与循环经济有关的科学知识和法律常识纳入宣传教育，利用奖励、补助政策促使企业积极建设循环经济。通过多渠道加大餐厨垃圾收运及处置的相关法律法规、政策等的宣传力度，加强垃圾分类培训，积极引导，加强监管，使广大餐厨垃圾产生单位及市民深入了解垃圾分类、餐厨垃圾集中收运处置的重要性和紧迫性。

作者：马海华[1]

1　马海华，浙江省永康市发展和改革局局长，在推进循环经济和工业绿色低碳发展方面研究较深，谋划提出并推动多项国家级、省级循环经济领域试点示范在永康落地实践。

从竹小汇到先行区——嘉善聚力打造长三角绿色生态一体化示范区绿色低碳最佳实践案例

在"双碳"目标指引下，嘉善县以"双示范"建设为载体，围绕"生态优先、零碳平衡、资源循环、建筑生长、科创联盟、数字赋能"，构建可示范、可推广、可操作性强的低碳试点示范高质量建设新路径，探索多跨协同融合的绿色低碳治理模式，聚力将竹小汇项目打造成为长三角绿色生态一体化示范区绿色低碳最佳案例，以竹小汇试点示范亮点经验助推先行区实现绿色低碳高质量发展。

一、引言

县域是经济高质量发展的主阵地，同时也是探索绿色低碳转型发展的重要载体。嘉善县承担着长三角生态绿色一体化发展示范区和县域高质量发展示范点两大国家战略，政治地位特殊、发展势头强劲。近年来，嘉善县全面贯彻落实国家碳达峰碳中和战略，充分发挥区域位置和政治地位优势，探索走出了"政策引领、以点带面、产业为主、区域协同、科创赋能"的绿色低碳发展"嘉善模式"，获得了国家生态文明建设示范县、省级低碳试点县、省级氢燃料电池汽车示范点、省级交通强国（绿色交通）建设试点县等20余项省级以上绿色低碳创建示范荣誉。作为在绿色低碳发展上的一个亮点，嘉善县统筹推进实施竹小汇科创聚落等一批低（零）碳示范项目建设，逐步构建了涵盖建筑、交通、能源等全领域低碳示范展陈链群，聚力打造了全国首个"真零碳"聚落样板。

二、主要做法

（一）以零碳聚落为引领，打造零碳模式新样板

1. 多能源互补，实现碳平衡

能源结构低碳化是生产端降碳的主要路径。竹小汇"零碳"聚落是中国第一个的零碳村落有机更新项目、全体系应用"低碳智慧城市设施"示范项目和光储直柔与传统电网有机融合项目。通过积极开发风能、地热能、太阳能、生物质能、氢能等可再生能源，进行多能互补，竹小汇科创聚落产生能源已远超消耗能源，且实现碳平衡。项目一期用能全部使用电能，每年建筑总耗电118万 kW·h，而建筑屋顶光伏发电量每年达 120万 kW·h（图 12-1），村落用能 100% 零碳化。此外，村落内电动汽车总耗电每年约 10万 kW·h，风力发电加上屋顶之外的光伏设备发电量每年约 10万 kW·h，用电和零碳发电实现平衡。

图 12-1　竹小汇零碳科创村落光伏俯瞰图

2. 多资源利用，实现碳循环

资源循环利用不仅有利于节约资源，同时也是推进节能降碳的有力举措。竹小汇"零碳"聚落聚焦生产生活多维度，全方位推进资源的有效循环利用。在建筑方面，将原有建筑拆除后产生的建筑垃圾，作为新建筑的装饰材料；以板式、瓦式的光伏板，进行太阳能采集，同时保障白墙灰瓦的江南水乡风貌；以地源热泵进行地热能采集，提供冷热源；聚落还采用发电风车等技术进行微循环能源补

充。在废弃物方面，采用先进技术实现污废水 100% 处理后回用、再排放，厨余垃圾等通过生物降解 100% 在本地处理，其他生活垃圾 100% 分类收集处理、回用。通过实时采集显示碳汇、碳平衡数据，实现整个聚落负碳运行。

（二）以生态修复为优先，谱写绿色生态新底色

1. 强化水生态治理，积极打造世界级滨水空间

作为长三角生态绿色一体化发展示范区，打造美丽宜人的生态环境对于嘉善来说至关重要，而水环境是其中重要部分。竹小汇生态岛通过生态沟渠和人工湿地净化农田退水，生态缓冲带削减面源污染，水下森林维护清澈水质，实现水质和生态的全面提升。同时，采用"精准分区 – 逆境改善 – 模块定植 – 稳态维持"沉水植物修复技术和"尾水 – 河网 – 湖荡"多源污染多级拦截与净化成套技术，解决低透明度、高风浪条件下沉水植被难以存活的技术难题，有效削减农业带来的面源污染。目前，祥符荡水质已达到 II 类水标准、透明度 2 m 以上，沉水植被覆盖度达 70%，初步实现"世界级滨水空间，人与自然和谐共生"的生态格局。

2. 保护生物多样性，完善河湖生态系统体验地

生态系统是碳汇的重要本底，而生物多样性是保持生态系统能力的关键参量。竹小汇生态岛总面积 107 亩，是一个天然孤岛。通过周边水贯通和"生态缓冲带 – 水下森林 – 人工湿地"组合工艺等生态湿地修复，岛上的乔木、灌木、芦苇、草地、水塘和浅滩形成了一个独特、平衡的岛屿生态系统。为精准捕捉动植物种类数量情况，在全国率先执行以先行启动区镇域为单位的水生态和生物多样性调查，监测点位遍布 11 个湖泊和数百条河流，形成科学完整的本底数据库。同时，不断深化竹小汇生物多样性保护经验，持续强化生物多样性保护，加强生境恢复和物种培育，持续开展萤火虫回"嘉"主题活动。

（三）以科创联盟为驱动，激活绿色低碳新引擎

1. 以零碳聚落为载体，组建长三角低碳生态创新联盟

作为长三角生态绿色一体化发展示范区，周边科技创新力量密布，而科技创新是促进实现碳中和目标的关键变量，嘉善也在聚力成为绿色低碳发展相关科技创新力量的吸引子。竹小汇科创联盟充分集聚中国生态城市研究院低碳生态研究中心、生态环境部土壤与农业农村生态环境监管技术中心长三角双碳研究中心、中国环境科学研究院示范区科创中心以及疏浚技术装备国家工程研究中心等国家级科研院所聚焦低碳、生态领域的科技研发和技术创新，并联合爱德曼氢能创新

中心、江苏英特飞、上海城建集团等长三角地区优秀企业进行成果转化及应用方面的探索。竹小汇零碳科创村落见图12-2。

图 12-2　竹小汇零碳科创村落俯瞰图

2. 以祥符荡创新中心为依托，深化绿色低碳产学研合作

竹小汇附近的祥符荡科创绿谷研发总部是示范区重大科创及产业转化平台，由嘉善县联合长三角域内院校合作共建，通过集聚浙大、复旦、清华长三院等长三角高端科研资源，致力于打造示范区科创高地。目前，浙大智慧绿洲 4 个未来实验室、复旦嘉善研究院、祥符实验室等已陆续投入运行，会聚起一批院士领衔的一流研发团队，为打造长三角前沿科创成果献计献策。

（四）以智慧稻田为示范，探索低碳农业新模式

1. 以"零直排"助力减污

农业虽在区域碳排放中所占比重不高，但由于其资源消耗较大、污染物排放较多，存在较大潜力的协同减排空间。竹小汇智慧田通过引入阿里云的数字技术和中国水稻研究所的植物低碳作业数字模型，打造了长三角地区首个 400 亩低碳智慧示范田。示范田以 5 亩为最小单元种植湿地型稻田，配套生态沟渠，构建分布式水稻生态环境系统。通过利用生长模型和物联装备进行田间灌排自动调控，让水位始终保持在水稻不同生长周期的最佳需水值，示范田较传统模式可节水 50%，结合生态沟渠自然净化，稻田退水氮磷削减 30%～40%，达到"零直排"效果。

2. 以"智慧田"助力降碳

农业的智慧化发展是挖掘节能降碳空间、降低资源消耗和全生命周期碳排放的重要路径。竹小汇"智慧田"聚焦间歇性精准灌排、北斗导航、绿色防控等功能，集成数字测碳、装备控碳、立体减碳三大技术，以及联动薄露灌溉、光谱分析、纳米气泡、自动巡航等技术模型，实现全方位和全生命周期的减排固碳。在不减产的前提下，竹小汇"智慧田"较传统模式可减少灌溉用水50%，减少肥料使用15%，减少燃油消耗10%，减少劳动力投入15%，亩均碳排放当量减少20%以上，取得经济、减污、降碳效益的有机合一。

（五）以多跨协同为支撑，彰显绿色低碳新风尚

1. 以氢能示范，引领交通绿色低碳

氢能既是重要的储能技术，同时也是一种清洁、零碳的能源，当前相关技术已趋于成熟，产业化示范不断涌现。位于嘉善县的长三角示范区跨省氢燃料公交示范线（西塘—黎里）作为浙江省首条氢燃料电池公交线（图12-3），目前累计推广各类氢公交100辆，配置于善枫线、西枫线以及城区、城乡公交，共覆盖20条线路，总行驶里程达900万km，累计减少二氧化碳排放约3 200 t。同时，作为浙江省氢燃料汽车推广应用示范点，嘉善县已统筹建成加氢站3座（图12-4），实现30 min社会化加氢网络圈。

图12-3　长三角示范区跨省氢燃料公交示范线（西塘—黎里）

图 12-4　浙江省首座加氢站——中石化嘉善善通加油加氢站

2. 以绿建标准，打造低碳建筑典范

示范区企业交流服务基地聚力打造三星级绿色低碳建筑典范，按照"百年烟雨，一叶扁舟"的设计理念，以一叶扁舟的形象呈现，集成会议、展示、数字化三大功能。建筑对照三星绿建标准，利用地源热泵、智慧路灯、隔热玻璃等各类低碳建筑技术集成，打造成为一体化示范区，践行"节能低碳 绿色可持续"理念的标志性建筑是示范区嘉善片区建筑领域绿色低碳引领的主窗口。

三、经验启示

作为长三角生态绿色一体化发展示范区和县域高质量发展示范点的"双示范"区域，嘉善县始终秉持绿色低碳循环发展理念，形成了较多可复制、可推广的经验。

（一）打造零碳示范标杆，形成零碳、无废、生长聚落

以聚落要素视野，通过低（零）碳技术集成输出，打造形成"零碳、无废和生长型"3 个集中展示生态绿色、零碳赋能的高质量成果单元，为全国持续性提供可复制、可推广的"竹小汇零碳模式"。零碳聚落上，利用太阳能、地热能、风能以及未来计划使用的氢能、生物质能 5 种清洁能源进行"多能互补"，实现"碳补偿"。无废聚落上，利用废旧砖瓦重建，采用污水处置系统和垃圾生物降解技术等进行降耗应用，实现废物零外运。生长聚落上，实行碳平衡数据实时监测

和定期评估，不断在二期、三期建设中整合和优化现有技术，实现全生命周期的零碳运行。

（二）强化绿色生态修复，共建人与自然和谐共生格局

坚持尊重自然、顺应自然、保护自然，统筹自然生态系统全要素系统治理，促进人与自然和谐共生。嘉善县聚焦加强重要生态系统保护与修复、重要生态空间保护监管，加大生物多样性保护力度，以全力提升生态系统质量和稳定性。同时，积极推进清水绿廊建设，串接淀山湖生态区与嘉善主城区、完善主要河流连接生境斑块等多元功能，打造伍子塘、太浦河、红旗塘、中心河等生态绿廊，夯实全县生态安全基底。此外，率先开展江南圩田展示园的水网整治，加强湖荡周边缓冲带林地建设，加强长白荡、汾湖、祥符荡等重要自然湿地的保护力度，加快建设湿地公园，构筑城乡一体化的生态绿地系统空间结构。

（三）加快绿色科创赋能，构建科技融合产业创新体系

科技创新是实现碳达峰碳中和的关键变量。嘉善县抢抓上海全球科创中心建设机遇，依托 G60 科创走廊、沪渝高速和通苏嘉甬高速两条功能创新轴，以祥符荡科创绿谷为极核引领，持续深化与国内外大院名校的科技创新合作，加快建设嘉善复旦研究院、上海大学（浙江）高端装备基础件材料研究院、浙江大学长三角智慧绿洲、祥符实验室等高能级创新载体，集聚更多科技创新力量。同时，加大新型研发机构引育力度，面向集成电路、智能网联汽车、生物医药等优势领域，支持有条件的载体争创省级新型研发机构、重点实验室、制造业创新中心、产业创新中心等，打造"成果＋市场""成果＋产业""成果＋资本"的科技产业融合发展体系。

（四）氢能领域融合发展，促进交通用能产业结构优化

氢能是当前广受关注的零碳能源。聚焦氢能"零碳"优势，作为浙江省氢燃料汽车推广应用示范点，嘉善县积极推动氢能交通与氢能产业融合发展，聚力打造以氢赋能"双碳"目标的"嘉善实践"。首发上线全省首条氢能公交线路，累计推广各类氢公交达 117 辆。集聚招引全链条氢能产业生态，出台"一揽子"氢能扶持政策，规划建设 230 亩嘉善氢能产业园。着力强化氢能科技创新领航，成立嘉善氢能产业创新联盟，连续举办三届中国（嘉善）氢能与燃料电池产业发展与应用论坛。

四、展望

下一步，嘉善县将立足现有绿色低碳发展优势，以竹小汇试点示范亮点经验助推先行区绿色低碳高质量发展。

（一）以竹小汇零碳聚落引领先行区清洁能源全覆盖

加快先行区嘉善片区清洁能源全覆盖，围绕南北祥符荡及沉香荡，充分依托并挖掘创新中心周边渔光互补、分布式光伏、氢能源生产等已有清洁能源供给能力和网络，探索打造清洁能源全覆盖片区。积极推进中心多元融合高弹性电网建设，促进源网荷储高效互动，实现新能源充分消纳和高效利用，构建源网荷储一体化的区域能源互联网。推进清洁能源绿色筑底，积极建设用户侧"光伏 + 储能"等新型储能项目，建设内河岸电水上服务区，搭建清洁能源数据治理平台，实现电能灵活调节和精准控制。有机嵌入 5G、数字互联基因，率先构建区域智慧车联网，引领全域绿色低碳交通。

（二）以竹小汇生态岛促进先行区生态综合治理示范

加快先行区嘉善片区生态绿色综合治理，建设引领示范区绿色创新发展的重要增长极和动力源。统筹生态环境保护提升与生态园区示范打造，围绕祥符荡科创绿谷的规划、建设和运营，全面调查区域生态基底与生态系统服务数量和质量，开展科创绿谷水系综合整治工程、圩区整治工程。以巩固提升水环境质量为目标，以全域推进水生态修复、联合开展跨界水体治理、整合提升智水大脑应用、深化污水零直排区建设、探索水生物多样性保护为重点，持续推进各项工作落地见效，努力打造先行区"三水融合"的嘉善样板。

（三）以竹小汇无废聚落促进先行区资源循环化利用

按照资源利用全生命周期管理理念，以产业发展能力提升为支撑，加快构建资源循环利用管理闭环，着力提升资源利用效率和水平。积极推动先行区大宗工业固体废物综合利用水平显著提升、固体废物产生强度下降、再生资源行业持续健康发展。与其他两区共同探索建设立足示范区、服务长三角、面向全国的循环经济交易中心，探索协同打造示范区静脉产业园区。推动建立完善的示范区废旧物资、再生资源、二手设备及二手商品的评估和分级标准，探索新兴固体废物一体协同综合利用路径，鼓励"互联网 + 回收"、区块链、碳普惠等先进技术和机制在循环经济市场交易中的推广应用。

（四）以竹小汇生长聚落带动先行区低碳建筑推广应用

积极推广光储直柔建筑技术，探索 5G、物联网、大数据、人工智能等新兴方向的新技术在建筑节能运维管理、智能化系统建设等方面的应用示范场景。利用大数据和云平台技术进一步拓展建筑能耗监测平台的监测范围和服务功能。在示范区推进绿色生态园区示范项目建设，积极示范实施热湿分离控制独立新风系统、高温高效末端辐射空调系统、防冷热桥高质量建筑热工系统等技术，实施风廊道优化、海绵园区、生物多样性保护等技术，打造舒适健康低碳建筑与园区（社区）的标杆。

（五）以竹小汇科创联盟推动先行区绿色低碳科创聚集

强力打造以祥符荡科创绿谷为核心的"北斗七星"世界级创新湖区生态圈，前瞻布局一批科技创新基础工程和重大战略项目，建设一批具有较强区域显示度和综合影响力的多级科创平台，形成梯次合理的创新体系，加速集聚一大批高层次人才集聚。构建形成"基础研究＋技术攻关＋成果转化＋科技金融＋人才支撑＋创新环境＋数字云服务"七环相联创新生态链；升级完善"政产学研金介用"七位一体创新机制，打造具有国际影响力和竞争力的世界级湖区科技创新策源地。

作者：马明[1]，王鹤霖[2]

1　马明，嘉兴市发展规划研究院能源低碳领域负责人，高级工程师。长期从事绿色低碳循环发展、应对气候变化、能源管理等研究和咨询工作。

2　王鹤霖，嘉兴市发展规划研究院能源低碳领域研究员，工程师。从事应对气候变化、绿色低碳发展等研究和咨询工作。

富春江镇深耕绿色发展　雕绘低碳高质共富新局

"天下佳山水，古今推富春。"桐庐县富春江镇始终是低碳理念的忠实践行者，作为国家级风景名胜区"三江两湖"黄金旅游线上的一颗璀璨明珠，自 2012 年成立全省首个慢生活体验区以来，富春江镇积极探索低碳发展模式，自然风光、人文底蕴、旅游产业、先进制造业在此深度融合，巨型绿色"充电宝"百亿级抽水蓄能电站开工，逐步实现了从"卖柴火"到"卖风景"、从"造耗能器械"到"造高端装备"的华丽转身，树起绿色事业和低碳产业良性发展新"标杆"。

一、引言

富春江镇享有全国特色小镇、国家级美丽宜居示范镇、全国重点镇、全国卫生镇、全国环境优美乡镇、中国水力发电设备制造基地等美誉，是国家级风景名胜区"三江两湖"黄金旅游线上的一颗璀璨明珠。2022 年，巨型绿色"充电宝"百亿级抽水蓄能电站在富春江镇落地开工（图 13-1、图 13-2），标志着富春江镇的绿色低碳发展迎来又一座里程碑。秉承着绿色低碳、系统集成的理念，富春江镇低碳发展促进共同富裕的新格局已初具雏形。

图 13-1　百亿级抽水蓄能电站开工	图 13-2　芦茨湾全貌

二、厚植生态资源本底

（一）河道资源丰富，水力发电站数量多

富春江镇镇域范围内共有富春江、清渚江、芦茨溪（图13-3）等9条河道，总长度达74.2 km，水电资源蕴藏量丰富。利用境内充沛的水资源，因地制宜建有多座水力发电站。境内七里泷峡谷出口处，建有低水头大流量河床式电站——富春江电站（图13-4），富春江水电站控制流域面积31 300 km²，总库容8.74亿m³，装机容量29.72万kW，兼有防洪减灾、航运、灌溉、水产、城市供水等综合经济效益。除富春江水电厂外，沿芦茨溪等溪流有多处小水电站，富春江镇东部山区还建有龙门水库电站、关里电站、南湖口电站、白云源电站等10座小水电站，装机容量6 035 kW。

图13-3　美丽河湖芦茨溪

图13-4　富春江水电厂大坝

（二）农产品资源丰富，森林覆盖率高

境内土壤较肥沃，生态条件较好，适宜多种用材林木、竹类及经济林的生长繁衍，主要有木、竹、茶、果、菜等作物，农产品资源丰富、品质优良。镇域内山脉连绵无尽，起伏有致，山间峰岗林立、林木苍郁，森林植被种类繁多，常见针叶林、针阔混交林和经济林等（图13-5）。全镇现有林业用地面积24.50万亩，生态公益林约19万亩，森林蓄积量88万m³，全镇森林覆盖率高达83%（图13-6）。

图 13-5　富春江绿道航拍图

图 13-6　大庄畲族村在高山采摘杭白菊

（三）空气质量优越，生物多样性高

富春江镇风光秀丽，拥有高品质的自然生态环境，其中芦茨慢生活区负氧离子每立方厘米平均值过万，空气质量达到国家一级标准，是一座名副其实的"天然氧吧"（图 13-7）。同时，富春江镇深入推进水环境治理、河长制和环境综合整治工作，不断加强生态环境保护，河湖生态得到有效保护和修复，生态环境不断改善，得益于富春江镇生态环境的持续向好，植被增加为野生动物提供了良好的栖息地，天目臭蛙、桃花水母、中国大鲵"娃娃鱼"（图 13-8）等珍稀物种频频现身、"定居"于此，这大大增加了富春江镇域内的生物多样性，生态系统的稳定性也不断增强。

图 13-7　慢生活体验区"天然氧吧"

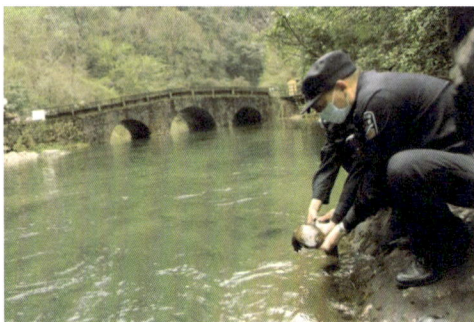

图 13-8　工作人员在白云源景区放生"搁浅"的中国大鲵"娃娃鱼"

三、发展美丽产业集群

（一）依托山水资源，推动低碳民宿集群发展

1. 加强基础设施建设

开展清渚江流域综合治理、小微水体改造、富春江镇路域环境提升改造、农

村生活污水的治理提升改造、垃圾中转站的改造与新增等 9 个项目建设，累计投资 6.77 亿元，加强了水生态保护修复，持续提升生态环境质量。同时开展富春绿道建设、白云源互通景观提升等项目建设，累计投资 4 959 万元。

2. 将"低碳"元素全方位融入文旅生态

青龙坞区块已吸引了风语筑、开满山野、天方夜谭、静庐澜栅、溪山深渡等 11 个高端产业入驻，"青龙坞"民宿品牌效应和经济效益快速凸显，青龙坞高端低碳民宿集群已经成为对外展示的旅游金名片。2016 年起，富春江镇与上海旅游公司合作促成了上海"直通车"项目，标志着一个以慢生活体验区为核心、辐射全镇区域内各主要乡村旅游景点的低碳旅游服务网络初步形成，将逐步打造成高端低碳艺术产业集群。据统计，直通车项目已为村集体增收 90 余万元。2020 年招引庆余良（原乡二期）、枕山溪谷民宿等特色业态项目 4 个，招引资金 4 500 万元，建成严陵坞慢村一期、云外民宿、明怀书院、隐逸瑜伽三期、石舍香樟咖啡馆等特色项目，全年新增民宿 7 家，新增企业 40 家。芦茨村成功申报浙江省旅游业"微改造、精提升"五年行动计划试点景区村，成为杭州地区唯一一个试点景区村（图 13-9）。

图 13-9　芦茨村高端民宿

（二）依托农业资源，凝聚低碳农业发展优势

1. 让优势农业承载更多绿色底蕴

着重发展红茶、水果、中草药、种猪等农业产业，成功打造"芦茨红"区域品牌，用心打造严陵铁皮石斛、里董林下经济、大庄杭白菊、上泗稻鳖共养等农业基地，改造提升象山桥种猪园；大力发展物业经济，打造渡济村"渡

舟同行"、大庄村"喜乐·巧手"等低碳共富工坊 10 个，加快形成"一村一业""一村一品"新模式，推动传统农业向现代农业转型、带动农业特色产业发展。

2. 迭代升级美丽乡村

围绕"五大乡村"建设理念，率先发布全省首个"民宿智脑"数字驾驶舱，建成"民宿智脑"数字平台，以数字化理念、技术、方式解决产业转型难、服务升级难、乡村治理难等问题（图 13-10）。稳步发展现代农业，2021 年新建高标准农田 1 000 亩，提升改造 300 亩，农业质效稳步提升。富春江镇切实投身"乡村振兴 + 双碳愿景"的新业态探索和实践，致力于推动现代科技与生态自然的融合发展，以绿色建筑技术为核心，以"双碳"减排成果转化为抓手，凝聚节能低碳、环境保护、人文关怀、空间高效使用等要素，打造低碳农文旅融合发展新模式，以数字化方式精准赋能乡村振兴。

图 13-10 数字乡村"民宿智脑"

3. 推广"公司 + 基地 + 农户"的一体化产业模式

深化蔬菜、水果、中药材、养殖、苗木、茶叶等效益农业基地。全面实施资源化利用，实现畜禽粪污高效精准利用，推进田间农产品加工副产品等资源化利用，减少畜禽粪污管理的温室气体排放；实施有机肥替代行动，加大商品有机肥推广力度，深化测土配方施肥技术，实施统防统治绿色防控行动，全面推进肥药减量化；全面提升农业综合生产能力，降低温室气体排放强度，提高农田土壤固碳能力，加快传统农业逐步向高效、生态、现代农业转变，提升综合生产能力和产业化水平，农村经济稳步增长。

158

（三）依托宜居环境，加快工业产业转型升级

1. 推进碳生产力优化布局

一方面，富春江镇依靠良好的生态环境，吸引更多低碳绿色企业入驻，成功招引一批优质项目及成长性好的公司落户，实现工业产值翻一番，规模以上高新技术产业产值达 15.9 亿元，占比从 35% 提升至 48%，并于 2021 年培育市级"未来工厂"企业 2 家。另一方面，凭借宜居环境倒逼落后的工业企业加速整改，下足功夫提升工业质效，针对镇域范围内不符合产业导向和能耗高、污染高、安全生产风险高、产出低的"三高一低"企业，坚决予以清退关停。"十三五"及2021 年累计关停低小散企业 78 家，仅 2021 年腾出产业空间近 50 亩，有效推动低碳发展。同时，坚持开展低效盘活工作，突出产业主导，针对土地集中连片、低小散集聚工业地块进行大刀阔斧式的收储盘活，"十三五"及 2021 年累计实现盘活 1 500 亩低效用地。

2. 打造"千亩百亿"高端装备制造产业集群

富春江镇不断加快规划产业梯度发展，积极推进工业结构战略性调整，大力实施产业集群战略，全力推进装备制造产业园二期落地建成，结合产业园一期及庄头工业园区，建设 610 亩装备制造产业园二期项目，北接 870 亩产业园一期、南联 320 亩庄头工业园，搭建 1 800 亩高端装备制造产业集聚新平台，打造"千亩百亿"高端装备制造产业集群（图 13–11）。

图 13-11　高端装备产业园规划图

四、促进百姓共同富裕

（一）实施风貌提升改造，乡村实现美丽蜕变

作为"三江两岸"的重要节点，富春江在城镇建设上不断完善功能设施、优化生态环境、提升城镇品位，先后创成 AAAA 级景区镇和省级工业特色型美丽城镇样板。以"富春慢生活·山居实景地"为创建主题，以富春山水作为文化内涵为底色，以一条马岭古道串联起四大隐逸场景和 25 个文化节点为核心，打造集乡村风情度假、富春文化体验、户外拓展运动、乡野栖居生活、文化艺术创作等功能于一体的新时代富春山居图样板区，并于 2022 年成功创建"富春慢居县域风貌样板区"。乐活富春江、游村芦茨、艺术青龙坞、原真茆坪、未来石舍……每一个节点的打造，充分展现出独具韵味的美丽富春山居村景，以点带面，努力构筑富春山水文化的感知缩影和文艺振兴乡村的典型示范。

（二）加强低碳科普教育，营造绿色生活氛围

利用世界环境日、全国低碳日等重要节点，广泛开展丰富多样的宣传活动，持续加强绿色低碳理念宣传。拓展公众参与机制，创新公众参与的形式和途径，提升市民低碳认知和低碳素养，推动全民低碳意识和低碳行动知行合一。积极开展低碳宣传工程项目，以慢生活体验区为主平台，"新村夜话"（图 13-12）等活动为抓手，通过举办慢生活体验节、青龙坞国际音乐节（图 13-13）、夏日会等国际知名活动，督促人们在文化生活及生产实践中，形成低碳消费、低碳排放的意识和行为，树立低碳文化发展观。同时承办哲学家论坛、富春江诗词达人争创赛（图 13-14）等高端文化节目，打造老少皆宜、雅俗共享的文化名地，进一步擦亮低碳文化品牌，走出一条富春江镇特色的低碳文化创意发展之路。

图 13-12　新村夜话

图 13-13　青龙坞国际音乐节

图 13-14　富春江诗词达人争创赛

（三）凝聚乡贤才智力量，助力低碳产业高效发展

实现"双碳"目标任重而道远，人才是低碳产业高速、健康发展的基石。富春江镇积极挖掘乡贤人才资源，聚焦"引、育、管、用"4个方面，深挖新乡贤文化的时代内涵，持续加强"先贤""今贤""新贤"的挖掘引入培育工作，推进落实乡贤联谊会的管理，尽最大努力激发新乡贤活力（图 13-15、图 13-16）。探索创新"乡贤＋低碳"模式，鼓励乡贤利用自身优势反哺乡村，主动参与村级治理，带动地方产业转型升级、降低能耗。充分利用新乡贤资源、人脉、资本优势，引导项目回归、资金回流、信息回传、技术回援、人才回乡，形成新乡贤驱动低碳发展的良好态势。通过乡情恳谈会、村民说事等形式，邀请新乡贤共商家乡特色产业发展，引回大批新乡贤投身家乡低碳建设，凝聚乡贤才智力量，携手同心共奏低碳发展和谐曲。

图 13-15　乡贤低碳共富讨论会

图 13-16　富春江镇乡贤合影

五、发展启示与展望

优质生态资源是一条"扁担"，一头挑着绿水青山，一头挑着金山银山，只

有畅通转化通道，才能真正成为支撑高质量发展的"金扁担"。富春江镇全力推动生态产业、生态生活、生态环境低碳发展，实现生态美、生产美和生活美"三美"融合，以"生态美"推动"共同富"，全方位全过程推行低碳规划、低碳设计、低碳建设、低碳生产、低碳生活，使发展建立在高效利用资源、严格保护生态环境、有效控制碳排放的基础上，统筹推进高质量发展和高水平保护，打造共同富裕示范区城镇样板，绘就新时代"富春山居图"。通过逐步将生态优势转化为经济优势，2022 年富春江镇全年接待游客达 110 万人次，旅游经营收入达1.55 亿元，老百姓年收入人均 10 万元以上。

下一步，富春江镇将全面加速建立健全生态产品价值实现机制，紧紧围绕已有绿色低碳资源基础，充分挖掘低碳资源转化、良好生态蕴含的经济价值，深入践行"两山"理念，让绿水青山颜值更高、金山银山成色更足，扎实推进共同富裕迈上新台阶。

作者：王雪晴[1]，韩大庆[2]，周云[3]

1 王雪晴，中共党员，浙江大学工学硕士，生态环境工程师，现任富春江镇人民政府副镇长，分管生态环境、旅游、民宿、服务业经济、慢生活体验区、低碳乡镇建设等工作。

2 韩大庆，中共党员，浙江大学工学学士，水利工程师，桐庐县作家协会会员，现任桐庐县富春江镇综合办主任。

3 周云，中共党员，天津城建大学管理学学士，社工师，现任桐庐县富春江镇环旅办一级科员。

下渚湖湿地全力做好生态修复
在全省率先推出湿地碳汇生态补偿模式

近年来，下渚湖湿地紧密围绕国家湿地公园和创5A级风景区建设，全力做好湿地生态修复和生物多样性保护，国宝朱鹮已成为下渚湖的标志性物种。2022年，下渚湖依托全省首批、全市唯一的林业碳汇先行基地试点，在全省创新推出湿地碳汇生态补偿交易，在绿色金融、司法修复和生态富民等领域先行先试，实现湿地生态功能显著增强、生态经济蓬勃发展和生态转化持续拓展的多赢局面。

一、引言

下渚湖位于"绿水青山就是金山银山"理念发源地——浙江湖州南部，紧邻杭州市，属德清县下渚湖街道行政区划范围，是国家湿地公园、4A级风景旅游区、省级风景名胜区。下渚湖湿地面积36 km²，中心湖区面积约1.26 km²，水域面积3.4 km²，是具有多样性景观的典型天然湖泊湿地，湖区内有港汊1 000余条，大小土墩600余处，形成湖中有墩（岛），墩（岛）中有湖，港汊纵横，水网交错的独特水乡景观，为江南最大湿地（图14-1）。下渚湖湿地生物多样性保持良好，2004年建立了国家级野大豆原生境保护点，2008年建立了朱鹮易地保护暨浙江种群重建基地，800多种动植物在此繁衍生息，下渚湖湿地资源保护项目获得2014年中国人居环境范例奖。

图 14-1 下渚湖湿地风貌

二、下渚湖湿地修复背景

曾经的下渚湖是一个令人扼腕的垃圾湖、大型水产养殖场，存在突出问题。

治理前，湖泊内水葫芦泛滥、围栏网箱养殖遍布、水产饲料投放、农家乐生活污水、内塘水产养殖废水直排入湖，水体富营养化严重。2014 年以前，下渚湖断面水质最好仅达到Ⅳ类，1/4 水域覆盖水葫芦，1/3 水域进行网箱和珍珠养殖，包含农家乐在内的环湖 105 户农户生活污水直排入湖。入湖支流两岸高污染水产养殖、生猪、鸡鸭等畜禽养殖和温室龟鳖养殖废水直排，环湖 7 个行政村农村生活污水无截污纳管。2013—2020 年下渚湖水质监测断面数据见表 14-1。

表 14-1 下渚湖水质监测断面（市控监测断面）

年份	2013	2014	2015	2016	2017	2018	2019	2020
年平均水质类别	Ⅳ	Ⅳ	Ⅲ	Ⅲ	Ⅲ	Ⅱ	Ⅱ	Ⅱ

注：数据来源于德清县环境保护监测站。

治理前，湿地和支流淤泥堆积，河流不畅通、岸边无护堤、防洪能力不足，水土流失严重，防洪标准不达标。农民填湖造塘、侵占水域面积时有发生，湿地红线范围内被侵占用于养殖的面积达 500 余亩，使蓄洪防旱功能大受损失。

人类活动的密集和生态环境的破坏，造成水生动植物、鸟类结构简单，湖泊内鱼类品种单一，一些对水质有要求的本土动植物，如鳑鲏鱼、土步鱼、螺蛳罕见踪影。

三、下渚湖湿地修复举措

2013 年年底，浙江省委、省政府实施了"五水共治"，下渚湖遵循保护优先、源头治理、科学修复、持续发展的原则，积极保护湿地良好的原生态湿地环境（图 14-2）。

图 14-2　下渚湖湿地修复

（一）清退红线范围内农业养殖

先后编制《下渚湖风景名胜区总体规划》和《下渚湖国家湿地公园总体规划》，明确了湿地生态保育区、恢复重建区、宣教展示区、合理利用区和管理服务区五大区块，湿地率达 59.86%。围绕规划的实施，先后对红线范围内农业养殖全部清退。其中，清退了外荡珍珠养殖 950 亩、清退了生猪养殖场 230 个，减少存栏 5 万头，清退养鸭等禽类养殖场 93 个，减少存栏 18 万羽（头），清退温室龟鳖养殖棚 12 个约 9 万 m^2，现在的下渚湖范围内，已见不到任何珍珠、畜禽、龟鳖等养殖。开展湿地水域内围网养殖清退，网箱取缔 16 万 m^2，回收水域 2 427 亩国有水面使用权。为彻底解决环湖农家乐生活污水排放问题，对一个自然村 105 户农户实行整体拆迁。

（二）打响渔业养殖尾水治理攻坚战

为了促进产业绿色可持续发展，下渚湖街道于 2016 年在全域范围内打响了渔业养殖尾水治理攻坚战，并建立了长效运维机制。推行"四池三 / 二坝式"（沉淀池、曝气池、生物净化池、湿地洁水池、过滤坝）渔业养殖尾水净化模式，确定了以村为治理主体，分片分区域集中治理的模式，并通过智能实时监控系统，实现养殖尾水全程监管，目前全街道 1 万亩左右的青虾养殖共建设尾水治理点 43 个，实现全覆盖。做好农村生活污水治理。全面推进"一根管子接到底"的农村生活污水治理模式，将卫生间污水、餐厨间污水、洗涤池污水、洗浴间污水纳入同一根管子，采用"县里统一考核，街道维护监管，村里设施维护，农户门前包干，企业负责运行"的"五位一体"模式，实现了农村生活污水治理运维规范化、专业化、长效化，环湖6个行政村生活污水全部纳管，受益农户10 432人。做好环境卫生治理。推行涵盖城区、公路、河道、集镇、村庄五大区域的"一把扫帚扫到底"的城乡环卫一体化管理新模式，通过资源整合，将分散在各部门的环卫职能集中到城管部门，城乡垃圾收集覆盖率和生活垃圾无害化处理率达100%，既提高了环卫作业的效率，又促使农村环境干净整洁。

（三）首创"水下森林"模式的水生态修复

下渚湖在持续优化水质的基础上，不断推进水环境生态修复，针对湖泊类型湿地，首创了"水下森林"模式的水生态修复技术。在水体中构建以沉水植物为基础，结合挺水和浮水植物，各类水生动物，多种有益微生物为一体的稳定水生态平衡系统，让水体有自净能力，进而改善水质，形成"水下森林"的生态景观。目前已建设环湖10万 m³的"水下森林"，经过检测，各项污染物指标明显降低，水质透明度明显提高，主要指标均达到地表水环境质量标准 III 类水以上，部分时间段已稳定在 II 类水，水体及周边景观效果也大幅提升。为补充和恢复生物资源的群体，改善水体藻类情况，提升水生态环境，下渚湖一直坚持进行增殖放流，几年来，共放流了中华鳖、鲢鱼、鳙鱼、草鱼等生态鱼种 7 000 万尾。

（四）开展中小流域综合治理工程

围绕提升湿地防洪能力，下渚湖投入资金 4 700 万元，开展了中小流域综合治理工程，对下渚湖周围大小 39 条河道，采取水系沟通、清淤疏浚、生态护岸、生态修复、闸坝修缮、亲水设施及景观节点建设等方式，共治理河道42.8 km，清淤疏浚 71 万 m³，生态护岸 22.8 km，植物护坡 1.34 km。

（五）建立生态补偿机制

为切实提高湿地范围农户生态保护意识，下渚湖建立了生态补偿机制，每年对相关行政村实施生态补偿 700 余万元。在全国率先实施"河湖健康体检"，对环湖 60 个水体以基础、水文、水质、生态、管理、病史等 6 类 18 个指标对河湖进行全面体检，成功经验在全省进行推广。实施"生态绿币"机制，用绿币基金奖励在治水、护水等环保工作中有突出贡献的个人或社会群体，带动全民自觉维护水体环境工作，目前生态绿币基金库折合人民币已达 134 万元。开展数字化治水，在全省首创"护水 e 站"，并更新升级成"公众护水平台"的基础上，不断探索创新生态环境保护新机制，将"五水共治"中的经验做法积极推广运用。推行垃圾分类智能化监管平台，日常通过芯片扫码评价考核民众家庭垃圾分类参与率、精准率。建立数字乡村一张图管理，以"一图感知"的方式实时掌握生产、生活和生态变化情况，并对接视频检测、五水共治、环境整治、垃圾分类等数据接口，在数据共享交互的基础上实现数字化管理。推进基层河长履职，围绕"一看、二查、三巡、四访、五落实"基层河长履职五步法，深入基层宣传走访，收集群众投诉反馈，发现问题及时处理，确保将河长制工作落地见效。

（六）开展湿地碳汇试点

2022 年年初，下渚湖街道被省双碳工作领导小组确定为全省第一批低（零）碳乡镇（街道）试点，下渚湖湿地被列入全省第一批、全市唯一的林业碳汇先行基地。据初步测算，下渚湖街道 2021 全年净固碳量达到 1.7 万 t，到 2025 年，预计可年新增湿地碳汇 3 万 t，湿地水质植被修复面积累计 2 250 亩，固碳增汇新品种新技术应用面积 2 960 亩以上，生态效益显著。

2022 年 4 月，下渚湖湿地抓住全省首批、全市唯一的林业碳汇试点机遇，通过两山合作社收储交易 1 万 t 湿地碳汇指标（金额 58.8 万元）（图 14-3），并向德清农商银行等 6 家金融机构和青春宝等 3 家工业企业出售完毕，推动部分金融机构和企业自主购碳，实现降碳（零碳）运行。

图 14-3　落地全省首笔湿地碳汇生态补偿交易

湿地碳汇生态补偿模式推出后，先后取得获评湖州市第一批生态文明建设改革创新典型案例、中英绿色金融课题采纳下渚湖湿地保护案例等多项成果。目前，全县各金融机构在下渚湖及周边区域已累计发放"湿地碳汇·共富贷""湿地碳汇两山贷"等湿地碳汇与生物多样性保护相关贷款 487 笔，金额 12.74 亿元。

在建立湿地碳汇金融闭环体系方面，湖州银行德清支行在下渚湖投放全国首笔以碳汇指标为核心的"湿地碳汇·共富贷"产品。德清农商银行基于拓宽生态资源价值转换路径、构建生态产品高水平实现机制，在碳汇生产（Production）端、收储交易（Transaction）端、企业需求（Demand）端形成"PTD"全封闭内循环资金支持体系，农商行已累计发放湿地碳汇信贷 382 笔，金额4.67 亿元。

在开展生态损害赔偿异地修复方面，全市生态环境案件集中管辖的南太湖新区人民法院在下渚湖建立生态损害赔偿异地修复"湿地碳汇生态修复基地"，将市域内发生的生态损害案件的部分赔偿金额补偿至下渚湖街道，用于湿地生物多样性保护、生态系统保护修复、湿地综合治理、水环境修复等工作。目前已确定3 笔修复资金 229 万元。

在创新推出碳汇共富专项产品方面，湖州银行德清支行创新开发并投放全国首笔以碳汇指标为核心的"湿地碳汇·共富贷"产品，依据农户湿地碳汇量等提供专属授信额度和优惠利率，探索出适合湿地生态修复和生物多样性保护的绿色金融支持路径。

在保险保障湿地碳汇方面，推动平安财险湖州分公司在下渚湖试点开展商业性湿地碳汇指数保险，以德清县自然资源资产经营有限公司为主体，把从事湿地生产经营的农民、湿地生产经营组织、从事湿地碳汇的生产经营组织作为投保人。对下渚湖湿地区域内湿地植物发生碳汇损失风险的，按照合同约定赔偿损失金额，该险种首期保费 50 万元，对应保障金额达 1.3 亿元。

四、成效与展望

（一）生态功能显著加强

下渚湖湿地景观体系、生态系统、生物多样性和抗洪排水能力明显优化，发挥了湿地的"绿肾"效应。湿地水质稳定在 Ⅱ～Ⅲ 类水，湿地生物多样性保持良好，800 多种珍稀动植物在此繁衍生息。鸟类中的"东方宝石"朱鹮，全球10% 种群在下渚湖，并已成功放飞，目前已在野外自然繁衍到第三代，被命名为朱鹮易地保护暨浙江种群重建基地，并获评获"中国最美湿地"称号。

（二）生态经济蓬勃发展

下渚湖二都小镇依托"水下森林"，打造了"湖色森鲜"夜市，游客数量比往年同期翻三番，带动了二都小镇的农户农产品销售和民宿业、餐饮业的发展。

下渚湖街道具有良好青虾生长条件，通过拓展青虾商业业态，延长青虾产业链，有效带动村民致富增收，获得"中国青虾之乡"的美誉。得益于下渚湖良好的生态资源，下渚湖成为长三角旅游休闲的重要目的地，下渚湖湿地公园年接待游客120万人，获评浙江省最值得去的50个景区之一。

（三）生态机制不断健全

下渚湖率先建立水产养殖尾水治理模式（"四池三/二坝式"净化模式）创新得到省委主要领导批示肯定，并在全省推广。并创新推出"生态绿币"机制、"河湖健康体检"机制、治微九式、数字化治水、治水实践体验馆等全国首创举措，获得全国人大调研肯定。

（四）生态转化持续拓展

下渚湖借助丰富的文旅资源和生态转化条件，积极拓展两山转化场景。如古代防风文化资源推出防风文化节，被命名为国家非物质文化遗产；每年由国家湿地保护管理中心、浙江省林业厅和浙江省体育总会在下渚湖湿地开展生存越野挑战赛；每年冬季举办民俗鱼汤饭活动，以3 187人同品鱼汤饭的纪录在下渚湖挑战成功吉尼斯——规模最大的鱼汤饭品尝活动。

下渚湖将坚定不移走好"绿水青山就是金山银山"的生态转化之路，继续做好下渚湖湿地修复和文旅开发，有效统筹湿地资源深化湿地碳汇生态补偿改革，积极树立湿地绿色开发导向引领湿地经济活动绿色化。并围绕下渚湖湿地零碳试点样本，开展湿地植物固碳、土壤排通量、湿地生态系统整体交换等方面研究，为湿地碳汇方法学研究提供可靠数据积累，为全省提供湿地碳汇改革"德清经验"。

作者：泉江东 [1]

1　泉江东，下渚湖街道党工委书记、下渚湖湿地风景区管委会主任，积极推动下渚湖湿地生态修复，促成全省首笔湿地碳汇生态补偿交易。

低碳湖滨　时尚未来

作为展示美丽杭州建设的重要窗口，湖滨积极践行绿色低碳的发展理念。在商圈打造中，通过引入低碳产业、实施步行街改造、开发智慧停车系统、升级银泰商城污染治理设施等方式，为游客和消费者构建绿色消费场景，增强低碳体验感。在生活圈建设中，将低碳景观融入老城改造，倡导居民节约用水、垃圾分类，通过各类特色活动构建绿色循环的生活氛围。未来，湖滨将继续深挖低碳之路，以生活、消费新风尚，引领时尚未来。

一、引言

湖滨街道因湖而名，因湖而兴，湖城一体是西湖门厅，杭城会客厅，是时尚、智慧、人文的新消费示范街区，城市品质提升的"醉杭州"样板（图 15-1）。2002 年，湖滨路改建为休闲步行街，主要机动车辆从西湖隧道穿行；2003 年，湖滨步行街正式启用。自那时起，绿色休闲、低碳环保的生活观和旅游观在湖滨深深扎根。湖滨开始了低碳环保的旅游发展模式。随着 20 年的发展和建设，湖滨已形成西面商圈繁荣，东部品质生活的发展格局。湖滨街道以平面、立体、空间的三维管理模式，从绿色商圈的打造和低碳生活圈的构筑两方面入手，通过产业转型、建筑升级、设施共享、智慧管理带动游客体验绿色消费、低碳旅游；在老城改造、节能节水、垃圾分类、社区活动中引导居民低碳思考、集约生活；构建了绿色商业圈、低碳生活圈，实现区域环境生态化、居民生活低碳化、政府管理智慧化，推动街道绿色低碳的高质量发展。湖滨成为展示杭州高质量建设和高水平发展的重要窗口。烟火气息十足的生活区，是城市中老城区改造的典范；繁华的商业街区，带来了自然生态、集约低碳的新时尚。湖滨的低碳之路，从步行街走来；杭州城的低碳未来，将继续沿着步行街走下去。

图 15-1　湖滨俯瞰图

二、打造低碳商业圈，引领绿色消费

（一）引入低碳产业，创新绿色消费场景

布局引入低碳生产力。湖滨引入了小鹏、蔚来、上汽奥迪新能源总部等新能源车销售产业，形成低碳产品销售一条街，打造新能源车总部经济新高地（图 15-2）。通过规模性地引入电动汽车销售品牌，在游客游览时不仅可以展示电动汽车，还能通过厂家专业的介绍，让游客提高对电动汽车的认识，沉浸式体验新能源汽车带来的便利与优势，认识各个品牌的特色与品牌间的差异，提高群众对电动汽车的认知度和认可度。结合亚运会的影响力，将辖区内的亚运特许零售商店打造成碳中和商店，在售卖亚运会周边产品的同时，向游客和消费者展示商品中的低碳元素。

图 15-2　新能源车销售产业

建设绿色商场。湖滨街道的各类商场严格设置商场空调温度，洗手间等用水

显著区域设置节水标识，鼓励顾客节约用水；合理设置机动车及电动自行车停车位置，引导标识明确，提供电动汽车和电动自行车充电设施。充分利用智慧化手段开展营销和服务，提高管理和运行效率。借助商场广告宣传，传播绿色消费、环保、节能的理念，鼓励消费者在商场内实施垃圾分类和使用可降解环保包装物。

（二）改造基础设施，打造绿色商圈典范

创建减污降碳示范银泰。湖滨银泰作为杭州最高端的商业体，银泰购物中心在 in77 A 区排水改造中，采用以真空为排水动力、全过程封闭化与智能化的排水系统（图 15-3）。利用真空设备使排水管路内产生一定程度的负压，依靠管路内负压和外部常压的压差，使空气推动污水进入污水管网进行输送的排水方式。污水以气水混合物的形式在管道内输送，极大改善了 in77 的排水环境，提升了排水水质，解决了商城新增污水难以进入污水管网、潜污提升泵堵塞维护难等问题。同时通过真空原理带走排水点附近 60 L 左右的空气，将空气中的有害悬浮物、细菌、异味一同带入真空管网，有效消除空气中的污水恶臭、细菌、悬浮颗粒及有危害颗粒。

图 15-3 银泰商城屋顶绿化、屋顶光伏、油烟废气处理设施一体图

改出全国首批低碳街区。2018 年 12 月，在被商务部确定为全国首批步行街改造提升试点后，湖滨步行街掀起了一波低碳改革浪潮。街道从步行街道路铺装、绿化有机更新、景观亮灯提升、城市家具更新、城市立面改造、节点景观提升六大方面对街区进行改造提升。一期工程完成道路铺装 3.5 万 m²、绿化有机更新 3 000 m²、景观亮灯提升 195 处（全部采用智慧灯杆）、城市家具更新 128 处、城市立面改造经营单位 30 多个、第五立面改造 10 个。二期工程完成景观铺装施工面积 1.3 万 m²、绿化提升面积 1 000 m²。通过整治沿街立面、增设城市家具、增设街区外摆等方式增加街区时尚气息，延伸智慧终端载体，扩大街区

"数"治覆盖面，完善街区无障碍设施，提升街区友好度和游客的环境体验感。在步行街的改造中，以东坡路改造为重头戏，把车行道改为全封闭的步行道，这在全国试点街区中是唯一的，也顺理成章地打造了全国首批低碳商圈——低碳街区（图 15-4）。

图 15-4 改造后的东坡路

（三）发展绿色交通，突破智慧管理"瓶颈"

为提高区域管理效能，湖滨街道打造了全市首个街道级城市大脑——湖滨智芯系统，建成湖滨步行街综合管理平台，通过深化街区治理应用场景建设，为辖区居民、游客和其他消费者带来绿色、舒适的体验。其中，群众直观感受最深的便是湖滨停车不再难，道路不拥挤。

步行街改造取消了 660 个停车泊位，这相当于使整个街区减少了 40% 的泊位配套。为弥补配套需求，湖滨街道采用了智能出行管理系统。系统将步行街周边各自独立的 9 个停车场 2 413 个泊位数据统一视作步行街配套，通过城市大脑接入实时校准在线。在进入街区的各路口安装了智能引导牌（图 15-5），使车主途中就能了解剩余空位、行车路线等关键信息，就近找到泊位。同时该智能出行管理系统也已经拓展到了湖滨街道全域范围，尤其是辖区内的医院。在医院周边各个路口，均可看见附近道路、综合体的空余泊位情况，为群众就医停车提供了极大的便利。通过从车主"四处找泊位"到"抬头见泊位"，同时通过提炼泊位指数（停车位的重复使用率）、停车指数（整个湖滨停车场的饱和度）向社会公开，既方便群众，也倒逼管理的能力提升。在解决停车问题的同时也有效缓解了各大医院、热门商圈周边的交通拥堵，减少了机动车低速行驶、排队等待期间的尾气排放。

图 15-5　车位引导牌

（四）升级公共设施，实现基础设施共享

　　湖滨采用智慧化设计，实现公共设施的升级，促进基础设施智慧共享，提升旅游体验。商业街区设置 A 级导视牌，通过扫描二维码形成电子无障碍地图，或者通过 App 应用商店下载使用已完成语音版集成的电子无障碍地图，为障碍人士在街区通行全程保驾护航。在东坡路的两侧，通过智慧灯杆建设，实现"多杆合一"。通过对 107 个路灯的改造建设，外观融入杭州特色元素，使用功能上，除夜间照明基础功能外，整合了广告、应急广播、Wi-Fi 接入等功能。智能灯杆可感应外界环境因素，自动调整灯光颜色及明暗。自带摄像功能，实时感知街区动态信息。游客可以通过交互屏幕获取周边停车指数，实时查看周边地铁、公交、游船路线与时间，还能获取餐饮娱乐、游玩路线等商家信息，得到更舒适便捷的游玩体验。同时，在近年的建筑改造和商业区翻新中，湖滨充分引入节能低碳技术，实现公共设施的升级；不断拓展公共设施的利用率，实现设施的高效共享。

三、构筑低碳生活圈，践行绿色生活

（一）老城改造，融入低碳景观

　　结合老旧小区改造和修缮维护工作，湖滨街道在公共设施改造中充分贯彻绿色低碳理念。老旧小区改造中以平改坡的形式，降低顶层用户能耗。采用智慧化停车管理系统，对老旧小区内的机动车辆进行管理和控制，实时展现高密度小区及周边区域停车位，调节周边交通流量，对停车饱和的老旧小区实施严格控制。

推动辖区内公共交通体系建设，构建十分钟步行圈。辖区内公共用房改造过程中，以安装集中充电装置、探索安装光伏发电、采用节能灯智能化设定亮灯时间等措施，实现公共建筑的节能低碳。充分运用海绵城市理念，采取植被、铺装、景观方式，改造提升基础设施的防护绿地。更有效地提供净化、抗噪、防尘等生态防护功能，打造海绵社区与节水示范社区。在污水管网维修养护的同时，加强街道生态环境用水集约、循环利用，合理布设雨水收集模块，建造贮水池、渗透池、调洪池，配置雨水回收设备，对雨水进行储存处理，用于区域绿化、景观用水、路面清洗等（图15-6）。

图 15-6　改造后的青年路社区

积极探索固碳增汇路径，重新规划街道土地资源，加强各社区生态环境规划设计，推动庭院绿化美化以及路旁、宅旁等有效空间绿化遵从自然规律，尽可能采用原生植物。充分利用绿化带隔声减噪，建设满足居民休闲需要的公共绿地和步行绿道。街区改造中始终坚持"最小干预、传承文化、合理利用、实施可行"的原则，既保留了原有的自然韵味，又融入了新颖的智慧化低碳元素，在新旧碰撞中让人有耳目一新的感觉。

（二）节约用水，提升资源利用

湖滨地处上城核心区域，在老城区的改造与建设中，湖滨注重绿色、环保理念，通过强化节水措施，增强全区水资源节约与保护意识，建立和完善科学用水体系和节约用水管理体系，有效地控制用水量的增长速度，保证各小区安全供水，使用水结构得到了有效调整。通过开展节水型社区建设，居民生活用水户表率达到100%，节水器具普及率达到100%，人均月用水水平3.05 m³/（人·月），年节水量可达60 t左右。在公共设施节水方面，小区公共场所（含绿化）采用节水装置，配置雨水回收设备，回收的雨水经过处理后可用于冲洗厕所，清洗路面、浇灌草坪、水景补水。

（三）垃圾分类，实现无废街区

自 2010 年开始实施垃圾分类以来，湖滨一直以"绣花"的精神，狠抓基础体系。街道大力开展老旧小区垃圾投放设施提升改造工程及撤桶并点工作，11 处露天垃圾房更新成带顶棚、带水池智能投放箱。共建设回收站（网）点 13 个（6 个小鹿再生资源回收网点，6 个企业自营 +1 个街道分拣集置点）、特殊垃圾堆放点 9 个。在日常管理中，号召辖区内公共机构、企业、学校，主动参与垃圾分类；执法检查中，重点对分类成效相对薄弱、市级考核排名落后的企事业单位开展普法宣传、开具整改单，甚至约谈责任人，以执法促整改。通过探索建立积分账户、红黑专榜，对正确分类的居民给予适当积分奖励等形式提高辖区居民垃圾分类的积极性和参与度。湖滨街道成功创建为浙江省生活垃圾分类示范片区，辖区内多个小区被评选为浙江省高标准生活垃圾分类示范小区。

（四）特色活动，潜移习惯行为

湖滨借助特殊节假日契机推广低碳理念，如在植树节期间，湖滨街道开展植树节相关活动的同时，创新开展同心"荟"力齐种树线上互动活动，携手上城发布微信公众号，以科普答题、邀请好友浇水等方式收集绿色能量 1.7 万点，35 人领取环保布袋、绿植等奖品。街道、社区召集社区干部、党员志愿者等共同种下"清廉树""孝亲树""友爱树"等主题绿植 120 多株，并现场宣传垃圾分类、节能种树等低碳、环保知识。结合众多特色活动，湖滨街道将会说话的垃圾桶、楼道垂直绿化、太阳能楼道灯、实名制垃圾分类等一系列低碳创新项目串联，推出一条极具特色的低碳生活体验路线。在日常生活中，湖滨率先推出《居民低碳生活宣传手册》、低碳家庭标准，建立青少年减碳工作室，推出生态旅游体验线，评选低碳家庭示范户和低碳达人，倡导居民写低碳日记等活动，潜移默化地影响居民的生活习惯和日常行为，构建浓厚的低碳氛围。

四、经验启示

湖滨的低（零）碳建设成果，是城市实践低碳路径的典型案例，验证了以生活和商业为主要功能的中心城区在城市减污降碳和低（零）碳建设中的可行性和可达性。充分展示了低碳建设与社会发展和经济发展的协同性，以低碳之路走向社会进步和共同富裕。

（一）注重场景构建，增强低碳体验感

社会发展和生活生产中涉及碳排放的领域范围广泛，降碳的路径多种多样，社会群众对"双碳"工作的认知程度也大相径庭。通过低碳场景的构建，让群众能够亲临其境，共同参与，切实践行湖滨的低碳之路，目睹湖滨的建设历程。如低碳步行街场景的构建，运用了城市大脑监控体系（图15-7），集成道路信息、设备资源等信息，建立数据库，实现对步行街环境卫生作业、泊车位等的监控、巡查、信息传输的同步性，提高交通通行效率和管理效能以及环境效益。

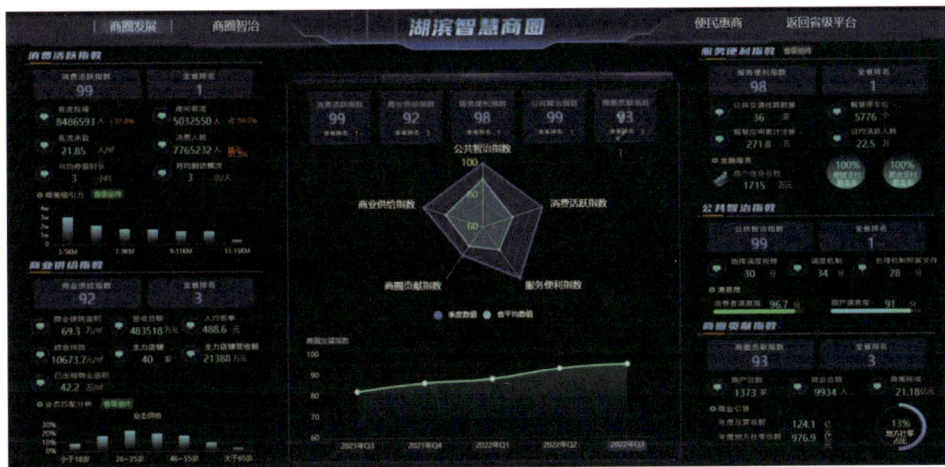

图 15-7　智慧湖滨管理系统

（二）注重思想教育，普及低碳理念

绿色集约的低碳理念，是社会低碳发展的重要基础。对于湖滨这样集历史悠久的老城区和繁华的旅游商业区于一体的街道，居民和游客的意识形态决定着湖滨的"碳"索之路能走多远。普及低碳理念，引导居民养成循环节约的生活习惯，带动游客文明游览、绿色消费是湖滨的建设重点。湖滨街道通过制作低碳生活手册等方式，指导老年人节约用水用电、选购节能家电以及简约包装商品，提高老年群体的参与度；积极开展低碳学习积极分子、低碳建设先进个人等评选活动，提高群众积极性和参与度，帮助群众建立节能降碳主人翁意识，逐步建立低碳意识全民普及的高素质街道。

（三）注重细胞建设，延伸低碳触角

城市的低碳化发展，需要各个领域全民践行。湖滨街道大力倡导低碳理念的

延伸，面向学校、社区、家庭、企业、商场等开展全面立体的"低碳"建设宣传教育，营造全街道共建共治共享的良好氛围，推动形成简约适度、绿色低碳、文明健康的生活理念和生活方式。结合上城区无废城市"一区一品"的建设目标，组织开展低碳社区创建，并逐步将低碳细胞延伸至低碳机关、低碳家庭、低碳学校、低碳商场、低碳餐馆、低碳酒店、低碳医院、低碳企业等类别，定期组织开展评估工作，让"低碳细胞"创建覆盖全街道。

五、展望

作为中心城区的代表，湖滨率先走出了低碳建设的第一步。作为"碳路"先锋，湖滨将继续沿着步行街走下去，深挖自身优势，不断突破创新，积极谋划，力争探索出更多高效可行的低（零）碳建设举措，为其他城区街道提供更多典型做法。借助西湖景区的吸引力，利用全国示范步行街的号召力，将湖滨的历史文化与"碳路"文化相融合，形成生活、消费新风尚，引领时尚未来。

（一）构建管理保障体系

湖滨街道将继续大力推进辖区的低碳建设工作，形成以街道办事处党委书记负责，分管环保、建筑、数字化的班子成员齐抓共管，横向联动、上下贯通的工作体系，不断加强街道低碳发展的重大战略研究。定期对街道管理人员及相关低碳建设工作人员开展培训，及时解读国家和省市的相关政策，学习其他地区的先进经验和做法，提高基层管理人员对低碳建设工作的认知和专业技术水平。邀请省市专家团队，对辖区内的低碳建设项目进行指导，帮助辖区范围内的居民培育和建立低碳意识，促进低碳项目的实施和落地。将低碳建设工作列入街道办事处和相关部门重要议事日程，定期对建设进展情况开展评估，重大变化及时调整，确保组织到位、责任到位、措施到位。

（二）构建低碳生活系统

围绕湖滨步行街的低碳发展理念和周边商圈绿色低碳的文化元素，持续构建步行街—商圈—景区的低碳生活系统。纵向深入实施低碳管理，贯彻高标准洁美养护理念；优化区域交通设置，完善街区、景区步行道和自行车道的衔接；构建智慧管理体系，以智慧系统和平台的建设，为慢行生活系统的建设提供保障，提升居民、游客和消费者的低碳体验感；横向持续拓展低碳商圈建设，鼓励解百、工联等商城在基础管理、设备设施更新维护、绿色供应链建设、实施绿色服务、引导绿色消费和资源循环利用等方面探索创新，建设成为节能减排、绿色产品销售和废弃物回收三位一体的实体零售企业。同时积极延伸低碳细胞建设，鼓励各类组织和群体开展低碳示范创建，从各个领域推动低碳技术的应用和推广，将低碳文化融入街区历史文化血液中。

（三）构建低碳展示场景

依托西湖景区、步行街、周边商圈等优势，探索建设向社会展示省市低（零）碳建设成果的平台。谋划组织和参加各类低（零）碳宣传和成果展示活动。推进街区范围内各项大型活动积极实现碳中和。探索引入碳标签产品售卖渠道，在步行街、商场等区域设置专区销售带有浙江省碳足迹、碳标签的特色商品。通过产品的售卖，向消费者展示产品碳足迹，引导消费者更多地选购环保、低碳的产品。运用数字化媒体主动传播和分享浙江低（零）碳故事，为杭州、为浙江搭建低（零）碳文化传播的桥梁。

作者：阮阆怡[1]

1 阮阆怡，湖滨街道办事处特约撰稿人。杭州市环境保护科学研究设计有限公司，工程师。主要从事环保、低碳等方面政策研究。

吉利全产业链碳中和实践

企业是碳排放的主要来源，同时也是推进碳达峰碳中和的主阵地。要确保实现碳达峰目标，离不开企业的全面参与，要提前布局实现碳中和目标，更离不开企业的创新引领。吉利汽车是我省新能源汽车生产龙头企业，同时也是民营经济的典范。在汽车制造竞争极为激烈，同时上下游产业关联甚广的情境下，吉利以全产业链碳中和为目标，在管理体系、设计制造、循环经济、绿色出行与绿色物流、绿色甲醇替代等方面开展了大量的实践探索，取得了较为明显的成效，或可为企业转向绿色低碳发展提供有效经验。

一、引言

汽车产业是国民经济的战略性和支柱性产业，也是碳排放的重要来源，涉及工业和交通运输领域。据清华大学能源环境经济研究所研究，未来我国交通业还将有 3 倍的增长空间，同时将带来巨大的碳减排压力。作为浙江汽车行业低碳发展的典型，吉利控股集团主动响应"双碳"国家战略，谋定而后动，以 2045 年实现全链路碳中和为目标，创新供应链端、制造端、使用端的原材料、工艺及用能方式，致力于打造成为中国和世界汽车行业可持续发展模式标杆。本章主要阐述吉利在推进全产业链碳中和上的实践做法与成效，以期为交通运输行业及企业的绿色低碳转型提供有益借鉴。

二、主要做法及成效

（一）创新碳管理机制，凝聚组织合力

要推进碳达峰碳中和，首先要在思维、理念上有所转变，而这最终又会反映到管理机制上。吉利通过将绿色低碳发展理念融入全公司、全流程，进而建立起

专门负责的工作机构、管理体系和数字化平台，有效地凝聚了干事的力量。

1. 成立统筹的碳中和工作组

为有效统筹碳中和管理相关事项，在集团董事会层面设立环境、社会及管治委员会（以下简称 ESG 委员会），ESG 委员会下设协同指导小组、ESG 工作组和碳中和工作组共同构成的 ESG 联合工作组。碳中和工作组主要负责研究碳中和相关政策趋势和行业态势，制定碳中和总体战略与目标，建立碳中和业务相关运行机制、流程，统筹规划集团的碳中和管理，推进跨业务集团 / 板块的碳中和相关工作和碳资产开发与交易等。与此同时，在各业务集团 / 板块对应设立碳中和工作组，负责相关决策的落地实施。吉利控股集团旗下各品牌碳减排目标见图 16-1。

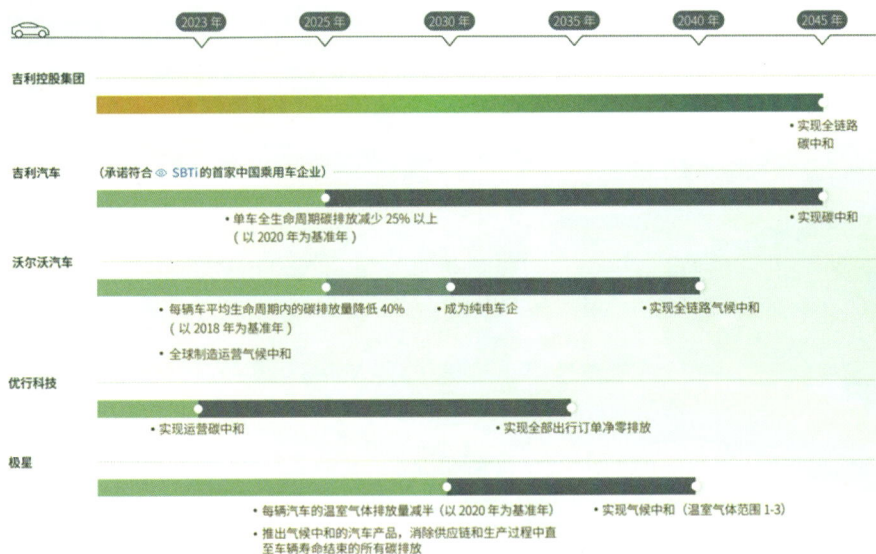

图 16-1　吉利控股集团旗下各品牌碳减排目标

2. 建立全覆盖的碳管理体系

"双碳"目标的有效落地实施，离不开相应管理机制的支持，这也意味着要对传统管理模式进行一定程度的更新。吉利在国内率先自主研发了从控股到各基地工厂全覆盖。以管理者、控股集团和子业务集团三个层级为主体的碳管理体系。管理者层面，主要是最高管理者制定碳管理方针，任命碳管理团队、提供所需资源，履行管理者代表相关职责。控股集团层面，主要是由碳中和工作组编制战略规划和管理体系文件，研发低碳技术和碳金融路径，管理各业务集团碳绩效。子业务集团层面，主要是执行碳管理体系文件，落实碳管理职责，反馈相关情况及数据。为有效强化相关管理机制的落地，吉利控股集团还编制了一系列配套的碳管理体系手册，明确术语和定义，按照 PDCA（策划、运行、检查、改进）过程建立二级程序文件和三级支撑文件，做到有章可循、有序配合。

3. 建设数字化的碳管理平台

碳排放管理涉及范围广泛、流程复杂，从最初的碳排放核算，到制定碳减排目标、执行碳减排举措、评价碳减排绩效，都亟须数字化的有力支持。吉利基于自身实际及目标导向，推出了自研的"一站式"碳管理平台——吉碳云（图 16-2）。该平台紧密结合业务场景，以区块链、大数据、隐私计算技术为支撑，内置丰富的核算模型、方法学以及碳排放因子数据库，具备智能识别企业排放源、自动关联碳排放因子、保障数据安全等特征，可实现碳盘查与监测、产品碳足迹核算、碳目标与绩效管理、碳资产开发与管理、碳普惠与运营等功能，以统一管理吉利及其供应链的碳排放数据和碳资产。该平台已覆盖吉利汽车集团上游供应商 800 余家，完成所有零部件碳排放核算以及重点碳排放供应商的场地数据收集。

图 16-2　吉利控股集团吉碳云平台架构

（二）注重绿色设计与制造，强化源头减排

作为一家典型的制造业企业，汽车制造是吉利最主要的碳排放来源，也是碳减排的潜力所在。但是，制造很大程度上是由设计所规范的，更加绿色低碳的设计无疑是更具低成本和竞争优势的做法。吉利通过强化在设计、生产运营以及产品阶段的绿色低碳导向，有效减少了企业边界内的碳排放。

1. 贯彻生态正向设计

对于汽车来说，轻量化设计不仅意味着产品的市场优势，同时也可以减少能源消耗与碳排放。吉利坚持生态正向设计理念，研发应用先进轻量化技术，优化材料、结构和工艺，提高动力性能及燃油经济性，同时优先采用环境友好型材料。比如，沃尔沃汽车与瑞典钢铁集团 SSAB 及其 HYBRIT 计划合作，致力于开发最先进的无化石钢铁；极氪 001 车身采用 15% 的可再生钢板材料和 25% 的可再生铝合金材料；远程 G3 重卡的前后顶杂物箱隔板计划使用生物基塑料，导风板、导流罩后侧支架均计划使用再生塑料，再生材料使用比例超过 10%。

2. 致力气候零负荷运营

汽车制造工厂的低碳化，由于其聚集了主要的碳排放活动，是至关重要且不可避免的环节。吉利秉持"建设对环境无害的绿色工厂，制造有益于人类的环保车辆"的原则，旗下吉利汽车、沃尔沃汽车、吉利商用车等多家整车制造基地通过 ISO 14001 外部审核，截至 2021 年，11 家制造基地获评国家级绿色工厂。其中，西安零碳工厂建成 52 MW 超级光伏电站，同时采购国际绿证 I-REC，实现电力碳中和，获得钛和认证颁发的 I 型零碳工厂五星级证书，成为国内整车企业的首个零碳工厂；截至 2021 年年底，沃尔沃汽车台州工厂持续提升自有发电能力，清洁能源利用率达 46%，同时全面推行可持续的绿色供应链管理战略，获评国家级绿色供应链；极星成都生产基地是中国首家获得全球绿色建筑评估体系 LEED 金级认证的汽车工厂（图 16-3），使用 100% 的可再生电力。

图 16-3　吉利控股集团极星成都生产基地

3. 生产低（零）碳汽车

当前新能源汽车替代传统燃油车进程大幅加速，如何推出适合当下、面向未来，符合绿色低碳潮流的汽车产品成为重要命题。吉利聚焦纯电动汽车，兼顾混合动力，同时前瞻布局碳中和汽车，建立起多层次错位互补的低（零）碳汽车品牌。混合动力方面，2022 年推出的星越 L 增程电动版，搭载 41.2 kW·h CTP 平板电池和 85 kW 直流快充，WLTC 工况的纯电续航里程达到 205 km。并且搭配热效率高达 43.32% 的增程器，使得 WLTC 工况全时增程电动里程高达 1 250 km。纯电动方面，2020 年发布全新自主研发纯电车型开发平台——SEA（Sustainable Experience Architecture，浩瀚智能进化体验架构），次年在该架构基础上推出首款智能电动汽车极氪 001（图 16-4）。前瞻布局方面，2021 年旗下极星宣布创新、可循环的碳中和汽车"Polestar 0 计划"，将使用可循环电池、可回收材料，并在整个供应链中使用可再生能源，以不依靠碳补偿的方式，在 2030 年前生产出真正气候中和的汽车。

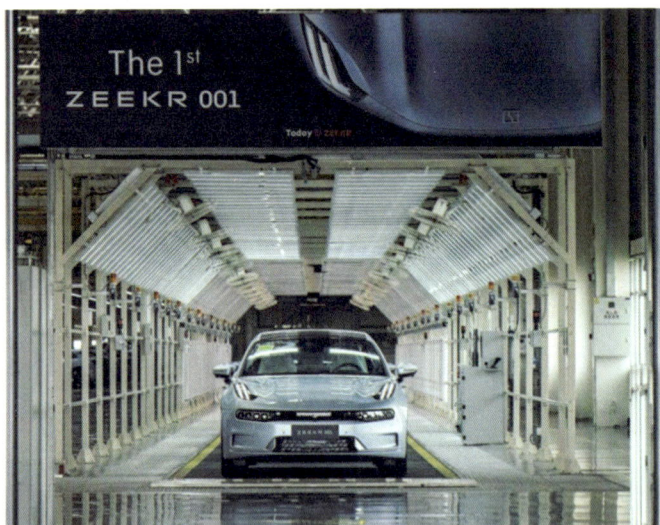

图 16-4　极氪 001 车型

（三）强化资源循环利用，降低全生命周期碳排放

作为节约资源、降本增效的重要手段，循环经济同时是降碳的重要路径，这在汽车等复杂物料生产体系中尤为突出。吉利主动践行生产者责任延伸制度，加入中国汽车生产者责任组织（PRO），探索易推广、可复制的资源循环利用闭环体系，有效降低车辆全生命周期碳足迹水平。2021 年整车报废材料可再利用率、可回收利用率分别达 92.8%、96.9%。

1. 使用可持续包装

包装历来是循环利用的重点方向，因为包装材料并不是产品本身，不会因被消费而不复存在，所以天然存在多次利用的可能，这无疑也是推进节能降碳、节约资源的重要举措。吉利主动推动对多元再利用包装材料的研发和推广应用，广泛采用纸质、木质以及可循环塑料等环保包装材料（图 16-5），加速循环包装理念和应用的普及。2021 年，全面梳理各生产基地一次性包装使用情况，制定一次性包装切换循环包装纳入年度推进目标，实施循环包装改善项目。该项目已推广至 12 个整车制造基地和 1 个动力制造基地，并完成 72 个项目 58 家零部件供应商入厂包装切换循环包装，有效减少一次性纸箱、木箱、一次性内衬等包装材料的使用。

图 16-5　使用循环材料制成的包装箱

2. 推行电池梯次利用

电池是汽车，尤其是电动汽车的关键部件，同时是能耗、物耗的主要来源，其在制造和运行过程中都持续地产生碳排放和污染物，电池的回收利用也因此成为推行节能降碳、降本增效的重要来源。通过建立流程健全的电池回收体系，吉利实现了关键零部件 100% 的追溯管理，整车厂试验后的报废电池和客户端产生的报废电池均被统一回收至售后站点。通过与第三方回收企业或电池生产商合作，根据残值价值对回收的电池进行分类处理，最大化地实现梯次利用，减少制造成本。

3. 开展零部件绿色再制造

作为同级循环的一种重要实现机制，零部件再制造通过对废旧产品的修复改造，实现了对原材料、零部件的高性能替代，在诸如汽车等现代装备制造业等零部件繁多复杂的领域具有极为可观的节约资源、减少能耗和碳排放潜力。吉利将汽车废旧零部件的再制造利用作为全产业链碳中和的重要一环，深入探索专业化修复，在保障质量特性和安全性能不降低的基础上，2021 年实现再制造零部件平均节能 60%、节材 70%、降碳 80%，并通过减少资源消耗实现降低成本

50% 以上，取得经济效益、环境效益和社会效益的有机统一。同时，吉利还探索开展整车低碳修复，通过将高新技术和传统整车制造工艺相结合，实施高价值维修保值、主动预防性维护和全面质量改善，延长整车生命周期。

（四）发展绿色出行与绿色物流，带动全社会碳中和

和汽车制造相比，在全生命周期中，汽车的碳排放更多发生在使用环节。以汽车制造为基础，分别对应客运、货运两大场景，吉利积极发展绿色出行、绿色物流，带动实现全社会的碳中和。

1. 大力推行碳中和出行方式

一方面，吉利布局"新能源汽车共享生态"战略性投资业务，打造建设了曹操出行，将全球领先的互联网、车联网、自动驾驶技术以及新能源技术创新应用于共享出行领域。用户通过使用曹操出行，每千米可获得约 142 g 碳减排量，并全部计入曹操出行个人 App 端的碳资产账户。成立 6 年以来，曹操出行累计节省燃油资源 5.34 亿 L，碳减排总量超 108.35 万 t。另一方面，吉利的另一出行品牌英伦电动汽车 LEVC，已实现全系产品均采用纯电、增程式的新能源动力系统。LEVC TX 车型在英国自下线以来，累计减少约 5 490 万 L 化石燃料消耗，相当于减少约 9 万 t 碳排放。

2. 聚力提供碳中和物流服务

物流体系已成为经济社会发展的重要基础设施，活动水平仍处于快速增长中。吉利聚焦于智慧互联、充换电补能基础设施、绿色能源服务提供等方面，开展了长足的探索。聚焦于城市绿色运力和智慧车联网，建设绿色慧联平台，向用户提供绿色运营、移动物联网共配的体系支持，以及新能源物流车全生命周期管理服务；2022 年绿色慧联绿色里程达 3.6 亿 km，累计减碳量达 18.6 万 t；荣膺《南方周末》"2021 年度特别关注奖——年度绿色产品"。聚焦建设、运营充换电站，管理电池银行，建设万物友好运力服务平台，服务重卡规划充换电补能方案，做到快速补电；2021 年打造的全球首座"风光储充换"一体化宁波绿色轿运重卡充换电站正式投运，可"一站式"解决企业购车成本高、充电时间长、运营低效、载货量少、里程焦虑等痛点，首批 50 台换电重卡预计 5 年可减少碳排放 1.84 万 t。聚焦电动重卡绿色能源服务，建设阳光铭岛平台，为换电重卡客户提供集设计、工程、运营等于一体的换电服务；在该服务模式下，可做到 48 h 内完成换电站的搭建、24 h 内完成移站、单车换电时间不到 5 min、一天最高可实现 200+ 换电服务，为换电站实现更低成本的电力供应。

（五）开发利用绿色甲醇，探索零碳能源新物种

汽车产业的低碳零碳转型已成为社会共识，新能源汽车发展大势业已成形。尽管电动汽车已逐步成为主流技术方案，考虑汽车制造及相关上下游规模庞大，且容易受碳酸锂等关键原料价格波动的影响，仍有必要探索多种可持续的能源技术路线。吉利选择全球公认的清洁可再生能源甲醇作为突破方向，从 2005 年起开展大量的创新探索和实践落地，构建起甲醇经济运营模式，形成醇、运、站、车、捕的循环生态。

1. 攻克甲醇汽车技术难题

2015 年，吉利以 2.8 亿元入股全球领先清洁甲醇生产商的冰岛国际碳循环公司（CRI），共同探索清洁甲醇燃料合成生产技术。2019 年，旗下远程商用车发布全球首款甲醇重卡，其搭载的甲醇发动机攻克低温启动难及涉醇部件的腐蚀两大技术难题，并突破了专用润滑油开发、专用添加剂开发、排放控制、甲醇电喷控制系统等多项关键技术，达到世界领先水平。通过解决甲醇发动机零部件耐醇、耐久性能等行业难题，吉利已掌握甲醇汽车的核心技术，形成专利 200 余件。

2. 发布甲醇汽车并推动落地

吉利深耕甲醇汽车 18 年，开发甲醇燃料车型 20 余款，累计行驶里程接近 100 亿 km，最高单车运行里程超过 150 万 km，成为全球首个实现甲醇汽车量产的主机厂。在工信部为期近 5 年的五省市甲醇汽车试点项目中，吉利投入甲醇汽车 908 辆，占试点车辆总数的近 90%。根据试点运行数据，甲醇车与汽油车相比，能效提高约 21%，碳排放减少约 26%。2021 年，旗下远程汽车推出 13 L 国六甲醇发动机，动力可达 430 马力 /460 马力，平均燃料成本相比柴油重卡可节省 18%，兼具可靠性、动力性和经济性。2022 年，吉利推出全球首款醇电混动轿车——第 4 代帝豪醇电混动轿车，搭载全球首款醇电混动发动机和 3 挡混动电驱 DHT PRO，百公里醇耗在 9 L 左右，每公里出行成本低于 0.3 元，实现"低能耗"与"强动力"兼得。

3. 布局甲醇生产基地

2023 年由吉利和河南省顺成集团共同投资的全球首个 10 万吨级绿色低碳甲醇工厂在安阳正式投产，这是我国首套、全球规模最大的二氧化碳加氢制绿色低碳甲醇工厂，预计每年将生产 11 万 t 甲醇，可直接减排二氧化碳 16 万 t，相当于增加森林种植面积 16 万亩，具有良好的社会效益和经济效益。

三、主要启示

（一）数智管理体系建设助力实现碳目标

一个以绿色低碳发展为导向、功能设置健全、运行状态良好的管理体系，是企业实质性推行碳中和的起点和重要一步。吉利以实现 2045 年全链路碳中和为总体战略目标，并明确到 2030 年、2035 年、2045 年的具体目标，致力于成为中国和世界汽车行业可持续发展模式标杆。为达成碳中和目标，率先实践自主研发的建立碳中和管理制度与体系、设置碳中和工作组工作架构和制定企业碳中和标准等碳管理模式，并具体落地为数字化的碳管理平台——吉碳云碳管理等平台，确保相关管理举措落地，实现工厂能源和碳排放数字化管理成效的大幅提升。

（二）产业链减排赋能碳中和

任何一个企业都处于产业链之中，且与外部、内部频繁发生物质、能源和信息的交换。在产业链的尺度上，推进碳中和，是企业追求更高层次绿色低碳发展的必然选择。吉利在探索车辆全生命周期碳中和路径的道路上卓有成效，已搭建起一套完整的绿色低碳产业链，包括从早期材料端的同步工程分析，到建立可持续绿色工厂节能增效制造和循环包装与绿色运输，再到多技术路径全面助力用户绿色出行解决方案和废物回收循环利用处置等环节，并倾力打造"车""出行""物流"三大碳中和场景，助力探索汽车行业全链路碳中和的解决方案。

（三）关键核心技术提升减碳能力

要实现碳中和目标，必然离不开科技创新这一关键变量，而要最大限度发挥科技创新的作用，就必然要攻克和掌握关键核心技术，确保不被"卡脖子"。吉利控股深耕甲醇领域 18 年，成功解决甲醇发动机零部件耐醇、耐久性能等行业难题，掌握甲醇汽车的核心技术，形成专利 200 余件，开发甲醇燃料车型 20 余款，累计行驶里程接近 100 亿 km，最高单车运行里程超过 120 万 km，成为全球首个实现甲醇汽车量产的主机厂，全面推动了甲醇能源和甲醇汽车的发展，也大大拓宽了厉行碳减排、推进碳中和的能力和路径。

四、展望

（一）借助碳市场发挥绿色金融优势

绿色金融是支撑实现碳达峰碳中和的重要助力。吉利旗下吉致汽车金融有限公司（以下简称吉致）秉持绿色发展理念，深耕绿色金融领域，通过将环保因素融入风险政策，以金融手段推动新能源汽车发展，目前正持续在新能源汽车金融领域发力，积极助力各新能源品牌销售。下一步，吉致考虑持续发挥其厂商汽车金融的优势，为新能源汽车、换电模式、充电桩建设等领域提供更加多元化、多样性的绿色金融产品，提升绿色金融的便利性、可及性和延展性，并推动绿色金融与普惠金融的有效衔接，为社会各阶层和群体提供适当、有效、可负担的绿色金融服务。

（二）有效提高公众碳普惠参与度

碳普惠是快速提升居民践行绿色低碳生活理念的重要机制。前期，吉利旗下曹操出行大力推进落实碳普惠项目，将上线碳积分兑换商城，通过多样化的奖品激励，让用户对低碳行为可知可感。此外，极氪也上线了碳普惠平台 Z-Green，通过数字科技计算出用户驾驶新能源电动车较同等运力燃油车产生的碳减排量，用户可直观地看到自己为碳中和所作贡献。下一步，吉利考虑将碳普惠相关应用进行整合，并推动与政府相关碳普惠平台贯通，加大碳积分的权益兑换力度，进一步有效提升相关普惠机制的覆盖面与用户活跃度。

作者：徐靓[1]，张伟[2]

1　徐靓，吉利控股数科板块双碳业务负责人，汽车行业十余年从业，有丰富汽车产业碳管理经验。
2　张伟，吉利控股集团碳中和负责人，高级工程师，跨国车企 10 多年碳管理经验。

第四部分　专项创新

地方立法推进发展方式绿色转型的思考与建议

随着碳达峰碳中和工作的深入推进，地方立法已成为我国实现"双碳"目标的重要手段与关键途径，为各领域发展方式的绿色转型提供了促进性与规范性支撑。本章通过对发展方式绿色转型领域法律、法规、规章及配套政策的研究，总结了目前绿色转型相关立法的现状和特点，从绿色金融、市场化机制等重点领域法治建设实际情况入手，分析了存在的难点与困境，并结合各地绿色转型相关地方立法实践，提出了推动完善绿色转型领域地方立法的若干建议。

一、我国推进发展方式绿色转型的法律制度现状与特点

作为指明党和国家事业前进方向的重要纲领，党的二十大报告明确指出，加快发展方式绿色转型是践行绿水青山就是金山银山理念的关键步骤之一，这标志着产业结构的调整优化与绿色发展的体系完善在顶层设计层面已经成为我国未来发展中必不可少的一部分。《中共中央 国务院关于完整准确全面贯彻新发展理念做好碳达峰碳中和工作的意见》（以下简称《意见》）则是明确了深度调整产业结构、持续巩固提升碳汇能力、健全法律法规标准和统计监测体系等一系列绿色转型实施路径与支撑保障体系，并在以《意见》作为核心的基础上，与国务院2021年10月印发的《2030年前碳达峰行动方案》，以及能源、工业、交通运输等各领域各行业的专项方案共同构成"1+N"政策体系。

同时，各地方的"双碳"实施意见也进一步将《意见》中提及的绿色转型途径与地方发展优势相结合，如《中共浙江省委 浙江省人民政府关于完整准确全面贯彻新发展理念做好碳达峰碳中和工作的实施意见》（以下简称《浙江双碳意见》）就提出了实施循环经济"991"行动升级版、推行绿色保险、打造碳中和技术线上交易平台等符合地方发展特点与实际需求的绿色转型具体实施手段。

（一）国家层面密集出台或修订一系列推进绿色转型发展政策法规

自习近平总书记于 2020 年 9 月在第七十五届联合国大会一般性辩论上的讲话中首次提出碳达峰碳中和目标以来，国家层面密集出台或修订了一系列与绿色低碳转型相关的法律法规与政策文件，不断推进改革与创新，为推动经济绿色转型发展增加相应制度供给。

在法律法规层面，2020 年 12 月，生态环境部发布《碳排放权交易管理办法（试行）》（生态环境部令 第 19 号），以及碳排放权交易配额分配、温室气体报告与核查等相关活动的技术规范，为全国碳市场建立运行提供法律依据；2021 年 11 月，生态环境部发布《企业环境信息依法披露管理办法》，要求企业建立健全环境信息依法披露管理制度，并将碳排放信息纳入企业应当披露的环境信息范围；2023 年 4 月，国家发展改革委发布了新修订的《固定资产投资项目节能审查办法》，重点突出了控制化石能源消费的导向；2023 年 2 月，最高人民法院发布了《最高人民法院关于完整准确全面贯彻新发展理念 为积极稳妥推进碳达峰碳中和提供法律服务的意见》（以下简称《最高法意见》），作为最高人民法院出台的第一部覆盖"双碳"领域问题的规范性文件，《最高法意见》解决了碳市场交易、保障产业结构深度转型等审判领域中的焦点法律适用问题，为各级人民法院在未来审理涉"双碳"领域案件提供重要指引。

在政策层面，2021 年 2 月，国务院印发《关于加快建立健全绿色低碳循环发展经济体系的指导意见》（以下简称《循环经济意见》），用全生命周期理念厘清了绿色低碳循环发展经济体系建设过程；2021 年 4 月，国务院印发的《关于建立健全生态产品价值实现机制的意见》是首个将"两山"理论落实到制度安排和实践操作层面的纲领性文件，通过"1+6"的制度框架明确了生态产品价值实现机制和战略方向；2021 年 10 月，国务院印发的《2030 年前碳达峰行动方案》是"1+N"政策体系中"N"的首要政策文件，相比《意见》在任务、指标等领域更加具体化，并成为各部门、各地方制定碳达峰实施方案的重要依据和参考；2021 年 10 月，国务院印发《关于推动城乡建设绿色发展的意见》，提出了发展零碳建筑、实施绿色建筑统一标识制度等措施，明确了推进建筑领域绿色发展的主要路径；2021 年 12 月，国务院印发《"十四五"节能减排综合工作方案》，确立了"十四五"期间推动节能减排的总体要求、主要目标、政策机制和保障措施。

（二）地方立法成为推进绿色转型发展的重要手段

地方立法同样发挥着通过试点为其他地方层面和国家层面绿色转型立法提供宝贵经验的作用。以《天津市碳达峰碳中和促进条例》（以下简称《天津条例》）为例，该条例在确立天津市"双碳"管理体制的基础上，进一步明确要求在地方立法、政策制定、规划编制、项目布局中统筹考虑"双碳"目标。其中，《天津条例》专设"绿色转型"一章，就调整能源结构、推进产业绿色转型和促进绿色低碳生活三大目标，提出了提高净外受电和绿电比例、推动城镇新建建筑全面建成绿色建筑、开展绿色生活创建活动等具体实施途径。

伴随我国绿色转型进程的快速推进，国家层面制定的法律法规往往不能及时回应"双碳"新市场新领域中产生的新问题。这时，地方立法因地制宜、形式灵活的立法方式能够快速有效地填补相关立法领域的空白。以绿色金融为例，2016 年发布的《关于构建绿色金融体系的指导意见》在国内首次明确了"绿色金融"的概念，并提出了发展绿色金融的路径，以及支持和鼓励绿色金融的激励措施。然而，该意见作为行政规范性文件缺乏法律强制力，同时《环境保护法》《商业银行法》等法律法规中缺乏绿色金融相关规定。作为回应，深圳市于2021 年施行了《深圳经济特区绿色金融条例》（以下简称《深圳条例》）、湖州市于 2022 年施行了《湖州市绿色金融促进条例》（以下简称《湖州条例》）以及上海市浦东新区于 2022 年施行了《上海市浦东新区绿色金融发展若干规定》（以下简称《浦东规定》），以上地方立法都充分体现了因地制宜的特点。比如在对绿色信贷支持这一点上，《深圳条例》就包含创新绿色信贷品种、降低绿色信贷资金成本、扩大绿色信贷规模等政策导向；《湖州条例》则是提出对绿色信贷在融资额度、利率定价等方面的支持；《天津条例》提出了增加对低碳节能项目的信贷支持；而《浦东规定》是探索通过提高绿色信贷不良率容忍度等方式支持绿色信贷业务。各地虽然确立的机制和措施各异，但都体现了对绿色金融的支持，并在实践层面推进了主管部门、金融机构以及相关企业在绿色金融领域的探索和实践，真正赋能金融领域的绿色转型发展。

在各地通过地方立法积极推进发展方式绿色转型这一进程中，浙江省也始终走在全国前列。2016 年 5 月施行的《浙江省绿色建筑条例》，是全国首个强制推广绿色建筑的地方立法，对绿色建筑的建设标准进行等级划分，并根据等级提供公积金贷款额度上调等激励措施。2022 年 8 月施行的《浙江省生态环境保护条例》则是充分体现浙江数字化改革走在前列的优势，通过建设生态环境综合协同管理平台和"浙里无废""问题发现·督察在线"等场景应用，为数字治污提供支撑。2023 年 1 月施行的《浙江省电力条例》为我国提出"双碳"目标后颁布的第一部综合性地方性电力法规，提出了创新性的新能源发展激励机制，规定新建公共机构建筑和工业厂房应当按照国家和省规定安装分布式光伏发电设施，允许其发电量可以按照规定抵扣建筑能耗量或者工业企业用能总量。此外，聚焦综合型绿色转型发展工作的《浙江省绿色低碳转型促进条例》也被列入浙江省 2023 年立法计划。

二、绿色转型法治建设中遇到的问题

（一）法律法规缺失导致"无法可依"

随着"双碳"工作的深入推进，各种节能、降碳、减污、增效的新技术、新机制应运而生，为政府、企业、公众等各类主体实施绿色转型发展提供了新的工具和手段。但由于立法存在一定滞后性，对于一些新兴领域，难免在初期会出现法律法规缺失的现象，导致相关主体在绿色转型过程中面临"无法可依"的困境。以碳排放权交易市场为例，作为通过市场机制控制温室气体排放的一项创新制度，碳排放权交易市场是我国实现"双碳"目标的重要政策工具。为了保障碳排放权交易市场的运行，国家和地方相继出台了一系列关于碳排放核算、报告、核查、碳排放权交易以及有关会计处理等事项的规范。尽管碳市场的法治建设正得到不断完善，但不管是国家层面还是地方层面，均未对碳排放权的法律属性作出明确界定，对于参与碳排放权交易的应税主体及相关税务处理，亦缺乏相关制度规定，这不仅在一定程度上影响了企业参与碳市场的积极性，也使得金融机构和企业在开展碳资产管理、碳金融及相关衍生品创新的过程中，缺乏法律依据，难以有效识别和防范可能存在的法律风险。

（二）立法间缺乏协调导致绿色转型相关政策有效性受限

推动发展方式绿色转型是一项复杂的系统性工程，相关政策法规涉及能源、交通、建筑、科技、金融等各个行业和领域，而不同行业及领域的法治建设进程、监管体系又各有不同，不同政策法规之间缺乏协调，限制了绿色转型政策措施有效性的发挥。以氢能发展领域为例，氢能不仅是未来国家能源体系的重要组成部分，更是用能终端实现绿色低碳转型的重要载体。尽管国家能源局在最新一稿《中华人民共和国能源法（征求意见稿）》中将氢能列入"能源"范畴，且《意见》和《浙江双碳意见》等政策也将促进氢能产业高质量发展作为构建清洁低碳、安全高效能源体系的重要组成部分，并出台了《氢能产业发展中长期规划

（2021—2035）》等专项规划，但尚未有法律法规明确将氢能的开发利用纳入能源监管范畴。与此同时，在现行法律框架下，氢气属于危险化学品的一种，涉及氢气的生产、储存和运输均受到危险化学品管控相关法律法规规制，制氢项目只能建在化工园区内。虽然应急管理部于 2020 年 10 月发布《中华人民共和国危险化学品安全法（征求意见稿）》，明确规定新建危险化学品生产建设项目应当进入化工园区，资源类和为其他行业配套的危险化学品建设项目除外，为解除氢能企业用地限制提供了可能性，但亦未正式生效。实践中，不同地区、不同主管部门可能对氢能制备、储运和加注等环节建设管理程序、安全监管责任，以及氢能基础设施的建设、审批流程和监管方式等方面提出不同的要求，导致涉氢企业无所适从或涉氢项目无法落地，难以满足氢能产业高质量发展的基本需求。

（三）"软多硬少"导致立法约束力较弱

虽然近年来在国家和地方层面均出台或修订了大量与绿色转型发展相关的法律、法规和规章，但就内容而言多以促进性、原则性的规定为主，旨在引导和激励相关主体调整和优化原有的经营和行为模式，禁止性、约束性的规定相对较少或处罚力度较弱，难以对违法违规行为形成有效威慑。例如《天津条例》中虽然针对调整能源结构这一目标规定了逐步扩大非化石能源消费等实施路径，但未对参与其中的主体作出强制性规定，也未设定对应的法律责任。《碳排放权交易管理办法（试行）》作为规范和调整全国碳排放权交易及相关活动的基本法律，对未按要求履行碳排放报告义务、未按时足额清缴碳排放配额的行为设定了相应罚则，但即使对未按时足额清缴这类严重违反碳排放权交易管理基本制定的行为，罚款金额仅为两万元以上三万元以下，相较于全国碳市场的配额价格，无法有力督促重点排放单位积极履行碳排放控制责任。又如《深圳条例》，对于未按照规定披露环境信息或者虚构、捏造数据或者信息的违规行为，只处以两万元以上十万元以下罚款，与企业通过"漂绿"从成本较低的绿色融资中获取的高额利益并不对称，不能有效预防"漂绿"等违规行为，从而背离激励绿色金融发展的意图和初衷。

（四）配套措施缺乏影响实施效果

尽管国家层面和地方层面通过立法创设和确立了很多创新性机制，但在实施初期往往因为配套措施的缺乏而面临实践困境。以绿色金融领域为例，虽然《循环经济意见》在国家层面提出了发展绿色信贷和绿色直接融资、发展绿色保险等要求，且《浦东规定》《湖州条例》《深圳条例》等地方立法分别明确了绿色金融的内涵，但在实践中，对于如何界定和判断贷款项目属于"绿色"，尚未建立和形成明确、统一、与国际标准接轨的技术和标准体系。除部分行业主管部门出台的基于绿色产业、绿色债券等指导目录外，金融机构缺少可量化的、被主管部门和监管机构认可的指标和评价体系，用以识别、判定绿色主体或绿色项目，并为其匹配对应的绿色金融产品和服务。同时，一些传统的高排放、高污染行业的企业虽然急需转型发展，但却难以获得绿色转型所需的资金支持。除此之外，即便人民银行针对利用碳减排支持工具的金融机构提出了信息披露与接受第三方专业机构核查的要求，但第三方机构需要具备哪些要求和条件，以及第三方机构适用哪些规则和方法对金融机构披露的信息进行核查等细则尚未得到规范。

三、推进地方发展方式绿色转型立法的几点建议

（一）确立地方绿色转型发展的主要目标和路径

在绿色低碳转型已经成为国际潮流的当下，欧盟、英国、法国、德国、韩国等 30 余个国家和地区先后出台了有关应对气候变化、控制温室气体排放、低碳绿色发展方面的法律法规。考虑到法律是对社会关系的长期性调整，而"碳中和"具有阶段性和时限性特点，虽然已有立法成果并未以"碳中和"命名，但大多把"碳中和"目标和相关管理制度一并纳入这些法律法规中，通过立法来保障气候中和目标的实现。在我国构建绿色转型发展相关法律体系的过程中，建议赋予绿色转型发展目标以法律地位，通过地方立法对参与绿色转型发展的各个主体形成约束力，为各领域的绿色转型发展提供驱动力，并让不同领域减排路径的制定与实施更加具有关联性和协同性。同时，绿色转型发展目标法律地位的确立，也能为对各个领域的绿色转型成效考核评估带来依据，从而保障目标设定的科学性和有效性。

（二）填补新技术应用和新市场诞生形成的法律空白

根据《意见》及各地实施方案，氢能、太阳能就地近地开发利用、碳捕集利用与封存等低碳、零碳、负碳和储能的新材料、新技术、新装备，以及碳普惠、生态产品价值实现、电力交易等新型市场化机制将得到快速发展和广泛应用，地方立法可以充分发挥其因地制宜、先行先试的特点和优势，打通企业在应用新技术、参与新市场、开展新业务中的堵点和难点，填补原有的法律空白，为各类主体在新形势下合法合规开展绿色转型的探索和创新提供制度保障。如浙江省在最新出台的《浙江省电力条例》中，对日益凸显的"隔墙售电"问题进行了回应，

规定分布式光伏发电、分散式风能发电等电力生产企业可以与周边用户按照规定直接交易，虽然具体规则尚需省电力管理部门制定，并报省人民政府批准，但依然为其他地区探索开展"隔墙售电"提供了有益的借鉴和参考。

（三）建立健全相应的配套政策和技术标准体系

国家层面构建了碳达峰碳中和"1+N"政策体系，除了《意见》这个发挥统领作用的"1"以外，还出台了行动方案，以及科技支撑、碳汇能力、统计核算、督察考核等支撑措施和财政、金融、价格等保障政策。在地方层面，仅靠一部综合性或者专项立法也难以适应新形势下推进发展方式绿色低碳转型的需要，还需要配套一系列的政策措施和技术标准。结合浙江省实际，可以通过地方立法确立碳普惠机制、绿色产品认证体系、"碳标签"认证机制，完善与生态产品质量和价值相挂钩的财政奖补机制，制定完善省级碳排放统计核算体系和市县级碳排放核算办法，并通过绿色金融改革创新试验区建设的深入开展，构建绿色金融的省级地方标准、行业标准，在保障浙江省发展方式绿色转型有效推进的同时，为国家健全完善相关技术标准体系先行先试。

（四）构建具有约束力的监管和惩罚机制

在地方立法中除了管理型、促进型的规定，还需要具有强制性、约束性规定，对相关主体的违法违规行为进行有效的威慑与惩戒，从而实现"刚柔并济"，保障关键制度能得到有效落实。同时，要明确监管部门及其职责权限，不仅要预防监管缺失现象的发生，还要避免监管部门之间的工作不协调与重复监管。如在绿色金融领域，浙江省可以在对《湖州条例》实施效果进行评估总结的基础上，通过正在制定的《浙江省绿色低碳转型促进条例》或专项立法，在对绿色金融的内涵进行界定的基础上，对存在"漂绿"或其他违反、破坏绿色金融基本管理制度的行为设定更严格的法律责任，为绿色金融的健康发展提供有力的法律保障。

（五）加强区域间的制度协调与联动

区域协同立法是实现长三角生态绿色一体化发展的重要途径，一方面有利于集中彰显长三角地区践行新发展理念、推动高质量发展的政策制度与方式创新，另一方面，还有利于率先将生态优势转化为经济社会发展优势，探索生态友好型发展模式，更好引领长江经济带发展。因此，为了探索从区域项目协同走向区域一体化制度创新，实现共商、共建、共管、共享、共赢，有效解决地方立法之间的功能定位冲突、地方立法碎片化、管控标准不衔接等问题，建议地方在推进发展方式绿色转型立法时充分考虑区域内不同地区法律制度和实施的实际情况，推动技术标准的互认，深化区域间的协调与联动，探索跨行政区域共建共享、生态文明与经济社会协同发展的新模式，实现可持续发展与经济、生活的平衡发展。

作者：宛图南[1]，唐玮[2]

1　宛图南，北京大成（上海）律师事务所律师助理，主要研究方向为欧盟政策与法律合规分析、WTO 争议解决机制、全球气候治理、绿色发展综合评估。

2　唐玮，北京大成（上海）律师事务所顾问，上海碳中和促进中心顾问专家、杭州市能源学会碳中和专委会委员、复旦大学环境资源与能源法研究中心研究员，致力于应对气候变化、资源环境等领域的政策研究，以及碳市场、绿色金融等创新业务实践。

加快节能降碳先进技术研发和推广应用，
促进绿色高质量发展

　　节能降碳技术推广应用在推动经济社会绿色化、低碳化转型和推动高质量发展等方面发挥着关键支撑作用。我国在推动节能降碳技术进步、推广绿色低碳先进适用技术方面开展了大量工作，但依然存在一些问题。具体表现为技术创新体系薄弱、研发供给不足，推广应用中选择难、落地难，技术推广配套制度不完善等。从加强技术创新体系、强化技术供给、搭建节能降碳技术推广平台和服务体系、完善技术推广配套政策措施等方面提出了对策建议。

　　节能降碳技术研发创新和推广应用是提高能源利用效率、降低碳排放的关键手段和重要抓手，也是实现"双碳"目标、促进绿色高质量发展的基础保障。党的二十大报告指出，加快节能降碳先进技术研发和推广应用，这为我们做好技术研发创新和推广应用工作指明了方向，并提供了根本遵循。

一、技术研发和推广应用迎来新机遇

　　当前，绿色低碳技术已成为全球新一轮科技竞争的重要领域，发挥着越来越重要的作用。习近平总书记在中共中央政治局第三十六次集体学习时强调，要狠抓绿色低碳技术攻关，加快先进适用技术研发和推广应用。绿色发展要有突破，科技创新是关键一环，这对绿色技术创新提出了更高要求，也带来了前所未有的发展机遇。

　　一是绿色发展为节能降碳先进技术创造了广阔市场需求。为加快推动绿色发展，国家制修订了一系列法律法规、政策和标准，出台了碳达峰碳中和"1+N"政策体系，强化了能耗强度、碳排放强度等指标约束，为节能降碳先进技术发展提供了巨大的潜在市场需求。据测算，我国 2030 年前实现碳达峰的总资金需求规模为 56 万亿元，2060 年前实现碳中和的投资需求将达 70 万亿元。

二是实现绿色高质量发展为节能降碳先进技术创造了巨大发展空间。节能降碳先进技术是推动经济结构优化升级的内在要求，也是培育形成绿色新动能的必然选择。改革开放以来，我国节能工作取得了显著成效，但能效水平仍较世界平均水平低 1/3，提升空间很大。节能降碳先进技术改造既是改造提升传统产业的重要支撑，也是催生新供给的重要领域，对绿色低碳循环发展经济体系的建立发挥着重要的带动作用。

三是建设美丽中国为节能降碳先进技术创造了持续动力。我国经济发展仍然面临着环境污染、能源资源利用效率低等重大问题，不断加强生态文明建设、满足人民群众对绿水青山美好生活的向往任重道远。节能降碳先进技术推广应用是提高能效、减少排放的源头性措施，也是推动美丽中国建设的重要基础性手段，并将在这一过程中获得源源不断的发展动力。

党的二十大报告指出，推动经济社会发展绿色化、低碳化是实现高质量发展的关键环节。浙江在高质量发展建设共同富裕示范区的背景下，需要持续深化绿色低碳在经济转型发展中的定位，加快传统产业改造升级，大幅提高经济绿色化程度，构建科技含量高、资源消耗低、环境污染少的产业结构。以绿色化、低碳化为特征的绿色转型，将通过技术进步、提升能效等降低资源消耗和污染物排放，从而形成资源高效利用、排放较少、环境清洁、生态安全的高质量发展格局。在迈向中国特色社会主义共同富裕先行和省域现代化先行的征程中，浙江仍需拥抱时势、抢抓机遇，率先走出一条省域层面推进绿色低碳经济转型发展、能源供应清洁低碳、能源利用高效化智慧化、促进经济高质量发展的新路子，打造国家乃至全球绿色低碳高质量发展的高地。

二、国家和浙江省在节能降碳技术推广的做法和实践

（一）国家绿色技术推广的做法

1. 技术推广政策框架逐步完善

一是法律法规层面有专项支持措施。如《中华人民共和国节约能源法》规定，中央财政和地方财政安排节能专项资金，支持节能技术研究开发、节能技术和产业的示范与推广、重点节能工程的实施等。对生产、使用国家推广目录的需要支持的节能技术、节能产品，实行税收优惠等扶持政策。在采购监管、金融信贷、价格政策等方面鼓励和支持节能技术改造等项目。《中国制造 2025》提出加强节能环保技术、工艺、装备推广应用，全面推行清洁生产。政策资金支持不断

深化，如《绿色债券发行指引》将节能减排技术改造项目、节能环保产业项目、低碳产业项目等作为重点支持方向。

2. 技术推广应用机制不断充实

一是节能技术推广目录涵盖面广。国家发展改革委发布的《国家重点节能低碳技术推广目录》《绿色技术推广目录》，工业和信息化部发布的《国家工业节能技术装备推荐目录》《"能效之星"产品目录》，国家机关事务管理局发布的《公共机构绿色节能技术产品参考目录》，住房和城乡建设部发布的《绿色施工推广应用技术公告》，以及农业农村部发布的《农业绿色发展技术导则（2018—2030年）》等目录几近涵盖国民经济各行各业，各省（自治区、直辖市）也在发布本地区的节能低碳相关的推荐目录等。二是节能技术应用案例示范性强。国际能效"十大节能技术和十大节能实践"、国家节能中心"重点节能技术应用典型案例""国家工业节能技术应用指南与案例""交通运输行业节能减排典型示范项目""建筑节能领域典型案例""农业和农村节能减排十大技术"等典型技术应用案例对本行业的节能技术应用起到关键的示范引领作用。三是节能技术推广应用平台不断完善。目前已建立了国家级节能中心、行业协会、社团组织、地方节能中心、地方节能协会等推广应用平台，形成平台推动、行业专家协助、技术企业参与的技术推广应用局面。

（二）浙江绿色技术推广的实践

浙江是长江经济带的重要一坏，创新资源丰富，产业优势明显，具有强大的技术研发力量和活跃的市场创新主体，是创新发展的"领头羊"。浙江省在探索市场化节能降碳技术推广机制方面做了有益尝试，取得了较为明显的成效。2021年5月，根据国家发展改革委办公厅《关于同意在浙江设立国家绿色技术交易中心的复函》，以国网浙江省电力有限公司双创中心为主体，设立国家绿色技术交易中心。交易中心聚焦"双碳"目标，对绿色技术供需双方进行撮合。专门组建了绿色技术专家经纪人团队，为交易者提供技术受理、公开交易、交易鉴证等服务，同时组织多方联合开发建成智能检索系统，储备了100余万项绿色技术专利，以大数据辅助技术经纪人决策交易。交易中心运行1年多来，已促成189项交易，交易额突破3亿元，撬动超百亿绿色产业投资。交易中心建设以绿色技术交易为驱动力，引导技术创新、促进成果转化，加快构建市场导向的绿色技术创新体系，努力建设成为具有国内引领性、国际影响力、全面开放的市场化绿色技术交易综合性服务平台。

国家绿色技术交易中心将立足浙江、辐射全国，紧紧围绕节能环保产业、清洁生产产业、清洁能源产业、生态环境产业、基础设施绿色升级等国家绿色技术推广目录进行技术攻关，培育一批绿色领域创新人才和龙头骨干企业，通过培育壮大绿色技术创新主体，增强我国在绿色技术领域的"造血功能"，大力推动重点行业和领域的绿色低碳化改造，构建以市场为导向的绿色技术创新体系，结合开展绿色技术示范推广、优化绿色技术创新环境及产业链等形式，加快绿色技术"引进来"和"走出去"，掌握绿色技术创新的主动权，提升国际竞争力，为培育壮大绿色产业和助力实现碳达峰、碳中和作出应有贡献。

三、技术研发和推广应用存在的主要问题

节能降碳等绿色技术面临重大发展机遇的同时，还要客观、清醒地看到在研发和推广应用中面临的问题。

（一）节能降碳先进技术研发亟待加强

首先，节能降碳技术整体水平亟待提升。与国际先进水平相比，我国绿色低碳技术领跑、并跑、跟跑的比例分别约为 10%、35%、55%，整体还处于跟跑状态。其次是技术成果转化率偏低，研发与推广应用亟待紧密结合。我国科研院所申请的绿色低碳技术专利占比约为 30%，虽高于国际平均水平，但失效和弃权比例高达 60%，相关投入没有形成现实的先进生产力。例如，新能源汽车基础软件、高精度传感器、计算芯片等严重依赖国外，这主要是由于高端技术研发供给不足、与应用结合不够造成的。

浙江省在围绕双碳科技领域的重大技术创新平台建设、关键核心技术攻关等方面开展了大量工作，目前建设能源清洁利用等国家重点实验室 5 家，培育认定太阳能利用及节能技术等省级重点实验室 71 家、省级新型研发机构 22 家，在可再生能源、储能、氢能、蓝碳等重点方向组织实施重大科技项目 48 项，但总体来看，仍然存在创新主体中龙头企业不强、自主创新能力弱、产业技术层次不高等问题，关键核心技术中储能电池、液氢储运等方面有待进一步突破，传统行业高效节能技术、碳捕集利用与封存（CCUS）等技术尚需加快迭代。

（二）技术供给和需求单位同时存在的"两难"问题突出

目前，节能降碳先进技术供给单位"推广难""获客难"以及技术应用单位"选择难""落地难"问题很普遍，究其原因，一是投资回报普遍周期长、收益低。节能降碳技改项目回收期多数在 3 年以上，且很多项目投资额度大、收益

回报小、不可预期风险高,导致企业"不愿用";二是技术落地缺少风险共担机制。相关方处于"各自为战"状态,对履行节能降碳社会责任、不能带来收益的部分尚未形成风险共担机制,电力、钢铁、石化等耗能量大、工艺流程长、安全系数要求高的行业企业存在"不敢用"的顾虑;三是缺乏公正客观的权威评价验证。新技术的成熟需要在应用中实现,而效果也需要依靠案例来验证,同时还需要权威机构给予公正客观的评价,但目前还缺少权威的评价测试验证手段,导致用能单位广泛存在技术"选择难"。

浙江省民营经济发达,中小企业数量多,但是企业规模总体偏小、技术相对薄弱、人才缺乏,使得企业作为技术创新的主体地位没有形成,而且也缺乏有力的节能降碳技术创新机制保障如产权激励、市场激励等,这都一定程度上削弱了企业的技术创新动力。同时,科技成果转化也仍然存在转化环节多、转化体制不对应等障碍,使得一些好的节能科技成果得不到有效转化和应用。

(三)管理制度不完善制约了节能降碳先进技术发展

一是部分现行法律法规和政策落实不到位。国家先后颁布了《中华人民共和国节约能源法》等多项法律法规,也相继提出了支持节能技术研发、示范和推广应用的财政、税收、金融等政策,但有的细化不够、操作性不强,有的偏于原则、刚性约束弱,导致落实不到位。二是在招投标制度方面的关键难点亟待突破。招投标制度是目前对先进技术应用具有普遍性、长期性和基础性影响作用的保障制度,但关键环节设计亟待完善,如未能明确设置"优先"使用节能降碳等新技术、新产品和新设备方面的具体条款。三是支持技术推广服务的手段缺失。技术推广服务是先进技术应用落地的桥梁纽带,需要政府、专业机构和企业等各方面共同发力、各司其职,不断丰富手段和载体,但目前提供技术推广服务的各类主体普遍存在定位不准、手段单一等问题,远不能满足发展的要求。四是标准引领不足。我国已发布终端用能产品设备强制性能效标准79项,近5年制修订的仅占其中的35%,部分标准指标已不同程度落后于市场实际情况,需要及时制修订发挥应有的倒逼引领作用。

浙江省在能耗双控目标落实、重点用能单位管理的制度创新、实践探索等方面开展了卓有成效的做法,取得了明显成效,但是在部分节能制度的落实尤其是用能企业的节能降碳意识提升、高能耗设备的淘汰使用等方面还需要强化,在节能标准方面也存在部分指标不科学、标准实施有待强化等情况,支持节能降碳先进技术推广应用的政策氛围和环境需要进一步优化。

四、深入推进技术研发和推广工作的对策建议

加强节能降碳等绿色先进技术研发和推广应用，需要从供给和需求两端发力，坚持问题导向和需求导向，突出关键环节问题的解决。结合浙江工作情况和具体实践，提出以下建议。

一是以通用领域关键技术研发为主导带动整体水平提升。锅炉、电机等设备耗能量大、用途广泛，技术突破更新应用后带动作用大，应紧紧抓住这些领域的关键性技术加以攻关并加快推广应用；同时对先导共性关键技术要加大联合攻关和投入支持力度，力争走在前列、掌握主动。要依托骨干企业、高校科研院所等现有资源载体，积极建设创新中心、工程中心、企业技术中心等，以突破关键技术为目标，形成各具优势、形态完备的研发服务体系。浙江省在绿色低碳基础前沿技术方面，围绕氢能、储能、二氧化碳捕集等领域，重点突破海上风电绿色制氢与输储、高效安全规模化储能、大规模二氧化碳捕集、生态碳汇等技术；在应用技术研究方面，针对锅炉、电机、泵、风机、空压机、低品位余热利用等通用高效节能技术、高效率太阳能光伏发电、规模化低成本海上风电、二氧化碳捕集与矿化利用等关键共性技术，分年度有序布局实施重大项目，加快攻坚突破。

二是加大政策措施对先进技术研发和推广应用的支持。加快制修订相关法律法规，明确定量化、持续增长的刚性支持要求，避免出现不应有的时有时无、时多时少问题；财税、价格等政策要更多地从普惠公益、加快发展的角度用力，金融主要以市场化为导向兼顾公益性用力。积极推动金融资本与节能降碳技术的对接，促进更多技术项目落地见效。要完善招投标等制度，着力解决招投标过程中如何优先使用先进技术问题。推动建立由政府主导、供需双方和金融保险等共同参与的技术应用风险共担机制，并通过改革的手段消除各种阻碍先进技术应用不合理的门槛和条件，特别要打破对中小企业技术应用的不合理限制。

三是完善评价检测和技术推广服务机制。建立完善政府、协会、企业等多层次参与的评价、检测服务机制，特别要加强服务中小企业、体现公益属性的共性检测，为技术发展提供支撑服务。要大力推动技术创新及技术推广交易等各类服务平台建设，探索形成政府支持、市场化运作、可持续发展的技术推广服务模式。加强技术交易机构建设，大力培育检测、评价、认证等中介服务机构。浙江省内各级行业协会、服务平台等应当做好政府和企业之间的桥梁，及时整理近期国家和省级政府发布的相关政策措施，定期为各类企业举办政策培训，搭建并丰富技术推广的渠道和手段。国家绿色技术交易中心更要充分发挥国家级平台的作

用，建立完善绿色低碳技术评估、交易体系，加快技术创新成果转化应用，为浙江经济绿色低碳转型发展贡献技术支撑。

四是强化相关标准制修订工作。按照"宜快则快、宜慢则慢、成熟一个实施一个"的原则，加快制修订一批节能降碳技术标准规范，完善重点用能领域和用能设备强制性节能标准，促进先进技术得到更大范围的推广应用。加强强制性节能标准节能监察执行力度和结果运用，提升用能主体节能降碳的自觉性。浙江省要充分深化节能降碳标准化工作联动机制，制定更加科学合理的地方能效标准，强化节能标准的实施，创造节能潜力空间，促进节能降碳技术的应用。

五是加强科研人才培养和节能降碳基础管理。充分发挥高校、科研机构、行业协会和企业等各方面的作用，建立完善多层次节能降碳人才合作培养模式，依托项目落地实践，培养学科交叉、复合多元、攻坚克难的研发人才队伍。持续推动用能单位建章立制、加强企业能源管理人才培训，不断提升节能降碳工作的基础管理水平。浙江省聚焦抢占绿色低碳科技创新制高点，以科技部门"鲲鹏计划"、领军型创新创业团队、"万人计划"、海外工程师计划等为依托，大力引进培育国内外高端人才和团队，力争新引育"双碳"领域领军型创新创业团队，为绿色低碳技术研发攻关和推广应用提供坚实的人才保障。

作者：辛升[1]

参考文献

[1] 国务院."十四五"节能减排综合工作方案（国发〔2021〕33 号）.

[2] 国家发展改革委，科技部.《关于进一步完善市场导向的绿色技术创新体系实施方案（2023—2025 年）》的通知（发改环资〔2022〕1885 号）.

[3] 国家发展改革委，工业和信息化部，财政部等 9 部委.关于统筹节能降碳和回收利用 加快重点领域产品设备更新改造的指导意见（发改环资〔2023〕178 号）.

[4] 国家发展改革委，市场监管总局.关于进一步加强节能标准更新升级和应用实施的通知（发改环资规〔2023〕269 号）.

第四部分 专项创新

---

1 辛升，高级工程师，国家节能中心推广处处长，主要研究方向为节能政策研究与分析、节能技术推广、节能市场化机制、重点用能单位管理等方面工作。

[5] 国瑞沃德（北京）低碳经济技术中心. 中国工业节能技术进展报告2015. 北京：中国科学技术出版社.

[6] 杭州网，关于《中华人民共和国节约能源法》和浙江省实施办法贯彻实施情况的报告. https：//z.hangzhou.com.cn/2022/rddschy/content/content_8291622.html.

[7] 蒋建平，童森军，林文都. 浙江省节能标准化现状分析及对策 [J]. 大众标准化，2014，2：51-53.

[8] 辛升，公丕芹. 节能技术推广存在的问题与对策研究 [J]. 中国能源，2018，40（12）：41-44.

标准化助力浙江省碳达峰碳中和行动

实现碳达峰碳中和，是以习近平同志为核心的党中央统筹国内国际两个大局作出的重大战略决策。标准是国家质量基础设施的重要内容，是资源高效利用、能源绿色低碳发展、产业结构深度调整、生产生活方式绿色变革、经济社会发展全面绿色转型的重要支撑，对如期实现碳达峰碳中和目标具有重要意义。本章梳理了浙江省的地方标准的发展现状，通过对比分析，总结了"双碳"背景下浙江省标准化工作面临的新机遇、存在的问题和挑战，并在此基础上针对性地提出了标准化建设建议，为标准化支撑浙江省碳达峰碳中和行动提供参考。

一、"双碳"标准体系建设的重要性

从 20 世纪 90 年代的《联合国气候变化框架公约》及《京都议定书》，到 2015 年达成《巴黎协定》，全球气候治理进程完成了从发达国家"自上而下"强制减排到各国"自下而上"提出与其国力相适应的气候变化行动目标的转变。在此背景下，采取各项减排措施以控制大气中的温室气体增加，已成为国际社会的共识。2020 年 9 月 22 日，习近平总书记提出了"30·60"目标，凸显了我国在应对气候变化和温室气体减排工作中决心和担当。此后，党中央、国务院高度重视"双碳"目标，层层部署"双碳"的各项工作和措施，保障"双碳"目标达成。

在推进应对气候变化工作及推进绿色低碳经济发展的进程中，技术标准已成为约束碳排、提质增效、缓解气候变化的一种公认技术途径，是绿色低碳转型升级、绿色低碳技术推广应用和推动碳达峰碳中和的重要依据，也是参与国际应对气候变化工作的重要支撑。

浙江省的"双碳"工作是一次广泛而深刻的社会变革，是一项要素众多、结构复杂、周期漫长的系统工程，需要构建全覆盖、多维度、多层次的"双碳"标准体系，作为"双碳"工作的必要补充和支撑。以标准的"定量"优势加强"双碳"工作开展的可操作性，发挥"补充细化"作用引领"双碳"工作向具体化、精细化的方向延伸，系统性推进浙江省经济结构绿色转型。

二、浙江省"双碳"标准建设现状

自"十二五"时期开展应对气候变化工作以来，浙江省持续推进"双碳"标准制定工作。据统计，浙江省目前已出台"双碳"标准 72 个，其中"十二五"期间出台标准 20 个，"十三五"期间出台标准 20 个，"十四五"开年以来出台标准 32 个。从 2012—2022 年各年的标准出台情况看（图 19-1），2019 年与 2021 年出台的标准数量较多。其中 2019 年出台了 10 项标准，主要由于 2018 年年末浙江省对能源"双控"工作的推动加速了节能降碳标准出台；2021 年作为"双碳"元年，受多个政策激励影响，浙江省出台了 23 项多领域标准，数量为历年最多。2022 年，随着"双碳"工作的回归理性，标准数量出现一定回落，共出台了 9 项标准。

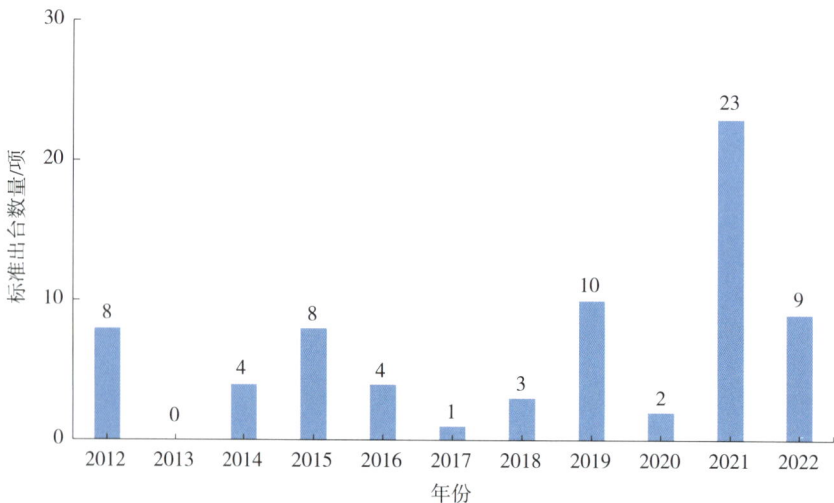

图 19-1　2012—2022 年各年度"双碳"标准出台数量

从涉及的领域看，出台的标准涵盖了浙江省"一总六分"领域。从各个领域的占比上看（图 19-2），能源领域的占比最高，达 51%；居民生活领域占比达 17%，位列第二；工业领域占比达 11%，位列第三；建筑领域占比达 8%，位列第四；综合领域占比达 7%，位列第五；交通和农业领域占比较低，均为

3%。从目前情况看，碳预算、碳足迹、碳捕集、运输与封存等多个领域的标准尚属空白，还需要进一步在这些领域发力，开展相关标准的研究。

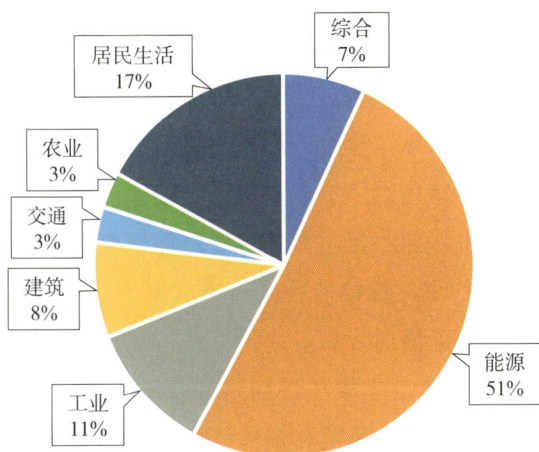

图 19-2　浙江省"双碳"地方标准分布及占比

2023 年，浙江省将拟出台低碳标准 33 个，包括新型储能、碳排放核算体系、碳普惠、长三角区域交通碳排放核算等多个创新领域标准，进一步完善浙江省"双碳"标准体系。

三、"双碳"标准体系建设面临的新机遇和新挑战

近年来，浙江省在节能、碳排放管理等领域标准化工作取得进展。但与碳达峰碳中和工作对标准化的迫切需求相比，"双碳"标准体系的广泛性、协调性、精准性都有待提升，在标准与政策衔接、推动标准有效实施的机制、标准跨区域互认等方面还存在不足。

（一）新形势下，"双碳"标准体系建设的新机遇

1."双碳"带来新问题，对标准体系建设提出新需求

自"双碳"目标提出以来，浙江省积极开展和推进相关工作。但由于"双碳"工作覆盖面广、层次多，在各项工作落实落细上会遭遇诸多新问题。"双碳"标准体系建设是建立健全"1+N+X"碳达峰碳中和政策体系的延续、细化和补充，具有强渗透性和广覆盖性，有利于推进"双碳"工作向深向实发展。为了如期实现碳达峰碳中和目标，浙江省印发《浙江省碳达峰碳中和工作标准体系实施方案》，要在 2024 年年底前形成覆盖重点领域重点行业的"一总六分"碳

达峰碳中和标准体系，提出了要夯实共性标准基础、扩大标准的覆盖面等建设要求。

2.绿色发展迎来新空间，对标准提升提出新要求

绿色低碳是高质量发展和新旧动能转换的内在要求，是经济社会可持续发展的必由之路。在此背景下，浙江省产业结构和消费模式将发生重大变化，企业转型升级意愿更强，对"双碳"标准的建设提出新要求。一方面，传统产业积极转型要求提高标准门槛。绿色经济的发展提升了传统产业的节能减排转型的积极性，已有标准的约束力度稍显不足，要提升对节能低碳转型技术、项目和企业认定标准，进一步形成硬约束，推动能耗高、排放高的产业转型升级。另一方面，优势企业发展要求标准创新高质发展。由于绿色市场竞争主体不断涌入，优势企业为了保证和提升竞争优势，需要先进前沿的标准来谋求更大的减排可能和机会，进一步降低温室气体排放的风险和责任，提升企业竞争力。

3.低碳技术不断研发创新，为标准应用提供新场景

低碳技术创新是推进"双碳"工作的核心驱动力。当下，浙江省正处于新一轮科技革命和产业变革当中，低碳技术不断创新发展，持续推进能源和产业绿色低碳转型，为实现"双碳"目标提供科技保障。然而低碳技术的落地应用需要与之相匹配的标准体系来保障，将技术真正转化成规范化、规模化、市场化的成果，实现技术在"双碳"工作中的创新引领作用。因此，低碳技术创新发展也带动新标准的研发与制定，为标准提供新的应用场景。

4.市场国际化程度提升，为标准国际化发展提供新动力

实现碳达峰碳中和是事关高质量发展大局中的重大任务之一，减碳工作更是全球共参的时代议题。浙江省作为外贸出口大省，更频繁、更紧密地与国际接轨，更深入参与国际绿色市场的竞争。亟需制定适应、领先于国际要求的"双碳"标准，提供浙江智慧，献出中国方案，提升我国在国际"双碳"标准制定中的话语权，进一步争取在国际标准化组织和活动中反映自身利益与诉求，有力开拓外贸出口市场。

（二）新目标下，"双碳"标准体系建设面临的新挑战

1."双碳"标准体系广泛性、精准性和系统性不足

目前浙江省已出台涵盖"一总六分"领域的 72 项"双碳"标准，但仍缺少分领域、分层级、分主体标准，现阶段覆盖面和深度有限。其次，省内研标制标组织对"双碳"标准化的需求识别不够敏感和精准，难以充分发挥能耗限额等标准的"硬约束"作用，难以深入落实落细减碳减排的各方各面。另外，省内的

标准化技术委员会存在"各自为政"的情况，研究系统性不足，存在标准多头制定，指标设置、技术要求不统一的问题，标准之间容易出现交叉和重复。

2."双碳"标准体系与政策的衔接性不足

由于标准制定过程较长，导致标准与政策之间衔接不紧密。标准的制定需要反复沟通、协调与调研，具有较长的制定周期，但政策具备动态调整的特性，在此前提下，如果遇到政策频繁调整，便会造成标准与政策间严重脱节，导致标准与政策发展不衔接、不协调，难以实现标准建设与政策发展有机结合，影响"双碳"目标实现。

3."双碳"标准体系实施有效性不足

由于"双碳"工作范围广，涉及职能部门多，在标准研制工作上各有侧重，立场和关注点都有所不同，导致标准要求不一，增加了企业的执行难度。其次，相关单位对标准解读、宣传、贯彻、培训力度不够，导致企业不能及时获取和掌握标准信息。再次，市场主体缺乏积极有效参与和配合，存在企业对已有标准执行不重视，对标准化意识不足，缺少相关标准专业人才，自我标准声明公开不足等问题，难以实现标准真正落地。此外，浙江省尚未形成统一的"双碳"标准化信息服务平台，企事业单位不能及时了解"双碳"领域的国内外标准、标准需求等信息。

4."双碳"标准跨区域互认不足

以碳中和为基础的区域互动新规则和以碳中和为逻辑的区域新合作正在全力展开。积极推进区域间标准互认成为顺利达成碳中和目标的重要保障。但是，由于存在区域间的壁垒，技术标准、评定准则等差异较大，导致标准间互认难度较大，在区域间的应用和推广问题多，阻碍跨区域的节能降碳管理与绿色产品流通，限制绿色低碳区域一体化发展。

四、浙江省"双碳"标准化工作对策建议

（一）加强标准与政策协同

标准的制定需要坚持"一个目标"，并有序推进"两个协同"。"一个目标"即建立最佳秩序、取得最佳效益，"两个协同"是指纵向要推动标准从制定到执行的上下全链协同拓展，横向要推动各标准主体与政策主体协同配合。始终围绕这一目标进行标准研制与体系构建，通过政策制定和标准谋划，形成共促高质量发展合力。

（二）完善"双碳"标准体系

明确标准化事业发展的"四个转变""四个目标""七大任务"[1]，立足"双碳"标准创新高地建设，围绕解决政府治碳、企业减碳和个人低碳的实际需求，按照"急用先行"原则研制一批关键亟需标准，完善"双碳"标准体系建设。要加快完善从基础研究、应用技术、标准制定到产业实现的全链条"双碳"标准，创新标准转化工作系统，支撑碳技术创新的落地转变。要强化数字技术融合，及时将应用在"双碳"工作中的人工智能、区块链、云计算等先进的数字化技术融入标准，提升标准水平。

（三）加强标准实施和监管

推动建立省级"双碳"标准化专家委员会，协调、推动"双碳"各项工作顺利开展，为如期实现"双碳"目标提供重要组织保障。研究搭建"双碳"标准化技术信息公共服务平台，提供快速了解研标需求、标准及时查新、国内外标准现状了解等服务的载体。另外，还需要提升宣贯力度，组织专业机构、行业协会、重点企业定时及时召开标准交流沟通会，做好标准宣贯、技术培训、指导交流与成果转化推广，推动标准与企业深入衔接。建立标准实施信息反馈机制，开展标准实施效果评价，探索建立标准实施情况统计分析报告制度，引入第三方评估机构及时跟踪和反馈；推动市场加强自主标准公开、实施与监督，引导高质量、原创性的团体标准和企业标准公开发布和推广，推动先进的团体标准和企业"领跑者"标准的应用落地，鼓励团体、企业对标准做好自律和互相监督工作，发挥市场优胜劣汰的作用。

（四）推动跨区域标准互认

立足区域间经济发展实际，促进"双碳"标准共建共享。要探索建立长三角区域标准化联合组织，负责统一标准的立项、发布、实施、评价和监督，联动区域间的相关部门、标准化研究院、企业等多方主体，定期会商解决标准制定和应用难题，助推"双碳"标准体系一体化发展。要建立区域低碳技术共享和再分配的协调发展机制，进一步完善区域间碳市场机制、碳金融机制、碳资产管理政

---

1 四个转变、四个目标、七大任务来自《国家标准化纲要》的说法。

策、财政补贴、税收减免以及科技创新支持等，调动开展参与跨区域"双碳"工作的积极性和主动性，推动标准互认。

1 蒋建平，浙江省标准化研究院 副院长，正高级工程师，主要从事标准化、质量与品牌建设等领域研究，持续服务于制造业绿色、低碳和高质量发展。近 10 年来，主持各级计划科研项目 15 项，出版专著 5 本，发表学术论文 67 篇；为主申请发明专利 3 项，获省部级奖项 3 次，副部级奖项 2 次，获省级领导批示 10 次。联合天通控股股份有限公司等筹建新型磁电和光电信息材料国家技术标准创新基地，为 ISO/IEC JTC1/SC7/WG7（系统软件工程领域）和 IEC/TC82/WG9（光伏领域）注册专家、国家标准技术评估专家、浙江省全域"无废城市"建设咨询专家委员会成员、浙江省市场监督制造业绿色低碳高质量发展创新团队学科带头人。

2 朱东锋，浙江省标准化研究院 标准化工程师，主要从事碳达峰碳中和、循环经济等领域标准化研究，承担全国气体标准化技术委员会（SAC/TC206/SC3）第二届含氟气体分标委委员、省居民生活领域碳达峰工作专班成员、省生态环境标技委（ZJQS/TC37）副秘书长、省可降解材料与制品（ZJQS/TC85）标技委委员、浙江标准在线入库专家等，累计主持省部级科技项目 1 项、厅局级项目 1 项，参与相关课题 4 项，参与国家标准制定 4 项，参与省级地方标准 3 项，主持或参与浙江制造团体标准 50 余项。

3 张天佑，浙江省经济信息中心能环部博士，长期从事应对气候变化相关工作，2017 年以来，主要承担全省能耗双控制度研究、双碳课题研究等课题，以及温室气体清单编制、碳报告管理等业务工作，近年来还参与了居民低碳出行、零碳公共机构相关标准起草工作。

浅谈企业碳资产管理

随着我国碳市场的启动，碳资产管理日益受到重视。碳资产管理包括碳配额、减排量的管理，碳资产的处置和金融产品等方式，目的是促进企业可持续发展和减少碳排放量。本章简要介绍了碳资产的概念，重点分析了企业碳资产管理的关键点，并简要梳理了碳资产交易与碳金融服务等内容。最后，本章以浙江省企业碳资产管理案例为例，为读者提供了相关建议。

一、碳资产的内涵及发展

随着全球各国对温室气体控制基本达成共识以及我国"30·60"目标的提出，越来越多的企业正意识到碳资产在企业生产经营过程中的重要性。目前，全球主流碳市场的交易流通标的为碳排放配额和核证自愿减排量。2022 年 4 月 12 日中国证监会发布的《碳金融产品》行业标准中指出碳资产是由碳排放权交易机制产生的新型资产。在具体分类上，主要分为政府发放的各类碳排放权配额，以及可能获得碳信用的碳减排项目等。

（一）碳配额的概念

碳配额是由政府机构监管的强制性制度，用以限制特定行业企业的排放量。基于《京都议定书》提出的机制，各国政府应在规定时间内实现承诺的碳减排目标。各国政府根据目标将本国的碳排放权按照规则分配给相关企业，最终分配给企业的碳排放权就是排放配额。1 个配额代表 1 t 二氧化碳排放量，单位以吨二氧化碳当量（tCO$_2$）计。中国的碳配额分为两类，一类是全国碳市场 CEA，另一类为试点碳市场下的碳配额。

（二）减排量的概念

基于项目的减排量交易是指在总量控制之外，对某个具体减排项目产生的减排量（又称碳信用），根据其产生机制又可分为与配额交易相关联的碳信用交易机制减排量以及其他自愿减排机制减排量。前者典型代表 CCER（国家核证自愿减排量）是在中国碳配额市场之外引入的自愿减排市场交易，是作为中国碳市场的补充，后者的代表国际上的自愿减排交易减排量（如 VCS），在这类市场中的碳信用额（Carbon Point）可以根据不同的标准进行核证产生，其项目主体一般没有履约义务，可以由那些自愿地想要抵销其排放的企业购买。

（三）我国碳市场的发展

在碳配额的管理上，生态环境部基于《全国碳排放权交易管理办法（试行）》制订配额分配方案，向纳入全国碳排放权交易市场覆盖范围的重点排放单位发放配额，配额用于交易，企业需根据实际排放情况在履约期保证其账户有足量配额进行履约清缴。在 CCER 的管理上，国家专门规定了林业碳汇、可再生能源发电、甲烷利用等多样化的自愿减排方法学，通过方法学来认定减排项目及其所产生的减排量，减排量可等量替代配额进行履约。自国家赋予碳资产强制履约的性质起，碳资产有了刚性需求，即有了资产价值，并可通过碳市场体现公允价格，具备与财会概念中无形资产类似的属性。

二、企业碳资产管理模式

从碳资产管理的主体出发，可以将碳资产管理模式分为两类。

（一）控排企业的碳资产管理

目前，在发电、石化、化工、建材、钢铁、有色、造纸、航空八大控排行业内生产过程中排放二氧化碳达到 2.6 万 t 或综合能源消费量折合 1 万 t 标准煤以上的企业均被纳入全国碳市场，通过强制配额履约及全国碳排放权交易的市场化手段来倒逼控排企业减少温室气体排放。加入全国碳市场对控排企业的高效碳管理提出新要求，特别是对属于集团公司类型的控排企业。由于其具有下属企业数量多、组织架构层级多等特性，导致碳排放及碳资产管理难度大。

控排企业提升碳资产管理质量的关键是通过减排措施优化配额管理。通过梳理企业生产流程，找准重点排放源，从能源结构、工艺、设备、能源管理等方面挖掘减排潜力，如使用可再生能源、能效提升技改、高效能源管理系统等，从源头上减少排放。此外，也要综合考虑能耗降低成本、配额收益增加、节能减排改造投入成本，优化配额管理质量。

（二）非控排企业的碳资产管理

非控排企业的碳资产主要是通过技改和投资节能减排项目来获取。非控排企业可利用 CCER（国家核证自愿减排量）方法学研究，对我国境内可再生能源、林业碳汇、甲烷利用等项目的温室气体减排效果进行量化核证，并在全国碳排放权交易市场进行交易获利。以控排企业 5% 的抵消配额的上限测算，目前 CCER项目年减排量的缺口在 1.5 亿 t 左右，非控排企业可通过参与减排量开发获利。

非控排企业的碳资产管理焦点是识别减排潜力。企业可从减排、碳汇两个角度出发分析国家各种减排项目方法学，明确项目适用的方法学，做好项目设计文件开发，记录好日常监测文件和台账记录，加强与第三方审核机构沟通，从而最大限度识别和挖掘项目最终减排量。同时，也要注意理论减排量与可开发减排量的区别，有很多理论存在减排的项目并不一定能成为可开发减排量。此外，要考虑理论减排量的方法学符合程度、减排量收益是否能覆盖开发成本等问题。

三、企业碳资产交易类型

碳资产的特点在于可以用于各主体的碳中和抵消以及控排企业的履约清缴，同时可以实现变现增收。国际市场上已将碳排放指标作为一种交易标的设计了与大宗商品类似的各种标准化金融产品。同时，为保障碳资产交易健康有序进行，国家也建立了统一的碳交易市场。在此，主要介绍我国市场目前常见的交易类型。

（一）现货交易

碳现货是碳金融原生工具。碳资产的现货交易是在碳资产的交付和转移的同时完成资金的结算，主要通过交易平台或者场外交易等方式完成交易。以全国碳排放权交易所为例，全国碳配额交易方式分为挂牌协议交易、大宗协议交易和单项竞价交易。

（二）远期交易

碳远期交易是买卖双方约定在将来某个确定的时间以某个确定的价格购买或者出售一定数量的碳单位（碳配额或者减排量）的非标准化合约，一般为场外交易。双方协商确定合约的价格、数量和交货时间等内容，最后以实物交割方式履约。远期交易因价格确定所以不存在价格风险，但由于监管结构较为松散，容易面临违约风险。

（三）期权交易

碳期权是在碳期货基础上产生的一种碳金融衍生品，是指交易双方在未来某特定时间以特定价格买入或卖出一定数量的碳标的的权利，其本质是一种选择权。碳期权的交易方向取决于购买者对于碳排放权价格走势的判断。以 CCER 期权为例，当预计未来 CCER 价格上涨时，CCER 的卖方会通过购买看涨期权对冲未来价格上升的机会成本，如果未来 CCER 价格下降，则通过行使看涨期权 CCER 卖方获得收益。

因此与碳期货一样，碳期权可以帮助买方规避碳价波动所带来的不利风险，具备一定的套期保值功能。期权的购买者能够通过区别购买看涨期权或者看跌期权锁定收益水平。此外，还可以通过对不同期限、不同执行价格的看涨期权和看跌期权的组合买卖来达到锁定利润、规避确定风险的目的。

（四）置换交易

置换交易是碳资产特有的一种交易类型。由于减排量可以抵扣配额进行履约，而减排量天然比配额价值略低，因此在市场上催生出了碳配额及 CCER 置换交易的业务。

碳配额及 CCER 置换交易业务本质是一种远期合约交易。交易双方通过签订合约，约定在未来确定的期限内，相互交换等量碳配额和核证自愿减排信用及其差价的交易。通过创新设计碳配额 /CCER 置换产品并开展交易业务，不但使两步独立交易简化为一个置换交易操作提高交易效率，还可实现远期交易，有利于企业和投资机构对利用产品锁定当下碳资产市场价格，降低日后交易成本，更好地对自身碳资产进行管理。特别是大型电力企业可用 CCER 抵消的配额量大，当配额与 CCER 市场价格差距大时，成本节约的效果将更显著。

（五）碳交易机构

碳交易机构是碳市场中的重要组成部分，是保障碳资产交易的关键。为了保障碳交易市场健康有序发展，交易机构要充分认识碳市场的各类风险预判涨跌趋势，分析碳排放权交易市场在准入、交易、金融产品等方面的政策规则并提出相应的预案，充分发挥市场导向功能，促进碳市场运行平稳有序。此外，也要明确碳排放交易市场是政府政策工具的本质，在推进碳市场健康发展的同时协同政府做好精准控碳工作。

四、面向企业的碳金融服务

随着碳资产作为资产的价值体现，催生出碳减排的直接投融资活动以及相关金融中介等服务，帮助企业盘活碳资产，获得减排项目融资，降低融资成本，提高经营效率。

（一）碳债券

碳债券是绿色债券的一种，主要是指以碳资产或碳资产收益作为债券还本付息的担保或资金来源，或是将所募资金用于碳减排项目活动的债券。碳债券主要有以下几种类型：一是以预期现金流作为附加利息收益。以 CER/CCER 的交易收益作为债券利息支付的部分资金来源，而债券发行主要还是依附于发行公司的信用与经营财务状况，并没有以碳资产或碳资产收益作为债权主体，碳信用的收益仅仅充当浮动利息的支付。二是以碳资产作为担保进行贷款。碳配额是政府行政分配获得，具有财产权的性质，这是碳资产可以质押性的基础。银行是否愿意参与质押交易的关键在于市场流动性，只有市场具有流动性，才能给银行信心，愿意给企业贷款。

以碳资产出发发行碳债券国内外都已有先例可循，但碳债券交易主要以交易双方发展长期合作关系为目的，且在具体利率优惠方面空间不大，因此在市场上的交易行为较少。此外，若以碳资产为担保发行债券直接融资，又会受 CCER 资产规模和碳配额存续期的限制，还存在适合的债券种类有限和估值困难等问题。要想解决这种局面，需要全国碳市场建立并逐步统一后，扩大市场覆盖范围，吸纳更多企业和机构，提升碳市场交易量，引入期货期权交易，有效对冲头寸风险，加强碳资产价格发现。这样才能为企业盘活碳资产提供更多可能性，为碳金融创新发展注入新的活力。

（二）碳基金

在众多碳金融创新工具中，碳基金是重要的投资类碳金融创新工具。碳基金专为碳排放权或减排量交易而设立，通过发行机构集中来自公共或者私人部门投资者的资金进行投资操作，以获得投资收益和资本增值收益，所得收益由投资者来分享。碳基金为应对气候变化、发展低碳经济引入了更加广泛的资金来源渠道。作为全球项目级碳信用的主要购买商，碳基金在全球碳市场发展初期是减排项目开发的重要资金来源。

目前国内运行的碳基金主要是参与国内试点碳市场的配额交易和 CCER 交易，以根据市场行情走势低买高卖，进而交易获取差额利润。我国的低碳基金早期大部分是专注于投资绿色低碳企业股权的私募基金，投资于国内碳市场的基金在 2014 年后才逐渐涌现，如中国清洁发展机制基金、中国绿色碳基金（China Green Carbon Fund）、"绿色1+1"专项基金、碳中和基金和生态城市发展基金等。

五、浙江省企业碳资产案例

某水泥制造企业是我国水泥行业最早的企业之一，被誉为中国水泥工业的摇篮。作为水泥行业的重要企业，其在自然资源的消耗降低以及二氧化碳减排方面存在一定的压力。为此，该企业于 2011 年便实施碳资产的管理，控制其碳排放并且优化公司的运营。该公司在实施碳资产管理之后，通过减少煤炭与水泥的使用量，并且在生产过程中利用废气余热等方法减少了二氧化碳的排放。同时，该企业还在推广节能、环保等生产理念，在不断优化生产流程的同时，满足了市场的需求，提高了公司的盈利能力。

某发电厂是一家大容量燃煤电厂。作为第一批纳入全国市场的控排企业，既要在煤价上行中保障电力供应，又要完成碳市场履约要求。为此，电厂将后续预发放配额通过碳配额远期交易形式提前变现，将获得的资金用于电厂节能改造，提高了单位能耗产能，降低了电厂排放水平，缩小了配额缺口，形成了碳资产交易—节能技改—减少排放—增加碳资产—降低履约成本的完美闭环。

某企业是一家提供 IT 技术服务的公司，其受数据中心和服务器运作影响碳排放量较大。为了解决碳排放问题，该公司在 2012 年实施了碳资产管理，优化数据中心和服务器的能源使用，通过提高能源效率和节省能源，降低碳排放。

某百货商场是一家全面架构在云上的互联网百货公司，其销售量位居中国百货零售业前列。因此，其在进货、运输、运营等活动中会产生大量的碳排放。为了控制其碳排放并提升社会责任感，该企业在 2013 年实施了碳资产管理。该公司通过货物的集中采购和分拣，并优化物流运输方式以及运作效率，缩短了运输时间，并且减少了碳排放。同时，该公司还利用可再生能源（如风能、太阳能和水能等）来产生对公司有益的收益。

六、启示和建议

目前国内碳市场已正式开启，但参与主体、交易品种、交易方式、监管规则仍在不断完善成熟过程中，对于碳资产管理的研究和模式也在不断地随之更新。在此对企业完善碳资产管理建设提出几点建议。

（一）坚持低碳发展理念

企业应该始终坚持低碳发展目标，引领公司向可持续发展道路上迈进，持续降低对环境的影响。同时，积极发展可再生能源，替代传统能源，在减少碳排放的同时给企业带来额外收益。

（二）开展碳资产管理

碳资产不同于一般传统资产，属于新兴事物，因此需要在公司内部就碳资产管理达成共识，按照低碳发展的需求，将碳资产的管理落实到制度层面。在我们越来越看重碳排放问题的现在，企业应实施碳资产管理，从而优化其生产运作流程，减少碳排放量，并带来经济效益。碳资产价值要通过交易才能充分体现，因此要做好交易过程中的交易流程设计、配套风控等方面的工作，保证碳交易的健康有序进行。

（三）灵活使用碳交易、碳金融等工具

低碳化转型必然带来相应的技改与管理的成本投入，要灵活使用碳交易、碳金融工具，制订合适的碳资产开发和交易方案，将转型成本通过市场化手段降到最低，形成正向推动。同时，在实施碳资产管理过程中，企业应灵活运用各类支持政策，并加强与其他公司的合作，共享经验和技术。

作者：黄虹飞[1]，周立颖[2]

1　黄虹飞，浙江浙能碳资产管理有限责任公司市场运营部主任，长期从事企业碳资产管理相关工作，2006 年以来，主要承担浙能集团 CDM 项目开发、温室气体编制、碳资产管理等系统内业务，并牵头方法学开发、温室气体清单编制、低碳标准申报等课题咨询项目。

2　周立颖，浙江浙能碳资产管理有限公司碳市场开发部专职，从事减排项目开发、低碳咨询、碳排放管理相关工作。承担浙能集团低碳产品开发、碳排放与资产管理等系统内业务，并参与低碳标准制定、方法学开发、低碳课题研究等咨询项目。

构建数智治理体系　助推"双碳"目标实现

"数智治理"作为数字时代技术赋能碳达峰碳中和治理的新模式、新趋势，对我国实现"双碳"目标具有支撑作用。本章通过分析当前碳达峰碳中和数智治理面临的主要问题，以浙江省为例，系统介绍了该省在推进碳达峰碳中和中的数智治理探索实践，并提出了相关的对策建议，为全国及其他地区提供了浙江样板。

一、引言

积极推进碳达峰碳中和治理体系和治理能力现代化，充分发挥数智治理在实现碳达峰碳中和目标中的关键作用，是贯彻落实总书记关于碳达峰碳中和重要论述精神的重要举措。但由于数据基础较差、碳统计核算体系薄弱、数智治理手段缺失等问题，"双碳"实现数智治理依然面临巨大挑战。

基础数据分散，数据共享共用困难。碳数据收集困难、滞后，碳数据统计不全面、不及时，是碳数据全周期高质量管理面临的主要问题。此外，碳数据的敏感性和封闭性，导致碳数据跨业务交换困难，形成了数据孤岛。提升数据质量，确保碳数据的真实、准确、全面，从而实现碳数据高质量管理和全流程共享，是实现"双碳"数智治理的关键基础。

统计核算体系薄弱，数据规范性不足。目前，国家尚未建立统一的碳统计核算体系，地方探索的区域、行业碳排放核算（速算）体系普遍存在数据更新偏慢、核算口径不一、基础排放因子滞后等问题。构建统一规范的碳统计核算体系，实现对基础数据的准确核算、深度挖掘、科学分析，是推进"双碳"数智治理的重要保障。

治理手段缺失，具体工作缺乏抓手。政府层面，政府缺乏有力抓手监测分析区域、领域、行业的"双碳"工作进展，无法支撑政府科学决策。企业层面，企业缺乏低碳转型路径指引，不能明晰减碳路径，难以实现生产过程的智能低碳管理，从而实现提质增效。个人层面，缺乏平台记录和量化个人的低碳行为，无法有效引导个人践行低碳生活。

以数字化改革为引领，是浙江特色所在，也是当前浙江助力碳达峰碳中和目标实现的重要途径。浙江省积极探索构建数智治理体系，通过建设"双碳"数字化智能管理平台，赋能政府精准控碳、企业低碳转型和个人低碳生活。

二、浙江碳达峰碳中和数智治理体系实践

（一）数智治理基础

2021年，浙江在全国率先启动数字化改革，实施数字化改革两年来，取得了显著成效，积累了丰富经验。浙江省数字化改革的标准路径是，通过V字模型迭代，逐步梳理完善核心业务，形成需求清单、场景清单和改革清单（以下简称3张清单）；根据3张清单，构建以"基础设施层、数据资源层、应用支撑层、业务应用层"为四横、以"政策制度体系、组织保障体系、网络安全体系、标准规范体系"为四纵的系统架构；最终形成数字化应用的顶层设计。浙江省数字化改革标准路径和丰富经验为"双碳"实现数智治理提供了科学的路径指引。

早在2014年，浙江省就建成了全国首个应对气候变化领域的省级碳排放管理平台——浙江省气候变化研究交流平台。该平台覆盖省市县三级和重点企业，实现了碳排放数据全流程在线采集、编制、审核、管理、分析和研判，形成了全省统一的应对气候变化基础信息数据库，为应对气候变化、实现"双碳"数智治理打下了很好的数据基础。

（二）数智治理顶层设计

1. 确立总体思路

实现碳达峰碳中和，是多重目标、多重约束的经济社会系统性变革，需要统筹处理好经济发展、能源安全、碳排放、和居民生活4个维度关系。

浙江省对标国际一流和通行规则，在4个维度平衡的基础上，系统分析能源消费总量、碳排放总量、能耗强度、碳排放强度4个核心指标；以能源、工业、建筑、交通、农业、居民生活六大领域绿色低碳变革为路径；利用科技创新这一变量，形成了"4+6+1"的工作思路（图21-1）。通过跟踪监测各领域核心指标、工作推进和实施效果的情况，保障实现全省碳达峰碳中和目标。

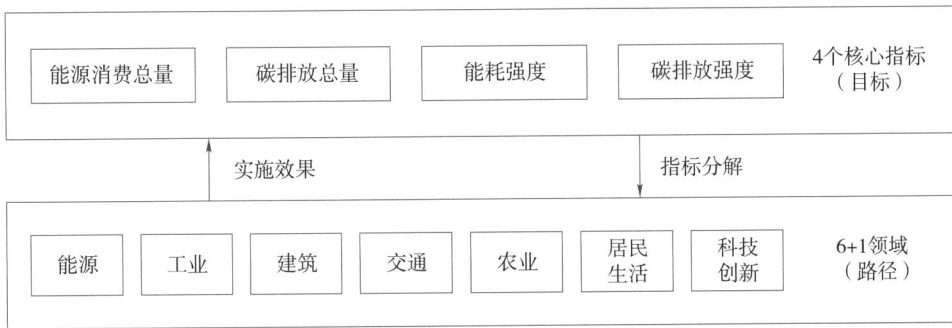

图 21-1 "双碳"工作总体思路

2. 梳理 3 张清单

政府、企业和个人是实现碳达峰碳中和目标的三大主体。政府是全面推动实现碳达峰、碳中和目标的行动主体,承担碳达峰碳中和顶层方案设计、任务目标分解等工作。企业是承担碳减排的直接主体,通过技术改进、转型升级等各种方式落实碳减排责任。个人是消费领域中最大的碳排放主体,也是承担碳减排的重要主体,个人通过选择绿色低碳生活方式、消费方式,可最大化减少碳排放。因此,实现数智治理的关键,就是针对政府、企业和个人的三方需求,借助数字化手段,寻求改革突破点,最终实现助力政府精准控碳,推动企业低碳转型,引导个人低碳生活。

对于政府治而言,需聚焦解决重点管什么、怎么管,以及管的成效怎么样的问题。对于企业而言,需聚焦解决企业为什么要减碳、怎么减,以及减的成效怎么样的问题。对于个人而言,需聚焦解决哪些行为可以减碳、减了多少碳,以及减碳的收益是什么。在需求清单的基础上,谋划一些数字化改革场景,在数字化改革场景中找到突破口,推进改革突破、流程再造和制度创新。可以说,3 张清单是浙江省数字化改革走实走深的核心抓手。

3. 建立数据归集机制

当前碳排放数据收集面临主体多、数据分散、数据采集困难、核算复杂度高等多重挑战,导致碳数据归集、管理困难。浙江省依托省大数据局一体化智能化平台,以碳排放数据仓为载体,建立跨区域、跨部门的数据归集机制,高频收集全省各领域、各区域、各行业能源消费数据,以及统计部门分地区、分行业碳排放核算数据、经济数据等;实现多源综合数据互补汇聚。

同时,基于地理信息系统构建碳账户体系,将企业、项目、个人等主体的碳排放核心数据归集到双碳数据仓,纳入统一碳账户管理,实现碳账户数据可监测、可查询、可追溯、可比较,为各层级政府部门推进"双碳"工作、建设数字化应用场景提供重要支撑。

4.健全统计核算体系

碳排放统计核算是实现"双碳"数智治理的重要基础，也为政府决策提供可靠数据依据。2021年，国家统计局将浙江省列为碳排放统计核算试点地区，承担省级地区分行业碳排放核算方法研究。目前，浙江省已按照核算方案实现对全社会六大领域和工业分行业碳排放量试测算，同时，积极推进设区市碳排放统计核算工作，为浙江省构建统一规范的碳统计核算体系奠定了坚实基础，也为实现"双碳"数智治理提供可靠、规范的数据基础底座。

（三）数智治理平台建设

1.助力政府精准控碳

政府既是全面推动实现"双碳"目标的行动主体，也是落实"双碳"目标任务的责任主体。监测碳达峰工作进展、监管重点用能数据、定位各类减碳主体是政府实现数智控碳的关键。

为高频跟踪监测全省分区域、分领域"双碳"工作进展，浙江省建设了碳达峰碳中和智治平台，实现了对区域碳排放总量、能源消费总量、碳排放强度、能耗强度等指标的动态监控、比对、分析、预警，对领域主要指标完成情况及主要工作的推进情况进行高频监测；为省、市、县各级政府主管部门动态掌控碳达峰工作进程，面向重点地区和用能对象开展实时预警提供了科学支持。

对重点用能单位的用能数据监管是推进节能工作的关键。杭州市通过打造"能源双碳数智平台"，实现对全市工业、交通运输等重点领域的2 000多家等重点用能单位的数智监管。通过制定精确的能源分配机制，提高了全市重点用能单位能源利用效率。

节能审查制度在遏制高耗能、高排放、低水平项目盲目发展中发挥重要作用。杭州市临安区通过构建天目"临碳"数智大脑，基于"固定资产投资能碳预评估"模块对新上项目进行能效评估，对高碳项目进行预警，提出整改意见，实现了对高碳项目的智能化管理。

总体来说，浙江省通过建设"双碳"数字化智能管理平台，帮助政府全面掌握"双碳"工作在总体管控、统筹分析和成效评定方面的进展情况，提升政府数智治理能力，助力政府精准控碳。

2.服务企业低碳转型

企业是碳减排的核心主体，在碳达峰碳中和工作中承担着重要责任。用能情况不掌握、碳家底摸不清、减碳路径不明晰是企业在减碳过程中面临的主要挑战。

为实现企业用能预算自主调配，浙江省谋划建设节能降碳 e 本账应用。通过建立"省—市—县—企业"的用能预算分级管理机制，支持企业查询自身用能信息、自主测算用能情况、实现用能预算管理等，给予企业自主调配生产计划和用能权限，最大限度地减轻用能空间限制对企业生产经营的影响，充分激发企业生产潜力。

为精准服务重点领域、重点行业率先实现碳达峰，引领企业精准降碳，湖州市首创"碳效码"应用。该应用创新构建碳效智能对标体系，为工业企业赋予碳效码。对评价为高碳企业，开展节能诊断服务，制订降碳减量计划，推动实施绿色技改项目。在省相关部门的联合推动下，全省共有 4.2 万家规模以上企业完成评价赋码。

企业推动技术创新，优化产品和管理方法，实现降碳增效，都需要强大的资金支持。衢州市创新构建碳账户金融体系，根据碳账户画像按月为企业生成碳征信报告。金融机构在获得企业授权后，可查询使用企业的碳征信报告，给予相应的金融服务支持。目前，该平台已上线 3 002 家企业的碳征信报告，累计发放碳金融贷款 533 余亿元。

总体来说，浙江省通过建设企业用能预算管理、碳效码、碳账户金融等数字化平台，帮助企业摸清碳家底，为企业提供金融贷款、节能技改等服务，提升企业自主减碳意愿，推动企业绿色转型。

3. 引导个人低碳生活

居民生活领域是实现碳达峰工作的重要一环，个人消费产生的碳排放量不容忽视。当前个人端碳减排面临数据分散、难以定量等问题，以数字化方式探索个人参与碳减排，形成全社会绿色生活方式，意义重大。

为积极引导个人践行低碳生活理念，浙江省建设了全国首个省级"碳普惠"应用，该应用与多家数据源单位合作建设 20 类数据场景，实现个人低碳场景的全面覆盖。通过构建"低碳行为获取—减排量核算—碳积分赋予—普惠权益兑换"闭环普惠流程，向个人普及绿色低碳理念，提高个人参与绿色低碳生活的意愿。

垃圾分类作为生活中的关键小事，也是个人走进低碳生活最简单有效的方式。余杭区创建"一键低碳回收（虎哥回收）"应用，利用"一站式"收集模式，培养用户垃圾分类习惯。通过上门回收的方式，把居民投放的生活垃圾按重量支付居民"环保金"，"环保金"可以在网上商城兑换商品或提现。目前该模式已经在浙江省逐步推广。

湖州通过搭建"碳达人"应用场景，将居民屋顶光伏、垃圾分类、绿色出行等有效低碳行为开发为减排场景。用户可以通过个人绿色行为获得碳积分，并在

"碳达人"积分商城兑换所需的实物、电子券等。

三、碳达峰碳中和数智治理启示和建议

综合浙江省在构建"双碳"数智治理体系的做法和成效，给全国及其他地区构建双碳数智治理体系提供了良好的思路和实践路线。

（一）建立科学有效的数据归集机制

建立科学、有效的数据归集机制，打通数据孤岛，是实现数智治理的关键基础。碳排放基础数据分散、数据质量较差、数据的时效性不高是目前"双碳"工作普遍存在的问题。因此，建议在安全规范的前提下，建立省、市、县三级数据归集机制，汇聚多源互补数据，提升基础数据准确性、时效性和共享性。同时，可以按照业务主题建设不同数据库，形成多种数据产品，实现碳排放精细化、智能化管理和全方位分析。

（二）研究统一规范的碳统计核算方法

建立统一、规范的碳排放统计核算体系，摸清碳排放家底，是实现数智治理的重要保障。碳统计核算体系涉及多个层级、多类主体和多个维度，其核算的边界和方法也各有差别。因此，建议按照急用先行、先易后难的顺序，逐步开展区域、行业企业、产品的碳统计核算方法与标准研究。为政府制定政策、监测评估工作进展提供可信的依据，为企业打造碳减排路径，形成低碳产品的提供重要支撑。

（三）谋划服务多元主体的数字化应用

建立服务政府、企业、个人等多元主体的数字化应用，是实现"双碳"数智治理的主要路径。碳达峰碳中和是一个多维、立体、系统的工程，涉及政府、企业、个人多方面的主体，需要政府全面主导、企业主动作为和社会公众积极参与。因此，建议立足多元主体实际需求，以需求为导向谋划建设数字化应用，支撑政府治理、企业服务和个人普惠。

作者：浙江省经济信息中心著作组

"双碳"背景下，浙江省绿色金融发展新使命

"双碳"背景下，绿色金融成为撬动市场要素、支持浙江省低碳高质量发展的重要抓手。绿色金融发展需要在绿色金融政策、信息披露、产品服务等方面共同发力。浙江省以绿色金融改革创新试验为契机，通过完善政策标准制度的完善、创新绿色金融产品服务、发展绿色金融数智化工具等路径，率先探索以碳效提升为核心的发展新思路、新举措，促进浙江省绿色金融全方位、多领域发展。

一、引言

绿色金融是现代经济的血液，是提振经济的关键变量，对推进绿色低碳经济发展具有乘数效应。2017 年以来，国务院批准在浙江湖州、衢州等地开展绿色金融改革创新试验。2019 年国家发展改革委牵头制定了《绿色产业指导目录》。2021 年中国人民银行（以下简称人行）发布了中国首批绿色金融标准《金融机构环境信息披露指南》和《环境权益融资工具》，规范了金融机构环境信息披露工作，引导金融资源更加精准向绿色、低碳领域配置。2022 年 4 月，人行在召开的电视会议中明确要求要实现绿色金融与转型金融的有效衔接，注重绿色金融、普惠金融融合发展。

"双碳"目标的提出，进一步为绿色金融赋予新的使命与内涵，绿色金融成为浙江省低碳高质量发展的重要抓手。一是引导浙江省资金要素配置。绿色金融通过鼓励绿色投融资、抑制高碳投资，引导资金流向绿色低碳领域，形成发展绿色低碳行业所必需的金融资本，有效降低资本筹集的成本，优化市场资源配置。二是支持低碳产业发展。绿色金融一方面可以加快传统产业转型升级。另一方面，绿色债券、绿色基金等绿色金融工具能够发挥金融系统的资金聚集功能，实现金融资源要素的有效配置。三是助力应对气候风险。尤其是在当前国际贸易市场变化和我国"双碳"目标提出的双重影响下，浙江省传统制造业、化石能源行

第四部分 专项创新

229

业等棕色资产容易遭受冲击。绿色金融具有对这些环境和气候风险的前瞻性，可以降低对棕色资产的影响。

浙江省积极推动"双碳"工作，对绿色金融提出了相关要求。自 2020 年起，中国银保监局浙江监管局牵头印发了《关于金融支持浙江经济绿色发展的实施意见》《浙江银行业保险业支持高质量发展建设共同富裕示范区工作方案（2022 年度）》《浙江银行业保险业支持丽水气候投融资试点建设的指导意见》《深化清洁能源全产业链金融服务的指导意见》等文件。同时，浙江省在绿色金融方面取得了显著成效，截至 2021 年年末，浙江省绿色贷款余额同比增长 46.3%，高于全国增速 13.3 个百分点；绿色债券发行量同比增长 128.57%，融资额同比增长 5.63%；绿色保险产品创新 20 余种，各类绿色保险年服务超过 50 万次[1]。

二、绿色金融在浙江省发展面临的挑战

（一）绿色金融的法规政策机制有待完善

我国绿色金融发展至今，仍存在绿色金融相关配套政策法规不完善的问题。一是法律条文缺失导致责权不清。监管部门相继制定了支持绿色信贷的政策与法律，但缺乏界定商业银行在绿色信贷方面权利义务的法律条文。绿色信贷政策多属于部门规章制度，其立法层次不高，强制力和权威性不够。二是政府配套政策措施缺位，绿色信贷风险补偿机制、绿色信贷担保、税收减免等配套政策还未完全建立。三是信贷投放与环评信息的联动机制不畅，部分企业存在故意瞒报信息、为应对环保检查做"表面工作"等问题，因此商业银行难以对企业环保信息的真实性作出准确判断，导致其绿色信贷的管理成本和风险增加。

（二）企业绿色信息披露不够充分

目前企业环境信息披露制度还存在一些问题。一是强制环境信息披露主体有限。浙江省民营企业发达，小微企业占比 75% 以上，大部分企业不属于环境信息强制性披露的企业之列，难以获取该类企业环境信息。二是披露内容不完整。依据有关法律法规等规定，所披露的指标不能全面反映企业遵守生态环境法律法规和环境治理情况。三是披露形式不规范、不统一。为取得环境披露信息，金融机构等需要采取多种方式，增加获取成本。四是缺乏信息真实性保障机制。企业的环境信息具有较强的专业性，金融机构等缺乏鉴别环境信息真伪的能力，在这种情况下，无法保证企业披露环境信息的真实性。因此，金融机构难以通过企业

1　数据来源《浙江省绿色金融发展报告（2021）》。

环境信息披露掌握企业完整的、有效的、合规的环境信息，不能在进行授信审批和贷后管理中作出准确的风险判断。

（三）绿色金融产品和服务亟需创新

在浙江省开发绿色金融产品时，金融机构通常面临着企业计量评估体系不健全、环保专业知识不足等问题，影响了金融机构有针对性地推出各种绿色金融产品与服务。一是企业绿色发展评价难定量。金融机构在分析企业生产经营情况时，往往面临着企业低碳相关历史数据缺失、数据记录不规范等问题。同时金融机构由于专业限制，对于无法满足 ESG 指标体系的企业难以灵活评价其绿色发展情况。二是绿色金融作用范围受限。虽然已有文件提出绿色金融要与普惠金融、转型金融相衔接和融合，但目前绿色金融碳减排支持工具的主要作用范围仍局限在《绿色产业指导目录》所提及的产业，对于国民经济支柱行业中传统和高耗能产业的低碳转型提效，缺少相应的转型金融产品支持。三是绿色金融贷款发放难。浙江省小微企业量多面广，短时间内难以大幅改善面向小微企业的计量体系和统计核算体系。此外，银行的发展水平参差不齐，面临着优化资产、风险控制等问题。因此市面上缺少面向小微企业的普惠绿色金融产品。

三、绿色金融在浙江省的实践

（一）形成了绿色金融相关标准制度

浙江省持续推动绿色金融行业标准落地实施，加快地方标准体系建设，完善绿色金融监管评价体系。在省级层面，相继立项了《小微企业绿色评价》《绿色建筑低碳项目贷款实施规范》等标准，发布了《长三角征信链征信一体化服务规范》《绿色低碳项目融资评价规范》《银行个人碳账户管理规范》等省级团体标准，推出了《关于金融支持碳达峰碳中和指导意见》《绿色债券支持项目目录》《金融赋能"双示范"建设 2021 年信贷指导意见》等推动绿色金融市场标准化、规范化发展的文件，出台了《浙江省银行业金融机构（法人）绿色金融评价实施细则》，提出强化环境信息披露等要求；在地市层面，湖州市发布了《绿色建筑项目贷款人的标准》《银行业客户 ESG 评价标准》《湖州市银行信贷碳排放计量方法指南》，衢州市形成了工业、农业、建筑、道路运输、能源生产等重点领域碳账户建设的地方标准以及《支持衢州市银行业保险业绿色专营机构发展的意见》等相关文件。

（二）创新了绿色金融产品服务

浙江省各地紧扣"双碳"目标，开展绿色信贷、绿色债券、绿色保险、碳排放权质押等产品服务创新，形成了多种绿色金融产品与服务，包括鼓励企业降碳提效的"碳效贷""碳价贷""低碳贷""积碳释放贷""碳衍生交易贷款"等；鼓励生态环境和碳汇保护的"碳汇共富贷""碳汇收储贷"等；面向农户或小微企业等固定对象的"长青贷""农户光伏贷"等。基于区域资源禀赋、产业特色、市场需求等地方特色，各地也开展了绿色金融产品服务实践：

湖州市：中行湖州分行结合碳效码应用，创新"工业碳惠贷"绿色金融产品，促成了"碳效码"推出以来在银行信贷领域的首次应用。

衢州市：农行衢州分行成功向企业发放"绿色减碳贷"，是首笔以"碳账户"为主要参考指标的专项贷款，助力企业实现固碳减排、绿色转型。

嘉兴市：人民银行嘉善县支行指导相关银行为本地纳入碳排放权交易企业，并通过中国人民银行征信中心动产融资统一登记公示系统质押登记和公示。

温州市：首单绿色金融债券落地乐清，发行规模 1 亿元，主要用于光伏发电相关设备制造、公共自行车、智慧停车建设等绿色低碳项目的融资需求投放。

金华市：在银行间债券市场成功发行全国首单民营企业可持续挂钩债和碳中和债，若实现挂钩目标，预测 2023 年可减排二氧化碳 60 余万吨。

台州市：创新"长青贷"小微绿色信贷，立足于普惠小微企业，降低担保门槛，实现绿色普惠金融产品定制化、定价差异化、成效跟踪常态化。

（三）研发了绿色金融支持工具

全省充分利用数字赋能的优势，完善绿色金融基础设施研发。人行杭州中心支行积极探索全省碳账户金融多跨场景建设，开发碳信息数字化共享和多跨场景应用；湖州市积极推进碳账户综合支撑平台建设，重点推进碳账户体系，开发ESG评价数字化系统；衢州市开发绿色金融服务信用信息平台（衢融通），通过信用信息收集、银企对接、数据分析等功能，推进金融机构绿色金融服务数字化发展；温州市大力推进碳信用平台建设，完善"碳信用 + 绿色金融"功能，按企业信用评级结果，为企业匹配提供金融减碳优惠服务；台州市探索开展浙江省碳账户金融多跨场景"微绿达"建设，推进小微绿色信贷识别与主体认定。

此外，立足于碳排放主体与产业发展现状，浙江省充分发挥数字化优势，开发全省企业碳效数据基础建设和企业碳效评估支持工具。依托省发展改革委牵头建立的浙江省碳达峰碳中和智治平台，浙江省碳账户、碳金融、碳普惠等重大应用取得成效，为绿色金融提供碳效相关数据基础。同时，积极开展企业碳效识别、评价工具构建，助力金融机构降低信贷发放风险、创新绿色金融产品，如浙江省工业碳效码对全省规上企业碳效情况进行分档、跟踪，浙江省经济信息中心推出面向小微企业的碳效评价模型，湖州创新企业五色码和 ESG 评价数字化系统等，为金融机构推进绿色金融工作提供多种支持工具。

四、推动"双碳"目标下浙江省绿色金融发展的启示

（一）企业多方位提升绿色低碳发展能力

充分认识全球碳中和形势和绿色转型趋势。企业既是绿色金融的实施对象，也是绿色资金的需求方。在气候突发事件、能源危机、绿色贸易壁垒等不利影响下，缺乏气候应对能力和防御能力的民营企业将面临严峻挑战。企业应提高对"双碳"目标重要性、必要性和紧迫性的认知，深刻理解"双碳"目标可能给企业带来的机遇与挑战，构建符合绿色低碳趋势的运营理念和经营规划。

积极采取绿色低碳发展行动。企业是我国经济复苏与可持续发展的重要支撑力量。企业应在新发展理念指导下顺势而为，根据自身实际情况调整经营目标与发展模式，充分发挥经营灵活、决策快捷的优势，抓住"双碳"带来的新机遇，在"窗口期"内完成低碳转型。

建立健全碳排放管理制度和工作机制。浙江省民营企业大多未建立专门的碳排放数据统计和管理制度，这不仅让企业缺乏低碳转型的决策依据，更干扰了企业的绿色融资。企业应加快建立碳排放信息统计、核算、披露等管理制度，并形成覆盖各个生产环节的碳排放管理工作机制，从而助力企业获得绿色金融支持，把消耗性投入转变为盈利性产出。

（二）金融机构多角度创新绿色金融服务

探索创新风险评价标准和量化工具。金融机构在"双碳"目标下，推出了一系列创新绿色金融产品，但由于部分企业碳管理较为粗放，数据可得性、真实性差，影响了金融机构服务的可行性和积极性。建议金融机构围绕"双碳"的工作要求，不断创新绿色金融业务模式，将"碳效"作为识别绿色主体、计算和评估企业或项目环境效益的关键指标之一，充分应用技术手段在风险可控的前提下服务更广泛的用户群体。

加强引导高质量发展的绿色普惠金融产品设计。企业在低碳转型过程中会产生新的融资需求，及时提供新的金融产品与服务，成为金融机构必须研究的新课

题。建议金融机构根据企业在"双碳"目标下不同阶段的转型特点，针对其低碳转型中的痛点，创新具有"碳"属性的普惠金融服务产品和服务渠道，提升融资便利度，更好地满足企业在低碳转型过程中的多元化资金需求。

持续提升绿色金融能力建设。随着我国碳达峰碳中和政策体系的出台，绿色普惠金融和转型金融将会发挥更大作用。建议金融机构加快建立健全企业环境信息尽职调查制度和流程规范，完善碳排放信息披露机制，加强绿色金融培训，培养兼具金融、环境等专业背景的复合型人才，提升绿色普惠金融产品创新路径、风险管理、运营服务的质效。

（三）政府多层级开展绿色金融支持工作

完善绿色金融顶层设计，强化监管。当前，我国绿色金融制度缺乏普适性和强制力，部门之间的政策关联性和协调性有待加强。建议政府部门结合当地产业转型和绿色经济的发展需要，加大财政支持力度，引导金融机构提升绿色低碳业务和资产规模比重，强化绿色金融监管，分层次、分步骤推动金融机构等相关主体公开披露绿色信息，加快构建与"双碳"目标相适应的绿色金融政策体制和机制。

通过数字化手段提升绿色金融的广度和深度。把数字化平台作为推进碳达峰碳中和的关键性、系统性举措，加强部门间协调合作，打破数据孤岛，强化企业碳效等绿色信息共享机制，持续推进企业环境信用体系建设，为构建"敢贷、愿贷、能贷、会贷"的长效机制提供科技支持，持续优化企业融资环境。强化大数据、物联网等数字化技术应用，有力支撑金融机构对企业在贷前、贷中、贷后碳效水平的持续跟踪。

构建以"碳效"为核心的多层次标准体系。让金融机构等市场主体准确把握"绿色"的内涵是绿色金融规范发展的前提。政府部门应加快构建以"碳效"为核心，覆盖行业、企业、产品与服务多个维度的标准体系，使金融机构能够轻松识别经济活动中的"绿色"活动，科学评估企业经营活动对环境产生的外部性影响，同时为绿色金融决策提供依据。

作者：浙江省经济信息中心著作组

第五部分　研究专论

全球碳中和进程下碳足迹碳标签制度发展动向

　　随着《巴黎协定》下全球绿色低碳转型大潮流的推动，碳减排及碳中和相关制度和政策体系正在逐步完善。不同于联合国主渠道下共同但有区别的责任原则，越来越多的重点行业和产品正在实施无差别化的碳标准标识制度，并在国际贸易、新经济和消费领域逐渐形成新的技术规范，这将深远地影响全球供应链及产业的发展。为此，建议应前瞻性开展制度性的比较研究，探索建立符合中国国情的碳足迹评价技术体系，推动关键产业产品碳标签试点示范，持续完善数据平台、标准制定、制度规章等绿色公共产品，培育第三方核查、认证、法律服务机构，主动应对碳贸易壁垒，锚定全球零碳产业发展"新赛道"，实施创新驱动的"双碳"行动。

　　随着联合国应对气候变化《巴黎协定》进入实施，目前全球已经有 130 个国家和地区以不同形式宣布了碳中和目标，经济总量、能源消费及温室气体排放占到全球的 90% 左右，特别是中国、美国、欧盟等主要经济体都提出碳中和目标后，接下来碳中和就会逐步成为全球产业投资、能源市场、资本流动和国际贸易等领域中的新规则。欧美、七国集团等正在或即将采取的基于单边措施的碳贸易壁垒和绿色技术"脱钩"政策，如碳边境调节机制、产品全生命周期碳足迹标准、绿色供应链"碳嵌入"管理、机构碳资信评级、敏感实体清单等，将对中国等发展中贸易大国产生较为深远影响。

一、碳足迹碳标签制度发展的国内外实践

　　碳足迹（Carbon Footprint）源于生态足迹（Ecological Footprint）的理念，主要以二氧化碳排放当量表示人类生产消费活动导致的温室气体排放。碳足迹可分为国家碳足迹、个人碳足迹、企业碳足迹、产品碳足迹四个层面。其中，产品碳足迹是应用最广的概念，即研究产品生命周期产生的温室气体排放量。根据

世界经济论坛的数据显示，电子产品、汽车、食品、建筑、时尚、快速消费品、专业服务和货运八条供应链的碳足迹就占据了全球排放量的 50% 以上。碳标签（Carbon Labelling）是指商品在全生命周期（一般包括从原料、制造、储存、运输、废弃到回收全链条）中所排放的温室气体，在产品标签上用量化的指数标示出来，以标签的形式告知消费者产品的碳信息。目前，国际主要的碳足迹估算是以自愿性参与为主，涵盖的产品主要为食品、电子消费品等。英国、加拿大和美国的碳标识市场发展较早，法国、德国、日本、韩国等国家近年来也加快了碳标识的发展。

尽管国际上有关碳标准标识制度在不断探索，但总体上仍呈现治理碎片化、标准不统一的特征。目前国际上关于碳中和、碳减排，具体到一家企业或者产品，在核算与认证方面并未建立统一的标准。相关认证管理工作处于分散化、碎片化态势。特别是在产品层面的碳排放标准（碳足迹）管理认证方面，目前主要是处在行业自治、企业自治的阶段，依靠苹果、宜家、大众等行业内的头部企业自行制定供应链管理标准对供应商提出碳管理要求，同时为满足头部企业开展碳排放管理标准互认和信用背书等方面的要求，一些非政府组织联合头部企业成立了一些非官方管理体系和行动倡议。关于产品碳足迹核算与认证，相关的技术标准主要有以下四个，跨国公司、头部企业、非政府组织成立的非官方体系，也主要是采用或者参照以下四个标准。

（1）ISO 国际标准。现有的 ISO 国际标准中，与单个产品或服务的碳足迹估算相关的是 ISO 14040（2009）和 ISO 14044（2006），ISO 14064（2006）与组织或企业尺度上的碳足迹测算相关，为组织和企业设定了碳足迹测量和验证的规范和指导。ISO 14065（2013）是对 ISO 14064 的补充，为采用 ISO 14064 或其他相关标准或规范进行 GHG 确认和验证机构的提供规范及指南，而 ISO 14067 标准，主要是为了解决碳足迹具体计算方法的问题，是由国际标准化组织参考 PAS 2050 编制的。

（2）PAS 2050 规范。《公众可获取的规范：商品和服务在生命周期内的温室气体排放评价规范》（PAS 2050:2011）是由碳信托（Carbon Trust）和英国环境、食品和乡村事务部（DEFRA）联合发起，英国标准协会（BSI）编制发布的一套公众可获取的规范，适用于多种类型的产品和行业，包括商品和服务；生产厂家、零售商和贸易商；企业到企业（B2B）以及企业到消费者（B2C）和国际供应链的碳足迹评估。产品碳足迹迄今运用较普遍的就是 PAS 2050 标准。

（3）IPCC 国家温室气体清单指南。IPCC 的《国家温室气体清单指南》提供了一种方法，可以分碳源和碳汇估算人为排放的国家清单。因此，研究系统的边界就相应地为国家的边界，因而并不遵循生命周期分析方法，但这些估算温室气体排放的排放因子和方法也能适用于生命周期评估的研究。

（4）WRI/WBSCD 的《产品和供应链标准》。世界资源研究所（WRI）和世界可持续发展工商理事会（WBCSD）于 2008 年年底拟定了《产品生命周期核算和报告标准》和《企业（范围 3/ 供应链）核算和报告标准》，合称《产品和供应链标准》。WRI/WBSCD 企业标准改变了产品碳足迹中完全使用生命周期评价方法的做法，开始允许甚至鼓励使用投入产出分析方法。

在这一领域需要特别关注部分有影响力的管理体系和倡议。在企业碳减排碳中和目标的制定和实施监督方面，主要靠企业自行制定目标并公开相关信息。目前，国际上也成立了一些为企业开展碳减排提供认证服务的非官方机构，如科学碳目标倡议（Science Based Target Initiative，SBTi），主要为企业制定碳减排目标提供信用背书，目前全球已有 4 151 家企业（包括中国 127 家企业）加入并接受 SBTi 的指导开展减排行动，其中 1 537 家企业作出了净零排放承诺。按照 SBTi 的原则，接受净零排放承诺的企业，最迟需要在 2050 年（电力行业为 2040 年）实现净零排放目标。百分之百可再生能源倡议（RE100）是由气候组织发起，与碳信息披露项目（Carbon Disclosure Project，CDP）合作，并联合了大众、苹果、微软等全球极具影响力的跨国企业，共同承诺将在尽可能短的时间（最晚到 2050 年）实现自身业务 100% 可再生电力，要求成员企业每年披露用电数据和目标进展。

欧盟在建立官方产品碳减排标准和管理体系方面走得比较靠前。欧盟正在加快开展相关立法，将开创先河，成为第一个对进入欧盟市场的产品（包括进口产品）提出碳排放认证管理，对相关产业的进出口贸易产生重要影响。欧盟是最早立法建立碳交易市场的政治实体，电力、钢铁、水泥、铝、化工、石化、航空等行业都被纳入碳交易市场，这些行业的企业都受到了碳排放配额管理，排放配额逐年收紧，并由免费向 100% 拍卖过渡，预计到 2030 年，所有排放配额都要通过拍卖有偿分配。近期，欧盟在《绿色新政》的框架下，陆续通过了新版电池法、碳边境调节机制及碳市场改革法案，并对能效指令、可再生能源指令进行了修订。按照电池法的要求，电池产业链从原材料的开采、采购和生产加工，到电池产品生产，再到废旧电池的回收与再利用，都要受到相关产品全生命周期碳足迹限额标准的管控。

我国碳排放统计核算标准体系刚刚起步。我国碳足迹认证管理方面起步比较晚，还未对产品市场准入提出碳足迹管理方面的要求。部分行业率先开展了探索和示范，如 2018 年《中国电器电子产品碳标签评价规范》《LED 道路照明产品碳标签》发布；2019 年"中国碳标签产业创新联盟"成立；2021 年中国电子节能技术协会发布《行业统一推行的产品碳标签自愿性评价实施规则（暂行）》；2022 年《企业碳标签评价通则》发布。我国正在构建完整统一规范的碳排放统计核算体系，正在逐步完善针对企业的碳排放统计核算体系，产品碳足迹认证管理方面，也将按照突出重点、梯次推进的工作节奏，聚焦于重点行业的原材料、半成品和成品，再逐步扩展至其他行业产品和服务类产品。在完善产品碳核算基础上，探索建立碳标签制度体系，引导消费者选择低排放产品和服务，倒逼全产业链减排。我国不少出口导向型企业已经受到来自供应链下游跨国公司（采购方）的约束，不得不按照采购方的要求开展相关管理，同时，随着欧盟电池法、碳边境调节税法的生效，以及新能源法完成修订，我国电池全产业链、光伏全产业链、钢铁、水泥、铝等行业不得不面临欧盟的碳排放管制。

二、碳足迹碳标签制度发展存在的突出问题

首先是企业应对被动。国际上官方没有达成共识，国内官方也未制定统一规范的技术标准，企业开展碳中和、碳减排缺乏规范的技术指引，提出碳中和、碳减排目标的企业"走出去"能否得到国际认可，在国内能否得到官方认可，都是未知数。与此同时，很多出口导向型企业不得不按照供应链下游采购方的要求开展企业或者产品层面碳足迹的管理，但因为出口市场不同，采购方不同，开展认证和管理的标准也不统一。随着欧盟相关立法的生效，国内涉及的电池全产业链、光伏全产业链、钢铁、水泥、铝等行业，需要针对对应欧盟的法规，进行相应碳排放管理，数据填报等方面的工作。目前欧洲采纳的标准体系，与国内企业目前正在采取的做法存在差异，也就是即使按照国内的相关要求在开展数据报送和管理，也有极大可能仍不满足欧盟对应标准体系的要求，国内企业需要重新去了解和适应。企业在这个过程中没有话语权，只能被动接受。标准不统一，标准之间缺乏协调和互认，使得我国的企业在工作中始终处在被动的地位，也给企业开展相应的碳排放管理和认证增加了难度和成本。

其次是制度性影响。我国部分绿色能源发达地区的资源优势不一定能转为规则优势。企业开展碳减排，对产品进行碳足迹认证，归根结底，底层的措施是一样的，主要包括提高能效、采用可再生能源、优化生产工艺、产品或原料替代

等，其中提高可再生能源的比例是公认的减排措施。但在实际操作中，因为具体技术标准和核算方法涉及如何认定、如何避免重复计算等问题，存在一家企业利用可再生能源或者采购绿色电力的做法，不一定能得到认可的问题。

（1）计算边界不同，很可能导致排放量被高估。以欧盟碳边境税相关制度为例，欧盟目前的核算标准，用的是欧盟碳交易市场对纳入企业的核算体系，按照这个体系，欧盟对进口的铝产品的碳含量是以纳入欧盟碳市场的氧化铝、预培阳极、电解铝、铸造几个工段的生产设施开展相应排放量核算，按照吨铝在各工段的平均排放量加总作为基准排放量。未来中国出口到欧盟的铝，即使国家碳市场即将纳入电解铝，实际上相比欧盟来说这也只是一个工序阶段，出口到欧盟，欧盟还是会计算四个工序的排放量。中国出口的铝的排放量的计算，实际比国内电解铝企业报告给国家主管机构的排放量要高。

（2）国内企业采购绿电、采购绿色电力证书，可能得不到国际认可。国内绿色电力市场处在发展期，相关政策协调不到位，目前国家对企业消耗电力产生的间接碳排放，会定期更新排放因子，排放因子的更新主要考虑的就是可再生能源比例的提升。电解铝生产企业在绿色电力丰富的地方设厂，通过采购绿色电力，能否在国家碳市场核算体系中得到完全的认可，目前也是一个未决问题，在欧盟看来，因为中国目前不能就如何避免绿色电力导致的减排的重复计算问题，因此欧盟目前也不认可企业采购绿电和绿证带来的减排效果，在计算铝的排放量的时候，仍然按照普通电力消耗量间接推算产品的碳排放量。

三、更好推动碳足迹碳标签制度发展的建议

未来无论是企业层面的碳排放管理，还是产品层面的碳排放管理，一旦上升到法律、标准、市场准入、供应链管理等维度，就会对行业、企业的市场竞争产生直接的影响，同时将对国家、区域和产业园的产业竞争力产生重大影响，需要提前谋划，积极应对。

一是应针对出口型企业进行深入摸底，识别容易受到国际供应链、欧盟等发达国家（地区）碳足迹管理认证影响的行业和企业，识别企业面临的主要问题。

二是深入研究和分析国际上主要的产品碳足迹认证标准和体系，找出关键点，对照我国碳排放核算体系的建设，积极参与我国碳排放核算体系标准的制定和讨论，确保国家相关标准体系能够兼容并发挥地方和产业的优势。

三是开展前瞻性研究，积蓄技术储备力量，为后续积极参与和推动国际相关

标准体系的互认作出地方和产业贡献。

四是基于国际供应链低碳化管理的趋势，以及国家"双碳"目标下产业发展新的形势，重新认识和定位地方优势产业，并对产业发展政策进行调整和优化，培育"双碳"目标下新的产业竞争优势。

作者：柴麒敏[1]

---

1 柴麒敏，国家应对气候变化战略研究和国际合作中心战略规划部主任、清华大学现代管理研究中心兼职研究员、中国环境科学学会碳达峰碳中和专委会副主任兼秘书长，主要研究方向为全球气候治理、应对气候变化综合评估及能源环境经济学。

建立碳排放"双控"制度的思考与展望

我国提出实现"双碳"目标要"统筹建立二氧化碳排放总量控制制度"。本章对碳排放总量控制制度的目标研判方法和分配方法进行了综述，调研国际相关制度实施并总结了对我国的经验借鉴，结合我国在行业、地方层面已实施的控制碳排放总量相关的制度和政策，提出建立碳排放"双控"制度的建议：①采用自上而下的宏观测算，通过设定未来经济、社会、能源发展、产业结构调整的不同情景，研判实现"2030 年前碳达峰并实现稳中有降"和"到 2035 年实现稳定下降"的碳排放总量的可能区间；②将"区域"和"部门"作为最主要的责任主体，合理采用目标分解方式；③对地方政府、部门行业、重点企业这三类不同的排放主体分别建立不同的配套制度；④建设相应的保障制度和数据支撑体系，保障好各项政策工具的顺利执行。

一、引言

我国已于 2015 年提出 2030 年前后碳排放达到峰值，2020 年将目标更新为力争 2030 年前达峰，并在 2021 年的"十四五"规划纲要中提出 2030 年要实现碳排放达峰后稳中有降。"十一五"以来，我国实施的是以碳强度和能耗强度作为约束性指标、能源消费总量为指导性目标的节能减排政策，并将相关目标以省级人民政府为对象进行分解和考核。这些措施虽然有效保障了我国 2009 年提出，到 2020 年单位 GDP 碳排放比 2005 年下降 40%～45% 的碳强度下降目标，但并未对碳排放总量的增长形成有效控制（图 24-1）。由于我国正处于工业化、城镇化的过程中，在 2030 年前控制碳排放增长速度、快速达峰并实现下降仍具有巨大挑战。

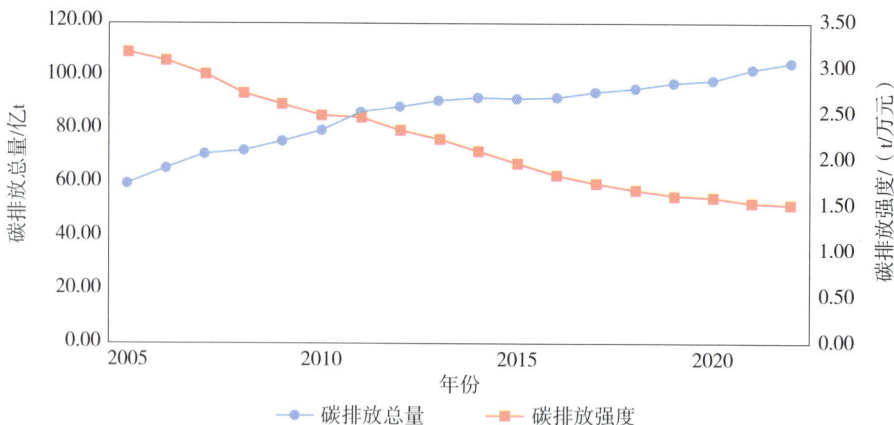

图 24-1　2005—2022 年我国碳排放总量和强度的变化情况[1]

　　碳排放总量控制指依据有关法律和规定，设定一个国家、地区或行业某一时间段的二氧化碳排放总量目标，使所有排放源实际的二氧化碳排放量总和控制在设定的目标之内。我国已将控制碳排放总量的思路纳入碳达峰碳中和的宏观政策文件，指出了碳排放总量控制制度的建设路径。中共中央、国务院印发的《关于完整准确全面贯彻新发展理念做好碳达峰碳中和工作的意见》强调中国将"统筹建立二氧化碳排放总量控制制度"，2021 年年底的中央经济工作会议提到出要创造条件尽早实现能耗"双控"向碳排放总量和强度"双控"转变，《国务院关于印发 2030 年前碳达峰行动方案的通知》提出对能源消费和碳排放指标实行协同管理、协同分解、协同考核。

　　然而，碳排放总量控制制度的基本要素和研究方法有哪些，如何将能耗"双控"向碳"双控"转变，目前还没有明确的政策安排。本章基于碳排放总量控制制度的相关研究综述、国际制度经验借鉴，以及我国已有实践的经验和挑战，提出符合我国国情的碳排放总量控制制度框架和政策建议。

二、研究方法综述

（一）目标研判方法

　　诸多研究机构、学者针对科学合理提出我国现阶段碳排放总量目标展开研究。清华大学《中国低碳发展转型战略及路径》报告提出，我国二氧化碳排放在2025 年前后进入峰值平台期，化石能源消费相关的二氧化碳峰值排放量控制在

1　指能源相关的碳排放总量和强度（2005 年 GDP 不变价），没有公开的统计数据，图中数据为作者根据能源和经济统计数据自行测算。

110 亿 t 之内 [1]。中国工程院《我国碳达峰碳中和战略及路径》报告指出，我国二氧化碳排放有望于 2027 年前后实现达峰，峰值控制在 122 亿 t 左右 [2]。张希良等 [3] 提出，能源相关碳排放在"十五五"中期达到峰值，峰值水平在 105 亿 t 以内，2035 年在峰值水平基础上下降 15% 左右。

从已有研究来看，确定碳排放总量目标的方法，包括自下而上、自上而下和混合方法三大类 [4-11]。基于宏观经济分析和政策规划方面的研究，较多采用自上而下模型，其典型代表是综合考虑人口、经济、社会与环境的 IPAT 模型、KAYA 模型、CGE 模型、系统动力学模型等。若较多关注能源系统则采用自下而上模型，以工程技术模型为出发点，对以能源消费和能源生产过程中所使用的技术为基础进行详细描述和仿真，并以能源消费、生产方式为主进行供需预测及环境影响分析，其典型代表是基于各种能源技术的 LEAP 模型、MARKAL 模型、MESSAGE 模型等。将自上而下与自下而上结合起来的混合模型，从能源的开采、转化、运输、市场到最终能源需求对排放过程进行模拟，通过系统仿真来预测各部门能源的供应能力、能源价格、需求量以及宏观经济参数。

从基年到目标年排放量预测，多采用趋势分析法、情景分析法、KAYA 分析法等，并结合国家或地区的减排责任和减排意愿等，综合考虑 GDP、人口、城镇化率、产业结构、能源结构等因素进行目标衔接，最终确定未来的排放目标，研究思路和方法如图 24-2 所示。

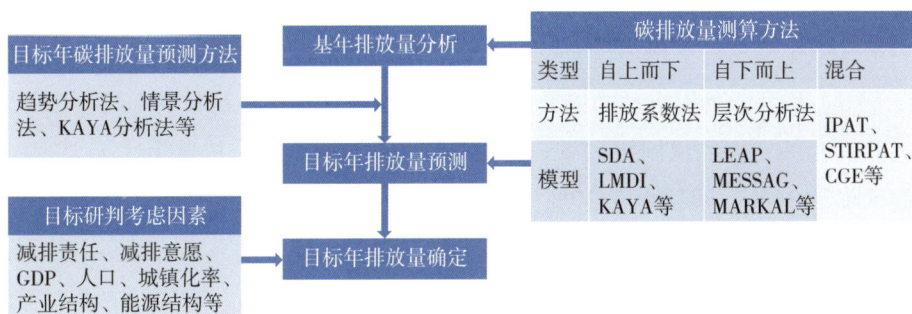

图 24-2　研判碳排放总量控制目标的框架

（二）目标分配方法

国家的碳排放总量目标需要分解到责任主体和排放主体进行落实，采取何种原则进行分配，以及采用何种方法进行测算，是制订分配方案的关键，本章对现有部分研究中的分配方案进行梳理。

1. 分配原则

在碳排放总量控制的前提下，公平和效率是碳排放分配的最主要原则 [12-13]。

其中，公平原则一般考虑地区之间人口数量和发展阶段的差异[14]，主要通过人均累积碳排放、人口、GDP、人均 GDP 和碳排放密度等体现[15]。效率原则的核心是产出最大化，指有利于使国家在既定的碳排放总量目标下产生更多的发展效益[14]，主要通过单位 GDP 能耗、单位 GDP 碳排放、碳生产力等体现[13]。除公平和效率原则外，部分学者在研究中还基于可行、能力、责任、有效、综合、偏重、经济指数、减排潜力等原则进行碳排放总量的分配[16-19]。

2. 分配方法

分配方法主要可分为指标体系法和模型分析法两类。指标体系法能够对影响碳排放总量的多个因素和指标进行全面考虑，指标选取较为灵活，是国内政策研究较多采取的一种省区间总量分配方法。另一类方法是构建多样化模型进行碳排放总量的分配，包括数据包络分析（DEA）模型、双寡头博弈模型、CGE 模型、双目标规划模型（BPM）等。还有部分学者对已有研究方法进行综合运用发展出混合模型，如综合调研、熵值法、K– 均值法、影子价格模型的多种分析方法[12, 14-26]。

三、国际经验借鉴

应对气候变化《京都议定书》签署后，主要发达国家为履行减排责任，积极采取多样化政策措施以实现温室气体减排目标，一些国家和地区建立了碳排放总量控制制度。例如，欧盟致力于做全球应对气候变化领军者，不断设定并强化以温室气体排放总量下降为核心指标的中长期气候目标，并以欧盟排放交易体系（EU ETS）和责任分担机制为主要抓手进行落实。在总量控制机制与可再生能源及能效等相关法规的协同推动下，欧盟 2020 年温室气体排放量相比于 1990 年大约下降了 31%，超额完成 20% 的目标，彰显出其总量控制体系的实效性。英国和法国都建立了分阶段的碳预算制度来支撑长期总量控制目标的落实，德国通过《联邦气候变化法》实现了总量目标在能源、工业、建筑、交通、农业等部门间的量化分配。美国加州、日本东京等也开展了次国家级的总量控制制度的探索和实践。国际相关制度的实施为我国开展相关工作提供了有益借鉴[27]。

（一）不断强化中长期温室气体总量控制目标，并通过立法增强约束性

2008 年，欧盟提出 2020 年前在 1990 年水平上在欧盟成员国范围内减排至少 20%；可再生能源占比上升至 20%；能效提升 20% 的具有法律约束力的气候目标（"20–20–20 目标"）[28]。2014 年，欧洲理事会在《关于 2030 的气

候和能源政策框架》中批准温室气体排放量到 2030 年至少在 1990 年基础上减少 40% 的约束性目标。2019 年，欧盟委员会发布的《欧洲绿色协议》提出更高的 2030 年气候目标，即将原降低 40% 提高到至少降低 55%，同时正式宣布 2050 年气候中和目标。2021 年 6 月通过的《欧洲气候法》，进一步提升了 2030 年和 2050 年气候目标的法律约束性[29]。

英国是全球立法应对气候变化的先行者之一，2008 年出台全球首部《气候变化法案》（Climate Change Act，CCA），规定英国 2050 年温室气体排放量在 1990 年基础上至少降低 80%，在目标调整机制下，2019 年 CCA 修订版，将目标提高至 100%，即英国将于 2050 年实现净零排放。CCA 设定了英国到 2050 年的具有法律约束力的气候目标，同时对目标的调整、阶段性目标的设定及目标实施进展评估等事项作机制性安排，即碳预算机制[30]。

（二）对总体目标进行区域、部门或行业分解，并建立制度促进各排放主体减排

欧盟以集体交付的方式实现温室气体减排目标[31]，如图 24-3 所示，将排放源（吸收汇）分为①电力、能源密集型工业、国际航空（2012 年纳入）等大型排放源，② EU ETS 之外的小型工业源、建筑、其他交通、农业、废弃物等其他排放源，③土地利用、土地利用变化和林业（LULUCF）部门，建立部门和国别结合的目标分解方案，并分别通过 EU ETS、责任分担机制和 LULUCF 条例等制度，支撑排放目标和分解方案的落实。

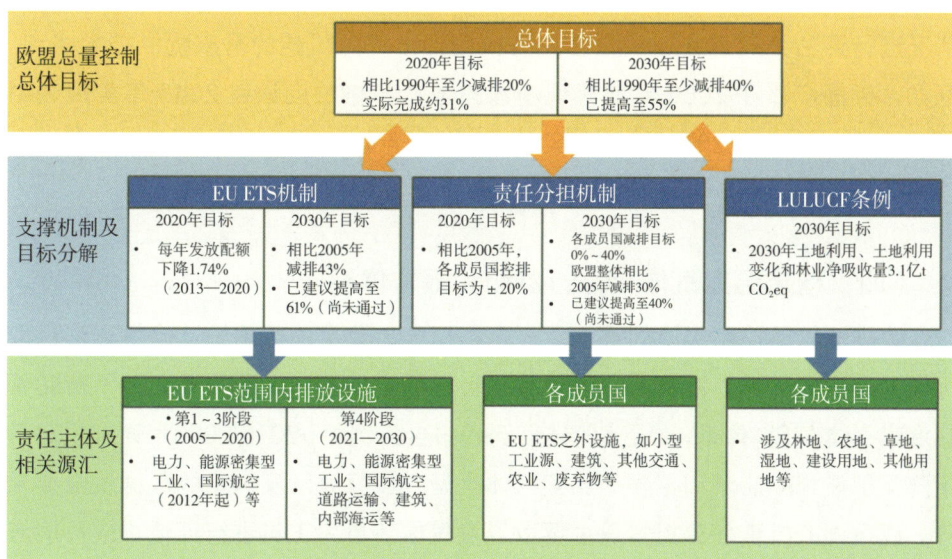

图 24-3 欧盟总量控制落实机制及目标分解方案

（三）在体制机制安排上，实施目标制定、分解落实到进展评估的闭环管理

英国碳预算工作机制[32]安排体现为目标制定、目标分解和开展落实行动、目标实施进展评估，以及更新目标等全流程，同时涵盖了英国议会、政府和气候变化委员会（Climate Change Committee，CCC）的不同职能，如图24-4所示。

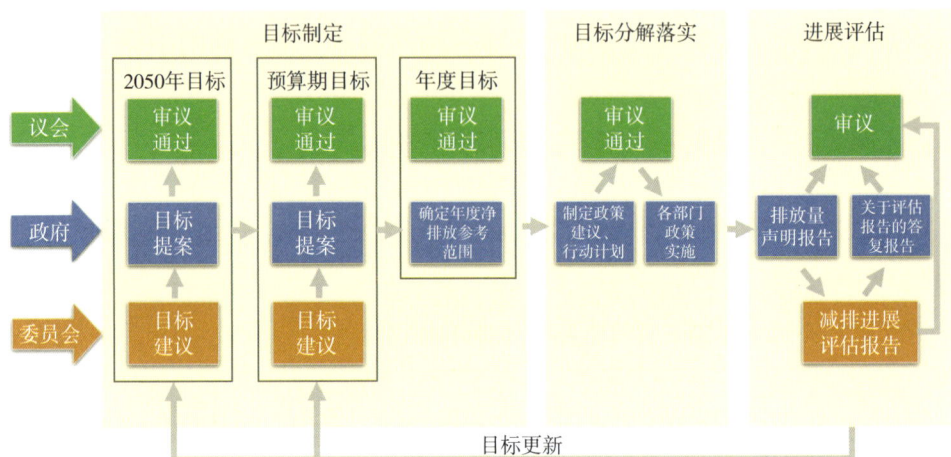

图 24-4　英国碳预算相关工作机制

值得注意的是，CCC 是英国根据 CCA 专门成立的、由专家构成的第三方机构，其主要职责包括：①就碳预算的目标向政府提出建议，②就碳预算的实施情况进行评估并向议会提供报告，③根据国家权力机构的需求提供技术咨询。例如，英国应该在 2050 年前实现净零排放、苏格兰应该在 2045 年实现碳中和，而威尔士应在 2050 年之前实现 95% 的温室气体减排等目标建议均出自 CCC[33]。

（四）构建温室气体核算、监测和报告体系

碳排放总量控制实施的难点之一是以统一、公平的数据统计核算方法获取可信的碳排放数据，以及准确评估减排目标的进展情况。欧盟建立并不断完善其温室气体 MRV 体系，《温室气体监测和报告条例》（2018/2066）详细规定了不同类型设施应监测和报告的温室气体类型、核算方法及满足的数据质量要求等。成员国减排责任分担情况主要以温室气体清单为工具进行评估，成员国应建立并运行国家温室气体清单系统，在 3 月 15 日之前提交其 X–2 年温室气体

清单，并配合欧盟汇总编制汇总的温室气体清单，以便及时向 UNFCCC 提交。同时，还应报告 X–1 年的估算清单，欧盟委员会应汇总后在当年 9 月向公众发布。

四、我国实践经验与挑战

我国在行业和地方层面实施了碳排放总量控制相关的政策。行业层面上依托碳排放权交易制度对重点行业、重点企业进行排放总量的控制。从 2011 年起启动了北京、上海、湖北等 7 个省市的碳排放权交易试点，2017 年起正式启动全国碳市场建设，2021 年起正式启动电力行业的碳排放权线上交易。

地方层面上支持低碳试点省市探索碳排放总量控制[34]。2016 年，北京市"十三五"规划《纲要》提出"十三五"碳排放强度累计下降 20.5%、碳排放总量达峰的双控目标，把全市节能减碳约束性控制目标纵向分解到各区，将能耗双控目标横向分解到各行业部门，还为 51 家重点用能单位、800 多家重点排放单位分别下达了能耗双控目标和碳排放双控目标[35]。上海提出全市碳排放总量与人均碳排放于 2025 年之前达到峰值，至 2035 年控制碳排放总量较峰值减少 5%，从目标、手段、政策、管理方面对碳排放总量控制进行探索[36]。武汉 2017 年以市政府文件形式出台了《武汉市碳排放达峰行动计划（2017—2022 年）》，把到 2022 年的碳排放达峰目标分三步走进行双向分解，既分到领域层面，如工业、建筑、交通、能源等，也分解到区县层面，还落实到责任单位，每两年对进展情况进行一次评估和考核[37]。

上述实践和探索为逐步建立国家二氧化碳排放总量控制制度提供了宝贵经验和制度实施基础。实施过程中也逐渐暴露出减排工作缺乏上位法律保障、落实机制和管理手段不足、数据核算体系不完善等问题。

五、建立碳排放"双控"制度的建议

从当前的能耗"双控"过渡到碳排放总量控制，需要结合碳达峰碳中和与高质量发展的需求，设立总量控制目标，即建立该制度的政策目标，并为此匹配相应的政策工具，从而将相关政策对象纳入实施，同时，为了保证目标和制度实施效果，还需要定期评估目标完成情况和制度实施进展、及时更新调整目标分解和制度设计，形成全过程管理的目标设立、制度体系、评估更新的管理流程。

基于上述研究，以总量控制制度作为支撑实现碳达峰碳中和的顶层制度为核心，提出落实碳排放总量控制全流程制度框架（图24-5），形成不同责任主体"共同但有区别"地规范和约束温室气体排放机制，提高温室气体排放空间作为稀缺资源的有效利用。具体如下：

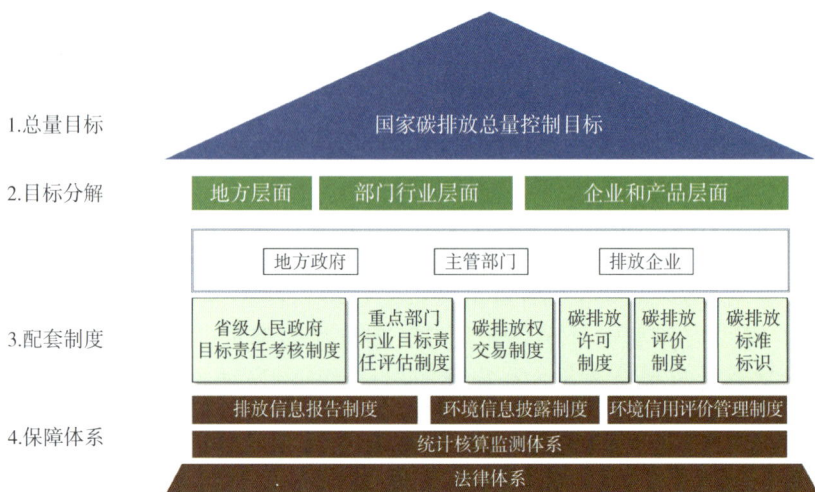

图 24-5　碳排放总量控制制度框架

（一）科学制定国家碳排放总量控制目标

针对国家碳达峰碳中和总体目标需求，研判未来一段时期（2030年、2035年等关键年份）的排放量控制目标，并进行每五年阶段性分解和年度分解。

科学制定总量目标，需要在宏观经济社会发展层面，将碳排放目标与高质量发展、能源革命等目标做好衔接。因此，建议采用自上而下的宏观测算，通过设定未来经济、社会、能源发展、产业结构调整的不同情景，研判实现"2030年前碳达峰并实现稳中有降"和"到2035年实现稳定下降"的碳排放总量的可能区间。再统筹考虑碳强度、能源消费、能源结构、环境保护等因素的变化趋势和转型难度，确定科学合理的总量控制目标。

（二）将碳排放总量目标进行科学分配

依据排放源特征及责任的不同，相关主体包括中央政府、地方政府、主管部门、企业和社会公众等，需要将总量控制目标进行差异化的分配，为其中主要的排放主体设置一定的排放目标。

参考国内外相关实践和研究，对碳排放总量目标进行分配，包括区域分解、行业分解、区域和行业分解相结合但不重复、区域和行业双分解且同时管理四类。其中，区域分解主要是指针对省、市或下辖区级人民政府的主体责任，根据指标体系法或构建模型，综合考虑公平、效率和能力原则，进行下辖区域分解；行业分解则是针对主管部门的相关责任，考虑工业、建筑、交通等部门的排放特点和排放趋势，确定工信、住建、交通和林业等部门的排放目标和管理措施。

（三）建立落实机制和配套制度

碳排放目标通过不同的落实机制和配套制度来推动相关责任主体的实施，参考国内外研究和实践经验，着重讨论适用于地方政府、部门行业、重点企业等责任主体的配套制度。

对于地方政府，将已有的以省级人民政府为主体落实碳强度目标和能耗双控目标的目标责任制，过渡为温室气体总量控制目标责任考核制度为主体的制度体系，总结国家层面碳强度下降目标考核、能源双控考核、地方层面碳排放总量控制考核等实践经验，发挥相关专业人员、能力和技术优势，加快过渡至碳排放总量目标考核。

对于部门行业，探索建立重点部门行业目标责任评估机制，并进一步扩大碳排放权交易制度的覆盖范围，加强对重点行业排放配额的管控。

对于重点企业，探索建立温室气体排放许可制度、评价制度及标准标识体系，利用温室气体排放许可制度推动形成归属清晰、权责明确、监管有效的排放权产权制度，推动生产要素低碳转型；利用重大建设项目碳排放评价制度，严格控制重大固定资产投资项目造成的温室气体排放增量，推动重大工程项目投资及建设的低碳转型；完善碳排放管理标准体系，通过行业排放标准、技术标准、产品标准等措施，促进工业、能源、建筑、交通的低碳发展。

（四）完善相关的保障体系

为保障好各项政策工具的顺利执行，需要建设相应的保障制度和数据支撑体系。一是要构建完善的应对气候变化相关法律法规体系，明确碳排放量的法律属性和各个主体的法律责任与义务，为制度实施提供法律依据。二是进一步完善温室气体 MRV 体系建设，提升基础数据的真实性和准确性，确保核算结果的科学性、可比性和可评估。三是加强信息公开工作，既有利于接受社会和舆论监督，也是顺应国际社会对透明度等相关要求的必要措施。例如，建立关于温室气体排放情况的定期公报制度，环境信息披露、环境信用评价等制度，为控制碳排放总量工作营造良好的社会环境。

作者：杨秀[1]，杨姗姗[2]，郭豪[3]

参考文献

[1] 项目综合报告编写组.《中国长期低碳发展战略与转型路径研究》综合报告 [J]. 中国人口·资源与环境，2020，30（11）：1-25.

[2] 中国青年报客户端. 中国工程院：我国有望 2027 年实现碳达峰，2060 年前 实现碳中和 [EB/OL]. https：//m.gmw.cn/baijia/2022-04-01/1302876708.html，2022-04-01/2022-08-12.

[3] 张希良，黄晓丹，张达，等. 碳中和目标下的能源经济转型路径与政策研究 [J]. 管理世界，2022，38（1）：35-66.

[4] 刘冬梅，陈颖，时进钢. 我国温室气体环境影响评价 CO_2 排放量估算方法研究 [C] // 2012 中国环境科学学会学术年会论文集（第一卷）. 北京：中国农业大 学出版社，2012：892-896.

[5] KAYA Y. Impact of carbon dioxide emission on GNP growth：Interpretation of proposed scenario[R]. Paris：IPCC Energy and Industry Subgroup，Response Strategies Working Group，1990.

[6] 朱宇恩，李丽芬，贺思思，等. 基于 IPAT 模型和情景分析法的山西省碳排放 峰值年预测 [J]. 资源科学，2016，38（12）：2316-2325.

[7] 李强，左静娴. 基于 STIRPAT 模型的长江经济带碳排放峰值预测研究 [J]. 东 北农业大学学报（社会科学版），2017，15（5）：53-58.

[8] 唐杰，崔文岳，温照杰，等. 基于 Kaya 模型的碳排放达峰实证研究 [J]. 深圳 社会科学，2022，5（3）：50-59.

[9] 陈丽君，吴红梅，范玲，等. 浙江省碳排放峰值判断及其对策研究 [J]. 中国能 源，2017，39（4）：43-47.

---

1 杨秀，清华大学气候变化与可持续发展研究院副研究员，主要研究领域为能源与气候变化。

2 杨姗姗，清华 - 力拓资源能源与可持续发展联合研究中心高级工程师，主要研究领域气候变化政策和 温室气体排放。

3 郭豪，清华大学气候变化与可持续发展研究院助理研究员，主要研究领域为能源与气候变化。

[10] 高新宇 . 北京市可再生能源综合规划模型与政策研究 [D]. 北京工业大学，
    2011.

[11] 洪竞科，李沅潮，郭偲悦 . 全产业链视角下建筑碳排放路径模拟：基于
    RICE-LEAP 模型 [J]. 中国环境科学，2022，42（9）：4389-4398.

[12] 程纪华 . 中国省域碳排放总量控制目标分解研究 [J]. 中国人口·资源与环
    境，2016，26（1）：23-30.

[13] 何永贵，闫家琦 . 基于效率与公平的我国区域碳排放权初始分配研究 [J]. 华
    北电力大学学报（社会科学版），2020（5）：26-32.

[14] 熊小平，康艳兵，冯升波，等 . 碳排放总量控制目标区域分解方法研究 [J].
    中国能源，2015，37（11）：15-19.

[15] 王文举，陈真玲 . 中国省级区域初始碳配额分配方案研究——基于责任与目
    标、公平与效率的视角 [J]. 管理世界，2019，35（3）：81-98.

[16] 田云，林子娟 . 巴黎协定下中国碳排放权省域分配及减排潜力评估研究 [J].
    自然资源学报，2021，36（4）：921-933.

[17] 裴晨雯，屈卓然，刘若彬 . 中国省际碳排放权的初始分配 [J]. 科学技术创新，
    2021（22）：25-27.

[18] Cheng Y L, Gu B H, Tan X C, et al. Allocation of provincial carbon
    emission allowances under China's 2030 carbon peak target: A
    dynamic multi-criteria decision analysis method[J]. Science of The Total
    Environment, 2022, 837: 155798.

[19] 张浩然，李玮 . 区域碳排放权减排分配机制设计——基于 1.5℃温升目标 [J].
    科技管理研究，2020，40（14）：227-236.

[20] 吴军，李曼，徐广姝，等 . 碳排放总量控制下行业间碳配额分配的博弈机制研
    究 [J]. 北京化工大学学报（自然科学版），2020，47（6）：115-120.

[21] 柴麒敏，傅莎，郑晓奇，等 . 中国重点部门和行业碳排放总量控制目标及政策
    研究 [J]. 中国人口·资源与环境，2017，27（12）：1-7.

[22] 杜莉，张云 . 我国碳排放总量控制交易的分配机制设计——基于欧盟排放交
    易体系的经验 [J]. 国际金融研究，2013（7）：51-58.

[23] 解瑞丽，郑彦强，苏旭东 . 关于实施碳排放总量控制制度的思考 [J]. 中国环
    保产业，2020（7）：13-17.

[24] 卞勇，刘宇 . 建立碳排放总量控制制度 [J]. 开放导报，2021（5）：14-20.

[25] 田丹宇，郑文茹，高诗颖 . 加快构建碳排放总量控制的长效机制 [J]. 环境保
    护，2020，48（12）：55-57.

[26] 王金南，蔡博峰，曹东，等 . 中国 CO_2 排放总量控制区域分解方案研究 [J].
环境科学学报，2011，31（4）：680-685.

[27] 杨姗姗，郭豪，杨秀，等 . "双碳" 目标下建立碳排放总量控制制度的思考与
展望 [J]. 气候变化研究进展 ，2023，19（2）：191-202.

[28] Official Journal of the European Union. Effort Sharing Decision[EB/OL].
http：//data.europa.eu/eli/dec/2009/406/oj，2009/2022-07-12.

[29] European Union. European Climate Law [EB/OL]. https：//climate.
ec.europa.eu/eu-action/european-green-deal/european-climate-law_en.
2021/2022-07-12.

[30] UK Parliament. Climate Change Act 2008 [EB/OL]. https：//www.
legislation.gov.uk/ukpga/2008/27/contents，2008/2022-07-12.

[31] Official Journal of the European Union. Effort Sharing Regulation[EB/OL].
http：//data.europa.eu/eli/reg/2018/842/oj，2018/2022-07-12.

[32] Climate Change Committee. The Sixth Carbon Budget The UK's path to
Net Zero [R/OL]. https：//www.theccc.org.uk/publication/sixth-carbon-
budget，2020/2022-07-12.

[33] Climate Change Committee. 2022 Progress Report to Parliament [R/
OL]. https：//www.theccc.org.uk/publication/2022-progress-report-to-
parliament/ 2022/2022-07-12.

[34] 杨秀，田丹宇，周泽宇，等 . 我国区域低碳发展的实践进展与建议 [J]. 环境
保护，2018，46（15）：15-21.

[35] 北京市人民政府 . 北京市 "十三五" 时期节能降耗和应对气候变化规划
[EB/OL]. http：//fgw.beijing.gov.cn/fgwzwgk/zcgk/ghjhwb/wnjh/202204/
t20220413_2676116.htm，2016-08-07.

[36] 上海市人民政府 . 上海市城市总体规划（2017—2035 年）[EB/OL]. https：
//www.shanghai.gov.cn/nw42806/index.html，2018-01-17.

[37] 武汉市人民政府 . 市人民政府关于印发武汉市碳排放达峰行动计划（2017—
2022 年）的通知（武政〔2017〕36 号）[EB/OL]. http：//fgw.wuhan.gov.
cn/zfxxgk/zfxxgk_1/zc/202001/t20200117_1477235.html，2018-01-04.

"双碳"背景下浙江蓝碳领域的机遇和挑战 [1]

海洋作为地球上最大的碳库与巨大的潜在碳中和场所，日益受到重视。本章聚焦于不同海洋生态系统特色及所处空间差异，分析了海洋碳汇的原理与现实意义，重点回顾了滨海湿地碳汇研究的国内外进展，指出了浙江省蓝碳研究的重点区域和重心工作。

海洋是高质量发展的战略要地。党的二十大报告提出"发展海洋经济，保护海洋生态环境，加快建设海洋强国"。地处长三角一体化发展国家战略区域的浙江省，正在为高质量发展中实现中国特色社会主义共同富裕先行和省域现代化先行而踔厉奋进。作为"两山理论"的萌发地，绿色低碳、人与自然和谐共生已经成为浙江全社会的共识。浙江有 4.4 万 km² 的海域面积，海洋碳汇工作部署，不仅是科技创新牵引下实现海洋生态系统保护修复的重要组成部分，也是深入贯彻落实党中央、国务院关于碳达峰碳中和的重大战略部署的省域探索。

一、海洋碳汇原理与现实意义

发展海洋碳汇是有效应对气候变化的重大战略。海洋储存了地球上约 93%（约为 40 万亿 t）的二氧化碳，是地球上最大的碳库，每年可清除 25% 以上排放到大气中的二氧化碳 [2]，对减少大气 CO_2、缓解全球气候变暖、支持生物多样性起到至关重要的作用，是碳中和重要的实现路径。海洋碳汇（又称"蓝碳"）指利用海洋对海洋化碳的溶解作用及海洋生物光合作用吸收大气中的二氧化碳，将其固定、储存在海洋中的过程，已成为全世界减缓和适应气候变化的重要抓手。为实现 2060 年碳中和的宏伟目标，减排的同时增强自然生态系统的碳汇功

1　本章内容系浙江省领雁计划：海洋"蓝碳"生态系统增汇关键技术与示范应用（课题编号：2023C03120）和东海实验室预研项目："舟山岛群海洋生态系统碳储量及'蓝碳'增汇潜力评估"（课题编号：DH2022ZY0006）的部分研究成果。

能是实现碳中和目标的必然途径[19]。我国在《中共中央　国务院关于加快推进生态文明建设的意见》《全国海洋主体功能区划》等文件中对发展海洋碳汇作出部署，提倡"充分发挥海洋碳汇的作用，发展海洋碳汇经济"。

巩固海岸带碳汇是实现碳中和目标的必要前提。地处陆海生态系统交错带的滨海湿地，生态环境的多样性造就了其丰富的生态系统生产力。滨海湿地中的红树林、盐沼、海草床等生态系统所固存的碳被称为海岸带"蓝碳"，海岸带蓝碳生态系统固碳速率极高，并具有长期持续的固碳能力[7]。从单位面积碳埋藏速率看，滨海湿地"蓝碳"系统的碳埋藏速率是陆地生态系统固碳速率的 15 倍，海洋生态系统固碳速率的 50 倍左右[15]。滨海湿地"蓝碳"碳汇功能是重要的基于海洋的气候变化治理手段，属于"基于自然的解决方案"[3, 22]，是解决人类目前所面临的气候变化问题的有效途径[6]。保护生态环境就是保护生产力，改善生态环境就是发展生产力。因此，对海岸带"蓝碳"来说，首先是要保护生态系统，保护千百年来自然界积累埋藏的碳库。

系统提升滨海湿地"蓝碳"功能是实现碳中和目标的有效手段。滨海湿地生态系统具有高人工可调控性和较强的恢复力[14, 20]。人类活动可以破坏这类"蓝碳"生态系统的固碳功能，也可以通过生态恢复来增加其"蓝碳"碳汇功能[5]。2022 年 6 月 24 日，科技部等八部委联合印发的《科技支撑碳达峰碳中和的实施方案（2022—2030）》在碳达峰碳中和管理决策支持行动中指出，加强科技创新对碳汇的技术体系和标准体系建设的支撑保障，为国家碳中和工作提供决策支撑。滨海湿地除固碳外，还具有防洪、侵蚀防治、食物供给、提供栖息地、清洁水质等多种生态功能，各生态功能间相互支持，构成滨海湿地生态系统的整体功能。全球范围滨海湿地生态服务功能价值高达数十亿美元[1]，特别是在固定大气 CO_2 和去除污染物方面的固碳除污功能显著，被誉为"地球之肾"。因此开展海岸带生态系统碳汇提升，需要在生态系统整体修复提升的总体框架下实现。

二、滨海湿地碳汇研究的国内外进展

滨海湿地虽然距离人类较近，但我们对滨海湿地"蓝碳"生态系统的碳汇分布格局、碳埋藏速率和过程机制还缺乏足够了解[13]。Macreadie 等总结了当前"蓝碳"研究尚未解决的十个重要问题[4]，其中涉及滨海湿地"蓝碳"功能的问题有 9 个，分别是：①气候变化如何影响"蓝碳"系统的碳累积？②人类干扰如何影响"蓝碳"系统的碳累积？③"蓝碳"生态系统的分布及其时空格局如何？④有机和无机碳循环过程如何影响碳排放？⑤如何估算"蓝碳"系统中碳的来源？⑥影响"蓝碳"系统中碳埋藏速率的因子有哪些？⑦"蓝碳"系统和大气的温室气体交换速率如何？⑧如何减少"蓝碳"估算中的不确定性？⑨管理措施如何维持并提升"蓝碳"固碳功能？这些科学问题既是当前研究热点，也是未来的主要研究方向。一项全球尺度滨海湿地"蓝碳"格局模拟预测的研究中预计：全球滨海湿地"蓝碳"系统碳埋藏能力到21世纪末将持续增加[15]。而我国由于缺乏国家尺度的滨海湿地"蓝碳"功能定量分析和预测评估，导致我国滨海湿地"蓝碳"资源尚未纳入国家碳汇交易和固碳减排体系中。

滨海湿地初级生产力高，且由于其地表常被水体浸没，沉积物通气性差，有利于有机质保存，因而被认为是有机碳的主要埋藏区域之一[12]。淤泥质滩涂在我国滨海湿地中比重突出，面积大大超过红树林和海草床湿地总面积之和，沉积物埋藏速率高、固碳潜力强。滩涂沉积物埋藏碳的主要来源是周边的盐沼湿地和红树林的碳输入，以及海水中颗粒有机碳和矿质结合碳组分的沉积，理应纳入滨海湿地"蓝碳"碳汇计量体系[22]。

滨海湿地中微生物作用影响着沉积碳的埋藏效率。滨海湿地被固定于沉积物中的有机碳因微生物活动发生降解，以温室气体形式释放到大气中，而剩余的部分有机碳最终会在沉积物中以难降解有机质的形式长期沉积和封存，计算这部分有机质的沉积速率和在沉积物中的周转时间，对于完善滨海湿地碳埋藏的模式具有重要意义。沉积有机碳的埋藏效率还受多种宏观因子影响，如盐度、沉积物温度、植被类型和生物量、土地利用方式、氧化还原条件等[16]。目前针对滨海湿地有机碳埋藏、转化的研究主要是利用有机碳总量来描述碳循环组成，但微观上从滨海湿地微生物与有机碳相互作用耦合过程角度的研究十分有限，限制了对滨海湿地有机碳埋藏机制的理解[8, 10]。其中一个尚不确定的重要问题是，滨海湿地沉积物中微生物群落的垂向分布及其对有机碳封存效率的影响因子是什么？是气候变化导致的，还是自然变化引起的？

焦念志院士等指出研究和实施海洋"负排放"是实现碳中和的重要途径[19]，并提出海洋"负排放"相关的基本途径与案例（图25-1）。唐启升院士、张继红等界定了碳汇渔业[21, 24]，是指通过渔业生产活动促进水生生物吸收水体中 CO_2，并通过收获把这些已经转化为生物产品的碳移出水体的过程。尽管渔业碳汇的量级、计量方法等还没有达成共识，但通过养护渔业和生物多样性，优化绿色养殖带来的碳汇提升应该是一条重要的途径。

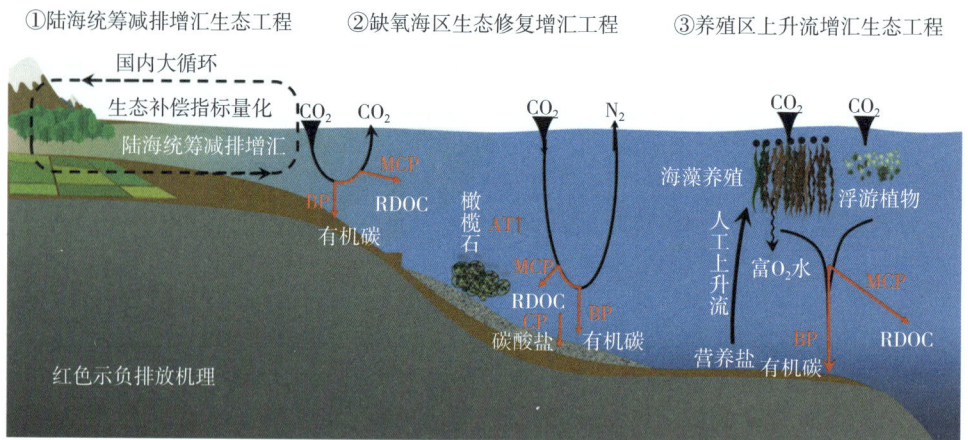

① 陆海统筹减排增汇生态工程　② 缺氧海区生态修复增汇工程　③ 养殖区上升流增汇生态工程

注：AT——碱度，BP——生物泵，MCP——微生物碳泵，CP——碳酸盐泵，RDOC——惰性溶解有机碳

图 25-1　海洋负排放生态工程案例示意图 [19]

相较于陆地绿碳，"蓝碳"的优势体现在封存时效长、捕获效率高、生态环境效益显著三个方面。IPCC 2019 年发布的《气候变化中的海洋与冰冻圈特别报告》强调"蓝碳"是易于管理的海洋生态系统所有生物驱动碳通量及存量。滨海湿地的"蓝碳"功能具有面积小、储量大的特点。其中的淤泥质滩涂湿地则由于具有较高的初级生产力、较低有机质分解速率及较高的物质埋藏速率，被称为缓解全球变暖的重要"蓝碳"资源，日益引起重视。如前文所述，淤泥质滩涂和盐沼是浙江省滨海湿地的主要类型，针对这一特点，海洋二所领衔在浙江省率先开展了淤泥质滩涂碳库研究，为自然资源部将淤泥质滩涂的碳汇功能推广到全国提供了先导性科技支撑。

滨海淤泥质滩涂的土壤有机碳库作为湿地碳库系统的一部分，其演变过程不仅与土壤、植被与人类活动等要素有关，而且受到水文潮汐系统以及沉积与埋藏条件等因素的影响（图 25-2），同时亦受到气候变化引起的海平面上升，互花米草入侵改变沉积物碳氮库，以及来自海上的其他海洋碳库的影响。加强滨海淤泥质海滩的科学研究，保护现存湿地生态系统结构与功能的完整性，停止破坏性的淤泥质海滩开发活动，恢复和新建滨海湿地生态系统，增强其"蓝碳"生态系统服务功能对中国早日实现碳中和目标具有重要意义。

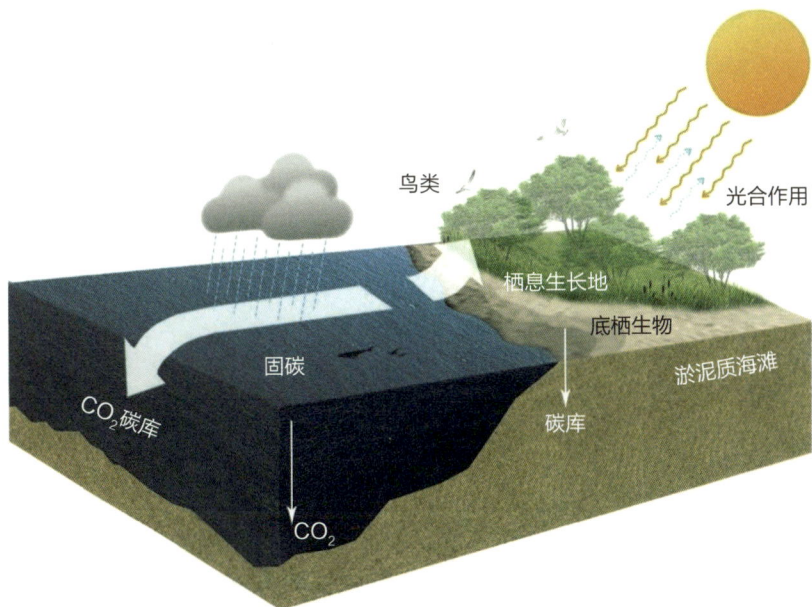

图 25-2 淤泥质海滩的碳汇功能 [23]

三、浙江省"蓝碳"工作的机遇挑战

浙江省滨海湿地总面积 295.06 km²，其中滩涂 217.40 km²，占 73.68%，盐沼 76.60 km²，占 25.96%，滩涂和盐沼是浙江省滨海湿地的主要类型，也是浙江省开展滨海湿地"蓝碳"研究应着重关注的生态系统。

对浙江省而言，在推动实现人与自然和谐共生高质量发展的进程中，海洋碳汇发展应遵循因地制宜、统筹兼顾的原则。包括在摸清全省"蓝碳"本底基础上，建立健全海洋碳汇监测体系、协调推进海洋生态保护修复与海洋碳汇优化提升、开展海洋碳汇基础研究、推动海洋碳汇价值实现、建设"蓝碳"示范基地试点等路径。从浙江省自身海洋地理与生态禀赋出发，本着尊重自然、顺应自然、保护自然的生态文明要求，未来"蓝碳"工作可着重关注如下几点：

（一）重视陆域物质输入和水文生态过程对盐沼及淤泥质滩涂的固碳能力影响

陆地入海河流带来的数以亿吨计的淤泥或粉砂随着海拔降低而逐渐堆积在河口海岸带，在潮水动力和水沙盐效应共同作用下，沿海岸线，特别是海湾区形成了坡度较缓的淤泥质海滩，同时也带来了大量的营养物质，为滨海"蓝碳"提供了空间和物质基础。河流是淤泥质海滩的生命源，海洋潮汐和波浪系统是塑造淤泥质海滩的主要动力。根据潮汐过程中海水能到达的位置将淤泥质海滩分为：①不受潮汐影响的潮上带海滩；②只有在大潮时才被海水淹没的高潮区；③小潮高潮线和小潮低潮线之间的潮间带地区；④只有在大潮落潮的短时间内露出水面的低潮区；⑤一直受潮汐影响的潮下带海滩（图 25-3）。周而复始的潮汐运动，再加上从陆地河流运移过来的丰富有机质和营养物质，使得淤泥质海滩逐渐生长了盐沼植物，植物的生长发育和演替逐渐构成了海边的绿洲。

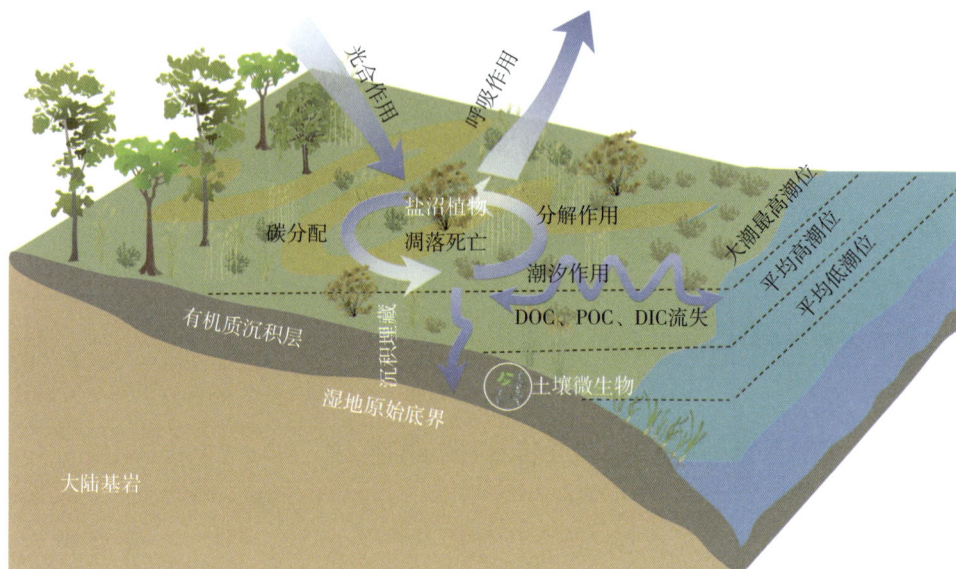

图 25-3　潮汐作用下盐沼湿地固碳关键过程[18]

注：包括盐沼植物的光合作用及光合产物分配、碳沉积埋藏、土壤碳矿化分解、DOC/POC/DIC 流失等。

在滨海湿地生态系统中，如果把红树林、海草床比作"影视明星"，那光滩就是"群众演员"。"明星"虽亮，但面积小，碳汇总量小，光滩看起来荒凉，但面积大，碳汇总量相当可观。与一般人的想象不一样，光滩实际也是充满生机的海洋高生产力区。淤泥质光滩表面生长着丰富的、肉眼不可见的底栖硅藻等微型生物，这些微型生物通过光合作用合成有机碳的能力与红树林、盐沼群落不相上下。同时，泥质光滩也截留了大量来自海上的藻类等有机物，因此有大量的泥螺、蛏子、弹涂鱼等海洋生物在此繁衍生息。

然而不合理的围填海或其他海洋开发等人类活动，以及受全球变化的影响，滩涂容易受到外来物种入侵影响，生态价值可能发生改变。因此，对盐沼、淤泥质滩涂湿地进行水—沙—植被—沉积一体的水文生态学和生物地球化学研究是系统认识滨海湿地的重要途径。

（二）兼顾海洋生态系统保护修复与固碳增汇的协同增效

维护和发展海洋蓝色碳汇、稳步提升海洋碳汇能力是助力我国实现碳达峰碳中和目标的重要工作。2021 年，《中共中央　国务院关于完整准确全面贯彻新发展理念做好碳达峰碳中和工作的意见》和《国务院关于印发 2030 年前碳达峰行动方案的通知》相继发布，均提出整体推进海洋生态系统保护和修复，提升红树林、海草床、盐沼等固碳能力。自然资源部、国家发展改革委、国家林草局联合印发《海岸带生态保护和修复重大工程建设规划（2021—2035 年）》，提出了整治修复滨海湿地和海岸带生态系统碳汇增量的工作目标。生态环境部正组织实施海洋碳汇监测评估、开展海岸带碳通量监测等，探索以增强气候韧性和提升蓝色碳汇增量为导向的海洋生态保护修复新模式。

"十四五"时期，我国将更注重科技创新与治理能力提升，特别是加快补齐基础性、关键性的能力短板，加强海洋生态环境领域能力建设，打造开放式科技创新平台等。在海洋碳汇方面，自然资源部、生态环境部等部门将会在沿海加强海洋应对气候变化监测与评估，组织海洋—大气二氧化碳交换通量监测评估、重点海域碳储量监测评估，加强缺氧、酸化等海洋生态环境风险的监测预警；增强海洋生态系统的气候韧性，将碳中和与适应气候变化指标纳入红树林、海草床、盐沼、淤泥质光滩等典型海洋生态系统保护修复监管范畴等。

浙江省布局盐沼、淤泥质滩涂蓝碳增汇技术研究将有力推动我国加快研发和布局前瞻性、颠覆性海岸带"蓝碳"增汇技术。将"蓝碳"与海岸带生态系统重大生态保护修复工程相结合，实现生态保护修复与固碳增汇协同增效。空间协调匹配的行业布局将在碳中和实现进程中日益受到重视。

（三）重视海洋保护地碳汇功能在碳中和目标实现进程中的引领作用

党的十九大提出建立以国家公园为主体的自然保护地体系的重大改革任务，构建以国家公园为主体、自然保护区为基础、各类自然公园为补充的自然保护地分类系统。党的二十大报告对生态文明建设作出了进一步战略部署，明确要提升生态系统多样性、稳定性、持续性。自然保护地是生态文明建设的核心载体，也是我国生态安全体系中最具多样性、稳定性和持续性的宝藏。海洋自然保护地在保护海洋生物多样性，提升海洋生态系统稳定性和生物量方面发挥着重要作用。通过生态环境保护、修复和生物多样性养护等人为努力，保护地生态系统结构与功能得到加强，生态系统碳库储量随保护地生物总量提升而得以增加，即碳汇功能得到提升。有效识别并充分发挥自然保护地碳汇功能，提升自然保护地在实现碳中和目标中的作用。推动自然保护地碳汇交易机制与交易平台建设，将兼具推动生物多样性保护和提升碳汇功能的双重作用。杭州湾国家湿地公园、洞头国家级海洋公园等自然公园是浙江省内重要的海洋自然保护地，也是浙江省重要的"蓝碳"载体。南麂列岛、韭山列岛两个国家级海洋自然保护区，中街山列岛、五峙山鸟岛等岛屿类型海洋保护地周边上升流生态系统发育。岛屿上升流生态系统碳载荷、存贮时间、碳垂直与水平通量等问题，是整体开展浙江海岛生态系统"蓝碳"潜力评估的领头阵地，也是中国为全球丰富"蓝碳"管理的重要平台。

（四）推动海洋碳汇价值实现机制和"蓝碳"示范基地试点

海洋"蓝碳"生态系统增汇的确定、核算与管理存在 3 个技术难题：一是基于多时空数据的滨海湿地生态系统的碳汇多维评估技术；二是基于自然的"蓝碳"巩固提升和工程负排放协同增汇修复技术；三是政策引导—空间管控—行业协作"三位一体"最优碳汇管理模式构建技术。

基于自然的解决方案着眼于长期可持续发展目标，为协调经济发展和生态环境保护，促进人与自然和谐共生提供了新思想。基于自然的解决方案有 8 个准则，其中基于尺度设计、生物多样性净增长和生态系统完整性、包容性治理、适应性管理、主流化与可持续性等准则都在国际环境治理方面取得了很好的成效。在提升盐沼、淤泥质滩涂滨海湿地"蓝碳"碳汇功能的研究与工程实践中，贯彻基于自然的解决方案将助力生态文明建设与高质量发展。

围绕"浙江海域蓝碳生态系统特点及固碳增汇关键驱动因子"和"浙江近海湿地生态系统保护修复与'蓝碳'增汇协同增效的科学原理"两个科学问题，瞄准"蓝碳"生态系统增汇的确定、核算与管理中亟待解决的瓶颈问题，通过自然科学认知难点突破与关键技术攻关，研发基于多源多时空数据的滨海湿地生态系统碳汇多维评估技术，发展基于自然的"蓝碳"巩固提升和工程负排放协同增汇修复技术，形成政策引导—空间管控—行业协作"三位一体"最优碳汇管理模式，架构基于自然的海洋生态修复与碳汇提升系统解决方案，提升海洋"蓝碳"生态工作绩效。

作者：陈建芳[1]，曾江宁[2]，金海燕[3]，于培松[4]，刘诚刚[5]

参考文献

[1] Costanza R，Pérez-Maqueo O，Martinez M L，et al. The value of coastal wetlands for hurricane protection[J]. *Ambio*，2008，37：241-248.

[2] Friedlingstein P，O'Sull Ⅳ an M，Jones M W，et al. Global Carbon Budget 2022，Earth Syst. Sci.Data，14，4811‒4900，https：//doi.org/10.5194/essd-14-4811-2022.

[3] Howard J，Sutton-Grier A，Herr D，et al. Clarifying the role of coastal and marine systems in climate mitigation[J]. *Frontiers in Ecology and the Environment*，2017，15：42-50.

[4] Macreadie P I，Anton A，Raven J A，et al. The future of Blue Carbon science[J]. *Nat Commun*，2019，10：3998.

[5] Macreadie P I，Hughes A R，Kimbro D L. Loss of 'blue carbon' from coastal salt marshes following habitat disturbance[J]. *Plos One*，2013，8：e69244

[6] Macreadie P I，Nielsen D A，Kelleway J J，et al. Can we manage coastal ecosystems to sequester more blue carbon?[J]. *Frontiers in Ecology and the Environment*，2017，15：206-213.

[7] McLeod E，Chmura G L，Bouillon S，et al. A blueprint for blue carbon：Toward an improved understanding of the role of vegetated coastal habitats in sequestering CO_2[J]. *Frontiers in Ecology and the Environment*，2011，9：552-560.

[8] Moran M A，Kujawinski E B，Stubbins A，et al. Deciphering ocean carbon in a changing world[J]. *Proc Natl Acad Sci*，113（12）：3143-3151.

[9] Olsson L，Ye S，Yu X，et al. Factors influencing CO_2 and CH_4 emissions

---

1 陈建芳，自然资源部第二海洋研究所研究员，自然资源部海洋生态系统动力学重点实验室主任，主要研究方向为海洋生物地球化学、海洋生态环境监测。

2 曾江宁，自然资源部第二海洋研究所研究员，浙江省近海海洋工程环境与生态安全重点实验室主任，主要研究方向为海洋区域生态学、自然保护地、生态修复。

3 金海燕，自然资源部第二海洋研究所研究员，主要研究方向为海洋环境科学与生物地球化学。

4 于培松，自然资源部第二海洋研究所副研究员，主要研究方向为海洋碳化学、海洋环境监测。

5 刘诚刚，自然资源部第二海洋研究所副研究员，主要研究方向为海洋初级生产力。

from coastal wetlands in the Lioahe Delta, Northeast China[J]. *Biogeosciences*, 2015, 12: 4965–4977.

[10] Pei L, Ye S, Yuan H, et al. Glomain-related soil protein distributions in the wetlands of the Liaohe Delta, Northeast China: Implications for carbon sequestration and mineral weathering of coastal wetlands[J]. *Limnology and Oceanography*, 65, 979–991.

[11] Raymond P A, Bauer J E. Use of ^{14}C and ^{13}C natural abundances for evaluating riverine, seturaine, and coastal DOC and POC sources and cycling: A review and synthesis[J]. *Organic Geochemistry*, 32: 469–485.

[12] Reddy K R, Delaune R D. Biogeochemistry of Wetlands[M]. *CRC Press*, 2008.

[13] Rogers K, Macreadie P I, Kelleway J J, et al. Blue carbon in coastal landscapes: A spatial framework for assessment of stocks and additionality[J]. *Sustainability Science*, 2018, 14: 453–467.

[14] Wang F, Eagle M, Kroeger K D, et al. Plant biomass and rates of carbon dioxide uptake are enhanced by successful restoration of tidal connectivity in salt marshes[J]. *Science of the Total Environment*, 2021a, 750: 141566.

[15] Wang F, Sanders C J, Santos I R, et al. Global blue carbon accumulation in tidal wetlands increases with climate change[J]. *National Science Review*, 2021b, 8（9）: 140–150.

[16] Ye S, Laws E A, Yuknis N, et al. Carbon sequestration and its controlling factors in the temperate wetland communities along the Bohai Sea, China[J]. *Marine and Freshwater Research*, 2018, 69: 700–713.

[17] 陈雪初, 高如峰, 黄晓琛, 等. 欧美国家盐沼湿地生态恢复的基本观点：技术手段与工程实践进展 [J]. 海洋环境科学, 2016, 35（3）: 467–472.

[18] 韩广轩, 王法明, 马俊, 等. 滨海盐沼湿地蓝色碳汇功能、形成机制及其增汇潜力 [J]. 植物生态学报, 2022, 46（4）: 373–382.

[19] 焦念志. 研发海洋"负排放"技术 支撑国家"碳中和"需求 [J]. 中国科学院院刊, 2021, 36（2）: 179–187. DOI: 10.16418/j.issn.11000–13045. 20210123001.

[20] 唐剑武, 叶属峰, 陈雪初, 等. 海岸带蓝碳的科学概念、研究方法以及在生态恢复中的应用 [J]. 中国科学：地球科学, 2018, 48（6）: 661–665.

[21] 唐启升，刘慧. 海洋渔业碳汇及其扩增战略 [J]. 中国工程科学，2016，18（3）：68-73.

[22] 王法明，唐剑武，叶思源，等. 中国滨海湿地的蓝色碳汇功能及碳中和对策 [J]. 中国科学院院刊，2021，36（3）：241-251.

[23] 曾江宁，韩广轩. 陆海拉链——滨海湿地 [M]. 北京：中国林业出版社，2022.

[24] 张继红，刘纪化，张永雨，等. 海水养殖践行"海洋负排放"的途径 [J]. 中国科学院院刊，2021，36（3）：252-258.

[25] 张瑶，赵美训，崔球，等. 近海生态系统碳汇过程、调控机制及增汇模式 [J]. 中国科学：地球科学，2017，47：438-449.

第五部分 研究专论

探索林业碳汇生态产品
市场补偿机制的浙江实践路径

林业碳汇高质量发展对碳达峰、碳中和战略目标的实现有着十分重要的作用。浙江森林覆盖率位居全国前列，具备林业碳汇高质量发展的天然禀赋和巨大潜力。参考国内外先进做法经验，聚焦浙江实际，探索构建基于林业碳汇生态产品市场补偿机制的浙江省林业碳汇交易体系，既是浙江省生态文明建设的现实选择，也是实现"绿水青山就是金山银山"的有效途径，更是主动践行习近平总书记赋予浙江的"干在实处永无止境、走在前列要谋新篇、勇立潮头方显担当"新期望和在高质量发展中奋力推进共同富裕先行区的生动体现。

一、引言

实现碳达峰碳中和，是党中央的重大战略决策，事关中华民族永续发展和人类命运共同体构建，党的二十大报告也明确提出积极稳妥推进碳达峰碳中和工作，确保"双碳"目标顺利实现。

森林作为陆地生态系统的主体，承担着陆地上最大的"储碳库"功能，发挥着生态系统增汇"吸碳器"的作用，是未来固碳增汇的重要对象。2022 年 3 月，习近平总书记在参加首都义务植树活动时指出，森林是水库、钱库、粮库，现在应该再加上一个"碳库"。据 IPCC 报告估算全世界森林生态系统储存了约 1.15 万亿 t 碳，占陆地生态系统的 57%，其年吸收量约占陆地生态系统年固碳总量的 2/3。林业碳汇是实现国家碳中和战略目标最经济的选择，具有投入少、成本低、生态附加值高等特点，对加快实现碳达峰碳中和目标具有十分重要的意义。

二、国内外先进做法

（一）国际林业碳汇先进做法

林业碳汇在应对气候变化中发挥着重要作用，其重要地位逐渐被国际社会普遍认可。1997 年，《京都议定书》首次提及"碳汇"一词，要求发达国家缔约方提出减排目标和措施，支持通过"造林、再造林、森林可持续经营"等措施增加碳汇。2001 年，《联合国气候变化框架公约》第六次缔约方会议续会和第七次缔约方会议，分别通过《波恩政治协议》和《马拉喀什协定》，提出土地、土地利用变化和林业（LULUCF）活动对气候变化的影响，允许发达国家通过开展造林、再造林行动，将吸收的碳汇量用于抵消一部分工业活动排放的二氧化碳。2007 年，《巴厘岛行动计划》把发展中国家通过减少砍伐和森林退化以降低温室气体排放（REDD）纳入林业碳汇项目范畴。2009 年，《哥本哈根协议》要求必须通过建立激励政策和机制，促使发展中国家尽快采取行动减少排放和增加碳汇，包括减少发展中国家毁林、森林退化，以及森林保护和可持续森林经营。2010 年，《坎昆协议》明确，要对这类经过核算的碳汇用于抵消工业、能源排放总量时设定上限。2013 年，华沙气候大会明确可以为发展中国家采取 REDD+ 行动提供激励机制，包括减少毁林、减少森林退化，实施森林保护、森林可持续经营、提高森林碳储量的具体行动。2015 年，巴黎气候大会达成的《巴黎协定》单设森林相关条款，确定了 2020 年后全球共同应对气候变化的框架性安排，特别是从 2018 年开始，对各国提出的目标进展情况进行预评估。

从国际市场来看，国际碳信用机制是指实体间通过自愿的减排行动创造可交易的信用额度。世界银行的报告根据碳信用的产生和管理方式将其分为三类：国际机制、国内机制和独立机制。2021 年碳信用市场总体增长了 48%，信贷总量从 3.27 亿增加到 4.78 亿，这是自 2012 年碳信用发行峰值以来的最大同比增长。2021 年碳信用市场的增长大部分来源于独立碳信用机制新发行项目，越来越多的公司通过独立的碳信用机制购买自愿减排量，独立信贷发放增长了 88%，总计 3.52 亿，占当年碳信用供应的 74%，而来自国际和国内信贷机制的发行量增长速度较慢。由于气候变化谈判进程的不断推进，林业应对气候变化的重要作用逐渐凸显，林业成为全球碳信用签发最大的行业。从全球碳信用机制项目注册总量和信用量来看，由于《京都议定书》第一个承诺期到期，注册总量和签发量在 2012 年迅速增加，2013 年金融危机和欧盟配额供过于求导致欧盟排放交易体系下项目注册总量和签发量下降，随之到 2015 年之后趋于稳定。从分行业领域来看，2015—2019 年林业碳汇项目签发了最多的碳信用，约占全球碳信用总量的 42%，可再生能源是第二大碳信用项目来源，约占全球签发碳信用的 33%。

（二）国内林业碳汇交易探索

我国积极参与全球气候治理行动，充分重视和发挥林业碳汇在应对气候变化和低碳绿色发展中的关键作用。2007 年 6 月，作为发展中国家，我国率先颁布了《中国应对气候变化国家方案》，决定通过植树造林、森林管理等方式最大限度地发挥森林的碳汇功能。2015 年 9 月，中共中央、国务院印发《生态文明体制改革总体方案》明确指出，建立增加碳汇的有效机制。2016 年 11 月，国务院办公厅印发《关于完善集体林权制度的意见》明确指出，着力破解生态保护与林农利益间的矛盾，促进碳汇进入碳交易市场。2019 年，九部门联合印发《建立市场化、多元化生态保护补偿机制行动计划》强调，将具有生态、社会等多种效益的林业温室气体自愿减排项目优先纳入全国碳排放权交易市场，充分发挥碳市场在生态建设、修复和保护中的补偿作用。党的二十大报告明确提出，完善碳排放统计核算制度，健全碳排放权市场交易制度，提升生态系统碳汇能力，积极参与应对气候变化全球治理。

我国是世界上最早开展林业碳汇计量监测体系建设的国家之一。自 2003 年起，国家林业局组织加强林业碳汇研究，组织编制碳汇造林系列标准和建设林业碳汇计量监测体系。2004 年，启动林业碳汇项目试点，2006 年注册的广西珠江流域再造林项目是世界上第一个清洁发展机制下再造林碳汇项目。2010 年发布《碳汇造林技术规定（试行）》《碳汇造林检查验收办法（试行）》，2011 年发布《造林项目碳汇计量与监测指南》，2012 年发布《林业碳汇项目审定与核查指南（试行）》，2019 年制定《全国林业碳汇计量监测体系建设工作方案》，编制《竹林低碳经营与碳汇计量监测技术规范》《森林生态系统碳库调查技术规范》等标准。目前已经在国家发展改革委备案的 CCER 林草碳汇项目方法学有五个，分别是《碳汇造林项目方法学》《森林经营碳汇项目方法学》《竹子造林碳汇项目方法学》《竹林经营碳汇项目方法学》《可持续草地管理温室气体减排计量与监测方法学》。此外，各试点省市也相继制定了一些地方标准，如北京市制定的《林业碳汇项目审定与术语技术规范》、上海市制定的《城市森林碳汇调查及数据采集技术规范》、广东省制定的《广东省林业碳汇普惠方法学》等，林业碳汇计量监测标准及方法学的开发为我国林业碳汇项目进入区域性和全国性碳交易市场奠定了坚实的技术支撑。

当前我国林业碳汇交易基本属于项目层面的交易，项目类型主要有四种：一是《京都议定书》清洁发展机制（CDM）下的林业碳汇项目；二是中国自愿核证减排机制（CCER）下的林业碳汇项目；三是省级自愿类项目，包括北京林业核证减排量项目（BCER）、福建林业核证减排量项目（FFCER）和广东省省级林业普惠制核证减排量项目（PHCER）等；四是其他项目，包括林业自愿碳减排标准（VCS）项目、非省级林业碳汇项目、贵州单株碳汇扶贫项目等。此外还有中国绿化基金会和中国绿色碳汇基金会开展的相关碳汇项目业务。

三、浙江实践可行性

浙江"七山一水二分田"，森林覆盖率位居全国前列，森林蓄积量的单位面积增长量、增长率全国领先。根据最新监测结果，2020年全省森林面积为622.72万hm^2，森林覆盖率达61.17%，森林植被总碳储量2.90亿t，森林植被年吸收二氧化碳7 294万t，具备林业碳汇高质量发展的天然禀赋和巨大潜力。

（一）浙江省林业碳汇研究与技术开发基础雄厚

在浙江省政府和相关部门的支持下，浙江农林大学建立了"亚热带森林培育国家重点实验室""国家林业和草原局竹林碳汇工程技术研究中心""浙江省森林生态系统碳循环与固碳减排重点实验室"等林业碳汇研究与技术开发重要平台，集聚形成了以浙江农林大学为主体，浙江省林科院、浙江省森林资源监测中心等单位协同的多学科研究群体和科技创新团队，在森林生态系统碳汇计量监测、增汇减排技术、碳汇交易与政策等方面取得重大创新与突破，尤其在竹林碳汇研究和相应碳汇项目方法学开发中走在世界前列，竹林碳汇研究成果获得国家科技进步二等奖1项、省科学技术进步一等奖2项。主持开发的《竹子造林碳汇项目方法学》和《竹林经营碳汇项目方法学》，通过了国家发展改革委备案，突破了竹林碳汇进入中国碳减排市场的技术和制度瓶颈，开发的《农户森林经营碳汇项目方法学》，可使亿万林农真正参与到林业碳汇项目中来，因此在林业碳汇建设和交易方面具有坚实的技术支撑。

（二）浙江省森林资源数据大平台建设基础雄厚

在浙江省森林资源监测中心、浙江农林大学等单位努力下，完成了浙江省资源本底数据库和全省林地一张图建设，使森林资源数据准确落实到每个山头地块；系统探明了浙江全省森林生态系统五大碳库碳储量与时空分布格局；建立了省、市、县多级联动的森林碳储量监测方法，实现了全省森林生态系统碳储量一体化监测和年际更新出数；建立了全省林业地籍综合管理、全省生态公益林管理等信息系统，这些都为林业碳汇功能评估、林业碳汇项目开发和林业碳汇交易奠定了坚实的数据基础。同时浙江拥有阿里巴巴等众多互联网世界知名企业，互联网技术、区块链技术发达，可为碳汇交易提供技术保障，有助于林业碳汇交易的广泛开展和推广。

（三）现有林业碳汇实践经验

依托浙江农林大学、浙江省林科院、浙江省森林资源监测中心等在林业碳汇计量监测、增汇减排技术、碳汇交易与政策等方面的技术优势，浙江省林业碳汇开发实践也走在全国前列。

1. 建立了全国首个"碳汇林业试验区"和全球首个"竹林碳汇试验示范区"

2010 年，浙江农林大学研制完成全国首个县级碳汇林业建设规划，并使杭州市临安区成为全国第一个"碳汇林业实验区"。2012 年，浙江农林大学、安吉县与国际竹藤组织等机构在多哈气候变化大会（COP18）上共同签署协议，使安吉县成为全球首个"竹林碳汇试验示范区"。2014 年，基于临安碳汇项目，开发了农户森林经营碳汇交易体系，开创了农户参与森林经营碳汇项目、出售森林碳汇的新模式，同年 10 月，临安区首批 42 户农民实现了森林碳汇交易。

2. 建立林业碳汇基金专项体系

2010 年 7 月，国务院批准建立中国绿色碳基金后，浙江省申请建立全国第一个省级基金——浙江碳汇基金；全国第一个市级基金——温州碳汇基金；全国第一个县级基金专项——浙江碳汇基金鄞州专项；全国第一个中央、省、县三级管理专项——浙江碳汇基金北仑专项，初步形成中国—浙江—市县的三级管理模式。

3. 启动林业碳汇交易试点建设

2011 年 11 月，全国林业碳汇交易试点平台落户浙江省华东林业产权交易所。试点平台成功交易国内首批碳汇造林项目产生的 14.8 万 t 碳信用额，开创我国林业碳汇交易先河。2013 年 6 月，黑龙江省伊春市森林经营增汇减排项目产生的碳减排量通过华东林业产权交易所成功交易。

4. 开展森林经营碳汇项目开发实践

2015 年以来，已在浙江安吉、景宁、诸暨、遂昌、临安等地率先开发竹林经营项目 40.6 万亩，涉及 2 万多户竹农，可产生国家自愿核证减排量 500 多万 t；并开展技术培训 20 多期，显著提高了广大林业技术人员和林农开展林业碳汇经营的意识、能力及水平，也使项目开发主体积累了丰富的实践经验。2016 年联合中国绿色碳汇基金会组织实施了 G20 杭州峰会碳中和项目，实现峰会的零碳排放。2021 年开化县推出"零碳相伴"绿色金融产品，发放全省首笔林业碳汇价值质押贷款 300 万元。

5.建立县级竹林碳汇收储交易中心

2021 年 12 月，安吉县"两山"竹林碳汇收储交易中心正式启用，运用数字化改革思路，构建了竹林碳本底、碳收储、碳增汇、碳交易、碳足迹、碳收益六大应用场景，实现了林地流转—统一经营—碳汇收储—平台交易—收益反哺的全链条闭环管理，打通了碳汇交易区域市场；同时引入"竹林碳汇价格指数保险"和"毛竹碳汇富余价值恢复补偿保险"，为平台和村集体（农户）碳汇交易的收益保底。

四、浙江实践路线图

浙江省现有林业碳汇资源丰富、林业碳汇科技支撑体系完备、森林资源数据大平台建设基础雄厚、林业碳汇计量监测与项目开发实践丰富，同时浙江省林业碳汇市场潜力巨大，市场前景较为看好。因此，浙江省可率先建立区域性林业碳汇交易中心，完善林业碳汇交易体系，既可为丰富我国碳交易市场体系作出贡献，又可为建设市场化、多元化生态保护补偿机制打造浙江样板，为生动践行绿水青山就是金山银山提供浙江示范，进一步彰显浙江在应对全球气候变化和碳达峰碳中和战略目标中的责任担当。

（一）提升浙江省林业碳汇能力

围绕森林扩面提质，做好森林增汇文章。森林数量增加、质量提高、结构优化是森林增汇的有效方法。要持续推进新增百万亩国土绿化行动，不断增加森林覆盖面积。启动千万亩森林质量精准提升工程，组织开展退化竹林生态修复试点，维持和提高竹林质量，增强森林碳汇功能。

围绕森林健康保护，做好森林减排文章。森林火灾、病虫害和非法征占用林地等都会使森林增加排放。要严格保护森林资源，加强林地利用管理，加强森林灾害防控体系建设，增强森林防灭火能力，持续推进松材线虫病综合防治，为保障森林健康提供坚实基础。

围绕森林资源合理利用，做好竹木产品固碳文章。森林树木随着生长和成熟，固碳能力在达到顶峰后会逐渐下降，为了维持和提高林地固碳效率，森林资源保育与采伐利用需要并重。要不断改进竹木产品加工工艺，促进产品碳转移，提高竹木产品固碳功能。

围绕林业碳汇技术创新，做好科技支撑文章。以森林碳汇发展共性技术和关键技术需求为导向，深入推进森林生态系统增汇减排技术研究，力争在高固碳树种选育、森林提质增汇、森林保护促汇、竹木产品固碳关键技术等方面取得新突破。完善推进森林碳汇计量监测、竹木产品碳足迹碳标签核算体系建设，为碳汇能力提升、碳汇精准监测和碳汇交易打好基础。

围绕林业碳汇先行示范，做好试点建设文章。重点在造林绿化、质量提升、竹木制品固碳、机制创新四个主要方向，开展全省林业固碳增汇试点建设。有效发挥森林、湿地生态系统固碳作用，加强生态保护修复，提升生态系统碳汇增量。探索竹木固碳产品"碳标签"应用示范，引导社会主体购买竹木制品，获得产品"碳积分"。探索推进以森林碳汇为主的区域性碳汇交易，引导全社会共同参与林业碳汇建设，助力碳中和目标实现。

（二）建设浙江省林业碳汇交易体系

1. 目标定位

建立浙江省林业碳汇交易中心，完善浙江省林业碳汇交易体系建设，在目标定位上主要有 3 个方面：一是为重点排放单位的配额抵消交易、非重点排放单位的碳中和交易、低"零"碳试点示范项目、"零碳"机关、会议及活动等提供林业碳汇产品，打通"两山"转化的林业碳汇通道，充分发挥林业碳汇交易平台作用，逐步实现其他林业生态产品交易。二是围绕市、县碳达峰碳中和行动方案与目标，提供市域、县域间林业碳汇横向交易服务，构建经济发达地区与林业碳汇富足地区间的总量平衡交易机制，为山区跨越式发展和全省梯次达峰提供机制支撑，推进省域碳中和战略目标实现。三是对接国际、国内碳排放权交易市场，统一开展林业碳汇项目方法学开发和项目培育工作，提供林业碳汇交易的金融、法律、政策及中介服务，服务浙江，辐射全国，努力成为国家统一碳排放权交易市场的有效补充。

2. 重点任务

一是制定管理办法。围绕区域性林业碳汇交易，研究制定管理办法，率先将低"零"碳试点示范项目、"零碳"机关、会议及活动等纳入林业碳汇交易范围，逐步建立市域、县域间碳净排放量与碳汇净增量挂钩交易机制，激发山区政府开发林业碳汇的积极性。参照国家碳排放权交易管理机制，研究建立浙江省重点排放单位（年排放量在 2.6 万 t 二氧化碳当量以下的，具体根据浙江省情况设定区间）配额管理与交易机制，并适当提高林业碳汇抵消碳排放权配额比例。二是搭建交易平台。华东林业产权交易所是浙江省唯一的全省性林权交易平台，2010年12月在杭州挂牌成立，现已开通华东林权交易网，主要从事林权交易、林业碳汇交易、原木（木材）等大宗林产品交易，目前已完成重组。鉴于当前国家有关部委对于试点外省份不再新批地方碳市场交易机构的政策，先期可依托华东林业产权交易所（为国务院交易场所部际联席会议核准备案的交易所之一）碳汇交易试点平台，建立全省林业碳汇交易中心。三是制定交易机制。基于不同的碳汇交易标的（林业减排碳、中和碳、国际标准林业碳等），开发符合浙江省省情、林情的林业碳汇交易方法学与快速计量监测方法。根据林业碳汇交易内容，细化完善交易标的、计量核证标准、交易价格等重点。借鉴广东、福建等省份先行经验，规范项目设计、第三方审核、合规性审核、实施监管、核证、登记、签发等环节。四是建立监管机制。按照政府主导、市场运作、协同合作的模式，完善林业碳汇交易监管机制。浙江省发展改革委、省生态环境厅、省林业局按职责承担碳达峰碳中和目标体系建立、碳排放权配额管理、林业碳汇项目开发、核证等工作，研究制定浙江省林业碳汇市场交易规则。加强大数据应用，建设浙江省林业碳汇交易数据平台，为林业碳汇需求方、供给方、中介服务方等企业、个人、团体提供开放服务。

3. 建设内容

一是落实交易中心运营主体架构。由丽水市人民政府牵头重组华东林业产权交易所，推动以华东林业产权交易所为林业碳汇交易中心的运营主体架构，建立行业主管部门、科研院所、交易机构、金融机构、重点减排企业等组成的林业碳汇交易综合性平台，打造立足浙江、辐射长三角、示范全国的林业碳汇交易中心。二是构建交易中心日常运行机制。建立由林业碳汇需求方、供给方和保障机构组成的林业碳汇交易中心运行模式。推进林业碳汇产品价值实现需要多部门协同，由浙江省发展改革委制定生态产品价值实现路径，搭建区域性林业碳汇交易平台，制定相关管理规则，由省生态环境厅研究制定区域碳排放权抵消办法，由省林业局组织开展林业碳汇项目申报与实施，由省自然资源厅加强国土空间规划管控，将生态碳汇价值赋予土地价值评估；由省林业部门开展林业碳汇能力提升工程，形成多部门多跨协同、多措并举的林业碳汇交易中心运行机制。三是强化交易中心科技支撑依托。依托浙江农林大学、浙江省林业科学研究院、浙江省森林资源监测中心等单位，继续加强林业碳汇计量监测体系建设，深化林业碳汇交易项目方法学研究与开发，形成我省林业碳汇交易核定的地方标准。依托浙江省数字化改革优势，加快构建林业碳汇"数智化"应用场景，切实降低林业碳汇开发与交易成本，支撑浙江省林业碳汇交易中心日常运作。

五、展望与政策建议

（一）林业碳汇交易产品类型创新

1. 加快建立林业碳汇交易市场

可将林业碳汇分为用于抵消国家碳排放配额的核证自愿减排量"CCER 碳汇"和用于抵消非强制性减排的"中和碳汇"两类，在积极做好国家强制减排抵消类碳汇交易的同时，大力推进"中和碳汇"交易机制建立。围绕区域性"中和碳汇"交易，研究制定林业碳汇交易办法，率先降低"零"碳试点示范项目、"零碳"机关、会议及活动等纳入区域性"中和碳汇"交易范围，逐步建立市域、县域间碳净排放量与碳汇净增量挂钩交易机制，激发山区政府建设林业碳汇的积极性。

2. 积极盘活现有林业碳汇产品

将造林、森林经营等成果转化为国家碳排放权抵消交易产品，将国土绿化、森林保护等成果转化为区域林业碳汇交易产品，推动林业碳汇交易实现，助力山区林农实现共同富裕。

（二）林业碳汇交易金融支持

1. 拓宽绿色金融通道

在原有林权证质押、山林经营权质押、绿色金融债券等基础上，积极推广林业碳汇价值质押贷款、林业碳汇期权质押贷款等模式，拓宽森林提质改造、山林抚育等项目融资通道，助力林业碳汇项目开发与碳汇交易。

2. 创新林业碳汇保险

建立林业碳汇创新性金融保险产品，增强林业抵御风险的能力，保证森林生态效益、森林在低碳减排中的作用发挥，为林木整个成长过程中可能遭受的自然灾害和意外事故所造成的减碳量的经济损失提供保障。

3. 构建碳汇金融新模式

积极推广安吉竹林碳汇"两山"银行收储、开化"零碳相伴"林业碳汇质押贷款等创新模式，在全省构建"森林险 + 碳汇贷"绿色金融新模式，提前兑现林业碳汇收益，真正让林农获得实实在在的林业碳汇收益。推动社会资本等各方主体投入林业碳汇发展，积极鼓励引导社会资本和社会各界积极参与林业碳汇建设，为企业、社会和个人自愿碳减排提供林业实践路径。

（三）林业碳汇交易配套政策措施

1. 开展试点探索

筛选具有发展林业碳汇优势的山区县为试点，结合山区26县高质量发展"一县一策"、低碳试点县等相关政策给予林业碳汇抵消机制扶持。推动高耗能高碳排放行业按碳排总量配置一定比例的林业碳汇，优先向山区26县、林业碳汇试点县等采购林业碳汇指标。

2. 强化考核激励

全面推行林长制，将林业碳汇发展工作纳入林长制考核。将林业碳汇纳入生态保护补偿范畴，建立与林业碳汇生态产品价值相挂钩的政府绿色发展财政奖补机制，将森林植被碳储量与财政转移支付资金挂钩。探索以碳减排约束性指标考核促进林业碳汇交易，未完成碳减排目标的地区或企业可以等额或者差异化配额购买林业碳汇来抵消。

3. 加强立法保障

积极推动林业碳汇交易法规建设先行先试，将林业碳汇交易相关规章、制度、职责纳入《浙江省绿色低碳转型促进条例》，切实保障林业碳汇交易顺利开展。

作者：周国模[1]，李翀[2]，顾蕾[3]

1 周国模，博士生导师，浙江省特级专家，浙江农林大学教授，浙江省重点科技创新团队"林业碳汇与计量创新团队"带头人。

2 李翀，硕士生导师，浙江农林大学副教授，浙江省重点科技创新团队"林业碳汇与计量创新团队"核心成员。

3 顾蕾，硕士生导师，浙江农林大学教授，浙江省重点科技创新团队"林业碳汇与计量创新团队"核心成员，杭州亿衡碳科技有限公司董事长。

PART ONE
COMPREHENSIVE
EVALUATION

Strategy and Practice of Responding to Climate Change and Low-carbon Development in Zhejiang Province— Fifteen-Year History Review and Future Prospects

Zhejiang Province has been practicing the green and low-carbon development concept, actively responding to climate changes, and taking the lead to set good examples across the country. Zhejiang has thus become a major promoter and practitioner of global climate governance. This study comprehensively analyzes the foundation of green and low-carbon development in Zhejiang Province and reviews the historical evolution of its response to climate change since 2007. From the "two main lines" of mitigation and adaptation, the implementation practice and work outcomes of Zhejiang Province is also summarized. Meanwhile, combining with the new development situation and requirements for responding to climate change under the context of "dual carbon" goals, this study gives several suggestions for Zhejiang to build a high-quality sustainable development pattern that facilitates green, low-carbon and circular development.

Climate change is a global challenge, and no country can stay out of it. In the post-epidemic era, economic recovery of all countries has faced mounting pressure, green trade barriers have emerged, and global challenges have grown, adding uncertainty and enormous challenges to responding to climate change. We need the international community to work together to address the challenges of climate change and build a community of life for man and nature. At the same time, the Report to the 20th National Congress of the Communist Party of China proposed "Working actively and prudently toward the goals of reaching peak carbon emissions and carbon neutrakity", which provides a new guideline for continuously promoting green and low-carbon transition, and needs to further coordinate the relationship between development and emission reduction, aiming to achieve synergy and efficiency in reducing pollution and carbon emissions. At present, Zhejiang Province is in the critical period of implementing the Double Eight Strategy, and strongly fostering the deepening of innovation, reform and opening up. It is therefore essential to practice the new development concept in a complete, accurate and comprehensive way, actively seize the high ground for low-carbon and zero-carbon industrial development and technological innovation and fully stimulate the green transition of economy and the society. Reviewing the past experience prepares us to face the future challenges. Under the new situation and new background, it is necessary to take stock of the province's work on climate change, clarify development ideas, strengthen development beliefs, effectively fulfill emission reduction commitments and green development obligations, and contribute to the realization of "two pioneer missions" in high-quality development of Zhejiang Province.

I. Development Foundation

Located in the south wing of the Yangtze River Delta on the southeast coast of China, Zhejiang Province borders the East China Sea in the east, Fujian province in the south, Jiangxi province and Anhui province in the west, and Shanghai and Jiangsu province in the north. With a total area of 105,500 square kilometers and a resident population of 65.77 million, Zhejiang Province consists of 11 municipalities, 90 counties (cities and districts).

A. Climate Characteristics

Zhejiang Province is located in the central subtropical zone. With a monsoon humid climate and moderate temperature, it enjoys four distinct seasons, sufficient light and abundant rainfall. Over the past five decades, the average temperature of Zhejiang Province has increased significantly, with a warming rate of 0.47℃/10 years, higher than the national warming rate (0.36℃/10 years) in the same period, and the average temperature of the year has been between 15 ℃ and 18 ℃ . Due to the influence of the ocean and Southeast Asian monsoon, Zhejiang Province experiences significant changes in the prevailing winds in winter and summer, and precipitation also has obvious seasonal changes, with the annual sunshine hours between 1,100-2,200 hours and the annual average precipitation between 1,100-2,000 mm, and with May and June being the period of concentrated rainfall. At the same time, under the dual influence of the westerly and easterly weather systems, meteorological disasters in Zhejiang Province are numerous, making it one of the hardest-hit areas in China from typhoons, heavy rain, drought, cold waves, high winds, hail, frost damage, tornadoes and other disasters.

B. Resource Endowment

As an important ecological barrier in East China, Zhejiang Province is rich in forest resources. As of the end of 2022, the province has 91.13 million mu[1] of forests, with a forest accumulation of 346 million cubic meters and a forest coverage rate of 61.15%, which is among the highest in the country. But at the same time, Zhejiang Province is also a province of limited resources, with 70% of its area covered by mountains, 20% waters and 10% farmlands. Zhejiang Province has more people and less land and its energy, arable land, metal and mineral resources endowment does not stand out. Hence, it is basically dependent on the resources of other provinces and foreign markets. The scarcity of coal, oil, gas and other primary energy makes its fossil fuel supply highly dependent on external sources. The province's external electricity accounted for nearly 36% of its total electricity consumption in 2022. Photovoltaic, offshore wind power and other renewable energy resources reserves are relatively abundant, but policies on land, sea, forestry and others tend to tighten, and renewable energy development is facing increasing constraints.

C. Industrial Basis

In 2022, Zhejiang's GDP is reached 7.771 5 trillion yuan, ranking fourth in the country and its GDP per capita is exceeded 110,000 yuan, reaching the level of high-income economies. The structure of the three industries is adjusted and optimized to 3.0 : 42.7 : 54.3, and a modern economic system is basically formed. The manufacturing industry structure has become more high-end,

---

1   Chinese unit of land measurement . One mu corresponds to about 666.67 square meters.

with the added value of strategic emerging industries and high-tech industries accounting for 33.5% and 65.3% of the added value of above-designated-size industries, respectively, and the "415X" advanced manufacturing clusters have taken shape. The contribution of the tertiary industry to the economy has continued to improve. The development of digital economy steadily ranks in the first echelon of the country and the added value of the core industry of digital economy accounts for 11.6% of GDP. Zhejiang Province is in a leading position in the country's green development.

Column 1 "415X" Advanced Manufacturing Clusters

Four world-class industrial clusters. Relying on the advantages of digital economy and industrial characteristics, Zhejiang Province will focus on building world-class industrial clusters, such as green petrochemicals, digital security, automobiles and modern textiles.

Fifteen advantageous industrial clusters. Combining with the transformation and upgrading of traditional manufacturing industries, Zhejiang Province cultivates special advantageous industrial clusters, such as modern hardware, pumps and valves, rubber and plastics, non-ferrous metals, stationery and sporting goods, electric motors, fiber-optic cables, green household supplies and green batteries, etc., in the traditional advantageous fields, such as consumer goods manufacturing, raw materials manufacturing, machinery and equipment manufacturing. It focuses on digital economy, bio-economy and other new economic areas and focuses on cultivating software and information technology services, life and health, intelligent manufacturing equipment, intelligent electrical, intelligent home appliances, photovoltaic equipment and other emerging manufacturing clusters.

X new star industrial clusters. It focuses on digital economy, life and health, new materials and other strategic emerging industries, future industries and industry chain to fill the gap. Leading enterprises take the role to drive the industry chain to collaborate, interact, innovate and co-develop around the industrial sub-sectors, cultivating more than 50 ten-billion-level new star industrial clusters with technological leadership and international competitiveness.

D. Ecological Environment

Zhejiang Province is the birthplace of the idea that "lucid waters and lush mountains are invaluable assets" or the "Two Mountains" theory and it is also the first place to practice this idea. In recent years, it has deeply practiced the "Two Mountain" theory, continued to promote the "Integrated Management of Five Water Issues" and the construction of "clean air demonstration zone" and "waste-free cities" in its region and also strengthened the whole chain of plastic pollution treatment. Zhejiang Province has built itself the first ecological province in China, and won a UN Champions of the Earth Award for its "Green Village Project", which has become its most well-known name card and has been praised by General Secretary Xi Jinping. In 2022, among the surface water quality monitoring points managed at the national level, the proportion of locations that achieve Class I to Class III good water quality reaches 99.4%, ranking first in the country and the proportion of locations that achieve Class I to Class III good water quality in provincial monitoring points reaches 97.6%, a year-on-year rise of 3.4 percentage points. The average concentration of $PM_{2.5}$ in cities in the region is 24 micrograms/m^3, and the ratio of good air quality days is 89.3%, continuing to lead the Yangtze River Delta.

II. History of General Strategies

As early as 2007, Zhejiang Province has established a leading group for climate change response, and it was one of the earliest provinces in the country to respond to climate change. Its climate change response over the past 16 years can be roughly divided into four stages:

A. The first stage (2007-2012), the initial stage of foundation building

The end of the 11th Five-Year Plan (2006-2010) and the beginning of the 12th Five-Year Plan (2011-2015) saw rapid economic development in Zhejiang Province. In 2012, Zhejiang Province's GDP exceeded 3.5 trillion yuan, with a total energy consumption of 181 million tons of standard coal equivalent and energy consumption per 10,000 yuan of GDP of 0.55 tons of standard coal equivalent, ranking third among the 31 provinces, autonomous regions and municipalities after Beijing and Guangdong province. The focus of its climate change response in this phase is to build a work structure and policy system for climate change response, strengthen basic capacity building, promote low-carbon innovative pilot projects according to local conditions, and actively participate in international cooperation and exchange.

1. Establishing a sound working mechanism. In July 2007, Zhejiang Province

established a leading group for climate change response with the governor in charge and 31 provincial departments as members, which was tasked with making overall plans and coordination for climate change response in Zhejiang Province. The leading group office was set under the Provincial Development and Reform Commission, which dealt with the daily affairs of the leading group. As required by the provincial government, municipalities with districts and some counties (cities and districts) also set up their own coordinating bodies for climate change response. By 2008, Zhejiang Province had built a work pattern for climate change response with the provincial leading group taking the lead in featuring the provincial, municipal and county level linkage. In addition, Zhejiang Province had built the first provincial-level research institution for climate change response, Zhejiang Center for Climate Change and Low-carbon Development Cooperation, which provided intellectual support for government decision-making.

2. Formulating and issuing policy documents. According to the national unified deployment, Zhejiang provincial government issued "Zhejiang Province Plan for Coping with Climate Change" (ZZF 〔2010〕 No.50, Figures 1-1) in October 2010, specifying the overall objectives, key areas and tasks of the province's climate change response until 2012. At the same time, a package of policies for climate change response, such as changing the mode of economic development, promoting energy conservation and carbon emission reduction, accelerating the promotion and utilization of new energy, promoting the construction of ecological civilization, and developing circular economy, were launched one after another, forming a policy system featuring "1+N" pattern with the provincial plan for coping with climate change as the core.

3. Actively promoting the construction of pilot zones. On greenhouse gas (GHG) inventory preparation, as one of the seven pilot provinces in China, Zhejiang Province issued and implemented "Work Plan for the Preparation of GHG Inventory in Zhejiang Province" (ZZ 〔2011〕 No. 140) in 2011, and established an inter-departmental and cross-disciplinary inventory preparation mechanism. The GHG inventory database was developed simultaneously, laying a solid foundation for the subsequent preparation of regular inventory reports. On local innovative practices, in July, 2010, Hangzhou was selected as one of the

first low-carbon pilot cities in China, and promoted its low-carbon development by developing a low-carbon economy, low-carbon buildings, low-carbon transportation, low-carbon life, low-carbon environment and low-carbon society. In November 2012, Ningbo and Wenzhou were selected as the second batch of low-carbon pilot cities by the National Development and Reform Commission.

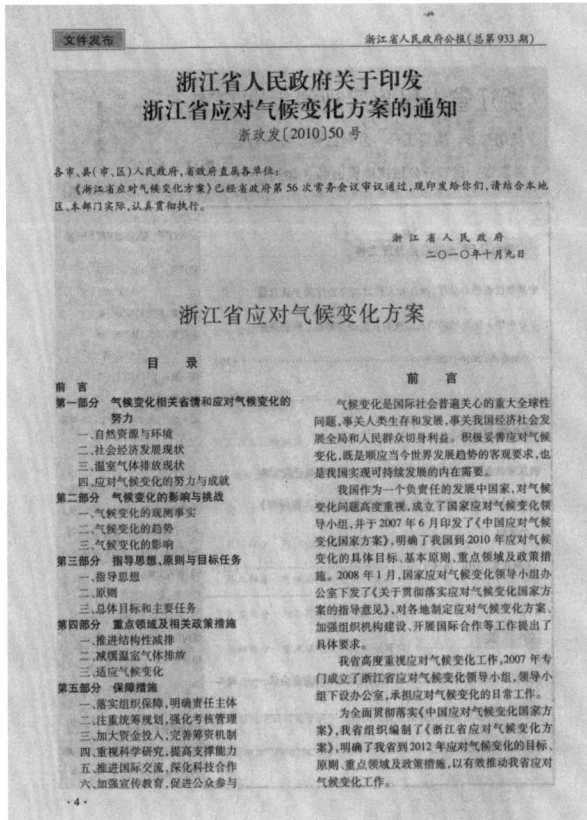

Figure 1-1　Zhejiang Province Plan for Addressing Climate Change

4. Engaging in practical cooperation and exchange. Zhejiang Province is one of the earliest provinces in China to participate in the Clean Development Mechanism (CDM), and the CDM projects it implemented feature various types, distinctive features, large emission reduction and wide geographical distribution. By the end of 2012, the province launched a total of 199 CDM projects, covering natural gas, wind power, biomass, waste heat and pressure power generation, etc., of which 55 projects were successfully registered and 24 projects were issued with certified emission reductions (CERs). The emission reduction issued was approximately 139.5 million tons of carbon dioxide equivalent, accounting

for 20.1% of the cumulative issuance volume in the country during the same period, ranking first in China in terms of both the number of projects and emission reduction issuance volume, and obataining international funds of nearly 10 billion yuan. At the same time, at the government level, the province carried out in-depth international cooperation in five major areas, namely low-carbon technology, low-carbon buildings, low-carbon transportation, low-carbon industrial parks and low-carbon financing. For example, Ningbo cooperated with the World Bank, the Asian Development Bank and other international institutions, and completed several major projects, such as a model project for urban household waste collection and recycling, a model project for comprehensive energy efficiency in low-carbon city, and a project for construction of early warning system for building energy consumption and low-carbon city planning.

B. The Second Stage (2013-2017), the Exploration Stage to Build up Momentum

During the 12th Five-Year Plan (2011-2015) period, Zhejiang Province vigorously developed its digital economy, the "No. 1 Project" and continuously pushed forward the decarbonization of its industrial structure. In 2015, carbon emissions per unit of GDP in Zhejiang Province dropped to 1.0 tons per 10,000 yuan, and the carbon intensity dropped by 24.68% compared with 2010, beating the target of 19% set by the state. The focus of its climate change response in this phase is to explore the establishment of an assessment mechanism for meeting carbon intensity reduction target, actively promote the construction of a multi-level pilot system, and push forward the preparation of GHG inventories at the provincial, municipal and county levels.

1. Exploring the establishment of a goal-led mechanism for meeting low-carbon targets. Zhejiang Province was the first in China to issue and implement the "13th Five-Year Plan" for low-carbon development, specifying the general idea, main objectives, and initiatives for low-carbon development of the province during the "13th Five-Year Plan" (2016-2020) period. It established a sound assessment mechanism for meeting carbon emission targets, broke down its carbon intensity control target which was subsequently assigned

to municipalities and completed the trial assessment of municipalities' performance in meeting carbon intensity reduction target during the 12th Five-Year Plan. It continuously improved the carbon emission statistical system, unified the statistical caliber of energy, agriculture, waste treatment and other fields, and developed a basic statistical reporting system for climate change response including 25 tables and 248 indicators.

Column 2   Methods for Assessing the Performance in Meeting the Targets and Fulfilling the Responsibilities for Controlling GHG Emissions during the 13th Five-Year Plan

In October 2017, with the consent of the provincial government, Zhejiang Provincial Development and Reform Commission issued "Trial Measures for the Assessment of Municipal People's Governments' Performance in Meeting the Targets and Fulfilling the Responsibilities for Controlling GHG Emissions in the 13th Five-Year Plan" (ZFGZH [2017] No. 854), officially launching the assessment of municipal people's governments' performance in meeting the targets and fulfilling the responsibilities for controlling GHG emissions.

The assessment mainly focused performances in nine aspects, namely the completion of carbon intensity targets, energy conservation and structural optimization, low-carbon industrial system construction, low-carbon development of urbanization, regional low-carbon development, carbon market construction and operation, low-carbon science and technology innovation, basic capacity support, and relevant safeguard measures. It evaluated municipal people's governments' performance in meeting annual temperature control targets and implementing policies and measures.

The assessment of the completion of carbon intensity targets includes two parts: one is the annual reduction target of carbon dioxide emissions per unit of gross regional product, as a veto indicator in the annual assessment; the second is the cumulative progress target of carbon dioxide emissions per unit of gross regional product, as a veto indicator in the assessment at the end of the five-year plan.

---

2. Accelerating the exploration of multi-level low-carbon pilot system. Zhejiang Province strengthened and expanded its construction of national pilot zones with significant improvement in both the quantity and quality of such pilot zones. The three approved pilot cities continued to make progress. For instance, Hangzhou demonstrated to the world its effort in building itself into a low-carbon pilot city from six aspects during the G20. Ningbo, a port city pressed for low-carbon transition to reach peak carbon emission and Wenzhou explored

low-carbon development based on financial reform. In February 2017, Lishui was selected as a national pilot climate-resilient city and in July 2017, and Jiaxing, Quzhou and Jinhua were selected as the third batch of national low-carbon pilot cities.

Zhejiang Province established its provincial-level low-carbon pilot system, issued the Notice on Launching *Provincial Low-carbon Pilot Program* and launched the construction of the first batch of eight low-carbon pilot counties (cities), with a focus on innovative practices in the total carbon emission control system, greenhouse gas emissions statistics and accounting system, etc.

Column 3　Key System Innovation in the First Batch of Low-carbon Pilot Counties (Cities)

Beilun District and Rui'an City: With the goal of creating a low-carbon pioneer area in a strong coastal industrial city, these two explored the establishment of an evaluation system for business carbon productivity, total carbon emission control system for key industries, etc.

Wencheng County: With the goal of creating a low-carbon poverty alleviation demonstration area, it explored the establishment of low-carbon mechanisms benefiting the people, an assessment and evaluation system for the low-carbon development of counties (cities and districts), etc.

Qingyuan County: With a focus on ecological industrial transformation, it explored the establishment of a resource factor conservation system with low-carbon development at its core, an assessment and evaluation system for the low-carbon development of counties (cities and districts), etc.

Jingning County: With the goal of creating a demonstration area for green economy in mountainous regions and a key ecological function area in the mountainous region of southern Zhejiang Province, it explored low-carbon mechanisms benefiting the people (photovoltaic projects), an assessment and evaluation system for the low-carbon development of counties (cities and districts), etc.

Longquan City: With the goal of creating a low-carbon development system innovation area, low-carbon economy demonstration area, low-carbon culture publicity area, carbon sink capacity building experimental area, it explored the establishment of a carbon sink mechanism that benefits the people, and vigorously promoted targeted poverty alleviation with photovoltaic projects.

Wuyi County: With the goal of creating a new model featuring low-carbon transformation of traditional industries and low-carbon development of emerging industries in central Zhejiang Province, it explored the establishment of a carbon emission standard for industrial park access and introduced policies to support the development of new energy.

Kaihua County: With the goal of creating a low-carbon poverty alleviation demonstration area, it launched a special fund plan for carbon sinks, developed carbon sink forests and other projects, and explored the establishment of low-carbon mechanisms benefiting the people.

3. Pushing forward the preparation of GHG inventory at the provincial, municipal and county levels. As the first province in China to require the regular preparation of GHG inventory at the provincial, municipal and county levels, Zhejiang Province took the lead in issuing local guidelines for inventory preparation in 2014, and formulated the first provincial inventory management approach in 2017 in China, based on which it completed the provincial GHG inventory for 2005-2017 and GHG inventory of 11 municipalities and 90 counties (cities and districts) for 2010-2017. Meanwhile, it upgraded its climate change research and communication platform, building it into an online system featuring climate change data collection, review, management, analysis and study and covering the provincial, municipal and county levels, the first of its kind in the country, which helped the provincial government have a better understanding of the emission of six greenhouse gases of four entities, namely, the province, municipalities, counties and enterprises and in five fields.

4. Solidly promoting the green and low-carbon transition of key areas. In terms of low-carbon economy, the traditional industry deepened its transition and upgrading, forming a preliminary industrial pattern of low energy consumption, low pollution and low-carbon emissions. In terms of energy structure, Zhejiang Province continued to accelerate the utilization of low-carbon energy, such as photovoltaic, natural gas and clean electricity outside the province, and the total consumption of coal continued to decline, and the proportion of non-fossil energy in the province's total primary energy consumption was increased to 16.7% in 2017. In terms of low-carbon buildings, it promulgated "Green Building Regulations of Zhejiang Province", formulated

"Green Building Design Standards", and continuously improved the regulations and rules on saving energy and reducing carbon in construction. In terms of low-carbon transportation, the province actively built itself to a model province for green transportation, focusing on improving the low-carbon transportation system, and energy consumption per unit of transport turnover and passenger volume continued to decline. In terms of carbon sinks, the province consolidated the capacity of forest carbon sinks, strengthened wetland protection, and promoted the "blue carbon sink" action.

5. Actively participating in the construction of national carbon trading market. Since 2014, the province has organized nearly 450 carbon trading enterprises and nearly 1,300 non-carbon trading enterprises to submit their carbon reports every year, and commissioned more than 10 third-party verification and review agencies to carry out verification and review of these reports in batches. It established a number of mechanisms, such as the assessment of the performance of verification and review personnel, the disclosure of performance evaluation of verification agencies and the practice of on-site review. It launched the study of "Interim Management Measures for Greenhouse Gas Emission Reporting of Key Enterprises and Public Institutions in Zhejiang Province" and improved the province's monitoring, reporting and verification (MRV) system.

6. Deepening external cooperation and exchanges. Zhejiang Province successfully held a series of activities, such as the "Zhejiang Climate Change South-South Cooperation Experience Sharing and Technology Seminar". It actively promoted the early stage of its low-carbon new energy cooperation project with California of the United States, and reached agreement on cooperation matters. In 2017, under the guidance of the United Nations Development Programme (UNDP), Zhejiang Cooperation Center for Climate Change and Low-carbon Development completed the report entitled "Developing Green Logistics, Zhejiang in Action", which was released at the United Nations Climate Change Conference in Bonn.

Figure 1-2　The UN Climate Change Conference Sharing
Session was successfully held in Hangzhou in March 2017

Figure 1-3　Training courses were held on Zhejiang Climate
Change South-South Cooperation in November 2017

C. The third stage (2018-2020), the transition stage of integrating the old and the new

In 2018, the duty of climate change response was shifted to the ecology and environment department. The focus of climate change response in this phase is to accelerate institutional restructuring, comprehensively strengthen capacity building, continuously improve the MRV system, actively participate in the construction of national carbon trading market, and explore new types of pilot zones, etc.

1. Strengthening capacity building. On September 26-27, 2019, Zhejiang Provincial Department of Ecology and Environment hosted a capacity building session for climate change response in Ningbo, which was the first large-scale and all-round professional training session organized by the province's ecology and environment system after the duty of climate change response was shifted to the ecology and environment department. The meeting called for analysis and assessment of carbon emission intensity and carbon emission dynamic prediction and early warning.

Figure 1-4　Capacity Building Session for Zhejiang's Climate
Change Response Held in Ningbo in 2019

2. Fully participating in the construction of carbon trading market. Zhejiang Province deeply implemented the model project of low-carbon big data for climate change and continuously optimized and upgraded its provincial climate change research and exchange platform. In 2019-2020, it organized more than 1,200 enterprises to submit their carbon emission data, verified the data of 290 enterprises and reviewed the data of 145 enterprises. It completed the preliminary work for power generation enterprises to participate in the carbon market and determined the list of 143 power generation enterprises to be included in the carbon market, laying a solid foundation for enterprises from Zhejiang Province to participate in national carbon market transactions.

3. Exploring the construction of new low-carbon pilot zones. Focusing on strengthening the R&D and application of "zero carbon" technology and

deepening carbon emission management, Zhejiang Province explored the creation of multi-level near-zero carbon emission pilot areas, including near-zero carbon cities, counties, townships, villages (communities) and enterprises and built a pilot system for deep emission reduction. It actively made coordinated efforts to explore emission reduction, carry out preliminary research on reducing greenhouse gases and air pollutants, and explore the construction of pilot zones for emission reduction. Based on analysis of the achievements and experience of pilot zones of various types at various levels, such as pilot cities, counties, industrial parks, communities and enterprises, it summarized low-carbon development paths and practices.

D. The fourth stage (September 2020-present), a collaborative and efficient development stage

On September 22, 2020, President Xi Jinping made a serious announcement at the 75th session of the United Nations General Assembly that "We aim to have CO_2 emissions peak before 2030 and achieve carbon neutrality before 2060". The focus of climate change response in this phase is to take carbon emission peak and carbon neutrality as the core, establish a "1+N+X" policy system, formulate a systematic plan for the "4+6+1" realization path, and comprehensively promote the green and low-carbon transition of the economy and society.

1. Building a work pattern featuring top-level leadership. On the one hand, Zhejiang Province focuses on its top-level institutional design. Since September 2020, it has started its plan to achieve carbon peaking and carbon neutrality. It has set up a leading group led by main leaders of the provincial party committee and the provincial government has formulated and implemented the province's carbon peaking plan and the carbon peaking plan of "6+1" areas and 11 municipalities and introduced a series of fiscal, financial, measurement and assessment policies. It also was initiated the drafting of regulations on the promotion of green and low-carbon transition and further built the target system, work system, policy system and evaluation system for carbon peaking and carbon neutrality. On the other hand, it was engaged in social mobilization. After the issuance of the provincial implementation opinions and plans, the provincial and municipal governments have been working together to carry out

PART ONE COMPREHENSIVE EVALUATION

in-depth publicity and reporting around the top-level design to achieve carbon peaking and carbon neutrality, experts and scholars were invited to publish theoretical and explanatory articles in provincial media and party newspapers, and held training courses for officials. Meanwhile, it developed and launched a carbon application to encourage the public to practice a green and low-carbon life, whose total number of users exceeded 1.3 million and low-carbon activities exceeded 24.13 million. Its effort to achieve carbon peaking and carbon neutrality gained widespread attention from the society.

Figure 1-5   Application of ZheJiang Tan Pu Hui

2. Formulating the "4+6+1" pattern for the carbon peaking and carbon neutrality path. On May 21, 2021, Yuan Jiajun, then secretary of the provincial party committee, emphasized at the meeting to strength the province's effort for peak carbon emission and carbon neutrality that we should take digital reform as the leader, scientific and technological innovation and institutional innovation as the driving force, and structural adjustment as the key to coordinate economic development, energy security, carbon emission, and residential life, and take the lead in achieving comprehensive green and low-carbon transition of economic and social development. The overall idea and path to achieve this

goal is the "4+6+1" pattern:

"4" refers to four core indicators to be targeted, namely total energy consumption, total carbon emission, energy consumption intensity and carbon emission intensity. Zhejiang Province delivers systematic analysis of the four indicators and formulates scientific plans for peak carbon emission. It focuses on the reduction of carbon intensity and energy consumption intensity, which drives down the total amount of carbon emission and energy consumption, leading to peak carbon emission in a scientific way.

"6" refers to six areas where green and low-carbon transition is promoted, namely energy, industry, construction, transportation, agriculture and residential life. Zhejiang Province strives for more progress in low-carbon transition on the basis of securing current achievement, pushes forward green and low-carbon transition in six key areas to reach peak carbon emission step by step.

"1" refers to a key factor, namely, science and technology innovation. Zhejiang Province develops a technology road-map for carbon peaking and carbon neutrality, takes the lead in building a green and low-carbon technology innovation system, seizes the high ground with technology and provides high-quality support for reaching carbon emissions peaking and achieving carbon neutrality.

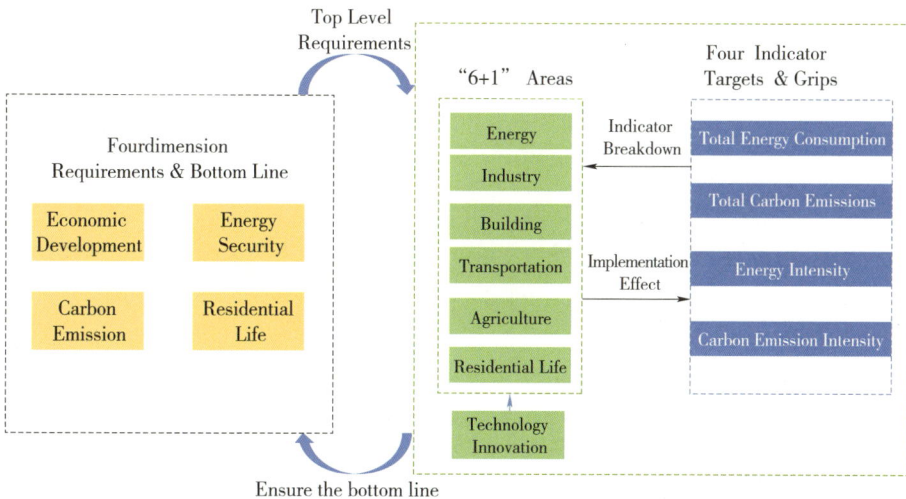

Figure 1-6 "4+6+1" Pattern for Carbon Peaking and Carbon Neutrality of Zhejiang Province

3. Taking the lead in building a smart governance platform for carbon

peaking and carbon neutrality. Taking advantage of its digital economy, Zhejiang Province empowers its low-carbon development with digital technology and has built the province's unified carbon emission database and the first carbon account application in China, making it possible for dynamic monitoring and study of carbon emission in six fields, 11 cities and more than 47,000 enterprises. The platform has been built around the needs of the government, enterprises and individuals and turned the reform results into practical application, launching major features, such as carbon emission statistics and prediction and early warning, energy saving and carbon reduction ebook, carbon pilot and carbon benefit, etc. Zhejiang Province's practice of building the first integrated management platform for carbon peaking and carbon neutrality in China was published and promoted by China's Work Brief on Carbon Peaking and Carbon Neutrality.

4. Building a low/zero carbon pilot system. In August 2021, Zhejiang Province issued the *Guidance on the Construction of Low/Zero Carbon Pilot Zone* (ZSTB〔2021〕No.5), proposing to build a muti-field, muti-tiered and diversified low/zero carbon pilot system that includes low-carbon pilot counties, townships, villages, industrial parks and factories, etc. By the end of 2022, 23 low/zero carbon pilot counties, 80 low/zero carbon townships (streets), 632 low/zero carbon villages (communities), 18 pilot projects for pollution and carbon

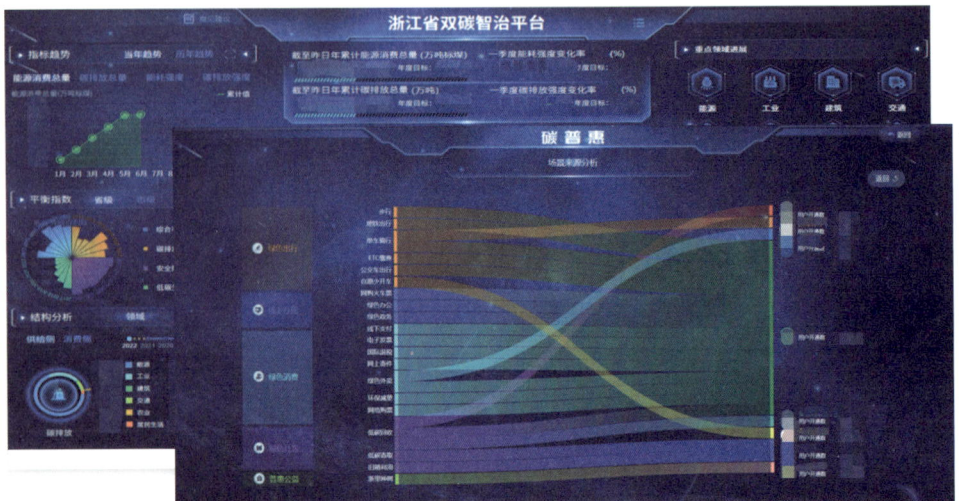

Figure 1-7   Interface of Smart Governance Platform for Dual Carbon Goals of Zhejiang Province

reduction synergy, 4 forestry sink pilot counties, 34 new energy storage model projects, 279 green and low-carbon factories and 20 green and low-carbon industrial parks and 279 low-carbon ecological farms had been built in Zhejiang Province. The first-batch 40 model cases for green and low-carbon transition in Zhejiang Province were selected.

Figure 1-8　Cases for Green and Low-carbon Model Transition at the Provincial Level

5. Coordinating efforts to reduce pollution and carbon emission. In September 2022, the Ministry of Ecology and Environment (MOE) replied to support Zhejiang Province in constructing the first innovation zone in China for pollution and carbon reduction synergy. In December 2022, Zhejiang Provincial Department of Ecology and Environment took the lead in issuing the *Implementation Plan for the Construction of the Pollution and Carbon Reduction Synergy Innovation Zone in Zhejiang Province*, proposing the goals of the zone, and sorting out 29 specific tasks in 8 aspects, such as source prevention and control, model innovation, and enhancing the synergy capacity. At the same time, Zhejiang Province had launched 26 model projects for pollution and carbon reduction synergy, and built 5 model cases, such as digital empowerment of pollution and carbon reduction synergy in Yuhang District and the digital and smart governance of pollution and carbon reduction synergy in Shangyu Economic Development Zone.

III. Mitigation Strategy and Major Practices

Mitigation is the human intervention to reduce greenhouse gas emission sources or increase carbon sink. In recent years, Zhejiang Province has adhered to the idea that "lucid waters and lush mountains are invaluable assets", and has successively implemented major strategies for ecological development including the strategies of building an ecological province, building a beautiful Zhejiang Province and building Zhejiang Province into a big garden. Also, it promotes green and low-carbon mode of production and lifestyle, and strives to mitigate the impact of climate change with its own green and low-carbon development. Over the years, Zhejiang Province has made positive progress in mitigation efforts on energy, industry, construction, transportation, residential life, and carbon sinks.

A. Low-carbon Transition in Energy Development Approach

1. Promoting leapfrog development of renewable energy. Renewable energy is the key for Zhejiang Province to solving energy constraints and achieving the transition of energy structure. The province attaches great importance to the development of renewable energy, and actively promotes large-scale development of wind, photovoltaic (PV), water and other renewable energy. Regarding the development of PV, Zhejiang Province supports commercial and industrial distributed PV projects, and carries out an action to install rooftop PV on a million of household buildings and launches a project to double its wind and PV capacity, as a result of which the installed PV capacity has grown rapidly in the province. Also, PV application in Zhejiang Province takes many forms, such as the rooftop PV, PV power combined with fishery industry, PV power combined with farming and floating PV, etc. At the same time, taking advantage of its marine resources, Zhejiang Province steps up the development of offshore wind power. As of the end of 2022, its installed wind and PV capacity exceeded 30 million kilowatts, accounting for more than a quarter of the province's total installed power capacity. In addition, Zhejiang Province accelerated the construction of pumped storage projects. The total installed capacity of pumped storage power stations that have been built and are under construction leads the country. It is worth mentioning that Zhejiang Province always insists on

promoting the development of nuclear power in a safe and orderly manner. In 2020, San'ao Nuclear Power Phase I Project, the first time private capital has invested in a civilian nuclear power project, officially started, and as of 2022, Zhejiang Province's installed nuclear power capacity reached 9.13 million kilowatts and cumulative power generation totaled 73.05 billion kilowatt-hours, both of which ranked third in the country.

2. Fully adjusting and optimizing the energy structure. In 2014, Zhejiang Province took the lead in building itself into a national model province for clean energy. By controlling the total amount and intensity of energy consumption, it effectively increased the proportion of clean energy consumption. Natural gas consumption increased significantly from 3.18 billion cubic meters in 2010 to 18 billion cubic meters in 2022 and non-fossil energy accounted for 19.0% of total energy consumption, an increase of 9.2 percentage points from 9.8% in 2010. At the same time, Zhejiang Province coordinates energy security and low-carbon development. It strictly has controlled the total amount of coal consumption, and reduced coal consumption in industrial production and residential life through the implementation of "coal-to-gas" and "coal-to-electricity" projects. The proportion of coal consumption in energy consumption dropped from 61.3% in 2010 to 41.7% in 2022, well below the national average. Measures, such as retrofitting coal power units with ultra-low emission technology have effectively improved the clean and efficient use of coal in Zhejiang Province and the average standard coal consumption for coal power generation has dropped from 312g/kW·h in 2010 to 294g/kW·h in 2022. In addition, Zhejiang Province strengthens the construction of projects transmitting external clean power into the province, and has successively put into operation Xiluodu-Zhejiang high-voltage direct current power transmission project, Baihetan-Zhejiang ultra-high voltage direct current (UHVDC) transmission project and other major projects. The share of low-carbon energy in its energy structure has been further improved.

3. Continuously improving energy efficiency. Zhejiang Province not only makes efforts to optimize the energy supply structure, but also attaches great importance to the improvement of energy efficiency on the consumption side. Since the "12th Five-Year Plan (2011-2015)", Zhejiang Province has aimed at controlling both energy consumption amount and intensity and pushed

forward the reform of energy consumption patterns. It focuses on transforming industries with high energy consumption and heavy pollution and forces the orderly exit of inefficient production capacity from the market. It steps up the energy-efficient renovation of enterprises and launches projects to encourage over 1,000 enterprises whose annual energy consumption totaling 10,000 tons of standard coal equivalent or above to meet energy saving targets. It strictly carries out requirements on energy efficiency evaluation of projects for market access. There has been a steady decline in energy consumption per unit of output. Meanwhile, Zhejiang Province actively promotes the reform of the allocation of energy factors, which is included in the first batch of pilot provinces for the paid use and transaction of energy use rights in the country. Through improving the energy use right trading system, a unified energy use right trading platform was established in Zhejiang Province, with the leading number of transaction projects and transaction scale in China. Zhejiang Province also formulates and regularly revises the Guide on Industrial Energy Efficiency in Zhejiang Province, and strictly implements the tiered electricity price policy for enterprises whose energy consumption exceeds the energy consumption limit standard for per unit product. In addition, the province vigorously promotes the digital transformation of energy conservation and carbon reduction management in public institutions, and builds a network for online monitoring of energy conservation in public institutions across the province. Remarkable results have been attained in energy conservation in public institutions. Since the "11th Five-Year Plan (2006-2010)", Zhejiang Province has reached the obligatory targets for energy conservation set forth by the state for three consecutive five-year plans. In 2021, the energy consumption per 10,000 yuan of GDP is 0.38 tons of standard coal equivalent (price in 2020), a cumulative decrease of 20.3% compared with that in 2012. The energy consumption per unit of the added value of industrial enterprises above designated size has been decreased by 23.8%, and the energy consumption per unit of the added value of enterprises whose annual energy consumption totaling 1,000 tons of standard coal equivalent and enterprises whose energy consumption is under key monitoring has been decreased by 26.9% and 26.5%, respectively. Remarkable results have been achieved in improving energy efficiency.

B. Effectively Enhancing Carbon Productivity in the Industrial Sector

1. Accelerating industrial upgrading and transition to low-carbon development. At the beginning of this century, in order to tackle the resource and environment constraints and extensive economic development, Zhejiang Province implemented an initiative to accelerate the transformation and upgrading of traditional industries and promote advanced development of industrial structure. The province set up a provincial leading group for industrial transformation and upgrading, and held meetings every year to deploy and promote its effort. In particular, since 2010, the province has launched a series of projects to eliminate enterprises with high energy consumption, heavy pollution and low efficiency, encourage the development of high-tech and high-added-value products in tertiary industry, improve production efficiency by technical transformation and equipment update, improve land use intensity, support the development of e-commerce and develop well-known enterprises, products and brands. During the 13th Five-Year Plan (2016-2020) period, a total of 8,250 enterprises with outdated and excess production capacity have been eliminated, and a total of over 6 million tons of standard coal equivalent has been saved. In recent years, Zhejiang has carried out new initiatives to improve industrial land use eco-efficiency and started the new round of further transforming the development model, optimizing the economic structure and changing growth drivers. In 2021, the Ministry of Industry and Information Technology officially agreed to support Zhejiang Province in building a national demonstration zone for the transformation and upgrading of traditional manufacturing industries. At the same time, the province continues to strengthen system and mechanism innovation, formulates and implements guidance on reforming regional energy conservation assessment and energy consumption standard, and on reforming environmental impact assessment and environmental standards. The newly approved industrial land is basically made sure to meet all the standards before being transferred to enterprises to ensure green and efficient industrial growth.

2. Promoting high-quality development of emerging industries. Accelerating the transition from old growth drivers to new ones and promoting the optimization and upgrading of economic structure are important countermeasures to mitigate climate change. Continuous optimization of

economic structure and steady improvement of the quality of development requires the leading and supporting role of strategic emerging industries. In 2020, Zhejiang Province proposed to make every effort to gain ground in high-tech innovation on Internet+, life and health and new materials, and accelerate the convergence of scientific and technological resources. Under the guidance of high-tech innovation in the three areas, and through implementing the digital economy - the "No. 1 Project", Zhejiang Province's "three new" economy, which refers to economic activities with new industry, new business format, and new business model, has seen rapid development. Statistics in 2022 showed that the added value of "three new" economy accounted for 28.1% of its GDP in Zhejiang Province, and the added value of the core industries of digital economy reached 897.7 billion yuan, an increase of 6.3% over the previous year. In particular, new growth drivers represented by high-tech industries continued to lead growth. The added value of high-tech industries in 2010 was 239.6 billion yuan, which is only 16.7% of that in 2022, and remarkable development has been achieved over the years.

3. Focusing on playing the exemplary role of pilot zones and projects for industrial low-carbon development. Zhejiang Province has built a series of pilot zones and projects in enterprises and industrial parks for the green and low-carbon development of industries, which play a leading and exemplary role for other businesses. In this process, the province has gained advanced experience for low-carbon development that can be replicated and promoted, and has then further boosted wide-range low-carbon development of industries. At the enterprise level, Zhejiang Province has continuously implemented three rounds of circular economy "991" action plan, and selected a number of key enterprise projects with demonstration significance that bring out social benefits of resources every year and supported them with provincial-level special fund. At the same time, it promotes the construction of a green manufacturing system, establishes green and low-carbon factories, formulates guidelines for the evaluation of green and low-carbon factory construction, specifying overall requirements for energy and resource input, products, and environmental emissions, and builds demonstration enterprises for green supply chain management and green design. Up to now, two batches of 200 provincial-

level green and low-carbon factories have been announced. At the level of industrial parks, Zhejiang Province mainly focuses on the transformation of industrial parks to circular development and promotes the transition to green and low-carbon development of massive economy. Since 2014, it has launched five batches of pilot projects for provincial industrial parks' transformation to circular development, and promoted the transformation of 70 parks above the provincial level to circular development, helping the park economy seize opportunities for green development under the pressure of resources and environment. At the same time, it formulates evaluation guidelines for the construction of green and low-carbon industrial parks, specifying the accreditation of green and low-carbon industrial parks, and it accelerates the transition to green and low-carbon development of industries. By the end of 2022, Zhejiang Province has established 20 provincial-level green and low-carbon industrial parks.

C. Steadily Building a Green and Low-carbon Transportation System

1. Continuously optimizing the transportation structure. Transportation sector accounts for 9% of the total carbon emissions in Zhejiang Province, and is one of the key areas for carbon emission control. In recent years, Zhejiang Province has made efforts to build a strong and high-quality transportation network and has continuously optimized its transportation structure through developing multimodal transportation and building a pattern featuring the linkage between seaports, dry ports, airports and information ports. The construction of green and low-carbon transportation has achieved remarkable results and Zhejiang Province is one among the first batch of pilot provinces for green transportation in the country. To set its transportation sector on a low-carbon path, Zhejiang Province focuses on building demonstration transportation lines and projects, vigorously develops multimodal transportation, and actively promotes the shift from "road-to-railway" and "road-to-waterway" for transportation of bulk cargo. According to statistics in 2021, a total of 551,000 TEUs (twenty-foot equivalent units) of containers were handled through river-sea combined transportation, 531,000 TEUs of containers through sea-river combined transportation, and 1.204 million TEUs of container through sea-

railway combined transportation, all showing an upward trend. At the same time, Zhejiang Province is actively building a pattern featuring joint development of four types of ports. In 2019, it issued the Proposal for Accelerating the Development and Construction of Seaports, Dry Ports, Airports and Information Ports, speeding up the connection between sea, land, and air transportation modes, aiming to bring out maximized benefits and to achieve comprehensive traffic system optimization, transportation efficiency enhancement, and logistics cost reduction.

2. Vigorously fostering low-carbon development of transportation equipment. Zhejiang Province has effectively promoted clean and low-carbon transportation equipment through various measures, such as promoting new energy vehicles, eliminating outdated commercial vehicles, and replacing energy sources for ships. Especially in public transportation, through the promotion of clean energy in urban public transportation, Hangzhou and Huzhou have a 100% clean bus fleet, and Ningbo, Huzhou, and Shaoxing have a 100% clean taxi fleet. At the same time, in the past two years, Zhejiang Province has successively formulated implementation plans for the construction of new transportation infrastructure and the construction of charging infrastructure along highways, and deployed the construction of charging and battery swap infrastructure and hydrogen refueling stations, further improving new energy infrastructure of transportation. Regarding the elimination of outdated commercial vehicles, Zhejiang Provincial Department of Transportation and other five departments jointly issued the *Implementation Opinions on Accelerating the Elimination of Outdated Commercial Vehicles* in 2019, promoting the early phase-out of diesel trucks with emission standards under national stage III. By the end of 2022, a total of nearly 70,000 outdated commercial diesel trucks with emission standards under national stage III have been eliminated in Zhejiang Province. In addition, during the 13th Five-Year Plan (2016-2020) period, the province vigorously promoted the application of LNG-powered transport ships and environment-friendly passenger ships, and the energy consumption per unit of transportation turnover of waterway commercial ships dropped by 22.7% in zhejiang.

3. Continuously improving the public transportation system. For a long

period of time, Zhejiang Province has always prioritized the development of public transportation over other patterns of transportation and has continuously improved the construction of public transportation infrastructure and the quality of public transportation services, making public transportation more attractive and competitive over other patterns of transportation and promoting green and low-carbon travelling modes. Data show that public transportation share in motorized travel mode in Zhejiang Province has been increased from 18.4% in 2010 to 36.7% in 2020. In terms of infrastructure construction, Zhejiang Province is striving to create a green travel system that integrates railway, bus and non-motorized transportation networks. Since the 12th Five-Year Plan (2011-2015) Hangzhou and Ningbo have launched subway services and Wenzhou, Shaoxing and Jiaxing have established the urban railway transit. Zhejiang Province has enriched its bus routes, and there have been nearly 6,000 regular bus routes, and 840 kilometers of bus lanes in the province. Urban greenway network and other non-motorized systems have been further improved. At the same time, Zhejiang Province has made great efforts to improve the quality of public transportation services. It launches diversified bus services for the "last mile" of urban public transportation and launches an application for one-stop online transportation service, which can be accessed through various channels, such as the WeChat official account. Flexible and diverse bus services, such as rush hour commuter buses, subway connecting buses, customized buses, and water buses, have been launched according to local conditions. The public bicycle system represented by Hangzhou's red public bikes has been further improved, providing great convenience for the public to travel by public transportation.

D. Solidly Pushing forward the Development of Green Buildings

1. Establishing a sound work system for green building development. Zhejiang Province has focused on continuous growth of energy consumption and carbon emissions in the construction sector in urban and rural development, and has always considered building green and energy-saving buildings as an important measure to deal with climate change and achieve low-carbon development. It has established and continued to improve the work system for the development of green buildings. It is the first province in China to establish

a complete green building development system covering the entire process of planning, design, construction, completion acceptance, and operation. Specifically, as early as 2011, Zhejiang Province issued the *Several Opinions on Actively Promoting the Development of Green Buildings* (ZZF〔2011〕No.56) to promote the development of green buildings in an all-round way. It continues to formulate special plans for green buildings, clearly requires local governments to speed up the formulation and implementation of special plans for green buildings, and coordinates efforts to promote the development of green buildings. At the same time, Zhejiang Province continues to improve regulations, standards, and other systems in this regard. In 2015, *Green Building Regulations in Zhejiang Province* was issued, which pushed forward the development of green buildings through legislation. A series of local standards, such as Guidelines for the Design of Solar Photovoltaic Systems for Existing Civil Buildings, were formulated, strengthening technical support for green building development. In addition, Zhejiang Province has established a supervision platform for public buildings' energy consumption covering all cities with districts, whose data are shared with the provincial supervision platform, realizing dynamic monitoring of public buildings' energy consumption in the province.

2. Effectively improving the low-carbon development of new buildings. In terms of the standard system, Zhejiang formulated and issued a series of standard guidelines in 2021, such as *Zhejiang Province Public Building Energy Conservation Design Standards*, *Zhejiang Province Green Building Design Standards* and *Zhejiang Province Residential Building Design Standards*, requiring energy conservation rate of residential buildings in the province to reach 75%. In the construction of new buildings, Zhejiang Province vigorously promotes new construction methods, such as prefabricated buildings. By the end of 2022, over 400 million square meters of prefabricated buildings have been built in the province, accounting for more than 30% of new buildings for three consecutive years. Four cities have been listed as demonstration cities for prefabricated buildings and 23 enterprises have been listed as demonstration industrial bases for prefabricated buildings. In addition, Zhejiang Province steps up its efforts to promote the application of renewable energy, and promotes renewable energy applications in building design, construction and installation. In 2022, 25 million

square meters of buildings were equipped with renewable energy applications, and a cumulative 140 million square meters of buildings were equipped with solar energy and other renewable energy applications. Urban newly-built green buildings account for more than 98% of all new buildings.

3. Steadily promoting the energy-efficient renovation of existing buildings. Zhejiang Province attaches great importance to the green and low-carbon development of all links in urban and rural construction, especially the improvement of the energy efficiency of existing buildings, and it has adopted a series of measures to steadily carry out energy renovations. Since the 12th Five-Year Plan (2011-2015) Zhejiang Province has launched key projects, such as the renovation on old neighborhoods, urban organic renewal, sponge city construction, and "future community" construction, during which external wall insulation, movable external shading, thermal insulation roofing, solar energy, ground-source heat pumps and other relatively mature energy-saving technologies were adopted, and green building materials were applied. The energy-efficient renovation on existing buildings have achieved remarkable results. By 2022, the province has completed energy-efficient renovation on a total of 12 million square meters of existing public buildings. At the same time, Zhejiang Province formulated and issued *Technical Regulations on Energy-Efficient Renovation of Existing Government Office Buildings*, which provides an important reference for guiding the energy-efficient renovation of public buildings.

E. Consolidating and Enhancing the Carbon Sink Capacity of Ecosystem

1. Promoting the development of forestry carbon sinks with all efforts. In recent years, Zhejiang Province has incorporated the development of forestry carbon sinks into the province's overall efforts to respond to climate change, and has initiated a project to develop high-quality forestry, realizing the enhancement of both the quantity and quality of forestry. In terms of quality improvement, Zhejiang Province has carried out key projects, such as planting rare tree species and colored tree species, precisely improving the quality of ten million mu of forestry, which help effectively optimizing the forest stand

structure and continuously improving the quality of forestry. In terms of quantity increase, Zhejiang Province has solidly promoted initiatives, such as planting ten thousand trees in each village and the afforestation of an increased million mu of land, which also help continuous improvement of forest quality. By the end of 2022, the forest coverage rate of Zhejiang Province reached 61.24% (including shrubs), forest stock volume reached 420 million cubic meters, and the annual growth rate of forest stock volume of high-forest per unit area continued to rank among the top in the country. At the same time, the forestry carbon sink management mechanism has been improved. Lishui City has set up the first municipal forestry carbon sink management bureau and Anji County has set up the first county-level forestry carbon sink management bureau. Chun'an County is the first in the country to set up a township forestry carbon sink service center. Zhejiang Province has made efforts to improve the local forestry management system and mechanism, and the overall protection and management of the forest ecosystem has been strengthened.

2. Enhancing the capacity of wetland and ocean carbon sinks. In addition to forestry carbon sinks, Zhejiang Province also has a large number of wetlands and marine carbon sink resources, which are also one of the development priorities. In terms of wetland carbon sinks, Zhejiang Province has successively issued Regulations on Wetland Protection in Zhejiang Province, Implementation Opinions on Strengthening Wetland Protection and Restoration Work and other policy documents to strengthen wetland protection and restoration, and the carbon sink has been continuously strengthened. By the end of 2022, the province has a wetland area of approximately 1.24 million hectares, with 2 wetlands of international importance, 2 wetlands of national importance, 87 wetlands of provincial importance, and 79 wetland-type nature reserves. At the same time, the province has steadily promoted the development of marine carbon sinks. It issued and implemented Blue Carbon Science and Technology Innovation Special Action Plan of Zhejiang Province and Blue Carbon Work Plan of Zhejiang Province in the Field of Natural Resources, strengthening the scientific and technological support for the development of marine carbon sinks. It also carried out a blue carbon survey in the province. It is worth mentioning that in 2023, Zhejiang Province issued the first provincial-level program in the

field of marine carbon sinks, Guidance on Enhancing the Capacity of Marine Carbon Sink in Zhejiang Province, which made a comprehensive deployment of the work related to carbon sequestration and sink increase in marine carbon sink ecosystem. At the municipal levels, some coastal areas are also actively promoting the protection and enhancement of marine carbon sinks, such as Wenzhou City, where mangrove restoration and planting are carried out in an orderly manner, and more than 200 hectares of mangroves have been planted in areas, such as Yueqing Bay and Oujiangkou, and Zhoushan City, which took the lead in issuing the Blue Carbon Economy Development Action Plan of Zhoushan (2021-2025), aiming to speed up the construction of an economic system with blue carbon capacity enhancement as the core.

3. Exploring and promoting the innovation on market-oriented mechanism of carbon sink. As early as 2010, under the approval of the then National Forestry Administration, Zhejiang Province established the East China Forestry Property Rights Exchange, which mainly engaged in forestry rights trading, forestry carbon sink trading and other services, and was the only forestry carbon sink trading pilot platform in China at that time. Research institutes in Zhejiang also actively promote forestry carbon sink-related methodological research. For instance, Zhejiang Agriculture and Forestry University led the research of methodology on the management of carbon sink projects in bamboo forest, methodology on carbon sink projects of bamboo afforestation and other standards, which were filed for record at the National Development and Reform Commission and were incorporated into the China Certified Emission Reduction (CCER) methodology system, setting a "Zhejiang standard" for the national bamboo forest carbon sink trading projects. In addition, some cities in Zhejiang Province actively carry out research on methodology and trading mechanism of forest carbon sink projects, yielding several achievements, all the first of its kind in the country. For instance, Wenzhou City developed the first Technical Regulations on Forest Carbon Sink Projects in 2013, and Lin'an district in Hangzhou launched the country's first forest carbon sink trading system for farmers in 2014. Zhejiang Province also focuses on local carbon sink resources endowment and builds demonstration pilot projects for carbon sink trading. It carries out pilot projects first, so that experience can gained and then shared.

Lishui City and Anji County were listed as the forestry carbon sink and bamboo forestry carbon sink trading pilot zones in Zhejiang Province, respectively. In particular, Lishui City formulated the Methodology on Forestry Carbon Sink Inclusion in Lishui of Zhejiang and Interim Measures on the Development and Trading Management of Forestry Carbon Sink in Lishui in 2020 and carried out carbon sink trading exploration. At the same time, Zhejiang Province issued the *Carbon Inclusiveness Emission Reduction Management Measures for Carbon Neutrality in Large-Scale Events* (*Meetings*) *in Zhejiang Province* (*Trial Implementation*), which clarifies the process of forestry carbon sink development, management, commission certification and registration. The market-oriented mechanism of carbon sink development has been continuously improved.

F. Green and low-carbon lifestyle has become a new trend

1. Strongly advocating green and low-carbon consumption. Climate change response and low-carbon development requires not only green and low-carbon transition on the supply side, but also green and low-carbon consumption on the consumption side. In recent years, Zhejiang Province has introduced a series of policies and measures to actively guide the whole society to adopt a green and low-carbon consumption idea. On the supply side, multiple departments of Zhejiang Province jointly issued the first provincial-level document on green product certification, Opinions on Accelerating Green Product Certification in 2019, which has strongly promoted effective supply of green products. On the demand side, the office of the leading group for domestic waste classification in Zhejiang Province and other nine departments jointly issued the Notice on the Restriction of Disposable Consumer Goods in 2019, which set off a wave of restrictions on the use of disposable consumer goods throughout the province. At the same time, Zhejiang Province has taken advantage of the development of digital economy, and promoted green consumption practices, such as electronic invoicing, online payment and second-hand recycling, etc. In addition, through regular publicity activities, such as "National Energy Conservation Publicity Week" and "National Low Carbon Day", low-carbon life styles, such as clean plate campaign and shopping with baskets and cloth bags, have become increasingly popular. Green and low-carbon consumption is becoming a

conscious choice of more and more consumers.

2. Pushing forward urban and rural domestic waste classification. Strengthening the management of domestic waste classification and promoting the front-end waste reduction and back-end waste recycling and harmless disposal help mitigating climate change. In recent years, especially since General Secretary Xi Jinping put forward the idea that garbage classification is the new fashion in 2018, Zhejiang Province has stepped up its efforts in urban and rural domestic waste classification, and has effectively improved the policies and system in this regard. In 2018, Zhejiang Province set up a leading group for domestic waste classification and built a work system featuring coordinated efforts of departments and the province, cities and counties. It then issued Management Measures for Urban Domestic Waste Classification, Management Regulations on Domestic Waste and other normative documents, and it issued the country's first provincial standard for urban domestic waste classification in 2019. A system of regulations and standards for domestic waste classification is basically established. In addition, in promoting the "garbage revolution", Zhejiang Province has produced typical cases, such as Huge Recycle, a company providing domestic waste treatment and classification services, and has obtained typical experience that can be replicated and promoted, such as the method of classifying garbage for two times and into four categories. Zhejiang Province leads the country in its waste classification effort and by the end of 2022, the province's urban and rural domestic waste classification and treatment coverage has reached 100%.

3. Exploring innovative carbon inclusiveness mechanism. To encourage and guide the whole society to actively participate in climate change response and low-carbon development, thus forming a green and low-carbon life trend which everyone can participate in and contribute, Zhejiang Province has been exploring innovative carbon inclusiveness mechanism, and a number of provincial and local typical practices have been created. At the provincial level, taking advantage of digital reform, Zhejiang Provincial Development and Reform Commission led the efforts to develop a carbon inclusiveness application, which was officially launched in 2022 on Zhejiang Province's government service platform and covered five major scenarios, such as green travel, green

consumption and online processing, etc. Residents can gain carbon points with their low-carbon practices in clothing, food, housing and transportation and exchange carbon points for rewards. Up to now, this application has over a million users, and it has become a provincial carbon inclusiveness platform that can be used in various scenarios and provides various rewards. At the local level, Huzhou City has built a carbon point system where financial institutions convert residents' green practices into carbon points through big data modeling, and develop green credit products with preferential interest rate. Xianju County proposed the concept of "green currency", encouraging tourists to exchange green currency by practicing green lifestyle and practice the consumption concept of carbon compensation and "carbon offset". Quzhou City takes the recycling and resource utilization of domestic waste as an opportunity and launches a digital application of "zero-waste life" where users can accumulates points for their carbon account through green and environment-friendly practices, and the points can also be exchanged for goods, forming an effective incentive mechanism for low-carbon behavior.

IV. Adaptation and Key Practices

Adaptation is an adjustment response made by nature or human systems under the stimulus of actual or expected climate change. In recent years, Zhejiang Province has been improving its climate change work mechanism. It focuses on infrastructure, forest ecology, marine environment, water resources, emergency response and disaster prevention and actively promotes the integration of climate change adaptation into the overall socioeconomic development. It released the first assessment report of Zhejiang Province's climate change adaptation and launched the construction of national-level climate-resilient pilot city. Its efforts in this regard yielded positive results.

A. Strengthening the adaptive capacity of economic and social systems

1. Strengthening the adaptive capacity of infrastructure. For a long time, Zhejiang Province has been committed to the construction of climate-resilient infrastructure that can effectively avoid climate-induced risks and losses.

To improve climate resilience of transportation facilities, Zhejiang Province, in its effort to build itself into a province with strong transportation network, focuses on building a modern comprehensive transportation system, enhances transportation system resilience, and builds a transportation system for natural disaster prevention and control. It issued and implemented the *Management Measures for the Construction of Highway Emergency Response Base* and built a number of emergency response bases. So far, five provincial highway emergency response bases have been built, providing full support to the highway sector's response to typhoons, floods, rain, snow, frost and other extreme weather and natural disasters. At the same time, it has strengthened the climate resilience of energy facilities. By using the "anti-typhoon and disaster-proof grid" system evaluation platform, Zhejiang Province carried out differentiated upgrading of the grid based on the diagnosis of the province's power supply grid, aiming to improve the grid's capacity to fight floods and typhoons. By carrying out long-cycle AI load forecast and flexibly adjusting the grid operation during peak hours, the power supply can be fully guaranteed under extreme high temperatures. Zhejiang Province strengthens the application of climate change adaptation technologies in energy projects. For instance, Putuo No.6 offshore wind power project in Zhoushan city adopted anti-typhoon design in marine booster stations and island mode of operation to ensure the safety of wind farms in extreme weather conditions. In addition, to strengthen the climate resilience of water conservancy facilities, Zhejiang Province made the overall plan for joint management of five water issues in 2013, and promoted key efforts in flood control and drainage to adapt to climate change. It has launched major landmark projects including over 100 flood control and drainage schemes with the total investment reaching over 100 billion yuan, and the Haitang Anlan 100-billion project for the maintenance and reinforcement of sea walls. Climate change resilience of water conservancy infrastructure has been significantly improved. Up to now, the flood control and drainage system of main river basins in Zhejiang Province has been basically built, and the proportion of main dikes reaching the standards has increased to 90%.

2. Strengthening the adaptive capacity of urban areas. Located in the Yangtze River Delta city cluster, Zhejiang Province has a high level of

urbanization and a high sensitivity to climate change, and has always focused on building the adaptive capacity of urban areas. Zhejiang Province takes the sponge city construction as an opportunity to strengthen urban drainage and flood control and enhance the adaptive capacity of cities. In 2016, the *Implementation Opinions on Promoting the Construction of Sponge Cities in Zhejiang Province* was issued to promote sponge city construction by building exemplary pilot sponge cities. It highlights the construction of climate-friendly urban ecosystems through the building of green roofs, rain gardens, water storage ponds and bioretention facilities, etc. Jiaxing, Ningbo, Hangzhou and Jinhua have been selected as the national pilot sponge cities, with strong financial support from central government, and they have built a number of pilot projects in pipe network upgrading, river governance and protection engineering, pipe gallery and underground space development. In provincial-level pilot cities, Shaoxing, Quzhou, Lanxi and Wenling created innovative sponge city construction models based on their own different geographical conditions including river plains, mountains, hills and coastal mudflats, providing exemplary experience for other counties and cities in Zhejiang Province. As of the end of the 13th Five-Year Plan (2016-2020) 25% of the built-up areas of municipalities with districts and more than 20% of the built-up areas of county-level cities in Zhejiang Province have reached the standard of sponge city, and the sponge city construction has achieved preliminary results. In addition, Zhejiang Province has issued a series of documents, such as *Implementation Plan for Urban Flood Control*, *Opinions on Further Strengthening Urban Drainage and Flood Control and Opinions on Enhancing the Flood Control Capacity of Urban Power Distribution Facilities*, which made systematic planning for urban flood control. Zhejiang Province has implemented six key projects including reinforcing river dikes, dredging river channels, creating new river channels, smoothing pipe networks, retrofitting areas susceptible to water logging and strengthening facilities, which have significantly improved urban flooding prevention and control. By the end of the 13th Five-Year Plan, Zhejiang Province has improved 876 urban rivers and constructed 6,861.8 kilometers of rainwater pipe networks, further enhancing urban drainage and flood control to adapt to climate change.

Figure 1-9　Model project of sponge city construction in Jinhua-Yanweizhou Park

3. Strengthening the adaptive capacity of public health. Zhejiang Province always puts people first and life first, and through the implementation of "Healthy Zhejiang" action, it has come up with a way for health improvement with Zhejiang characteristics. In particular, to strengthen the adaptive capacity of public health, Zhejiang Province focuses on improving the government's public service and management level to adapt to climate change. In view of the extreme weather, it promotes the establishment of health monitoring, surveying and risk assessment system and standard system, and properly performs in providing medical and health services in high temperature weather. At the same time, it has strengthened disease prevention and control, epidemic dynamic monitoring and research on influencing factors that are closely related to climate change, and formulated public health emergency plans and rescue mechanisms closely related to climate change. It is worth mentioning that Zhejiang Province has actively improved the monitoring and early warning system of the impact of climate change on human health and strengthened the health warning of extreme events and epidemics warning. It carries out pilot monitoring of health hazards in public places in each city, and establishes an early warning system for high temperature, heat waves and health risks. In addition, scientific research institutions in Zhejiang Province have further strengthened research on the health of the population in climate change adaptation, carried out projects for human health protection in climate change adaptation, and enhanced the

public's ability to cope with extreme weather, such as high temperature and heat waves.

B. Enhancing the adaptive capacity of key areas

1. Improving the adaptive capacity of agriculture. Zhejiang Province is located in the southeast coast of China. It boasts excellent light, heat, water, soil and other agricultural endowments, and is a comprehensive agricultural region of farming, forestry, animal husbandry and fishery, known as a "land of fish and rice" and the "home of silk and tea". Therefore, strengthening climate resilience of agriculture has been the main focus of Zhejiang Province to promote the modernization of agriculture and rural construction. Efforts in this regard cover both overall planning and concrete practices, which significantly enhanced the adaptive capacity of agricultural sector. On overall planning, Zhejiang Province formulated and issued a five-year plan for the development of modern agriculture and related action plans and other policy documents. It made great efforts to build itself into a pilot province for modern ecological and circular agriculture and a model province for high-quality and safe agricultural product, and actively responded to adverse effects of climate change-induced regional droughts and floods, sudden outbreaks of plant pests and diseases, and extreme weather events on agricultural production. On concrete practices, especially on practices promoting climate smart water-saving agri-technologies, Zhejiang Province issued the *Opinions on Accelerating the Construction of Efficient Water-Saving Irrigation Projects* in 2015, and vigorously promoted efficient water-saving irrigation technology. It carried out the construction of four one-million worth projects for efficient water-saving irrigation, and the province's farmland water conservancy facilities continued to be improved. The modernization of large and medium-sized irrigated areas was promoted. Farmland irrigation and flood control and drainage capacity continued to be improved. By the end of 2022, there were 122 irrigated areas of over 10,000 mu, with an 85% intact rate of key facilities. At the same time, Zhejiang Province enhanced the selection and promotion of crop varieties that can adapt to climate change, and introduced and promoted drought-resistant and water-saving rice. In 2021, approximately 60,000 mu of drought-resistant and water-saving rice were planted in Zhejiang

Province. In addition, Zhejiang Province took advantage of digital reform and created a smart agriculture cloud platform. This platform integrates agricultural business applications and data at all levels, which is a data center of modern agriculture, featuring integrated management of modern agriculture, emergency command and disaster warning and effectively enhancing the adaptive capacity of agricultural production.

2. Improving the adaptive capacity of forestry. With 61.24% forest coverage, Zhejiang Province has regarded the enhancement of adaptive capacity of the forestry sector as an important part in its overall climate change adaptation efforts, and it has been devoted to maintaining ecological security and climate security. To strengthen the climate resilience of forests, in accordance with the requirement set by the *Action Plan for Forestry to Adapt to Climate Change* (*2016-2020*), Zhejiang Province orderly increases the proportion of forestation of fire-resistant, drought/wet-tolerant, disease- and insect-resistant, extreme cold/heat-resistant tree species, and promotes climate resilient forest cultivation and management models. It increases the protection of forests and natural forest resources, and it enhances the adaptability and resilience of forest ecosystems to climate change by strengthening the monitoring and control of forest disasters, such as fires and pest invasions, etc. In addition, Zhejiang Province continues to strengthen the protection of forest land. It is the first in China to create a new model of the construction of roads that can serve both as patrol lanes for forest fire monitoring and rural highways. It also strengthens the application of information technology in forest disaster prevention and builds an application system for forest fire prevention, control and rescue, realizing effective early warning of forest fire risks. Since the 13th Five-Year Plan (2016-2020), Zhejiang Province has seen a 45% reduction in forest fires year-on-year. In addition, Zhejiang Province issued the *Implementation Opinions on Establishing Nature Reserve System in Zhejiang Province*, and vigorously promoted the construction of the nature reserve system. It expanded the scale of nature reserves and promoted the standardization and capacity building of nature reserves. The pilot project of Qianjiangyuan national park system was carried out, and Zhejiang Province actively explored the vertical management model of national nature reserves by the provincial government, which improved the protection and

management of nature reserves.

3. Improving the adaptive capacity of water resources. Zhejiang Province is densely populated with rivers and lakes, and it also has access to sea. Its water production per unit area is among the highest in China. However, its per capita water resources is far below the national average, and water resources security is still under tremendous pressure. Especially under the combined impact of climate change and other factors, it is particularly important to strengthen the adaptive construction of water resources. Zhejiang Province took the joint management of five water issues as the guidance and further enhanced the climate resilience of water resources by optimizing water resources allocation, strengthening water pollution control, promoting the construction of a water-saving society. In the optimization of water resources allocation, it focuses on the construction of key water sources projects and water diversion projects and optimizes water resources allocation network. It successfully completed Eastern Zhejiang Water Diversion Program, Qiandao Lake water distribution project and other key projects. By the end of 2021, Zhejiang Province had a total reservoir capacity of 44.9 billion cubic meters. On water pollution control, Zhejiang Province took water treatment as an opportunity to speed up industrial transformation and upgrading, significantly improving water environment quality. In particular, it launched the river chief system, and effectively promoted the protection of water resources, water pollution control and water environment management. By the end of 2022, the share of water resources with Class V poor water quality was completely eliminated and among the surface water quality monitoring points managed at the national level and managed at the provincial levels, the proportion of locations that achieved Class I to Class III good water quality reached 99.4% and 97.6%, respectively, reaching a record high. At the same time, Zhejiang Province strengthened the construction of water resources analysis and evaluation and forecasting system, and established an early warning mechanism of water resources' carrying capacity, significantly enhancing the binding force of water resources' carrying capacity. In the construction of a water-saving society, Zhejiang Province issued and implemented the *Water Conservation Action Implementation Plan* and promoted the construction of a water-saving society by building counties into water-saving

units in batches and with the government playing a major role in this process. It built a number of national and provincial water-saving cities. In addition, Zhejiang issued and implemented the *Water Network Construction Plan* in 2022 and built a water network featuring eight major water systems as the basic vein, Xin'an River and other important lakes and reservoirs as the nodes. A number of new water resources allocation channels and flood water drainage channels were built in eastern, central and northern Zhejiang Province. The natural water system and water conservancy facilities were intertwined in a network and an overall pattern featuring three water resources allocation channels, eight water system and ten reservoirs was formed, effectively enhancing the resilience of water resources to adapt to climate change.

C. Strengthening the Efforts of Climate Change Adaptation in Key Areas

1. Improving the adaptive capacity of mountainous regions in southwest Zhejiang Province. Zhejiang Province is mainly covered by mountains, with 70% of its area covered by mountains, 10% by waters and 20% by farmlands. In particular, the southwestern Zhejiang Province is highly mountainous and it is the highest-altitude area in the province. It boasts abundant ecosystem types and is an important ecological barrier in East China. With global warming, sensitive areas, such as the mountainous regions in southwestern Zhejiang Province are facing development challenges, such as changing precipitation patterns and intensifying natural disasters. Lishui is a typical mountainous city in southwestern Zhejiang Province with 90% of its area covered by mountains, 5% by waters and 5% by farmlands, which is an area prone to disastrous weather. To mitigate the impact of climate and reduce climate disasters, Lishui has actively explored practices for climate change adaptation and has achieved remarkable results. In 2017, Lishui became one of the first climate-resilient pilot cities in China. It established a leadership mechanism for climate-resilient city construction and clarified the overall plan for its climate change adaptation effort. It focuses on identifying the prominent problems and key issues under climate change, and mainly carried out research on climate change adaptation in geological disaster-prone areas and research

on ecological water utilization system. In particular, Lishui has been actively improving the capability of mountainous cities to adapt to climate change. It created an urban space utilization model that combines underground and overground space and space in and out of the mountains, improved the comfort level of urban climate environment, and enhanced the city's capacity in emergency response and disaster prevention and mitigation to extreme weather, such as high temperatures and heavy rains. At the same time, it sped up the improvement of water conservancy infrastructure, such as water diversion projects, strengthened the energy-efficient renovation of buildings and improved the ability of buildings to adapt to climate change. As a key ecotourism area in Zhejiang Province, Lishui established a tourism safety warning system, formulated tourism emergency plans and built emergency response systems, effectively improving the climate comfort level and safety coefficient of the tourism industry in Lishui.

In addition to Lishui, Quzhou city, also located in the mountainous region of southwestern Zhejiang Province, has continued to improve its capability to adapt to climate change. As the birthplace of the Qiantang River, the mother river of Zhejiang Province, Kaihua County in Quzhou has taken the pilot construction of Qianjiangyuan National Forest Park as an opportunity to actively promote the ecological protection and restoration of the water source region of Qiantang River and enhance the response and adaptation of the forest ecosystem to climate change. On watershed management, Quzhou implements total watershed volume and intensity control, develops cross-regional water allocation schemes for major watersheds, clarifies the upper limit of water resources utilization and the bottom line of ecological flow, effectively enhancing the adaptive capacity of water resources. In terms of institutional innovation, Quzhou has constructed a system for water consumption amount and intensity control at the municipal and county levels, and clarified the main responsibility for water conservation. In urban and rural construction, the impact of climate change is fully considered, and new city sites, urban expansion and township construction are subject to climate change risk assessment. Regarding disaster prevention and mitigation, Quzhou is the first in China to establish a work model of disseminating weather forecast and early warning through community grid management system and an efficient coordinated emergency response mechanism with information sharing among departments has been built. It is worth mentioning that Quzhou provides direct weather services for agriculture-related departments and large planters, and launches policy-supported weather index insurance for tea and tea oil tree. The application for online quick purchase of weather index insurance was selected as one of model projects of the province's digital reforms, which can be shared and promoted across the whole province.

2. Improving the adaptive capacity of the Northern Zhejiang Plain. The Northern Zhejiang Plain, consisting of Hangzhou-Jiaxing-Huzhou plain and Ningbo-Shaoxing plain, is the region with the highest population concentration and urbanization level in Zhejiang Province, and is well equipped with transportation, energy and water conservancy infrastructure. It is the most economically-developed area in Zhejiang Province. Strengthening flood prevention and drainage infrastructure is the key to climate change adaptation in plain areas. To this end, Zhejiang Province has implemented a series of major water conservancy projects, such as the Taijia River project, the improvement project of the river channel of Shaoxi River, the improvement project of inlet and outlet river channels of Taihu Lake in Hangzhou-Jiaxing-Huzhou area, the expansion of the drainage project in southern Hangzhou-Jiaxing-Huzhou area, and Xixian Datang reinforcement project, effectively improving the adaptive capacity of the Northern Zhejiang Plain and minimizing the losses caused by floods. A drainage frame of "northward to Yangtze River, eastward to Huangpu River and southward to Hangzhou Bay" has been formed. On the time dimension, Zhejiang Province issued *Management Measures for Polder Improvement Projects in Hangzhou-Jiaxing-Huzhou Region*, *Technical Guidelines for Polder Improvement in Hangzhou-Jiaxing-Huzhou Region* (Trial Implementation) and other policy documents in 2011, providing comprehensive guidance to the construction of polders in this area and enhancing the flood prevention and control and ecological environmental protection of polders. In 2013, Zhejiang Province made the overall plan for joint management of five water issues, promoting flood control and drainage as the focus of water management, and a number of key flood control and drainage projects were launched. In 2016,

Zhejiang Province held a mobilization meeting for the efforts to build over 100 flood control and drainage projects worth a billion yuan, proposing to upgrade the flood protection level of all plains in Zhejiang Province to 20-year flood. The weak links in flood prevention and drainage has been strengthened. The proportion of main dikes reaching the standards was increased from less than 50% to 90%.

At the same time, in order to solve the problem of uneven spatial and temporal distribution of water resources in the Northern Zhejiang Plain and further enhance the adaptive capacity of water resources, Zhejiang Province has been optimizing the allocation of water resources. In 2021, the Eastern Zhejiang Water Diversion Program, which took 18 years to build, was completed. It is the strategic water resources allocation project that covers the largest number of basins and regions with the longest water diversion line and benefits the largest number of population in Zhejiang Province. It is a reconfiguration of the water network in eastern Zhejiang Province and brings out huge social and economic benefits in water resources security, flood control and other aspects.

3. Improving the adaptive capacity of coastal areas in eastern Zhejiang Province. As a major marine province with 43,700 square kilometers of sea area and more than 7,500 kilometers of coastline, Zhejiang Province has been improving the resilience of coastal areas and coastal zones to adapt to climate change by scientifically implementing sea-related development activities, strengthening the protection and restoration of marine ecosystems, and enhancing the capacity building of marine disaster prevention. In 2011, the State Council approved the construction of Zhejiang ocean economic development demonstration zone, which is the first sea-related national strategy carried out in Zhejiang Province, setting off a new climax of scientific implementation of sea-related development activities. Coastal areas formulated implementation plans of the demonstration zone planning and programs for the development, utilization and protection of important sea areas, islands and other marine resources to coordinate the efforts for the demonstration zone construction. An adaptive and sustainable marine economy development model has been established in this process.

In terms of marine ecological environment protection and improvement,

Zhejiang Province has carried out water quality real-time monitoring by buoys in near-shore waters, built a three-level network of marine environment monitoring stations of national, provincial and municipal control. A coordinated land and sea pollution control system was basically built. Especially since the 13th Five-Year Plan (2016-2020), Zhejiang Province has carried out "Blue Bay" comprehensive improvement action, ecological coastal zone construction and other projects. The ecological environment of Hangzhou Bay, Sanmen Bay, Taizhou Bay and other bay areas has undergone comprehensive improvement. Pollution control and ecological protection projects in Qiantang River, Ou River, Jiaojiang River and other major rivers flowing into the sea have yielded remarkable results. The average proportion of good quality seawater in Zhejiang Province reached 42.7% at the end of the 13th Five-Year Plan. At the same time, Zhejiang Province has continued to improve the marine ecological environment protection system. It formulated plans for the development of marine main functional areas, the protection and utilization of the coastline, the protection of uninhabited islands and others. It set up effective control of marine development intensity and established a red line system for marine ecological protection, defining a marine ecological protection red line zone of 14,000 square kilometers, accounting for 31.72% of sea area under provincial control. The marine blue ecological barrier has also been consolidated, with a total of 4 national-level marine ecological civilization demonstration areas approved and 18 national and provincial-level marine reserves built, with a total area of more than 4,000 square kilometers.

Apart from enhancing the climate resilience of the sea and coastal zones through the protection and enhancement of marine ecological environment, Zhejiang Province also attaches great importance to the capacity building of marine disaster prevention. During the 12th Five-Year Plan (2011-2015), Zhejiang Province followed the idea of joint efforts in disaster control with the focus on disaster prevention. It implemented five major projects such as comprehensive marine disaster observation network, early warning network, information service network, emergency command system, risk assessment and zoning, etc., and initially built the province's emergency management system for marine disasters. It took the lead in China to carry out the delineation of marine disaster key defense areas, marine disaster potential risks identification, marine meteorological observation network construction, marine disaster risk assessment and others. Especially in recent years, Zhejiang Province has promoted Haitang Anlan 100-billion worth project, issued and implemented *Planning on the Construction of Haitang Anlan 100-Billion Worth Project*. It has dealt with problems, such as seawall subsidence along the coastline and seawall structural damage and improved the safety standard of seawalls, further improving coastal areas' capacity for typhoon and storm tide control.

D. Improving the Climate Disaster Prevention and Mitigation System

1. Further improving disaster prevention and relief mechanism. In recent years, affected by global warming, climate risks have continued to increase, and extreme weather and climate events, such as heavy rainfall, flooding, super typhoons, high temperature and heat waves, have occurred frequently. Zhejiang Province has established and continued to improve a disaster prevention and relief mechanism by conducting climate disaster assessments, building disaster planning systems, and improving emergency management systems, which effectively strengthen its ability to adapt to climate change. Regarding climate disaster assessment, Zhejiang Province has formulated the *Implementation Rules for Meteorological Disaster Investigation and Risk Assessment*, and completed the meteorological disaster survey in five pilot counties and cities (three national pilot counties). At the same time, Zhejiang Province has collected data on the province's population, economy, rice and other refined hazard-bearing body to provide strong support for meteorological disaster risk assessment in different areas. In terms of disaster emergency planning system construction, Zhejiang Province issued the first government-level marine disaster emergency plan in China as early as 2009, *Marine Disaster Emergency Plan of Zhejiang Province*, specifying regulations on the prevention and emergency response to storm surges, tsunamis, red tides and other marine disasters within Zhejiang Province. Meantime, Zhejiang Province strengthened the construction of digital disaster prevention applications, launching the forest fire monitoring system using geostationary satellite and its App which provides forest fire real-time monitoring across the whole province with updates every

10 minutes and 85% accuracy rate. Notably, Zhejiang Province focused on the institutional construction of disaster risk emergency management, effectively strengthened the legalization of disaster risk management, and built a natural disaster emergency relief system that integrates joint efforts of the province, cities, counties and townships. It developed a natural disaster risk prevention and control and emergency relief platform, and created a five-color map mechanism for natural disaster prevention and control, providing support to local governments' decision-making for disaster prevention and mitigation.

2. Continuously improving disaster early warning system. Zhejiang Province has been attempting to shift the focus from post-disaster relief to pre-disaster prevention, and strengthen the construction of a comprehensive disaster risk monitoring and early warning system. With the advantages brought by its digital reform, Zhejiang Province developed an information management system and an early warning and forecast release platform for extreme weather events, which are connected to 18 departments and have been put into operation. The two systems can be accessed by community officials through Zhejiang Province's government service platform, effectively enhancing disaster warning service. Statistics from the early warning and forecast release platform showed that Zhejiang Province had 31 major weather events in 2021, activated emergency response 15 times for a total of 1,514 hours, including 111.5 hours of first-class response, issued 1,395 warnings of geological hazards, flash floods, urban flooding and other disaster risks, and ranked second in the country with 95.4 points of satisfaction with early warning services. In addition, Zhejiang Province strengthened research and judgment of risk situations based on the early warning platform, carried out disaster risk surveys and key hidden danger identification projects, strengthened the overall planning and coordination of key projects for natural disaster prevention and control, and also carried out scientific research on extreme weather and climate events, as well as research on disaster prevention and mitigation measures for high temperature, heat waves, heavy rainfall, typhoons, forest fires and other disasters, aiming to develop new long-term plans for comprehensive disaster defense.

3. Establishing a sound post-disaster supporting system. For a long time, Zhejiang Province has been actively improving its disaster prevention and

post-disaster relief capacity and has built a diversified disaster risk sharing mechanism and livelihood protection system, significantly improving its major disaster risk management level. In terms of system construction, Zhejiang Province issued the *Implementation Opinions on Reforming Disaster Prevention, Mitigation and Relief Mechanism* in 2021, which proposed to improve the post-disaster recovery and reconstruction work mechanism and clearly required the establishment of sound organization system, planning system, policy system, implementation system and supervision system for post-disaster supporting efforts. Moreover, Zhejiang Province introduced financial insurance mechanism. The introduction of agricultural weather insurance mechanism, weather index insurance products, weather insurance services and other initiatives has effectively protected farmers' property security in extreme weather events. Specifically, in terms of agricultural weather insurance, Zhejiang Province issued the *Implementation Opinions on Accelerating the High-quality Development of Agricultural Insurance*, *Action Plan to Further Accelerate the High-quality Development of Agricultural Insurance* and other policy documents to strengthen guidance in this regard. In 2021 alone, plantation insurance provided 34.2 billion yuan of risk protection for farmers in the province and paid out 800 million yuan in compensation. Besides, Zhejiang Province launched new types of weather index insurance, such as low temperature/high temperature weather index insurance, rainfall weather index insurance and drought index insurance to provide farmers with strong risk protection against extreme weather disasters. In 2021, weather index insurance provided 46,000 farmers with 1.1 billion yuan of risk protection. In addition, Zhejiang Province launched a provincial-level pilot catastrophe insurance, and utilized big data and other technologies to make it possible for farmers to file the claim online with no file needed to be submitted, simplifying the claim settlement process and creating green channels for claim settlement.

V. Conclusion and Future Prospects

Zhejiang Province has the fourth largest economy in China and has a large private economy. It is a big greenhouse gas emitter and faces severe challenges in energy saving and carbon reduction. It suffers from severe impact of climate change, and has an urgent need for green and low-carbon transition. For more than ten years, Zhejiang Province has been practicing the idea that lucid waters and lush mountains are invaluable assets and maintaining the strategic determination to cope with climate change. It has mobilized the whole province to engage in the construction of Ecological Province, Green Zhejiang Province, Ecological Zhejiang Province, Beautiful Zhejiang Province, Big Garden and other initiatives. Its climate change response has undergone historic changes both in its understanding, philosophy and practices to deal with climate change. The target system, work system, policy system and evaluation system for the goal of "carbon peaking and carbon neutrality" have been basically built.

In 2020, General Secretary Xi Jinping clearly pointed out that Zhejiang Province should play an exemplary role in ecological civilization construction during his visit to Zhejiang Province. The report of the 15th Party Congress of Zhejiang CPC points out that it is imperative to promote high-quality modernization of man and nature in harmony and build a model province of ecological civilization. At present, Zhejiang Province is in the decisive decade to deal with climate change, reduce disaster risks and achieve sustainable development goals and it still has a long way to go in climate governance. Zhejiang Province must fully and accurately apply new development philosophy, adhere to the principle of promoting high-quality development, achieving energy security, controlling carbon emissions and improving people's quality of life. It shall incorporate climate change response into its overall economic and social development plan and make efforts on the five major strategies including transition from dual control of total energy consumption and intensity to dual control of total carbon emissions and carbon emission intensity, digital and intelligent carbon emission control, green finance, market standard access and green technology leadership, and focus on five paths including carbon reduction in energy structure, carbon reduction in industrial structure, carbon control in construction and transportation, decarbonization powered by science and technology, and carbon sequestration in ecosystem. A climate change and low carbon development system with Zhejiang Province characteristics featuring five strategies plus five paths should be built. Zhejiang Province should coordinate efforts in pollution and carbon reduction, and achieve green, low-carbon, circular and high-quality sustainable development.

A. Strategically, Zhejiang Province highlights system innovation and builds itself into a national demonstration province for green, low-carbon and circular development

First, building a pioneer area for transition from dual control of total energy consumption and intensity to dual control of total carbon emission and intensity. The transition from dual control of total energy consumption and intensity to dual control of total carbon emission and intensity is the policy-oriented guidance for a period of time in the future. Zhejiang Province as a demonstration area for Beautiful China Initiative, should take this initiative as the focus and take the lead in building a systematic and complete carbon emission policy system. It should take steps to establish a carbon emission budget management system, give full play to the role of market-based resource allocation and trading mechanism, and promote the transformation and upgrading of industrial and energy structures to low-carbon and high-end ones in a more flexible and efficient manner. It should also establish a carbon emission evaluation system for fixed asset investment projects, study and develop carbon emission evaluation standards and methodologies for key industries, helping reduce energy consumption and carbon emissions of investment projects from the source. It should establish a more mature system for breaking down and supervising carbon emission reduction target and carbon emission statistics monitoring system to provide basic data support for scientific decision-making.

Second, building a pilot area for digital and intelligent carbon control. The digital reform in Zhejiang Province's carbon control had an early start and gained rapid development. In the future, Zhejiang Province should work on this foundation, upgrade the basic applications and comprehensive application scenarios and build an intelligent carbon emission monitoring and dynamic accounting system. It should step up its effort to build a digital and intelligent carbon control system, and form a closed-loop management model of "target setting - target breaking down-tracking and warning-service control-assessment and rectification", building the one-stop carbon control management for government, a network of clear carbon reduction goals for enterprises and carbon inclusiveness engagement for individuals at one button. At the same time, these platforms can help to guide and limit all parts of Zhejiang Province to plan economic and industrial development in accordance with carbon-carrying capacity, strengthening the layout of carbon productivity, and realizing digital and intelligent carbon control.

Third, building a model area for the transition to green finance. Transition to low-carbon development of high-carbon industries is crucial for Zhejiang Province to achieve carbon neutrality, and transition finance is a new area that can contribute to the transformation of high-carbon industries. As a pilot zone for green finance reform and innovation, Zhejiang Province needs to realize the orderly and effective connection between green finance and transition finance in the future, and accelerate the construction of an efficient synergy system between transition finance and green finance. It should build a climate change investment and financing system, build new and diversified climate investment and financing models, improve the quality and efficiency of climate investment and financing services and provide more digital and intelligent services. It should also actively launch and apply new carbon finance products, and play the supporting role of investment and financing for climate change mitigation and adaptation. It shall launch transition finance-related bonds to channel more social funds to support high-carbon economic activities, including the transition of enterprises, projects and financial assets to low-carbon and zero-carbon development, promote emission reduction and business transformation of the real economy, and accelerate carbon peaking and carbon neutrality of the whole society.

Fourth, building a model area where "carbon peaking and carbon neutrality" standards can be applied. The establishment of a sound "carbon peaking and carbon neutrality" standard system serves as a specific measure to improve the standardized green development of key areas and to ensure standardized ecological benefits. Zhejiang Province has issued an implementation plan for carbon peaking and carbon neutrality standard system, and these standards should be applied in all key areas in the future. Zhejiang Province will focus on six major areas including industry, energy, construction, transportation, agriculture and residential life, and set the standards for market access from various dimensions, including intensity, total amount, spacial distribution, business formats and technology. Zhejiang Province will develop classified and hierarchical carbon emission criteria fit with international and domestic advanced levels, regulate carbon emission activities, and build a comprehensive carbon peaking and carbon neutrality standard system featuring "one general system plus six sub-systems" that is compatible to Zhejiang Province's construction of an ecological civilization exemplary zone.

Fifth, building a demonstration area for the promotion of green technology. Green technology innovation is playing a key role in responding to climate change and reducing carbon emission. Zhejiang Province is one of the provinces with the strongest science and technology innovation capacity, and it needs to further strengthen the guidance of green technology innovation with the "315" innovation system project in the future. It will build a comprehensive green and low-carbon technology innovation system for carbon neutrality. By using digital technologies, such as AI, Big Data and Internet of Things, it will promote key core technologies, such as renewable energy, energy storage, hydrogen energy, carbon capture, utilization and storage (CCUS) and ecological carbon sink to reach international advanced level, and coordinate efforts to promote deep decarbonization in key areas, such as energy, industry, transportation and construction. It will actively give full play to the role of national green technology trading center, promote the commercialization and trading of green technology achievements across regions, and properly perform green development and innovation.

B. On the work path, Zhejiang Province rationally controls the pace of its carbon emission efforts, vigorously and orderly promotes carbon peaking and carbon neutrality

First, promoting deep decarbonization of the energy structure. Zhejiang Province focuses on developing green and low-carbon energy and keeping supply and price stable, and promotes the transition of energy structure by launching sophisticated clean energy projects, improving the quality of external energy resources, building projects with leading energy efficiency, promoting green consumption and deepening market reform. Zhejiang Province puts its focus on giving priority to the development of new energy. It successively implements projects to double its wind and PV capacity, develops nuclear power in a safe and orderly way, develops pumped storage in a scientific way, arranges the development of clean and efficient thermal power, and actively strives for external clean electricity. It steps up its efforts to build a high-standard energy facility network. It strengthens clean and efficient utilization of coal, upgrades coal-fired power generating units to reduce carbon emissions, renovates their heating supply facilities and allocates coal-fired power generating units for flexible purposes. It gives full play of the leading role of energy efficiency standards, and strictly applies the energy efficiency standard of 0.52 tons of standard coal per 10,000 yuan for market access to new projects. It carries out energy efficiency diagnosis to approximately 4,000 enterprises in 7 major industries in batches and by industries, and adopts the access mechanism featuring regional energy conservation assessment and industrial energy efficiency technical standards. It actively promotes green power trading and accelerates the application of green power certificates. It improves the four-level energy budget management mechanism covering province, municipalities, counties and enterprises. It deepens the reform of energy-use rights trading and explores the establishment of spot market for energy-use rights trading. It also promotes the use of electricity to replace coal, fuel oil and other traditional energy sources.

Second, promoting the decarbonization of industrial structure. Zhejiang Province focuses on industrial structure adjustment, builds a green, low-carbon and circular modern industrial system, promotes the upgrading of the industrial scale and structure, and forges new industrial competitive advantages in its effort to achieve the dual carbon goals. Zhejiang Province puts its focus on cultivating emerging industries, builds four trillion-level world-class advanced industrial clusters, fifteen 100-billion-level provincial industrial clusters and a number of 10-billion-level new star industrial clusters, and develops new energy industries, such as PV, wind power, hydrogen energy and energy storage. Besides, it continuously promotes the construction of demonstration areas for traditional manufacturing industry transformation and upgrading, implements carbon peaking special action in seven key industries with high energy consumption, and promotes the green and low-carbon transition of key industries. It improves the green manufacturing grading and cultivation mechanism, promotes energy-efficient renovation of process systems, and builds a green manufacturing standard system. Moreover, it promotes industrial energy saving and carbon reduction with digital technology, vigorously develops the new paradigm of industrial brain plus future factory, and promotes the digital transformation of industrial enterprises, subdivided industries and industrial clusters.

Third, promoting carbon reduction in construction and transportation. In terms of construction, Zhejiang Province puts its emphasis on reducing buildings' energy consumption and optimizing buildings' energy structure. It promotes the upgrading of green and low-carbon buildings, formulates and further revises the *Energy-Efficient Design Standards for Residential Buildings with Ultra-Low Energy Consumption* and *Evaluation Standards for Green and Ecological Urban Area*. It accelerates the industrialization of new-type buildings, promotes the application of green building materials and green construction. It strengthens the application of renewable energy in new buildings, especially the application of solar PV power, air-source heat pumps and solar thermal. Regarding transportation, Zhejiang Province promotes the upgrading of its transportation structure, traffic equipment, organization efficiency and other factors on the transportation chain. It puts the focus on the co-development of four types of ports, strengthens the construction of railway-highway-waterway, river-sea and other multimodal transportation hubs and promotes the construction of the Yiwu-Ningbo-Zhoushan Great Channel. In addition, Zhejiang Province steps up its efforts to build Ningbo-Jinhua city cluster to strengthen the national comprehensive freight hub chain, build a East China hub for China-Europe freight trains, build Quzhou into a multimodal transportation hub across borders of four provinces, and build Jiaxing into a sea-river multimodal transportation hub. Through comprehensive policy guidance, Zhejiang Province accelerates the replacement of frequently-used public transportation vehicles and elimination of outdated business vehicles. It promotes comprehensive urban traffic management, and vigorously develops non-motorized transportation and sharing transportation modes, such as sharing bicycles.

Fourth, promoting the application of science and technology in low-carbon development. On the one hand, Zhejiang Province should seize the high ground of green and low-carbon science and technology innovation. It puts its focus on the implementation of four key initiatives for cutting-edge technology innovation, and focuses on innovation in zero-carbon power, zero-carbon non-electric energy, zero-carbon process remodeling, zero-carbon system coupling, carbon universal utilization and storage, carbon sinks and other areas. It establishes innovative mechanisms for scientific research. For instance, it adopts open competition mechanism, the "horse racing" mechanism, merit-based commission mechanism and other ways to select the best candidates in science and technology projects. In addition, Zhejiang Province speeds up research on cutting-edge low-carbon technology. It accelerates the construction of provincial laboratories in the field of energy, strengthens the construction of state key laboratories for clean energy use, fluorinated greenhouse gas substitution, control and treatment, and creates a leading low-carbon technology innovation cluster in China. It deepens the construction of national green technology trading center, and promotes the transformation and utilization of carbon peaking and carbon neutrality technology. It implements the "10-100-1,000" Initiative for green technology innovation to strengthen the coordinated development of technology industry. On the other hand, Zhejiang Province should take advantage of its digital reform and deepen the construction of its platform for smart governance of carbon peaking and carbon neutrality. It should explore the construction of a products' carbon footprint database, which can include statistics and data on electricity, energy use and others. It should also guide Quzhou to improve the quality of its carbon account system and expand the coverage of this system, strengthen carbon emissions dynamic monitoring and prediction and early warning of key regions and fields, improve the service features and help enterprises reduce carbon and individuals lead a low-carbon life.

Fifth, promoting effective carbon sequestration of the ecosystem. Zhejiang Province has abundant natural and ecological resources, such as forests, oceans and wetlands, which have great potential for carbon sequestration. Zhejiang Province should give full play to its green ecological advantages, strictly adhere to the red line of ecological protection, strengthen the spatial planning and usage control of its land, and build a land spatial development and protection pattern that is conducive to carbon peaking and carbon neutrality. It shall continue its efforts to clear the sky, water and soil, control pollution from the source in a targeted and scientific way and in accordance with the law. It will focus on solving prominent environmental problems, and build a solid ecological security barrier. It will strengthen the construction of a living community of mountains, water, forests, fields, lakes, grasses and sands, and step up its efforts to implement major projects for the protection and restoration of important ecosystems. It will carry out major actions for the greening of land, forest quality improvement, biodiversity conservation and others, develop a nature reserves system mainly composed of national parks, give full play to the role of forests, oceans, wetlands, lakes, soil in carbon sequestration, and enhance the overall increase in carbon sinks in the ecosystem.

Author: The writing group of Zhejiang economic & information centre

Assessment of Zhejiang's Progress in Climate Change and Low-carbon Development from the Perspective of "Four Dimensions" Balance

The national strategy of carbon peaking and carbon neutrality has put forward new requirements for regional low-carbon development evaluation. Centering on the four dimensions of economic development, energy security, carbon emissions, and resident living, an evaluation system for climate change and low-carbon development covering multiple dimensions such as carbon emissions reduction, economic and social development, especially the just transformation dimension, is constructed, and empirical analysis is conducted on the provincial benchmarking and municipal comparison. Zhejiang's climate change and low-carbon development are found to have achieved steady improvement, similar to Guangdong Province, and all dimensions are continuously improving, except for energy security and carbon sink enhancement, which are heavily affected by resource endowment. The level of low-carbon and high-quality development of the 11-districted city continues to improve, with Hangzhou, Wenzhou, and Lishui topping the list. In the future, it can be improved by expanding and perfecting the evaluation indexes, expanding the evaluation scope and improving the evaluation methods.

I. Introduction

The evaluation of regional low-carbon development is a common academic research topic, and there are mature paradigms in both the selection of evaluation indexes and methods. However, there are still three differences in the study of this paper, i.e., the Assessment of Zhejiang's Progress in

Climate Change and Low-carbon Development from the Perspective of "Four Dimensions" Balance. First, as the birthplace of the "Two Mountains Theory", Zhejiang has always attached importance to green and low-carbon development. However, the evaluation of low-carbon development taking Zhejiang as the object is still relatively rare, especially the unprecedented comparison between provinces and cities in parallel. But there is no doubt that the comparison itself is necessary and meaningful. Second, the evaluation of this study is labeled as "four dimensions", which means that Zhejiang continues to emphasize the comprehensive balance of four dimensions, i.e. economic development, energy security, carbon emissions and resident living, in promoting carbon peaking and carbon neutrality. Therefore, the evaluation in this paper is no longer confined to the evaluation of carbon emissions reduction, but focuses more on its interaction with socioeconomic development, such as employment, disposable income and other items related to the just transformation. Third, as the work of carbon peaking and carbon neutrality has been promoted for more than two years, the understanding of carbon emissions and carbon emissions reduction has progressed. As the practice of Zhejiang, it is necessary to refine carbon emissions to energy, industry, construction, transportation, agriculture and resident living, and investigate the characteristics of total volume, efficiency, quality and other dimensions respectively, which together constitute the main characteristics of regional carbon emissions, and these characteristics are the starting point for conducting low-carbon development evaluation.

The recent literature related to low-carbon development evaluation can be divided into two main directions. One is in the selection of indexes, which can be divided into three categories. First, it evaluates the economic and social situation, and also evaluates the indexes related to just transformation, such as [1]. Second, it evaluates carbon emissions only, without economic and social development, such as [2], [3], [8] and [9]. Third, on the basis of evaluating carbon emissions, economic and social evaluation indexes are included, but the indexes related to just transformation are not involved, such as [4], [5], [6], [7] and [10]. Therefore, studies that jointly consider and evaluate the indexes related to just transformation and the performance of carbon emissions reduction are relatively rare. By combining with the aforementioned studies, the selection of indexes in this paper will expand the evaluation indexes to the characteristics of each sector based on carbon emissions and will include evaluation indexes related to economic and social development at the same time, especially those closely related to just transformation. The other is in terms of evaluation methods, it can be summarized into two categories. First is the adoption of TOPSIS and its improved related methods. [3], [4], [7], [8] and [9] all belong to this category. Second, other methods are adopted, which are slightly differentiated, mainly including the coupling coordination degree model[1], the method combining Dagum Gini coefficient and its decomposition, Kernel density estimation and quadratic assignment program[2], fuzzy evaluation method[5], simple weighting method[6], and the method combining the dynamic integrated measurement model with the regional difference[10]. It can be seen that TOPSIS is still a relatively mainstream method. But it is worth noting that the TOPSIS method involves the problem of determining the weights of indexes, and relevant studies have more often used the entropy weighting method and its improved method [3, 4, 7, 8, 9] because of its objectivity in determining the weights. Being more familiar with the actual situation, subjective weights will be used in this paper.

This paper mainly focuses on the four dimensions of economic development, energy security, carbon emissions, and resident living, analyses the characteristics of the carbon emissions sector, introduces indexes related to just transformation, and constructs a low-carbon development evaluation index system. Meanwhile, a two-level TOPSIS evaluation method system is constructed in an innovative manner. The subsequent contents are arranged as follows: Part II introduces the evaluation indexes and evaluation methods; Part III introduces the evaluation results and comparison between Zhejiang and Jiangsu, Shandong, Fujian and Guangdong; Part IV introduces the evaluation results and comparison among the 11 districted city in Zhejiang; Part V summarizes the conclusions and gives the prospect for the next step.

II. Evaluation index system and method

A. Evaluation index

With reference to relevant studies and combining them with the actual situation of Zhejiang, a two-level evaluation index system of dimensions-indexes has been established. There are 10 dimensions: the first dimension is the economic development; the second dimension is energy security; the third to ninth dimensions are related to sectors under carbon emissions; and the tenth dimension is resident living, which will be discussed in the following separately.

1. Economic development

It mainly includes three indexes.

The carbon decoupling index, i.e. the ratio of carbon emissions growth rate to GDP growth rate, measures the dependence of economic development on carbon emissions. In the case of economic development with a positive GDP growth rate, the smaller the index, the better. When greater than 1, it means that the growth rate of carbon emissions is faster than that of GDP, and the economy is in the process of high carbonization. When between 0 and 1, it means that the growth rate of carbon emissions is slower than that of GDP, and the economy is in the low-carbon transition. When equal to 0, it means that carbon emissions are no longer growing; when less than 0, it represents a decline in carbon emissions.

R&D expenditure intensity, i.e. the ratio of R&D expenditure to GDP. Scientific and technological innovation (STI) is the key variable that drives the achievement of carbon peaking and carbon neutrality, and strong STI input is required to ensure STI output.

The growth rate of the number of enterprise legal persons, i.e. the year-on-year growth rate of the number of enterprise legal persons, measures the impact on the business environment in the process of achieving carbon peaking and carbon neutrality. If there is a negative impact, the number of enterprise legal persons may decrease.

2. Energy security

It mainly includes two indexes.

The utilization rate of renewable energy, measured by non-water renewable energy generation to installed capacity, mainly reflects the degree of low-carbon energy system. As the country is at the height of building renewable energy, its utilization level will be evaluated to avoid stranding of related assets.

Electricity self-sufficiency, measured by imported power to total power consumption, mainly reflects the extent to which electricity can be self-supplied within a region.

3. Carbon emissions reduction in the energy sector

It mainly includes three indexes. There are generally three carbon emissions reduction indexes for each sector, representing the efficiency of carbon emissions, the structure of carbon emissions, and the impact on employment in the sector respectively. The latter is a concrete depiction of just transformation.

Carbon emission per unit of energy, measured by regional carbon emissions to energy consumption, mainly reflects the degree of low-carbon energy system.

The coal consumption ratio, measured by the carbon emissions to carbon emissions of terminal coal consumption in a region, mainly reflects the energy structure of carbon emissions. To avoid the impact of large power supply projects, only the proportion of coal used in the end consumption is considered.

Employment growth in the energy sector, measured by the growth rate in the energy sector to permanent resident population growth, mainly reflects the impact of carbon emissions reduction on employment in the energy sector. In order to keep the employment ratio of the whole society from falling, the growth rate of the employed population cannot be lower than that of the permanent resident population. If the growth rate of the employed population is lower than that of the permanent resident population, it indicates that the employment rate of the whole resident population will be reduced by the employment rate of this sector.

4. Carbon emissions reduction in the industry sector

It mainly includes three indexes.

Carbon emissions per unit of industrial value added, measured by regional industry sector carbon emissions to industrial value added, mainly reflects how much carbon emissions is required for the output of a unit of value added.

The growth rate of value added of strategic emerging industries, which mainly reflects the low-carbon extent of industrial structure. Compared with other industry sector, strategic emerging industries have higher carbon productivity, and the expansion of their scale will drive down carbon emissions per unit of value added in the industry sector.

Employment growth in the industry sector is the same as the corresponding index in the energy sector.

5. Carbon emissions reduction in the construction sector

It mainly includes three indexes.

Carbon emissions per unit of value added in the construction sector, measured by the regional carbon emissions in the construction sector to industrial value added, mainly reflects how much carbon emissions is needed for the output of per unit of value added. As the construction sector includes the construction and public buildings sectors, carbon emissions and value added are also expressed as the sum of the two sectors.

The proportion of carbon emissions from electricity in the construction sector mainly reflects the low-carbon extent of the building energy utilization structure. Compared with other energy sources, electricity has a relatively low-carbon emission factor, and is still in the process of continuous decline. Increasing the proportion of electricity utilization will reduce carbon emissions without reducing energy consumption.

Employment growth in the construction sector is same as the corresponding index in the energy sector.

6. Carbon emissions reduction in the transportation sector

It mainly includes three indexes.

Carbon emissions per unit of transportation turnover, measured by regional transportation carbon emissions to cargo transportation turnover, mainly reflects in the amount of carbon emissions required for the output of per unit of cargo transportation turnover. The transportation sector includes operational transportation and non-operational transportation, and only operational transportation is considered here.

The proportion of carbon emissions from electricity in the transportation sector mainly reflects low-carbon extent of transportation energy utilization structure.

Employment growth in the transportation sector is same as the corresponding index in the energy sector.

7. Carbon emissions reduction in the agriculture sector

It mainly includes two indexes. Emissions in agriculture sector are relatively small, so structural indexes are no longer considered.

Carbon emissions per unit of agricultural value added, measured by the agricultural carbon emissions of the region to goods agricultural value added, mainly reflects how much carbon emissions are needed for the output of per unit of agricultural value added.

Employment growth in the agriculture sector is same as the corresponding index in the energy sector.

8. Carbon emissions reduction in the residential living sector

It mainly includes three indexes.

Per capita living electricity consumption, measured by the resident living electricity consumption to resident population in the region, which mainly reflects the living quality of residents. The consumption of residential power can represent the quality of life to some extent, given almost all the non-mobile energy used by residents is electricity.

The urbanization rate of resident population mainly reflects the low-carbon extent of resident population structure. According to available studies, urban residents usually have lower per capita living carbon emissions due to greater agglomeration. Under a certain total resident population, an increase in urbanization rate can help reduce carbon emissions.

The overall employment growth of residents, measured by the growth rate of employed population to that of resident population, which have same significance as that of energy and other sectors, and mainly measures the impact of carbon emissions reduction on the employment of all residents.

9. Carbon sink enhancement

It mainly includes two indexes.

Per capita forest area measures per capita forest resources mainly.

Forest coverage rate measures forest resources mainly.

10. Resident living

It mainly includes three indexes.

Per capita disposable income mainly reflects the impact of carbon emissions reduction on the value of income.

The sharing degree of economic development achievements, measured by the proportion of per capita disposable income to per capita GDP, mainly reflects the impact of carbon emissions reduction on the sharing of economic development achievements. Carbon emissions reduction is usually characterized by scale effect and intensive capital. It is very likely that with the promotion of carbon emissions reduction, the proportion of wage income in GDP will decrease, which is contrary to just transformation.

$PM_{2.5}$ reflects the impact of carbon emissions reduction on the ecological environment mainly.

There are a total of 10 dimensions and 27 indexes as listed above (Table 2-1).

Table 2-1　Index system of the assessment of Zhejiang's progress in climate change and low-carbon development from the perspective of "Four Dimensions" balance

Dimension	Index	Significance	Calculation method	Remark
Economic development	Carbon decoupling index	The dependence of economic development on carbon emissions	The ratio of carbon emissions growth rate to economic growth rate	
	R&D expenditure intensity	Support of STI to carbon emissions reduction		
	Growth rate of the number of enterprise legal persons	The impact of carbon emissions reduction on the business environment	The year-on-year growth rate of the number of enterprise legal persons	
Energy security	Utilization rate of renewable energy	Energy low-carbon	The ratio of non-water renewable energy generation to installed capacity of non-water renewable energy	Not applicable to districted city
	Electricity self-sufficiency	Energy security and supply guarantee	The ratio of imported in electricity to total electricity consumption	Not applicable to districted city

Dimension	Index	Significance	Calculation method	Remark
Carbon emissions reduction in the energy sector	Carbon emissions per unit of energy	Quality of low-carbon energy development	The ratio of carbon emissions to energy consumption	
	Coal consumption ratio	Low-carbon of energy consuming structures	the carbon emissions of terminal coal consumption to total carbon emissions	
	Employment growth in the energy sector	The impact of carbon emissions reduction on employment in the energy sector	The ratio of employment growth rate in the energy sector to resident population growth rate	
Carbon emissions reduction in the industry sector	Carbon emissions per unit of industrial value added	Quality of low-carbon industrial development		
	Growth rate of value added in strategic emerging industries	Low-carbon of industrial structure		
	Employment growth in the industry sector	The impact of carbon emissions reduction on employment in the industry sector	The ratio of industrial employment growth rate to resident population growth rate	
Carbon emissions reduction in the construction sector	Carbon emissions per unit of value added in the construction sector	Quality of low-carbon development in construction		
	Proportion of carbon emissions from electricity in the construction sector	Low-carbon of building energy consumption structure		

Dimension	Index	Significance	Calculation method	Remark
Carbon emissions reduction in the construction sector	Employment growth in the construction sector	The impact of carbon emissions reduction on employment in the construction sector	The ratio employment growth rate in the construction industry to resident population growth rate	
Carbon emissions reduction in the transportation sector	Carbon emissions per unit of transportation turnover	Quality of low-carbon transportation development		
	The proportion of carbon emissions from electricity in the transportation sector	Low-carbon of transportation energy consumption structure		
	Employment growth in the transportation sector	The impact of carbon emissions reduction on employment in the transportation sector	The ratio of employment growth rate in the transportation sector to resident population growth rate	
Carbon emissions reduction in the agriculture sector	Carbon emissions per unit of value added in the agriculture sector	Quality of low-carbon development in rural areas		
	Employment growth in the agriculture sector	The impact of carbon emissions reduction on employment in the agriculture sector	The ratio of employment growth rate in the agriculture sector to resident population growth rate	
Carbon emissions reduction in residential living sector	Per capita living electricity consumption	Quality of residential lives		
	Urbanization rate of resident population	Low-carbon of residential structure		

Dimension	Index	Significance	Calculation method	Remark
Carbon emissions reduction in residential living sector	Overall employment growth of residents	The impact of carbon emissions reduction on overall employment	The ratio of employed population growth rate to resident population growth rate	
Carbon sink enhancement	Per capita forest area	Per capita forest resources		
	Forest coverage rate	Forest resource		
Resident living	Per capita disposable income	The impact of carbon emissions reduction on income		
	Degree of sharing of economic development achievements	The impact of carbon emissions reduction on the sharing of economic development achievements	Per capita disposable income as a percentage of per capita GDP	
	$PM_{2.5}$	The impact of carbon emissions reduction on the ecological environment and the synergistic reduction with atmospheric pollutants		

B. Evaluation method

The two-level TOPSIS method is used.

1. The first-level calculation

The relative proximity of each dimension is calculated separately. In this case, the ideal solution and the negative ideal solution adopt the combination of the maximum or minimum values of each evaluation unit. The index number is denoted by i and the evaluation unit number is denoted by j, and the main steps are as follows.

(1) Standard

For the positive index,
$$x_{ij} = \frac{X_{ij} - \min_j(X_{ij})}{\max_j(X_{ij}) - \min_j(X_{ij})} \tag{2-1}$$

For the negative index,
$$x_{ij} = \frac{\max_j(X_{ij}) - X_{ij}}{\max_j(X_{ij}) - \min_j(X_{ij})} \tag{2-2}$$

(2) Select the ideal solution and the negative ideal solution

The ideal solution
$$Z^+ = (x_1^+, \cdots, x_n^+), \tag{2-3}$$

of which
$$x_i^+ = \max_j(x_{ij}) \tag{2-4}$$

The negative ideal solution
$$Z^- = (x_1^-, \cdots, x_n^-), \tag{2-5}$$

of which
$$x_i^- = \min_j(x_{ij}) \tag{2-6}$$

(3) Calculate the distance value of each unit to the ideal solution and negative ideal solution

Distance to the ideal solution
$$d_j^+ = \sqrt{\sum_i w_i (x_{ij} - x_i^+)^2} \tag{2-7}$$

Distance to the negative ideal solution
$$d_j^- = \sqrt{\sum_i w_i (x_{ij} - x_i^-)^2} \tag{2-8}$$

(4) Calculate the relative proximity of each evaluation unit

The relative proximity of each evaluation unit is
$$s_j = \frac{d_j^-}{d_j^- + d_j^+}. \tag{2-9}$$

Notes that
$$d_j^+ \、 d_j^- > 0, \forall j$$

Therefore
$$\frac{0}{d_j^- + d_j^+} \leqslant s_j = \frac{d_j^-}{d_j^- + d_j^+} \leqslant \frac{d_j^-}{d_j^- + 0}, \tag{2-10}$$

That is $0 \leqslant s_j \leqslant 1$. When taken as 0, the evaluation unit coincides with the negative ideal solution, i.e., it is the worst value in all dimensions; when taken as 1, the evaluation unit coincides with the ideal solution, i.e., it is optimal value in all dimensions.

2. The second-level calculation

The main steps are the same as the first-level calculation. Since the relative proximity is theoretically in the interval of [0, 1], the ideal solution is fixed as 1 and the negative ideal solution is fixed as 0 for each subdivision, and the relative proximity of each integrated dimension is calculated again as the comprehensive evaluation result of climate change and low-carbon development of each province, city and districted city.

III. Provincial-level evaluation and comparison

A. Overall evaluation results and its evolution

Four coastal provinces with similar economic scale and development processes as Zhejiang Province, including Jiangsu, Shandong, Fujian, and Guangdong, were selected as evaluation objects to conduct provincial-level evaluation of low-carbon development progress.

In terms of the overall trend, the five provinces can be divided into three types—stable type, steadily rising type, and fluctuating growth type. Fujian Province belongs to the stable type, whose low-carbon development relative proximity stabled between 0.6-0.62, consistently maintaining an advanced level among the five provinces. The steadily rising type includes Zhejiang Province and Guangdong Province. From 2016 to 2020, their relative proximity is similar and has consistently increased. In 2020, Zhejiang Province ranked first in relative proximity, surpassing aFujian Province, which had ranked first for the past four years, while Guangdong Province ranked third. The fluctuating growth type includes Jiangsu Province and Shandong Province. The relative proximity of the two provinces was the lowest in 2018, but it significantly increased in 2020, with no change in ranking among the five provinces.

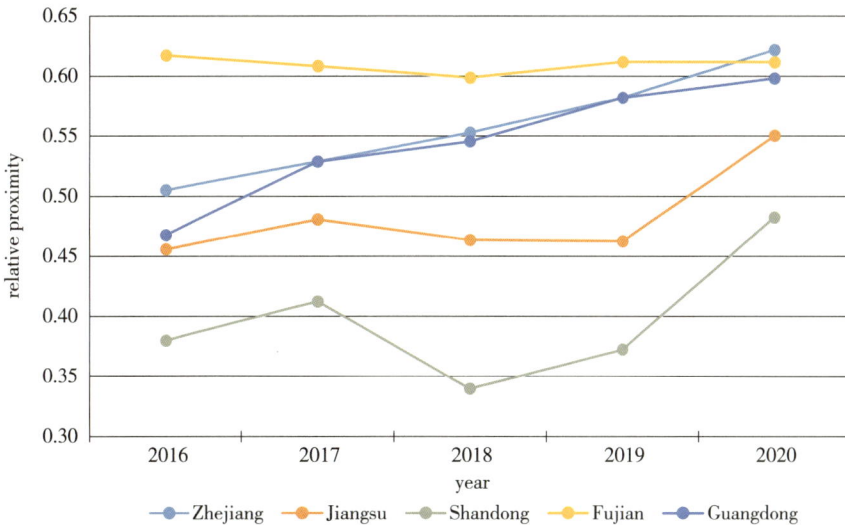

Figure 2-1   Trend of relative proximity among the five provinces

The reasons for the fluctuations in relative proximity may be due to different development strategies chosen by each province. Fujian has chosen a conservative development model, maintaining a stable development in carbon emissions reduction. Its relative proximity by dimensions fluctuates slightly and maintains an overall stable upward trend. The steadily rising provinces have achieved continuous increases in relative proximity in most dimensions, which promoting persistently overall low-carbon development. Zhejiang Province has achieved continuous green low-carbon development in all areas except for energy security and carbon sink enhancement, while Guangdong Province has achieved steady low-carbon development in all areas except for carbon emissions reduction in the industry sector. The fluctuating growth type has chosen a mode of aggressive development followed by governance, especially in 2020, when the overall level of low-carbon development significantly increased.

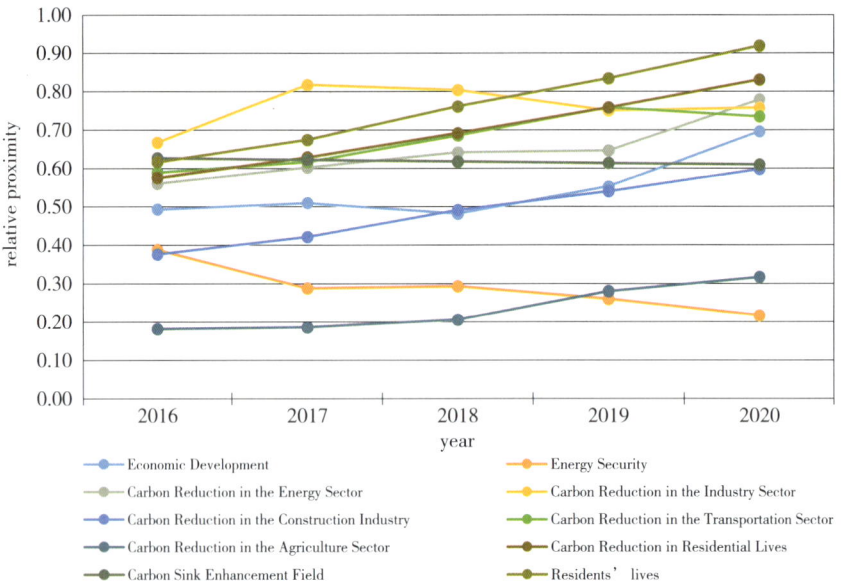

Figure 2-2   Trend of relative proximity by dimensions of Zhejiang Province

B. Evaluation results and its evolution by dimensions

From the perspective of economic development, there are significant fluctuations among the five provinces. Zhejiang and Jiangsu provinces have similar development patterns, showing a "U" shape during the "13th Five-Year Plan" period, with a continuous decline in relative proximity from 2016 to 2018, followed by continuous growth, and the overall situation has improved compared

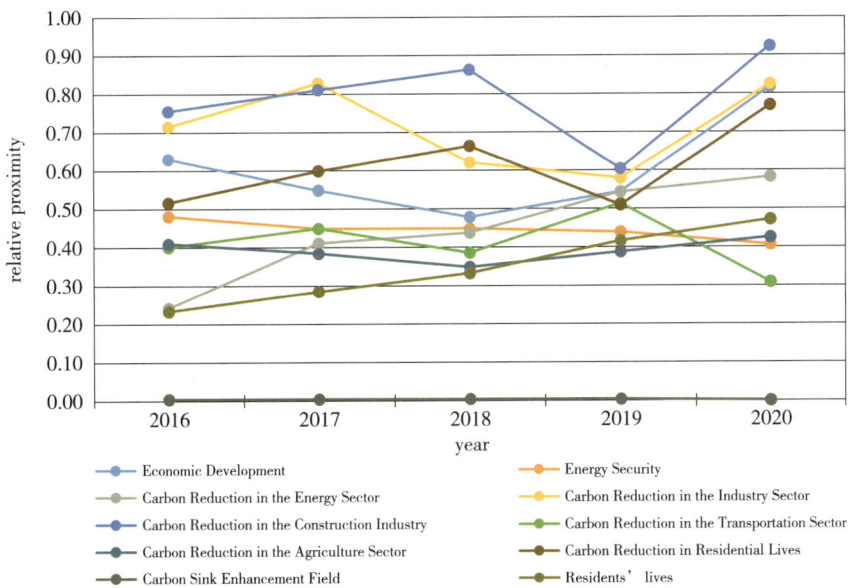

Figure 2-3   Trend of relative proximity by dimensions of Jiangsu Province

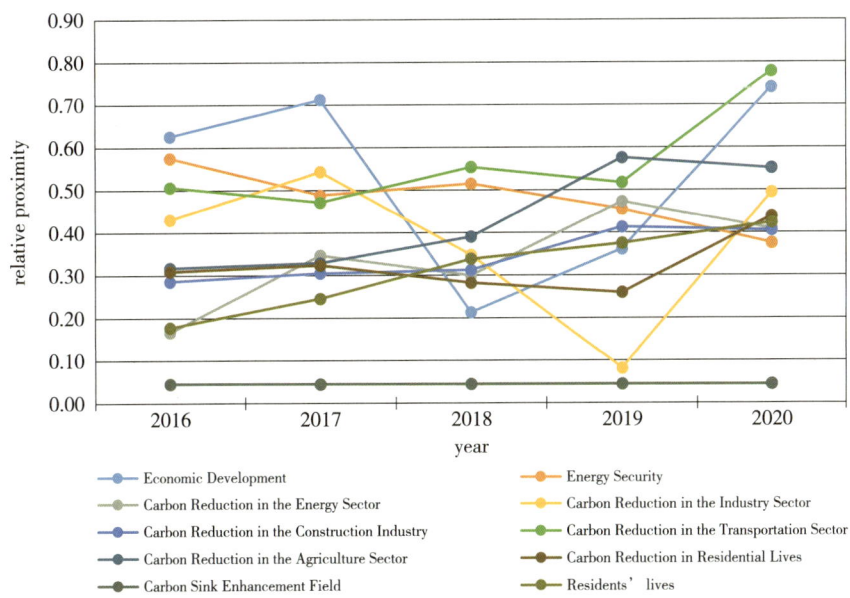

Figure 2-4   Trend of relative proximity by dimensions of Shandong Province

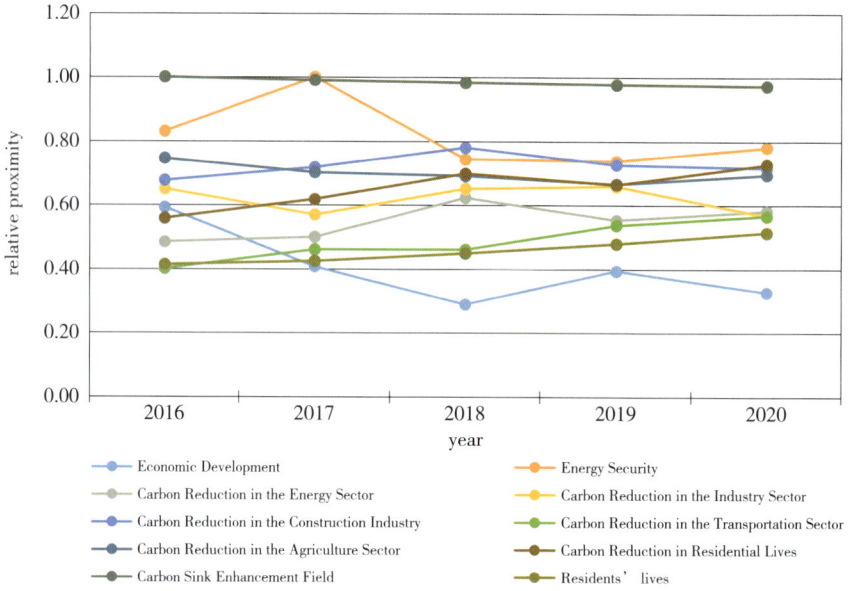

Figure 2-5　Trend of relative proximity by dimensions of Fujian Province

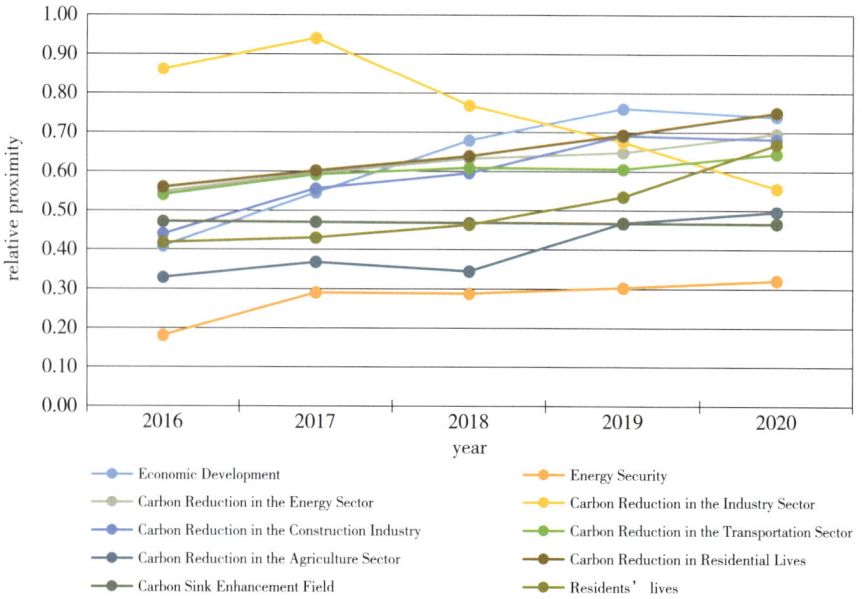

Figure 2-6　Trend of relative proximity by dimensions of Guangdong Province

to 2016. This is related to the weak or even strong decoupling of carbon emissions in the two provinces. Guangdong, on the other hand, showed an inverted "U" shape, with the relative proximity of economic development increasing continuously before 2019, and slightly decreasing in 2020. However, the overall growth rate was the highest, which is closely related to its optimization of the business environment and investment in scientific research so more advanced enterprises have been attracted to develop in Guangdong. Shandong Province showed a trend of growth-decline-growth, although the fluctuations were large, the level of green economic development has still improved during the "13th Five-Year Plan" period, which is also close to the overall trend of low-carbon development in Shandong Province. Unlike other provinces, the level of green economic development in Fujian Province fluctuated and declined during the "13th Five-Year Plan" period, dropping from third place in 2016 to last place in 2020, which is related to the insufficient decoupling between its economic development and carbon emissions. Especially in 2020, due to the impact of the epidemic, its carbon emissions growth rate exceeded the economic growth rate, resulting in a relatively low overall relative proximity.

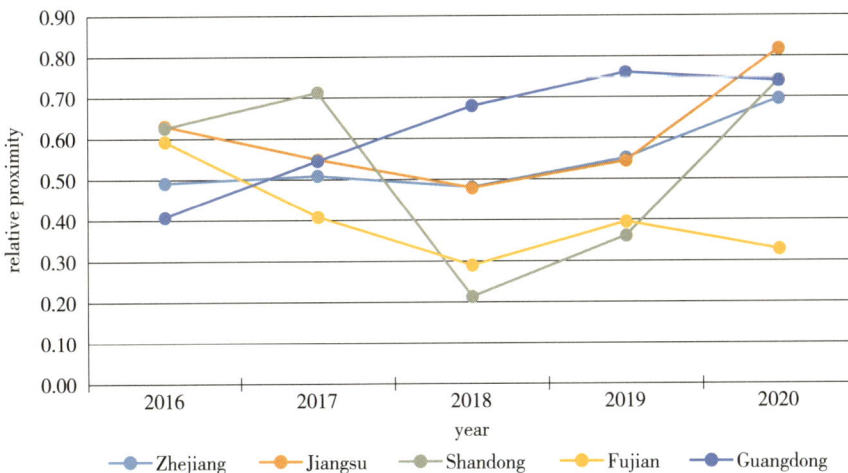

Figure 2-7   Trends in relative proximity of economic development

In terms of energy security, except for Guangdong, other regions show a downward trend in the development of energy security. The development of energy security mainly considers the development of renewable energy and the degree of electricity self-sufficiency. Only Fujian province has achieved electricity self-sufficiency through the construction of nuclear power and other projects, while other provinces still partially rely on external power. Fujian province has consistently ranked first in terms of energy security. For Zhejiang, Jiangsu, and Shandong provinces, although the overall generation and installation capacity of renewable energy has been continuously increasing, due to the constraint of the coal consumption control target, the supply of thermal power is insufficient, which leads to the need to introduce a large amount of external power to ensure the safety of residents' livelihood and industrial development security. The proportion of external power consumption has continued to increase from 2016 to 2020, and the degree of external dependence has continued to deepen, leading to an increase in the risk of power supply. Guangdong province has vigorously developed renewable energy, thereby reducing its reliance on external power supply. The proportion of external power supply has decreased from 33% in 2016 to 22% in 2020, and energy security has been well safeguarded.

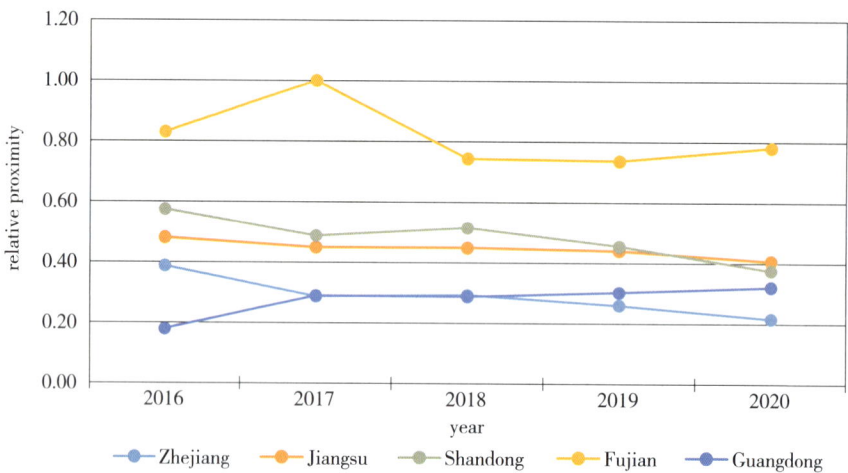

Figure 2-8   Trends in relative proximity of energy security

All provinces have achieved overall optimization in carbon emissions reduction in the energy sector. The optimization of energy structure is the key to achieve carbon emissions reduction in the energy sector. With the deepening and optimization of policies such as dual control of energy consumption and coal consumption control, the proportion of coal consumption in all provinces has continued to decrease, high-carbon energy consumption has decreased, and the energy carbon emissions per unit in most regions have continued to decrease. In

2020, the proportion of coal consumption in Zhejiang Province dropped to 6.38%, which is the lowest among all provinces, and the energy carbon emissions per unit also continued to decrease, ranking first in the evaluation of energy carbon emissions reduction. While promoting orderly carbon emissions reduction in the energy sector, it is also necessary to consider its impact on industrial development. The proportion of employees in the energy industry decreased in some years when applying the ratio of industry employment changes to changes in the resident population as a measuring index.

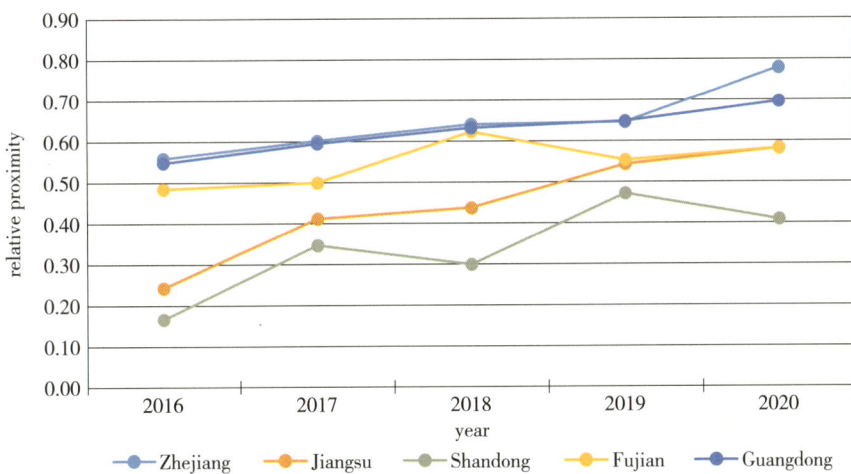

Figure 2-9   Trends in relative proximity of carbon emissions reduction in the energy sector

For industrial carbon emissions reduction, there are differences among provinces due to differences in industrial structure and development direction. Zhejiang, Jiangsu, Fujian, and Guangdong have all achieved overall reduction in industrial carbon emissions intensity, and carbon efficiency has been significantly improved, which is beneficial to industrial carbon emissions reduction. However, the industrial energy consumption intensity in Shandong Province increased significantly from 2016 to 2019, and although felling slightly in 2020, it still increased overall. This is related to the overall industrial structure in Shandong Province, which is why Shandong ranks last in terms of industrial carbon emissions reduction. The evaluation of industrial carbon emissions reduction in Guangdong Province has been continuously declining since 2017, which is related to the continuous decline in the growth rate of added value of strategic emerging industries since 2017. Strategic emerging industries are generally low-carbon and high-efficiency industries, which are conducive to the overall optimization of the industrial structure, but the slowing industrial growth may not be enough to drive low-carbon development. At the same time, with the optimization and adjustment of the overall industrial structure and technological upgrading, the number of employees in the industry sector continues to decrease, and with the increasing demand for carbon emissions reduction, the ability to accommodate employment may decrease.

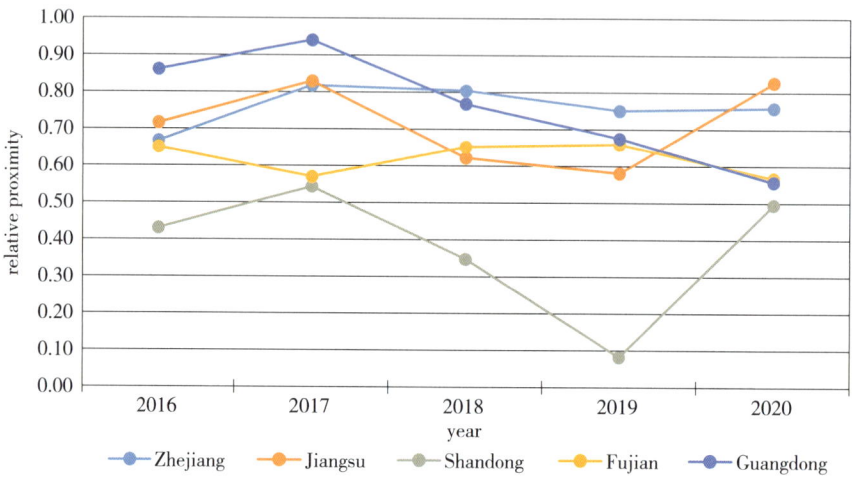

Figure 2-10   Trends in relative proximity of carbon emissions reduction in the industry sector

Looking at carbon emissions reduction in the construction sector, all provinces are continuously optimizing their carbon emissions reduction efforts in this area with the improvement of electrification and carbon efficiency. From the perspective of carbon emissions per unit of value added in the construction industry, it is constantly reducing for all provinces, indicating a continuous improvement in carbon efficiency in the industry. However, due to the large differences in electrification levels between provinces, there are significant differences in their relative proximity. Among the five provinces, Jiangsu has the highest proportion of electric power carbon emissions in the construction industry, reaching over 90%, while Shandong province, whose average level is the lowest, only reaches up to 58.1% (in 2019). Meanwhile, looking at changes in relative proximity, Guangdong province has seen the greatest improvement. On the one hand, the proportion of electric power carbon emissions in the construction industry in Guangdong province increased by about 9.2 percentage points from 2016 to 2020, with a significant growth rate. On the other hand, in the process of continuously promoting emissions reduction in the construction industry, the employment growth rate in the construction industry of Guangdong province has exceeded the growth rate of its permanent resident population, indicating that the development in this industry is expanding and achieving a coordinated development of emissions reduction and growth.

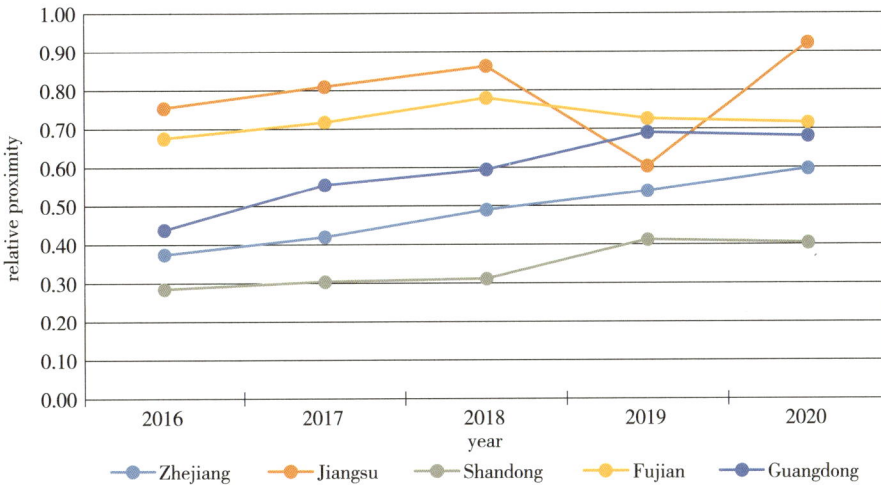

Figure 2-11   Trends in relative proximity of carbon emissions reduction in the construction industry

Looking at carbon emissions reduction in the transportation sector, except for Jiangsu, the relative proximity of all other provinces has improved. Carbon emissions reduction in the transportation sector mainly considers the carbon emissions per unit of transportation turnover and the proportion of electricity emissions in the transportation sector. The relative proximity of carbon emissions reduction in Zhejiang's transportation sector has increased significantly and has always maintained a leading advantage before 2020, mainly due to the relatively low overall carbon emissions per unit of transportation turnover and the continuous increase in the electrification rate of transportation. In 2020, the proportion of electricity carbon emissions reached 10.3%. Guangdong, which is also a major express delivery province, has a similar situation to Zhejiang, and its relative proximity is constantly improving but is lower than that of Zhejiang. The main difference is that the growth rate of electrification in the transportation sector is lower than that of Zhejiang, which results in a lower ranking than Zhejiang. Shandong's relative proximity fluctuates the most, with the highest increment, especially in 2020, when the carbon emissions per unit of transportation turnover in Shandong increased by 23% compared to 2019. The level of transportation cleanliness has significantly improved, resulting in effective carbon emissions reduction. Although the carbon emissions per unit of transportation turnover and electrification level in Jiangsu have continuously improved, transportation was severely affected by the epidemic in 2020, leading to a significant loss of employment and a contraction of the industry, resulting in a decrease in relative proximity in 2020.

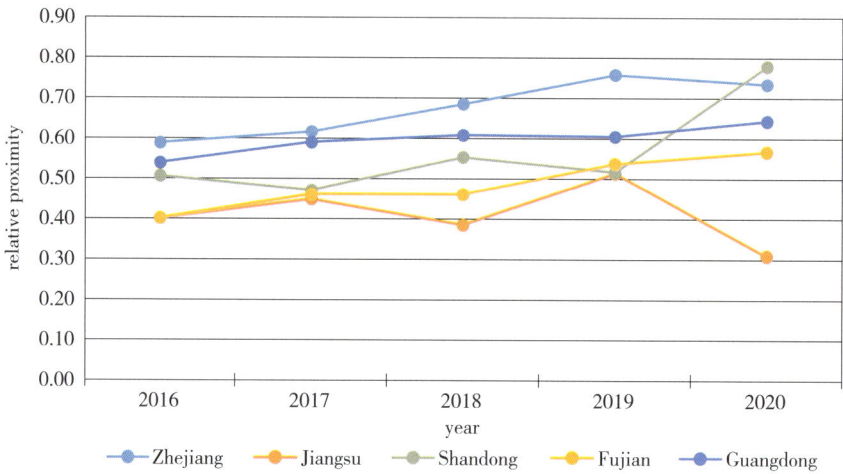

Figure 2-12   Trends in relative proximity of carbon emissions
reduction in the transportation sector

In terms of carbon emissions reduction in the agriculture sector, preliminary results have been achieved with the renewal of agricultural machinery and the construction of high-standard farmland. From the perspective of relative proximity ranking, Fujian Province has always ranked first, mainly due to its excellent resource endowment and rich and high-quality agricultural products with high added value, resulting in its unit carbon emissions for agricultural value-added being much lower than other provinces. However, in recent years, the number of people engaged in agricultural production has continued to decrease, leading to inadequate agricultural security assurance, resulting in a decrease in its relative proximity. Shandong Province has shown the most significant growth in relative proximity, with its unit carbon emissions for agricultural value-added decreasing by approximately 25.9%, making it the province with the most significant decrease. On the other hand, Zhejiang Province has the lowest relative proximity raking in terms of carbon emissions reduction in the agriculture sector, with the highest unit carbon emissions for agricultural value-added. This is closely related to Zhejiang Province's less farmland, complex terrain, and high demand for mechanical operations. Therefore, continuous renew of agricultural machinery is irreversible to improve the carbon efficiency level in the agriculture sector.

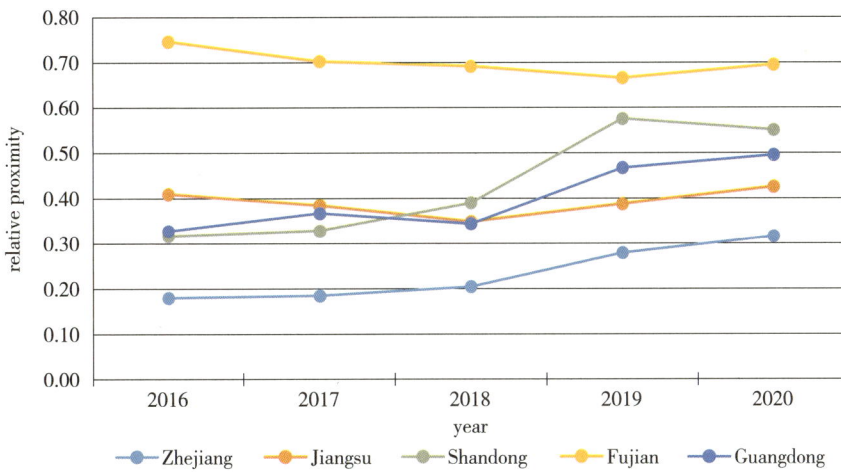

Figure 2-13   Trends in relative proximity of carbon emissions reduction in the agriculture sector

From the perspective of carbon emissions reduction in the residential living sector, except for Shandong Province, the other four provinces have close relative proximity. The relative proximity of carbon emissions reduction in the residential living sector in these five provinces has generally increased. By 2020, except for Shandong Province, the relative proximity of carbon emissions reduction in the residential living sector in other provinces has reached above 0.7. The low relatively proximity of Shandong Province is mainly due to two reasons. Firstly, urbanization can promote the aggregation of living and industry, and bring improvement in energy efficiency. However, the urbanization rate in Shandong Province is relatively low compared to other provinces. Secondly, the poor employment situation in Shandong Province influences the resident living. The relative proximity of carbon emissions reduction in the residential living sector in Zhejiang Province has increased the most, and ranked first in 2020. This is related to the high urbanization rate in Zhejiang Province and the high level of electricity consumption in resident living.

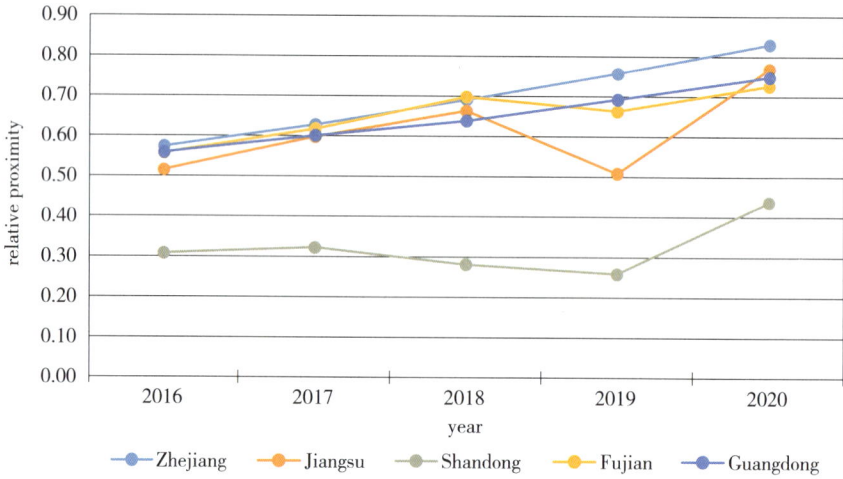

Figure 2-14　Trends in relative proximity of carbon emissions reduction in the residential living sector

From the perspective of carbon sink, regional resource endowment basically determines the situation of carbon sink enhancement. The per capita forest area in Fujian Province reaches 0.2 hectares, nearly twice as much as that in Zhejiang Province, and nearly nine times as much as that in Jiangsu Province which has least per capita forest area. Moreover, the forest coverage rate is as high as 66.8%, so Fujian has the highest relative proximity in terms of carbon sink enhancement. Zhejiang Province ranks second in terms of per capita forest area and forest coverage rate, and second in relative proximity in terms of carbon sink enhancement. The situation of urban construction land in Fujian and Zhejiang has led to a decrease in per capita forest area and a decrease in relative proximity. The relative proximity ranking of carbon sink enhancement in other regions is also consistent with the ranking of forest area and coverage rate. Due to slow growth in forest area, the change in relative proximity is relatively small.

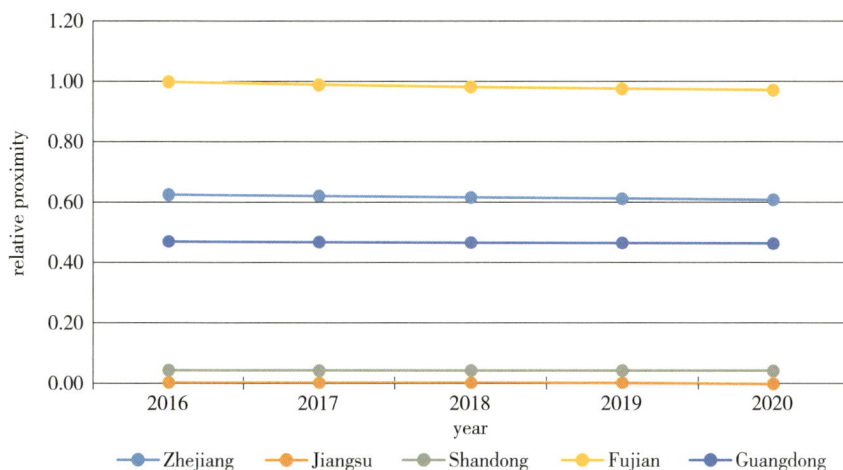

Figure 2-15　Trends in relative proximity of carbon sink enhancement sector

From the perspective of resident living, economic development and improvement of ecological environment have brought continuous improvement in resident living standards. Zhejiang Province ranks first in relative proximity in resident livelihood, and the increase of relative proximity is the most significant. As a demonstration area for common prosperity, it adheres to the principle of "hiding wealth among the residents". The per capita disposable income of residents reached 54,000 yuan in 2020, accounting for more than 50% of per capita GDP. The relative proximity rankings of other provinces in terms of resident living are Guangdong, Fujian, Jiangsu and Shandong in proper order, among which Jiangsu is the second-ranked province in terms of per capita disposable income, but due to its low proportion of per capita GDP and poor air quality ranking among provinces, the resident living ranking falls behind.

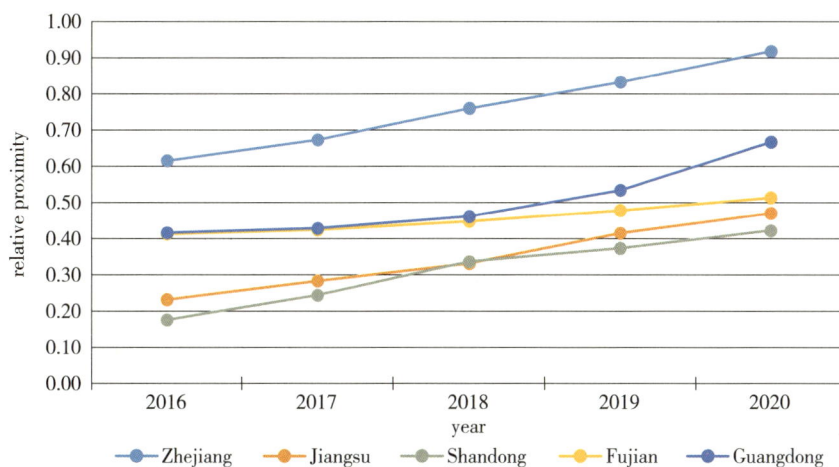

Figure 2-16　Trends in relative proximity of resident living

IV. Assessment and comparison of districted city

A. Overall evaluation results and its evolution

The annual assessment results of 11 districted cities in Zhejiang Province from 2016 to 2021 is analyzed. Over the past six years, although there has been a significant fluctuation due to the impact of economic development change during the COVID-19 pandemic, the level of low-carbon and high-quality development in all districted cities in the province has continued to improve on the whole.

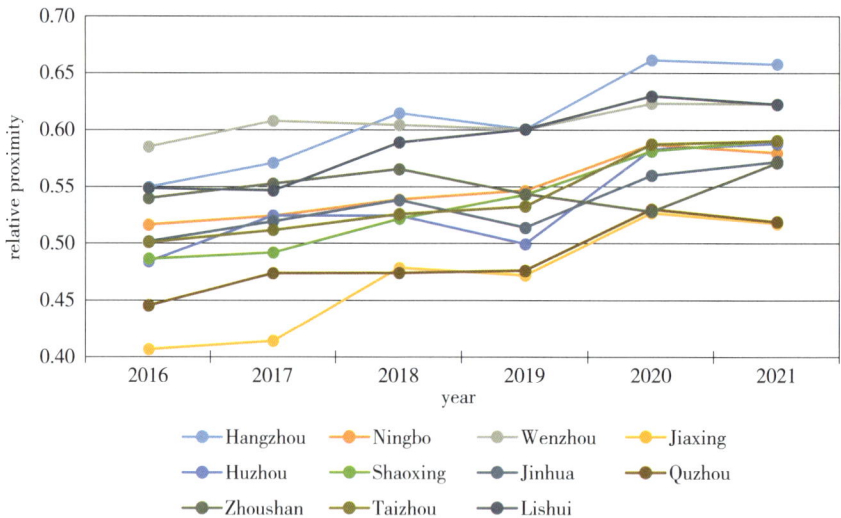

Figure 2-17   Changes in the assessment of low carbon and high-quality
development in districted cities from 2016 to 2021

From the overall evaluation results, currently, Hangzhou, Wenzhou, and Lishui rank higher in the overall low-carbon and high-quality development level among the 11 districted cities in Zhejiang Province, while Quzhou and Jiaxing are in relatively lower positions. Hangzhou, as the provincial capital city, has high-quality economic development and residents' living. Its energy structure and carbon productivity in important sectors such as energy, industry, construction, and transportation are relatively good. Wenzhou has a solid foundation in economic development, and the carbon emission structure in the energy sector has gradually improved, with the proportion of coal consumption in the energy sector decreasing year by year. Lishui has outstanding advantages in the carbon sink enhancement sector and energy structure. At the same time, the carbon productivity in the industry sector and the employment rate in the industry sector both perform well in low-carbon and high-quality development. Although Jiaxing has a significant advantage in economic development and service industry employment, its coal consumption accounts for a large proportion, and the quality of resident living is somewhat affected by environmental pollution. There is also room for improvement in energy conservation awareness, and the electrification level in sectors such as construction and transportation lags behind other cities. In addition, the ability to accommodate employment in the industrial and energy sectors needs to be strengthened. Quzhou needs to improve its carbon emissions reduction in the sectors of energy, industry, and resident living.

In terms of low-carbon and high-quality development, Hangzhou, Huzhou, and Jiaxing have made significant progress and ranked among the top three in all districted cities in Zhejiang. Hangzhou has achieved significant results in reducing emissions in the construction and agriculture sectors, improving the quality of life of its citizens, and optimizing its urban energy structure. Over the past six years, the per capita disposable income of Hangzhou has significantly increased, the effectiveness of environmental pollution control has been remarkable, and the service industry has developed rapidly. Huzhou has made significant achievements in improving the quality of life of its citizens, reducing emissions in the transportation sector, and promoting new energy in transportation. The income of its residents has greatly improved, and the environmental governance industry has made remarkable achievements. Jiaxing has made significant achievements in improving the quality of life of its residents, reducing emissions in the construction and household sectors. Similar to Hangzhou, the service industry has brought economic development while continuously improving its energy structure. As the urbanization rate has increased year by year, the awareness of energy conservation among residents has also increased synchronously, and the living environment and economic level of its residents have improved. Other districted cities have generally made significant progress in the quality of life of their residents and the electrification level of the service industry.

B. Evaluation results and evolution in various dimensions

Through the evaluation of 11 districted cities in different dimensions such as economic development, energy emissions reduction, industrial emissions reduction, building emissions reduction, transportation emissions reduction, agricultural emissions reduction, residential emissions reduction, carbon sink enhancement, and improvement of residents' living quality, the results show that the low-carbon and high-quality development of these cities has improved in most dimensions over the past six years.

From the perspective of economic development, Hangzhou, Jiaxing, and Huzhou have a higher level of attraction to enterprises and are among the top in the province in terms of investment in scientific and technological development. Jiaxing, Wenzhou, and Quzhou have a better degree of decoupling between carbon emissions and economic development. The degree of decoupling in Ningbo and Zhoushan needs to be improved. The economic development of most districted cities in the province has improved in the past six years. Relatively, Wenzhou and Zhoushan have more room for improvement of economic development due to relatively low R&D investment and overall slow growth of enterprises.

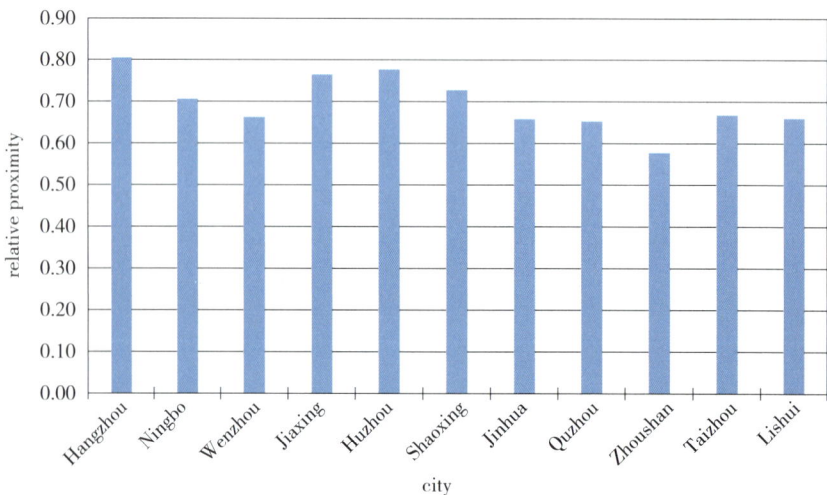

Figure 2-18   Dimensions of economic development in districted cities

From the perspective of carbon emissions reduction in the energy sector, Wenzhou and Hangzhou are among the top in the province with a rational energy consumption structure and a high degree of absorption of talent in the energy sector. Quzhou, Ningbo, and other areas have a relatively high proportion of coal consumption, and their energy carbon emission structure needs to be improved, ranking lower in the province. The energy carbon emission structure of Ningbo, Wenzhou, Taizhou, Lishui, and other areas has declined in ranking in the province in the past six years.

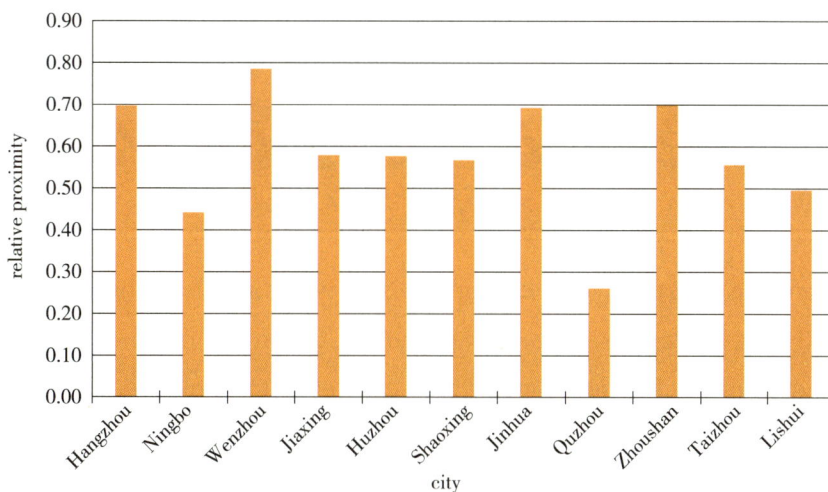

Figure 2-19   Dimensions of emissions reduction in the energy sector of districted cities

From the perspective of carbon emissions reduction in the industry sector, Jinhua, Lishui, and Hangzhou have vigorously developed high-tech industries, reduced carbon emissions per unit of industrial value-added, accelerated the absorption of talent in the industry sector, and achieved significant carbon emissions reduction. Zhoushan's industrial carbon emissions reduction assessment results need to be improved due to the production of high energy-consuming industries such as Zhejiang Petrochemical. Quzhou's industrial energy carbon emission structure is not sufficiently low-carbon. At the same time, Huzhou, Hangzhou, Lishui have relatively low-carbon emissions per unit of industrial value-added, while Shaoxing and Jiaxing have fast-growing high-tech industries, and these cities are in a mid-level position in the province considering comprehensive factors. In the past six years, Taizhou has experienced a decline in its ranking in the industry sector carbon emissions reduction due to the shrinking proportion of employment in the industry sector and a relatively low increase rate in high-tech industry value-added, similar to Zhoushan.

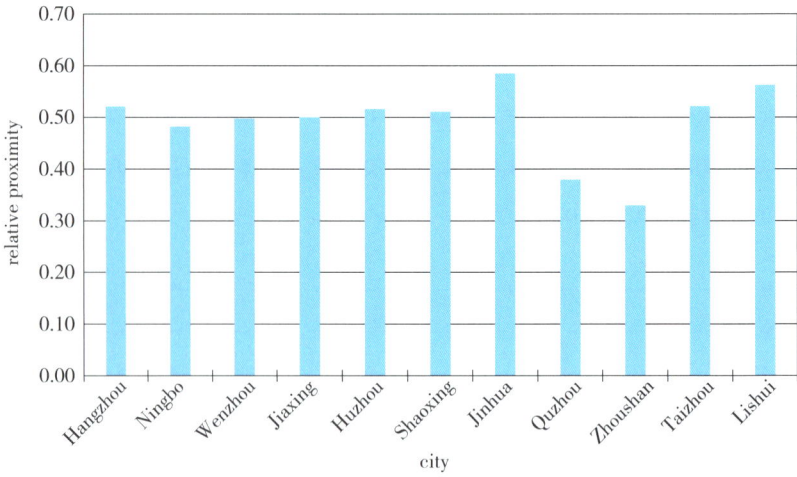

Figure 2-20   Dimensions of emissions reduction in the industry sector of districted cities

From the perspective of carbon emissions reduction in the construction sector, Hangzhou and Ningbo rank in the top tier in the province due to their high degree of electrification in the construction sector, high value-added and carbon productivity in the service and construction industries. Taizhou and Zhoushan also have relatively balanced development and rank in the second tier. Although Jiaxing has a high growth rate in employment in the tertiary industry, its carbon emissions per unit of value-added and electrification level are relatively low. Similarly, Wenzhou ranks lower in the province due to a low level of electrification in the service industry and a shrinking employment population in the industry. In the past six years, the ranking of carbon emissions reduction in the construction sector has declined in Wenzhou, Jinhua, and Lishui.

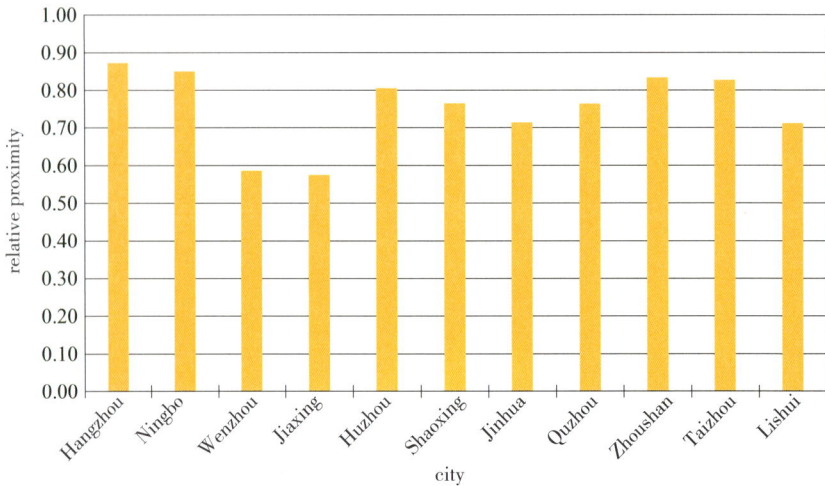

Figure 2-21   Dimensions of emissions reduction in the construction sector of districted cities

Looking at carbon emissions reduction in the transportation sector, Huzhou, Hangzhou, and Quzhou have relatively high carbon emissions from electricity use in transportation, and their carbon emissions per unit of transportation turnover and the employment situation are in a higher position, ranking in the top tier of Zhejiang. Ningbo and Taizhou have low carbon emissions per unit of transportation turnover, but the use of new energy in the transportation sector is relatively low. The situation in Zhoushan and Jiaxing is similar to that in Ningbo and Taizhou, but the employment situation in the transportation sector is improving. Lishui and Jinhua are affected by higher carbon emissions per unit of transportation turnover, with Jinhua having a low proportion of new energy in transportation, and Lishui having a poor employment situation in the transportation sector. Therefore, their rankings are relatively low in the province. In the past six years, the rankings of Ningbo, Jinhua, and Lishui in the transportation sector have declined.

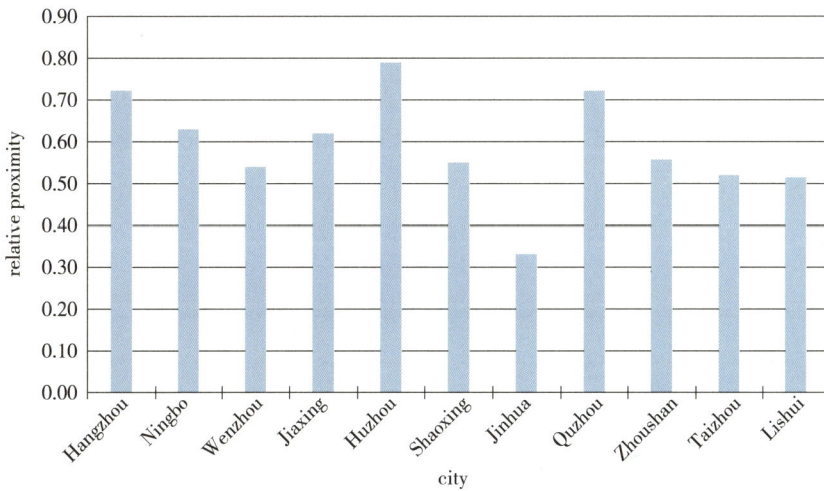

Figure 2-22   Dimensions of emissions reduction in the transportation sector of districted cities

Looking at the carbon emissions reduction dimension in the Agriculture sector, Zhoushan, Lishui, Wenzhou, Shaoxing, and Hangzhou all have excellent performance, with improvements in agricultural employment and carbon productivity. Jiaxing and Quzhou need to improve their efforts to reduce carbon emissions in the Agriculture sector, with significant losses in agricultural employment, and therefore rank lower. However, in the past six years, each city has achieved significant carbon emissions reduction in the Agriculture sector, and the overall level of carbon emissions reduction has improved.

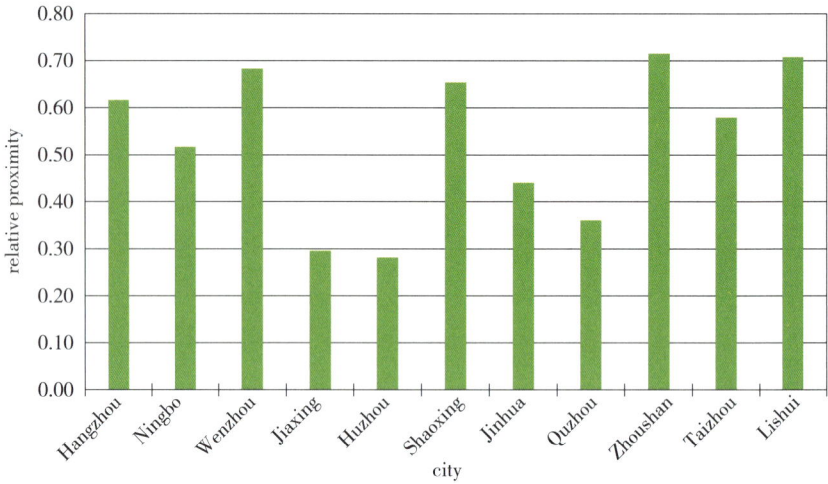

Figure 2-23   Dimensions of emissions reduction in the agriculture sector of districted cities

Looking at carbon emissions reduction in the residential living sector, Hangzhou, Ningbo, and Wenzhou have done a good job in meeting the electricity needs of residents, with urbanization rates increasing year by year and the residential sector being well protected, ranking in the top tier. Quzhou needs to improve its level of urbanization and employment rate, which affects its ranking. Over the past six years, all 11 districted cities have achieved remarkable results in reducing carbon emissions in the Agriculture sector.

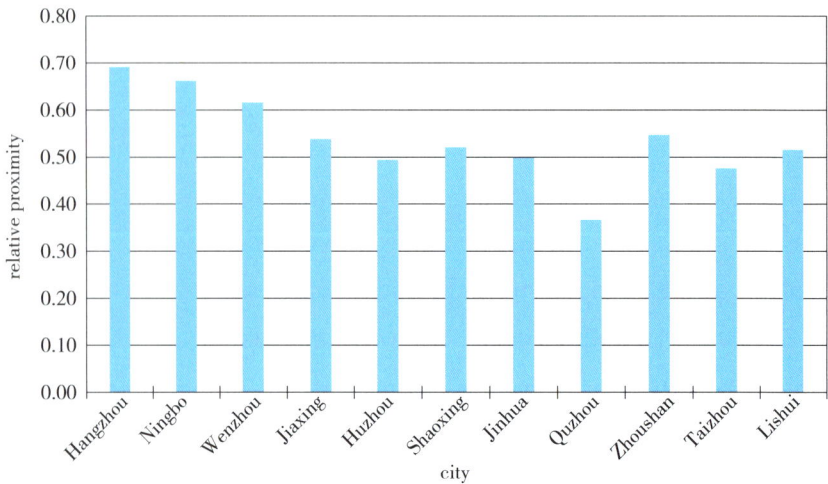

Figure 2-24   Dimensions of emissions reduction in the residential living sector in districted cities

From the perspective of carbon sink enhancement, Lishui and Quzhou have abundant natural resources and have carried out ecological and environmental protection work, as well as having a high per capita forest area, giving them an advantage in the carbon sink sector and ranking them at the forefront of the province. Other districted cities have been scored in order due to population growth, resource endowment limitations, and the protection of carbon sink resources in the past six years.

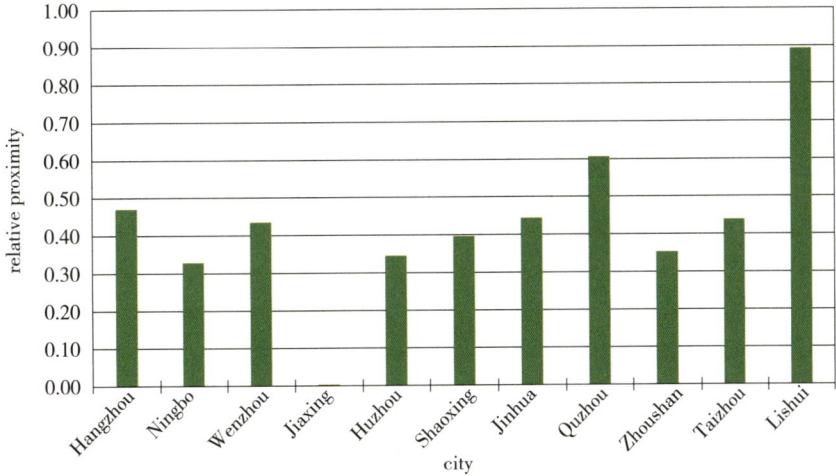

Figure 2-25   Dimensions of carbon sink enhancement sector in districted cities

From the perspective of the quality of resident living, Wenzhou, Jinhua, Taizhou, and Huzhou are among the top cities in the province due to their control of environmental pollution and balance between per capita disposable income and GDP. Although Hangzhou has a higher per capita disposable income, its ranking in terms of the quality of resident living is lower due to the impact of high levels of environmental pollution such as $PM_{2.5}$ Quzhou ranks lower due to relatively lower resident incomes. However, overall, the quality of life for residents in all districted cities in the province has improved over the past six years.

C. Evolution of districted city clustering

As a simplest exploration, the comprehensive relative proximity of each districted city in 2021 is firstly clustered, as shown in Figure 2-27. According to the figure, the 11 districted cities clearly fall into three categories. In terms of relative proximity from high to low, Hangzhou, Wenzhou and Lishui fall into the first category, with the best performance in the low-carbon development; Jiaxing and Quzhou fall into the third category, with the poor performance in the low-carbon development; the remaining six districted cities fall into in the second category.

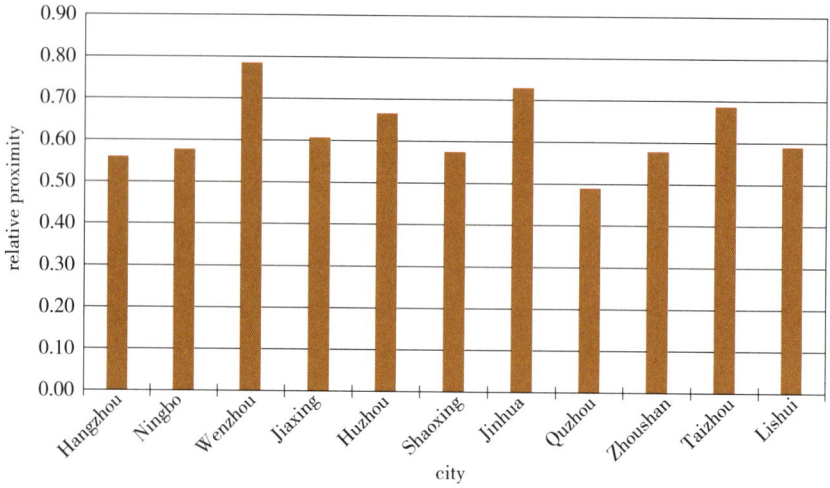

Figure 2-26   Dimensions of resident living sector in districted cities

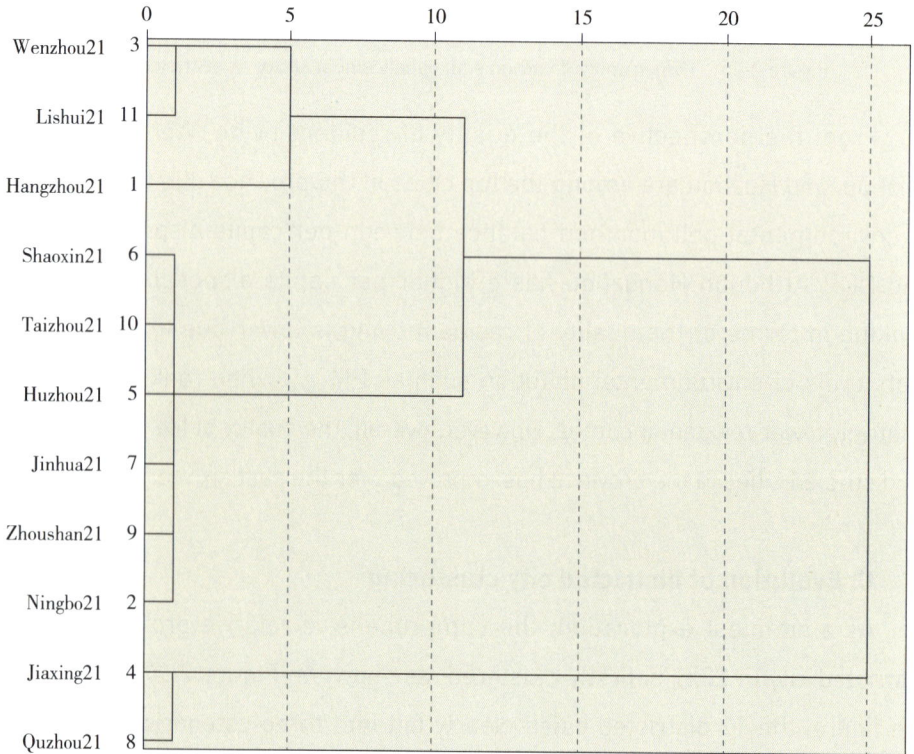

Figure 2-27   Comprehensive relative proximity of each districted city in 2021

Although the comprehensive relative proximity can be used to classify districted cities, it can only characterize the level of low-carbon development, and it is difficult to generalize their key characteristics. Therefore, the second round of cluster analysis is conducted to cluster the relative proximity with each dimension as an object, as shown in Figure 2-28. As can be seen from the figure, the 11 districted cities clearly fall into four categories, the first category includes Lishui and Quzhou. The second category includes Huzhou and Jiaxing. The third category includes Shaoxing, Taizhou, Ningbo, Zhoushan and Hangzhou. The fourth category includes Wenzhou and Jinhua. They are described below, respectively.

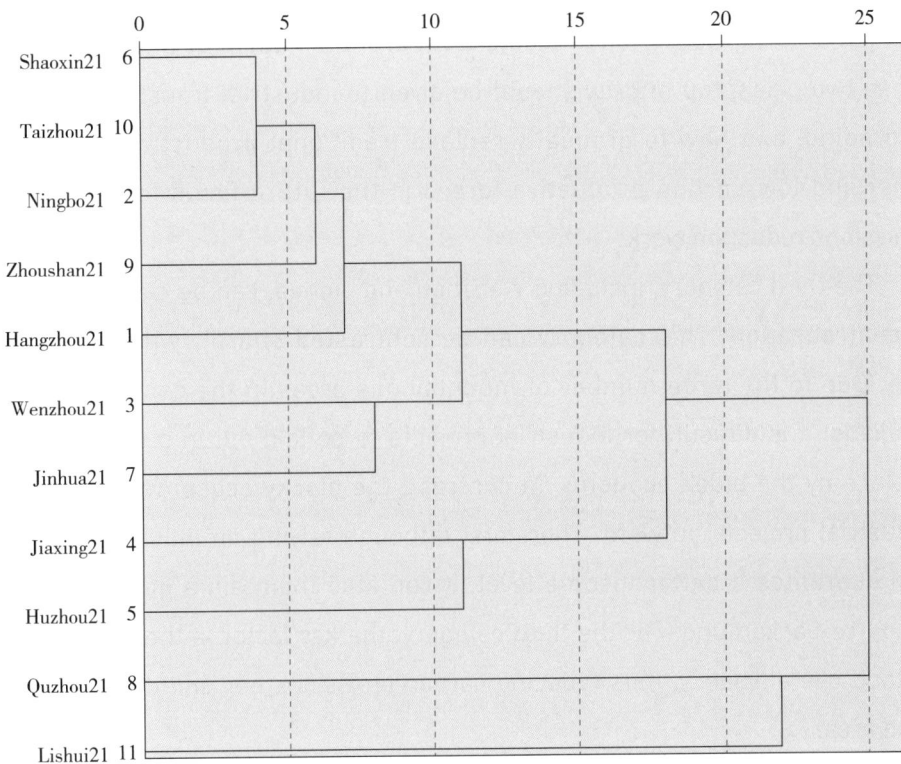

Figure 2-28   Cluster diagram of relative proximity for 9 dimensions of districts cities in 2021

The first category, including Lishui and Quzhou, can be called economic late-mover. The common characteristic is their backward economy, resulting in the negative impact on technological innovation support, people's quality of life and income level, as well as related industrial structure. However, there are still significant differences between the two. Quzhou is a typical region from high carbon to low carbon, where energy efficiency improvement and low-carbon industrial structure have always been the focus of carbon emissions reduction, and will continue to maintain. Lishui is a typical region with low-carbon development all the time, and more is spent on attracting investment in industrial projects, especially on projects related to the value transformation of green ecological resources in the future.

The second category, including Huzhou and Jiaxing, can be called industrial agglomeration. Due to the advantage of natural plain, industrial enterprises and industrial projects are highly densely distributed, which leads to greater pressure on the consumption of energy resources and the maintenance of ecological resources. However, due to a large number of industrial projects, residents' living quality and income level are maintained at a high level. For these two cities, top priority should be given to industrial transformation and upgrading, and how to gradually replace traditional productive forces with emerging low-carbon productive forces is the future focus for the carbon emissions reduction work.

The third category, including Wenzhou and Jinhua, can be called industrial decentralization. This category can be contrasted sharply with the second one. Due to the large number of mountainous areas in the central-southern Zhejiang, it is difficult for industrial projects to be laid out in succession, and replace by the block economy. In contrast, the blocky economy has very few industrial projects outward. Therefore, although relying on industrial projects can guarantee a better income level, it can also maintain a good ecological resource background. For the third category, the key factor is the improvement of land use efficiency, thus reducing carbon emissions per unit of construction land area.

The fourth category, Shaoxing, Taizhou, Ningbo, Zhoushan and Hangzhou, can be called comprehensive type. This category is featured by complexity, which is more likely to be grouped together as a result of multiple dimensions offsetting each other.

V. Main Conclusions and Future Prospects

Centering on the four dimensions of economic development, energy security, carbon emissions and resident living, an evaluation system for climate change and low-carbon development covering carbon emissions reduction, economic and social development, especially the just transformation dimension is constructed in the study, and an empirical analysis is conducted on the comparisons between provinces and cities. The main conclusions are as follows:

(1) In the comparison of provinces, the actions on climate change and low-carbon development in Zhejiang has achieved steady improvement, which is similar to Guangdong. In addition, Fujian is at a stable and high level, while Shandong and Jiangsu show the characteristics of unstable fluctuation. In 2020, Zhejiang ranked the first among the five provinces in history. In terms of different dimensions, except for energy security and carbon sink enhancement, which are greatly affected by resource endowment, the remaining eight dimensions of Zhejiang are characterized with continuous improvement.

(2) In the comparison of municipal level, the low-carbon and high-quality development in the 11 districted cities shows a trend of continuous improvement. In terms of absolute value, Hangzhou, Wenzhou and Lishui top the list, while Quzhou and Jiaxing relatively lag behind.

(3) From the classification analysis of districted cities, it can be divided into four categories. Lishui and Quzhou can be called the category of backward economic development. The former is suggested to focus on improving energy efficiency and low-carbon industrial structure, while the latter is suggested to focus on the value transformation of green ecological resources. Huzhou and Jiaxing, which can be called the industrial agglomeration category, should lay emphasis on the approach that how to gradually replace traditional productivity with emerging low-carbon productivity. Wenzhou and Jinhua, which can be called the industrial decentralization category, should mainly to improve the efficiency of land use and reduce per unit carbon emissions of construction land area. Shaoxing, Taizhou, Ningbo, Zhoushan and Hangzhou, which can be called comprehensive category, should consider promoting the green and low-carbon transformation of economy and society from six sectors.

Although the evaluation indexes and methods are innovative, the green low-carbon transformation development of economic society is an extremely comprehensive and complex macrosystem. This study is just a preliminary attempt. Subsequently, it can be considered to selectively refine from the perspective of expanding and improving evaluation indexes, especially from the perspective of integrating just transformation, common prosperity and other strategies closely with green and low-carbon development transformation. It also can expand the scope of the evaluation, including increasing the number of subjects of evaluation on both spatial and temporal scales, and improve the evaluation methods, including the operation of weight determination, and the handling of individual outliers.

Author: The writing group of Zhejiang economic & information centre

Reference

[1] Pan Qingjie, Zhao Shouguo. Measurement and Evaluation of Coupling Coordination Between Green Innovation and Economic Development in China[J]. *Science and Technology Management Research*, 2023, 33(1): 124-136.

[2] Li Xuhui and Tao Yitao. Measurement, regional differences, and causes of China's green and low-carbon innovation development under the "dual carbon" goals[J]. *China population, resources and environment*, 2023, 33(1): 124-136.

[3] Li Tongshan, Wang Yanrui. Evaluation of regional agricultural carbon neutralization capacity based on entropy weight TOPSIS model[J]. *Regional Economic Review*, 2022, 57(3): 92-98.

[4] Sun Qi, Wu Qiaosheng, Siyao Li, et al. Measurement on China's Urban Low-carbon Development Performance Index[J]. *Statistics & Decision*, 2021,37(17): 75-79.

[5] Chen Jing. Evaluation of regional low-carbon transportation based on Object-Process-Subject analysis method[J]. *Ecological Economy*, 2021,37(3): 38-42.

[6] Fu Lin, Cao Ying, Guo Hao, et al. China's low-carbon development progress and policy evaluation since the 12th Five-Year Plan period[J]. *Chinese Journal of Environmental Management*, 2021, 13(1): 16-24.

[7] Tang Decai, Zhang Yan, Wang Luxia. Research on Comprehensive Evaluation

of Carbon Emissions reduction Ability in the Yangtze River Economic Zone[J]. *Ecological Economy*, 2021, 37(6): 44-50.

[8] Wang Jingjing, Li Qifen, Yang Yongwen. Comprehensive evaluation of nearly zero carbon emission parks based on variable weight theory[J]. *Science Technology and Engineering*, 2021, 21(1): 334-340.

[9] Li Chunhua, Sun Zhenqing. Research on evaluation of regional green design capability under the target of carbon peak[J]. *Science and Technology Management Research*, 2021, 41(19): 177-183.

[10] Liang Gang. Measurement on the construction level of China's green, low-carbon and circular development economic system[J]. *Statistics & Decision*, 2021, 37(15): 47-51.

PART TWO
SECTOR
ACTIONS

Reform Practice of the New Power System Promoting the Transformation toward Clean and Low-carbon Development in Zhejiang Province

Zhejiang Province, a receive-end region with limited energy resources, is faced with the challenge of striking a balance between security, low-carbon development, and economic growth. In the context of rising economic indicators, restricted energy consumption targets, and the strong demand for stable prices from private businesses, practitioners in the energy and power industry have been looking for ways to achieve a regional low-carbon transition. This paper examines the opportunities and challenges to the transformation toward low-carbon development in Zhejiang Province and outlines a path to achieving this goal by building the new power system. Related practical cases are cited to provide ideas and experience for Zhejiang to build a provincial modernized demonstration.

I. Opportunities and Challenges to the Transformation toward Clean and Low-carbon Development in Zhejiang Province

Zhejiang is a major economic and industrial province with limited resources, including virtually no reserves of fossil energy resources such as coal, oil, and gas, and is therefore completely reliant on external sources. In terms of electric power, even with the use of locally developed conventional and new energy sources, more than one-third of its energy needs still have to be met by external sources. It has become increasingly prominent that we are not entirely rely on ourselves for power supply as a result of the need to increase the energy supply to resume production after the epidemic, the complex and changing international energy supply situation, and frequent extreme weather disasters in some areas. Consequently, the issue of how to maintain a balance between energy security and self-sufficiency has become an urgent problem that needs to be addressed. Moreover, Zhejiang does not have any advantages in the development of clean energy. Its water resources have already been almost completely utilized, its wind and light resources are limited in terms of quality and spatial conditions, and its light resources rank third in China, placing it at a lower level than other areas. Furthermore, wind power is restricted by land resources and geographical conditions, making it economically unfeasible for large-scale, centralized development. Therefore, it is essential to find a suitable pathway and development model for transforming Zhejiang into a low-carbon province in order to build a clean energy model.

On March 15, 2021, General Secretary Xi Jinping proposed the building of the new power system at the 9th meeting of the Central Financial and Economic Affairs Commission of the Communist Party of China Central Committee. This is another systematic exposition on the development of energy and power since General Secretary Xi Jinping put forward a new energy security strategy featuring "Four Reforms and One Cooperation" in June 2014. It outlines the basic role of the new power system in achieving the "dual carbon" goals and provides a scientific direction and fundamental guidance for the development of energy and power.

II. Building the New Power System Is the Only Way for Resource-limited Receiving-end Regions to Achieve the Transformation toward Clean and Low-carbon Development

Electric power is the major form of clean energy development and utilization, including wind power, solar energy, nuclear energy, hydropower, and other sources. The power grid in the province links 13 types of energy, such as water, nuclear, wind, solar, and biomass, which cover the whole process of energy production, supply, storage, and consumption. It meets different energy requirements such as cooling, heating, electricity, and hydrogen from the consumption side, and serves more than 20 million commercial, industrial, and residential consumers in the province. Consequently, the electric power system is the core backbone of the energy system in Zhejiang Province.

The new power system is a concept that is yet to be widely accepted, but it can significantly improve power distribution on a large scale, facilitate access for different energy users and suppliers, adapt to the efficient conversion of multiple energy sources, and maintain a high level of resilience in the case of accidents and disasters. Overall, the new power system is a major upgrade from the traditional power system, an essential part of a clean, low-carbon, safe and efficient energy system, and is tasked with the significant responsibility of energy transition.

Building the new power system has four significant implications for both China and Zhejiang Province. First, it accelerates the building of ecological civilization. In 2021, the National Development and Reform Commission of the People's Republic of China proposed that China's ecological civilization construction has entered a new stage with carbon reduction as the key strategic direction. Zhejiang Province vigorously develops non-fossil energy such as wind and solar power generation, which is the primary means of reducing carbon emissions in the energy sector. Second, it ensures national energy security, which is a key factor for regional economic development and national security. Achieving the transformation towards clean and low-carbon development will substantially reduce Zhejiang's dependence on external oil and gas, and significantly improve its capacity to ensure energy security. Third, it builds the new development paradigm by having end-user energy consumption electrified, which will improve energy conservation and energy efficiency, enhance the endogenous drivers for green development, and provide strong support and sustained momentum for Zhejiang to become a leading province in building socialism with Chinese characteristics. Fourth, it promotes the transformation and upgrading of the energy industry chain. Through independent innovation, we aim to make breakthroughs in core and disruptive technologies in the energy and power sector, eliminate dependence on key technologies, and promote the entire energy and power industry chain to be self-sufficient and controllable, and transformed and upgraded. Thus, establishing the new power system is a necessary course for Zhejiang Province to achieve the goal of power supply guarantee and reduce dependence on external resources, which is a critical step to promote the province's transformation towards clean and low-carbon development.

III. Reform Practice of Building the New Power System in Zhejiang Province

Since 2021, Zhejiang has been at the forefront of actively creating a model for the transformation toward clean and low-carbon development in the energy sector, and has implemented a variety of reforms in terms of development goals, system construction, and cross-border integration.

A. Formulating the development goals of the new power system in Zhejiang Province, which aims to "take a step forward every five years and achieve a leap in development every fifteen years"

Zhejiang Province may explore a path for receiving-end regions with limited energy resources to achieve the transformation to low-carbon development by building the new power system, which helps to achieve a balance between security, reliability, cleanliness, low-carbon, and economic efficiency. In terms of goals, the development goals of Zhejiang's new power system can be summarized as "a step forward every five years and a leap in development every fifteen years".

By 2035, the Zhejiang New Power System Provincial Demonstration Zone will be fully constructed, signifying a qualitative upgrade from the quantitative development between 2021 and 2035. By 2025, the proportion of new energy installed capacity will be 27%, and the demand-side response capacity will reach to 8% of the peak load, creating a large receiving-end power grid pattern with "ultra-high voltage AC ring grid as the main backbone and ultra-high voltage DC as the main active receiving artery". By 2030, the proportion of new energy installed capacity will be 34%, and the demand-side response capacity will be 10% of the peak load, forming a large receiving-end power grid pattern of "One Ring and Four DCs", and the provincial demonstration zone will be mostly established, helping Zhejiang to reach carbon peaking in a high-quality manner. By 2035, new energy will dominate power output, forming a large hybrid AC/DC receiving-end grid structure, and enabling the integrated development of the large power grid with distributed power sources and micro-grids throughout the area. The provincial demonstration zone will be entirely completed, supporting Zhejiang's progress in attaining common prosperity.

From 2036 to 2050, the new power system in Zhejiang Province will undergo a qualitative change to an innovative leap, reaching an international advanced level in terms of security, reliability, green and low-carbon, and cleanliness and efficiency. The source-grid-load-storage will be coordinated and develope sustainably, with new energy becoming the main source of power supply and external power resources obtained through continuous efforts. The power distribution network will be highly integrated with power flow, data flow, and value flow, with mutual backup of AC and DC power supply and mutual assistance among multiple supply areas in the large receiving-end grid. This will create a low-carbon energy network for energy complementarity and energy efficiency improvement, and become a value creation center for resource sharing and mutual benefit, in support of Zhejiang's effort to push forward socialist modernization.

B. Building the "Four Carriers" of the New Energy System i.e., Production, Supply, Storage, and Transportation

Zhejiang Province takes the new power system as the core carrier, implements the important directives and spirit of the 20th CPC National Congress on building the new energy system, and actively builds the "four carriers" of the energy system i.e., production, supply, storage, and transportation.

The first carrier is independent energy supply. The conversion of the secondary energy in the downstream segment of fossil fuels in the energy system are promoted, while changing to increase the use of clean energy and gradually increasing the proportion of energy supply from less than 1% 10 years ago to about 20% at present and over 50% in the future.

The second carrier is coordination of improving energy transportation and layout. The marine transportation characteristics of incremental oil and gas resources have consolidated the foundation for the intensive layout of large power supply in coastal areas of Zhejiang Province. The advantages of power interconnection and coverage provide an efficient means for reducing fossil fuel storage and transportation costs and improving congestion.

The third carrier is multilateral energy storage. The multilateral storage capacity is formed by switching from relying on 5-10 days of thermal coal stocks and around 5% natural gas reserve capacity for power regulation to carrying out pumped storage, new energy storage, and virtual power plants for storage and regulation.

The fourth carrier is market linkage. Fossil fuels are closely coupled with power in terms of quantity and price, and a feedback mechanism for power quantity and price fluctuations will be established to comprehensively manage the power market and fossil energy market, systematically ensuring energy security. By accelerating the price and cost transparency and information disclosure of power sales companies, Zhejiang Province has promoted orderly competition in the industry market.

IV. Promoting the "Six Integrated Developments" in the Consumption Side

First, promoting the integrated development of complementation and competition in the energy sector. Under the background that electricity, gas, and coal should be used as appropriate, a stable supply of fossil fuels and increasing the production of primary electricity can stimulate the energy market, enhance the synthetic utilization of energy sources, and promote the mutual reinforcement and development of energy technologies. Ultimately, clean energy can replace fossil fuels in terms of market price and technological advancement, enabling the integration of safety, cleanliness, and cost-effectiveness.

Second, promoting the integrated development of the industrial sector. It is suggested that the fossil fuel consumption should aggregate towards raw material utilization, industrial energy improves its cascade utilization mode, green electricity trading and the carbon market change tracks together and get coordinated, which can promote industrial enterprises to adjust emissions flexibly and meet energy development needs through market-based approach. Industrial production efficiency will be enhanced by implementing two-part tariffs in electricity pricing and guiding coal-fired and natural gas-fired electricity capacity pricing based on supply adequacy, which can improve energy system efficiency. Interactive energy use will be enhanced and fixed proportions of controllable loads will be formed among industrial enterprises, improving cascade response capability.

Third, promoting the integrated development of ecological economy in the agricultural sector. The acceleration of adopting electric agricultural machinery and the connection between rural new energy sources, plug-and-play interfaces and agricultural machinery can reverse the current situation in which over 90% of energy consumption in the agricultural sector is from oil products. This will reduce operating costs and improve the cleanliness of end-use energy.

Fourth, promoting the integrated development of smart and low-carbon technologies in the transportation sector. The orderly charging mode and sorting network mode is to be prepared in advance after the proportion of electric vehicles is raised. The integration of vehicle network, road network and charging network will be sped up, while a household back feeding mechanism and technical support will be built for the car batteries.

Fifth, promoting the integrated development of energy conservation and carbon reduction in the construction sector. The proportion of short process steelmaking will be increased. Equipment replacements with high efficiency and low operating cost such as induction furnaces will be applied. The use of waste heat recovery, CCUS and other technologies will be increased in cement production. Research and development of temporary transformers adapted to the construction, supporting equipment, and emergency support equipment will also be conducted to promote the electrification of construction machinery.

Sixth, promoting convenient and intelligent integrated development in the sector of people's livelihood. Residential electricity safety and security will be enhanced by utilizing energy storage and biomass flexibly to foster common prosperity. Besides, Zhejiang has accelerated the use of air conditioners, so as to increase the capacity of large-scale non-inductive regulation. Furthermore, the demands for flexible heat sources will be explored, and upstream waste heat and energy will be used in a distributed manner.

V. Cases and Achievements of Promoting Regional Clean and Low-carbon Transformation

As the main construction unit of the new power system, State Grid Zhejiang Electric Power Co., Ltd. has been actively promoting the construction of the new power system demonstration zone since 2021. Over the past two years, it has accumulated rich experience in multiple aspects, such as building the backbone grid network with strong AC and DC, the panoramic monitoring of the Energy Big Data Center, local consumption of high-proportion distributed new energy and so on.

A. Case 1: The UHV Backbone Grid of "One Ring and Four DCs" Guarantees the Core Carrier of Clean Energy Supply

During the 14th Five-Year Plan period, Zhejiang will build the provincial UHVAC ring network consisting of three 1,000kV AC UHV substations in Wujiang, Ningshao and Taiwen, as well as the existing west Zhejiang Channel. The network will create conditions for a large number of coastal power access in southeast Zhejiang Province in advance, greatly promotes the power interconnection in the Yangtze River Delta region, and spurs the integrated development of four provinces and one municipality in East China. Combined with the three UHVDC stations of ± 800kV (i.e., Bingjin, Lingshao and Baihetan) and the Gansu-Zhejiang Fourth DC Station to be built, Zhejiang will form a backbone grid structure of "One Ring and Four DCs". The structure will provide a strong support carrier for the reliable input of external clean energy and the development and consumption of local clean energy in Zhejiang. Also, it will meet more than 35% of high-proportion external power supply, over 50% of high-proportion non-fossil power installation safe consumption, as well as the medium and high-speed growth of Zhejiang Province and the demand of "doubling" in the medium and long-term.

B. Case 2: Dynamic Monitoring of Zhejiang Energy Big Data Center for Panoramic View of Zhejiang Energy Operation

To effectively guide and standardize the panoramic energy data business, State Grid Zhejiang Electric Power Co., Ltd. and the People's Government of Zhejiang Province have jointly established a provincial energy big data center featured by multi-function coupling, data fusion, service sharing, value co-creation, and win-win cooperation, aiming to promote the whole-process energy industry data aggregation and fusion, sharing and exchange, quasi-real-time monitoring, analysis and application, ADM (Aid in Decision Making), and planning support to digitally boost energy conservation and carbon reduction, serving the "dual carbon" goals.

The Energy Big Data Center collects all kinds of energy data such as coal, oil, gas, and electricity in the province, carries out the analysis of energy flow and carbon flow in all links, and builds an energy information interconnection platform connecting government units, the general public, the energy industry, and energy-using enterprises. By the end of 2022, the Center had covered 342 indicators from more than 10 provincial departments, and aggregated carbon account information involving 46,770 enterprises above designated size, 2,168 provincial key projects, and 430,000 individuals. Besides, the Center has fostered hundreds of digital applications.

C. Case 3: Jiaxing Haining Source-grid-load-storage Integration Project Achieves Local Consumption of High-proportioned Distributed New Energy

In the Jianshan area of Haining, local clean energy accounts for 50.2% of primary energy, clean electricity accounts 57.0% of total social electricity consumption, and electricity consumption in end-use accounts 57.48%. Jianshan is the most intensive area of distributed new energy in the province. The instability brought by a large number of intermittent new energy sources is in contradiction with the power consumption demands of local precision manufacturers in Jiaxing. To cope with this issue, the State Grid Zhejiang Electric Power Co., Ltd. has built a new power system prototype to meet the local consumption of high-proportion distributed new energy by building a new AC-DC hybrid distribution network and applying new technologies and equipment such as SiC energy routers. Under the high growth expectation of "14th Five-Year Plan" economic growth and energy consumption of 9%, Haining has achieved remarkable results, such as clean energy consumption accounting for more than 59%, local consumption of distributed photovoltaic energy consumption 98%, and power supply reliability increased to more than 99.995%.

D. Case 4: Air Conditioning Load Interactive Response Improves System Flexibility

By changing the traditional regulation mode of "source moving with load", giving full play to the favorable factors of market flexibility, user sensitivity and daring to change, and carefully investigating the structure and volume of air conditioning load in the whole province, State Grid Zhejiang estimates that the maximum air conditioning load of residents in summer accounts for 40%, and the total amount exceeds the installed capacity of two Three Gorges. Based on this huge base, State Grid Zhejiang and Zhejiang Government systematically promotes the flexible load management of air conditioning. Firstly, the application system of "digital drive and classified implementation" has been built. According to the types of air conditioning, application scenarios and response effects, 4 categories and 14 sub-categories of terminal sensing technology schemes have been formed. Secondly, a management and control mechanism of "government-enterprise linkage and administration by competent authority of industry" have been established. To assist the Provincial Development and Reform Commission in issuing the *Guiding Opinions on Further Strengthening the Flexible Regulation and Control of Air Conditioning Load and Promoting Energy Conservation and Efficiency Improvement in the Whole Society*, Zhejiang has reached the intention of air conditioning load control in public institutions with the Provincial Bureau of Organs Affairs, and 7 cities and 45 district and county governments have issued supporting policies simultaneously. Third, the promotion path of "pilot breakthrough from point to area" has been implemented. Aiming at public institutions, commercial buildings and household appliances cloud platforms, Zhejiang has formulated a three-year action plan for air conditioning load management. At present, more than 30,000 households have been surveyed on the spot, and more than 3,000 households have been transformed and accessed, of which 643 households are connected to the cloud platform of household appliances. After a year's work, a regulation resource pool consisting of 9.1 million kW load has been established, with a maximum regulation capacity of 3.8 million kW.

E. Case 5: Pinghu Refined Power Consumption Improves System Energy Efficiency

Under the extensive mode of "high growth, high energy consumption and high cost", Zhejiang Province seeks to change and explore a way to enhance system energy efficiency and fine power consumption, without reducing the production capacity of enterprises. This not only reduces the energy consumption of enterprises and saves production costs, but also balances the three demands of production balancing demand, power consumption restrictions, and energy conservation and consumption reduction. In 2022, the State Grid Zhejiang, in cooperation with the Pinghu Government of Jiaxing, issued the *Notice on Amendment of the City's Orderly Power Consumption Plan in 2022* on March and clearly carried out the pilot work of energy efficiency improvement. By making a detailed analysis of the energy demand of 1,174 industrial enterprises during the summer peak of 2022, going deep into the internal process and adopting the standardized accounting method, the State Grid Zhejiang proposed a refined power consumption mode for enterprises in the region. From July to August in 2022, local enterprises saved more than 100 tons of standard coal per day, increased the social output by nearly 3 million yuan, and reduce carbon dioxide emissions by 39,500 tons per year.

F. Case 6: Green Electricity Trading Contributes to Green Asian Games

In 2022, State Grid Zhejiang Electric Power Co., Ltd. steadily promoted the green electricity trading market and normalized its trading, achieving a cumulative volume of 2.576 billion kilowatt-hours, a 600% increase from 2021. Under the guidance of *Implementation Plan for Promoting Green Consumption* and *Opinions on Improving the System Mechanism and Policy Measures for Green and Low-carbon Transition* issued by the National Development and Reform Commission and other departments, in regard to the power quota, Zhejiang Provincial Government organized regular green electricity trading in a combination of "annual + monthly + intra-month" to continuously open the provincial green electricity trading market. Users in Zhejiang Province were guided to purchase and consume green electricity, and more than 600 retail users were served. Twenty-nine aggregators were accelerated to act as agents for nearly 2,000 distributed power sources in Zhejiang Province, reaching 239 million kilowatt-hours of green electricity trading. Moreover, the green trading was promoted through multiple channels. Through the green power certificate trading platform of the Beijing Power Exchange Center, 21,000 certificates were traded for two provincial power companies, achieving 100% green electricity supply for all venues of the Asian Games.

Currently, the construction of the new power system has entered the development stage from pilot demonstration to in-depth promotion. Through more than two years of construction, Zhejiang's new power system consumes an average of 190 billion kilowatt hours of clean electricity each year, reducing carbon dioxide emissions by more than 140 million tons, which is equivalent to providing 100 million ordinary households with a full year of clean and pollution-free energy. The province's clean electricity has accounted for more than 2/3 of the total power. While achieving the transformation, Zhejiang withstood the test of many super typhoons such as Hagupit and Chanthu, and pulled through the structural power shortage difficulties caused by the rise of national coal price, and generally kept the electricity price of Zhejiang Province stable and orderly. In the future, with the construction of the new energy system, Zhejiang's new power system will show its leadership and demonstration more comprehensively, and will make new power contributions to Zhejiang's provincial modernized demonstration.

Author: Sun Yikai[1], Wang Xiran[2], Sun Ke[3]

1　Sun Yikai, deputy senior engineer, Secretary of the Think Tank of the Economic and Technological Research Institute of State Grid Zhejiang Electric Power Co., Ltd. He has been engaged in research on power grid planning for a long time.

2　Wang Xiran, engineer, engaged in research on power grid transmission and substation engineering design, provincial power grid planning, energy economics, and carbon peaking and carbon neutrality strategy.

3　Sun Ke, senior engineer, chief expert of the Think Tank of the Economic and Technological Research Institute of State Grid Zhejiang Electric Power Co., Ltd. He has been engaged in research on power grid planning, energy economics, low-carbon transformation and other fields for a long time, and has been awarded many honorary titles such as Zhejiang Province's 151 Talents, Excellent Expert Talents of State Grid.

Design and Practice of Industrial Carbon Efficiency Code in Zhejiang Province

In the current work of carbon peak and carbon neutralization, deep adjustment of industrial structure is an important task. Therefore, it is necessary to timely and accurately understand the carbon productivity of key carbon emission industries in manufacturing field, and take carbon efficiency as an important scale to measure the low-carbon development of the industry to guide their the green, low-carbon and high-quality development. Zhejiang Province takes the lead in actively exploring the green and low-carbon development in manufacturing field, and takes the initiative in putting forward the "carbon efficiency code" in China, which provides replicable and scalable "Zhejiang experience" for the promotion of carbon peak and carbon neutrality in manufacturing field throughout the country.

I. Carbon Code Helps Accurately Identify the Breakthrough in Carbon Reduction

A. Background of Low-carbon Development in the Manufacturing Field in Zhejiang Province

Achieving carbon peak and carbon neutrality is a major strategic decision made by the CPC Central Committee, a solemn commitment to the international community, and an intrinsic requirement to promote high-quality development. The manufacturing field consumes the most energy among all sectors, and is also the largest source of carbon emissions, accounting for about 60% of the total carbon emissions in Zhejiang Province. The effectiveness of carbon emission control in the manufacturing field will greatly affect the smooth achievement of carbon peak goals.

At present, the proportion of industries with high carbon emissions in the manufacturing field of Zhejiang Province is relatively high. From 2015 to 2021, the proportion of carbon emissions of various industries was constantly changing, but the proportion of carbon emissions of the seven major high-carbon industries such as textiles and chemicals was always much higher than the proportion of their value-added output. Meanwhile, the level of carbon productivity needs to be improved urgently, and the establishment of a high-quality and low-carbon industrial system is imminent.

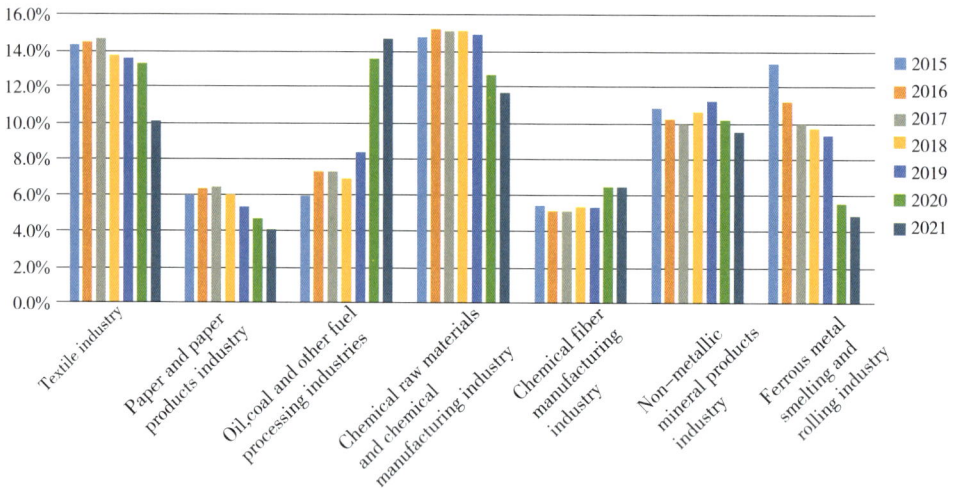

Figure 4-1   The proportion of carbon emissions from the seven major high carbon industries to industrial carbon emissions above designated size from 2015 to 2021

B. Identifying Carbon Reduction Breakthroughs in Manufacturing Field

In 2021, Zhejiang Province launched the "Industrial Carbon Efficiency Code" for the first time nationwide. Carbon efficiency, also known as carbon emission intensity, refers to the amount of carbon dioxide emitted by a company per unit of economic output. As a comprehensive indicator, "carbon efficiency" can reflect both the production efficiency of enterprises and the low-carbon level of energy structure. The carbon efficiency of enterprises is benchmarked and graded, and then given the corresponding symbols, which is the "carbon efficiency code".

Carbon efficiency code can provide an important foundation for accurately implement policies of carbon peak in manufacturing field of Zhejiang Province[1]. Zhejiang Province proposes to strive to develop low-carbon-efficient industries, and push forward the low-carbon transition in high-carbon-efficient industries. Based on carbon efficiency codes, industrial regulatory authorities can adopt unified evaluation methods and standards to identify key industries and enterprises that need carbon reduction, accurately implement policies based on different classification results, identify key breakthroughs in low-carbon-efficient industries and high-carbon-efficient industries, and accelerate the low-carbon transformation of industrial structure.

Carbon efficiency codes can provide effective benchmarking information for industrial enterprises to carry out energy-saving and carbon-reduction actions. The lack of basis for enterprises to formulate energy consumption and carbon emission control targets will affect the effectiveness and enthusiasm of enterprises to carry out energy-saving and carbon reduction actions. As the unified and authoritative carbon efficiency bench-marking information throughout the province, the carbon efficiency code can assist enterprises in taking low-carbon actions independently. Financial institutions can accurately evaluate the carbon efficiency level and carbon reduction potential of enterprises, and continuously track their carbon reduction performance; At the same time, green finance products based on carbon efficiency can be developed to support low-carbon transformation and green development of enterprises.

Carbon efficiency codes can provide support for regulatory authorities to optimize factor allocation and adopt differentiated policies. In the future, carbon efficiency will likely become an important evaluation indicator. Energy, capital, land, and other factors are likely to give priority to low-carbon and high-efficient industries and enterprises. Services such as green financial services, energy-saving technical transformation services, carbon trading, energy use rights trading, and market-based mechanisms will differ for industries and enterprises

1 2021, Zhejiang Provincial Party Committee and Provincial Government, *the Opinions of the Central Committee of the CPC and the State Council on Carbon Dioxide Peaking and Carbon Neutrality in Full and Faithful Implementation of the New Development Philosophy.*

with different carbon efficiency levels. The relevant regulatory authorities can introduce targeted policies and systems to promote the optimal allocation of resource elements and assist in promoting low-carbon transformation of high-carbon enterprises and green development of low-carbon-efficient enterprises.

II. Design of a Unified and Accurate Carbon Efficiency Evaluation Model

A. Overall Consideration of Methodology

To build an operational, scalable, and highly accurate carbon efficiency evaluation system, standardized data sources, accurate carbon efficiency evaluation methods, and intelligent carbon efficiency applications should be considered.

1. Standardized Data Sources

As the basic source of greenhouse gas emissions, enterprises have always faced problems in obtaining carbon emission related data, such as diverse data sources, questionable data accuracy, and lagging data update frequency. To address these issues, a stable and reliable data source is needed to ensure accurate and timely access to carbon emission related data of enterprises.

The industrial carbon efficiency code data is sourced from industrial enterprises above designated size in Zhejiang Province. The collected indicators include data on terminal consumption, processing and conversion consumption, raw material consumption, and energy recovery of major energy sources such as coal, electricity, oil, and gas. In terms of data authority, the collection and accounting of industrial carbon efficiency code data in Zhejiang Province is mainly led by Zhejiang Provincial Bureau of Statistics, which conducts carbon efficiency accounting and evaluation for above designated industrial enterprises that have been in the database for more than two consecutive years and operate normally. In terms of data accuracy, the statistical department will review, verify, and confirm the basic data before conducting carbon efficiency evaluation. For example, relying on the statistical platform, more than 30 indicators related to various energy consumption varieties can be audited on and off the table. In terms of data timeliness, the carbon efficiency of the carbon efficiency code data is comprehensively measured in the middle of each year, and the evaluation results of carbon efficiency level are formed based on the standard. In the future, with the further consolidation of the data foundation, various indicators may be updated monthly to achieve higher timeliness.

2. Accurate Carbon Efficiency Evaluation

Zhejiang Province has numerous industrial industries with significant differences. Therefore, it is necessary to establish a unified set of carbon efficiency evaluation standards and models for industrial enterprises, which can reflect both the differences between industries and the situation of enterprises with different carbon efficiency levels in the same industry.

(1) Calculation of Carbon Efficiency Level

$$C = \frac{CE}{EVA} \tag{4-1}$$

Among them, C—Enterprise carbon intensity, i.e., the carbon emissions per unit of added value of the enterprise;

CE—Enterprise carbon emissions;

EVA—Enterprise Value Added.

The higher the carbon emissions per unit of added value, the lower the carbon efficiency level, and vice versa, the higher the carbon efficiency level.

(2) Carbon Efficiency Level Classification

Based on the situation in Zhejiang, the industrial carbon efficiency code classifies the carbon efficiency of enterprises from the two dimensions of industry and manufacturing. The grading setting of manufacturing dimension in the carbon efficiency code is in line with the target of reaching the carbon peak in the manufacturing field of Zhejiang Province. The grading standards of industrial carbon code manufacturing and industry dimension are 0.6 tons/10,000 yuan of carbon intensity and 20,000 tons/10,000 yuan of carbon intensity, which are respectively the reference standards for the division of low-carbon industry and high-carbon industry in Zhejiang Province. In terms of manufacturing dimension, according to the distribution of carbon efficiency levels of manufacturing enterprises in the industries above designated, it can be divided into three levels. In terms of industry dimension, the carbon efficiency level of enterprises in the industry is determined by comparing the carbon efficiency of enterprises with the average carbon efficiency of their industries, and enterprises are divided into five grades. In order to reflect the carbon efficiency level of enterprises in their respective industries more accurately, the carbon efficiency code subdivides the seven major high-carbon industries and non-high-carbon key industries in the industrial field of Zhejiang Province into small categories (4-digit industry codes) in the industry dimension, enabling enterprises in these key industries to carry out carbon reduction work more accurately. The specific standard classification of carbon efficiency intelligent is shown in Table 4-1.

Table 4-1   Schematic diagram of intelligent benchmarking and grading of carbon efficiency of Zhejiang industrial carbon efficiency code

			Intelligent benchmarking of manufacturing carbon efficiency		
			1st Grade	2nd Grade	3rd Grade
			$C \leqslant 0.6$	$0.6 < C \leqslant 2.0$	$C > 2.0$
Intelligent benchmarking du stry carbon efficiency	1st Grade	$C \leqslant 0.5K_i$			
	2nd Grade	$0.5K_i < C \leqslant 1K_i$			
	3rd Grade	$1K_i < C \leqslant 1.5K_i$			
	4th Grade	$1.5K_i < C \leqslant 2K_i$			
	5th Grade	$C > 2K_i$ 或 $C < 0$			

Note: K_i represents the average carbon intensity of the industry i to which the enterprise belongs. The green part indicates that the enterprise belongs to the first grade of manufacturing and the first and second grade of industry, as a low-carbon-efficient enterprise; The blue part represents all enterprises with first and second-grade carbon efficiency except low-carbon-efficient enterprises, as low-carbon-inefficient enterprises and enterprises with general carbon efficiency level; The yellow part indicates that the enterprise belongs to the third level of manufacturing and the first to fourth level enterprises of industry, as high carbon efficient enterprises; The red part indicates that the enterprise belongs to the third level of manufacturing and the fifth level of the industry, as high carbon inefficient enterprises.

When considering carbon efficiency level grading, there are mainly two types of parameters that affect the carbon efficiency rating results. One is the manufacturing dimension grading parameter, which can be used as a reference for the optimization and transformation of the entire industrial structure when comparing the overall carbon efficiency level of the industry in the province; another is the classification of industry dimensions, which varies with industry differences, helping enterprises improve carbon efficiency by comparing standards within the industry.

3. Intelligent Carbon Efficiency Applications

The digital reform of Zhejiang Province is at the forefront of China. By combining with the digital platform, the application scope of carbon efficiency evaluation can be further expanded, and the promotion and application of industrial carbon efficiency code can be accelerated. Based on the Carbon Peak and Carbon Neutral Intelligent Governance Platform of Zhejiang Province, it can efficiently obtain carbon emission related data and quickly assign uniform codes to industrial enterprises in the province. Financial institutions can also provide enterprises with different types of green finance or transformation financial products refer to as the industrial carbon efficiency code. The competent authorities can track the low-carbon development of key enterprises, such as the transformation of energy-saving technical and improvement of carbon efficiency, through the enterprise carbon efficiency code.

Application in Policy Field. Through key applications such as the enterprise carbon account of Zhejiang Carbon Peak and Carbon Neutral Intelligent Governance Platform, the industrial authorities improve the proportion of carbon efficiency index in the evaluation systems such as "hero according to the average benefit per mu" and green low-carbon factories and take the carbon efficiency evaluation index and carbon efficiency index as the basic index of enterprise and regional evaluation. Promote carbon effect evaluation result application covering the differential land, energy, water, etc.

Application by Financial Institutions. Industrial carbon efficiency code is an important index to evaluate the degree of green and low-carbon development of enterprises and their future carbon reduction potential. Financial institutions can design financial products based on the carbon efficiency evaluation, and support the development of green and low-carbon enterprises with differentiated credit and financing. The People's Bank of China, the Banking and Insurance Regulatory Bureau and other departments integrate the application of industrial carbon efficiency code in the financial field, carry out the carbon account finance work, and launch a variety of green financial services based on carbon efficiency in the form of online and offline combination, such as Carbon efficiency Credit in Zhejiang, energy saving and carbon reduction technical transformation credit, industrial carbon preferential credit, etc.

Application of improving efficiency through technological transformation. When sorting out and screening the list of high-carbon and low-efficiency enterprises in various industries, the industrial regulatory department combines carbon technology transformation with the assignment of industrial carbon efficiency codes to carry out energy-saving diagnosis online services on mobile terminals such as "carbon diagnosis" and "carbon technology transformation" for enterprises and focus on enterprises with low-carbon efficiency to provide targeted technical support. In particular, "carbon efficiency + energy efficiency" energy conservation and emission reduction diagnostic services will be carried out for high-carbon enterprises in the "third level of manufacturing dimension and the fifth level of industry dimension" to help enterprises scientifically formulate and implement green technological transformation projects, and improve their management ability of energy conservation and carbon reduction.

B. Establishment of a Working Mechanism

In order to effectively promote the implementation and promotion of industrial carbon efficiency codes, it is necessary to establish a collaborative working mechanism among multiple departments, unify and standardize carbon efficiency evaluation technical standards, and establish an efficient collaborative mechanism of application promotion.

1. Establishing a Collaborative Work Mechanism among Multiple Departments

Zhejiang Province has made clear requirements for work related to "carbon efficiency" in top-level documents such as *The Opinions of the Central*

Committee of the CPC and the State Council on Carbon Dioxide Peaking and Carbon Neutrality in Full and Faithful Implementation of the New Development Philosophy, *Implementation Opinions on Accelerating the Establishment and Improvement of the green and low-carbon circular economic development system.* In this context, departments such as the Provincial Development and Reform Commission, the Provincial Bureau of Statistics, and the Provincial Department of Economy and Information Technology, in accordance with their respective responsibilities, collaborate to promote work related to the carbon efficiency code.

Statistical department. The Provincial Bureau of Statistics takes the lead in the accounting and rating of carbon efficiency evaluation throughout the province. Through the Zhejiang Statistical Digital Platform and a set of online reporting platforms, it collects data on the consumption and processing conversion consumption of major energy varieties such as coal, oil, natural gas, electricity, and heat, as well as production data such as enterprise added value, as the basis for carbon efficiency level accounting. Provincial Development and Reform Commission, the provincial Department of Economy and Information Technology, and other departments have cooperated to clarify the classification principle and related parameters of carbon efficiency level, rationally classify the enterprises in both manufacturing and industrial dimensions, and transmit the evaluation results to relevant departments to help carry out green finance, energy-saving technology transformation, green manufacturing system construction, etc.

Economic and information department. As the leading unit of carbon peaking and carbon neutrality in the industrial field of the province, the Provincial Department of Economy and Information Technology sorted out the industry of the enterprise, the average carbon efficiency level of the industry, the industry standard, and the intensity standard level, and further clarified the carbon efficiency evaluation standard with the provincial Bureau of Statistics and other departments. To further improve the application of carbon efficiency evaluation, research and formulate industrial carbon efficiency code management methods and operational rules of industrial carbon efficiency code related platforms; in the application of green industrial parks, factories, energy-saving, and carbon reduction technical transformation projects, the application scenarios of carbon efficiency codes should be promoted.

Development and Reform Department. The Provincial Development and Reform Commission, as the leading unit of carbon peaking and carbon neutrality work throughout the province, cooperates with the statistical, economic and information, financial departments, etc. to carry out the construction and application promotion of industrial carbon efficiency codes. The carbon efficiency code is integrated into the enterprise carbon accounts of Zhejiang Carbon Peak and Carbon Neutral Intelligent Governance Platform through integration with statistical departments and other platforms, achieving synchronous updates and multi-end access. At the same time, through the pilot work of carbon account finance in Huzhou, Quzhou, and other places, we will enrich the diversified application scenarios of industrial carbon efficiency codes.

2. Standardizing the Technical Standards for Carbon Efficiency Evaluation

The carbon efficiency evaluation method is the core of carbon efficiency codes, and its scientific, accurate, and reasonable nature will determine the application and promotion scope of carbon efficiency codes. In order to further enhance the authority and standardization of industrial carbon efficiency evaluation, with the Zhejiang Provincial Bureau of Statistics as the centralized management department, Zhejiang Economic and Information Center led the compilation of Zhejiang provincial standard *Specification for Comprehensive Assessment and Coding Management of Industrial Enterprises' Carbon Efficiency* (hereinafter referred to as the "Standard"), officially determining the carbon efficiency evaluation and grading methods in the form of a standard. The "Standard" unifies the accounting methods for carbon dioxide emissions, carbon efficiency level evaluation, carbon efficiency level grading, and coding of industrial enterprises throughout the province, and has passed the expert review at present.

In the process of studying and drafting the Code, in order to ensure the feasibility of the standard, we conducted sufficient research on enterprises and solicited opinions from relevant industry associations and key enterprises in the province. In order to ensure the scientificity and accuracy of the standard, in addition to extensively consulting the opinions of various research institutions and relevant experts, the standard verification work was carried out, including trial calculation verification and third-party data verification. With the trial calculation results of the scheduled industrial enterprises in 2021, enterprises were successfully quickly classified, and more than 5,000 enterprises in Zhejiang Province that need to focus on carbon control were identified. At the same time, we compared the "14th Five-Year Plan" outline of Zhejiang Province, and the low-carbon industry considered as first class was verified to be consistent with the low-carbon industry areas supported by Zhejiang Province. In order to ensure the applicability of the standard, we also extensively consulted the opinions of relevant government departments and then focused on the application of carbon efficiency codes in "carbon monitoring", "carbon benchmarking" and other directions.

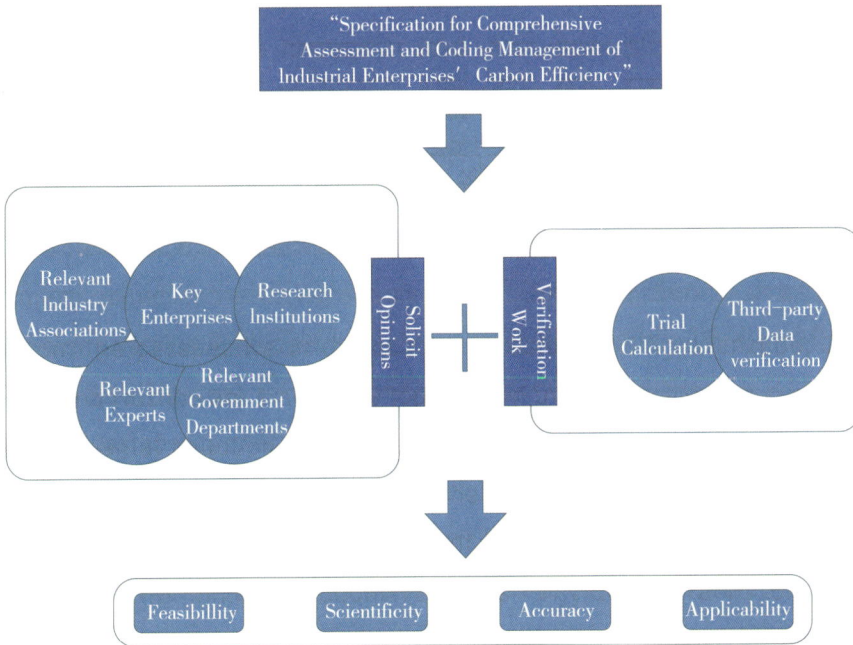

Figure 4-2   Research and Development Process of *Specification for Comprehensive Assessment and Coding Management of Industrial Enterprises' Carbon Efficiency*

3. Establishing an Efficient and Collaborative Application Promotion Mechanism

As a carbon efficiency evaluation tool for industrial enterprises, the ultimate goal of the industrial carbon efficiency code is to help promote the green and low-carbon development of the industrial field. Therefore, the design and application of carbon code should be coordinated with the related work of carbon peak and carbon neutralization in the province. Through the multi-scenario application of the carbon efficiency code, it promotes the efficient allocation of resources, effectively links with the goal of promoting the low-carbon industrial structure in Zhejiang Province, and helps relevant departments in various regions to realize the demands of carbon peaking and carbon neutrality for priority support of resource elements such as land, energy consumption, pollutant discharge, and finance to low-carbon emerging industries.

The economic and information technology departments establish a green manufacturing system under dual carbon goals linked by the carbon efficiency code, improve the evaluation system for green and low-carbon industrial parks and factories, and use the carbon efficiency evaluation results as the basic condition to force industrial parks and enterprises to undergo a green and low-carbon transformation, forming a broad consensus on green and low-carbon development throughout the province. Carbon efficiency codes promote the implementation of energy-saving and carbon reduction technology transformation projects. The government implements "carbon efficiency + energy efficiency services" for enterprises through carbon efficiency codes, organizes professional institutions to carry out more targeted energy-saving diagnoses, and promotes high-carbon-inefficiency enterprises to implement energy-saving and carbon reduction technology transformation. The carbon efficiency code deepens green finance and transformation finance to help enterprises achieve carbon peak carbon neutrality, identifies the current situation and potential of enterprise carbon efficiency development through the carbon efficiency code, gives differential treatment such as credit lines and interest rates to low-carbon enterprises to expand capacity and high-carbon enterprises to energy-saving technological transformation, and guides and assists enterprises in green and low-carbon development.

III. Application Practice of Carbon Efficiency Code to Promote Low-carbon Development of Economy and Society

Industrial carbon efficiency codes are used in different scenarios to promote low-carbon economic and social development in multiple aspects. In the process of promoting the application of industrial carbon efficiency codes in Zhejiang Province, carbon efficiency benchmarking and intelligent coding provides a strong foothold for the government to identify the carbon efficiency of key industries and enterprises and implement precise policies. Enterprise entities use carbon efficiency codes to understand their own carbon efficiency levels and formulate low-carbon development strategies. Meanwhile, industrial carbon efficiency codes provide efficient and accurate support for guiding the rational allocation of social resource elements with a focus on carbon efficiency.

A. Assisting the Government in Precise Carbon Control

For the competent departments of carbon peaking and carbon neutrality, they can accurately identify the key industries and subjects of carbon reduction and introduce targeted policies.

Identifying the carbon efficiency of key industries. Due to the intelligent coding of the industrial carbon efficiency code, the carbon efficiency of industrial industries above designated size in Zhejiang Province can be clearly clustered and divided. Carbon efficiency data effectively helps the government to clarify the status of the industry and provides future direction. Among the 38 industrial categories above designated size in Zhejiang Province, 14 industries are in the first grade of manufacturing dimensions, such as automobile manufacturing and pharmaceutical manufacturing, which are low-carbon industries emphatically supported by Zhejiang Province. The vigorous expansion of these industries will help Zhejiang Province achieve the "14th Five-Year Plan" carbon intensity target. Meanwhile, through the industry analysis of the industrial carbon efficiency code, carbon efficiency features of high industry concentration ratio of carbon emission, high carbon intensity and significant overlap in energy consumption intensity industries are shown in Zhejiang. Thus, accurate identification of key industries in different regions that require targeted carbon efficiency improvement is needed.

Accurately benchmarking the carbon efficiency of enterprises. Accurate benchmarking of industrial carbon efficiency codes enables rapid classification of industries and enterprises. In the manufacturing dimension, high-carbon and low-carbon industries can be quickly identified based on the production characteristics and differences among various manufacturing industries; in the industry dimension, efficient and inefficient enterprises within a certain industry can be quickly identified. To achieve precise benchmarking of the comprehensive dimensions of enterprises, based on the carbon efficiency and production level of the enterprises, manufacturing, and industry benchmarking are combined to accurately position the carbon efficiency of the enterprise in multiple dimensions. Enterprises can be further divided into four grades: high-carbon-inefficiency, high-carbon-efficiency, low-carbon-efficiency, and low-carbon-inefficiency in the two dimensions of industrial carbon efficiency intelligent benchmarking and manufacturing carbon efficiency intelligent benchmarking. The government can more accurately identify enterprises at advanced carbon efficiency levels in different industries, and avoid implementing "one size fits all" policies for enterprises due to industry restrictions. For low-carbon-inefficiency and high-carbon-efficiency enterprises, targeted special actions will be carried out to improve carbon efficiency, compliance inspections will be carried out, improvement plans will be formulated, and "one enterprise, one policy" benchmarking and improvement will be implemented according to the code.

B. Promoting low-carbon development of enterprises

At present, more than 40,000 industrial enterprises in Zhejiang Province have synchronized access to information. For enterprises, in an environment of "low-carbon with dividends, high carbon with pressure", carbon efficiency codes can enhance their low-carbon awareness, and understand the level of green development, and the direction of future improvement.

There are a large number of private enterprises widely distributed in all industries in Zhejiang Province, with high carbon emission industries such as textiles, chemical fibers, and non-metallic minerals accounting for a relatively high proportion. Simultaneously, many enterprises have problems such as an insufficient understanding of the emission situation in their industry and an unclear understanding of their own carbon efficiency development level. The pilot of industrial carbon efficiency codes in typical cities will be further promoted to the industrial field throughout the province to provide a strong driving force for the low-carbon development of enterprises.

A company in Jiangshan

The enterprise belongs to the traditional chemical industry, and the main raw material is hydrogen peroxide. In this process, a lot of carbon dioxide will be inevitably produced. According to carbon efficiency assessment, such as carbon efficiency code, the chemical industry belongs to the key industry of saving energy and reducing carbon in the province. The enterprise proposes a clear low-carbon transformation goal and wants to reuse the carbon dioxide generated by the conversion equipment. It is estimated that 75,000 tons of carbon dioxide can be reduced annually after the equipment is formed. According to the actual situation of carbon efficiency changes of the enterprise and its carbon reduction target, Agricultural Bank Quzhou Branch grants loans with preferential interest rates to help the enterprise set up carbon reduction equipment, and will continue to track the completion of the carbon reduction target of the enterprise after the loan.

A Technology Co., Ltd. in Changxing

This enterprise is mainly engaged in non-metallic mineral products. When the code was initially assigned, the industrial carbon efficiency intelligent benchmarking of the industrial carbon efficiency code was displayed as the fourth grade, and the carbon emission per unit added value was 1.5 times of the average value of the industry. The assignment of the industrial carbon efficiency code set off alarm bells for the carbon efficiency situation of the enterprise, and subsequently, the enterprise carried out low-carbon technology transformation. Ultimately, it prompted the enterprise to implement a carbon efficiency improvement project, replacing the distribution room with a new transformer, and carrying out energy-saving and green transformation of the mill and supporting equipment that have exceeded their service life. It is expected that after the renovation, the annual output value can be increased by 6 million yuan and carbon emissions can be reduced by 184 tons.

C. Channeling more resource elements

For third-party institutions such as financial institutions, industrial carbon efficiency codes provide accurate and authoritative carbon efficiency evaluations of enterprises required for carbon finance. Based on the intelligent benchmarking and coding of enterprises in the manufacturing and industry dimensions, banks and other financial institutions can provide targeted financial element support to the applicant enterprises based on the carbon efficiency evaluation results of industrial carbon efficiency codes to help the low-carbon development of enterprises. On the one hand, it helps financial institutions and others to identify enterprises that can be supported by financial and other elements. On the other hand, long-term tracking of carbon efficiency improvement of the enterprises can be conducted after the support.

A steel group in Huzhou

The enterprise is mainly engaged in the deep processing of special steel products, and the steel industry is one of the seven key industries of energy saving and carbon reduction in Zhejiang Province, which belongs to the high carbon industry in the intelligent benchmarking of industrial carbon efficiency. In the industry dimension, the carbon efficiency intelligent benchmarking and initial coding were in the fifth grade, which was in the middle or lower level among the same industry. The assignment of industrial carbon efficiency codes has warned and urged enterprises to increase their efforts in energy-saving and low-carbon transformation. The enterprise introduces graphene motors and renovate heating furnaces to reduce energy consumption, and cooperates with leading enterprises such as Baosteel, Huaxing, and Yongxing to develop high value-added products and achieve product transformation and upgrading by increasing the level of unit added value; By establishing a subsidiary for the recycling of renewable resources, the enterprise has realized the clean scrap steel and the high-efficiency transformation into a green steel enterprise. After the completion of a series of carbon reduction transformation, the enterprise timely updates the industrial carbon efficiency code, and the enterprise industrial carbon efficiency intelligence standard has been upgraded to the fourth level.

A bamboo company in Anji, Huzhou

The enterprise mainly produces bamboo, rattan and other furniture, furniture manufacturing industry. According to the carbon efficiency index of manufacturing dimension, bamboo and rattan furniture manufacturing industry in Zhejiang Province belongs to low-carbon industry. Meanwhile, in industry dimension, according to the carbon efficiency benchmarking result, the carbon efficiency of the company has reached the advanced level of the industry. The products produced by the company are certified green products, with a high level of green and low-carbon development. According to the carbon efficiency evaluation of the enterprise, such as the carbon efficiency code, Huzhou Bank identified the enterprise as a low-carbon-efficient enterprise, which met the conditions of preferential support and gave low-carbon growth loan to green enterprises for the turnover of daily funds. Meanwhile, the bank will continue to track the change of carbon efficiency of the enterprise.

IV. Enlightenment from the application of carbon efficiency codes

In the process of data acquisition, practical application, and promotion of industrial carbon efficiency codes in Zhejiang Province, some common problems that may exist widely at the national level have also been encountered. Through the practical application of industrial carbon efficiency codes in Zhejiang Province, some inspirations are formed for the future promotion of carbon efficiency codes nationwide.

A. Unified and standardized data acquisition

There are many private enterprises in Zhejiang Province, but the mechanism of corporate environmental information disclosure is lacking, and the accumulation and record of data are not comprehensive. There are problems such as difficulty in quickly obtaining unified caliber and accurate data related to corporate carbon emissions.

In order to ensure data standardization and uniformity, the basic data of industrial carbon efficiency codes are uniformly filled and summarized on the platform of the National Bureau of Statistics. The existing energy consumption data and value-added data of industrial enterprises above designated size can be directly obtained from the statistical department without secondary reporting. Due to the high frequency of data collection, electricity energy consumption data can be directly obtained through collaboration with the power sector. In order to ensure the authenticity and accuracy of data, before carbon efficiency code evaluation, basic data need to be reviewed, verified and confirmed, including data verification of energy-related reports filled in by enterprises on the online reporting platform of the Provincial Bureau of Statistics, and then compared with the third-party on-site verification report; Also, it is necessary to clarify the requirements for obtaining the basic data of carbon efficiency codes in terms of frequency, region, and coverage, including time requirements, which are the data continuously generated by enterprises in the past year; In terms of regional requirements, data should be collected from the regions where actual corporate carbon emissions occur; In terms of completeness requirements, the collected data should cover all data within the accounting scope.

B. Connecting with green finance and transformation finance

In the process of low-carbon transformation, enterprises urgently need funds to support technological transformation or product transformation. However, under the traditional green finance model, the coverage of enterprises is very limited, lacking targeted financial product support. Financial institutions urgently need to support such high-carbon enterprises to carry out low-carbon transformation through transformation finance, and also need to accurately evaluate the carbon efficiency level and transformation potential of enterprises. However, they often face the problems of strong professionalism and high service cost.

Accurately identify enterprises with financial transformation needs. Based on the results of multi-dimensional coding of industrial carbon efficiency codes, banks and other financial institutions can classify enterprises into four different types: high-carbon-inefficiency, low-carbon-efficiency, high-carbon-efficiency and low-carbon-inefficiency according to the multi-dimensional carbon efficiency code assignment, and accurately identify the high-carbon-efficiency and low-carbon-inefficiency enterprises with the potential of low-carbon transformation. Design different financial products for different types of enterprises, such as granting inclusive loans to already low-carbon-efficient enterprises to support their daily production and operation; For enterprises with high-carbon efficiency and low-carbon-inefficiency, guide enterprises to design future low-carbon paths based on carbon efficiency codes, provide financial support for transformation, help enterprises to carry out technological transformation or product transformation and upgrading, and continuously track and supervise the changes of carbon efficiency codes.

C. Raise the low-carbon awareness of market players

Some enterprises do not have a deep understanding of the carbon efficiency improvement in carbon peaking and carbon neutrality work. Under the requirements of low-carbon and high-quality industrial development, some enterprises have the mentality of "low energy consumption, no need to change", and "too much investment, unwilling to change". Meanwhile, some third-party institutions have concerns about supporting the low-carbon transformation of enterprises due to a lack of understanding of low-carbon related professional technology, relevant policy, and investment risks.

Government departments should formulate policies related to carbon efficiency, expand the application scope of enterprise carbon efficiency assessment results, and guide enterprises to attach importance to carbon efficiency improvement; By improving the measurement and evaluation system and utilizing powerful tools such as carbon efficiency codes, establish a full process carbon efficiency tracking and supervision system; Meanwhile, increase financial support for the low-carbon transformation of enterprises. Leading enterprises should play a leading role by formulating low-carbon management plans based on the coding conditions of carbon efficiency codes, promoting the green transformation of production methods, and actively disclosing environmental information related to carbon efficiency. Third-party institutions should continuously innovate green business models, use "carbon efficiency" as one of the key indicators to identify green entities, calculate and evaluate the environmental benefits of enterprises or projects, and innovate transformation financial service products and technological transformation service channels aimed at guiding enterprises to improve carbon efficiency.

Author: The writing group of Zhejiang economic & information centre

Pursing the Development of Green and Low-carbon, and Jointly Creating the Future of Low-carbon Buildings

In order to better adapt to the new situation of carbon peaking and carbon neutrality development, green and low-carbon buildings have become an inevitable trend for the high-quality development of the building industry. Based on the current status of building carbon emissions in Zhejiang Province as well as the main practical exploration and effects of technical paths, energy-saving and carbon reduction in the building sector, it is concluded that building energy conservation must follow the principle of "prioritizing passive technologies and optimizing active technologies" . At the same time, due to the establishment of the closed-loop management mechanism in Zhejiang for the entire construction process, it provides important support and guarantee for achieving energy-saving and carbon reduction targets in the building sector, which is an important experience in construction management in Zhejiang Province. Finally, further prospects are proposed for the overall planning and layout of energy-saving and carbon reduction in the building sector of Zhejiang Province.

I. Introduction

In November 2015, President Xi Jinping proposed the requirement of "developing green buildings" at the United Nations Climate Change Conference. In September 2020, President Xi Jinping proposed for the first time that "China aims to have CO_2 emissions peak before 2030 and achieve carbon neutrality before 2060". In March 2021, General Secretary Xi Jinping clearly required at the 9th meeting of the Central Financial and Economic Affairs Commission of the Communist Party of China Central Committee that "improving energy efficiency standards in the construction industry". Besides, it also emphasized that carbon peaking and carbon neutrality should be included in the overall layout of ecological civilization construction. Carbon peaking has become a key phase in the 14th Five-Year Plan, however, the carbon emissions of the entire life cycle of buildings account for about 40% of society's total carbon emissions.

According to the inconsistency between the described objects and boundaries, the scope of carbon emissions in the construction field can be divided into three dimension: large, medium, and small. The large range refers to the carbon emission of the whole life cycle of the building, including embodied carbon emissions and operational carbon emissions, in which embodied carbon emissions include physical and chemical carbon emissions of building materials production, transportation, and construction, as well as carbon emissions from building renovation and demolition; operational carbon emissions include carbon emissions from the operation of public buildings and residential buildings. Compared with the large range, the medium range does not include carbon emissions from the production and transportation of building materials. Compared with the medium range, the small range would be classified according to carbon emissions by sector, and carbon emissions of residential buildings will be included in residents' daily life.

According to the energy balance sheet of the Zhejiang Provincial Bureau of Statistics, the total carbon emissions of construction and public building operations in the building sector of Zhejiang Province in 2019 accounted for approximately 11.4% of the total carbon emissions. Wherein, the total carbon emissions of construction in the building industry accounted for about 2.1%, while the total carbon emissions of public building operations accounted for about 9.3%. During 2010-2019, the total energy consumption in the building sector of Zhejiang Province expanded by 1.81 times, and the total carbon emissions expanded by 1.43 times, with the highest average annual growth rate of 4.2% in public buildings. Overall, the average annual growth rate of carbon emissions is lower than that of energy consumption, indicating an annual decrease in the overall indirect carbon emission factors in the building sector of Zhejiang Province. This also means that increasing its use of energy with low emission factors in the construction industry of Zhejiang Province, meanwhile conversely the proportion of fossil fuels with high emission factors were reduced used.

The building sector exhibits a trend of increasing before decreasing in terms of the total amount of direct carbon emissions. The overall direct carbon emissions and proportion of the building industry and public buildings showed a downward trend year by year after 2014, which was a turning point, with the public building sector showing the most significant change. This means that the direct application of fossil fuels such as coal and oil in the building sector is gradually decreasing, and the energy structure on the consumption side is gradually transforming to higher-quality development. In 2010, the proportion of electricity consumption in the building industry was one-third, which increased to nearly half by 2019; the proportion of electricity consumption in public buildings was close to four-fifths by 2019. The electrification level of terminal device in the building industry has steadily improved, continuously promoting the low-carbon development level of the building sector.

According to the intensity analysis, the per capita carbon emission intensity of public buildings in Zhejiang Province in 2019 was 0.67 tons of CO_2/person, and the per capita carbon emission intensity of residential buildings was 0.7 tons of CO_2/person, totaling 1.37 tons of CO_2/person. In the past decade, the carbon emission per capita in the building sector and the carbon emission intensity per unit GDP of the service sector have shown a significant upward trend. Based on the year-end resident population and urbanization rate from 2010 to 2019 in Zhejiang Statistical Yearbook 2020, it can be found that the growth rate of per capita emissions from public buildings is much faster than the average annual population growth rate, i.e., the number of people remains the same, while the average growth rate caused by the household energy consumption habits per unit of population has a greater impact. If the intensity is calculated by the service sector GDP growth rate, taking into account the price increase factor, and at comparable prices in 2015, it can be found that the average annual GDP growth rate of the service sector in the last ten years is much faster than the average annual growth rate of carbon emissions per unit of service sector GDP.

II. Low-carbon Technology Pathways in the Building Sector

Low-carbon technologies in the building sector can be divided into three paths, which are carbon reduction, decarbonization, and carbon-free technologies. Carbon reduction technologies include energy-saving technologies for high energy consumption and high carbon dioxide emission links in the building operation process. Decarbonization technologies include CO_2 capture, utilization, and storage technologies applied in the buildings. For example, the carbon sink effect of plants and oceans, and the CO_2 absorption, capture, sequestration, and storage of materials. However, the current decarbonization technologies in the building sector are still in the research stage in the domestic and foreign industry and have not been able to achieve a large-scale application stage in the building sector. Carbon-free technologies include the applications of clean energy technologies such as nuclear energy, solar energy, wind energy, biomass, etc. in the building sector.

Building energy conservation, green performance, and low-carbon technology in the building sector are intertwined, overlapped, and different from each other. For low-carbon technology, building energy saving is the most important carbon reduction path, besides, the use of renewable energy in buildings also belongs to the carbon-free part of low-carbon technology. The green performance of buildings includes safety and durability, health and comfort, the convenience of life, a livable environment, and resource conservation. The safety and durability of buildings can reduce the emboied carbon emissions of building construction; the convenience of life and livable environment of buildings could reduce carbon emissions from transpotatio; the resource-conserving buildings could reduce carbon emissions in building operations and materials for building construction and use.

China's work on building energy conservation started in the 1980s with a three-step approach. The first step set the target of reducing energy consumption by 30% compared with the local structures generally designed in the 1980s. Subsequently, the second step aimed to achieve an additional 30% energy conservation compared with the first step, resulting in a total of about 50% energy conservation compared with the structures in the 1980s. Finally, the third step sought an additional 30% energy conservation on top of the second step, amounting to an approximate 65% energy conservation in comparison to buildings in the 1980s.

After the three-step stage is completed, the objective of energy-efficient building design aims for low, ultra-low, nearly zero, and zero energy consumption. Low-energy buildings must reduce their energy consumption by 25%-30% based on the third-step requirements, resulting in a design energy-saving rate of around 75%. Buildings classified as ultra-low energy need to cut their energy usage by more than 50% to about 82.5% based on the standard set by the third step. To be considered as nearly zero-energy buildings, the energy consumption must be decreased by a minimum of 60%-75% compared with the requirements of the third step and reach a design energy-saving rate of about 90%. Zero-energy buildings must fully utilize renewable energy sources from within and outside of the building so that the annual renewable energy production can be equal to or higher than the total energy consumption of the building for the year.

Carbon-free technology in buildings is mainly achieved through the integration and application of renewable energy sources. In Zhejiang Province, the promotion of renewable energy sources mainly focuses on solar photovoltaic and solar thermal utilization, as well as air-source heat pump hot water systems. Ground source heat pumps, surface water source heat pumps, and solar light-induced systems are encouraged in suitable areas. Renewable energy sources such as wind energy, biomass energy, and tidal energy can be used in some suitable areas.

With the development of solar photovoltaic systems, the initial investment in solar photovoltaic systems has greatly decreased, and the annual power generation has greatly improved. Solar photovoltaic systems have already achieved good economic benefits of Zhejiang Province. Building Integrated Photovoltaics (BIPV) is to install solar photovoltaic arrays on the outer surface of the building envelope to provide electricity. BIPV can be divided into two categories: one is the combination of photovoltaic arrays and buildings, such as the photovoltaic panels are placed on the roofs, which is the best installation practice for distributed photovoltaic power generation systems in urban areas; the other is the integration of photovoltaic arrays and buildings, such as photovoltaic tile roofs, photovoltaic curtain walls, and photovoltaic daylighting roofs. This also requires the photovoltaic components not only need to meet the functional requirements of photovoltaic power generation but also take into account the basic functions of the building, such as sun-shading requirements.

The ideal application mode of distributed photovoltaic power generation system is the application of PEDF (Photovoltaic, Energy storage, Direct current, and Flexibility). Photovoltaic refers to fully utilizing the building surface to develop photovoltaics. Energy storage refers to storing electricity in batteries which will be connected to the grid during the peak demand period and stored during the valley power period. Direct current refers to the internal direct current distribution, transmitting the demand for load electricity through changes in direct current voltage. Flexibility refers to being used as a flexible load in application strategy on the basis of the above technical configuration, achieving flexible power consumption.

In the process of integrating renewable energy into buildings, the effects on the urban ecology, urban wind environment, and urban geomorphic environment must be taken into account. For instance, when incorporating solar energy into urban buildings, the effect of the reflection of solar modules and components on the urban landscape must be considered, as well as any potential consequences of connecting solar photovoltaic systems to the power grid. The application of wind energy in urban buildings must consider the impact of the wind speed field on urban ventilation corridors, the impact of noise on the acoustic environment, and the impact of wind turbine blades on bird flight. Due to the risks and impacts of geological collapse, ground subsidence, and groundwater pollution caused by groundwater exploitation, the use of ground water heat pump (GWHP) should generally be used with caution or restricted.

III. Main Practices and Effects of Energy-Saving and Carbon Reduction in the Building Industry of Zhejiang Province

Zhejiang Province has adopted a strategy of system development and top-level design to promote energy-saving and carbon reduction in the building sector. For more than 20 years, Zhejiang Province has been actively working in this regard. This process began in 1998 with the Standing Committee of the People's Congress of Zhejiang Province passing the Measures for the Implementation of Law of the People's Republic of China on Energy Conservation in Zhejiang Province. Since then, several policies have been taken, including the formulation of Several Opinions on the Implementation of Solar Energy Utilization in Buildings in 2007 and the introduction of Several Opinions on Actively Promoting the Development of Green Buildings in 2011 by the People's Government of Zhejiang Province. In the same year, the Zhejiang construction management department issued normative documents like the Measures for Energy Conservation Assessment and Review of Civil Building Projects. This created a green building supervision system and reinforced the supervision of the implementation of mandatory green building design standards for new civil buildings. In May 2012, the Eleventh People's Congress of Zhejiang Province adopted the Regulations on the Promotion of Renewable Energy Development and Utilization in Zhejiang Province. Subsequently, in 2014, Zhejiang Province issued the Notice on the Comprehensive Promotion of Green Building Action in the Construction of Government-Invested Public Welfare Buildings and Large Public Buildings. This was further strengthened in 2015 when the Twenty-fourth Meeting of the Standing Committee of the Twelfth People's Congress of Zhejiang Province adopted the Regulations of Zhejiang Province Green Building.

In Zhejiang Province, energy conservation in the building sector is led by the continuous improvement and iterative update of technical standards. In 2003, the Design Standard for Energy Efficiency of Residential Buildings (DB 33/1015) was published with a design energy-saving rate of 50%. This was revised in 2015 to 65% and was revised again in 2021 to over 75%. Similarly, the Design Standard for Energy Efficiency of Public Buildings (DB 33/1036) for local engineering and construction standard was set at 60% in 2007 and updated in 2021 to more than 75%. These iterative improvements in the design energy efficiency rate of civil buildings have made a significant contribution to reducing building carbon emissions.

Zhejiang Province has issued the local engineering construction standard Design Standard for Green Building (DB 33/1092), which combines green building technology. The design standard incorporates elements from the national standard Green Building Evaluation Standard (GB/T 50378), and has been tailored to the local economic development conditions, climate, geographical conditions, and technological improvement level. The clauses that would normally require a large amount of simulation analysis and evaluation have been pre-simulated and analyzed during the preparation of the design standard, and expressed design technology provisions that designers can use in accordance with local conditions.

Zhejiang Province has issued a range of local engineering construction standards, regulations, and guidelines, including the Accounting Standard for Renewable Energy Application of Civil Building (DBJ 33/T1105), the Guideline for Special Planning's Compilation of Green Building in Zhejiang Province, and the Technical Specification for Energy-Saving Assessment of Civil Buildings, to guide the construction process towards energy-saving and carbon reduction.

As of November 2020, a total of 990 million square meters of new buildings have been constructed according to green building standards in Zhejiang Province, and a total of 897 buildings have been voluntarily certified with the national Green Building Label (GBL), with a total construction area of about 100 million square meters, including 465 public buildings, 426 residential buildings, and 6 industrial buildings. Two-star projects account for the largest proportion, up to 67%, while one-star and three-star projects account for a relatively small proportion, 19% and 14% respectively.

IV. Major Implications

Zhejiang Province is located in a hot summer and cold winter region, so building energy efficiency must follow the principle of "prioritizing passive technologies", That is, passive technology is used first, and then active technology is used for optimization. In the practice of building energy conservation in Zhejiang Province, it is important to fully adapt to the local climate features, focus on building indoor environment and health while reducing energy consumption and carbon emissions, emphasize the design concept of people-oriented, and pay attention to the transformation and application of natural resources. This is the technical experience of building energy conservation in Zhejiang Province.

Passive energy conservation measures are aimed at reducing the energy demand of buildings which can be achieved without the use of mechanical or electrical device. Active energy conservation, on the other hand, involves improving the efficiency of energy-using equipment and systems to reduce energy consumption after energy demand arises. This approach is preferred due to the longer lifespan of buildings associated with passive energy conservation than the lifespan of the equipment and systems associated with active energy conservation, as well as the high equipment and technology requirements, the large one-time investment, and energy consumption associated with active energy conservation. Consequently, passive technologies should be used whenever possible to design buildings with satisfactory environmental quality without using the equipment. Only when the environment is harsh and passive technologies are inadequate for the building's needs should equipment engineers provide active technologies to supplement and assist.

The climate features of Zhejiang Province are different from other climate zones, mainly characterized by short spring and autumn seasons, long winter and summer seasons, hot summers, and cold wet winters. With people's aspirations for a better life and higher requirements for the indoor environment, the indoor thermal environment of buildings is mostly improved by installing heating and air conditioning facilities to regulate indoor temperature and humidity. The energy consumption of air conditioning accounts for about 30%-50% of the energy consumption for maintaining the building environment. Through the analysis of the impact of various factors of building envelope on air conditioning energy consumption and energy-saving rate, the window-to-wall ratio of buildings in Zhejiang Province has a significant impact on air conditioning load and energy-saving rate, followed by the heat transfer coefficient of external wall>heat transfer coefficient of the roof>shading coefficient>heat transmission coefficient of the outside wall. Therefore, when implementing energy conservation measures for buildings in Zhejiang Province, it is necessary to consider selecting appropriate window-to-wall ratios in the building design stage, especially regulating the use of large-area transparent curtain walls, fully considering the mutual influence of shading, lighting, and ventilation and reasonably designing external windows. When setting up the building envelope for insulation, it is important to ensure the thermal performance of the exterior windows and roof and to fully consider the optimal shading. Wall insulation optimization should be considered secondary.

Buildings in Zhejiang Province also need to consider the free use of natural resources for passive energy conservation. Most buildings in Zhejiang Province have a natural ventilation demand during use, especially in spring and autumn or when the air conditioning is not in use at night. The use of natural ventilation can eliminate indoor heat accumulation and achieve "free cooling", thereby reducing air conditioning energy consumption and improving indoor air quality. According to a survey conducted by Tsinghua University nationwide, more than 80% of people prefer natural wind. Opening the outer window can satisfy people's desire to be close to nature, thereby improving their subjective satisfaction with the indoor environment. Natural wind and mechanical wind have significant differences in physical characteristics such as frequency spectrum and turbulence intensity. The physical characteristics of natural wind cannot be replaced in terms of the comfort it brings to humans' physiological and psychological stimulation. The utilization of natural resources also includes the utilization of natural light resources. Indoor lighting in buildings accounts for approximately 20%-30% of building energy consumption. When considering energy conservation measures, increasing the external window area and using natural lighting can reduce lighting energy consumption, but natural lighting should also consider the impact of increasing the window-to-wall ratio on air conditioning energy consumption.

From the perspective of active technologies, building energy-saving and carbon reduction are achieved through optimizing energy consumption structure and iterating and updating energy-using equipment and system efficiency. In terms of energy consumption, buildings in Zhejiang Province are still using fossil fuels with high carbon emission factors. Under the same standard equivalent coal condition, coal has the highest carbon emission factor, followed by oil, and natural gas has the lowest carbon emission factor. The carbon emissions factor of electricity varies depending on the type of power generation during electricity production. With the future trend of vigorously developing clean energy generation, the carbon emission factor of power energy will gradually decrease.

Therefore, improving the electrification level of building is one of the technical paths for carbon reduction in the building sector of Zhejiang Province. Taking the data of Zhejiang Province in 2019 as an example, if the energy use structure in the building sector is optimized by replacing coal and oil use in public buildings with electricity, coal and oil use in urban buildings with electricity and oil, coal use in rural buildings with electricity, and the oil use in rural buildings with natural gas, an estimated 485,600 tons of carbon can be reduced annually.

The iteration and update of energy-using equipment and system efficiency include two aspects. On the one hand, the efficiency level of energy-using equipment products will be improved, and energy-using equipment with an energy efficiency level of level 2 or above will be adopted. Especially for the prominent problem of high energy consumption and low comfort in the public buildings constructed before 2,000, the iteration and update of energy-using equipment and timely elimination of low-efficiency equipment can promote the energy efficiency improvement of energy-using equipment in existing buildings. On the other hand, energy-using equipment cannot be viewed in isolation, it is necessary to comprehensively balance and consider the efficiency improvement of energy-using systems in the design process. For example, the role of an energy hub or grid aggregator can be developed by decentralizing building energy, complementing energy through energy bus technology, and integrating and aggregating dispersed resources of different spatial distributions into the bus for sharing. By analyzing different energy demands and utilizing energy by quality and quantity, residual and waste energy can be recovered and utilized.

In addition to the energy-saving characteristics of buildings as products, the construction of buildings also has the potential for energy-saving and carbon reduction in. Prefabricated construction, the application of green building materials, the recycling of building materials, and the use of recyclable materials will be promoted in the building construction process. Prefabricated buildings shift much of the on-site work in traditional construction mode to mechanized production on assembly lines in factories. Building components and fittings (e.g. floor slabs, wall panels, stairs, balconies, etc.) are processed and manufactured in factories, transported to construction sites, and assembled and installed with reliable connection methods, greatly reducing labor and improving efficiency and reducing energy consumption in the building sector. Compared with traditional construction mode, prefabricated buildings could save about 10%-30% of energy consumption. According to a study comparing and analyzing prefabricated concrete building projects in 11 cities, including Beijing, Shanghai, Shenyang, Shenzhen, Hefei, and Jinan, prefabricated concrete buildings can reduce carbon emissions by 24.31kg per unit area during the construction phase.

In addition to the technical aspect, energy conservation in the building sector of Zhejiang Province has formed a complete closed-loop work system from the policy mechanism perspective. The refined top-level design provides a good guarantee for achieving building energy conservation and low-carbon. Zhejiang Province has established a system for building energy conservation in planning, design, construction, and operation. An energy-saving evaluation and drawing review management system is established at the design phase, while a construction, energy efficiency evaluation, and completion acceptance management system is established during the construction phase. In the operational phase, an energy consumption monitoring system is established to form a closed-loop management system, thus reinforcing the supervision of energy-saving and low-carbon buildings.

In the planning phase, green carbon reduction goals are determined through planning guidance. Special Planning of Green Buildings in Zhejiang Province specifies the development goals of green buildings and determines the green building levels, renewable energy application requirements, and carbon emission reduction requirements for various newly-built civil buildings. In the use rights, auction or listing announcement of urban construction land, the construction goals of the land are required to follow the Special Planning of Green Building in Zhejiang Province.

During the design phase, the green carbon reduction targets are divided up through design supervision. Green, low-carbon, energy conservation, and other relevant technical components will be implemented in specific projects, and a special energy conservation assessment and review will be carried out in the design phase. The review of the construction drawing design documents will ensure their compliance with mandatory green building standards and their implementation of energy conservation review opinions. Failing to meet these requirements will result in the withholding of the construction drawing design document review certificate.

During the construction phase, green carbon reduction targets are implemented through construction supervision. The construction organization must adhere to the construction drawing design documents and mandatory standards for green buildings, and conduct an energy efficiency assessment of the project before completion to assess whether indicators such as the thermal insulation performance of the building envelope and the efficiency of the energy-using system comply with the requirements of energy conservation assessment and review. This ensures that green energy conservation and low-carbon indicators are effectively implemented in the construction process.

In the operation phase, green carbon reduction targets are achieved through operational regulation and adaptation. The provincial and municipal urban and rural construction authorities establish energy consumption regulatory information system of public buildings to implement dynamic monitoring and information sharing of energy consumption in public buildings. Newly constructed office buildings for state agencies and public buildings with building areas larger than 10,000 m^2 should be set up with building energy usage classification and measurement and data collection devices. By monitoring the energy usage of the building during operation, the effectiveness of energy-saving measures can be ensured.

At present, a closed-loop management mechanism for energy-saving and low-carbon building construction supervision has been basically established in Zhejiang Province, covering the process from planning, design, and construction to acceptance. This provides important support and guarantee in achieving energy-saving and carbon reduction in the building sector and is a significant experience in construction management in Zhejiang Province.

V. Future Prospects

Guided by the overall planning and layout of energy-saving and carbon reduction in the building sector, Zhejiang Province is making progress in building energy conservation from the old three-step approach to the new three-step approach. Demonstration projects such as high-star green buildings, nearly zero (zero) energy buildings, and low-carbon buildings will be created, resulting in a batch of exemplary achievements with Zhejiang characteristics. The focus on energy-saving and carbon reduction in buildings has shifted from building products and building product construction to their use, operations, and management. Digital means and platforms are used to facilitate full-process management, work coordination, data analysis, and information sharing of building projects. According to the three dimensions of promoting integrated urban-rural development, transforming the urban-rural construction and development model, and improving the level of green development management, urban-rural construction will lead to a new era of green development.

Author: Ding De[1], Wu Jiayan[2]

1   Ding De, technical director of the Architectural Design & Research Institute of Zhejiang University Co., Ltd., director of the Green Building and Ecological Urban Area Branch of the China Association for Engineering Construction Standardization, member of the Standardization Working Committee of the China Association for Survey and Design, and main author of the Implementation Plan for Carbon Peak in the Construction Industry of Zhejiang Province. His main research directions include building energy conservation and carbon emissions, green performance of building, green building and low-carbon digitization, etc.

2   Wu Jiayan, deputy chief engineer of the Architectural Design & Research Institute of Zhejiang University Co., Ltd., mainly focuses on climate adaptive building performance research, green and low-carbon buildings, and digitization. She is the main author of the implementation plan for carbon peak in the construction field of Zhejiang Province.

A Review on the Reform and Innovative Explorations of Zhejiang Province on Promoting High-quality, Green and Low-carbon Development in Transportation

Focusing on the overall implementation of carbon peaking in Zhejiang Province, this study, based on innovation in data, management, service, technology and application, systematically summarizes the experience and practice of promoting carbon peaking and carbon neutrality in the transportation field over the past few years. Then it briefly introduces the logic and core contents of such innovative results at provincial level on carbon emission database, transportation carbon index, corporate carbon efficiency code, digital platform and demonstrative application examples. Finally, this study also makes an outlook on the precise conversion and application by implementing three "No.1 projects" in carbon peaking and carbon neutrality in transportation.

I. Introduction

As an efficient instrument, transportation is not only a solid foundation for promoting socioeconomic development in Zhejiang Province but also the main frontier for responding to climate change and facilitating green development, in which its carbon emission covers 9% of the overall amount in the whole province. Recent years saw Zhejiang Province taking a leading position around China in integrated network mileage, transportation scale and equipment, marking a great leap forward in history. The transportation industry has highly valued energy conservation and emission reduction and kept putting low-carbon development strategy as the basis of the transportation system. Especially since the 19th CPC National Congress, under the guidance of General Secretary

Xi Jinping Thought on Socialism with Chinese Characteristics for the New Era, the transportation system has accelerated the transformation of development concept, proactively adjusted the transport structure, vigorously promoted the application of new energy and clean energy, and strengthened low-carbon governance capacity. Therefore, remarkable results have been achieved in building a low-carbon transportation system and important contributions have been made to responding to climate change and fostering ecological advancement. From five perspectives on the "innovation of data, management, service, technology and application", reforms have been carried out after practical explorations in recent years. See the text below for brief descriptions.

II. Practice and Effect

A. Innovating the Method of Collecting and Calculating Carbon Emissions in the Transportation Sector

Since transportation is a giant complex system. Policies and speeding up the working process mainly depend on the statistical calculation of carbon emissions. At present, the "top-down" IPCC method is the mainstream to calculate carbon emissions in the transportation sector in the province[3]. Its merits lie in easy access to data and simple calculation to handle while its demerit is no access to the subledger of carbon emission in terms of data range and update frequency in the transportation sector. In order to solve this question, it is necessary to innovate the method of collecting carbon emissions in the transportation sector.

1. Identifying the Main Components of Carbon Emissions in the Transportation Sector of the Province through "Top-Down" Method

Through identification and analysis, it is found out that transportation in business is the major contributor of carbon emissions in the transportation sector, and it covers 70% of the overall amount, among which road transportation accounts for about 70% in the transportation in business[4]. Road transportation is four times as much as railway and ten times as much as ships in carbon intensity of per unit turnover, thus the key parameter to realize carbon peaking in the transportation in business hinges on road transportation. The carbon emission sorted out from people's living to transportation (mainly from private cars) continues to increase over the past decade, covering more than 50% of carbon emissions in non-business transportation. Therefore, the key parameter of carbon peaking in non-business transportation depends on private cars.

2. Collecting Carbon Emissions of Road Transportation across the Province in the Top Priority Areas

A special survey has been initiated on the carbon emission of road transportation around the whole province in relevant prioritized areas. The objectives of the survey involved all vehicles in business in 11 regions and cities of road freight transport, highway passenger transport, bus passenger transport, and cab passenger transport. The data on their transportation production, mileage, and energy consumption were collected and investigated. The survey integrated the three methods of monitoring and investigating equipment, the investigation by the enterprises themselves, and questionnaires on the vehicles to realize mutual complementation and adjustment, which is a breakthrough innovation. It turned out to be the first in the country to establish a provincial level 100 km unit consumption calculation model and build a per 100 km consumption standard as well as an oil consumption database of different models, different fuel types, different emission standards, different vehicle ages, and different working conditions. The results show that the 100 km actual energy consumption of heavy-duty road freight vehicles in the province is generally lower than the standard limit, the 100 km actual energy consumption of mini-trucks is generally higher than the standard limit, the 100 km actual unit consumption of buses and cabs in business is close to the standard limit, and the 100 km energy consumption of city buses is basically lower than the national standard limit.

3. Carrying out Data Calculation of Carbon Emission in the Transportation Sector across the Whole Province in a Comprehensive and Precise Way

Based on the provincial 100 km unit consumption standard database, an energy consumption calculating model is built respectively through incorporating the province's vehicle approval system, vehicle trajectory, and transport information under special conditions respectively, to create a set of road transport energy consumption measurement rules that can achieve real-time, dynamic and high-frequency monitoring. The annual energy consumption in the subfields around the province and in various cities is calculated in an extended way to achieve detailed accounting of the energy consumption of different segments of the road transport industry (road passenger transport, road freight, city buses, and cabs, etc.) and create a unified book of energy consumption in the road transport industry in the province. Through comparison among the database, in 2022, the province's annual energy consumption of trucks in business was 6.1 million tons of standard coal, cabs (online car-hailing) nearly 700,000 tons of standard coal, buses 530,000 tons of standard coal, and passenger buses in business nearly 300,000 tons of standard coal.

B. Innovating the Model of Managing the Strategic Objective on Carbon Emission Reduction in the Transportation Sector

Focusing on the 14 initiatives on emission reduction in 6 major areas of the transportation sector in the province, research and evaluation on the low-carbon index are first initiated at the provincial level. As a quantitative tool to track and assess the overall effect of the work on carbon peaking at both provincial and municipal levels, the index is of great importance for providing reference in decision-making.

1. Identifying the Methods and Principles of Building the Low-carbon Index in the Transportation Sector in the Province under the Guidance of Quantitative Application

When the transportation sector develops and reaches at a level with certain economic and production scale and both the internal and external demands shift to the green and low-carbon development, the low-carbon index is able to maximize the energy efficiency of the industry by adopting a series of energy-saving and carbon-reducing measures. The evaluation system has three characteristics. First, it is quantitative evaluation through selecting quantifiable evaluation indicators, reducing the shortcomings of qualitative indicators in the vertical comparison, and evaluating the final score to achieve horizontal and vertical comparison of low-carbon development of transportation. Second, it is a hierarchical system to evaluate the low-carbon development of transportation at provincial, municipal, and county levels with the core conclusions and core indicators that can be mutually verified at different levels. Third, it is a flexible evaluation with timely adjustment of some indicators and regular updating of indicator weights to reflect the highlights of work at different stages. The index system of evaluation includes transportation development quality, transportation energy consumption and emission, and transportation low-carbon management.

2. Building an Index System Responding to the Low-carbon Index in the Transportation Sector in the Province to Make the Index Produce Real Effect

A pool of evaluation indicators on low-carbon development in the transportation sector is built by centering on transportation development quality, transportation energy consumption and emissions, and transportation low-carbon management, of which the indicators are 13[5], 8[6] and 36 respectively. After several rounds of iterations, 13 specific indicators are finally selected for the calculation. Indicators for transportation development quality reflect the intensity of the regional traffic economy and production activities, those for traffic energy consumption and emissions reflect the energy conservation and carbon reduction of the regional transportation sector, and those for low-carbon management reflect the progress made in carbon peaking and carbon neutral-related work of in the region. The final result of the regional carbon index is jointly affected by the above-mentioned three factors.

3. Formulating a Checklist on Carbon Peaking According to Different Cities and Areas to Boost the Index

With the goal of improving the index, the implementation of the key and difficult tasks for promoting carbon peaking in the transportation sector in various cities is prioritized. Hangzhou makes continuous efforts in the shift of freight transport from road to waterway and shore power and strives to become a pilot city for demonstrating low-carbon development in the transportation sector in the province. As such areas developed in waterway transport as Jiaxing, Huzhou, Zhoushan, and Ningbo have a natural geographic advantage in energy conservation and emission reduction in the transportation sector with their carbon emissions intensity generally low, they focus on increasing the use of non-fossil energy in the transportation sector, accelerating the upgrading of low-carbon equipment, and improving efficiency inside the organization and such underdeveloped areas as Lishui, Jinhua, and Quzhou are smaller in the transportation sector scale and equipment quantity, thus the difficulty of upgrading the transport equipment and adjusting the transportation structure is reduced to a certain extent, and the upgrading of transport equipment is prioritized.

C. Providing Innovative Tools for Low-carbon Transformation of Enterprises Served in the Transportation Sector

Transportation enterprises are the main providers of transportation services and have become a key variable affecting the carbon peaking of the transportation sector. The transportation sector creatively develops the application tool of carbon efficiency code to characterize the carbon emission intensity of transportation enterprises by industry and sub-sector so as to serve the green transformation of transportation enterprises.

1. Focusing on the Base of Enterprises and Formulating the Rules of Code-Assignment

In the *Carbon Efficiency Classification and Grading Method for Road Freight Transport Enterprises on the Standardized List* (*Trial Implementation*) *of Zhejiang Province* released by the provincial competent department in June 2022, the carbon efficiency coding and promotion for road freight transport enterprises above designated size have been officially launched throughout the province. In terms of enterprise classification, according to the operating scope of the enterprise's vehicles, all the relevant enterprises in the province are divided into four types, i.e., general cargo transport enterprises, cargo-specific transport enterprises, dangerous goods transport enterprises, and comprehensive transport enterprises for coding respectively. In terms of company grading and coding, the carbon efficiency code is composed of three parts: enterprise carbon emissions intensity, enterprise low-carbon development foundation, and additional points. According to the carbon efficiency code score of road freight transport enterprises, green, blue, and red codes are assigned from high to low for each type of the enterprise, which are updated quarterly.

2. Promoting Enterprise Development and Evaluating the Green Base

At present, the carbon efficiency code has been assigned to all freight enterprises above designated size in the province, covering about 100,000 trucks in business. Generally speaking, the average score of enterprises was upgraded from 70 to 80 in the first quarter of 2022; the green code rate of enterprises rose from less than 50% in the first quarter to 60% in the fourth quarter; the average carbon emission intensity per unit turnover of enterprises dropped significantly, and the overall level of green and low-carbon development of the industry was improved. Among the four major categories of road freight enterprises, the highest can be seen in the comprehensive transport enterprises and the lowest in dangerous goods transport enterprises. The highest green code rate is found in comprehensive transport enterprises and general cargo transport enterprises the lowest. Therefore, the work on road freight industry carbon emission reduction management should focus on the general cargo enterprises and lead them to develop to a large scale in a professional way. The cargo special transport industry is found the lowest average unit turnover of carbon emission intensity, which can be ascribed to the fact that containers and other special transport vehicles are relatively high in organization efficiency. The dangerous goods transport industry shows the highest intensity because of the strict management on those vehicles that affects the loading of backhaul goods and at the same time reduces the efficiency.

3. Serving for Enterprise Transformation and Perfecting the Policies to Form a Close Loop

In order to make the carbon efficiency code to play a greater role in helping local authorities to connect the code with the policies to build a closed-loop system, in term of financial policies for green development, in May 2022, the Shaoxing Central Branch of People's Bank of China (PBOC), Shaoxing Branch of China Banking and Insurance Regulatory Commission (CBIRC) and Transport Bureau of Shaoxing jointly issued the *Guidance on Financial Support for Green Transportation and Low-carbon Circular Development*, which allows enterprises assigned with the green code to apply for higher loans and lower interest rates. At present, a total of RMB 18 million yuan of credit and RMB 7.84 million yuan of low-interest loans have been granted to green code enterprises. In term of policies on granting epidemic prevention subsidies, in July 2022, Transport Bureau and Finance Bureau of Shaoxing issued the *Implementation Rules of the*

Shaoxing Road and Waterway Transport Enterprise Epidemic Prevention Subsidy Policy, which gave an additional subsidy of RMB 10,000 yuan to the above-mentioned road freight enterprises that have applied for the carbon code and have been assigned with green code, and a total of RMB 400,000 yuan were granted for green code enterprises.

D. Innovating Digitized Governance of Low-carbon Development in the Transportation Sector

In response to the difficulties and obstacles such as large amounts and high mobility of carbon emission sources in the transportation sector, as well as the difficulties in accounting and monitoring, a pioneering provincial-level digital platform for carbon peaking in the transportation sector has been established, which targets three key users, i.e., the government, the enterprises, and the public. This digital platform realizes a comprehensive intelligent control system for carbon tools, namely the regional carbon index, the corporate carbon efficiency code, and public carbon point, so as to achieve online management of carbon emissions reduction tasks in the transportation sector, promote awareness, quantitative accounting and closed-loop supervision of carbon emissions in the industry.

1. Identifying the Platform Position based on a Question-oriented Concept

The following main issues are identified. Firstly, application construction has not been considered yet at the national level, and there is currently no nationwide plan for the construction of unified digital applications. It is Zhejiang that takes the lead in planning the construction and building a demonstrative model. Secondly, there are no substantive application results at the provincial level, and the construction of digital applications related to carbon emissions has relatively little experience to draw on. Thirdly, the carbon peaking system in the transportation sector needs to be reconstructed, and the statistics and accounting system for carbon emissions in the transportation sector is still in the exploratory stage. The positioning of the application is identified. It is an overall platform for promoting green and low-carbon transformation in the transportation sector, and the key application of digital reform in the transportation sector. In response to the issues such as multiple carbon management entities, diverse transportation equipment, broad regulatory scope, and difficult data monitoring, Zhejiang will focus on the "four values" of carbon emissions, energy consumption, carbon intensity, and energy intensity. The province will serve three types of entities, namely, the management departments, the transportation enterprises, and the public, and strive to achieve the transformation of carbon emission management from "invisible" to "visible", the transformation of carbon emission accounting from "rough estimates" to "detailed records", the transformation of carbon emission policies from "rough rules" to "detailed and accurate guidelines", and the transformation of enterprises and individuals from "not caring" to "indispensable".

2. Identifying Major Tasks of the Platform Through Three Lists

The first list identifies six major problems. The first is the rough perception of carbon emissions and the lack of details in data. The second is the non-transparency and lack of standards in carbon accounting, which makes the result lack of authority. The third is the lack of systemic carbon policies and insufficient accuracy in implementation. The fourth is the gaps that existed in carbon source management and the incomplete coverage of responsibilities. The fifth is the cross-sector carbon supervision that leads to low centralized management. The sixth is the lack of motivation and attractiveness in carbon emissions reduction, which results from insufficient participation by the main body.

The second list highlights three cross scenarios. The first is the multiple cross-scenario facing the government side. Upgrading transportation equipment and adjusting transportation structures are the two key variables, requiring coordination among environmental protection, public security, transportation, and other departments. The second is the multi-cross-scenario facing the enterprise side. The main issue is to solve the problems of corporate carbon point accounting and link to government-related carbon emission policies and to realize the closed loop of policy formulation, carbon point accounting, and policy evaluation. The third is the multiple cross-scenario facing the public side. The main issue is to solve the problems of personal carbon footprint reduction and carbon point trading and to realize the closed loop of footprint monitoring, platform accounting, and point exchange.

The third list proposes five major reforms. The first is to reform the existing data statistics mode and establish a set of unified tables (statistical system) for carbon emission. The second is to reform the existing business management mode and build a unified work system for carbon peaking. The third is to reform the existing policy incentive system and achieve accurate policy closed-loop force. The fourth is to reform the existing market access system and establish a normative standard system guided by emissions reduction for industries. The fifth is to reform the existing main body supervision mode and guide enterprises to participate in the transportation sector carbon emissions reduction.

3. Implementing the Scenario of the Platform Based on the Overall Structure of 133X

The overall structure of the digital application on carbon peaking is summarized as "133X", i.e., "One Traffic Brain, Three Types of Users, Three Tools and X Application Scenarios". "One Traffic Brain" refers to the algorithm rules of carbon peaking in the traffic field. "Three Types of Users" refer to the key applicable management departments of carbon peaking digital application (at the county, municipal and provincial levels), transportation enterprises, and the public. "Three Tools" refer to the carbon index, carbon efficiency code, and carbon points. The following five major functions will be realized by this structure.

Monitoring through one-screen perception: A carbon peak smart map is drawn to display the completion progress and status of carbon peak work in various regions of the province, and promote the integration of carbon peak data collection and reporting systems at the provincial, city, and county levels by establishing a set of updatable, reusable, and highly efficient data collection and reporting system. Accounting by one-table settlement: A unified table of carbon peak data is created in the province, integrating industry data, and forming a standardized data integration system and accounting system. Automatically calculate the total energy consumption, carbon emissions, energy consumption intensity, and carbon emission intensity by city, industry, and enterprise. Warn by the one-graph analysis and judgment: A carbon emission map is drawn in the transportation field to achieve assessments of the total energy consumption, carbon emissions, energy consumption intensity, and carbon emissions intensity. Track the indicators of 14 measurements in 6 areas in the action plan by region, and provide support for the closed-loop management system of indicator issuance, tracking warning, and indicator evaluation for provincial industry management departments. All can be handled in decision-making through one network. A digital application network for carbon peaking is established to predict and evaluate the before-and-after carbon reduction effect of carbon reduction work according to the carbon reduction tasks of each city and guide the formulation and optimization of future carbon reduction policies to achieve a closed-loop management of effect prediction, result evaluation, and policy optimization. Credit for one-code access: Enterprise carbon efficiency code and social public carbon points are established to link them to government subsidies, corporate operations (financing costs, operating permits, etc.), road rights allocation, vehicle insurance rates, subsidies, and rewards, etc., and embed them in the production and life processes of enterprises and individuals.

E. Innovating the Close Loop of Application Scenario of Low-carbon Policies in the Transportation Sector

Centering on key fields such as transportation equipment upgrading and transportation structure adjustment, taking digitalization as the tool, and combining with local realities, the transportation sector has carried out digitized application scenarios closed-loop design in Quzhou, Taizhou and other regions, and achieved phased results.

1. Promoting the "Shift of Freight Transport from Road to Waterway" of the Bulk Goods First by Centering on the Structure Adjustment in the Transportation Sector

From the perspective of transportation structure, waterway transport is the main way for long-distance transportation of bulk goods in developed countries, while the province still relies mainly on road transportation, leaving much room for optimization of transportation structure. In terms of carbon emission intensity, per unit turnover of waterway transport is only one-tenth that of road transportation, which has significant advantages in emission reduction. The logical loop is to convert the carbon emission reduction of bulk goods from "shift of freight transport from road to waterway" into energy consumption and use it as an increment of enterprise energy quota to stimulate internal dynamics and guide cargo owners to choose waterway transport actively.

For the improvement of the supporting policies for the "shift of freight transport from road to waterway", two practices are proposed. First, the energy saved therefrom is linked with enterprise energy consumption budget indicators and related incentive policies are drawn up. With carbon emission as a link, the correlation between the volume of "shift of freight transport from road to waterway" and the energy consumption indicators is established. Carbon emission reductions from the "shift of freight transport from road to waterway" are taken as an incentive for total energy consumption in the energy dual control index, which is applied directly to cargo owners. Second, subsidy policies for "shift of freight transport from road to waterway" are introduced. Subsidies are granted for containers linking the river and the seas, river shipping enterprises engaged in waterway transport, connected terminals, shipping companies, and other subjects.

2. Exploring and Promoting Green Urban Distribution by Centering on Equipment Upgrading in the Transportation Sector

In terms of equipment ownership, there are 1.73 million trucks around the province, nearly 80% of them are light or mini trucks and most are urban distribution vehicles. Moreover, it is relatively vague in which industry the authority and responsibility of the management should fall. In terms of carbon emissions, the amount from heavy-duty freight vehicles in Zhejiang Province accounts for 42% of carbon emissions in the transportation sector, which is the key carbon emission source in the entire road transportation. To form the closed logic loop, differentiated guidance policies are introduced by centering on the carbon emission reduction of heavy cargo enterprises and taking carbon efficiency code classification as a means to help enterprises to carry out new energy upgrade of transport equipment and guide enterprises to improve transport efficiency.

For the improvement of the supporting policies for green distribution, three practices are proposed. The first is to implement the financial subsidy policies, such as updating the new energy vehicle operation subsidies, linking the subsidy standard with the enterprise carbon efficiency code, and implementing differentiated subsidies. The second is to implement the right-of-way management policy, such as optimizing the rules of urban distribution vehicles in the restricted area. At first, the new energy vehicles in the restricted area will remain unrestricted and the non-new energy vehicles according to the enterprise carbon code will be graded right-of-way management. The third is to implement parking management policies, such as optimizing the differential parking management methods for the existing vehicles, continuing to implement free parking for new energy vehicles in government-operated public parking spaces, and giving corresponding preferential treatment to those which are not new energy vehicles according to their carbon code.

III. Major Implications

Firstly, it is a systematic project to promote carbon peaking in the transportation sector, which should be done in accordance with the general trend of high-quality social-economic development, the advantages of highly compatible development in the transportation sector, the development of high efficiency in the transportation market, and the development of high standard of green technology. Secondly, the government should actively build the policy instruments and upgrade methods of carbon target management in the transportation field to adapt to the actual situation in the province, promote the structural emission reduction in a step-by-step way, improve the matching degree between the policy and market demand, and optimize the policy through effect evaluation. Thirdly, the government should actively promote the construction of digital applications of carbon peaking, innovate data collection methods, create data processing standards, and create digital applications to help achieve the goal of carbon peaking in the transportation sector.

IV. Future Prospects

2023 marks the first year for the comprehensive implementation of the spirit of the 20th CPC National Congress, and it is also a critical year for deepening and implementing carbon peaking and carbon neutrality. In the field of transportation, the government will further make good use of the toolbox of reform and innovation, make efforts to use the dual-carbon strategy in transportation as a work of priority, and implement the "Three No. 1 Projects" of the Provincial Party Committee, firmly implement the concept of green sustainable development, innovate the work system and development mode, and continuously promote the high-quality development of transportation to achieve new results. Meanwhile, the government will firmly grasp the goal of achieving the peak of carbon emissions in the transportation sector before 2030, tackle the key and difficult tasks, take multiple measures to pragmatically promote change and advancement, and open up and promote the "transportation + energy" economies, and provide targeted strategies to accelerate the transformation of integrated governance for green transportation according to local conditions. The government will comprehensively promote the precise transformation and implementation of the "Three No. 1 Projects" in the field of dual-carbon transportation.

Author: Bai Hongyu[1]

References

[1] Xie S H, Wang L X, Shao Z L. Review on carbon emission researches at home and abroad[J]. Arid Land Geography, 2014(4): 720-730.

[2] Cao, C Y. Report on the study of carbon peaking in transportation in Zhejiang Province[R]. Zhejiang: Zhejiang Institute of Transportation Science, 2021:

---

1 Bai Hongyu, deputy director of Traffic Development Research Center of Zhejiang Academy of Communications and Transport Science (in charge of the work), head of Traffic Economic Operation Monitoring Center (part-time), member of Traffic Low-carbon Working Committee of China Society of Highway and Transport. He has been responsible for provincial and municipal projects such as the *"Research Report on Carbon Peak in the Transportation Sector of Zhejiang Province"*, and participated in the compilation of several policy documents. He has been responsible for the international cooperation projects *"Study on the Carbon Neutral Path and Countermeasures of Transportation in Zhejiang Province"* and *"Study on the Transformation of Road Freight Transportation in Zhejiang Province under the Vision of Carbon Neutrality"*, and formulated standards such as *"The Guidelines for Accounting and Evaluation of Carbon Emissions from Carbon Accounts of Road Transport Enterprises"* (DB 3308/T099-2021).

27-28.

[3] Tang W Q. Analysis of the pathways to peak energy-related carbon emission in China and its provinces[D]. Hangzhou: Zhejiang University, 2020.

[4] Wang B M, Feng D H, Liu Y L, et al. On the freight structure adjustment of Zhejiang province under the carbon peak background[J]. China Transportation Review, 2021(43): 103-108.

[5] Ouyang B, Zhang Y J, Guo J. The comprehensive evaluation indicators for low-carbon transport and applications[J]. Journal of Beijing Institute of technology (Social Sciences Edition), 2014(16): 7-13.

[6] Zhang Y H. Study on regional differences and impact factors of transportation carbon emissions under the background of high-quality development[D]. Xi'an: Chang'an University, 2021.

"Zhejiang Experience" and Prospect of Carbon Peaking in the Agriculture Sector

The agriculture system is both ecosystem and production system, with both functions of carbon emissions and carbon sequestration. In 2005, Xi Jinping, then the Secretary of Zhejiang Province, proposed to "vigorously develop high-efficiency ecological agriculture", and since then Zhejiang has been promoting green and sustainable development of agriculture, through coordinating pollution control, industrial transformation and carbon emission reduction and sequestration. This report analyzes the main paths has been taken for Zhejiang's agricultural sector to first achieve carbon peak, summarizes the "Zhejiang experience" in carbon emission reduction and sequestration, predicts the trend of carbon emission in the next decade, and some suggestions for further development are put forward.

I. Introduction

Carbon emissions reduction and sequestration in the agriculture sector have extensive and profound impacts. Agriculture production involves the largest land area and population in the world. The 3rd National Land Resource Survey shows that China's cultivated land area has reached 1.918 billion mu, which feeds 18% of the population with less than 13% of the global cultivated land area. As a form of land use that accounts for 1/8 of China's total land area, agricultural emission reduction and carbon sequestration on farmland are closely related to people's daily lives, and have the most extensive and far-reaching impacts. It is not only an important means of achieving "carbon peak", but also has huge potential in the "carbon neutrality" stage. With the eco-friendly transformation of China's agricultural production mode, carbon emissions in the crop production sector have begun to decline in the past five years. Zhejiang Province has already reached its peak and will play a leading role as the first one to reach peak emissions. In view of the goal of "carbon neutrality", it is necessary to plan ahead for carbon emission reduction and sequestration in the agricultural sector to tap its substantial potential.

Agricultural production is both a source and a sink of carbon. Agricultural production is not only a production system, but also an important part of the ecosystem. In this process, carbon emissions are complex, with various cropping systems and production modes having different effects on the environment. On one hand, all the activities in agriculture production, including energy consumption, livestock and poultry breeding, agricultural material inputs, rice planting, and soil itself, can emit greenhouse gases, most notably carbon dioxide, methane and nitrous oxide, which is the main source of non-CO_2 greenhouse gas emissions. On the other hand, agricultural production also has the potential to act as a carbon sink, with farmland soil, oceans, and other supporting materials acting as large ecosystems that can capture and store carbon. The increase of organic matter in the farmland soil can enhance the soil's carbon absorption capabilities and contribute to carbon sequestration. Therefore, while agricultural production must prioritize stabilizing food production and ensuring sustainable agricultural development, it is also important and irreplaceable to recognize its wider benefits in terms of resource cycling, ecological purification, carbon sequestration and sink enhancement .

Carbon reduction and sequestration in the agriculture sector have multiple values in a coordinated way. From the perspective of its connotation and the systematic route, it has coordinated significance with green development, pollution control and industrial growth.

In terms of curbing emissions by eliminating high-energy-consuming agricultural machinery, and using renewable energies, the sector can co-promote the adjustment of agricultural industrial structure and green development. Tke the construction of Zhejiang Provincial Coordinated Innovative Zone of Pollution and Carbon Reduction for instance. Through a focus on works with the strongest synergy between emission reduction and pollution control, such as reducing agricultural inputs and utilizing waste resources, it can identify the "greatest common divisor" of the agricultural ecological environment protection and exert the dual benefits of preventing and treating non-point source pollution and reducing carbon emissions.

By promoting emission reduction technologies and ecological models, practical actions can be taken to explore agricultural carbon sinks, which could effectively coordinate carbon reduction and sequestration and industrial growth without sacrificing productivity.

II. Main Practice and Achievements

Looking back on the development of high-efficiency ecological agriculture in Zhejiang Province, we can see that over the past two decades, the province has persistently pursued innovation while balancing high-quality agricultural development and ecological sustainability. As early as 2005, Xi Jinping, then the Secretary of the Zhejiang Provincial Party Committee, made the significant decision to "vigorously develop high-efficiency ecological agriculture." By the year 2010, Zhejiang had become the only pilot province in China for modern ecological and circular agriculture. In 2017, Zhejiang Province was designated as the first pilot province for whole-province green agricultural development by the former Ministry of Agriculture. In 2019, Zhejiang Province initiated the "dual control of fertilizers and pesticides" reform as a major means of promoting green agricultural development. Since the digital reform in 2021, green agricultural development in Zhejiang has entered a stage of integrated reform for high-efficiency ecological agriculture characterized by reduced input, efficient resource use, sound eco-environment, and high-quality products. In 2023, Zhejiang Province proposed to "build a strong province of high-efficiency ecological agriculture" towards advancing the province as a frontrunner in China's campaign to become an agricultural power. Over the years, Zhejiang Province has taken effective measures to eliminate outdated and inefficient production capacity, promote transition to renewable energies, improve agricultural production efficiency, recycle resources, and explore agricultural carbon sinks, playing a significant role in promoting the agricultural sector to peak first.

A. Major Practical Efforts

1. Effective measures to eliminate outdated and inefficient production capacity

In terms of phasing out outdated agricultural machinery, with improved agricultural mechanization in Zhejiang Province, a growing number of old and inefficient agricultural machines with high energy consumption, heavy pollution, and low safety performance had accumulated. To tackle this problem, Zhejiang Province has strengthened its guidance on purchasing policies and revised the agricultural machinery scrapping subsidy policy, encouraging and guiding organizations and individuals engaged in agricultural production in the province to voluntarily scrap inefficient and old agricultural machinery. For example, all the products currently benefiting from subsidy policies comply with the National III diesel engine emission standard. A special rectification campaign on modified tractors was also launched. In June 2021, the stock of over 50,000 modified tractors in the province was completely eliminated, accomplishing the provincial goal one year ahead of schedule and the national goal four and a half years ahead of schedule.

Reducing carbon emissions from fishing vessels is crucial for mitigating carbon emissions in the agricultural sector and protecting the marine ecosystem. Since 2014, Zhejiang Province has been carrying out a law enforcement campaign known as "one strike, three rectifications" to crack down on illegal, unregistered, and unlicensed fishing vessels, as well as to address issues of banned fishing gear, invalid licenses and marine environmental pollution. During this period, a range of regulations have been formulated and implemented to standardize fishing vessel management and control, fishing moratoriums, and eco-environmental improvement. For example, the province has maintained and deepened the "dual control" (power and quantity) system for marine fishing vessels, while also providing subsidies as a safety net to fishermen for reducing fishing vessels and shifting to other industries. As a result, over 19,000 illegal, unregistered, and unlicensed fishing vessels have been eliminated along the coast of Zhejiang Province, which accounted for nearly half of the total number eliminated in the entire country.

2. Effective measures to promote transition to renewable energies

The province is actively promoting the improvement of the energy mix among agricultural production entities, advocating electrification transformation of protected agriculture, and encouraging rational development and utilization of clean and renewable energies such as biomass and solar energy. The province also encourages the construction of livestock and poultry manure biogas power generation projects in large-scale breeding farms and densely populated breeding areas, and the implementation of centralized biogas supply in areas with favorable conditions to replace fossil fuels. Additionally, grain drying equipment that utilizes biomass pellets as a heat source has been included in the agricultural machinery subsidy policy. By the year 2021, of more than 5,700 grain dryers in Zhejiang Province, about 43.63% of them, or 2,502, were using clean biomass as their heat source.

The province has been guiding and promoting "agriculture-photovoltaic complementarity" to make reasonable use of the roofs of agricultural facilities, cold storage for processing agricultural and sideline products, and fishpond surfaces for developing photovoltaic agriculture without affecting agricultural production and the protection of agricultural land. For instance, the "fish-photovoltaic complementarity" project in Sandu Town of Jiande has been able to supply approximately 20 million kW · h of clean electricity annually to the Jiande area of Hangzhou since the completion of the Sandu PV Power Station, roughly equivalent to the annual electricity consumption of Sandu Town, resulting in a savings of about 8,000 tons of standard coal and a reduction of 17,000 tons of CO_2 emissions per year.

3. Effective measures to improve agricultural production efficiency

Reducing agricultural input and decreasing their inappropriate use play the most fundamental and crucial role in non-CO_2 emissions reduction in the agricultural sector. Under the overall framework of "dual control of fertilizers and pesticides", measures have been taken to reduce emissions at the source, optimize the supply-side structure of agricultural materials, and promote the recycling of agricultural waste. These efforts have laid a solid foundation for the green and low-carbon development of Zhejiang Province, with the amount of chemical fertilizers and pesticides used decreasing for nine consecutive years.

For example, in 2021, Zhejiang launched the "balanced fertilizer replaced with formulated fertilizer" action on the supply side, breaking the dominance of balanced fertilizer in the agricultural inputs market for over a decade. In 2022, formulated fertilizers accounted for 77.5% of the total fertilizer sales volume, and over 1 million tons of various types of organic fertilizers such as animal manure were applied.

The intensification of land use and the scale of operation are the prerequisites for cutting costs, increasing efficiency, and improving energy utilization. In order to improve the efficiency of agricultural operations, idle arable lands are being systematically transformed into family farms and cooperatives. Zhejiang Province is actively promoting the construction of modern agricultural service centers that are large-scale, specialized, and one-stop-shop, and enhancing their comprehensive services through the "1+X" approach, which includes mechanical services throughout the entire process, centralized seedling cultivation, and agricultural technology services. By the end of 2021, there had been 311 modern agricultural comprehensive service centers, 313 industry-agriculture cooperation alliances, and 1,097 crop hospitals established throughout the province, basically forming a socialized agricultural service network that covers all towns in the province.

In order to improve the mechanization level, efficient, energy-saving, multi-functional, and intelligent agricultural machinery has been included in the agricultural machinery purchase subsidy program. Combine harvesters and rice transplanters that meet national emission standards have been actively adopted and promoted, and agricultural machinery equipment such as aerial spraying and track laying to cultivate mountainous areas that have good fertilization and pesticide reduction effects and high transportation efficiency have been put into use. Since 2018, subsidies have been provided for unmanned aerial vehicles for crop protection, and a total of 3,402 units have been subsidized from 2020 to 2022. The comprehensive mechanization rate of crop cultivation and harvesting in the province has reached 77.2%. In addition, 278 digital agricultural factories (bases) and 20 future farms have been established.

In terms of scaling up livestock farming, the province proposes to lead the construction of high-level modernized breeding farms with the "six measures" (standardization, greenization, scaling, circularity, digitization, and basing), and to construct or upgrade facilities for precise feeding, water-saving, and livestock manure resource re-utilization in large-scale livestock farms, while promoting the application of comprehensive livestock odor control technology and equipment. This has pushed livestock farming towards a more intensive mode of transformation and upgrading with higher standards, lower emissions, and higher efficiency. By the end of 2022, the province has built and put into operation 124 pig farms with more than 10,000 pigs each in line with the "six measures" standard.

In terms of agricultural digitization, efforts are being made to promote the digitization of regulatory services, implement full-cycle, full-process service management and monitoring and early warning, and create digital applications such as "*Zhe Nong You Pin*" (Zhejiang Agricultural Excellence), "Animal Husbandry Brain", and "Fishery Industry Brain", integrating digital and intelligent means throughout the entire agricultural production process. The standardization level of agriculture is being improved, and the construction of digital agriculture factories and the digital transformation of large-scale farming and breeding bases are being promoted. The digitization of organized production is being promoted, and cross-regional scientific agricultural machinery scheduling and dynamic operations are being carried out based on digital applications such as "*Zhe Nong Ji*" (Zhejiang Agricultural Machinery). Pilot projects such as shared cold storage have been promoted in places like Cixi City of Ningbo to avoid seasonal idle resources, with the comprehensive utilization rate of cold storage increasing by more than 15%.

4. Effective measures for resource recycling

The comprehensive utilization of agricultural wastes, especially the full-scale and high-value utilization of crop straws, has been the most intensive field of agricultural low-carbon technology innovation, with great potential for emission reduction and carbon sequestration. Crop straws can be used to produce organic fertilizers, biochar, and compressed boards, and can also provide energy as a molded fuel. Returning straws to the farmland is an important measure for soil carbon sequestration. Around the "five utilizations" including fertilization and feedization, Zhejiang Province has strived to vigorously promote the multi-path and high-value utilization of straws, optimize the structure of straw utilization, and enthusiastically develop technology models such as biomass molding fuels and gasified clean energies. Zhejiang has also established pilot counties for full-scale utilization of crop straws in Deqing, Yongkang, and Tiantai, with their comprehensive utilization rate of crop straws exceeding 95%.

Zhejiang Province has been actively promoting the deep integration of agriculture and animal husbandry to further the efficient use of resources. Every year, 20% of livestock manure is collected through sewage interceptor during peak and slack periods, while the remaining 80% is utilized through returning biogas slurry to the fields. Through rationally allocating fields for waste disposal and strengthening distribution chains and field storage facilities, a modern ecological cycle mode has been established, closely linking livestock farmers, service organizations and planting entities. Organic fertilizer processing plants have been constructed in major livestock and poultry production areas. For example, in Longyou County of Quzhou City, biogas is recycled to eliminate pollution caused by animal waste. Through taking advantage of the hilly terrain around the breeding grounds, a cycle system of "biogas pool - biogas slurry pool - pipeline – fertilization" has been put in place to make full use of resources.

Zhejiang Province has been promoting ecological farming practices such as "rice-shrimp rotation" and "mushroom cultivation using straws", as well as 50 types of advanced and ecologically efficient new agricultural systems in four categories, including vertical farming, rotational farming between wet and dry seasons, multiple cropping on dry land, and intercropping in orchards. According to research, for example, the rice-fish symbiosis system emits less greenhouse gases and leads to a smaller environmental impact and higher ecological and economic benefits compared to the rice monoculture system. The rice-fish symbiosis ecological cycling model in Qingtian County was selected as a typical case for green and low-carbon transformation in 2022.

5. Effective Measures to Explore Agricultural Carbon Sequestration and Sink

To tap the potential of agricultural carbon sequestration, various measures have been taken to promote high-standard farmland construction. Actions have been taken to improve the quality of cultivated land and promote conservation tillage. Soil has been improved through the application of organic fertilizers, the return of crop straws to the soil and other technologies. In addition, shallow-water seaweed shellfish and seaweed farming have been developed to enhance the carbon sequestration function of marine fisheries. For instance, the research projects of new straw charcoal-based fertilizers, carbon dioxide fertilizers, collection and treatment of odor from pig farms, and Biochar have been included in the "three rural and nine directions" Technology collaboration strategy. Biochar is firstly one of the methods to remove carbon dioxide from the atmosphere. Secondly, it can improve soil structure and promote the growth of soil microorganisms. And lastly, due to its strong alkalinity, it can also improve soil acid-base balance and reduce the need for chemical fertilizers.

In terms of exploring agricultural carbon monitoring, reporting, and verification systems, Zhejiang province has collaborated with universities and research institutions such as Zhejiang university, china agricultural university, Xhejiang provincial academy of agricultural sciences, Tongji university, and Zhejiang A&F university, to advance the research on the assessment standards for agricultural carbon emissions and promote the development of digital models for agricultural carbon accounts. At the end of 2021, Quzhou city took the lead in issuing local standards for agricultural carbon account emission verification and assessments, conducting carbon emission accounting for more than 1,000 entities in industries such as rice, pigs, organic fertilizers and grapefruits.

B. Effects of Carbon Emission Reduction in the Agricultural Sector

Due to the goal of carbon peaking, China's "net-zero emissions" mainly highlight CO_2, and so the measurement of carbon emissions in Zhejiang's agricultural sector mainly focuses on CO_2 emissions. Based on data from statistical yearbooks, energy balance sheets and fishing vessel fuel consumption records, the carbon dioxide emissions in Zhejiang's agricultural sector have been calculated.

In terms of total emissions, CO_2 emissions from the agricultural sector of Zhejiang Province had already reached a peak of 6.57 million tons in 2017. Subsequently, thanks to actions such as "clearing out modified tractors" and the "One Strike, Three Rectifications" Campaign in the fishery, there has been a significant decline in emissions. In terms of proportion, carbon emissions from the consumption side of the agricultural sector account for 1.44% of total carbon emissions in society as a whole.

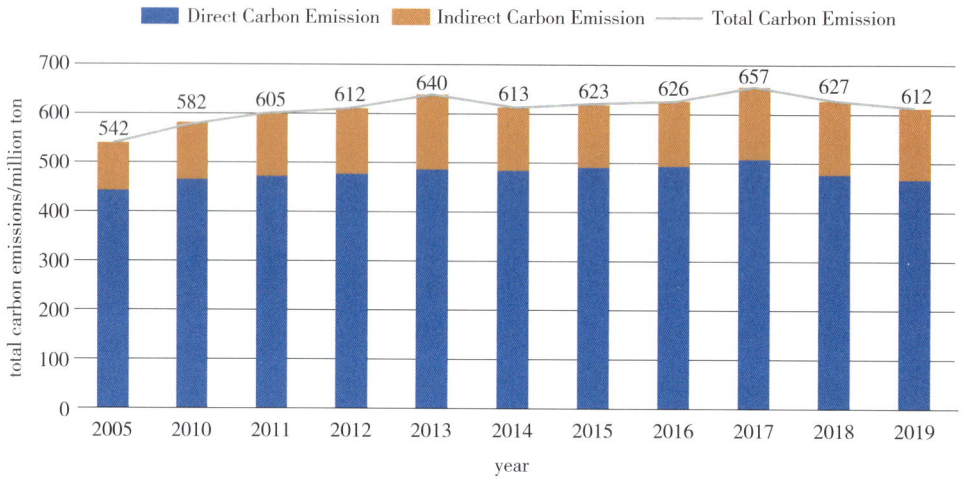

Figure 7-1   Trend of total carbon emissions in Zhejiang agricultural sector from 2005 to 2019

Looking at the energy consumption structure, agricultural machinery and fishing boats mainly consume gasoline and diesel, while large-scale breeding farms mainly use electricity. Since 2018, thanks to the elimination of grain dryers that use coal as a heat source, coal consumption has been reduced to almost zero. In terms of emissions, agricultural machinery, fishing boats, and large-scale breeding (including protected agriculture) are the main sources of carbon dioxide emissions, accounting for 27.42%, 48.75%, and 23.83% of total emissions, respectively.

III. Major Implications

A. Combining Traditional Ecological Methods with Modern Agricultural Technologies

Zhejiang Province's transition from eco-circular agriculture to high-efficiency ecological agriculture is rooted in its rich agricultural cultural heritage, which can be traced back to the traditional Chinese philosophical system of "harmony between man and nature." For thousands of years, agricultural production methods have been continuously inherited and continued, culminating in the development of ecological, organic and circular agricultural production technologies and agricultural knowledge concepts. Today, Zhejiang Province continues to develop a range of traditional eco-circular agricultural technologies for low-carbon production, such as using straw returning, deep burial, and centralized treatment to solve crop straw and other issues. Additionally, it actively promotes various new low-carbon agricultural technologies, including the demonstration and application of integrated water and fertilizer management, deep placement fertilization, physical and chemical control, and biological pest control technologies. Relying on agricultural science and technology alliances and other platforms, the province promotes low-carbon agricultural technology innovation research through the "Three Rural and Nine Directions" technology collaboration projects. The province has also hosted low-carbon agriculture forums, inviting academicians, experts and research institutes to participate in technology exchanges, so as to promote solid implementation of technologies and assist energy-saving and emission reduction efforts.

B. Giving Low-carbon Related Policies a Full Play

Zhejiang Province has been giving full play to policy guidance in low-carbon agricultural development. As part of the campaign to become a national pilot province for modern eco-circular agriculture, a national demonstration province for green development of animal husbandry, a national demonstration province for "machine substitution for human labor" in agriculture, and a pilot area for national green agricultural development, Zhejiang has made significant efforts to promote low-carbon agriculture. Notably, thanks to actions such as clearing out converted tractors, the "one strike, three rectifications" campaign in the fishing industry, and the "dual control of fertilizers and pesticides" reform, Zhejiang has become a pioneer in achieving carbon peaking and fostering low-carbon, eco-friendly agricultural sector. With the establishment of new policy systems, Zhejiang actively integrates the requirements for carbon neutrality development, takes the creation of low-carbon ecological farms as the starting point, and proactively focuses on promoting the improvement of agricultural production standards and the coordinated control of carbon dioxide and non-carbon dioxide greenhouse gases.

C. Highlighting the Introduction and Application of Market Mechanisms

Since agriculture was included as one of the "6+1" fields for carbon peaking and carbon neutrality, Zhejiang Province has actively encouraged local governments to take the lead in exploring the introduction of market mechanisms, aiming to spur the transformation and upgrading of main players, apply low-carbon and ecological technologies, and form low-carbon cooperative groups on the basis of low-carbon ecological farm creation, so as to facilitate the value realization in aspects such as integration of low-carbon ecological farm production and sales. In 2022, Quzhou City issued loans and financial credits totaling 200 million yuan based on the carbon footprint labeling of 1,000 agricultural entities. Wenzhou City completed 10,000 tons of marine fishery carbon sink trading. According to accounting, the carbon sequestration amount from local shellfish and seaweed farming reached 23,000 tons over the course of three years. Hangzhou and Jiaxing cities, after conducting a full-lifecycle carbon footprint survey of agricultural products including grape, Red Delicious apple, navel orange, dryland rice and strawberry, formed the first batch of agricultural carbon labels conforming to international standards, as part of various attempts to explore market value realization of low-carbon agriculture and promote low-carbon development to benefit farmers.

D. Driving the Utilization and Support of Digital Technology

Agricultural carbon emissions have unique characteristics and belong to diffuse source emissions, which means difficulties in accurately quantifying them. In the achievement of Zhejiang Province's carbon peaking and carbon neutrality targets, digital technology has played an important role in agriculture, which could be viewed as a result of inevitability and possibility. It is inevitable in the sense that the methodological characteristics of agricultural carbon emissions mean they can be modeled intelligently, using digital means to improve accounting efficiency. Quzhou and Zhoushan have already established agricultural carbon accounting models after introducing local accounting standards. Since the launch of Zhejiang's agricultural carbon peaking and neutrality, on the other hand, the "*Zhe Nong*" (Zhejiang Agriculture) app has accumulated increasing data, and the highly integrated applications have played a valuable role in data analysis. Production records, output and other data in the "*Zhe Nong*" app have provided important support for the accounting of agricultural carbon accounts and the calculation of carbon labels for agricultural products. Digitalization has forward-looking significance for reducing the costs of agricultural carbon emissions accounting, facilitating the application of market mechanisms, and improving the mechanism of carbon peaking and carbon neutrality-integrated farming and agriculture development.

IV. Future Prospects

First, Total Emission Control should be implemented. On enhancing climate change adaptation and ensuring food security, we should insist on reducing emission intensity and controlling total emissions at the same time. During the "14th Five-Year Plan" period, the carbon emissions of energy activities in agriculture and forestry in the province will reach a relative peak of 6.5 million tons and then steadily decline. The province will include peaking agricultural carbon emissions in important documents such as the province's plan for promoting high-quality rural revitalization and agricultural modernization. Key measures will be closely connected with the central tasks such as ecological civilization construction, digital reform in agriculture and rural areas, and rectification of issues found in central environmental protection inspections. A task list and a closed-loop management mechanism will be established for achieving a carbon emissions peak.

Based on the analysis and prediction of ensuring agricultural production and supply and industrial development, further optimization of energy consumption structure, and continuous improvement of energy efficiency, the carbon peak in the agricultural sector of Zhejiang Province has been forecasted. Carbon emission from energy activities in the agricultural sector of the province is expected to continue to grow slowly, reaching a relative peak of 6.5 million tons in 2025, and then entering a plateau, followed by a slow decline.

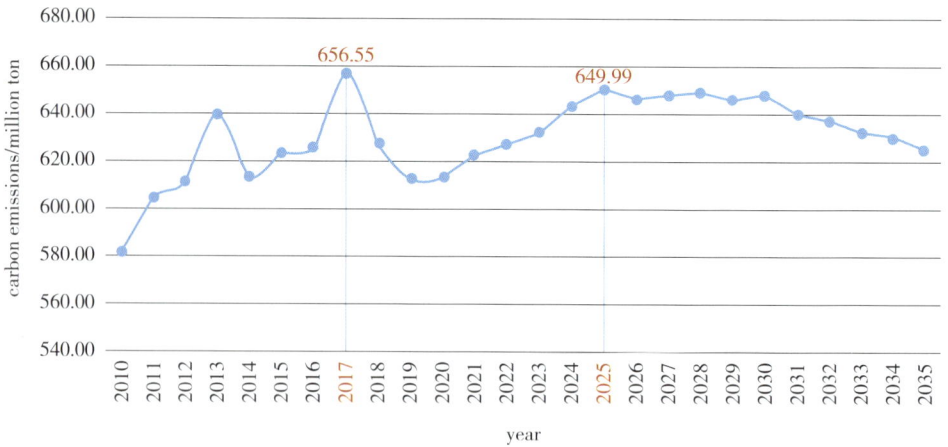

Figure 7-2   Carbon Emissions in the Agricultural sector in Zhejiang Province and Prediction

Second, the focus should be on new key areas. We should take low-carbon ecological farm construction, reduction of fishing boats and transition to other industries, and mechanized agriculture as the main areas of focus. Based on the distribution of industries and energy consumption structure, efforts will be made to reduce emissions from fishing boats in coastal areas, reduce emissions from agricultural machinery in plain areas, and pilot low-carbon (zero-carbon) agriculture in mountainous and hilly areas. The construction of low-carbon ecological farms will serve as the foundation for establishing the *Zhe Nong You Pin* Ecological Low-Carbon Farm Joint Development Alliance, an innovative platform that fosters communication and cooperation among production entities, and between production entities and the market for sales.

Third, technological innovation should be encouraged. It is essential to fully leverage the advantages of government-industry-university-research integrated platforms, such as the "Three Rural and Nine Directions" technology collaboration and the agricultural technology alliance, to guide the participation of multiple stakeholders including research institutions, industry associations, agricultural cooperatives, and leading enterprises, organize joint efforts in reducing emissions and sequestering carbon in agriculture, promote the establishment of a monitoring and accounting standard system for agricultural carbon sink, innovate the methodologies for reducing greenhouse gas emissions in agriculture, and implement training programs for professionals in the low-carbon agriculture.

450

Fourth, digital empowerment should be deepened. Data and decision-making flows should be established in core business and execution processes in apps such as "*Zhe Nong You Pin*" (Zhejiang Agricultural Excellence), "*Zhe Nong Mu*" (Zhejiang Agriculture and Animal Husbandry), and "*Zhe Nong Yu*" (Zhejiang Agriculture and Fishery). Through business integration, data integration and technology integration, the province will promote high efficiency in low-carbon ecological farm construction and precise business supervision.

Fifth, capacity building should be strengthened. It is vital to coordinate various agricultural-related funds from the central and local governments, increase financial input from cities and counties, and support agricultural carbon reduction and sequestration projects. It is also essential to explore the establishment of an ecological compensation mechanism for agriculture based on the evaluation of green development of entities and carbon accounting, and facilitate the implementation of policies, such as those involving electricity prices for agricultural production.

Author: Zhang Xiling[1], Gu Xingguo[2], Wu Lianghuan[3], Zhou Zhilin[4], Dai Jianfei[5]

---

1   Zhang Xiling, a cadre seconded by the Agriculture and Rural Affairs Department of Zhejiang Province, China, focuses on studying green agriculture development and carbon emissions in the agricultural field.
2   Gu Xingguo, a deputy researcher at the Zhejiang Academy of Agricultural Sciences, specializes in ecological agriculture.
3   Wu Lianghuan, a professor in the Department of Resource Science at the School of Environment and Resource Sciences of Zhejiang University, concentrates on plant application environmental ecology, organic agriculture, and food safety.
4   Zhou Zhilin, a chief staff member of the Agriculture and Rural Affairs Department of Zhejiang Province, is in charge of promoting green agriculture development and carbon emissions reduction.
5   Dai Jianfei, the head of the Rural Revitalization Service Center in Hangzhou, China, is an engineer who mainly engages in rural construction, rural industrial development, and rural governance.

References

[1] The World Statistics Pocketbook 2022 edition (Series V, No. 46).

[2] Jin S Q, Lin Y, Niu K Y. Driving green transformation of agriculture with low carbon: characteristics of agricultural carbon emissions and its emission reduction path in China[J]. Reform, 2021, 5: 29-37.

[3] Zhang W J, Yan S J, Zhang J, et al. Win-win strategy for national food security and agricultural double-carbon goals[J]. Scientia Agricultura Sinica, 2021, 54(18): 3892-3902.

[4] Tan Q C. Greenhouse gas emission in China's agriculture: situation and challenge[J]. China Population, Resources and Environment, 2011, 21(10): 69-75.

[5] Li B, Zhang J B, Li H P. Research on spatial-temporal characteristics and affecting factors decomposition of agricultural carbon emission in China[J]. China Population, Resources and Environment, 2011, 21(8): 80-86.

[6] IPCC. Climate change 2013: The physical science basis. Contribution of Working Group I to the fifth assessment report of the intergovernmental panel on climate change (STOCKER T F, QIN D, PLATTNER G K, TIGNOR M, ALLEN S K, BOSCHUNG J, NAUELS A, XIA Y, BEXV, MIDGLEY P M, Eds.). Cambridge: Cambridge University Press, 2013.

[7] Cheng Q Q, Shen C D, Yi W X, et al. Progresses in soil carbon cycle researches[J]. Advance in Earth Sciences, 1998, 6: 46-54.

[8] Pan G X, Zhao Q G. Study on evolution of organic carbon stock in agricultural soils of China: facing the challenge of global change and food security[J]. Advance in Earth Sciences, 2005, 4: 384-393.

[9] Cui W C, Jiao W J, Min Q W, et al. Environmental impact assessment on traditional agricultural systems based on carbon footprint: a case study of Qingtian rice-fish culture system[J]. Acta Ecologica Sinica, 2020, 40(13): 4362-4370.

Zhejiang's Carbon Inclusiveness Leading Carbon Peaking in Residents' Lives

Carbon emission in residents' lives is one of the main sources of carbon emissions and maintains a rigid growth trend. On the premise of meeting people's yearning for a better life, it is not only necessary to fully guarantee the use of energy of residents in their lives but also necessary to guide residents to use energy reasonably and actively practice low-carbon living. This chapter mainly introduces the impact of carbon inclusiveness on the carbon peaking in residents' lives, proposes ideas for promoting carbon inclusiveness in Zhejiang Province, and sorts out the effectiveness and existing problems of carbon inclusiveness application construction in Zhejiang. Finally, based on the actual situation and existing problems in Zhejiang Province, several suggestions are proposed for the next step of deepening carbon inclusiveness.

With the rapid development of the economy, the living standards of residents have been greatly improved, and the consumption level has significantly increased. As a result, carbon emissions in residents' lives continue to increase and become an important factor in driving the increase of carbon emissions. In the context of carbon peaking and carbon neutrality, at the beginning of promoting carbon peaking, Zhejiang Province has proposed to handle the relationship between carbon emissions and residents' lives. In accordance with the requirement of "meeting people's aspirations for a better life while achieving carbon peaking", Zhejiang Province has actively explored carbon inclusiveness to promote the formation of green production and lifestyle.

I. Introduction

A. Current situation and trend analysis of carbon emissions in residents' lives

1. Characteristics of carbon emissions in residents' lives in Zhejiang Province

At present, per capita GDP, per capita disposable income, and per capita consumption expenditure are positively correlated with carbon emissions in residents' lives. According to the seventh national population census, the permanent population of Zhejiang Province maintains rapid growth, with the current permanent population exceeding 65 million. With the improvement of residents' living standards, per capita carbon emissions will continue to maintain a high level. With the continuous growth of the population base, the carbon emissions in the residents' lives will continue to increase within a certain period of time. During the 13th Five-Year Plan period, the average annual growth rate of per capita GDP in Zhejiang Province was 8.12%, the per capita disposable income increased by 8.86%, the per capita consumption expenditure increased by 7.35%, the consumption propensity index remained at 0.64 and the average annual growth rate of carbon emissions from residents' lives in Zhejiang Province was 4.70%.

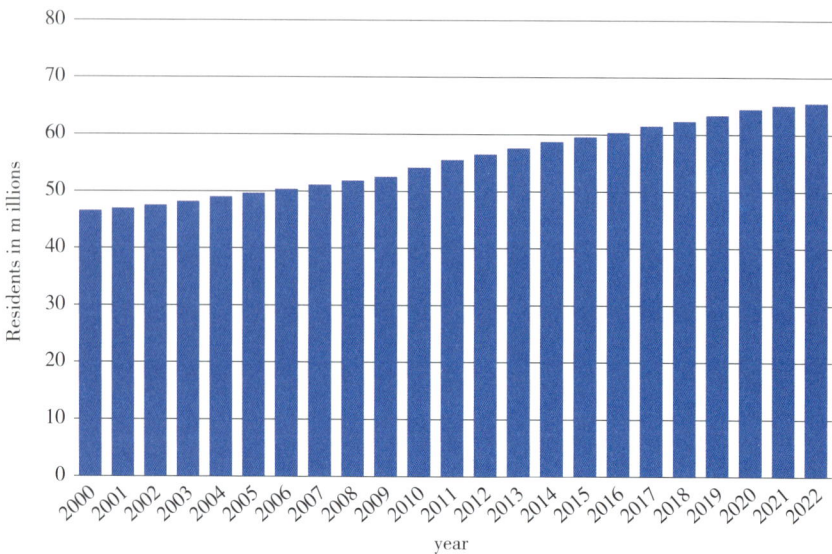

Figure 8-1　Population of Zhejiang Province in the Last 23 Years

From the perspective of energy consumption structure, the energy consumption in residents' lives mainly includes electricity, natural gas, oil products (liquefied petroleum gas), and a small amount of coal. According to historical trends, coal consumption in residents' lives has been decreasing year by year, and the proportion of natural gas consumption has significantly increased. During the 13th Five-Year Plan period, the average annual growth rate of natural gas consumption reached 13%, and it will become the main source of carbon emissions in residents' lives in the future. Electricity is the most important energy source in the field of residents' lives. In 2019, the consumption doubled compared to 2010, and during the 13th Five-Year Plan period, the average annual growth rate of electricity consumption reached 7.8%. Especially in the past 2022, the growth rate of electricity consumption in the field of residents' lives exceeded 22.46% compared to 2021. As the proportion of clean energy such as wind power, solar power, and nuclear power increases, the carbon emissions of electricity continue to decrease, and the total carbon emissions generated by electricity consumption will eventually show a downward trend.

2. Analysis of carbon emission trends in residents' lives in Zhejiang Province

The prediction of future carbon emissions in the field of residents' lives is mainly based on the analysis of the future development trend of Zhejiang Province. According to the relevant content of the *Outline of the 14th Five-Year Plan* (*2021-2025*) *for National Economic and Social Development and Vision 2035 of Zhejiang Province*, the average annual growth rate of GDP during the 14th Five-Year Plan and 15th Five-Year Plan periods is set at 5.6% and 4.8%, and the population of Zhejiang Province is mainly set at 0.8% per year (during the 14th Five-Year Plan period) A natural growth rate of 0.5% (during the 15th Five-Year Plan period). The urbanization level is initially set at around 1% annual growth.

Based on the analysis of historical trends in carbon emissions and the assessment of future development, it is expected that the total energy consumption and per capita energy consumption of residents in Zhejiang Province will continue to grow for a long time in the future. However, with the low-carbon transformation of residents' lifestyles, energy consumption in the field of living has shifted from high emission factor energy such as coal and oil to low emission factor energy such as natural gas and electricity. Moreover, with the development of renewable energy, the power emission factor continues to decrease. The carbon emissions directly generated in the field of residents' lives will continue to grow in the short term. Subsequently, the carbon emissions are expected to enter the plateau period after 2035. The expected levels of key indicators such as per capita electricity consumption when achieving carbon peaking in the residential sector of Zhejiang Province are shown in Table 8-1.

Table 8-1   Comparison of Energy Consumption Indicators of Residents' Lives in Zhejiang and Residents' Lives in Advanced Countries during Peak Years

Index	Zhejiang	Korea 2018	Japan 2018	England 2018	France 2018	Germany 2018	America 2018
Per capita GDP (ten thousand dollars)	2.9-3.1	3.12	4.02	4.30	4.16	4.78	6.30
Electricity consumption (kilowatt per person)	1,600-1,700	1,305	2,077	1,581	2,361	1,546	4,474
Gas consumption (kgce per person)	130-180	263	98	514	227	384	513
Energy consumption (tce per person)	0.55-0.63	0.71	0.72	1.02	1.06	1.01	1.84

Note: The key indicators are estimated.

B. The role of carbon inclusiveness in leading carbon reduction in residents' lives

Residents' lives is an important emission source among the six major fields. In promoting the carbon peaking of residents' lives, there is a lack of effective measures to cultivate low-carbon behaviors such as green travel and green consumption among residents, which mainly rely on guidance and encouragement.

1. Introduction to carbon inclusiveness mechanism

Carbon inclusiveness refers to the calculation of carbon emission reduction from public low-carbon behaviors and the conversion of it into carbon points that can be used to exchange for benefits. Carbon inclusiveness is a mechanism for green and low-carbon development. By establishing public low-carbon positive guidance mechanisms such as policy incentives and commercial incentives and taking them as mediums for consumption and production, individuals who practice green and low-carbon behaviors are cohered as a whole to implement the dual carbon strategy. By doing so, such mechanisms will gradually become an important way to guide the public to participate in green life.

The main implementation idea of carbon inclusiveness is to use technologies such as mobile internet, big data, and blockchain to quantify various low-carbon behaviors according to the carbon emission reduction methodologies or standards of low-carbon behaviors, form individual "carbon accounts", and reward carbon emission reduction behaviors through measures such as emission reduction trading, policy incentives, and market-oriented incentives.

2. The significance of conducting carbon inclusiveness exploration

Carbon inclusiveness is an important means of promoting the formation of a green and low-carbon lifestyle and facilitating changes from small things in production and living habits to the whole society. It is of great significance for accelerating the formation of green production and lifestyle, promoting the construction of ecological civilization and modernization of ecological environment governance, and promoting the achievement of the dual carbon goal.

For the government, the carbon inclusiveness mechanism can promote the carbon peaking in the lives of regional residents, and positively guide and motivate residents' low-carbon living behaviors, and establish a long-term mechanism, which is conducive to achieving precise and refined social governance. It is a positive exploration for practicing the concept of ecological civilization. Focusing on reducing carbon emissions at the consumer end, carbon inclusiveness integrates various resources of the entire society, which is conducive to forming synergy, achieving positive social interaction, and continuously consolidating the achievements of energy conservation and carbon emission reduction.

For enterprises, under the promotion of the carbon inclusiveness mechanism, residents are more inclined to purchase products with green certification, which will cultivate residents' consumption habits on green products, thus to promote enterprises to produce more green and low-carbon products and promote low-carbon transformation of the supply chain, achieving the effect of encouraging enterprises to voluntarily reduce emissions.

For the public, with the increasing willingness of residents to participate in green living and integrate into low-carbon development, the carbon inclusiveness mechanism covers various fields such as transportation, housing, and consumption, providing an effective channel for public participation in achieving the "dual carbon" goal. At the same time, residents' low-carbon behaviors can be converted into carbon points and exchanged for corresponding benefits, optimizing public resource allocation through digital and market-oriented means, transforming green and low-carbon behaviors into further green and low-carbon rights, achieving dual benefits for the environment and economy.

II. Carbon Inclusiveness Practice

Other countries and other provinces and cities in China have carried out a large amount of practices on carbon inclusiveness, which provide valuable experience for Zhejiang Province to carry out carbon inclusiveness.

A. Domestic and foreign practices of carbon inclusiveness

1. Foreign practices of carbon inclusiveness

The practice of public participation in carbon emission reduction in foreign countries started early. Although a clear concept of carbon inclusiveness was not proposed, a large number of mechanisms similar to carbon inclusiveness were explored. In 2011, the Ministry of Environment of South Korea established a green credit card system, including carbon points and green card credits, to encourage the public to practice green and low-carbon behavior and expand the green consumption market. Anyone who uses a green card to purchase products with a green logo or carbon label at a specific store, chooses public transportation or pays at a bank can receive corresponding green card points, discounts, and consumption refunds. In addition, Gwangju, South Korea has implemented a "carbon banking system", which converts the amount of water and electricity saved in daily life into "carbon points" with functions such as consumption and discounting, on a household basis, in order to encourage households to reduce carbon emissions.

From May 2009 to the end of March 2010, in order to promote the sales and use of energy-saving and environmentally friendly home appliances, the Japanese government implemented the "Environmental Protection Point System" nationwide. Under this system, residents who purchase energy-saving air conditioners, refrigerators, and televisions with four-star and above "unified energy saving label" can obtain corresponding environmental protection points according to specific specifications. Residents who purchase energy-saving and environmentally friendly appliances generally earn environmental protection points equivalent to 5%-20% of the product's price, which can be used to redeem 271 energy-saving products or services such as product vouchers, ride cards, and local specialties. Since 2011, Japan had launched a new "Environmental Protection Points" project to include practices like public hazard prevention and management, 3R (such as garbage disposal), and nature conservation into the scope of environmental protection, and expand the scope of use of environmental protection credits.

Except for similar mechanisms implemented in South Korea and Japan, from 2010 to 2013, Australia launched the Norfolk Island Personal Carbon Trading Scheme, that is, a certain carbon quota was allocated to individuals for their purchase of gasoline and use of energy, and the remaining quota, if any, can be used to exchange for cash. From 2002 to 2005, the port city of Rotterdam in the Netherlands implemented a green reward point system, under which individuals who purchase products from energy-saving program stores or other designated environmentally friendly products can earn point for public transportation and exchanging scenic spot tickets. However, due to a lack of long-term financial support, it didn't last long.

2. Domestic practices of carbon inclusiveness

(1) Carbon inclusiveness practices in Shanghai

In 2022, Shanghai publicly solicited opinions on the *Shanghai Carbon Inclusiveness System Construction Plan*, which proposed that from 2022 to

2023, Shanghai will develop the top-level design of the carbon inclusiveness system, construct relevant institutional standards and methodological systems, and build a carbon inclusiveness platform to conduct pilot demonstrations of projects with good statistical foundation and strong data availability in representative regions with good foundations, connect with the Shanghai carbon market, explore multi-level consumption channels, establish regional personal carbon accounts, and create a model of carbon inclusiveness in Shanghai. From 2024 to 2025, the coverage areas and project types of carbon inclusiveness will be gradually expanded. The construction of carbon inclusiveness platforms will be improved, and a standardized and orderly carbon inclusiveness operation system will be formed. As a result, a carbon inclusiveness ecosystem with clear rules, rich scenarios, and sustainable development will be formed gradually by using commercial incentive mechanisms.

(2) Carbon inclusiveness practices in Guangdong Province

In 2015, Guangdong Province launched the pilot work of the carbon inclusiveness, making it one of the first pilot areas in China to implement the carbon inclusiveness. In July 2015, the Guangdong Provincial Development and Reform Commission issued the *Implementation Plan of the Guangdong Provincial Carbon Inclusiveness Pilot Work* and the *Guidelines for the Construction of the Guangdong Provincial Carbon GSP Pilot Work*, which clearly defined the need to build a unified carbon inclusiveness promotion platform, a carbon inclusiveness certified emission reduction trading mechanism and a commercial incentive mechanism in the province, develop corresponding carbon inclusiveness methodologies, and select communities (neighborhoods), public transport, tourist attraction, energy saving, and low-carbon products as pilot fields for the carbon inclusiveness system. Registered users can obtain carbon coins through water conservation and bus travel on the carbon inclusiveness website, WeChat official account, carbon inclusiveness App and other carbon inclusiveness platforms. In April 2022, the Department of Ecology and Environment of Guangdong Province issued the *Management Measures for Carbon Inclusiveness Trading in Guangdong Province* (Y.H.F. [2022] No. 4), further deepening and improving the voluntary emission reduction mechanism, clarifying the content of carbon inclusiveness management, trading, and supervision, etc.

(3) Carbon inclusiveness practices in other regions

In June 2017, based on innovative research on the "carbon coin system", Wuhan launched the "Carbon Treasure Package" App and WeChat platform that advocates for low-carbon public travel. Citizens can obtain corresponding carbon points by walking, cycling, and renting new energy vehicles, and a certain amount of carbon points can be exchanged for movie tickets, catering vouchers, and other goods. At present, the "Carbon Treasure Package" is invested by interested enterprises and persons to gradually improve its functions.

In March 2020, the Chengdu Municipal People's Government issued the *Implementation Opinions on Building a "Carbon Benefiting Tianfu" Mechanism* to establish a "Carbon Benefiting Tianfu" carbon inclusiveness mechanism. This mechanism covers two paths: Firstly, by exchanging carbon points, rewards are given to the public for their energy conservation, carbon emission reduction, and related environmental protection behaviors; Secondly, the economic value of environmental benefits generated by carbon emission reduction projects is present, thus the enthusiasm to reduce emissions of the public and small and micro enterprises is stimulated by improving project carbon emission reductions (hereinafter referred to as "CDCER") according to relevant methodologies and absorbing them by carbon neutrality.

In November 2021, the General Office of the Shenzhen Municipal People's Government issued the *Work Plan for the Construction of Shenzhen's Carbon Inclusiveness System*, which pointed out the need to promote cross-regional cooperation in the carbon inclusiveness system. In March 2022, the Shenzhen Ecological Environment Bureau issued the *Shenzhen Carbon Inclusiveness Management Measures* to standardize the construction, operation, and supervision of the Shenzhen carbon inclusiveness system, and further clarify the management process and usage rules for the reduction of emissions generated by energy-saving and carbon emission reduction activities of the public and small and micro enterprises.

Establishment of the "Carbon Inclusiveness Cooperation Network"

On the National Low-carbon Day on June 15, 2022, in order to gather the joint efforts of the society, advocate the public to practice a green lifestyle, promote pollution reduction and carbon reduction at the consumer end, and give full play to the role of digital means in "forming a green lifestyle", the Publicity and Education Center of the Ministry of Ecological Environment, together with the All-China Environment Federation, the China Internet Development Foundation, the International Cooperation Center of the National Development and Reform Commission, and the China Ecological Civilization Research and Promotion Association jointly initiated the establishment of the "Carbon Inclusiveness Cooperation Network", and the network operation of which is supported by the Energy Foundation. The "Carbon Inclusiveness Cooperation Network" is committed to gathering various social forces and promoting green and low-carbon actions for all by innovative carbon inclusiveness.

B. Zhejiang Concept for Implementing Carbon Inclusiveness

Taking digital applications as the starting point for promoting carbon inclusiveness and individuals as the main body, Zhejiang Province will promote the formation of a low-carbon culture in society through motivating individuals' extensive participation in low-carbon life.

1. Overall Process

The process of carrying out carbon inclusiveness is generally divided into three stages, namely practice of individual low-carbon behaviors, carbon emission reduction quantification of individual low-carbon behaviors, and acquisition of benefits from individual low-carbon behaviors, which are achieved through digital tools.

(1) Practices of individual low-carbon behaviors

This is the foundation of the carbon inclusiveness mechanism. Any behavior of residents in fulfilling their need on clothing, food, housing, transportation, and daily necessities that can achieve the goals of energy conservation, carbon emission reduction, ecological environment protection, and resource conservation can be defined as low-carbon behavior. For example, in the carbon inclusiveness plans of Shenzhen and Chengdu, it is proposed to create various types of low-carbon scenarios such as travel, consumption, life, and public welfare, which is the process of defining low-carbon behavior and encouraging the public to practice it.

(2) Carbon emission reduction quantification of individual low-carbon behaviors

The carbon emission reduction of low-carbon behaviors is quantified to identify the contribution of such behaviors to carbon emission reduction, thus determining the public's contribution to carbon emission reduction. At present, in practice in various regions, the method of converting carbon emission reduction into carbon points is used in quantifying carbon emission reduction of the public's low-carbon behaviors.

(3) Acquisition of benefits from individual low-carbon behaviors

By converting quantified carbon emission reduction into benefits, carbon benefits are achieved and the public is given a sense of gain and achievement in practicing low-carbon behavior. Guangdong has adopted a commercial incentive approach, bridging the channel between carbon points and goods, achieving physical and service incentives, and promoting more people to participate in low-carbon activities.

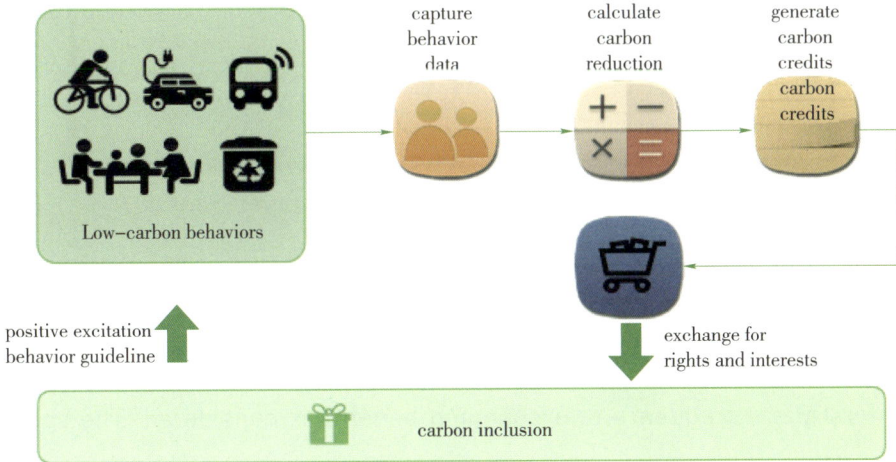

Figure 8-2　Operation Process of Carbon Inclusiveness Mechanism

2. Design ideas for low-carbon scenarios

When designing a low-carbon scenario, designers of the Zhejiang Carbon Inclusiveness System take full account of the actual situation of the province and build the carbon inclusiveness application scenario system through a model of government and enterprise cooperation based on the principle of "doing the easy things first, then the hard things, and then gradually expanding". In terms of data collection methods, based on the basic conditions of developed mobile internet in Zhejiang, by taking full account of the existing data foundation and cooperating with existing low-carbon applications such as Ant Forest, Cainiao, and Huge Recycle, the carbon inclusiveness scenario system in Zhejiang Province are combined with existing green and low-carbon activities to comprehensively integrate personal low-carbon data, and minimize data collection costs as much as possible. In terms of data collection dimensions, personal low-carbon data are collected from multiple dimensions such as the scenario side and payment side, so as to improve the efficiency and accessibility of data collection and achieve "senseless collection" of personal low-carbon data without increasing personal burden.

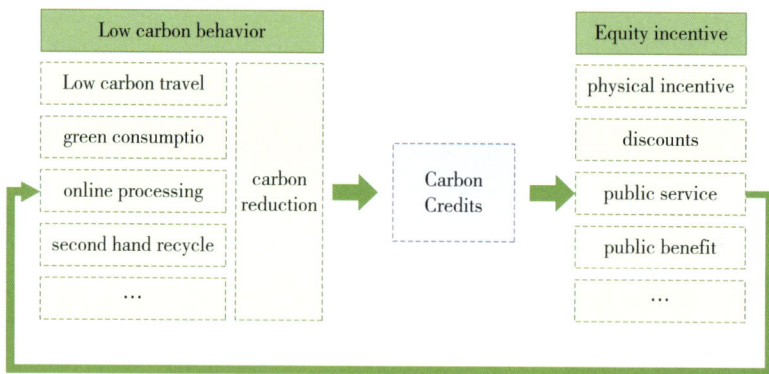

Figure 8-3   Zhejiang Carbon Inclusiveness Scenario System

3. Design ideas for carbon point system

The construction of a carbon inclusiveness point system mainly considers the following three factors:

Firstly, the frequency of exchanging benefits is considered. The specific value setting of points takes into account the frequency of exchanging benefits from the perspective of active users. Secondly, the contribution of carbon emission reduction is considered. For the carbon points generated for each specific sub-scenario, the contribution of the emission reduction brought by that scenario is mainly considered. Currently, emission reduction is mainly based on existing methodologies, empirical data from other provinces and cities, and relevant literature. An accurate credit setting will be gradually developed with the improvement of the carbon inclusiveness methodology in Zhejiang Province. Finally, the direction of government guidance is considered. For scenarios where quantification of emissions reduction is difficult, the emission reduction effect generated by related behaviors and the driving effect on the overall carbon emission reduction atmosphere in society are key points of consideration, and behaviors worthy of encouragement are granted with higher points.

4. Design concept of benefits system

The designer of the benefits system mainly considers the "low-carbon" attribute of benefits in designing. On the one hand, the benefits can be low-carbon products, such as consumer goods with obvious green labels (such as carbon labels); On the other hand, benefits can be something that further promotes low-carbon behaviors, such as bus and subway coupons, and the use of benefits is one kind of low-carbon behavior. When considering benefits design, it is also necessary to fully consider the public's acceptance of consumption methods and preferences for incentives.

(1) Designing a reasonable and feasible method to consume and absorb carbon points

During the process that the public participates in the carbon inclusiveness mechanism to exchange carbon points based on their own carbon emission reduction and then use the carbon points to exchange benefits, the sustainability of one-way public exchange for benefits is poor, making it difficult to bring more benefits to merchants, ultimately leading to a decrease in benefits and activity. Therefore, it is necessary to absorb public carbon points through multiple channels. Considering the circulation of carbon points among individuals and merchants, the emission reductions corresponding to individual carbon points can be used to achieve carbon emission reduction and carbon neutrality of merchants and commodities through point exchange and increase the enthusiasm of merchants to supply carbon inclusiveness products and services.

(2) Expanding carbon inclusiveness incentive methods

A single carbon inclusiveness incentive method may not be attractive to most users, but continuously expanding incentive methods and strengthening incentive effects from multiple aspects such as participation, sense of achievement, and sense of honor can achieve long-term operation of the carbon inclusiveness mechanism. Such methods include, but are not limited to, conducting low-carbon behavior collection activities to encourage users to identify low-carbon behaviors and enhance their sense of participation; increasing more physical product incentives, enriching product categories, covering the needs of more age groups, and meeting the sense of acquisition of various groups of people; establishing carbon inclusiveness level certification, and granting individuals, institutions, or enterprises having more points with corresponding honorary titles to motivate more users to participate with honors.

5. Design ideas for Zhejiang Carbon Inclusiveness Application

Relying on the development and construction of the mobile terminal application "Zheli Office" of the Zhejiang government affairs service network integration platform, Zhejiang Carbon Inclusiveness Application is developed and operated in the way of provincial unified construction, which is open to all residents of Zhejiang Province and can be used through the Zhejiang Government Service App or small programs (Alipay, WeChat, etc.). Zhejiang Carbon Inclusiveness Application remains open to the development of personalized zones in various regions. According to the principle of "hierarchical management", each region's government can plan "local zones" based on local characteristic needs, plan and promote application scenarios in the whole province, launch local characteristic rights or activities, and build a personalized carbon point consumption system.

III. The Achievements and Shortcomings in the Construction of Zhejiang Carbon Inclusiveness Application

A. Construction Achievements

1. Overall Achievements

Zhejiang Province takes "low-carbon action, points accounting, and benefits exchange" as its core, transforms residents' carbon emission reduction behaviors into carbon emission reduction, and assigns carbon points based on the carbon emission reduction. The carbon points can be used to exchange commercial benefits and other products. Through those incentives, the whole society is promoted to practice low-carbon action, a new model of building a green and low-carbon society that takes the lead in the country and is guided by the government, oriented by market, and supported by the participation of the whole people is set up, and a carbon inclusiveness system with "Zhejiang characteristics" in terms of application scenarios, benefits exchange, and other aspects is preliminarily formed.

Figure 8-4   Zhejiang Carbon Inclusiveness Application Home Page and Scenario Page

Since its official launch on March 29, 2022, the number of users has continued to increase. On July 25, 2022, the number of users of Zhejiang Carbon Inclusiveness Application exceeded 500,000, becoming one of the mainstream carbon inclusiveness platforms in China; On October 18th, 2022, the number exceeded 1 million, becoming the first provincial-level carbon inclusiveness platform in China owning 1 million users; At the end of April 2023, the number exceeded 1.35 million, becoming the "golden name card" that leads the low-carbon life of residents in Zhejiang.

2. Building a unique application scenario system with Zhejiang characteristics

At present, 5 major categories and over 20 subcategories of low-carbon application scenarios have been developed and constructed in Zhejiang Carbon Inclusiveness Application mainly in collaboration with enterprises and institutions such as Ant Forest, Huge Recycle, Cainiao, Zhejiang Tree Planting, and Zhejiang Commercial Insurance, of which the sources of carbon points are continuously expanded and the application scenarios are enriched. In terms of hierarchical design, the application scenario system includes five primary scenarios: Green Travel, Online Processing, Green Consumption, Green Communities, and Inclusion Public Welfare. Each major category is subdivided into secondary sub scenarios, for example, Green Travel is subdivided into six secondary sub scenarios: Walking, Bus Travel, Bicycle Travel, Subway Travel, Drive Less, and ETC Payment. In the future, Zhejiang Carbon Inclusiveness Application will also collaborate with more enterprises and entities to develop other low-carbon scenarios.

Table 8-2　List of Current Carbon Inclusiveness Application Scenarios in Zhejiang Province

Number	Major Category	Subcategory
1	Green Travel	Walking, Bus Travel, Bicycle Travel, Subway Travel, Drive Less, ETC Payment
2	Online Processing	Green Office, Online Train Tickets, Green Government Affairs
3	Green Consumption	Online Payment, Electronic Invoice, International Tax Refund, Online Delivery, Green Takeout, Plastic Reduction, Online Ticket Purchase
4	Green Communities	Low-carbon Recycling, Carton Secondary Utilization, Low-carbon Delivery
5	Inclusion Public Welfare	Zhejiang Tree Planting

3. Establishing a coordinated carbon inclusiveness cooperation model with government-enterprise cooperation

The low-carbon behavior data of residents are scattered across various departments and multiple platforms. While ensuring data security, Zhejiang Province has positioned Zhejiang Carbon Inclusiveness Application as an open platform and conducted application scenario cooperation with multiple market entities such as Ant, Union Pay, and Cainiao in accordance with the "government-enterprise cooperation" model. In terms of benefits exchange, provincial departments have carried out communication and cooperation with enterprises, social organizations, etc., and have received support from multiple scenic spots such as the "Yaoyan Mingzhu" in the province, as well as multiple enterprises such as the Zhejiang Provincial Energy Group and Union Pay Zhejiang Branch, providing residents in the province with concrete discounts.

The innovative "online + offline" model is adopted in carbon inclusiveness promotion. On the one hand, online promotion is carried out jointly with the Forestry Administration of Zhejiang Province, Alipay, Cainiao among others. With the in-depth cooperation on content, a series of public welfare activities such as "I plant trees for the Asian Games" and "travel blind box" are launched to promote carbon inclusiveness in Zhejiang and various users' access to and understanding on carbon inclusiveness are constantly improved through government-enterprise cooperation. On the other hand, offline promotion is carried out by relevant departments at the provincial level through multiple offline activities such as "Energy Conservation Promotion Week" and "Green Travel Promotion Month" to encourage users to use Zhejiang's carbon inclusiveness system. In addition, diversified incentive methods are used to expand their user base. For example, in some offline activities, users can use their carbon points to exchange scenic spot tickets, canvas bags, and other benefits.

B. Existing Shortcomings

1. Zhejiang Carbon Inclusiveness Application users in is in a relatively low activity degree, and the value of personal "carbon assets" has not been fully reflected

Since the launch of the Zhejiang Carbon Inclusiveness Application before one year ago, the number of users has exceeded 1.35 million, but it took 4 months for the number of users to increase from 0 to 500,000, and 3 months to increase from 500,000 to 1 million. However, with the decrease of the heat, especially after the decrease of the promotion, the number of carbon inclusiveness users has increased slowly. In September of last year, the number of monthly active users exceeded 250,000, and nearly 240,000 new users were added in a single month. However, after entering 2023, the number of monthly added users was less than 20,000, with an average daily active number of only around 10,000. Users generally reflect that the attractiveness of carbon inclusiveness benefits is insufficient. Furthermore, the data collection capacity is insufficient to cover all low-carbon data of users.

The reasons for the low user activity is that, on the one hand, the benefits are not rich and attractive enough, and on the other hand, the value of personal "carbon assets" has not been given full play, and the difference of services available to users of different levels or carbon points of Zhejiang Carbon Inclusiveness is not really reflected. At present, the diversified transformation path or mechanism for individual carbon point value has not been established, and it needs to be compensated by strengthening the operation and resource connection and other channels.

2. The impact of carbon inclusiveness is mainly reflected in the consumption side of residents, and the impact on the production side of enterprises is relatively shallow

The Zhejiang Provincial Development and Reform Commission has taken the lead and joined hands with multiple departments to carry out extensive cooperation with numerous enterprises in the development of scenarios and the supply of benefits, and has received support from multiple platforms such as Ant Forest, Huge Recycle, Cainiao, and Ele Me, which have contributed to the collection of personal low-carbon behavior data. Zhejiang Carbon Inclusiveness have had a certain positive impact on the development of low-carbon habits among residents, but the current impact is mainly reflected in the consumption side. Due to the incomplete construction of carbon footprint and carbon labeling systems, it is difficult to accurately identify the "low-carbon" attributes of many consumer goods, and the impact on the production side of enterprises has not yet been reached, so it is necessary to further strengthen the role of green consumption in driving low-carbon production.

3. The carbon inclusiveness standard system is not yet sound, and the calculation of carbon emission reduction is not yet supported

At present, other provinces and cities in China have conducted certain research on group standards and methodology in promoting carbon inclusiveness. In recent years, in terms of the group standards, *Technical Specifications for Evaluating Greenhouse Gas Emissions Reduction through*

Alternative Travel of New Energy Vehicles, *Accounting Methods for Carbon Emission Reduction in Electric Vehicle Travel*, and *Technical Specifications for Evaluating Greenhouse Gas Emissions Reduction in Private Passenger Car Joint Travel Projects* have been released. These standards provide a certain reference for conducting carbon emission reduction accounting related to carbon inclusiveness. However, at present, in addition to research on local travel standards, the group standards include more accounting norms rather than standards in areas such as green consumption and low-carbon living, so it is not yet possible to conduct systematic calculations on the carbon emission reduction of various low-carbon behaviors of residents in the province, and it is not possible to truly quantify everyone's contribution to carbon emission reduction.

IV. Future Prospects

A. Improving top-level design and promoting the establishment of a carbon inclusiveness standard system

At present, many of the problems that arise in the operation of carbon inclusiveness mechanisms are due to unreasonable or incomplete institutional design. When formulating institutional documents, the government must fully consider the various entities and links involved in the actual operation of carbon inclusiveness, and mobilize the participation of the entire society. At present, in accordance with the idea of "practicing while summarizing", Zhejiang Province has issued the *Opinions on Carbon Neutrality and Carbon Inclusiveness Management of Large Events* (*Conferences*) *in Zhejiang Province* to standardize the management of certified carbon emission reductions of carbon inclusiveness of large events (conferences). Next, Zhejiang Province needs to continue to improve the construction of a carbon inclusiveness system. In promoting consumer carbon emission reduction and supporting carbon inclusiveness models, systematic guidance should be issued as soon as possible to clarify the direction of encouragement and guidance, and guide innovative practices in various regions.

The carbon inclusiveness standard & specification system is a huge project that requires the joint efforts of all sectors of society. It needs to organize the development of carbon emission reduction accounting methodologies in areas such as green travel, green consumption, and green communities, strengthen the application of methodologies, and promote the upgrading of mature methodologies to local standards for carbon emission reduction accounting. It needs to develop a carbon inclusiveness scenario evaluation system to scientifically evaluate the carbon emission reduction effectiveness of different low-carbon behaviors, and establish a carbon inclusiveness low-carbon scenario evaluation standards. It is also needs to establish norms for the construction of carbon inclusiveness platforms, clarify platform construction architecture, technical standards, interface specifications, etc., establish unified data standards and scenario access norms, encourage local planning for local characteristic applications, and access to Zhejiang Carbon Inclusiveness Application according to unified standards and specifications.

B. Innovating carbon inclusiveness operation methods and expanding the diversified value of personal "carbon assets"

Based on the principles of "provincial-level coordination, government-enterprise cooperation, joint contribution and shared benefits, and public participation", with the help of a market-oriented carbon inclusiveness operation, green and low-carbon production and lifestyle will be formed. Under the coordination and management of provincial-level competent departments, professional operating companies will be selected to give third-party entities the lead in Zhejiang's carbon inclusiveness operation. Without harming user interests, independent operational activities will be carried out to continuously improve the activity of carbon inclusiveness operation.

In addition, it is necessary to establish a personal carbon account, which comprehensively covers functions such as personal carbon emission data collection, accounting, carbon rating, and scenario application. After the establishment and maturity of the voluntary emission reduction carbon market in the future, the value of personal carbon assets will be further strengthened. At present, in the Zhejiang Carbon Inclusiveness Application, users with carbon points in different ranges are awarded different levels of medals and rewards, and personal carbon ratings are reflected on their avatars. In addition, the

Zhejiang Carbon Inclusiveness Application is also connected with personal credit and credit reporting systems to link the green performance with other policies and commercial resources and effectively enhance the value of personal carbon assets.

C. Gathering the power of the whole society and leading low-carbon production and green consumption in the whole society

Enterprises and social organizations need to further play a role in promoting the carbon inclusiveness mechanism. For enterprises, they can actively provide preferential goods or services as rewards for low-carbon behaviors based on their own business, and produce low-carbon products to actively fulfill their corporate social responsibilities. International organizations, industry associations, social organizations, and other social organizations, can actively mobilize the public to participate in carbon inclusiveness activities, disseminate carbon emission reduction information in the field of daily consumption, tell the story of low-carbon life in Zhejiang, and comprehensively enhance the public's awareness of green consumption.

With the transformation of consumer awareness, products that pass green certification or have carbon labels will become more attractive in the market. Relying on the low-carbon product supply chain & industry chain system gradually constructed, a new supply of green product services will be continued to promote and expand, which, in turn, will force and guide enterprises to transform their production methods into green production, and ultimately achieve a virtuous cycle model of benefiting the public, increasing enterprises' revenue, and reducing the whole society's emissions. All parties will work together to promote the establishment of green product standards and labeling systems, gradually build a low-carbon product supply system, force the green transformation of production methods with green consumption, and establish a consumption production mutual promotion model.

Author: The writing group of Zhejiang economic & information centre

PART THREE
REGIONAL
TYPICAL CASES

Quzhou's Practice and Exploration of "Carbon Peaking and Carbon Neutrality" based on the Carbon Account Reform

Carbon peaking is not only a macro national strategy, but also a result practiced by enterprises and individuals. How to stimulate and mobilize the enthusiasm of enterprises and individuals for carbon reduction, and implement customized and precise carbon reduction policies, has become a hot and difficult issue. Quzhou City pioneered the setting up of 2.396 million carbon accounts, covering six fields: industry, agriculture, energy, construction, transportation, and residents' lives. Its carbon account system can dynamically calculate and record the carbon emissions and reductions of enterprises and individuals, so as to automatically generate carbon assessments, and accurately draw "carbon portraits". On the basis of carbon accounts, Quzhou City plans to implement investment expansion to promote transformation, reduce carbon costs for enterprises and increase efficiency, and promote carbon inclusiveness to help the public increase income and other application scenarios, and explore market-oriented promotion mechanisms, so as to embark on a new track of win-win development and emission reduction.

I. Introduction

Located in the west of Zhejiang Province and at the source of Qiantang River, Quzhou is an ecological barrier for the whole province and even East China, with 69.66% of forest coverage rate and the outbound water quality maintaining above Class II. Meanwhile, relying on Juhua, one of the eight major chemical bases in China, it has developed into a national fluorosilicone new material industrial base and an electronic chemical material industrial base in

China. The output value of heavy chemical industry has remained above 70% for a long time, and the energy consumption per RMB 10,000 yuan GDP and industrial added value in the whole city are 1.95 times and 2.42 times that of the whole province, respectively. Quzhou has a good foundation in green and low-carbon work, and has carried out a total of 9 national-level circular economy pilot projects, becoming the only "Grand Slam" city of circular economy pilot demonstration in China. Taking "carbon peaking and carbon neutrality" as a valuable opportunity to solve the deep-rooted contradictions inherent in development, Quzhou leverages the green and low-carbon development of economy and society with carbon account reform, forms intelligent monitoring and dynamic accounting of carbon accounts, carbon account finance to leverage green and low-carbon investment, enterprise carbon reduction to reduce costs and increase efficiency, carbon inclusiveness to boost common prosperity and other characteristic models, to realize the "four-in-one" good development trend of carbon reduction, pollution reduction, green expansion and growth, stable total carbon emission, continuous declination of carbon emission intensity, and the better quality of ecological environment.

II. Major Practices

The idea of building a "carbon peaking and carbon neutrality" digital intelligence platform in Quzhou City is to take carbon accounts as a digital governance tool to explore the carbon trajectory of six key carbon-related fields: industry, agriculture (forestry), energy, construction, transportation and residents' lives in a chain manner so that a carbon emission measurement system that runs through production to consumption is established to make the multi-dimensional carbon assessment that reflects the industry level, regional contribution and historical decline, which can be applied to various aspects such as carbon finance, energy consumption budget management and "carbon peaking and carbon neutrality" technology.

A. Establishing Carbon Accounts by Sector and Carrying out Carbon Assessment

Complying with the requirements of "accurate data, scientific accounting and fair assessment", a total of 2.396 million carbon accounts covering 7 major fields, i.e., industry, agriculture, energy, construction, transportation, residents' lives and forestry carbon sinks, are set up by using the new generation of information technology with the coverage rate of enterprises and residents reaching 100% and 93% respectively.

1. Industrial Carbon Accounts

Based on the energy big data center, 1,077 industrial enterprises above designated size and 1,695 enterprises below the designated size are accessed, and all types of energy data such as electricity, coal, gas and heat are collected and aggregated at high frequencies, among which the data on energy consumption (except coal) of enterprises above designated size are collected automatically. The research team of Northeast Electric Power University is entrusted to establish the methodology to automatically calculate the total carbon emissions and carbon emission intensity of enterprises. The enterprises are evaluated and labelled with four colors, i.e., "red, yellow, light green and dark green", by benchmarking the carbon efficiency benchmark value of the industry and the city's average tax carbon intensity and industrial added value carbon intensity.

2. Energy Carbon Accounts

According to the classification of non-zero-carbon units and zero-carbon units, 98 energy production enterprises are accessed and a research team from Northeast Electric Power University is entrusted to establish the methodology to collect and calculate data on power supply, heat supply, desulfurizer usage, fuel consumption, carbon emissions, carbon emission intensity and so on, develop evaluation standards, and implement four-color labeling management according to the carbon emission intensity per unit of power(heat) supply.

3. Building Carbon Accounts

According to the classification of existing buildings and new buildings, 119 existing buildings and 10 new buildings are accessed and a research team from Architecture Design & Research Institute of Zhejiang University is entrusted to establish the methodology to collect data such as basic information of pilot projects, information of envelope insulation system and information of building energy consumption system, and label and evaluate according to carbon emissions by centering on the upgrading standards of new buildings, promotion of renewable energy, improvement of energy efficiency of existing buildings and transformation and upgrading of green buildings.

4. Transportation Carbon Accounts

Guided by the application demand, 73 transportation enterprises in the city are accessed and data on the number of vehicles, mileage, freight completion, turnover and energy consumption of transportation vehicles of urban public transport, urban and rural public transport, intercity passenger transport, cruise taxis, freight transport enterprises above designated size and other main bodies are collected on a monthly basis to build "carbon accounts" in the transportation field with the methodology developed by the research team from North China Electric Power University and Zhejiang Institute of Transportation Planning and Design.

5. Agricultural Carbon Accounts

Supported by the theory of agricultural carbon neutrality rate of the research team of China Agricultural University, agricultural carbon accounts are established and 1,000 agricultural enterprises are accessed. Taking traditional breeding production, husbandry recycling, fertilizer use and other links as the key points of emission reduction, three carbon neutrality paths, i.e., comprehensive utilization of crop straw, soil carbon sink mechanism and resource utilization of livestock and poultry manure, are identified in converting carbon neutrality values.

6. Forestry Carbon Accounts

Supported by the carbon sink accounting method of Zhejiang Forest Resources Monitoring Center, forestry carbon accounts are established, 2,135 forestry business entities are accessed, and data information on forestry resources, regional carbon sink quality, carbon sink projects and carbon sink applications in Quzhou are statistically analyzed from three dimensions: resource accounts, carbon sink projects and carbon sink applications.

7. Resident Carbon Accounts

With the theoretical support from the Zhejiang Financial Association and other professional institutions, individual carbon reduction is measured in terms of electricity & water saving, green travel, and green payment and the system of carbon accounts for residents is set up, which covers three core areas (green payment, green life and green travel) and residents' basic necessities of life (clothing, food, housing and transportation) and other aspects.

B. Multi-scenario Utilization of Carbon Assessment Applications

Concentrating on the high-frequency needs of the masses, the common needs of enterprises, and the difficulties in "carbon peaking and carbon neutrality" governance, multiple cross-application scenarios in various fields are developed and integrated into the "one-stop carbon governance services" at the government level, "one-network carbon reduction" at the enterprise level, and "one-step enjoying low-carbon benefit" at the individual level.

1. Financial Field: Carbon Account Finance

The closed-loop system comprised of carbon emission e-book, carbon credit e-report, carbon policy e-release, carbon finance e-supermarket, and carbon benefit e-assessment ("5e") is built to realize government's intelligent carbon governance, enterprises' intelligent carbon reduction, and financial institutions' intelligent support. Up to now, 33 financial institutions in the city have 55 carbon financial products on their shelves, and the total amount of loans issued to enterprise carbon accounts is RMB 54.383 billion yuan, with a balance of RMB 40.957 billion yuan.

2. Energy Field: Energy Consumption Budget Management

The whole-process budget management of energy consumption is carried out in 1,087 industrial enterprises above designated size in the city by digital means. The annual energy consumption budget of enterprises is reasonably allocated and the allocation of energy elements is optimized through the "energy consumption dual control adjustment coefficient" and "energy optimization allocation coefficient" to facilitate energy elements favorable to high efficiency, low consumption, and emerging industries.

3. Industrial Field: Application of Product Carbon Footprint Accounting

The energy required and carbon emissions over the product life cycle are calculated to provide export-oriented enterprises with carbon footprint accounting reports. The carbon data of enterprises and products are visually monitored and the product carbon emissions are evaluated through comparison within the enterprise and analogy with similar products, which helps enterprises to explore their own carbon reduction potential and assists the government to monitor the carbon emission trend level of industry and accurately release carbon reduction policies.

4. Transportation Field: "Shift of Freight Transport from Road to Waterway"

Relying on the "four links" smart logistics cloud platform in Zhejiang Province, the transportation chain, the information chain, management chain and service chain of the whole logistics transportation process is fully interconnected to enable the real-time monitoring of the operational status, logistics efficiency, cargo structure, and flow direction of inbound enterprises. By scientifically calculating the incremental carbon emissions reduction of the "shift of freight transport from road to waterway" for cargo owners and enterprises, and linking it with enterprise energy consumption budget indicators in a closed-loop manner, the carbon reduction benefits of the transportation process of the cargo owners & enterprises are converted into incremental energy consumption indicators.

5. Construction Field: Promotion and Application of Prefabricated Buildings

With the support of the Provincial Academy of Construction Sciences and based on the cooperation with Baoye Group and other market entities, a low-carbon demonstration base for the production of prefabricated members and a low-carbon science museum are built and a low-carbon "century-old house" demonstration community is being planned in Quzhou after identifying methodological demonstrations, studying policies for the promotion of prefabricated buildings, and establishing a digital platform to verify the theoretical system and construction results.

6. Agricultural Field: Low-carbon Farms

Production data generated in the production process from sowing to harvesting on the farm is collected and calculated. Through the collection and analysis of data on the fertilizers and pesticides consumed in key points, the key links of carbon sequestration and emission reduction are precisely identified, the grading evaluation standards are developed, and the agricultural green production technology model of "low cost & high efficiency, quality & safety, and environmental protection" is promoted.

7. Forestry Field: Forestry Carbon Sinks for Common Prosperity

The original seven links in the development of the CCER forestry carbon sinks project are optimized into four links: planning management, project layout, project monitoring, and audit & filing, and the 29 documents originally required are integrated into 9 so that the whole process can be processed online. The data is connected with the provincial "one map of forest resources" to realize automatic land audit, the automatic layout of sample plots, automatic carbon sink calculation, and automatic report generation.

8. Resident Field: "Zero-waste Living"

Through applications such as "One-Click Recycling", "Data Collection in One Database", "One Set of Calculation Standards", and "One Package of Incentive Policies", the problem of "how to obtain, calculate and use" carbon points are solved. Residents are encouraged to participate in the resource utilization of domestic waste to promote pollution reduction and carbon reduction. Their work is quantified and evaluated thereby, which will advocate a green and low-carbon lifestyle in the whole society.

9. Technology Field: "Dual Carbon" Technology

The "dual carbon" technology consists of three application scenarios: carbon achievement promotion, carbon technology breakthrough, and carbon think tank. The "carbon achievement promotion" has brought together over 17,000 scientific and technological achievements, collecting enterprise technical needs and achieving intelligent matching in one stop. In the "carbon technology breakthrough" scenario, the system intelligently generates a "breakthrough due diligence report" after enterprises fill in the breakthrough requirements. The "carbon think tank" scenario brings together over 450,000 large-scale instruments, over 1,000 experts, and over 640 innovative carriers.

III. Main Achievements and Empirical Mode

The practices and experience of Quzhou's carbon accounts were approved by 12 cadres at or above the vice-provincial level, including Zheng Shanjie, then Governor of Zhejiang Province, and Yi Gang, Governor of the People's Bank of China, and were written into the *Notice on Issuing the First Batch of Typical Experiences of High-quality Development and Construction of Demonstration*

Zones for Common Prosperity issued by the National Development and Reform Commission and the *2022 Annual Report on China's Policies and Actions to Address Climate Changes* issued by the Ministry of Ecology and Environment. These practices and experience presented as case study at the 2022 UN Climate Change Conference (UNFCCC COP 27).

A. Figuring out the "Carbon Background" by Innovating Carbon Monitoring & Accounting System

1. Real-time Data Monitoring by "Automatic Data Collection and Full-Quantity Data Collection"

Automatic carbon-related data collection and full-quantity data collection mechanism for various entities is being explored and established, and energy data on electricity, natural gas and steam consumed by enterprises are directly collected on site at the collection rate of 15 minutes per time, so as to accurately grasp the carbon consumption points and carbon emission cycle of enterprises in the jurisdiction. The data barriers among and between various units relating to, including but not limited to, development and reform, economy and information technology, ecology and environment, agriculture and rural areas, housing and urban-rural development, statistics, taxation, finance, and state grid electric power are broken down and the data channels at provincial, municipal, county, park and enterprise level are vertically connected, so as to uniformly summarize and collect basic data on energy consumption, product output, value-added, and taxation scattered across various systems.

2. Integrating the Accounting System in Accordance with "Existing Regulations or Newly Enacted Regulations"

With the support from the research teams of colleges and universities, six theoretical methodologies which fill the gaps in China are established and seven local standards for carbon account accounting and evaluation construction covering production to consumption are released according to "existing regulations and newly enacted regulations". The six theoretical methodologies are the agricultural carbon neutrality accounting method, industrial carbon emission data continuous monitoring method, energy carbon emission data continuous monitoring method, building carbon account evaluation method, environmental information disclosure, and carbon credit reporting system, among which agricultural carbon neutrality accounting method is put forward for the first time in China.

3. Objective and Fair Evaluation Based on "3D Evaluation + Four-color Labeling"

The four-color labeling of "dark green, light green, yellow and red" is applied to the carbon reduction of enterprises based on three dimensions of industry progressiveness, regional contribution and historical decline method. Specifically, the carbon emission intensity per unit of industrial value added and carbon emission intensity per unit of tax revenue is used to reflect the regional contribution, the carbon emission intensity per unit of product output is used to reflect the industry progressiveness, and the annual change curve of indicators is used to reflect the efforts of enterprises to reduce carbon emissions. The labeling evaluation method of product output is the first of its kind in China.

B. Improving "Carbon Efficiency" by Innovating "Dual Carbon" Precise Governance Tool

1. Precise Financial Support

Carbon account evaluation results are converted into corporate carbon credit reports, supporting financial preferential incentive policies are introduced and low-carbon enterprises and carbon reduction projects are given support in terms of loan amount and interest rate pricing. For example, Jiangshan Hydrogen Peroxide Company plans to invest RMB 15 million to implement the "Technical Transformation of Carbon Dioxide Storage Equipment". As the enterprise was rated as "light green enterprise", Quzhou Branch of Agricultural Bank of China granted 30 BP reduction in loan interest rates and issued a loan of RMB 5 million. After the completion of the project, the enterprise captures an average of 2,500 tons of carbon emissions per month, and the CO_2 neutralization rate increases from 20.3% to 38.6%. A total of 13 financial institutions have imported the carbon credit reports into their core systems, and 10 cities have fully replicated the carbon account financial model.

2. Precise Guarantee of Energy Consumption

Differentiated energy budget allocation is implemented for enterprises by two coefficients, so as to promote energy elements and lean towards industries and projects with high output efficiency per unit of energy consumption. In 2022, Quzhou transferred 454,500 tons of standard coal from 184 inefficient enterprises to support 974 enterprises. The comprehensive energy consumption of comparable clinker in the cement industry in the city has reached the forefront; The energy consumption per unit product of the coke process, sintering process, and converter process in the steel industry (Yuanli) has reached the advanced level in the same industry nationwide.

3. Precise Services for Enterprise

According to the diagnostic report on energy efficiency (carbon efficiency) of enterprises with carbon accounts, carbon butler "one-stop" services are provided for enterprises, and a "dual carbon" research center is set up, which facilitates 11 "dual carbon" technology transactions. Based on the objective evaluation of enterprises by carbon accounts, 241 high-carbon and inefficient enterprises are rectified, freeing up 120,000 tons of standard coal energy; 223 enterprises are promoted to benchmark with the advanced level of domestic and foreign industries, and more than RMB 6 billion has been invested in the transformation and upgrading of production processes; reduction and replacement work has been carried out in cement and steel industries, and 78 chemical enterprises were eliminated.

C. Realizing "Carbon Revenue Increase" by Innovating "Dual Carbon" Market-oriented Promotion Mechanism

1. Innovating Synergies Effect Model of Enterprise Carbon Reduction and Cost Reduction

By closely following the rigid demand of enterprises to reduce costs, the relevant department comprehensively sort out the entry points of carbon account application in various fields and innovate the synergistic mode of carbon reduction and cost reduction. In the energy field, the real-time accurate monitoring function of carbon accounts is applied to analyze the needs of enterprises for energy saving & carbon reduction, utilization of green energy to realize carbon reduction and energy storage arbitrage, and explore the third-party investment method of "Energy Conservation + Green Energy + Energy Storage + Carbon Assets". At present, pilot construction is being carried out in 26 enterprises, which is expected to achieve energy conservation, carbon reduction, and cost reduction of over RMB 100 million. In the field of transportation, the online application of "shift of freight transport from road to waterway" for bulk goods is developed and launched, providing 123 enterprises with market-oriented solutions for the whole logistics of "shift of freight transport from road to waterway", which has reduced comprehensive logistics costs by 15%, saved transportation costs by about RMB 100 million, and achieved a carbon reduction of 12,000 tons.

2. Innovating Model of Carbon Inclusiveness for Common Prosperity

A low-carbon life incentive mechanism for residents centered on individual carbon points is established, and carbon inclusiveness activities such as "low-carbon rural living", "low-carbon parking" and "low-carbon public transport" are carried out. A total of RMB 8.968 billion in loans have been issued for individual carbon points, with a balance of RMB 6.485 billion. The linkage development of primary and secondary accounts of forestry carbon accounts has been creatively carried out. Six primary accounts and more than 600 secondary accounts are opened in the city, and forestry carbon sink (carbon inclusiveness) projects are developed for about 30,000 mu of forest land in the city, generating 49,400 tons of carbon sinks. At the centralized trading meeting of the first batch of forest carbon sink emission reduction development in Zhejiang Province, 1,750 tons were traded at the price of RMB 100 yuan per ton.

3. Innovating the "Dual Carbon" Industrial Development Model

By seizing the "critical window period" of industrial transformation before carbon peaking, the relevant departments vigorously develop the "dual carbon" benefiting industries such as new energy, new materials, energy conservation and environmental protection, striving to double the city's industrial output value and double the per mu benefit through five years' efforts, with a view to promoting the extended development of lithium ion battery materials towards energy storage batteries and power batteries, the photovoltaic industry towards integrated of wind, solar and storage, and fluorosilicone materials towards circular economy. By 2025, a "dual carbon" industrial base, with a total output value exceeding RMB 200 billion, will be built. Since last year, a large number of major projects, such as Times Lithium Battery, Geely Power and Energy Storage Battery, have been successively launched, and five pumping and storage projects have been included in the "Medium and Long-term Development Plan of Pumped Storage" of the National Energy Administration, of which four are key projects in the "14th Five-Year Plan". furthermore, one life-cycle service system for the whole industrial chain has been built and eight green low-carbon industrial projects with an investment of over RMB 10 billion have been introduced.

IV. Future Prospects

It is necessary to adhere to the transition to green and low-carbon development of the whole society led and pried by the construction of the carbon account system, closely follow the main line "expanding green investment, promoting green consumption, serving green exports, and developing green industries", continue to consolidate the foundation of carbon account construction, improve the effectiveness of carbon account application, and create hardcore achievements in carbon accounts.

First, the foundation and the quality of the carbon account should be improved. It is vital to strive to work with the Zhejiang Provincial Development and Reform Commission to formulate and release the provincial standard of *Zhejiang Carbon Account Construction Specifications* and upgrade the "zero-waste life" accounting evaluation standard and the accounting standard of carbon emission reduction of "shift of freight transport from road to waterway" to the provincial standard and the bank's personal carbon account standard to National Gold Standard; the comprehensive interconnection of personal carbon accounts and provincial carbon inclusiveness platforms should be improved; it is essential to jointly plan with the Department of Forestry of Zhejiang Province to build forestry carbon accounts into the base of provincial forestry carbon inclusiveness transactions; the legislation of carbon account data management regulations should be furthered; it is important to improve the full collection and automatic collection mechanism of carbon account data, establish a regular spot check and review mechanism for data quality, and promote the practical and effective closed-loop application of carbon accounts in various fields and blocks.

Second, the "Double Hundred" demonstration of green and low-carbon investment. About 100 industrial enterprises are organized to participate in the demonstration projects of carbon reduction, cost reduction, and efficiency improvement invested by third parties, aiming to implement the EMC model of "energy saving + green energy + energy storage + carbon assets" and promote energy-saving technology, low-carbon technology, energy storage technology and charging and replacing technology; it is necessary to implement about 100 major "carbon peaking and carbon neutrality" projects such as energy saving and carbon reduction, green energy and carbon reduction, low-carbon industries, circular economy, pollution reduction and carbon reduction, and ecological carbon sink, among which more than 20 major landmark projects such as new energy storage, hydrogen energy, and virtual power plants are planned. Innovative project carbon account financial products should be developed to be included in the central bank's carbon emission reduction support tools.

Third, a carbon labeling industrial base should be built. Relying on the carbon footprint accounting of industrial products to serve green exports, the "carbon peaking and carbon neutrality" companies cooperate with third parties to establish China (Quzhou) Carbon Labeling Industry Base, establish a mutual recognition mechanism between the application of carbon footprint accounting of industrial products and third-party certification agencies, create carbon footprint labeling laboratory and data center, standard center, evaluation center, and technology transformation center with national influence, promote the integration of carbon accounts and carbon labeling, enrich and improve the carbon footprint labeling database, formulate carbon footprint carbon labeling standards that are conducive to international trade and industrial competition, explore the market-oriented operation mode of carbon account carbon labeling empowerment enterprises, and create a carbon labeling supply chain and industrial application system.

Fourth, a pilot city with joint action on green and low-carbon life should be created. Relying on personal carbon accounts to promote green life and green consumption, it is vital to coordinate major shopping malls, scenic spots, theaters, hotels, and other consumption venues in the city, establish a joint action alliance for green and low-carbon life, issue a joint action initiative for green and low-carbon life, establish a green and low-carbon living (consumption) guidance and promotion mechanism using personal carbon accounts as the medium, and create the first pilot city for a joint action on green and low-carbon life in China.

Fifth, green and low-carbon national pilot demonstrations in various fields should be set up. A national green financial reform and innovation demonstration plot is to be built. It is important to promote the establishment of national forestry carbon sink pilot city, national green low-carbon agricultural pilot area, national green travel pilot city, and other pilot demonstration areas, strive for the first batch of national carbon peaking pilot parks, national climate investment, and financing pilot city and the transformation from "dual control" of energy consumption in Zhejiang Province to the national pilot project of "dual control" of carbon emissions landed in Quzhou, focus on exploring the establishment of carbon budget management and project carbon evaluation mechanisms, achieve the full coverage of provincial-level and above pilot demonstrations in various fields, and make efforts to build the city with the most national-level pilot demonstrations in the green and low-carbon field.

Author: Liu Hongfei[1]

---

1   Liu Hongfei, director of the Environment and Resources Department of the Development and Reform Commission in Quzhou, Zhejiang Province, has a deep research on the "Two Mountains" transformation and carbon peaking and carbon neutrality transformation, and has planned and promoted several national pioneering mechanisms in Quzhou.

Global Green and Low Carbon Transformation Efforts through Carbon Efficiency Reform in Huzhou City

Enterprises are the vitality of economic and social development, but they are also the absolute subject of energy consumption and carbon emissions. After the proposal of the national strategy of carbon peaking and carbon neutrality, the enterprise management model focusing on separating management has been unable to meet the needs of the government due to its lack of accuracy, so the carbon efficiency reform came into being. Huzhou City is the pioneer of carbon efficiency reform in China, and the industrial carbon efficiency reform has been selected as a "typical case of comprehensive deepening of local reforms in China". In addition to industry, Huzhou City also continues to explore carbon efficiency reform in areas such as residential life and public buildings, continuously expanding the application scenarios of carbon efficiency evaluation, and promoting the effectiveness of carbon emission reduction in various fields from both governance and services.

I. Introduction

Under the goal to reach "carbon peaking and carbon neutrality", a systematic and effective carbon productivity evaluation system is the foundation for achieving precise governance and efficient services. In recent years, Huzhou City has adhered to the principle of small entry points and large traction, taking the industrial field as a breakthrough point, and explored the establishment of an evaluation and application system that takes "carbon efficiency" as the carbon productivity level of enterprises. Through the model of "studying carbon emission methodology-formulating carbon efficiency evaluation standards-

collecting data to establish platform-developing policies to expand application",
Huzhou City has realized the "from 0 to 1" carbon efficiency evaluation system,
and it is approved as the only pilot city of carbon efficiency code in the province,
and industrial carbon efficiency reform has been selected as a typical case of
comprehensive deepening of local reforms in China. On the basis of replicating
the construction model of the industrial carbon efficiency system, Huzhou City
continues to explore and innovate in other fields. Up to now, a carbon efficiency
evaluation system covering enterprises, individuals, public institutions (subjects
responsible for public buildings) and other carbon emission behavior entities
has been established, and carbon efficiency practice has been carried out in finance,
energy conservation renovation, carbon emissions trading and other aspects, laying
a solid foundation for low-carbon transformation in the whole field.

II. Main Practices and Achievements

A. Three-Dimensional Depiction of Industrial Enterprises' "Carbon Portrait" with "One Code and Three Logos"

In response to the problems of scattered data, lack of coordination,
unclear base numbers and lack of accurate evaluation of carbon efficiency of
enterprises, an industrial carbon efficiency evaluation system focusing on the
key links such as "measurement, evaluation, use, and governance" of carbon
emissions is built in an innovative manner. The first industrial carbon platform
in China is launched and the industrial "carbon efficiency code" was created
for the first time to evaluate the carbon emission level of enterprises in carbon
emission per unit of added value, the comparison of carbon emissions in
the same industry and the use of green power in the form of "One Code and
Three Logos"; at the same time, 19 relevant institutional norms are introduced
to establish a complete set of regulations, standards, policies, and other
theoretical and institutional systems for the application and promotion of carbon
efficiency code.

Figure 10-1 "Industrial Carbon Efficiency Code" 2.0

1. Focusing on Action Goals and "Building" the System with a Strong Team

A special team for industrial carbon efficiency reform was set up with the secretary-general of the municipal government as the leader, integrating 8 departments such as economics and information, electricity, statistics, ecology and environment, and many professional forces from districts and counties to create a rapid response chain across departments, levels and businesses. Experts and scholars from Tsinghua University Energy Institute, Low Carbon Laboratory, China University of Petroleum and other local enterprises are invited to conduct expert certification and improvement on the "carbon efficiency code" evaluation system. The evaluation model has been recognized by a number of experts, including Academician Jiang Yi of Tsinghua University, and professional institutions such as the Dual Carbon Research Center of the Ministry of Industry and Information Technology and China National Institute of Standardization.

2. Sorting out Core Business and "Building" the Platform by Collecting Data

Through the IRS platform, more than 23 million data of 14 categories from statistics, tax, power, and other departments were collected in an interface way to form an industrial carbon efficiency data warehouse. Big data analysis is conducted on the consumption of 39 kinds of energy products in 5 categories, such as kerosene, gas, and electricity, in 381 sub-sectors of 33 industries in the city. The first "industrial carbon platform" is launched in China, and the core modules of "carbon monitoring", "carbon benchmarking", "carbon neutrality" and "carbon application" are built, and the "carbon map" of the city by region and industry is drawn, realizing data matching and fusion to form the "carbon efficiency index"; the industrial carbon platform cockpit is developed, creating an integrated digital platform for carbon management and carbon assessment. Version 2.0 of the industrial carbon platform is officially launched as the provincial industrial carbon platform.

3. Optimizing the Evaluation Model and "Drawing" Identification by Integrating Dual Codes

Focusing on the enterprise's carbon emissions, carbon utilization efficiency, and carbon neutrality, intelligent "benchmarking" of the three major indicators is carried out, and a "carbon efficiency code" that integrates the three labels in one is generated. The innovative dual-code integration of "enterprise code + carbon efficiency code" is developed with five service modules, carbon diagnosis, carbon technological transformation, carbon finance, green factory declaration, and green power trading, realizing "one-click processing". Industrial carbon efficiency codes have been fully promoted throughout the province. At present, all 42,000 industrial enterprises above designated size in the province have been assigned codes; evaluation and coding of over 5,000 enterprises below designated size have also been completed which can be dynamically updated quarterly.

4. Strengthening Institutional Norms and Compiling Standards for Long-Term "Management"

Nineteen relevant institutional norms have been developed and introduced in the province, including the *Management Measures for Industrial Carbon Efficiency Benchmarking* (*Carbon Efficiency Code*) *in Huzhou City* (*Trial Implementation*), the *Data Collection and Results Release Mechanism for Carbon Efficiency Evaluation in Huzhou City*, and the *Work Plan for Promoting Industrial Carbon Efficiency Reform in Huzhou City*, and a complete set of theoretical systems such as norms, standards, and laws are established. For Huzhou City's local standard, the *Standard for Carbon Efficiency Evaluation of Industrial Enterprises* is released to provide a "yardstick" for carbon monitoring, carbon measurement and carbon evaluation. The carbon efficiency code is incorporated into the *Huzhou City Green Finance Promotion Regulations*, and for the first time, a carbon emission information disclosure mechanism is established in the form of local legislation.

B. "Carbon Points+Carbon Emission Reduction" Empowers Individuals to Realize the Value of Carbon Emission Reduction

There are many scattered behavior subjects (individuals) in the field of life, and it is difficult to collect and quantify the low-carbon behavior data. Therefore, the carbon efficiency evaluation system in this field focuses on positive incentives and guidance, with voluntary participation as the principle, and selects behaviors with strong leadership, high frequency of occurrence, and data availability among individual carbon reduction behaviors as evaluation indicators. "Carbon emission reduction" is assigned to behaviors that are easier to calculate carbon reduction, and "carbon points" are assigned to behaviors whose methodology is temporarily unapproved and difficult to calculate carbon reduction. "Carbon points + carbon emission reductions" are assigned to measure the carbon reduction contribution of individual behavior. By creating the "Carbon Master ·Benefiting Huzhou" digital intelligence platform, establishing a carbon reduction trading mechanism, and establishing a carbon point exchange system with various forms, Huzhou has constructed a sustainable operating mechanism with "accurate identification, convenient participation, rich scenarios, and powerful inclusion" to promote realizing the value of personal green behavior in carbon reduction. At present, the platform has more than 20,000 users, accumulatively generating more than 581,600 carbon points and reducing carbon emissions by more than 4,136.33 tons.

1. Establishing the System and Standards and Carry out Work with Relevant Basis

Strengthen the top-level design. The *Work Plan of Huzhou City for Establishing "Carbon Benefiting Huzhou" Regulating Mechanism* is developed and implemented to clarify the responsibilities of construction, transportation, electricity, publicity and other departments, and to clarify the arrangement and division of responsibilities for data collection and platform publicity. Methodological research should be carried out. More than 50 kinds of green behaviors with high frequency, such as green travel, green consumption, recycling, paper and plastic reduction, energy efficiency, are comprehensively sorted out, and behavior maps are drawn one by one to provide strong support for effective identification of green behaviors. Standards and policies should be developed. A series of standards such as the Carbon Inclusiveness *Certification Specification for Carbon Reduction of Roof Distributed Photovoltaic Power Generation* should be developed and introduced to scientifically measure the carbon reduction of various green behaviors.

2. Establishing the Green Scenario System for the Masses Participation

The "Carbon Master · Benefiting Huzhou" digital intelligence platform is launched, through setting up green behavior scenarios such as green consumption, green travel, waste classification, residential photovoltaic, zero-carbon car owners, and smart air conditioners and modules such as "earning points", "points redemption", "public welfare", "earning cash", "personal carbon neutrality", "carbon benefits", and "master assistants", it is planned to build a comprehensive interactive platform that integrates carbon calculation, carbon sink, carbon sale, carbon exchange and carbon discussion. At the same time, it integrates the data resources of green and low-carbon behaviors such as Ant Forest, Huzhou Public Travel Platform, Huzhou Garbage Classification, and New Energy Cloud Platform to form a green life "database" and realizes automatic collection and real-time sharing of green behavior data of platform users. Since its launch, the platform has collected 16.51 million pieces of data on various green lifestyle behaviors.

3. Establishing the Market Trading System and Forming a Closed Loop for Carbon Reduction and Consumption

By opening up the closed loop of carbon emission reduction trading, the platform realizes the self-development function and promotes the sustainable operation of the whole system. For green behaviors, such as residential photovoltaic and new energy vehicle travel, which refer to accurate algorithms and easy collection of quantitative data, a series of local standards for carbon inclusiveness certification are formulated, and the process of carbon emission reduction accounting and certification are standardized, which lays the foundation for carbon emission reduction trading. An online one-stop transaction process with platform users as the main suppliers of carbon emission reductions, public institutions, enterprises, green demonstration entities as the main demanders, and digital RMB and smart contracts with enhanced value and efficiency is established to realize the transformation of carbon emission reduction flows within the municipal area. At present, more than 20,000 households have been accessed to distributed photovoltaics, and it is estimated that an average of 126,000 tons of photovoltaic power generation carbon emission reduction can be provided each year; more than 280 tons of carbon emission reduction transactions have been completed.

4. Establishing an Inclusion Feed-back System to Guaranteed Points Redemption

An inclusion model combining material incentives and spiritual incentives is established, aiming to attract the public to practice green behaviors through rich forms of carbon point redemption. Green low-carbon business alliance is formed to promote the exchange of carbon points for commercial discounts and public services, and the total value of carbon points redeemed for scenic spot tickets, coupons and public transportation vouchers is about RMB 100,000. Honor mechanisms such as carbon point rankings and "green and low-carbon experts" are designed. In 2022, five annual "carbon experts" were selected as typical representatives of practicing green low-carbon behaviors. The Yangtze River Delta Eco-Energy Carbon Sink Fund is established to call on enterprises and the public to support carbon sink public welfare projects such as afforestation and wetland protection in a low-carbon way by "purchasing carbon sinks", and to continuously enhance the public's sense of self-realization in participating in green behaviors. Since its establishment, the fund has received nearly 200 donations from individuals and enterprises and promoted the construction of 10 cooperative bases, such as Huzhou Liangxi National Forest Park, with a total afforestation area of 23.5 mu.

C. Accurately Controlling Carbon Emissions from Public Buildings through Building "Carbon Efficiency Codes"

The same responsible entity (such as schools, hospitals, etc.) often includes multiple buildings. It is not of practical value to evaluate the carbon emission level of a single building if it is divided into individual buildings, and it is more difficult to obtain data such as energy consumption. Therefore, in the construction field, building groups composed of the same unit are used as the basic unit for carbon efficiency evaluation. By clarifying the method of collecting basic data and carbon emission grading standards for public buildings, establishing a digital comprehensive platform and studying policy tools based on building "carbon efficiency codes", a carbon efficiency reform system is established in the building sector. In March this year, the research results of "carbon efficiency code" for public buildings in Huzhou City and the launch of the Digital Intelligence Platform were held, marking that Huzhou took the lead in extending "carbon efficiency code" to the construction field in China.

Figure 10-2   Research Results of "Carbon Efficiency Code" in Huzhou Public Buildings and Conference of Digital Intelligence Platform

1. Conducting Basic Surveying and Ensuring Scientific Calculation of "Carbon"

With Tsinghua University, the evaluation and application research of buildings "carbon efficiency code" should be carried out. The development overview, energy consumption data collection and standard status of local public buildings in Huzhou City should be investigated. And the carbon emission data collection methods and mechanisms of public buildings in typical cities in China (such as Beijing, Shanghai, Shenzhen, Hangzhou, etc.) should be combined to study the cost-efficient scale collection methods and mechanisms that are suitable for the energy consumption and carbon emission management of public buildings in Huzhou City; information and energy consumption data from over 600 public buildings covering three districts and three counties should be used as samples to conduct accounting and analysis on the carbon emissions of public buildings in Huzhou City. By verifying information such as building area, energy consumption over the years, building usage habits, correcting building information errors, green power usage, and "multi-household one meter" issues, the carbon efficiency calculation model is further optimized.

2. Developing Classification and Grading Standards and Promoting Reasonable Evaluation of "Carbon"

The grading methods and standards for building operation energy consumption (quota) and carbon emission data are benchmarked against the existing domestic ones, and the grading standards are developed around the management needs such as carbon emission reduction targets and key carbon emission reduction objects in the construction field in Huzhou. After research, demonstration and optimization, public buildings in Huzhou are divided into eight common types: office buildings, hotels and restaurants, commercial complexes, medical buildings, educational buildings, cultural and tourism buildings, scientific research buildings, and sports venues. Carbon efficiency is classified into five levels A to E, corresponding to five energy-saving and emission reduction management ideas, excellent, relatively excellent, with emission reduction potential, with great emission reduction potential, and requiring emission reduction renovation. The data collection method and standard, carbon emission calculation method and graded management scheme of the "carbon efficiency code" for buildings in Huzhou have been unanimously recognized by leaders and experts in the field of energy conservation and carbon reduction from the Ministry of Housing and Urban-Rural Development, Zhejiang University, Tongji University, Chongqing University, and other units.

3. Building a Digital Platform and Achieving Dynamic "Carbon" Measurement

A digital management platform based on GIS+ big data analysis is built, which is endowed with six major functions, "public building data access in the city, integration of all types of energy data, full-dimensional scientific carbon efficiency evaluation, full life cycle operation management, intelligent diagnosis and decision-making in the whole process, and comprehensive carbon construction asset management. Through rapid data collection and intelligent algorithm analysis, carbon efficiency evaluation is automatically formed so as to realize the dynamic "actual operation data" from the static "design energy saving rate" in the construction field. At present, data of housing and urban-rural development, economic and information, electricity, statistics, development and reform, financial institutions, etc. have been interconnected, penetrating the "carbon-power-electricity" data chain. A total energy consumption database for public buildings has been established, with a cumulative access to 11.7375 million square meters of public buildings and 300,000 pieces of data obtained. It is expected to access 127 million square meters of existing public buildings in the city.

4. Building a Policy System and Promote Efficient "Carbon" Management

Code for Certification and Management of Carbon Efficiency Codes for Public Buildings in Huzhou City should be formulated, and a benchmarking, disclosure and sharing mechanism for data and technology related to building energy consumption/carbon emissions based on the "carbon efficiency code" is established to ensure the implementation of five management strategies corresponding to the five carbon efficiency levels of A-E, namely, "recognition and incentive funding, recognition but no incentive funding, need to strengthen operation and management, need to carry out energy audits, and need to carry out mandatory energy-saving and carbon-reducing renovations". According to Tsinghua University's calculation, if the building "carbon efficiency code" is fully implemented during the 14th Five-Year Plan period, the public buildings in the city can save about 300 million kW · h of electricity which is equivalent to reducing carbon emissions by about 148,000 tons.

D. The "Carbon Efficiency +" Application System Releases Strong Momentum for Carbon Efficiency Reform

Carbon efficiency evaluation is not an end but a measure of the main carbon productivity level, reflecting its potential for further energy conservation and carbon reduction. But what is more important is how to turn this potential into reality, that is, how to substantively apply carbon efficiency evaluation. Huzhou City has also made diversified explorations in this regard.

1. Providing "Carbon Efficiency + Energy Efficiency Service" and Advancing Energy-Saving Transformation of Various Entities

Energy-saving diagnostic services for enterprises rated as Grade 4 and 5 in the industrial "carbon efficiency code" and with high carbon efficiency level are carried out, and green technological transformation projects are implemented. A total of 360 companies have been provided with energy-saving diagnostic services, and 380 energy-saving and carbon-reduction technological transformation projects have been promoted, with an estimated saving of 200,000 tons of standard coal. Energy conservation renovation of public buildings corresponding to Grade C, D and E in the building "carbon efficiency code" is carried out, which is expected to exceed the energy conservation renovation of existing public buildings in Huzhou during the 14th Five-Year Plan period by managing only 600 sample buildings covered by the current "carbon efficiency code".

2. Developing the "Carbon Efficiency + Green Finance" and Guiding the Green and Low-carbon Upgrades in Various Fields

Innovative financial products such as "carbon efficiency loan" and "carbon preferential loan" have been launched to provide credit support and preferential interest rates to low-carbon and high-efficiency enterprises and a total of 1,285 loans have been issued, totaling RMB 13.2 billion. Based on the energy consumption data of the "carbon efficiency code" in the building sector, point-to-point financial support is provided for green energy conservation renovation projects in existing buildings through "inventory management" to ensure that they are willing and able to change and should be changed immediately. The *List of Key Financial Support Projects* (*First Batch*) *for Green and Energy Conservation Renovation of Buildings* has been issued, with an energy conservation renovation area of 1.8589 million square meters, and a total of RMB 411 million of credit has been provided for the projects on the list.

3. Developing the Carbon Efficiency + Collaborative Evaluation and Forcing Enterprises to Implement Low-carbon Transformation

The carbon efficiency evaluation results of industrial enterprises are incorporated into the "Green Factory Star Management" evaluation system, which has been applied to 3,466 star-rated green factories, promoting 126 enterprises to complete clean production audits, and completing the "quality improvement and star upgrading" action for 450 green factories. Version 3.0 of "Heroes per mu" was first introduced in the province, and the results of carbon efficiency evaluation are included in the evaluation system of "Heroes per mu", with a weight of 15 points. "Green and low-carbon" has become an important scoring point for enterprises in the "Heroes per Mu" evaluation. According to calculations, after adding carbon efficiency indicators, there are 337 industrial enterprises above designated size whose evaluation results have changed, accounting for 11.04%.

4. Developing the "Carbon Efficiency + Market Transactions" and Promoting Cross-sector Collaborative Carbon Reduction

By trading the carbon emission reduction generated by personal green behaviors with enterprises and public institutions (responsible entities of public buildings) with carbon reduction needs, Huzhou not only improves the carbon efficiency level of enterprises and public institutions but also promotes the sustainable operation of carbon emission reduction trading. The *Implementation Rules for the Application of Carbon Emission Trading Results in Industrial Carbon Efficiency Evaluation in Huzhou City* has been introduced, which incorporates business transactions into carbon efficiency evaluation, and it encourages enterprises to actively purchase carbon reduction emissions. Currently, the industrial carbon efficiency code platform has been connected with the "Carbon Master · Benefiting Huzhou" platform, and enterprises have been promoted to subscribe to 4,000 tons of certified carbon reduction emissions. Carbon neutrality specifications for large-scale events (conferences) are developed, which help the "two sessions" and the China Green Low Carbon Innovation Conference achieve carbon neutrality by purchasing carbon emission reductions.

III. Major Implications

A. Promoting carbon efficiency reform in a step-by-step and phased manner

The two key points of carbon efficiency reform are generating the results of carbon efficiency evaluation and using the results to promote carbon reduction, but both need to be done step by step. In generating carbon efficiency evaluation results, data availability and methodological maturity should be fully considered. In terms of Huzhou City experience, the three categories that have been built so far are industrial carbon efficiency codes dependent on the industrial energy consumption statistical system of enterprises above the designated size, individual carbon points realized through authorization mechanisms and public buildings mainly using electricity, with relatively good data foundation. Except for individual carbon emission reductions without full-quantity accounting, the other two carbon emission accounting methods are relatively simple. In contrast, the fields of transportation and agriculture, where data sources and accounting methods are more complex, can be directions for further exploration. In the application of carbon efficiency evaluation, more efforts have been made to provide more accurate subject-level carbon portraits for energy, finance, economy and information technology and other competent departments to formulate and implement more targeted policies. If the departments fail to carry out these work, these application scenarios will also be difficult to be implemented.

B. Guiding and pushing carbon efficiency reform for enterprises

Enterprises are the vitality of economic and social development, but they are also the absolute subjects of energy consumption and carbon emissions. To carry out carbon efficiency reform, an important goal is to further achieve classified management within the industry and improve accuracy on the basis of the previous rough separate management. However, if the focus is still placed on management, it will not be able to meet the actual needs of enterprises. In fact, enterprises need not only the goal of carbon reduction but also the guidance of corresponding capabilities and the rendering of services to ensure the feasibility of carbon reduction, which is the goal of carbon efficiency reform. From Huzhou City experience, it can be seen that a large number of application scenarios related to finance, technology, and other aspects provide elements and capabilities for enterprises, which are indispensable for attracting their participation and ensuring the smooth implementation of the reform.

C. Implementing carbon efficiency reform through digital reform

Carbon efficiency reform requires a digital platform, which has become a consensus in almost all areas where this reform is carried out. However, there are still some disagreements on what kind of digital platform should be built. In terms of Huzhou City experience, it is mainly aimed at innovation and reform, gathering multi-source data to build carbon accounts and promoting governance and service functions simultaneously. These are essentially the contents of digital reform in Zhejiang Province. From this point of view, the digital platform is just a carrier and its input and output are more critical with more content other than digitization. Therefore, to build digital platforms related to carbon efficiency in other places, the complete process and normative paradigm of digital reform shall be implemented and progressed step by step.

IV. Future Prospects

Carbon efficiency reform has been promoted in many places across the country, which is also an effective verification of its vitality. However, this reform itself is far from over. Facing the future, the evaluation and application of carbon efficiency still need to be further strengthened and explored.

When it comes to carbon efficiency evaluation, on the one hand, the calculation methods related to carbon emissions and carbon efficiency can be further optimized, the accuracy and authority of the data can be improved, and the promotion of the methods can be strengthened; on the other hand, the coverage of carbon efficiency reform can be further expanded, especially in areas such as transportation and agriculture, small and medium-sized enterprises, and rural areas.

Referring to carbon efficiency application, it mainly refers to expanding the application of carbon efficiency evaluation in carbon emission budget management, green finance, carbon emissions trading and other aspects, deepening the interconnection mechanism between "carbon efficiency code" and evaluation systems of green buildings, green factories and so on and constantly expanding the scope and scenarios of carbon efficiency evaluation; at the same time, typical selection and publicity such as "carbon efficiency leader" can also be carried out to persistently enhance the public appeal and social influence.

Author: Hu Chang[1], Lu Qiaoling[2]

1   Hu Chang, deputy director of the Development and Reform Commission in Huzhou, has long been engaged in the field of resource and environment, and mainly responsible for research and practice on green and low-carbon development planning, carbon peaking and mechanisms to realize the market value of ecosystem goods and services, etc.

2   Lu Qiaoling, graduate student, has published 6 papers, including 4 SCI journal papers, and works in the Development and Reform Commission in Huzhou, mainly engaged in the field of resource and environment.

"Yongkang Model" of Circular Economy to Assist in Carbon Reduction

The hardware handicraft industry in Yongkang City has a long history and has enjoyed the reputation of that "hardware craftsmen go everywhere, and prefectures and counties cannot be separated from Yongkang". Craftsmen such as "mending pots and kettles, making copper and repairing locks" have achieved the most primitive resource recycling. With the continuous promotion of a circular economy, the resource recycling industry has transformed from extensive sorting to precision manufacturing, forming a circular system of small circulation of enterprises and systemic circulation of parks, taking the lead in developing a new path of circular economy in areas with a high degree of industrialization, high efficiency of resource utilization, relatively developed economy and small environmental capacity, and providing a "Yongkang Model" for the development of circular economy in Zhejiang and other regions in China.

I. Introduction

Yongkang City is a well-known hardware capital in China with well-developed hardware industry clusters, but relatively weak natural resources. It is a typical strong industrial city and a small resource county. To better practice the concept of "lucid waters and lush mountains are invaluable assets" and boost the modernization of hardware to create the "Hardware Capital of the World", Yongkang City explored the formation of a circular industrial chain of "recycled metal-hardware products-waste metal recycling-recycled metal" by taking a number of pilot projects as an opportunity, such as the establishment of a national circular economy demonstration city, the only pilot county for the construction of renewable resource recycling system in China, and the demonstration pilot project for the circular transformation of provincial-level parks. The Yongkang Model of "recycling system-raw material base-production and utilization-specialized market" is constructed, which takes the waste metal material market and recycling center of recycled materials as raw material supply bases, economic development zones and provincial-level high-tech industrial parks as production bases, and China Science & Technology Hardware City and online shopping malls as product distribution and sales centers. It is the first in China to carry out research on the development index of county-level circular economy, explore and establish the first statistical accounting system of county-level resource output rate, and has embarked on a unique and mature "Yongkang Path" for developing circular economy, becoming a model for Zhejiang Province and even the whole country.

II. Main Approaches and Results

A. Establishing a modern circular industry system

1. High-quality development of recycling-based manufacturing

The industrial circular economy is vigorously developed. A resource-saving, clean production and eco-friendly circular industrial system framework has gradually been formed through measures such as creating green factories to promote green manufacturing, demolishing small and micro-enterprise parks with inefficient land use, promoting the transformation and upgrading of low-efficiency enterprises through the "hero per mu yield" reform and promoting enterprise transformation and upgrading through differentiated policies. The clean production audit rate of enterprises above designated size is nearly 40%. There are 3 national-level green factories, 2 green design products, 2 provincial-level green factories, and 33 provincial-level water-saving enterprises.

2. Enhancing the development of circular service industry

Relying on the high degree of agglomeration of the existing hardware industry, the construction of the headquarters center of the hardware industry is promoted, and a productive service industry system that gathers various services and supporting facilities such as finance and insurance, creative information, information technology, accounting and law, and e-commerce is set up. Relying on the construction of the National Hardware Tools and Doors Product Quality Supervision and Inspection Center (Zhejiang Province), the hardware industry service industry chain will be lengthened and the market vitality will be further stimulated. Relying on the Hardware Industry Cluster in Yongkang City, with the theme of hardware culture, combined with the existing landscape tourism resources, a new pattern of industrial tourism development of "scenery + industry" has taken shape.

3. Developing modern ecological recycling agriculture

Taking the construction of the first modern agricultural equipment high-tech industrial park in the province as the entry point and breakthrough point for the "upgraded version" of Yongkang City modern agricultural machinery equipment, modern agricultural machinery equipment is promoted to develop in a large-scale, integrated and intelligent direction. Following the principle of "reduction, recycling and reuse", wastes such as livestock and poultry manure and crop straws are recycled and reused, forming a circular agricultural ecological chain of "resources-waste-renewable resources".

B. Improving the material recycling system

1. Improving the recycling system of renewable resources

Taking the construction of a "zero-waste city" as a starting point, the construction of various circular economy projects is accelerated, and a renewable resource recycling system based on one renewable resource sorting center and 54 renewable resource recycling outlets is set up. It is necessary to return renewable resources such as metal scraps, scraps, waste paper and waste plastics generated by metal-related processing and manufacturing industries to waste recycling enterprises, promote the recycling and reuse of renewable resources, greatly reduce production costs, save a lot of energy resources, reduce carbon dioxide, methane, nitrogen oxides, smoke and dust and other major pollutant emissions, and the environmental quality of air, water and soil will be significantly improved.

2. Improving the utilization level of renewable resources

The first waste-free industry alliance in the province is established, basically forming a solid waste disposal industry cluster for the resource utilization and recycling of industrial solid waste, construction waste, and household waste (kitchen waste). By 2021, through benign operation, the Waste-Free Industry Alliance has disposed of 81,000 tons of general industrial solid waste, collected and disposed of more than 60,000 tons of kitchen waste, and recovered more than 250 tons of pesticide packaging wastes. Domestic waste incineration and expansion projects are promoted and implemented, the construction of rural domestic waste "three-in-one" treatment centers, kitchen waste comprehensive utilization and harmless disposal centers is deepened, and the ability to dispose and utilize domestic waste has been significantly improved. As of 2021, the recycling rate of waste plastic and rubber is 78%, the recycling rate of waste paper is 84%, the recycling rate of waste agricultural film is 96%, and the comprehensive utilization rate of crop straw is 96.3%. By improving its own technology, construction wastes and waste incineration residues are fully utilized for production, and the recycling of building materials is realized. At the same time, the utilization level of various solid waste resources is enhanced, achieving a recycling rate of 96.5% of main non-ferrous metals, and the solid fuels and fertilizers generated effectively reduce the consumption of natural resources and fossil energy such as coal.

3. Improving the quality and efficiency of domestic wastes classification

The construction of "two fixed and four separated" centralized disposal points for domestic wastes is vigorously promoted, and the level of waste recycling and treatment is constantly enhanced. The "4+1" intelligent treatment method of "waste source classification, renewable resource recycling, resource utilization of kitchen waste, on-site reduction treatment of non-recyclable waste + intelligent recycling platform" is explored, creating a "Yongkang Model" for the classification, recycling and disposal of rural domestic wastes. Through the transformation and upgrading of the solar composting room, it is estimated that about 212 tons of domestic waste is disposed of every day, and the "Yongkang Model" of wastes classification has initially formed. Since its operation, more than 2,300 tons of kitchen waste have been disposed of, more than 690 tons of primary fertilizer have been generated and more than 700 tons of low-value renewable resources have been recycled, with a harmless disposal rate of

100%. As of 2021, the classification coverage of domestic wastes in urban areas reached 100%, and the recycling rate of domestic waste exceeded 60%.

C. Promoting resource conservation and intensive utilization

1. Deepening the recycling transformation of parks

The recycling transformation of development zone parks is actively carried out to realize the agglomeration and development of enterprises in the park through industrial transformation and upgrading, rectification of small and scattered hazardous enterprises and transformation of inefficient industrial land; through enterprise technology upgrading, process transformation, strengthening waste recycling, upgrading circular economy technology and equipment, extending circular economy industrial chain, reducing raw material consumption, enhancing the level of material reuse and recycling, raw material cost and energy consumption of enterprise production are greatly reduced, the output of industrial solid wastes continues to decline, the comprehensive utilization level of industrial solid wastes continues to maintain 100%, the output rate of water resources continues to rise, the reuse rate of industrial water reaches over 90% and pollutant emissions are greatly reduced. By 2020, the annual growth rate of industrial solid waste generation intensity in Yongkang City had achieved negative growth. In 2021, the energy consumption per unit GDP of the park was 0.38 tons of standard coal/10,000 yuan, the park achieved zero discharge of solid waste, and the industrial sewage discharge, chemical oxygen demand, ammonia nitrogen and other environmental indicators exceeded the emission reduction indicators issued by the superior.

2. Deepening the evolution in energy consumption

The reform of regional energy assessment is promoted, new high-energy consuming projects are strictly controlled, energy conservation management in key areas and units is strengthened, rectification of the "five furnaces" of highly polluting fuels is comprehensively promoted, and energy consumption per unit of GDP continues to decline. Coal-to-gas conversion work in enterprises is gradually implemented, 80 enterprises have realized coal-to-gas conversion, and the coal-fired boilers in the development zone have been basically eliminated. Rooftop solar distributed power generation is vigorously promoted with a total installed capacity of 20MWp. The *Implementation Plan for Management of Charging Pile Infrastructure for Electric Vehicles in Yongkang City* was issued, and 730 new public (special) charging piles were built. The energy consumption per unit of GDP in Yongkang City dropped to 0.35 tons of coal per 10,000 yuan, which is better than the average level in the province. The coal consumption of enterprises above designated size is 0.04 million tons, a decrease of 158,700 tons compared to 2012, and the coal consumption has decreased significantly; the proportion of clean energy consumption in the city has been increasing year by year. In 2021, the city's energy output rate reached 28.600 yuan/ton of standard coal, which is 1.5 times that of 2012 when circular economy work was launched.

3. Implementing of water conservation actions in high standard

By strengthening the implementation of the *Measures for Planned Water Use of Water Users in Yongkang City*, the allocation and management of water resources is reasonably optimized, the management of car washing industry, bathing industry, swimming pool and other industries are strengthened, and the construction of water-saving society through measures such as construction of water-saving units, water balance testing, cumulative price hikes for over-planned water use, and renovation of water-saving appliances, urban water conservation and emission reduction efforts have been significantly enhanced. 33 provincial-level water-saving enterprises and 15 water-saving units have been established. In 2021, the output rate of water resources reached 450 yuan/ton, 1.6 times higher than that in 2012; the water consumption per unit industrial added value is 0.0007 tons/yuan which is nearly 80% lower than that in 2012.

4. Comprehensive promoting the land conservation and intensive land use

A restraint evaluation mechanism of "hero per mu yield" in the industrial field is established, which rewards "efficient land use" by calculating "account per mu yield", squeezes out "inefficient land occupation" and develops high value-added industries with "space for land" intensive land use to achieve an overall increase in the taxation per mu of industrial enterprises. The *Implementation Opinions on Encouraging Enterprises to Renovate Inefficient Plants to Improve Intensive Land Use* was issued to strengthen the concept of yield per mu and reduce the pressure on the development of model enterprises, and the *Standards for Guiding the Construction of Land Use Planning for Industrial Construction Projects* is resolutely implemented which sets per mu investment bottom line to realize the transformation and upgrading of a large number of low-efficiency enterprises while ensuring intensive land use. Elimination of outdated production capacity is continuously promoted, and the rectification and improvement of "small, low efficiency and poorly managed" small enterprises is accelerated. In 2021, 1,164 "small, low efficiency and poorly managed" enterprises (workshops) were rectified, and 33 enterprises are involved in the elimination of outdated production capacity.

D. Improving the system and mechanism of circular development

1. Strengthening the leading role of digital reform

A zero-waste city management platform is established in Yongkang City which is established simultaneously with the kitchen waste information management platform and kitchen waste account system to realize the management, sharing and supervision of collection and transportation data, and the information management platform conducts unified monitoring and scheduling, command, real-time monitoring of the treatment process, real-time input of materials, sewage, and finished product quantities to realize dynamic management. Collaborative application of precision intelligent control closed-loop supervision for industrial solid waste is established, forming a digital, traceable, early warning, and closed-loop intelligent centralized disposal system for the entire process of industrial solid waste and achieving comprehensive, multi-level, three-dimensional, refined, and intelligent closed-loop monitoring and management of industrial solid waste output, transportation, and disposal.

2. Improving the policy system for circular economy

A national leading group for the creation of a circular economy was set up, a sound target responsibility assessment system for the construction of a circular economy was established, and normative documents such as the *Implementation Opinions on Promoting the Development of Circular Economy in Yongkang City* and the *Implementation Opinions on Strengthening Energy Conservation and Consumption Reduction in the Development of Circular Economy* was introduced. And 13 policy opinions on recycling of renewable resources and classified disposal of garbage were successively issued, providing institutional guarantees for recycling of renewable resources. A series of relevant policies and measures have been formulated, such as upgrading of manufacturing level, cultivation of key enterprises, drive of technological innovation, and green and clean production. A circular economy development index evaluation system is constructed which integrates evaluation, assessment and early warning functions, and scientifically evaluates the level of circular economy development in the city.

3. Improving the green finance system

It is vital to vigorously support the participation of different economic components and investment entities in the development of circular economy in various forms. *Opinions on Establishing Yongkang Industrial Development Guidance Fund* was issued to improve the combination of "five billion" industries and circular economy in financing, reduce the financing difficulty of key industries and operate funds in the modes of sub-fund, direct investment, benefiting equity investment and investment linkage to reduce investment risks. At the same time, relevant policies such as the *Opinions on Promoting the Development of Circular Economy in Yongkang City* and *Guiding Opinions on Intensifying Financial Support to Promote the Development of Circular Economy* (YYF [2014] No. 74) have been issued which further improve and innovate financial services from four aspects: giving play to the guiding role of credit funds, improving the financial service level of circular economy, perfecting the financial service system to support circular economy, building a long-term mechanism for credit supply in circular economy and solidly promoting the "1445" action plan for circular economy.

III. Major Implications

A. Strengthening and consolidating organization, policy, and finance element guarantees

It is essential to establish effective organizational structures such as work leadership groups, set up coordination and cooperation mechanisms among relevant departments such as development and reform, economy and information technology, environmental protection and land, efficiently promote the construction and implementation of circular economy projects and strengthen guidance on industrial transformation and upgrading, energy conservation and emission reduction, and inefficient land use transformation so as to promote efficient cooperation among multiple departments; it is vital to strengthen policy guarantees, carry out top-level design and joint promotion of policy formulation and project planning and introduce a series of policies to promote the development of circular economy to provide policy support for follow-up work and efficient operation of projects; it is important to promote the improvement of the financial service system that supports the development of the circular economy, improve the level of financial services for the circular economy, and continuously innovate financial services.

B. Establishing and improving the circulation chain of parks, industries and enterprises

With the comprehensive utilization of waste resources as the core work, it is vital to focus on improving the efficiency of resource reuse, extending the production chain of enterprise products, creating a circular economy information service platform, promoting the formation of a closed loop of material and energy flow between and within enterprises and building a three-dimensional recycling system at the park, industry and enterprise levels. The steel scrap, cable scrap and parts scrap generated during the manufacturing process must be self-recycled within the enterprise or unified resource utilization by third party resource comprehensive utilization enterprises; it is necessary to encourage enterprises to invest in resource recycling industries and strengthen the recycling and reuse of different types of equipment manufacturing products in the consumer field. In addition, it is important to encourage enterprises to carry out technological innovation, improve processes and update equipment, improve the utilization efficiency of steel, plastic devices, metal copper wires, etc., to reduce material loss, and guide enterprises to develop various efficient, environmentally friendly, and energy-saving products.

C. Building a complete supporting, production, and recycling system

It is essential to improve the infrastructure supporting system, follow the principle of pilot infrastructure in development and construction and ensure the basic realization of "five supplies and one leveling"; it is vital to form the framework for infrastructure construction such as roads, power supply, and water supply; it is key to standardize the cleaner production system, actively promote cleaner production and green enterprise creation in enterprises, cultivate demonstration models, reduce pollutant production from the source through recycling transformation, and promote the development of circular economy by drawing upon the experience gained on key points; it is necessary to innovate the garbage collection system, adopt the method of "government guidance, enterprise payment, and third-party service" and establish a digital, traceable, and closed-loop industrial solid waste processing system throughout the entire process of "classification, recycling, transportation, and terminal disposal".

D. Promoting the realization of smart manufacturing, energy utilization, and industrial efficiency upgrades

It is important to take the promotion of smart manufacturing transformation in traditional industries as the starting point, implement the special action of "machine replacing human", carry out the construction of intelligent unmanned factories (workshops), steadily promote the transformation and upgrading of traditional manufacturing industries, the reduction of energy consumption, waste emission reduction, and cost reduction and efficiency improvement; it is vital to push the upgrading of energy utilization, accelerate distributed photovoltaic power generation projects, improve the utilization rate of clean energy, and promote energy conservation in production through the utilization of geothermal energy; it is necessary to facilitate the technological transformation of clean production in enterprises focusing on energy-saving technological transformation and encourage enterprises to actively implement waste heat and pressure utilization to enhance economic and emission reduction benefits; it is good to promote the upgrading of circular industries, carry out circular transformation of parks and effectively build a circular industrial chain.

E. Developing overall plans to build a supporting platform for science and technology, governance and service

It is essential to establish a technology innovation platform guided by the government and dominated by enterprises, integrate the advantages of the government, research institutes, enterprises, industry associations, professional institutions and other parties, build an information-sharing scientific and technological service platform and comprehensively improve the modern production level of the industry by drawing upon the experience gained on key points; it is vital to build a platform for source remediation, establish a "hero of per mu yield" constraint evaluation mechanism, take modern small and micro enterprise venture parks and ecological parks as platforms for governance of "small and scattered hazardous" enterprises, continue to deeply promote the rectification of "small and scattered hazardous enterprises", effectively crack the land used by "zombie enterprises", dispose of "fenced land" and "inefficient land", make use of land that has been approved but not utilized, and maximize the output rate of industrial land; it is important to build a public service platform, establish multi-functional industrial information service platforms such as talent training, information services, and logistics services, and timely release market, technology, and talent information within the industry based on the actual needs of the industrial park and enterprises to provide information query services for enterprises; it is good to establish and improve government service centers, establish and improve one-stop service windows for project approval and enterprise tax declaration, attract social intermediary agencies, set up professional consulting teams, and provide enterprises with the ability to provide comprehensive services such as technology, economy, talent, policy, and law in a timely manner.

IV. Future Prospects

The history of industrial development in Yongkang is the history of exploration of the development of circular economy. From the practice of traditional hardware techniques going across the country to the current era of big hardware and big data, it has laid a profound foundation for the development of circular economy. Next, Yongkang City will continue to expand and extend

PART THREE   REGIONAL TYPICAL CASES

515

the "Yongkang Model" of circular economy development, explore Yongkang practices, Yongkang City materials and Yongkang City experience for the development of national circular economy, accelerate the establishment of advanced manufacturing bases and realize the transformation from traditional "small hardware" to modern "big hardware" and the iterative leap from "Hardware Capital in China" to "Hardware Capital in the World".

A. Strengthening the organizational leadership and improving the construction of the assessment system

It is important to give full play to the role of the leading group for the creation of a circular economy demonstration county, optimize the business environment and provide good guarantees for the healthy and sustainable development of enterprises. With the experience of demonstration creation, it is vital to do a good job of guiding the direction of enterprise construction and development, improving the assessment and evaluation system for the circular economy, taking the development goals of the circular economy as the basic content and taking economic transformation and upgrading, industrial integration and ecological development as the special evaluation focus to form a multi-level and three-dimensional evaluation system.

B. Strengthening departmental coordination and innovating the incentive and supervision mechanism

It is essential to strengthening cooperation among multiple departments, further clarify requirements for relevant departments, authorities, responsibilities and content and comprehensively improve the establishment of a circular economy development mechanism; it is vital to introduce relevant policy support programs and optimize the scope and intensity of support from the circular economy special development fund; it is important to improve corresponding supervisory local regulations and policies and form measures that encourage and supervise the development of circular economy in parallel; it is good to promote the construction of "Zero-waste Yongkang City" information supervision platform, promote the modernization of the whole category of solid waste governance system and governance capacity and strive to create a "network" for supervision.

C. Strengthening element support and improving technical service platform

It is necessary to further guide and encourage enterprises to intensify development and research of common technologies and key supporting technologies of circular economy and actively introduce and absorb the world's advanced circular economy technologies, strengthen the promotion and application of advanced technologies for the circular economy, and reward the government for innovative achievements; it is essential to optimize and improve the technical consulting service platform, information exchange platform, etc., organize and carry out technical consulting and technology promotion in a timely manner and release information about circular economy technology, management and policies to the society in a timely manner; it is important to explore the establishment of a circular economy expert consultation system and regularly organize experts to guide the circular transformation of parks; accelerate the construction of solid waste disposal terminals, promote the expansion of domestic waste incineration projects and fill the gap in domestic waste disposal capacity; it is vital to improve the disposal and utilization rate of existing perishable waste terminals (urban kitchen waste disposal centers and rural "three modernizations" centers) and reduce the pressure on terminal incineration disposal; it is good to implement the renovation and upgrading project of standardized domestic waste sorting center.

D. Strengthening publicity and education and cultivating and promoting typical models

It is vital to summarize typical experiences in the development of circular economy, promote mature models in the creation of a circular economy in various departments and enterprises through channels such as news and publication, radio, film, and television, and social organizations, lead the development of circular economy through typical demonstrations, further incorporate scientific knowledge and legal knowledge related to circular economy into publicity and education, and use incentives and subsidies to urge enterprises to actively build circular economy. It is essential to strengthen the publicity of relevant laws, regulations, and policies on the collection, transportation and disposal of kitchen waste through multiple channels, strengthen garbage classification training, and actively guide and strengthen supervision so that the majority of kitchen waste-generating units and citizens can deeply understand the importance and urgency of garbage classification and centralized collection, transportation, and disposal of kitchen waste.

Author: Ma Haihua[1]

1 Ma Haihua, director of the Development and Reform Bureau of Yongkang City, Zhejiang Province. He has conducted in-depth research on promoting circular economy and industrial green and low-carbon development and plans to propose and promote the implementation of multiple national and provincial pilot demonstrations in the field of circular economy in Yongkang.

Zhuxiaohui Village as Trailblazer Exemplifying Jiashan County's Effort to Build Eco-green Integrated Development Demonstration Zone in the Yangtze River Delta

Guided by "emission peak and carbon neutrality strategy" in promoting "double demonstration", Jiashan County in Zhejiang Province focuses on green development that highlights zero carbon balance, resource recycling, architectural growth, digital empowerment and science and technology innovation alliance. In this way, Jiashan County has blazed a feasible new path for low-carbon pilot demonstration and high-quality construction, a model that can be replicated and promoted. Through such a collaborative and integrated low-carbon model, Jiashan County aims to build up the Zhuxiaohui Project as a prime example in its effort to forge the eco-green integrated development demonstration zone in the Yangtze River Delta. The Zhuxiaohui Project offers practical experience for us to promote green, low-carbon and high-quality development in pilot zones.

I. Introduction

The county region has long been recognized as the main arena of high-quality economic development and the frontline to explore green and low-carbon transformation of development. With a vital role to play in the pursuit of two national strategies: eco-green integrated development demonstration zone in the Yangtze River Delta and high-quality development demonstration sites at the county level, Jiashan County possesses a strategic political position that provides tremendous momentum. Over the recent years, Jiashan County has taken solid steps toward the national goals of achieving emission peak and

PART THREE REGIONAL TYPICAL CASES

519

carbon neutrality. A distinct Jiashan County model in eco-green development is now taking shape through regional coordination and technological innovation with national strategies as guidance with enterprises as the leading support. Jiashan County has thus won more than 20 provincial and even national awards as an exemplary area for remarkable achievements in ecological progress, low-carbon pilot trials, hydrogen-fueled electric vehicles, and green transportation. As one of the highlights in green development, Jiashan County has pushed forward the construction of Zhuxiaohui sci-tech hub and many other low- or zero-carbon demonstration projects in a coordinated and all-round way, and gradually built a chain of low-carbon demonstration areas including architecture, transportation and energy, and made great efforts to create the first "Real Zero" model in China.

II. Major Practices

A. Building a new zero-carbon model led by the zero-carbon hub

1. Multi energy complementary helps achieve carbon balance

Low-carbonized energy mix is the main approach to carbon reduction in production. The "zero-carbon" hub in Zhuxiaohui Village represents China's first urban organic renewal project of zero-carbon villages, a demonstration project of "low-carbon smart city facilities" across the spectrum, and a project that integrates PEDF (Photovoltaic, Energy storage, Direct current, and Flexibility) into traditional power grid. Zhuxiaohui Village has taken proactive steps to develop wind, geothermal, solar, biomass, hydrogen and other renewable energy sources for multi energy complementary. Consequently, the energy production has far exceeded the energy consumption in the Zhuxiaohui sci-tech hub, thus carbon balance has been achieved. For instance, in the first phase of the project, the annual consumption of 1.18 million kW · h completely comes from electric power and has been offset by the 1.2 million kW · h photovoltaic power generated on the building roof per year, achieving 100% zero-carbon energy consumption in the village. In addition, the total power consumption of electric vehicles in the village—approximately 100,000 kW · h per year—is equivalent to that generated by wind and photovoltaic equipment beyond the roof, therefore, the balance has been maintained between electricity consumption and zero-carbon power production.

Figure 12-1   Aerial view of photovoltaic equipment in the Zhuxiaohui
Village's zero-carbon sci-tech hub

2. Multi Resource Utilization Enables Carbon Cycling

Recycling not only helps save resources, but also contributes to energy saving and carbon reduction. The "zero-carbon" hub in Zhuxiaohui strives for effective resource recycling throughout people's working and living space. Taking architecture as an example, the construction waste originated from demolition will be reused as decoration materials for new buildings. With the distinctive flavor preserved, Jiangnan watertown-styled houses in the village have their white walls topped with gray plates or tiles of photovoltaic panels for solar energy collection. Geothermal energy, which is collected by ground-source heat pumps, can heat and cool. Power generation windmills and other technologies have also been implemented in the hub for supplement to energy through micro-circulation. Apart from architecture, Zhuxiaohui also manages waste in a green way. It fully processes sewage and wastewater through advanced technology before they can be reused or discharged. Kitchen waste in the village is all treated locally through bio-degradation, while other sorts of waste are classified, collected and reused. The data on carbon sink and carbon balance is automatically updated and displayed in a real-time manner to monitor carbon-negative operation across the whole hub.

B. Composing a new ground in green ecology with priority in ecological restoration

1. Enhancing aquatic ecosystem conservation to create world-class waterfront

As a demonstration zone of eco-green integrated development in the Yangtze River Delta, Jiashan County is bound to create a beautiful and pleasant ecological environment, of which aquatic environments constitute an important part. Zhuxiaohui Ecological Island has purified farmland backwater by building ecological ditches and wetlands, to reduce non-point source pollution through ecological buffer zones and to maintain clear water through underwater forest, thus delivering all-round improvement in water quality and ecology. At the same time, the submerged vegetation restoration technology has been adopted, involving a series of steps: accurate zoning, improvement of local conditions, plantation by zone, and routine maintenance. And the complete multi-tiered control and purification technology has been applied to wasterwater, watercourses, and marshlands to technically ensure the survival of submerged vegetation in turbid water and rough waves, effectively reducing the non-point source pollution from agriculture. The water quality in Xiangfudang has reached Class II water quality standard, with over 2 meters deep in water transparency and 70% in the submerged vegetation coverage rate. Thus, initial success has been recognized in achieving harmony between man and nature at the world-class waterfront.

2. Protecting biodiversity to improve freshwater ecosystems

Biodiversity plays a key role in maintaining the capacity of ecosystems, an essential support for carbon sink. Zhuxiaohui Ecological Island is a natural island with a total area of 107 mu (7.13 hectares). As wetlands have been restored through watercourse connection and the combined measures of designating ecological buffer zones, planting underwater forests, and constructing man-made wetland, the trees, shrubs, reeds, grasslands, ponds and shoals on the Island have formed a unique and balanced island ecosystem. With a view to accurately record the number of species and population of flora and fauna, people at Zhuxiaohui have led the way across China in implementing a survey of water ecology and biodiversity in the pilot towns, with monitoring points covering 11 lakes and hundreds of rivers, forming a scientific and complete natural database. Steady improvement has been made based on previous experience in biodiversity protection in Zhuxiaohui and relevant efforts are stepped up from this perspective by strengthening habitat restoration and species cultivation, including the theme activities of attracting fireflies back to their home in Jiashan County.

C. Creating a new engine of eco-green growth drived by the Science and Technology Innovation Alliance

1. Establishing the low-carbon ecological innovation alliance of the Yangtze River Delta that begins with the zero-carbon hub

As an ecological and green integration development demonstration zone in the Yangtze River Delta, Jiashan County enjoys a wide range of scientific and technological innovation forces in the proximity, which underlie the efforts to achieve carbon neutrality. People in Jiashan County are also working hard to become an attraction of such forces, especially those related to green and low-carbon development. Zhuxiaohui Science and Technology Innovation Alliance is home to national scientific research institutes, such as Low Carbon Ecological Research Center of China Eco-city Research Institute, Yangtze River Delta Carbon Peaking and Carbon Neutrality Research Center of Soil and Agricultural Rural Ecological Environment Supervision Technology Center under the Ministry of Ecology and Environment, Science and Technology Innovation Center of Demonstration Zone under Chinese Research Academy of Environmental Sciences, and National Engineering Research Center of Dredging Technology and Equipment. This has positioned Jiashan people well to focus on scientific research and technological innovation in low-carbon and ecology. Besides national organizations, Jiashan County has also been exploring the commercialization and application of innovation outcomes with outstanding enterprises in the Yangtze River Delta, such as Edelman Hydrogen Energy Innovation Center, Jiangsu-based Interfero, and Shanghai-based Urban Construction Group.

Figure 12-2   Aerial view of Zero-carbon Science and Technology
Innovation Hub in Zhuxiaohui Village

2. Enhancing industry-academia-research cooperation in green and low-carbon development, with Xiangfudang Innovation Center as the platform

Close to Zhuxiaohui Village is the R&D Headquarter of Xiangfudang Science and Technology Innovation Green Valley, a platform for sci-tech innovation and commercialization of technological advances in the demonstration zone. It was jointly created by Jiashan County government and some universities in the Yangtze River Delta. With modern research resources channeled through Zhejiang University, Fudan University, and Yangtze Delta Region Institute of Tsinghua University, the Green Valley will be converted into a new powerhouse for sci-tech innovation in the demonstration zone. Fudan-Jiashan Research Institute, Xiangfu Laboratory, and four of the future labs by the Smart Oasis of Zhejiang University all have been put into operation, bringing together first-class R&D teams led by academicians who will offer constructive input on making further cutting-edge scientific and technological advances for the development of the Yangtze River Delta.

Figure 12-3   Utilization of Wind Power and Photovoltaic Energy in Zhuxiaohui Village

D. Exploring a new approach to low-carbon agriculture based on "Smart Field"

1. "Zero direct discharge" helps reduce pollution

Although agriculture does not account for a high proportion of regional carbon emission, there is significant potential for collaborative emission reduction considering its large resource consumption and large pollutant emissions. Zhuxiaohui Smart Field has made itself the first 400-mu low-carbon smart demonstration field in the Yangtze River Delta by introducing digital technology and digital model of plant low-carbon operations from Alibaba Cloud and the China National Rice Research Institute respectively. The demonstration field is a wetland type rice field with a minimum unit of 5 acres equipped with supportive ecological ditches, thus forming a distributed rice ecological environment system. By using growth models and IoT equipment for automatic regulation of field irrigation and drainage, the water level always maintains at the optimal water demand value for different growth cycles of rice. Compared with traditional fields, the demonstration field saves 50% in water usage, and thanks to natural purification of ecological ditches, the nitrogen and phosphorus in the paddy field are reduced by 30%-40%, thus making "zero direct drainage" possible.

2. "Smart Field" helps reduce carbon emission

Smart agriculture is an important way that gives us the scope to explore the possibilities of energy saving and carbon reduction, and to reduce resource consumption and carbon emissions throughout the entire life cycle. Zhuxiaohui "Smart Field" project features intermittent precise irrigation and drainage, Beidou navigation, and green prevention and control, and integrates carbon footprint measurement, carbon-control equipment, and comprehensive carbon reduction. Such technical models have also been adopted as connected thin-spray irrigation, spectral analysis, nano-bubbles, and automatic cruise. This makes it possible to achieve all-round and life-cycle carbon reduction and sequestration. "Smart Field" project is quite a contrast to the traditional mode in that while maintaining the yield, it helps reduce irrigation water, fertilizer, fuel, labour input and carbon emission equivalent per mu by 50%, 15%, 10%, 15% and over 20% respectively, thus achieving win-win results in economic gain, pollution control, and carbon reduction.

E. Fostering a green living culture through synergized collaboration

1. Hydrogen fuel plays a leading role in low-carbon transportation

Hydrogen is an energy carrier that allows to store energy and also a clean, carbonless energy source itself. There are a large number of emerging demonstration industries based on mature hydrogen-related technologies. The inter-provincial bus line from Xitang to Lili in the Yangtze River Delta Demonstration Zone in Jiashan County is the first hydrogen fuel cell-powered public buse in Zhejiang Province. Up to now, 100 hydrogen buses of various types have served in 20 lines, including Shanfeng Line, Xifeng Line and urban-rural buses. The buses have produced cumulative reduction of approximately 3,200 tons of carbon dioxide emission in their 9-million-kilometer mileage. As a demonstration area for the promotion and application of hydrogen-fueled vehicles in Zhejiang Province, Jiashan County government has built three hydrogen refueling stations to create a hydrogen refueling network with a 30-minute drive's radius.

Figure 12-4   Shantong Sinopec hydrogen refueling station in Jiashan
County—first of its kind in Zhejiang Province

2. Low-carbon construction programs target green building standards

The Enterprise Exchange Service Base in the demonstration area has made great efforts to create a three-star green building. Specially designed to project an image of a boat bracing the drizzle, it serves as a digitized place for meeting and exhibition. By three-star green building standards, the building is composed of such low-carbon building technologies as ground-source heat pumps, smart street lamps, and insulating glass. It has become a landmark in the integrated demonstration area that reflects Jiashan people's efforts to practice the philosophy of green, energy saving and sustainability through architecture.

III. Major Implications

As an eco-green integrated development demonstration zone in the Yangtze River Delta and one of the high-quality development demonstration sites at the county level, Jiashan County has long been embraced a green, low-carbon and circular development vision, and has accumulated the following valuable experience that can be replicated and promoted.

A. Creating a zero-carbon demonstration site: zero-carbon, waste-free and growing hub

"Zhuxiaohui zero-carbon model" provides replicable and applicable experience for other places to achieve sustainability. It integrates low- or zero-carbon technology in its green hub to create "zero-carbon, waste-free and growing" models, which highlight eco-green and zero-carbon achievements. The zero-carbon model features multi energy complementary between solar energy, geothermal energy, wind power, and to-be-used hydrogen fuel and biomass energy, achieving "carbon compensation". In the waste-free hub, no waste will be transported outside—waste bricks and tiles are going to be utilized for reconstruction, and sewage disposal system and garbage bio-degradation technology are adopted to reduce water consumption. In the growing model, real-time data monitoring and periodic data assessment of carbon balance are ensured, and technology developments are continuously integrated in the second and third phases of construction to realize zero-carbon operation throughout the entire life cycle.

B. Strengthening green ecological restoration for harmony between man and nature

Guided by the philosophy of respecting, adapting to and protecting nature, it is necessary to coordinate the governance of all elements of the natural ecosystem and promote harmonious coexistence between humans and nature Jiashan County government aims to improve the quality and stability of ecosystems by strengthening ecosystems protection and restoration, tightening supervision of natural ecological spaces, and promoting biodiversity conservation. In the mean time, active steps are taken to push forward the construction of ecological green corridors, such as Wuzi Pond, Taipu River, Hongqi Pond and Zhongxin River, to better link habitat patches in major rivers by connecting Dianshan Lake Ecological Zone with Jiashan main city, thus consolidating the ecological security of the county. In addition, Jianshan County have taken the lead in carrying out the water network renovation of Jiangnan Weitian Exhibition Park, moreover, the construction of buffer zones and forests around the lake, combined with the protection of important natural wetlands such as Changbaidang, Fenhu, and Xiangfudang, plus the construction of wetland parks, help build an integrated ecological green space system spatial structure between urban and rural areas.

528

C. Accelerating green technology innovation to build an industrial system empowered by science and technology advances

Scientific and technological innovation goes a long way toward the goals of achieving emission peak and carbon neutrality. Supported by G60 Science and Technology Innovation Corridor, Shanghai-Chongqing Expressway and Nantong-Suzhou-Jiaxing-Ningbo Expressway, Jiashan County has seized the strategic opportunity of building Shanghai Global Science and Technology Innovation Center to enhance innovation cooperation. Guided by the Xiangfudang Science and Technology Innovation Green Valley, Jiashan County government continues to interact collaboratively with leading universities within China and abroad in scientific and technological innovation as part of its efforts to bring together more innovation drivers by accelerating the construction of innovation powerhouses such as Jiashan-Fudan Research Institute, Shanghai University High-end Equipment Basic Materials Research Institute (Zhejiang), Zhejiang University Yangtze River Delta Smart Oasis, Xiangfu Laboratory. At the same time, by continuously enhancing the attraction for new R&D institutions, capable organizations are encouraged to create provincial-level R&D institutions, key laboratories, manufacturing or industrial innovation centers, etc., in a bid to enhance the strength of the areas where they lead, including integrated circuits, intelligent networked automobiles, and bio-medicine, aiming to create a scientific and technological industry integration development system that involves commercialization and capitalization of technological advances.

D. Promoting the improvement of energy mix for transportation through integrated development of hydrogen fuel

Hydrogen fuel is a zero-carbon energy source that has broadly drawn extensive attention. As a demonstration point for the promotion and application of hydrogen-fueled vehicles in Zhejiang Province, Jiashan County has taken active steps to promote the integrated development of hydrogen-fueled transportation and hydrogen energy industry in pursuit of "emission peak and carbon neutrality" strategy of hydrogen empowerment. The first hydrogen-fueled bus route within the province was launched with a cumulative promotion of 117 hydrogen-fueled buses in service. Jiashan County government has also attempted to attract businesses to build a complete hydrogen energy industrial ecosystem by introducing a package of favorable policies for hydrogen energy, and planning to build a 230-acre hydrogen energy industrial park. Furthermore, to strengthen the leadership of hydrogen energy technology innovation and establish the Jiashan Hydrogen Energy Industry Innovation Alliance, and have held three consecutive China (Jiashan) Hydrogen and Fuel Cell Industry Development and Application Forum.

Figure 12-5   Inter-provincial hydrogen-fueled bus line from Xitang to Lili in Yangtze River Delta Demonstration Zone

IV. Future Prospects

Going forward, Jiashan County will build upon what it has achieved in green and low-carbon development to promote green, low-carbon, high-quality development in pilot zones with practical experience the Zhuxiaohui Project has offered.

A. Achieving complete coverage of clean energy in the pilot zones with Zhuxiaohui zero-carbon hub as an example

To accelerate the full coverage of clean energy in Jiashan County by making the best use of the existing clean energy supply capabilities and networks around the innovation center based on the South and North Xiangfudang, and Chenxiangdang, such as fishing-solar complementary, distributed photovoltaic, and hydrogen energy production. Extensive attention will be diverted to pushing forward integrated construction of highly-elastic power grid in the center and promoting the synergy between source, network and storage, thereby achieving full consumption and efficient utilization of new energy, and building a regional energy network integrating source, network and storage. The projects of clean energy will be promoted, including new energy storage projects, such as "photovoltaic + energy storage" on the user side. Besides, to build inland riverside power and water service areas and establish a clean energy data governance platform, ending up with achieving flexible adjustment and precise control of power. Organic embedding of 5G and digital connectivity genes take the lead in building a regional smart vehicle network and lead to global green and low-carbon transportation within the county.

B. Promoting comprehensive ecological management in the pilot zones with Zhuxiaohui Ecological Island as an example

To accelerate comprehensive eco-green governance in Jiashan County and foster new growth pole and driving force that lead the development of green innovation in the demonstration area. Coordinated efforts will be made to improve ecological protection and build ecological parks. According to the plan, based on construction and operation of Xiangfudang Science and Technology Innovation Green Valley, the quantity and quality of regional ecological conditions and ecosystem services will be comprehensively investigated, and comprehensive improvement project for the water system and the polder area in the Green Valley will be carried out. In a bid to consolidate and improve the quality of water environment, it is necessary to enhance the ecological restoration of water in the whole region, jointly carry out inter-county water body governance, integrate and upgrade the application of intelligent water brain, promote the construction of zero direct sewage discharge area and explore aquatic biodiversity protection. It is expected that the implementation of these measures could help strive to set an example for the pilot zones in the efforts to improve aquatic environments, water resources, and aquatic ecosystems.

C. Promoting the resource recycling in the pilot zones with Zhuxiaohui waste-free hub as an example

In accordance with the concept of full lifecycle management of resource utilization, supported by the improvement of industrial development capacity, the construction of a closed loop of management system for resource recycling is expected to be accelerated, aiming to improve the efficiency and level of resource utilization. To actively promote the significant improvement of the comprehensive utilization level of bulk industrial solid waste in the pilot area, the reduction of solid waste generation intensity, and the sustained and healthy development of the renewable resources industry. To explore the construction of a circular economy trading center based on demonstration zones, serving the Yangtze River Delta and the whole country together with the other two districts, besides, to explore the collaborative creation of demonstration zone vein industrial parks. Complete evaluation and grading standards will also be designed for waste materials, renewable resources, and second-hand equipment and commodities. Then, new ways will be explored to make the best use of solid wastes by encouraging application of advanced technologies and mechanisms to recycling market, such as "internet+ recycling", block chain, and inclusive carbon markets.

D. Promoting the popularization of low-carbon buildings in the pilot zones with Zhuxiaohui growing model as an example

To actively promte the application of PEDF (Photovoltaic, Energy storage, Direct current, and Flexibility) in mansion construction, and explore the application demonstration scenarios of new technologies in emerging directions such as 5G, Internet of Things, big data, and artificial intelligence in building energy-saving operation and maintenance management, intelligent system construction, etc. It is beneficial for further expansion in the monitoring scope and service functions of building energy consumption monitoring platforms by utilizing big data and cloud platform technology. To promote the construction of green ecological park demonstration projects in the demonstration area. Moreover, to actively demonstrate the implementation of technologies such as heat and humidity separation control independent fresh air system, high temperature and efficient end radiation air conditioning system, and high-quality building thermal system with cold and hot bridges. Furthermore, technologies including wind corridor optimization, sponge park, and biodiversity protection will be employed to create a benchmark for comfortable, healthy, low-carbon buildings and parks (communities).

E. Promoting the concentration of green and low-carbon science and technology innovation projects in the pilot zones with Zhuxiaohui Science and Technology Innovation Alliance as a support

The "Big Dipper" world-class innovative lake ecosystem will be vigorously built based on Xiangfudang Science and Technology Innovation Green Valley. Multiple basic and strategic projects for scientific and technological innovation will be launched, while a batch of multi-dimensional platforms will be established for science and technology innovation with strong regional presence and comprehensive influence, forming an innovation force with talents from different echelons. In this way, a galaxy of high-caliber talents will be gathered. The seven-linked innovation chain will be formed: from basic research, technical breakthrough, outcome commercialization and technology financing, to talent-pool building, innovative environment and digital cloud services. It is projected that an innovation mechanism could be upgraded, involving government-industry-academia-research collaboration, financing support, intermediary agents, and end-users to create a world-class scientific and technological innovation powerhouse with international influence and competitiveness.

Author: Ma Ming[1] and Wang Helin[2]

1 Ma Ming, responsible for energy and low-carbon field in the Jiaxing Development Planning Research Institute, senior engineer. He has long been engaged in research and consulting work on green, low-carbon and circular development, climate change response, energy management, etc.

2 Wang Helin, engineer, a researcher in the energy and low-carbon field of the Jiaxing Development Planning Research Institute, engaged in research and consulting work on climate change response, green and low-carbon development, etc.

Fuchunjiang Town is Deeply Committed to Green Development, Striving for New Progress on the Low-Carbon, High-Quality Path to Common Prosperity

Fuchunjiang Town in Tonglu County, Zhejiang Province, is hailed as a place with "the most magnificent scenery ever seen across the country" as an ancient Chinese poem reads. Fuchunjiang Town, a brilliant pearl shining in the necklace of the "Three Rivers and Two Lakes" tourist route, always champions the philosophy of low-carbon development. The town government has proactively explored a low-carbon development model since 2012 when it established the first slow-paced life-experiencing area in the province, a model that integrates natural scenery, cultural heritage, tourism and advanced manufacturing industry. A case in point is a huge green "battery charger" of the pumped storage power station that is under construction. The green development model has empowered Fuchunjiang Town to transform itself from a "firewood seller" to a "scenery provider", from a "manufacturer of cost-inefficient machinery" to one of "cutting-edge equipment", thus setting a good example of how to promote eco-environmental development while stimulating low-carbon industry.

I. Introduction

Fuchunjiang Town is celebrated nationwide as a town with distinctive features, one of the most livable towns, a picturesque town of strategic importance and with the cleanest environment, and a town that serves as a nation-level hydropower equipment manufacturing base. It lies as a brilliant pearl shining in the "Three Rivers and Two Lakes" tourist route (Qiantang River, Fuchun River, Xin'anjiang River, West Lake, and Qiandao Lake). In 2022, the town government started the construction of the giant "battery charger"—a pumped storage hydropower station of billion-scale capacity, marking another milestone in its green, low-carbon development. Based on the belief in "green and low-carbon development with system integration", Fuchunjiang Town's new model of low-carbon development for achieving common prosperity has taken shape.

Figure 13-1   Groundbreaking ceremony of the billion-scale pumped storage power station

Figure 13-2   Panorama of Luciwan Scenic Spot

II. Consolidating Ecological Resource Base

A. Hydropower Stations above the Extensive River System

Nine rivers running through the town seat, including Fuchun River, Qingzhu River and Luci Creek, with a total stretch of 74.2 kilometers, provide abundant hydropower for Fuchunjiang Town. This put the town in a favorable position to build a number of hydropower stations. One of them is Fuchunjiang Hydropower Station, a riverbed power station with low head and large flow, built at the exit of Qililong Gorge. The Station controls a drainage basin of 31,300 square kilometers, with a total storage capacity of 874 million cubic meters and an installed capacity of 297,200 kilowatts. It brings comprehensive economic benefits through flood control, disaster reduction, shipping, irrigation, aquatic products and urban water supply. There are also some hydropower stations built along Luci Creek and other streams. Other ten small hydropower stations are founded in the eastern mountainous area of Fuchunjiang Town, including Longmen Reservoir Power Station, Guanli Power Station, Nanhukou Power

Station and Baiyunyuan Power Station, with an installed capacity of 6,035 kilowatts.

Figure 13-3   Scenery of Luci Creek

Figure 13-4   Fuchunjiang Hydropower Station Dam

B. A Wide Range of Agricultural Products and High Percent of Forest Coverage

The fertile soil and favorable ecological conditions are perfect for the growth of timber forests, bamboo, and economic forests, with abundant, high-quality natural resources to access, including wood, bamboo, tea, fruits, and vegetables. A range of rugged, thickly forested mountains with towering peaks is home to a wide variety of forest vegetation, such as coniferous forests, mixed coniferous forests, and economic forests. The town has a forestry land of 245,000 mu, an ecological public welfare forest of about 190,000 mu, and a forest stock of 880,000 cubic meters, with a forest coverage rate as high as 83%.

Figure 13-5   Villagers in Dazhuang She Ethnic Group Picking Chrysanthemum Morifolium in the Mountain

Figure 13-6   Aerial Photo of Fuchunjiang Greenway

C. Excellent Air Quality and High Biodiversity

Fuchunjiang Town offers beautiful scenery and a high-quality natural ecological environment. Its Luci Slow-paced Life Experiencing Area is well-known as a natural oxygen bar with an average negative oxygen ion per cubic centimeter of over 10,000, its air quality reaches China's highest standard. At the same time, Fuchunjiang Town has further promoted aquatic environment management, the river chief system and comprehensive environmental improvement, and continuously strengthened ecological environment protection. Through such efforts, it has effectively protected and restored the rivers and lakes and achieved continuous improvement in the ecological environment. The ever-better natural environment in Fuchunjiang Town leads to the increase of vegetation, which has provided a good habitat for wild animals—even such rare species as the Tianmu Sharp-nosed Frog (Odorrana tianmuii), peach jellyfish and Chinese giant salamander have often appeared or even settled down there.

Figure 13-7   "Natural Oxygen Bar" in Slow-paced Life Experiencing Area

Figure 13-8   A stranded Chinese giant salamander being released in Baiyunyuan Scenic Spot

III. Development of Scenic Industry Clusters

A. Promoting the Development of Low-carbon Homestay Clusters Based on Local Landscape

Firstly, strengthening infrastructure development. Nine projects have been initiated, including comprehensive management of Qingzhu River Basin, renovation of small and micro water bodies, improvement of the environment along roads in Fuchunjiang Town, enhanced management of rural domestic sewage, renovation, and construction of garbage transfer stations, etc., with a total investment of 677 million yuan. This helps strengthen water ecological protection and restoration and continuously improve the ecological environment. Meanwhile, the projects of Fuchun Greenway Construction and Baiyunyuan Inter-connected Landscape Improvement are carried out, with a total investment of 49.59 million yuan.

Secondly, pursuing all-directional integration of "low-carbon" elements into cultural tourism. Qinglongwu has attracted 11 high-end B&B brands to operate there, including Fengyuzhu Hostel, Kaiman Shanye Hostel, Tianfang Yetan Hostel, Jinglu Lanshan Hostel, and Xishan Shendu Hostel. The brand effect and economic benefits of Qinglongwu are becoming increasingly prominent so the high-end low-carbon B&B cluster there has made the area known across the country. Since 2016, Fuchunjiang Town has cooperated with Shanghai Tourism Company to promote the "through train" scheme in Shanghai, which means a low-carbon tourism service network has taken shape that incorporates the major rural tourist attractions in the whole town with the slow-paced life-experiencing area as the core. Going forward, it will be built into a high-end low-carbon art industry cluster. Up to now, the through-train project has increased the villagers' income by more than 900,000 yuan in total. In 2020, four distinctive business projects were invested there, including Qingyu Liang (Phase II in Yuanxiang) and Zhenshan Xigu Hostel, with a capital of 45 million yuan; and such projects as Yanlingwu Slow-paced Village Phase I, Yunwai Hostel, Minghuai Shuyuan Hostel, Yinyi Yoga Phase III, and Shishe Xiangzhang Café were completed. In the year 2020 alone, 7 B&Bs and 40 businesses started there. Luci Village has its application granted for the pilot scenic village for the five-year plan of Zhejiang Province aimed at "minor adaptation for notable promotion" in tourism. Thus, Luci Village is the only pilot scenic village across Hangzhou City.

Figure 13-9　High-end B&B in Luci Village

B. Exploiting the development strengths of low-carbon agriculture based on agricultural resources

Firstly, incorporating green elements into strong agriculture industries. Efforts are concentrated on the development of black tea, fruits, Chinese herbal medicines, and breeding pigs. The local brand of "Luci Red" has been created; distinctive agricultural bases are formed, such as the dendrobium candidum base in Yanling, forest-dependent industries in Lidong, the chrysanthemum morifolium base in Dazhuang, and the rice-turtle co-cultivation base in Shangsi; and Xiangshanqiao Breeding Pig Center is upgraded. Vigorous action is taken to develop the property-management economy; 10 low-carbon workshops are set up for villagers' income increase, such as Duzhou Tongxing in Duji Village, and Xile Qiaoshou in Dazhuang Village. Work are accelerated to create a new model of "one strong industry for each village," and "one competitive product for each village", so as to promote the modernization of traditional agriculture, and stimulate the development of agricultural industries with local advantages.

Secondly, upgrading rural village life. Guided by the vision to build powerful villages, livable villages, clean and beautiful villages, culturally advanced villages, and dynamic villages, we have taken the lead in the province in building the first operating room, and the first intelligent management platform of the "Smart B&B System". It is designed to help facilitate industrial transformation, service upgrading, and rural governance with digital theories, technologies, and approaches. We have made steady progress in developing modernized agriculture. In 2021, we built 1,000 mu of high-standard farmland and upgraded and transformed 300 mu of farmland; this effort has led to the improvement of agriculture in both quality and efficiency. Fuchunjiang Town has devoted time and energy to exploring and practicing new business forms of "achieving both rural revitalization and dual carbon vision", and has been committed to promoting the integrated development of modern technology and the natural environment. Based on the achievements in "dual carbon" reduction and green building technology advances, we will work on energy conservation, environmental protection, humanistic care, and efficient use of space to create a low-carbon development model that integrates agriculture, culture, and tourism, and promote rural revitalization with digital and smart technologies.

Thirdly, promoting the industrial model that connects enterprises, bases, and farmers. Further efforts are made to develop profitable agricultural bases of vegetables, fruits, Chinese herbal medicines, breeding, seedlings, and tea. We have pushed forward efficient transformation of livestock manure into resources, and utilization of by-products in agricultural produce processing. We have reduced greenhouse gas emissions from livestock manure. We have taken steps to replace chemical fertilizer with organic fertilizer by intensifying efforts to promote commercial organic fertilizer. We have coordinated prevention and control efforts in eco-green protection. We have improved the soil testing and formulated fertilization methods and comprehensively reduced the fertilizer and agricultural chemicals. We have taken comprehensive steps to expand the overall agricultural production capacity, cut greenhouse gas emissions, and improve the carbon sequestration in farmland soil. In this way, we will accelerate the transformation of traditional agriculture into efficient, ecological, and modern agriculture, and improve the comprehensive production capacity and industrialization level, so as to sustain economic growth in rural areas.

Figure 13-10   Conference on Digitalized Village and Smart B&B System

C. Accelerating industrial transformation and upgrading based on a livable environment

Firstly, improving the configuration of carbon productivity. With its favorable natural environment, Fuchunjiang Town has attracted more low-carbon life enterprises, worthwhile projects, and companies with great potential. Therefore, we have doubled our industrial output value, with the output value of 1.59 billion yuan coming from high-tech companies with annual revenue of 20 million yuan, whose contribution has risen from 35% to 48%. In 2021, we developed two municipality-level "future factories". Meanwhile, the livable environment creates pressure for backward industrial enterprises to speed up rectification. We have made great efforts to enhance industry quality, improve its efficiency, and resolutely shut down local enterprises with high energy consumption, heavy pollution, serious workplace safety risks, and low output, or those that go against the general trend. During the "Thirteenth Five-Year Plan" and in 2021, a total of 78 "small-scattered-slow" businesses (small, scattered businesses that were slow to adopt new technology) were shut down, and nearly 50 mu of industrial space was vacated in 2021 alone, thus effectively promoting low-carbon development. At the same time, we have stepped up efforts to make good use of idle industrial land, with enterprises playing the leading role. We have taken bold steps to expropriate contiguous industrial plots that house "small-scattered-slow" businesses. During the "Thirteenth Five-Year Plan" and in 2021, we put a total of 1,500 mu of idle land to good use.

Secondly, creating a high-end equipment manufacturing cluster of "Thousand-mu Land with Ten Billion Investment". Fuchunjiang Town has accelerated the planning of gradient industrial development, promoted the strategic adjustment of industrial structure, implemented the industrial cluster strategy, and pressed ahead with the construction of the second phase of the equipment manufacturing industrial park. By connecting the first phase of the industrial park and Zhuangtou Industrial Park, we will build the second phase of the 610-mu equipment manufacturing industrial park. With the first phase of the 870-mu industrial park lying in the north and the 320-mu Zhuangtou Industrial Park in the south, the whole area will be built into a 1,800-mu high-end equipment manufacturing industry cluster.

Figure 13-11　Rendered Image of High-end Equipment Manufacturing Industrial Park

IV. Promoting Common Prosperity

A. Shaping rural landscapes to enable transformation into a beautiful countryside

Sitting at a crucial junction of the golden cruise routes along the "Three Rivers and Their Banks" (Xin'an River, Fuchun River, Qiantang River, and the landscape along the banks), the Fuchunjiang Town government has made constant efforts to upgrade its public facilities, improve its natural environment, and increase the town's cultural vitality. It has made itself an AAAA scenic town and a provincial-level beautiful town with local industrial advantages.

Based on Fuchun rural landscape and culture and with the underlying theme of slowing-living in mountain retreats, Fuchunjiang Town is constantly building the Fuchun Slow-living Area into an area integrating "rustic vacation, cultural experience, outdoor sports, Arcadian life, and art creation"; and "Fuchun Slow Living County" was successfully established in 2022. Four serene scenes and 25 idyllic spots have been constructed along the Malin Ancient Road, the spots including Easy Fuchunjiang, Luci Resort, Artistic Qinglongwu, Homely Maoping, and Futuristic Shishe, all of which speak volumes about the rural charm of Fuchunjiang Town. Based on this, we will strive to build more models that will reflect Fuchun rural culture and make Fuchunjiang Town the epitome of promoting rural revitalization through art and literature.

B. Working to popularize low-carbon science as part of efforts to promote green living

We have taken the occasion of such important celebrations as World Environment Day and National Low-carbon Day to conduct massive campaigns to publicize green and low-carbon lifestyles. We have provided more effective mechanisms for public participation, and diversified the forms and ways thereof, in a bid to enhance citizens' low-carbon attitude and awareness and motivate them to play their part. With Slow-paced Life Experiencing Area as the main platform, we held "New Village Late-night Talk", Slow-paced Life Experiencing Festival, Qinglongwu International Music Festival, Summertime Fairs and other world-known activities to foster people's low-carbon awareness in consumption and their behaviors in minimizing carbon emission in their cultural lives and daily routines and help people relate to the philosophy of low-carbon development. At the same time, we also carried out high-end cultural programs such as the Philosopher Forum and Fuchunjiang Poetry and Culture Seminar, as part of efforts to create a place of culture that appeals to all ages and social groups. In this way, we will better project an image of a place with distinctive local culture, and blaze a new trail that features creative low-carbon development with Fuchunjiang characteristics.

Figure 13-12   New Village Late-night Talk

Figure 13-13   Qinglongwu International Music Festival

Figure 13-14   Fuchunjiang Poetry Talent Comtest

C. Pooling efforts and ideas from local talents to facilitate low-carbon industries' development

We still have a long way to go in achieving the goal of "carbon neutrality and carbon peak". Against such a backdrop, we have to make the best use of talents, who serve as the cornerstone of the rapid and healthy development of low-carbon industries. Fuchunjiang Town government has worked actively to discover and make the most of local talents. We have focused on the introduction, training, management, and use of human resources and tried to fully unlock their potential in new contexts. We have made continuous efforts to discover, introduce, and train more home-grown talents, either young or old, established or emerging. We have expedited the actual implementation of the management mechanism of Local Talents' Association, and tried our best to stimulate their creative energy. We keep exploring new ways of applying local talents' wisdom to low-carbon development mode by encouraging them to harness their advantages to foster village development, play a proactive role in village-level governance, and guide the transformation and upgrading of local industries and help with their energy consumption reduction. We have made full use of local talent's advantages in resources, interpersonal networks, and capital to attract projects, investment, information, technical assistance, and talents back to our town, thus creating a favorable low-carbon development trend. Local talents are also invited to attend "Villager Get-together" and "Villager Confabulation", where they will offer their constructive input on the development of industries with Fuchunjiang characteristics. With a large number of young talents attracted back to join us, we will pool their wisdom and strength for our low-carbon development in Fuchunjiang Town.

Figure 13-15　Local Talents at Seminar on Low-carbon Development for Common Prosperity

Figure 13-16　Group Photo of Local Talents in Fuchunjiang Town

V. Major Implications and Future Prospects

High-quality environmental resources help translate "lucid waters and lush mountains" into "invaluable assets". Only by making the most efficient use of these available resources will they be turned into new dynamism of high-quality development. Fuchunjiang Town government vigorously pushes forward the low-carbon development of eco-friendly rural industries and green life for the good of the natural environment, thus achieving the balance between the development of a sound environment, profitable industries, and better life, with a sound environment as a support to bring prosperity to all. We must be committed to a green, low-carbon path in every stage and aspect of development, including overall planning, design, construction, production, and daily life. We will make sure that economic growth is resource-efficient and environment friendly with low-carbon emissions by adopting a holistic approach to high-quality development and maximum environmental protection, in order to build a model town in the demonstration zone of common prosperity and to write a magnificent chapter in the development of Fuchunjiang Town in the new era. In the process of translating ecological strengths into economic gains, the tourism industry in Fuchunjiang Town generated 155 million yuan in 2022 from 1.1 million tourists, and the average per capita annual income of the villagers exceeded 100,000 yuan.

Looking ahead, Fuchunjiang Town government will step up its efforts to further improve the mechanism for the commercialization of ecological products by focusing on the available low-carbon and environmental resources and fully tapping their economic potential. We must uphold and act on the principle that lucid waters and lush mountains are invaluable assets on our path to common prosperity so that our assets will be able to increase in tandem with environmental benefits and more progress will be achieved in bringing prosperity to all.

Author: Wang Xueqing[1], Han Daqing[2], Zhou Yun[3]

---

1 Wang Xueqing, Communist Party member, Master of Engineering in Ecology and Environment, is currently the deputy mayor of Fuchunjiang Town People's Government, responsible for ecological environment, tourism, homestay, service industry economy, slow living experience zones, low-carbon rural construction, etc.

2 Han Daqing, Communist Party member, Bachelor of Engineering from Zhejiang University, hydraulic engineer, a member of Tonglu County Writers Association, and now the Director of Comprehensive Office of Fuchunjiang Town, Tonglu County.

3 Zhou Yun, Communist Party member, Bachelor of Management from Tianjin University of Urban Construction, social worker, is currently the first-level clerk of the Environmental and Tourism Office in Fuchunjiang Town, Tonglu County.

Ecological Restoration of Xiazhu Lake Wetland: Province-first Ecological Compensation Mechanism for Wetland Carbon Sinks

In Xiazhu Lake Wetland, the recent efforts have been focused on building it into a national wetland park and a 5A-level scenic spot through ecological restoration and biodiversity protection, with crested ibises—China's national treasure—as one of the symbolic species at Xiazhu Lake. In 2022, based on the pilot base of forestry carbon sinks, among the first batch in the province and the only one across the city, we launched the eco-compensation mechanism of wetland carbon sink trading, which has been piloted in green financing, judicial restoration and ecological prosperity. This has delivered a win-win result of the enhanced ecological function of wetlands, thriving ecological economy, and expanding ecological transformation.

I. Introduction

Xiazhu Lake National Wetland Park is located in southern Huzhou of Zhejiang Province, where the principle "lucid waters and lush mountains are invaluable assets" was proposed. The Lake is adjacent to Hangzhou and jurisdictionally belongs to the Xiazhuhu Community of Deqing County. It is a national wetland park, 4A-level scenic spot, and provincial-level tourist resort that spans 36 square kilometers, with the main lake covering about 1.26 square kilometers in the entire 3.4-square-kilometer water area. As a typical natural lake wetland with diverse landscapes, Xiazhu Lake Wetland Park is the largest one of its kind in the south of the Yangtze River that has more than 1,000 branches and 600 mounds, thus forming a special water landscape with mounds (islands) dotted in the lake crisscrossed by branches. Xiazhu Lake Wetland also boasts well-conserved biodiversity. In 2004, a national-level site was established for the protection of wild soybean original habitats; in 2008, the crested ibis ex-situ conservation base and Zhejiang species rebuilding base were established, where more than 800 species of animals and plants are thriving here. Such achievements in its protection project have won the Xiazhu Lake Wetland Park a national award in 2014 for its distinguished contribution to improving living environments.

Figure 14-1   Xiazhu Lake Wetland Landscape

II. Historical Background of Xiazhu Lake Wetland Restoration

Xiazhu Lake used to be a garbage lake and large aquaculture farm miserably fraught with serious problems:

The water hyacinth was raging out of control across the lake, the cage culture sprawled along the side of the lake, and the water body got seriously eutrophic thanks to the aquatic bait, the domestic sewage from farmhouses, and the wastewater produced in inner-pond aquaculture. Before 2014, Xiazhu Lake was classified as Class IV water body by China's Environmental Quality Standards for Surface Water, with 1/4 water area covered with water hyacinths, 1/3 left for cage culture and freshwater pearl farming, and inflow of domestic sewage from 105 households nearby. At that time, wastewater from highly-polluting aquaculture, livestock and poultry (including pigs, chickens, and ducks) breeding, and greenhouses turtle breeding on both sides of the tributaries all sluiced straight into the lake, and domestic sewage from seven surrounding villages were also discharged into the lake without being processed.

Table 14-1　Xiazhu Lake Water Quality Classification
(Municipal Water Quality Monitoring Section)

Years	2013	2014	2015	2016	2017	2018	2019	2020
Annual average water quality category	IV	IV	III	III	III	II	II	II

(Data source: Deqing County Environmental Protection Monitoring Station)

Before restoration, branches were blocked due to silt accumulated in wetlands and tributaries; no pier was built on either side, leading to serious soil erosion and ineffective flood control. There were frequent occurrences of farmers encroaching on public water areas by making private ponds in the lake for aquaculture, with the size of the wetland reduced below the redline by 500 mu, because of which the wetland was incapacitated from flood storage and drought prevention.

The environmental disturbances and damages made by humans like these resulted in biodiversity loss of aquatic wildlife and birds and a decline in fish biodiversity in the lake. Some native water quality-sensitive animals and plants, such as pomfret, bream, homespun fish, and freshwater snails, were hard to see.

III. Restoration Measures for Xiazhu Lake Wetland

Since the end of 2013, the CPC Zhejiang Provincial Committee and the provincial government have implemented the "Co-governance of Five Waters" strategy, which refers to wastewater treatment, floodwater prevention, water drainage, water supply protection, and water conservation. People at Xiazhu Lake Wetland Park have worked actively to restore and preserve the ecological wetland environment by prioritizing environmental protection and strengthening source-targeted environmental governance based on scientific approaches for sustainable development.

Figure 14-2   Wetland Restoration in Xiazhu Lake

A. Stopping Aquaculture and Animal Husbandry Beyond the Redline

The local authorities promulgated Master Plan on Xiazhu Lake Scenic Area and the Master Plan for Xiazhu Lake National Wetland Park, which designate five specific zones respectively for wetland ecological conservation, restoration, outreach, utilization, and management, and define the goal of raising the percentage of lake area covered by a wetland to 59.86%. In the implementation of the plans, the relevant authorities have stopped all aquaculture operations beyond the redline, including 950 mu of pearl farming in streams, watercourses, or tributaries, 230 pig farms with a total of 50,000 pigs, 93 duck and other poultry farms with a total stock of 180,000, and 12 greenhouse turtle breeding sheds covering about 90,000 square meters. Today, Xiazhu Lake is free from livestock, turtle, pearl farming, or any other forms of animal husbandry. the relevant authorities have stopped purse seining cultivation in the wetland, prohibited the use of net sets of 160,000 square meters, and reclaimed surface use rights of 2,427mu state-owned water areas. In order to completely stop domestic sewage discharge from nearby farmhouses, the relevant authorities have relocated a village with 105 households as a whole.

B. Mobilizing Concerted Effort for Tail Water Control in Fishery Farming

For green, sustainable development of the fishery, Xiazhu Lake Community launched a massive operation in 2016 for tailwater management in fishery farming, and started a long-term regulatory regime. The relevant authorities advocated "Four Ponds plus a Dam" tail water purification mode for fishing farms that involves a sedimentation pond, an aeration pond, a biological purification pond, a wetland cleaning pond, and a filter dam, with the villages playing the leading role in the region-specific management mechanism. In addition, the intelligent real-time system enabled whole-process monitoring of aquaculture tailwater. So far, 43 tailwater management sites have been set up across the community that fully cover the about 10,000mu culture water of freshwater prawn farming. We properly addressed rural domestic sewage treatment by comprehensively promoting the "one-pipe-for-all" approach, through which wastewater from the toilet, kitchen, washing pool and showering room would be discharged from the same pipe. We adopted the "five-in-one" mode in which the county government does assessment, the community exercises supervision, the village provides facility management, farmers play their part, and enterprises ensure effective operations, thus making the sewage treatment procedure-based, specialized and consistently effective. All domestic sewage in six villages around the lake has been well managed, delivering benefits to 10,432 farmers. We effectively ensured a clean environment by carrying out a new integrated management mode for a clean environment in downtown, towns, villages and highways and waterways. Through resource integration, we concentrated the scattered responsibility for environmental cleaning on the urban management department, and ensured all of domestic garbage in urban and rural areas were gathered and processed in an eco-friendly way, an achievement that not only facilitates clean-up efforts, but also helps create a clean, pleasant rural environment.

C. Adopting the Groundbreaking "Underwater Forest" Model for Aquatic Ecological Restoration

Besides continuous efforts to increase water quality, we have also worked consistently to restore aquatic environment in the Xiazhu Lake and pioneered the water ecological restoration with the "underwater forest" mode. This mode features a stable aquatic eco-system that enables self-purification processes and water quality improvement. Based on submerged plants, the eco-system consists of emergent and floating plants, aquatic animals and various beneficial microorganisms, which together form the ecological landscape of "underwater forest". Up to now, an "underwater forest" of 100,000 square meters has been built along the lake. Testing data show that all pollutant indicators have significantly reduced, and water transparency also increased. The main indicators all reached Class III by the Surface Water Quality Standards, and even Class II in some periods, and the water body and surrounding landscape also greatly improved. In order to replenish and restore aquatic life population and control algal blooms to improve aquatic environment, we at Xiazhu Lake has made consistent efforts on fish reproduction and release. Recent years has seen 70 million fish released into the lake, including softshell turtle, silver carp, bighead carp and grass carp.

D. Carrying out Comprehensive Watershed Stewardship for Small- and Medium-sized River Basins

We at the Xiazhu Lake carried out a comprehensive management project of 47 million yuan for small- and medium-sized watersheds to enhance flood control capacity in the wetland. We connected water networks, dredged up to 710,000 cubic meters, enriched ecological revetment of 22.8 kilometers (including 1.34 kilometers of tree revetment), undertook ecological restoration, repaired dams, upgraded hydrophilic facilities and created scenic spots, protecting and improving 39 waterways of totally 42.8 kilometers around the Xiazhu Lake.

E. Establishing Ecological Compensation Mechanism

In order to raise local farmers' environmental awareness, we at Xiazhu Lake has established an ecological compensation mechanism, which annually brings more than 7 million yuan as ecological compensation to relevant villages. We also took the lead in China in conducting the "river and lake health assessment" for 60 water bodies around the Xiazhu Lake, with 18 indicators in six categories, namely general situation, hydrology, water quality, aquatic eco-system, routine management, and past problems. The experience gained from such "assessment" has been promoted throughout the province. We have adopted "eco-green currency" mechanism, a specialized fund of 1.34 million yuan so far, to reward individuals or social groups for their outstanding contributions to environmental protection in water management or conservation, thus motivating the public to take initiative to safeguard the aquatic environment. We have applied digital technology to water management through "public platform for water conservation" that was built upon the province-leading "water protection e-station". This represented part of our efforts to break new ways in environmental protection and to promote the valuable experience and good practices in the "Co-governance of Five Waters". "Intelligent Monitoring Platform for Garbage Classification" is another advance in digitalized management, which records and evaluates residents' participation and accuracy rate in garbage classification with a microchip scanner. We applied a "smart screen" to village management, which displays real-time dynamics in production, daily life and ecology, and retrieves data on environmental improvement and garbage classification from video detection and "co-governance of five waters" system. The data sharing has made digitalized management possible. We made efforts to ensure "community-level river chiefs" properly perform their duties, which are summarized into "five steps", including observing water quality, checking necessary signs, patrolling, visiting and enquiring residents, identifying and rectifying problems. In the implementation of the river chief system, the chiefs are supposed to stay engaged with local residents and their communities, improve communication and outreach, seek their complaints, inputs and feedbacks, and address relevant problems with dispatch.

F. Carrying out Wetland Carbon Sink Pilot

At the beginning of 2022, Xiazhuhu Community was designated as the first batch of low (zero) carbon townships (communities) in Zhejiang Province by the provincial leading group for double-carbon work, and Xiazhuhu Wetland was included in the first batch of forestry carbon sinks in the province and the only one in Huzhou City. Preliminary calculation shows that the net carbon sequestration of Xiazhuhu Community in 2021 reached 17,000 tons, a number that will rise to 30,000 tons annually by 2025 from wetland carbon sinks. Totally 2,250mu wetland vegetation has been restored, and new varieties of vegetation and cutting-edge technologies for improving carbon sequestration and increasing carbon sinks have been applied to more than 2,960mu water areas, which has brought about remarkable environmental benefits.

Figure 14-3　The first wetland carbon sink ecological
compensation transaction in the whole province

In April, 2022, among the first batch of pilot forest carbon sinks in the province and as the only one in the city, Xiazhu Lake Wetland traded 10,000 tons of wetland carbon sinks valued at 588,000 yuan through Liangshan Cooperative, and sold them to Deqing Rural Commercial Bank and other five financial institutions and to three industrial enterprises including Qingchunbao. This helped promote some financial institutions and enterprises to take initiative in purchasing carbon offsets for low- or zero-carbon operations.

The ecological compensation model of wetland carbon sinks, since its introduction, has been listed among the first batch of typical cases of ecological progress reform in Huzhou, and been emphasized in Xiazhu Lake Wetland protection case taken by the Sino-British Green Financing Project. At present, financial institutions across Deqing County have issued 487 loans related to wetland carbon sequestration and biodiversity protection in Xiazhu Lake and its surrounding areas, with an amount of 1.274 billion yuan.

In establishing a closed-loop system of wetland carbon finance, Deqing Sub-branch of Huzhou Bank launched the nationwide first loan for wetland carbon sinks in Xiazhu Lake. Deqing Rural Commercial Bank has identified new ways of commercializing environmental resources and developing better ecological products by adopting a "PTD" closed-loop fund supporting system that involves carbon capture "production", carbon "transaction" and enterprises' "demands"). The Bank has issued 382 wetland carbon sink loans with an amount of 467 million yuan.

In pushing for ecological compensation to offset natural values elsewhere, the People's Court of Nantaihu New District, which takes charge of ecological environment cases across the city, has established an "ecological restoration base for wetland carbon sinks" for ecological compensation in Xiazhuhu Lake. Through the base, the Court will earmark the compensations in ecological damage cases across the city for wetland biodiversity protection, ecosystem protection and restoration, comprehensive wetland management, and aquatic environment restoration in Xiazhu Lake. As of now, 2.29 million yuan in three sums for restoration have been allotted.

In launching new products of carbon sinks for co-prosperity, Deqing Sub-branch of Huzhou Bank developed and launched the nationwide first wetland carbon sink loan, through which the Bank will provide farmers with exclusive credit allowance and preferential interest rates according to their wetland carbon sinks. This is part of our efforts to forge a new path to integrate green financial support into wetland ecological restoration and biodiversity protection.

In arranging insurance for wetland carbon sequestration, we have facilitated the process for Ping An Property Insurance Huzhou Branch to pilot commercial wetland carbon sinks insurance in Xiazhu Lake, with Deqing County Natural Resources Asset Management Co., Ltd. as the owner. The insured are the farmers living off the wetland, and the organizations engaged in wetland production and operation and carbon sinks. In case of any risk to carbon sink loss of wetland plants in Xiazhu Lake Wetland, the insurer shall pay compensation in accordance with the signed contract. The first premium of such an insurance is 0.5 million yuan, with the insured value of 130 million yuan.

IV. Achievements in Wetland Restoration and Protection in Xiazhu Lake and Future Measures

A. Enhanced Ecological Function

Great improvement has been seen in the landscape, ecosystem, biodiversity and flood control and drainage capacity, which allows Xiazhu Lake Wetland to play a better role as the planet's "green kidney". The water quality stays at Class II or Class III, and the biodiversity remains well preserved, with more than 800 rare animals and plants thriving here. Crested ibises, dubbed "the Oriental Gem", ten percent of whose population around the world has settled down in Xiazhu Lake, have been returned to nature there and reproduced to the third generation in the wild. This has made Xiazhu Lake known as the crested ibis ex situ conservation base and Zhejiang species rebuilding base, and has earned it the honorary title of "China's most beautiful wetland".

B. Thriving Ecological Economy

Based on the "underwater forest", a "Lakeside Natural Forest" night market was established at Erdu Town near Xiazhu Lake, and tourist arrivals tripled year-on-year, which has brought about more sales of agricultural products and spurred the development of local hotel and catering industries. The enabling environment for freshwater prawns in Xiazhu Lake Community has put it in a good position to create new forms of business and extend the industrial chain, which has helped increase the villagers' income and won it the reputation of "Land of Prawns in China". Thanks to its valuable environmental resources, Xiazhu Lake has become an important destination for tourism and leisure in the Yangtze River Delta. With 1.2 million tourist arrivals every year, Xiazhu Lake Wetland Park is rated as one of the 50 most worthwhile scenic spots in Zhejiang Province.

C. Improved Ecological Mechanism

We at Xiazhu Lake took the lead in establishing the aquaculture tail water management mode ("Four ponds plus three or two dams" mode), which was recognized by the Party chiefs of the CPC Zhejiang Provincial Committee and thus got promoted throughout the province. And we first created the eco-green currency mechanism, the river and lake health assessment mechanism, the "Nine-pronged Management Approaches for Small- and Micro-sized Waters", digitalized water management, Water Management Hands-on Experiencing Center and other trailblazing contributions, which were recognized by the

National People's Congress in their field trips.

D. Continued Commercialization of Environmental Resources

Based on its abundant cultural tourism resources and relevant favorable conditions, we at Xiazhu Lake worked actively to promote the commercialization of environmental resources in more scenarios. For example, based on legends of Fangfeng (a primeval Chinese water management hero) we launched the Fangfeng Cultural Festival, which was listed as a national intangible cultural heritage. An annual event of Cross-country Survival Challenge is co-organized in Xiazhu Lake Wetland by the National Wetland Protection and Management Center, Zhejiang Provincial Forestry Department and Zhejiang Sports Federation. In addition, a folk activity of "Fish and Rice Soup Tasting" is held every winter in Xiazhu Lake, which once attracted 3,187 participants and made it a Guinness record holder—the worldwide largest fish and rice soup tasting activity.

We at Xiazhu Lake will keep committed to translating "lucid waters and lush mountains" into "invaluable assets" and renewing our efforts in wetland restoration and cultural tourism development in Xiazhu Lake. We will effectively coordinate wetland resource enrichment and the reform of ecological compensation for wetland carbon sinks, and actively steer wetland development to see wetland-based economic activities develop in an eco-friendly way. Based on the zero-carbon pilot of Xiazhu Lake wetland, we will conduct research on the carbon sequestration of wetland plants, soil emission flux, and overall exchange of the wetland ecosystem. In this way, we will provide reliable data for future methodological research and share Deqing people's approaches and solutions to the reform of wetland carbon sinks with the whole province.

Author: Quan Jiangdong[1]

---

1 Quan Jiangdong, secretary of the Party Working Committee of Xiazhu Lake Street and director of the Management Committee of Xiazhu Lake Wetland Scenic Area Management Committee, actively promotes the ecological restoration of the Xiazhu Lake Wetland and has facilitated the province's first wetland carbon sink ecological compensation trade.

Low-carbon and Fashionable Hubin Subdistrict

As an important window to showcase the construction of beautiful Hangzhou, the Hubin Subdistrict actively practices the concept of green and low-carbon development. The shopping districts have built by introducing low-carbon industries, renovating the pedestrian streets, developing smart parking systems and upgrading the pollution control facilities in the Intime Mall, thus forming a green consumption scene for visitors and consumers and enhancing the sense of low-carbon experience. Besides, the low-carbon landscape have been incorporated into urban renewal and residents are advocated to save water and sort waste. In this way, a green and circular living atmosphere can be built via featured activities. In the future, Hubin Subdistrict will continue to advance the low-carbon path and lead a fashionable future with new lifestyle and consumption.

I. Introduction

Hubin Subdistrict, which literally means the West Lake area, is named after the lake and has been developed around the lake. It has become interdependent with West Lake. As "the foyer of West Lake, the living room of Hangzhou", it is "the most fashionable, intelligent and humanistic new consumption demonstration area, the 'Attractive Hangzhou' model of urban quality improvement". In 2002, Hubin Road was converted into a pedestrian street, with cars going through the West Lake Tunnel instead, and was officially opened in 2003. Since then, the concept of green leisure, low-carbon living and tourism has taken deep root. We then took advantage of the momentum to launch a low-carbon, green tourism development model. With two decades of development and construction, Hubin Subdistrict has formed a development pattern of "prosperous commercial areas in the west and quality life in the east". With the "three-dimensional management" model of flat planning, three-dimensional architecture and spatial structure, Hubin Subdistrict has adopted two aspects: the creation of a green business circle and the construction of a low-carbon living circle; guiding tourists to experience green consumption and low-carbon tourism through industrial transformation, building upgrading, facility sharing and intelligent management; guiding residents to live a low-carbon and intensive life through urban renewal, energy and water conservation, waste sorting and community activities. With these efforts, we have established a green business circle and a low-carbon living circle to achieve an ecological regional environment, low-carbon living and intelligent government management, and to promote the high-quality development of a green and low-carbon subdistrict. As a result, Hubin Subdistrict has become a key window to showcase Hangzhou's high-quality construction and advancement. The vibrant residential area is a model for the transformation of the old city, while the prosperous commercial streets bring a new fashion with natural ecology and intensive low-carbon living. Hubin Subdistrict has started its low-carbon journey from Hubin Pedestrian Street and will also start the low-carbon future of Hangzhou city.

Figure 15-1   Overhead View of Hubin Subdistrict

II. Establishing a Low-carbon Commercial Circle and Leading Green Consumption

A. Introducing Low-carbon Industries and Creating Green Consumption Scenes

Bringing in low-carbon productivity to the urban layout. Hubin Subdistrict has attracted new energy vehicle sales industries such as Xiaopeng, NIO and SAIC Audi new energy headquarters, forming a low-carbon product sales street and creating a new highland of new energy vehicle headquarters economy. These large-scale electric vehicle sellers not only showcase electric vehicles to visitors but also raise their awareness of electric vehicles through professional presentations, enabling them to immerse themselves in the convenience and advantages brought by new energy vehicles and recognize the characteristics of each brand and their differences, as well as increase the awareness and recognition of electric vehicles. By taking the advantage of hosting the 19th Asian Games in Hangzhou, Hubin Subdistrict turns the Asian Games licensed retail stores into carbon neutrality stores that sell Asian Games-related products and showcasing low-carbon elements to visitors and consumers.

Figure 15-2　New Energy Vehicle Sales Industry

Developing green shopping malls. The air-conditioning temperature of Hubin's shopping malls is set as per energy-saving requirements. Water-conservation signs are set especially in restrooms and other water-consuming areas to encourage customers to conserve water. Parking spaces for motor vehicles and electric bicycles are also reasonably planned, with clear guidance signs. Charging facilities for electric vehicles and electric bicycles are provided. The relevant departments have made full use of intelligent means to conduct marketing and services and to improve management and operational efficiency. Through advertising and publicity in shopping malls, Hubin spreads the concept of green consumption, environmental protection and energy conservation, and encourages consumers to carry out waste sorting and use biodegradable environmental packaging in shopping malls.

B. Improving the Infrastructure and Creating a Model of Green Business Circle

Making the Yintai Shopping Center a model of pollution control and carbon reduction. As one of the highest-end commercial complex in Hangzhou, the Yintai Shopping Center *in77A* adopts a vacuum drainage system, which is closed and intelligent in the whole process of the drainage renovation. The vacuum equipment generates a certain degree of negative pressure in the drainage pipeline, so that the air pushes the sewage into the pipelines relying on the pressure differences between the negative pressure inside the pipeline and the external atmospheric pressure where the sewage is transported in the form of air-water mixture. It greatly improves the drainage environment of *in77* and enhances the drainage water quality, thus ensuring that the sewage enters the pipelines and lifting pump unblocked and maintained. At the same time, it carries away about 60 liters of air near the drainage point by means of the vacuum principle, removing harmful suspended solids, bacteria and odours from the air together into the vacuum pipe network, effectively eliminating sewage odour, bacteria, suspended particles and harmful particles from the air.

Figure 15-3   Rooftop Greening, Rooftop Photovoltaic and Grease Exhaust
Treatment Facilities of Yintai Shopping Center

Building one of China's first low-carbon subdistrict through transformation. In December 2018, Hubin Pedestrian Street, identified by the Ministry of Commerce as the first batch of national pilot pedestrian street renovation and upgrading, has launched a wave of low-carbon transformation. The streets were renovated and upgraded in six aspects: road paving, organic renewal of greenery, landscape lighting enhancement, urban furniture renewal, urban facade renovation and focal point landscape upgrade. The first phase of the project involved 35,000 square meters of road paving, 3,000 square meters of organic greening renewal, upgrades of 195 landscape lighting (all using smart light poles), renewals of 128 urban furniture and renovation of over 30 business units' facade and 10 building roofs. The second phase of the project features a landscape paving construction area of 13,000 square meters and a greening enhancement area of 1,000 square meters. Through improving the facade of the buildings on the street and adding urban furniture and street stalls, the pedestrian streets have become more fashionable, with the extension of intelligent terminal carriers, the extension of the "digital" governance coverage, and the improvement of barrier-free facilities to enhance the "friendliness" of the business districts and the "sense of experience" of visitors. In the renovation of the pedestrian street, we topped it off with the renovation of Dongpo Road where we replaced the motor vehicles roads with a fully enclosed pedestrian walkway, which is unique among pilot subdistricts in the country, and thus logically created one of the first low-carbon business districts, the low-carbon streets, in the country.

562

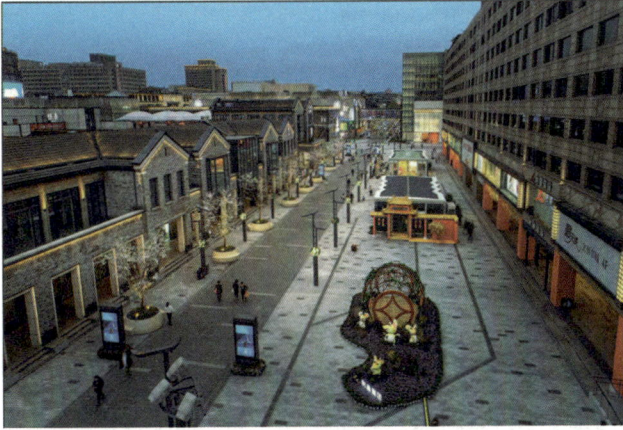

Figure 15-4   Renovated Dongpo Road

C. Developing Green Transportation and Breaking Through the Bottleneck of Intelligent Management

To improve the efficiency of regional governance, Hubin has built the city's first subdistrict-level city brain - "Hubin Smart Core" system and established the "Comprehensive management platform for Hubin pedestrian street". By continuing to build the "block governance" application scenario, it brings green and comfortable experience to residents, visitors and other consumers in the district. Among other things, the most striking experience for the public is that it is no longer difficult to park in Hubin and the roads are now less congested.

Hubin Subdistrict has removed 660 parking spaces from the pedestrian street, 40% reduction in parking support for the entire area. An intelligent traffic management system has been implemented in Hubin Subdistrict to manage parking demand. Data from 2,413 parking spaces in 9 separate parking lots around the pedestrian street are unified as a pedestrian street package and calibrated online in real time through City Brain access. With the installation of smart guidance signs at each intersection entering the streets, drivers will be able to find out important information such as vacancies and driving routes on their way to find a parking space surrounding them. This system has also been expanded to cover the entire Hubin Subdistrict, especially the hospitals within the district. The availability of parking spaces on nearby roads and complexes can be seen at all intersections in the vicinity of the hospital, providing great convenience for people to park for medical treatment. Drivers have experienced a shift from "looking around for a parking space" to "looking up to see a parking space". The system can calculate the parking space index (the repeat usage rate of parking spaces) and the parking index (the saturation of the parking lot) and make them available to the public, which will bring both convenience and force a higher capacity of management. In addition to solving parking problems, it also helps effectively reduce traffic congestion around major hospitals and popular shopping areas, and lower exhaust emissions during low-speed driving and waiting.

Figure 15-5   Parking Guidance

D. Upgrading Public Facilities and Sharing Infrastructure

Smart design has been adopted to upgrade public facilities, promote smart infrastructure sharing, and enhance tourism experience. The commercial area is equipped with A-grade guide signs, and digital maps of barrier-free facilities can be found out by scanning QR codes or downloaded and used through the application store, which has been integrated with the voice version, to guide the handicapped through the whole area. On both sides of Dongpo Road, it has built smart light poles to achieve "multi-functionality". The renovation and construction of 107 street lights incorporates the characteristic elements of Hangzhou in its appearance, and integrates functions such as advertising, emergency broadcasting and Wi-Fi access in addition to the basic function of night lighting. The smart light pole can automatically adjust the light color and shade by detecting external environmental factors. With its self-imposed camera function, the poles can sense the dynamic information of the surrounding area. On the interaction screen, visitors may access the surrounding parking index, view the routes and times of nearby subway, bus and boat in real time, and also get information on restaurants and entertainment, tour routes and other business information to get a more comfortable and convenient touring experience. During the renovation of buildings and commercial areas in recent years, Hubin Subdistrict has fully introduced energy-saving and low-carbon technologies to upgrade public facilities, and has constantly expanded the utilization rate of public facilities to achieve efficient sharing of facilities.

III. Developing a Low-carbon Life Cycle and Living a Green Life

A. Renovating the Old Communities and Incorporating Low-carbon Landscapes

Combined with the renovation, repair and maintenance of old urban residential communities, Hubin Subdistrict fully practices the green and low-carbon concept in the renovation of public facilities. The renovation of old buildings from flat roofs to sloped roofs is reduced the energy consumption of residents on the top floors. The intelligent parking management system is used to manage and control motor vehicles within residential areas, displaying parking spaces in high-density residential communities and surrounding areas in real-time, regulating traffic flow around the area, and imposing strict controls on those with saturated parking spaces. Hubin Subdistrict also promotes the development of a public transport system in the area and establishes a ten-minute walking circle. In the process of renovating public facilities in the subdistrict, measures such as the installation of centralized charging facilities attempted photovoltaic power generation, and energy-efficient lamps with intelligent lighting hours are used to achieve energy conservation and low-carbon in public facilities and buildings. Besides, the Subdistrict fully applies the sponge city concept and adopts vegetation, paving, and landscaping approaches to transform and improve the green infrastructure protection areas, which can better provide purification, noise reduction, dust prevention, and other ecological protection, to build sponge and water-efficient living communities. Furthermore, the Subdistrict repairs and maintains the sewerage system while collecting water to maintain the ecological environment in the district, by reasonably routing rainwater collection modules, constructing storage ponds, infiltration ponds, and flood control ponds, and configuring rainwater recycling equipment to store and treat rainwater for regional greening, landscape watering and street cleaning.

Hubin Subdistrict actively explores ways to sequester carbon and increase sinks, re-plans land resources, strengthens the ecological planning and design of communities, and promotes the greening and beautification of courtyards and effective spaces such as roadsides and werf in accordance with the laws of nature by using native plants whenever possible. Also, the Subdistrict makes full use of green belts for sound insulation and noise reduction and builds public green spaces and walking paths to meet the leisure needs of residents. The principle of "minimal intervention, cultural heritage, rational use, and practical implementation" has been adhered to in the urban renewal process, preserving the original natural flavor and incorporating new, intelligent, and low-carbon elements, thus giving people a refreshing sense when old and new elements come together.

Figure 15-6   Renovated Qingnian Road Community

B. Conserving Water and Using Resources More Efficiently

Hubin Subdistrict is located in the core of Shangcheng District. During the renovation and construction of the old urban area, Hubin focuses on the concept of green and environmental protection, strengthens water conservation measures, raises awareness of water conservation and protection, and thoroughly establishes the scientific water use systems and water conservation management systems. As a result, it has effectively controlled the growth rate of water consumption, ensured a safe water supply in all communities, and effectively adjusted the structure of water use. Through the construction of water-saving communities, the installation rate of meters per household for residents' domestic water consumption has reached 100%, the popularity rate of water-saving devices has reached 100%, and the monthly per capita water consumption level is 3.05 cubic meters per person per month, with an annual water conservation of about 60 tons. As for public facilities, water-saving devices are used in public places in the community (including greening) and rainwater recycling devices are configured. The recycled and treated rainwater can be used for flushing toilets, cleaning roads, watering lawns, and replenishing water in water features.

C. Sorting Wastes for Zero-Waste Neighborhoods

Since the introduction of waste sorting in 2010, Hubin Subdistrict has been carefully and meticulously building up the basic system. We have vigorously renovated the waste disposal facilities in the old living communities, replacing the scattered traditional bins with fixed sorting bins under central management, which means that 11 open-air waste rooms have been replaced with roofed smart bins with water tanks. A total of 13 recycling stations and 9 hazardous waste disposal sites were built (6 Xiaolu recycling stations, 6 enterprise-operated and 1 subdistrict-operated collective disposal site for sorting). Public institutions, enterprises, and schools in the subdistrict are encouraged to actively participate in waste sorting for daily management, and administrative inspections are carried out to facilitate improvement, with emphasis on popularizing the law, issuing correction requests, and even interviewing the leaders of enterprises and institutions with relatively weak performance and those lagging behind in the evaluation rankings among all districts in Hangzhou. We have set up point accounts, honor rolls, and black lists to reward residents with points for correct sorting, to increase the residents' enthusiasm and participation in waste sorting. Hubin Subdistrict has been designated as a demonstration area for household waste sorting in Zhejiang Province, and a number of residential communities have been modeled as high-standard demonstration communities.

D. Organizing Special Activities and Influence Habitual Behaviors

The low-carbon concept is also promoted via special festivals. For example, the Subdistrict launched traditional activities to celebrate Arbor Day, and also conducted joint online tree-planting activities with the Shangcheng District's Official WeChat account "Shangcheng News". The participants collected 17,000 green energy points by answering science quizzes and inviting friends to water. A total of 35 people received prizes such as cloth bags and green plants. Government officials and Party members were encouraged to plant over 120 trees themed "integrity trees", "filial piety trees" and "fraternity trees", and to promote low-carbon environmental protection knowledge and measures such as waste sorting, energy conservation and tree planting. Combined with featured activities, Hubin Subdistrict has integrated a series of innovative low-carbon projects such as "Talking Bins", "Vertical Greening of Buildings", "Solar Powered Corridor Lights" and "Real Name Waste Sorting Systems", with a view to creating a distinctive low-carbon living experience route. In daily life, it took the lead in launching the *Low-carbon Living Handbook for Residents*, the "Low-carbon Family Standard", the "Youth Carbon Reduction Workshop" and the "Ecotourism Experience Line". Also, it awarded "Low-carbon Family Demonstration Households" and "Low-carbon Achievers" and encouraged residents to keep a "Low-carbon Diary". These activities have influenced residents' living habits and daily behaviors in a subconscious manner and created a strong low-carbon atmosphere in Hubin Subdistrict.

IV. Major Implications

The achievements of low/zero-carbon construction in Hubin Subdistrict are typical examples of cities practicing low-carbon paths, proving the feasibility and accessibility of reducing pollution and low/zero-carbon construction in city centers, where living and business are the main functions. In addition, Hubin's success has also fully demonstrated the synergy between low-carbon construction and social and economic development by embarking on a low-carbon path toward social progress and common prosperity.

A. Focusing on Scene Structuring to Enhance the Low Carbon Experience

There are a wide range of fields in which carbon emissions are involved in social development and production, varied ways to reduce carbon emissions, and different levels of public awareness of efforts to achieve low carbon and carbon neutrality. The construction of low-carbon scenes allows the public to know and participate in the process, effectively practice the low-carbon approach and witness its development. For example, the low-carbon pedestrian street scene is established by using the "City Brain" monitoring system to integrate road information, equipment resources and other information. We have created a database to achieve synchronization of monitoring, inspection and information transmission for environment management and parking space in pedestrian streets, so as to improve traffic flow efficiency and management effectiveness, as well as environmental benefits.

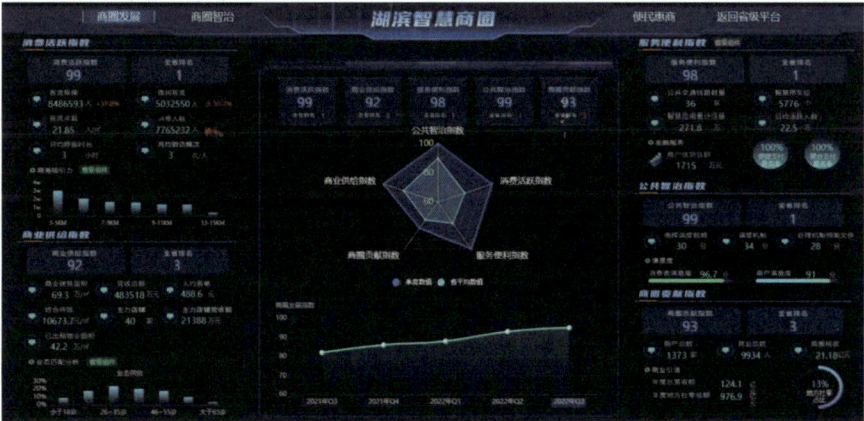

Figure 15-7　Smart Hubin Management System

B. Raising the Awareness and Popularizing Low-Carbon Concepts

The green and intensive low-carbon concept is an important foundation for low-carbon social development. In Hubin subdistrict, where the historic old downtown meets bustling tourist and commercial areas, the awareness of residents and visitors determines how far Hubin's "carbon" path can extend.

Therefore, Hubin has focused on guiding residents to develop a life habit of recycling and saving, and promoting civilized tourism and green consumption by popularizing the low-carbon concept. We have distributed low-carbon living manuals and conducted other measures to guide the elderly to save water and electricity and purchase energy-saving home appliances and simple packaging goods, thus improving the participation of the elderly groups. Activities such as awarding low-carbon learning activists and outstanding low-carbon residents are actively carried out to increase the public's enthusiasm and participation and to help them develop a sense of ownership of energy conservation and carbon reduction, so that a high quality subdistrict with popularized low-carbon awareness is gradually formed.

C. Building Low-Carbon Units Through the Concept Extension

A city's low-carbon development requires the practice of all people in all fields. Hubin Subdistrict has made great efforts to extend the concept of "low-carbon" to schools, communities, families, enterprises, shopping malls and so on to carry out a comprehensive "low-carbon" publicity and education on all fronts. Through broad participation and joint efforts in management, we can share the low-carbon fruits and form simple and moderate, green and low-carbon, civilized and healthy living concepts and lifestyles. Combined with the zero-waste construction goal of "each district with characters" in Shangcheng District, we have organized the development of low-carbon communities, gradually expanded low-carbon units to institutions, families, schools, shopping malls, restaurants, hotels, hospitals and enterprises, etc., and regularly assessed them to ensure that the "low-carbon units" are spread throughout the subdistrict.

V. Future Prospects

As a model for the urban area, Hubin has taken the first step towards low-carbon construction. As a pioneer of low-carbon development, we will continue to fully play the role of the pedestrian street, dig deep into our own advantages through continuous innovation and active planning, and strive to explore more efficient and feasible low/zero-carbon construction initiatives, so as to provide more typical practices for other subdistricts of Hangzhou. By leveraging the attraction of the West Lake scenic spot and the appeal of the national model pedestrian street, the historic culture and the "carbon road" will be integrated to form a new lifestyle and consumption trend, leading a fashionable future.

A. Building a Management and Guarantee System

Hubin Subdistrict will continue to vigorously promote low-carbon construction by forming a linkage working system with the Party Secretary in charge, the Party Committee members in charge of environmental protection, construction and digitalization respectively, and constantly strengthen the major strategic research on low-carbon development. Regular training is provided to the staff of management and related low-carbon construction in the subdistrict, including timely interpretation of relevant national and provincial policies, learning the advanced experiences and practices of other regions, and improving the awareness and professional skills of community-level management staff in low-carbon construction. We have invited municipal and provincial-level professional teams to provide guidance on low-carbon projects, help residents cultivate and build their low-carbon awareness, and promote the implementation and settlement of low-carbon projects. These projects were included in the priorities of the subdistrict office and relevant departments, with regular evaluation of progress and timely adjustments for major changes to ensure proper organization, clear responsibilities and timely action.

B. Establishing Low-Carbon Living System

Based on the development concept of the pedestrian street and the green and low-carbon cultural elements of the surrounding business areas, the low-carbon living system of a pedestrian street-business areas-scenic areas will be continuously built. We will implement an in-depth management and high-standard maintenance concept of cleanliness and beauty, optimize regional traffic settings, improve the connection of pedestrian and bicycle paths in neighborhoods and scenic spots. Moreover, Hubin will build an intelligent management system and provide guarantees for the construction of a slower living system through the development of intelligent systems and platforms, aiming at enhancing the sense of low-carbon experience for residents, tourists and consumers. Continuous efforts will be made to expand low-carbon shopping areas. We also encourage shopping stores such as Jiebai and Gonglian to innovate in basic management, upgrading and maintaining equipment and facilities, building green supply chains, implementing green services, guiding green consumption and recycling resources, etc., so as to become a 3-in-1 off-line retail enterprise involving energy saving and emission reduction, green product sales and waste recycling. In addition, we will proactively develop more low-carbon units by encouraging various organizations and groups to carry out low-carbon demonstration projects, promoting the application of low-carbon technologies in various fields, and integrating low-carbon culture into the historical and cultural blood of the neighborhoods.

C. Creating Low Carbon Display Scenes

Relying on the West Lake scenic spot, the pedestrian streets and the surrounding business areas, we will explore a platform to showcase the achievements of low/zero-carbon construction in the municipal and provincial levels, organize and participate in various low/zero-carbon publicity and demonstration activities and promote carbon neutrality in major events within the residents' communities. We will seek sales channels for carbon-labeled products and set up special zones in pedestrian streets, shopping malls and other areas to sell special products with carbon labels of Zhejiang Province's carbon footprint. These products can reveal their own carbon footprint and guide consumers to buy more environmentally friendly and low-carbon products. Digital media will be deployed to proactively communicate and share Zhejiang's low/zero-carbon story, building a bridge for Hangzhou and Zhejiang to spread a low/zero-carbon culture.

Author: Ruan Tianyi[1]

1 Ruan Tianyi, special contributor from the Hulin Street Office, engineer at Hangzhou Environment Protection Science Research and Design Co., Ltd., mainly engaged in policy research on environmental protection and low-carbon development.

Carbon Neutrality Practice of Geely Holding's Whole Industry Chain

Enterprises are a key contributor to carbon emissions and are integral to achieving the goals of carbon peaking and carbon neutrality. To meet the objectives of carbon peaking and neutrality, the full involvement and innovation of enterprises is essential. Geely Auto is the leader in new energy vehicle production in Zhejiang Province and serves as a model for private enterprise innovation. Geely Holding has set the goal of achieving carbon neutrality covering the whole industry chain in the competitive automobile manufacturing industry under the context that the upstream industries are widely connected with the downstream ones. To achieve this, the company has conducted extensive exploration in management systems, design and manufacturing, circular economy, green travel and logistics, and green methanol substitution, yielding impressive results and offering valuable experience for transitioning toward green and low-carbon development.

I. Introduction

The automobile industry is a strategic and pillar part of the national economy, as well as an important source of carbon emissions, involving the industrial and transportation sectors. According to research by the Institute of Energy, Environment, and Economy, Tsinghua University, China's transportation industry has the potential to grow threefold in the future; however, this could lead to immense pressure of reducing carbon emissions. As a typical example of low-carbon development in the Zhejiang automobile industry, Zhejiang Geely Holding Group (hereinafter referred to as "Geely Holding") has taken the initiative to respond to the national strategy of "dual carbon". By planning accurately and thoroughly before taking action, Geely Holding is committed to becoming a benchmark for sustainable development in China and the world automobile industry by innovating raw materials, processes, and energy usage at the supply chain, manufacturing, and use phase, with the goal of achieving carbon neutrality throughout the entire value chain by 2045. This paper focuses on the practice and effectiveness of Geely Holding in promoting carbon neutrality in the whole industry chain, with a view to providing a useful reference for the green and low-carbon transition of the transportation industry and enterprises.

II. Main Practices and Effectiveness

A. Innovating Carbon Management Mechanism to Consolidate Organizational Efforts

In order to reach carbon peaking and neutrality, a change in thinking and approach is necessary, which will be reflected in the management mechanism. Geely Holding has shifted its thinking and approach, integrating green and low-carbon development into the whole company and all the processes. This has resulted in the formation of a dedicated work mechanism, management system, and digital platform, all of which serve to motivate its employees to work together to reach the desired objectives.

Establishing an integrated carbon neutrality working group. In order to effectively coordinate matters related to carbon neutrality management, an Environmental, Social and Governance Committee (hereinafter referred to as the "ESG Committee") was established at the BoD level, and a joint ESG working group consisting of the Coordination Steering Team, the ESG Working Team, and the Carbon Neutrality Working Team. The Carbon Neutrality Working Team is mainly responsible for studying the policy and industry trends related to carbon neutrality, formulating overall strategies and goals for carbon neutrality, establishing operational mechanisms and processes related to carbon neutrality, coordinating the carbon neutrality management of the group, promoting cross-business group/sector work related to carbon neutrality and carbon asset development and trading, etc. At the same time, carbon neutrality working teams are set up in each business group/sector to be responsible for the implementation of relevant decisions.

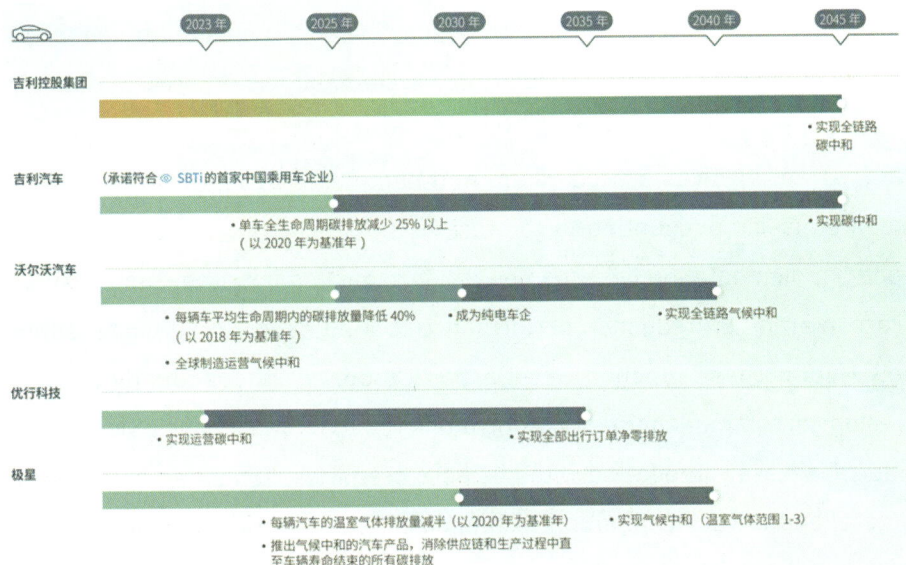

Figure 16-1　Carbon emission reduction targets of brands under Zhejiang Geely Holding Group

Establishing a comprehensive carbon management system. The effective implementation of the dual carbon strategy requires the support of corresponding management mechanisms, which also means that traditional management models need to be updated to a certain extent. Geely Holding has independently developed a carbon management system that covers all its holding companies and production bases in China. The carbon management system is mainly composed of three levels i.e., management, holding group, and subsidiary business groups. At the management level, the top management mainly formulates carbon management policies, appoints carbon management teams, provides required resources, and performs duties related to management representatives. At the holding group level, the carbon neutrality working team mainly prepares strategic planning and management system documents, develops low-carbon technologies and carbon finance pathways, and manages the carbon performance of each business group. At the level of the business groups, the main tasks include implementing the carbon management system documents, fulfilling carbon management responsibilities, and providing feedback on relevant situations and data. In order to effectively strengthen the implementation of relevant management mechanisms, Zhejiang Geely Holding Group has also developed a series of supporting carbon management system manuals to define terms and definitions and established second-level procedural documents and third-level supporting documents according to PDCA (Plan, Do, Check, Act) process, ensuring a systematic and orderly approach.

Building a digital carbon management platform. Carbon emission management involves a wide range and complex processes, from the initial carbon emission accounting to the formulation of carbon emission reduction targets, implementation of carbon emission reduction initiatives, and evaluation of carbon emission reduction performance that all need strong digital support. Geely Holding has launched Gee-Carbon Cloud, an independently developed one-stop carbon management platform tailored to its reality and objectives. The platform is closely integrated with business scenarios, supported by blockchain, big data, and privacy computing technologies, and has rich built-in accounting models, methodologies, and carbon emission factor databases. It has features such as intelligent identification of enterprise emission sources, automatic association of carbon emission factors, and data security guarantee, which can achieve functions such as carbon inventory and monitoring, product carbon footprint accounting, carbon target and performance management, carbon asset development and management, carbon inclusiveness and operation, etc. for the unified management of the carbon emission data and carbon assets of Geely Holding and its supply chain. Up to now, the platform has covered more than 800 upstream suppliers of Geely Holding, completing carbon emission accounting of all components as well as site data collection of key carbon emission suppliers.

B. Focusing on Green Design and Manufacturing, Strengthening Emission Reduction at Source

As a typical manufacturing enterprise, automobile manufacturing is the main source of carbon emissions for Geely Holding, thus also providing potential for carbon reduction. However, manufacturing is largely regulated by design, and greener and more low-carbon designs are undoubtedly a more cost-effective and competitive approach. Geely Holding effectively reduces carbon emissions within the enterprise boundary by strengthening its green and low-carbon orientation in design, production and operation, and product stages.

Figure 16-2　Gee-Carbon Cloud Platform Architecture of Zhejiang Geely Holding Group

Implementing ecological top-down design approach. For automobiles, lightweight design not only means market advantages, but also reduces energy consumption and carbon emissions. Geely Holding adheres to the ecological top-down design approach, develops and applies advanced lightweight technology, optimizes materials, structures, and processes, improves power performance and fuel economy, and prioritizes the use of environmentally friendly materials. For example, Volvo plans to collaborate with Swedish steel group SSAB and its HYBRIT technology to develop the most advanced fossil-free steel; the body of ZEEKR 001 adopts 15% renewable steel plate materials and 25% renewable aluminum alloy materials. It's planned that the front and rear upper glove compartment baffle plate of the long-haul G3 heavy truck will use bio-based plastics, and the air guide plate and the rear support of the air deflector will use recycled plastics, with the proportion of recycled materials exceeding 10%.

Commitment to zero-carbon climate operations. The decarbonization of automobile manufacturing plants is a vital and inevitable link as it gathers the main carbon emission activities. Geely Holding adheres to the principle of "building green factories harmless to the environment and manufacturing environmentally friendly vehicles beneficial to human beings", and the subsidiary Geely Auto, Volvo Car, Geely Commercial Vehicle, and other vehicle manufacturing bases have passed ISO 14001 external audit. As of 2021, 11 manufacturing bases were rated as national green factories. Among them, the Xi'an zero-carbon factory has built a 52 MW super photovoltaic power plant, procured the International Renewable Energy Certificate (I-REC) to achieve carbon neutrality in electricity, and received a Type I Zero-carbon Plant Five-star Certificate issued by Ti Testing and Certification Group, making it the first zero-carbon plant of a domestic vehicle manufacturer. By the end of 2021, Volvo Cars Taizhou plant had increased its in-house power generation capacity and achieved a utilization rate of 46% of clean energy. Additionally, the plant had fully implemented a sustainable green supply chain management strategy, earning the plant a national green supply chain award. The Polestar Chengdu production base is the first automobile plant in China to receive LEED Gold Certification, using 100% renewable electricity.

Figure 16-3　Polestar Chengdu production base of Zhejiang Geely Holding Group

Manufacturing low (zero) carbon cars. As the process of replacing traditional fuel vehicles with new energy vehicles is significantly accelerating, it is important to launch car products that are suitable both for the present and future, and conform to the trend of green and low-carbon. Geely Holding focuses on pure electric vehicles, while also considering hybrid power, and looks ahead to carbon neutrality vehicles to establish a multi-level, complementary low (zero) carbon vehicle brand. In terms of hybrid power, the Xingyue L extended-range electric version, launched in 2022, is equipped with a 41.2kW · h CTP flat plate cell and 85kW DC fast charging, with a pure all-electric range of 205km under WLTC conditions. In addition, the range extender with 43.32% thermal efficiency makes the full-time electric range of WLTC conditions up to 1,250km. In terms of pure electric vehicles, SEA (Sustainable Experience Architecture), a new self-developed pure electric vehicle development platform, was released in 2020, and the following year, ZEEKR 001, the first intelligent electric vehicle, was launched based on this platform. Looking ahead, in 2021 Polestar announced the "Polestar 0 Project", an innovative and recyclable carbon-neutral vehicle that will use recyclable batteries, recyclable materials, and renewable energy throughout the supply chain to produce truly climate-neutral vehicles by 2030, without relying on carbon offsets.

Figure 16-4   ZEEKR 001 of Geely Holding

C. Strengthening Resource Recycling and Reducing Carbon Emissions Throughout the Entire Lifecycle

As an important access of saving resources, reducing costs, and increasing efficiency, the circular economy is also a key pathway for reducing carbon emissions, particularly in the complicated production system like automobile. To this end, Geely Holding has actively practiced the extended producer responsibility system, joined the China Automobile Producer Responsibility Organization (PRO), and explored a closed-loop recycling system that is easy to promote and replicate, effectively reducing the carbon footprint of the vehicle's entire life cycle. In 2021, the reuse rate and recycling rate of scrap materials of the whole vehicle were 92.8% and 96.9% respectively.

Using sustainable packaging. Packaging has always been a key focus of recycling, as these materials can be reused multiple times and are essential for promoting energy and resource conservation, as well as reducing carbon emissions. To this end, Geely Holding has taken the initiative to promote recyclable packaging materials such as paper, wood, and recyclable plastic, accelerating the spread of the concept and application of recyclable packaging. In 2021, the company conducted an extensive assessment of the use of single-use packaging across its production plants and set a target to replace it with recyclable packaging. To achieve this target, Geely Holding launched an improvement project for reusable packaging, which has now been implemented in 12 whole-vehicle and 1 powertrain manufacturing plants, with 58 parts suppliers in 72 projects adopting recyclable packaging, effectively reducing the use of single-use cardboard boxes, wooden boxes, liners, and other materials.

Figure 16-5   Packing boxes made from recycling materials in Geely Holding

Promoting the cascading use of batteries. Batteries are essential components of automobiles, especially electric vehicles, which cause a major source of energy and material consumption. Battery production and operation processes continouslly produce carbon emissions and pollutants. Recycling batteries is important for conserving energy, reducing carbon emissions, lowering costs, and improving efficiency. Geely Holding has established a battery recycling system with 100% traceability management of key components. Both scrap batteries from factory testing and those generated by customers are collected and recycled at after-sales sites. Geely Holding works with third-party recycling companies or battery manufacturers to classify and process recycled batteries by their residual value, maximizing cascading use and minimizing manufacturing costs.

Carrying out green remanufacturing of parts. As an important implementation mechanism of the same-level cycle, parts remanufacturing achieves high-performance substitution of raw materials and parts through repair and transformation of waste products, and has considerable potential for resource conservation, energy consumption reduction, and carbon emission in complex fields such as automobile and other modern equipment manufacturing industry. Geely Holding takes remanufacturing and utilizing used automobile parts as an important part of achieving carbon neutrality throughout the industrial chain. By ensuring that quality characteristics and safety performance remain uncompromised, Geely Holding will achieve an average energy conservation of 60%, material savings of 70%, a carbon reduction of more than 80%, and a cost reduction of more than 50%. This will result in an organic unity between economic, environmental, and social benefits. Meanwhile, Geely Holding is exploring ways to reduce the carbon footprint of the whole vehicle and extend the life cycle. This is achieved by combining cutting-edge technology and traditional vehicle manufacturing processes in order to implement high-value repair and value preservation, preventive maintenance, and comprehensive quality enhancement.

D. Developing Green Transportation and Logistics to Drive Carbon Neutrality in the Whole Society

Compared with automobile manufacturing, the carbon emission generated during the use of automobiles throughout their entire life cycle is greater. To address this, Geely Holding is actively developing green travel and green logistics solutions corresponding to passenger and freight transportation scenarios based on automobile manufacturing, with the aim of achieving carbon neutrality in the whole society.

Vigorously promoting carbon-neutral travel. On the one hand, Geely Holding is implementing its "new energy vehicle sharing ecosystem" strategic investment plan, building and developing Cao Cao Mobility, and applying leading global Internet, IoV, autopilot system, and new energy technology innovations to the field of shared travel. By using Cao Cao Mobility, users can earn about 142 grams of carbon emission reduction per kilometer, which will be fully credited to their personal carbon asset account on the Cao Cao Mobility app. Since its establishment six years ago, Cao Cao Mobility has saved a total of 534 million liters of fuel and reduced carbon emissions by over 1.083, 5 million tons. On the other hand, LEVC, another electronic vehicle brand of Geely Holding, has achieved the use of pure electric and range-extended new energy power systems across its entire product series. Since the launch of the LEVCTX model in the UK, it has reduced fossil fuel consumption by about 54.9 million liters, equivalent to a reduction of about 90,000 tons of carbon emissions.

Focusing on providing carbon neutrality logistics services. The logistics system has become an important infrastructure for economic and social development, and it is still in rapid growth. Geely Holding has focused on and made considerable explorations on smart interconnection, charging, battery swap and power replenishment infrastructure, and green energy service ,etc. Geely Holding is committed to urban green transport services and Intelligent Connected Vehicles, and has focused on the construction of a Green Intelligent Link platform to provide users with green operations, mobile IoT co-distribution system support, and new energy logistics vehicle whole life cycle management services. The green mileage contributed by the Green Intelligent Link platform had amounted to 360 million kilometers, reducing 186,000 tons of cumulative carbon emissions by 2022. It was awarded the "2021 Special Attention Award— Green Product of the Year" by Southern Weekly. Geely Holding focuses on building and operating charging and battery swap stations, managing battery banks, building the Farizon transport service platform, and planning charging, battery swap and power replenishment solutions to serve heavy trucks for rapid power replenishment. Built in 2021, the world's first "wind, solar, storage, charging and swap" integrated Ningbo green car transporter truck charging and battery swap station was officially put into operation, which can provide a one-stop solution to the pain points of high purchase cost, long charging time, inefficient operation, low cargo capacity, mileage anxiety, etc. The first batch of 50 heavy-duty trucks is expected to reduce carbon emissions by 18,400 tons in five years. Centering on green energy services for electric heavy trucks, Geely

Holding builds the Solisand platform to provide battery swap services integrating design, engineering, and operation for battery swap and heavy truck customers; under this service model, the construction of battery swap stations can be completed within 48 hours, the relocation of stations can be completed within 24 hours, the battery swap for a single vehicle can be done within 5 minutes, and up to 200+ battery swap services can be realized in a day, providing more cost-effective power supply for battery swap stations.

E. Developing and utilizing green methanol to explore new species of zero-carbon energy

The automobile industry's low-carbon and zero-carbon transition has become a social consensus, and electric vehicles are emerging as the mainstream technology solution. However, considering the scale of automobile manufacturing and related upstream and downstream industries, as well as the impact of price fluctuations of key raw materials such as lithium carbonate, exploring multiple sustainable energy technology routes is still necessary. Geely Holding has chosen globally recognized clean and renewable methanol as a breakthrough direction, and since 2005 the company has conducted numerous innovative explorations and practical applications to build a methanol economic operation model and form a cycle of methanol production, transportation, station, vehicle, and capture.

Overcoming technical challenges of methanol vehicles. In 2015, Geely Holding invested RMB 280 million in Iceland-based Carbon Recycling International (CRI), a world leader in clean methanol production, to jointly explore clean methanol fuel synthesis and production technology. In 2019, Yuan Cheng commercial vehicle division launched the world's first methanol heavy truck, which overcame two major technical challenges of low-temperature starting and corrosion of components contacting methanol in its methanol engine, and made breakthroughs in several key technologies, including specialized lubricant and additive development, emission control, and methanol electronic fuel injection control system, reaching a world-leading level. Geely Holding has mastered the core technology of methanol vehicles and acquired more than 200 patents by solving industry problems such as the methanol resistance and durability of methanol engine parts.

Launching methanol vehicles and promoting their implementation. Geely Holding has long been engaged in methanol vehicles for 18 years, developing over 20 methanol fuel vehicle models, with a total mileage of nearly 10 billion kilometers and a maximum single vehicle mileage of over 1.5 million kilometers. It has become the world's first automaker to achieve mass production of methanol vehicles. In the five-year methanol vehicle pilot project in five provinces and cities organized by the Ministry of Industry and Information Technology of the People's Republic of China, Geely Holding contributed 908 methanol vehicles, accounting for nearly 90% of the total number of pilot vehicles. According to the pilot operation data, compared with gasoline vehicles, methanol vehicles can improve energy efficiency by about 21% and reduce carbon emissions by about 26%. In 2021, Yuan Cheng Auto launched a 13L National VI methanol engine with a power of up to 430 horsepower/460 horsepower. The average fuel cost can be reduced by 18% compared with diesel heavy trucks, while maintaining reliability, power, and economy. In 2022, Geely Holding launched the first methanol-electric hybrid sedan in the world—4th-generation Emgrand methanol-electric hybrid sedan equipped with the world's first methanol-electric hybrid engine and a 3-speed hybrid electric drive DHT PRO. The methanol consumption per 100 kilometers is about 9 liters, and the cost per kilometer is less than 0.3 yuan, achieving both "low energy consumption" and "strong power".

Establishment of methanol production base. In 2023, the world's first 100,000-ton green and low-carbon methanol plant invested by Geely Holding and Henan Shuncheng Group will be officially put into operation in Anyang. This is China's first and the world's largest CO_2 hydrogenation-based green and low-carbon methanol plant which is expected to produce 110,000 tons of methanol annually and directly reduce carbon dioxide emissions by 160,000 tons, equivalent to increasing the forest planting area by 160,000 mu, bringing good social and economic benefits.

III. Main Insights

A. Digital intelligence management system construction to help achieve carbon targets

A management system oriented to green and low-carbon development, with sound functional settings and good operation status, is the starting point and an important step for the company to substantially implement carbon neutrality. With the overall strategic goal of achieving carbon neutrality across the entire value chain by 2045 and identifying specific targets by 2030, 2035, and 2045, Geely Holding is committed to becoming a benchmark for sustainable development models in China and the world automobile industry. To achieve carbon neutrality goals, Geely Holding takes the lead in practicing carbon management models such as establishing the independently developed carbon neutrality management system and framework, setting up a carbon neutrality working team structure, and formulating enterprise carbon neutrality standards, etc. These measures are specifically implemented through digital carbon management platform - Geely Carbon Cloud to ensure effective management and significant improvement in the digital management of energy use and carbon emissions in plants.

B. Empowerment of carbon neutrality through emission reduction in the industry chain

Every enterprise is a part of the industry chain and frequently exchanges materials, energy, and information with external and internal parties. On the scale of the industry chain, promoting carbon neutrality is an inevitable choice for enterprises to pursue higher-level green and low-carbon development. Geely Holding has made remarkable progress in exploring the carbon neutrality path of the vehicle's entire life cycle by establishing a complete green and low-carbon industry chain, including synchronous engineering analysis from the early material development, establishment of sustainable green factories, energy-saving and efficiency-enhancing manufacturing, recyclable packaging, and green transportation. Geely Holding also provides comprehensive technical solutions to help users achieve green travel and waste recovery, recycling, and disposal. Efforts are made to create three carbon-neutral scenarios for vehicles, travel, and logistics, in order to explore solutions for carbon neutrality across the entire automobile industry value chain.

C. Key core technologies to enhance carbon reduction capability

To achieve carbon neutrality, technological innovation is a key variable. To fully leverage the role of technological innovation, it is necessary to overcome and master key core technologies to avoid stranglehold problems. For 18 years, Geely Holding has been committed to tackling industry issues such as methanol resistance and durability of methanol engine parts. As a result, the company has mastered the core technology of methanol vehicles and gained over 200 patents. More than 20 methanol fuel vehicle models were developed, with a total mileage of nearly 10 billion kilometers and a maximum single vehicle mileage of over 1.2 million kilometers. Geely Holding has become the world's first automaker to achieve mass production of methanol vehicles, comprehensively promoting the development of methanol energy and methanol vehicles, and greatly expanding their ability and path to implement carbon reduction and promote carbon neutrality.

IV. Future Prospects

A. Leveraging carbon markets to expand the advantages of green finance

Green finance is an important driving force to achieve carbon peaking and carbon neutrality. Genius Auto Finance Co., Ltd. (Genius AFC), a subsidiary of Geely Holding, upholds the concept of green development, focuses on the sector of green finance, integrates environmental protection factors into risk policies, and promotes the development of new energy vehicles through financial means. Geely Holding has been making progress in the sector of new energy vehicle finance, boosting the sales of various new energy brands. To look ahead, Geely Holding will continue to leverage its advantages in automobile finance to provide more diversified and varied green finance products for areas such as new energy vehicles, battery swapping models, and charging pile construction, enhancing the convenience, accessibility, and scalability of green finance. It will also promote the effective connection between green finance and inclusive finance, providing appropriate, effective, and affordable green finance services for all social classes and groups.

B. Effectively increasing public participation in carbon inclusiveness

Carbon inclusion is an important mechanism to quickly promote residents' practice of green and low-carbon lifestyles. In the early stage, Cao Cao Mobility, a subsidiary of Geely Holding, vigorously promoted the implementation of the carbon inclusiveness project. An online carbon points exchange mall will be launched to incentivize users to adopt low-carbon behaviors and provide a tangible and perceptible way to do so. In addition, Z-Green, a carbon inclusiveness platform, is launched by ZEEKR, which uses digital technology to calculate the carbon reduction generated by users driving new energy electric vehicles compared with fuel vehicles of the same traffic capacity, allowing users to visually see their contribution to carbon neutrality. Next, Geely Holding will consider integrating carbon inclusiveness-related applications and promoting connectivity with government-related carbon inclusiveness platforms, increasing the equity exchange of carbon points, and effectively enhancing the coverage and user activity of corresponding carbon inclusiveness mechanisms.

Author: Xu Liang[1], Zhang Wei[2]

1 Xu Liang, Geely Holdings' Dual Carbon Business Manager in the Digital Technology Sector, has worked in the automotive industry for more than a decade, possessing extensive experience in carbon management within the automotive sector.

2 Zhang Wei, Geely Holdings' Carbon Neutrality Manager, is a senior engineer with over 10 years of experience in carbon management within multinational automotive companies.

PART FOUR
SPECIAL
INNOVATIONS

Reflection and Suggestions on Local Legislation to Promote the Green Transformation of Development Methods

With the deepening of carbon peak and carbon neutrality efforts, local legislation has become an important means and critical pathway for China to achieve its "dual carbon" goals, supporting, promoting, and regulating the green transformation of development methods in all fields. Through research on the legal, regulatory, and policy frameworks supporting the green transformation of development methods, this article summarizes the current status and characteristics of relevant legislation, analyzes the difficulties and challenges posed in current legal system developments in critical areas such as green finance and marketization mechanisms, and provides several suggestions to improve local legislation for green transformation based on relevant local legislative practices.

I. The Current Status and Characteristics of Legal Systems for Promoting the Green Transformation of Development Methods in China

As an important guideline for guiding the orientation of the Party and the country, the report of the 20th CPC National Congress specifies that "accelerating the green transformation of development methods" is one of the key steps to implement the "lucid waters and lush mountains are invaluable assets" concept, which signifies that the adjustment and optimization of industrial structure and the improvement of the green development system has become an essential part of China's future development at the top-level design. The *Opinions of the*

Central Committee of the CPC and the State Council on Carbon Dioxide Peaking and Carbon Neutrality in Full and Faithful Implementation of the New Development Philosophy (hereafter referred to as the *Opinions*) clearly defines a series of implementation paths and support system for green transformation, such as profound adjustment of the industrial structure, sustained consolidation and improvement of carbon sink capacity, and improvement of legal standards and statistical monitoring system, and constitute the "1+N" policy system, serving as the core, together with the *Action Plan for Carbon Dioxide Peaking Before 2030* issued by the State Council in October 2021, as well as special plans for various sectors and industries such as energy, industry, and transportation.

Meanwhile, local opinions on the implementation of "dual carbon" goals also further combine the green transformation approach mentioned in the *Opinions* with the advantages of local development. For example, the *Implementation Opinions of the CPC Zhejiang Provincial Committee and the People's Government of Zhejiang Province on Completely, Accurately, and Comprehensively Implementing the New Development Concept and Doing a Good Job in Carbon Peak and Carbon Neutrality* (hereafter referred to as the *Zhejiang Double Carbon Goals Opinions*) propose specific implementation methods of green transformation that meet local development characteristics and actual needs, such as the implementation of upgraded "991" action plan for the circular economy, promoting green insurance, and building a carbon-neutral technology online trading platform.

A. Series of Policies and Regulations Have Been Issued or Revised at the National Level to Promote the Green Transformation of Development

Since President Xi Jinping first proposed the goals of carbon peaking and carbon neutrality during his speech at the 75th United Nations General Assembly in September 2020, a series of laws, regulations, and policy documents relevant to green transformation have been intensively enacted or revised at the national level, continuously promoting reforms and innovation, and increasing corresponding institutional supply for promoting green economic transformation and development.

At the level of laws and regulations, in December 2020, the Ministry of Ecology and Environment issued the *Administrative Measures for Carbon Emissions Trading (Trial Implementation)* (Decree No.19 of the Ministry of Ecology and Environment), as well as technical specifications for carbon emission allowance trading, quota allocation, greenhouse gas reporting and counting, and others, providing legal basis for the establishment and operation of the national carbon market; in November 2021, the Ministry of Ecology and Environment issued the *Administrative Measures for Legal Disclosure of Enterprise Environmental Information*, which require enterprises to establish and improve an administrative system for the legal disclosure of environmental information and include carbon emission information within the scope of environmental information required to be disclosed by enterprises; in April 2023, the National Development and Reform Commission issued the newly revised the *Measures for Energy Conservation Review of Fixed Asset Investment Projects*, which highlights the guiding direction of controlling fossil energy consumption; in February 2023, the Supreme People's Court issued the *Opinions of the Supreme People's Court on the Full, Accurate, and Comprehensive Implementation of the New Development Concept and Providing Legal Services for Actively and Prudently Promoting Carbon Peaking and Carbon Neutrality* (hereafter referred to as the *Supreme Court's Opinions*), which is the first normative document covering field of "dual carbon" goals issued by the Supreme People's Court. The *Supreme Court's Opinions* solves the key legal application issues in judgement, such as carbon market trading, safeguarding the deep transformation of industrial structures, and providing important guidance for people's courts at various levels in the future trial of dual carbon goals-related cases.

At the policy level, in February 2021, the State Council issued the *Guideline to Accelerate the Development of a Green and Low-carbon Circular Economic Development System* (hereafter referred to as the *Guideline on Circular Economy*), which uses the whole life cycle concept to clarify the construction process of a green, low-carbon, and circulatory development economic system; in April 2021, the *Guideline on Setting Up and Improving the Mechanism to Realize the Value of Ecological Products* issued by the State Council was the first programmatic document to implement the "Two Mountains" theory at the institutional arrangement and practical operation level. Through the "1 + 6" institutional framework, it clarifies the mechanism and strategic direction for realizing the value of ecological products; in October 2021, the State Council issued the *Action Plan for Carbon Dioxide Peaking Before 2030* issued by the State Council is a primary policy document for "N" in the "1 + N" policy system and is more specific in terms of tasks and targets compared to the *Opinions*, becoming an important basis and reference for various departments and local governments to prepare action plan for carbon dioxide peaking. In October 2021, the State Council issued the *Opinions on Promoting Green Development of Urban and Rural Construction*, which proposed measures such as developing zero-carbon buildings and implementing a unified green building identification system, clarifying the main path for promoting green development in the construction field. In December 2021, the State Council issued the *Comprehensive Plan for Energy Conservation and Emission Reduction During the 14th Five-Year Plan Period*, which establishes the overall requirements, major goals, policy mechanisms, and guarantee measures for promoting energy conservation and emission reduction during the 14th Five-Year Plan period.

B. Local Legislation Has Become an Important Means of Promoting Green Transformation and Development

Local legislation also plays an important role in providing valuable experience for other local and national green transformation legislation through pilot projects. Taking the *Tianjin Carbon Peak and Carbon Neutrality Promotion Regulation* (hereinafter referred to as the "*Tianjin Regulation*") as an example, the regulation further clarifies that the "dual carbon" goals shall be considered macroscopically in local legislation, policy setting, planning, and project layout based on the establishment of the management system of dual carbon goals in Tianjin. Among them, the "Green Transformation" chapter is specially designed in the *Tianjin Regulation* to propose proposes specific implementation methods such as increasing the proportion of net extraneous electricity and green electricity, promoting the all-round construction of green buildings in new urban areas, and conducting green life building activities, so as to achieve three goals, i.e., adjusting the energy structure, promoting green industrial transformation, and promoting green and low-carbon life.

With the rapid progress of China's green transformation, the new problems produced in the new market and field of carbon peaking and carbon neutrality cannot be responded to in a timely manner through laws and regulations formulated at the national level. At this time, local legislation, with its flexible legislative approach, can quickly and effectively fill the gaps in relevant legislative areas based on local conditions. Taking green finance as an example, the *Guidelines for Establishing the Green Financial System* was released in 2016, which first clarified the concept of "green finance" in China and proposed the development path and incentive measures for supporting and encouraging green finance. However, as an administrative normative document, it lacks legally binding force, and the *Environmental Protection Law*, the *Law on Commercial Banks*, and other laws and regulations lack relevant provisions on green finance. In response, Shenzhen implemented the Regulations of Shenzhen Special Economic Zone on Green Finance (hereinafter referred to as the *Shenzhen Regulations*) in 2021, Huzhou implemented the *Regulations of Huzhou on Promoting Green Finance* (hereinafter referred to as the *Huzhou Regulations*) in 2022, and Pudong New Area of Shanghai implemented the *Pudong New Area Green Financial Development Regulations* (hereinafter referred to as the *Pudong Regulations*) in 2022. These local legislations are all fully characterized by adapting to local conditions. For example, regarding the support for green credit, the *Shenzhen Regulations* include policy guidance such as enriching green credit varieties, reducing the cost of green credit funds, and expanding the scale of green credit; the *Huzhou Regulations* provide support for green credit in financing amount and interest rate pricing; the *Tianjin Regulations* proposes an increase in credit support for low-carbon energy-saving projects, while the *Pudong Regulations* support green credit business by exploring ways of increasing the tolerance of non-performing loans for green credit. Although each place has established different mechanisms and measures, they all reflect support for green finance and promote exploration and practice of supervisory authorities, financial institutions, and related enterprises in the field of green finance at the practical level, truly empowering the green transformation and development of the finance industry.

In the process of actively promoting the green transformation of development models through local legislation, Zhejiang Province has also been at the forefront of the country. In May 2016, the *Zhejiang Province Green Building Regulations* were implemented, which was the first local legislation in China to promote green buildings in a mandatory manner, classify the construction standards of green buildings, and provide incentive measures such as raising the loan limit for provident fund according to the level. The *Zhejiang Province Ecological Environment Protection Regulations* implemented in August 2022 fully embodies the leading superiority of Zhejiang's digital reform. It provides support for digital pollution control by building an integrated platform for ecological environment comprehensive coordination management and applying scenarios such as "no waste in Zhejiang" and "problem discovery and supervision online". The *Zhejiang Province Electricity Regulations* taken effect in January 2023, is the first comprehensive local electricity regulation issued after the dual carbon goals were proposed in China. It proposes innovative incentives for the development of new energy and stipulates that newly built public buildings and industrial plants should install distributed photovoltaic power generation devices in accordance with national and provincial regulations, allowing their electricity generation to offset building energy consumption or the total energy consumption of industrial enterprises according to relevant regulations. In addition, the *Zhejiang Province Green Low-carbon Transformation Promotion Regulations*, which focuses on comprehensive green transformation and development, is also included in Zhejiang Province's 2023 legislative plan.

II. Problems in the Legal Construction of Green Transformation

A. Lack of Legal Regulations Leads to "Lawlessness"

With the increasing efforts in achieving the dual carbon goals, various new technologies and mechanisms for energy conservation, carbon reduction, pollution reduction, and efficiency improvement have emerged, providing new tools and means for various entities such as governments, enterprises, and the public to implement green transformation and development. However, due to a certain lag in legislation, there will inevitably be a lack of legal regulations at the dawn of the progress for some emerging fields, resulting in a dilemma of "lawlessness" for related entities in the green transformation process. Taking the carbon emission allowance trading market as an example, as an innovative system that controls greenhouse gas emissions through market mechanisms, the carbon emission allowance trading market is an important policy tool for China to achieve the "dual carbon" goals. In order to guarantee the operation of the carbon emission allowance trading market, the central and local governments have successively promulgated a series of regulations on carbon emission accounting, reporting, verification, carbon emission allowance trading, and related accounting treatment. Although the legal framework of the carbon market is continuously improving, both the central and the local governments have clearly defined the legal attributes of carbon emission allowances, and there is a lack of relevant institutional regulations for the taxable entities participating in carbon emission allowance trading and related tax treatment. This not only affects the enthusiasm of enterprises to enter the carbon market to a certain extent but also makes it difficult for financial institutions and enterprises to identify and prevent possible legal risks in the process of carrying out carbon asset management, carbon finance, and related derivative product innovation due to lack of legal basis.

B. Lack of Coordination Between Legislation Limits the Effectiveness of Green Transformation Policies

It is a complex and systematic project to promote the green transformation of development methods, with related policies and regulations involving various industries and fields such as energy, transportation, construction, S&T, and finance. The legal construction progress and regulatory system of different industries and fields are different, and the lack of coordination between different policies and regulations limits the effectiveness of green transformation policy measures. Taking the hydrogen energy development field as an example, hydrogen energy is not only an important part of the future national energy system but also an important carrier to realize green and low-carbon transformation for energy end-users. Although the National Energy Administration listed hydrogen energy under the "energy" category in the latest draft of the *Energy Law of the People's Republic of China* (*Exposure Draft*), policies such as the *Opinions* and *Zhejiang Double Carbon Goals Opinions* have regarded promoting the high-quality development of the hydrogen energy industry as an important part of building a clean, low-carbon, safe, and efficient energy system, and several special planning documents are issued, such as the *Plan on the Development of Hydrogen Energy for the 2021-2035 Period*, there is no legal regulation that clearly includes the development and utilization of hydrogen energy in the energy regulatory scope. At the same time, under the current legal framework, hydrogen gas is a kind of hazardous chemical and is subject to relevant laws and regulations on hazardous chemicals for its production, storage, and transportation. Hydrogen production projects can only be built in chemical park areas. Although the Ministry of Emergency Management issued the *Hazardous Chemicals Safety Law of the People's Republic of China* (*Exposure Draft*) in October 2020, which stipulated that "new construction projects for hazardous chemicals manufacturing should be implemented in chemical industrial parks, except for resource-based projects and hazardous chemical construction projects for other industries". It provides the possibility of lifting land restrictions for hydrogen energy enterprises but has not yet come into effect officially. In practice, different regions and different regulatory departments may have different requirements for the construction management procedures in processes such as hydrogen preparation, storage, and refueling, safety supervision responsibilities, and construction, approval processes, and regulatory methods of hydrogen energy infrastructure, resulting in a lack of guidance for hydrogen users or difficulties in implementing hydrogen projects, making it difficult to meet the basic needs of high-quality development of the hydrogen energy industry.

C. "More Soft Constraints and Less Hard Constraints" Leads to Weaker Legislative Binding Force

Although many laws, regulations, and rules related to green transformation development have been issued or revised at the national and local levels in recent years, in terms of their content, they are mainly composed of promotional and principled provisions aimed at guiding and encouraging relevant entities to adjust and optimize their original operating and behavioral models, with relatively few restrictive provisions or weak punishment measures, which cannot effectively deter illegal and irregular behaviors. For example, although the *Tianjin Regulations* stipulate several implementation methods, including "gradually expanding the consumption of non-fossil energy" for the goal of "adjusting the energy structure," there are no mandatory provisions or corresponding legal responsibilities set for participating entities. As the basic law for regulating and adjusting national carbon emission allowance trading and related activities, the *Administrative Measures for Carbon Emissions Trading (Trial Implementation)* sets corresponding punitive provisions for behaviors such as failing to fulfill carbon emission reporting obligations or failing to pay carbon emission quotas on time and in full, but even for serious violations of the basic regulations for carbon emission allowance trading management, such as failing to pay on time and in full, the amount of fines is only between 20,000 and 30,000 yuan, which cannot effectively urge key emission units to fulfill their carbon emission control responsibilities compared to the quota price in the national carbon market. Similarly, the *Shenzhen Regulations* impose a fine of only between 20,000 and 100,000 yuan for violations such as failing to disclose environmental information as required or falsifying data or information, which is not symmetric with the high profits obtained by enterprises from low-cost green financing through "greenwashing," and cannot effectively prevent illegal behaviors such as "greenwashing" thus deviating from the intention and original purpose of incentivizing the development of green finance.

D. Lack of Supporting Measures Affects the Implementation Effect

Although many innovative mechanisms have been created and established through legislation at the national and local levels, in the early stages of implementation, there are many practical difficulties due to the lack of supporting measures. Taking the field of green finance as an example, although the *Guideline on Circular Economy* has proposed many requirements at the national level, such as developing green credit and direct financing as well as green insurance, and the *Huzhou Regulations*, *Pudong Regulations*, *Shenzhen Regulations*, and other local regulations have all defined the connotation of "green finance," the technical and standard systems that are clear, unified, and aligned with international standards for defining and judging loan projects as "green" have not yet been established. In addition to the guidance catalogs based on green industries and green bonds issued by some industry regulatory departments, there is a lack of quantifiable indicators and evaluation systems in financial institutions recognized by regulatory departments and regulatory authorities, which are used to identify and determine green subjects or green projects and match them with corresponding green financial products and services. Some traditional high-emission and high-pollution industries urgently need to transform and develop, but it is difficult for them to obtain the necessary financial support for green transformation. In addition, even though the People's Bank of China has put forward requirements for information disclosure and third-party professional organization verification for financial institutions using carbon emission reduction support tools, regulations on what requirements and conditions the third-party organizations need to meet and what rules and methods they should apply to verify the information disclosed by financial institutions have not been standardized yet.

III. Recommendations for Advancing Legislation for Local Development To Transform Towards Green Sustainability

A. Setting Main Goals and Pathways for Local Green Transformation Development

In the current era where green and low-carbon transformation has become an international trend, more than 30 countries and regions, including the European Union, the United Kingdom, France, Germany, and South Korea, have successively introduced laws and regulations related to responding to climate change, controlling greenhouse gas emissions, and promoting low-carbon and green development. Considering those laws can chronically adjust social relations, and "carbon neutrality" has phased and time-limited characteristics, although there have been legislative achievements that have not been named with "carbon neutrality", most have included the "carbon neutrality" goal and related management systems in these laws and regulations. Through legislation, it can ensure the realization of climate neutrality goals. In the process of constructing a legal system related to green transformation development in China, it is recommended to give legal status to the goal of green transformation development, to form constraints through local legislation for all participants engaged in green transformation development, provide a driving force for the green transformation development in various fields, and make the formulation and implementation of emission reduction methods in different fields more related and collaborative. At the same time, the establishment of the legal status of green transformation development goals can also provide a basis for the evaluation of the effectiveness of green transformation in various fields, thus ensuring the scientific and effective establishment of goals.

B. Filling the Legal Gaps Formed in the Application of New Technology and the Birth of New Market

According to the *Opinions* and the implementation plans in various regions, new materials, new technologies, and new equipment for low-carbon, zero-carbon, negative-carbon, and energy storage, such as local development and utilization of hydrogen energy and solar energy, carbon capture, utilization, and storage, as well as new market mechanisms such as carbon inclusiveness, value realization of ecological products, and power trading, will be developed rapidly and widely used. Local legislation can fully bring into play its characteristic advantages of being flexible and taking pioneer initiatives in accordance with local conditions, solving the blockages and difficulties for enterprises in applying new technologies, participating in new markets, conducting new businesses, filling the original legal gaps, and provide institutional guarantees for various entities to legally and compliantly explore and innovate green transitions in the new situation. For example, the latest *Zhejiang Province Electricity Regulations* issued by Zhejiang Province has responded to the increasingly prominent issue of "selling electricity through walls" by stipulating that "The power production enterprises for distributed photovoltaic power generation, decentralized wind power generation, and other ways, can directly trade with surrounding users according to regulations". Although specific rules still need to be formulated by the provincial power management department and reported to the provincial government for approval, it still provides useful references and guidance for other regions to explore "selling electricity through walls".

C. Establishing a Complete Set of Supporting Policies and Technical Standards

At the national level, a "1+N" policy system for carbon peaking and carbon neutrality has been constructed. Other than the *Opinions* that play the leading role of the "1", there are also action plans formulated, as well as support measures, such as S&T support, carbon sink capacity, statistical accounting, inspection and assessment, and guarantee policies in finance and pricing. At the local level, it is difficult to meet the need to promote the green and low-carbon transformation of development methods under the new situation without a series of policy measures and technical standards" in addition to comprehensive or specialized legislation. Based on the actual situation in Zhejiang Province, a carbon inclusiveness mechanism, a green product certification system, and a carbon labeling certification mechanism can be established through local legislation, and the fiscal awarding and subsidy mechanism linked to the quality and value of ecological products can be improved. A provincial carbon emission accounting system and city- and county-level carbon emission accounting methods should also be developed and improved, and the construction of a green finance reform and innovation pilot zone should be carried out to establish provincial and industry standards for green finance. This can not only effectively promote the green transformation of Zhejiang Province's development mode, but also provide a pilot for the country's efforts to improve relevant technical standards.

D. Establishing a Binding Regulatory and Punitive Mechanism

In local legislation, there also needs mandatory and regulatory provisions in addition to management-oriented and promotion-oriented provisions, to effectively deter and punish violations and irregularities of relevant parties, to balance soft constraints and less hard constraints, and to ensure that key systems can be effectively implemented. At the same time, the responsibilities and powers of regulatory departments should be defined clearly to prevent the absence of supervision and avoid work being uncoordinated or overseen multiple times by different regulators. For instance, in the field of green finance, Zhejiang Province can establish stricter legal responsibilities for behaviors that are "greenwashing" or violate or undermine the basic management system of green finance based on the definition of the connotation of green finance through the formulating *Zhejiang Province Green Low-carbon Transformation Promotion Regulations or* specialized legislation on the basis of evaluation and conclusion of the implementation of the *Huzhou Regulations*, so as to provide powerful legal protection for the healthy development of green finance.

E. Strengthening Institutional Coordination and Linkage Between Regions

Regional coordinated legislation plays a critical role in the green integrated developments of Yangtze River Delta region. It not only helps to intensively demonstrate the political, institutional, and methodological innovations for implementing the new development concept and promoting high-quality development in the Yangtze River Delta region, to lead the development of the Yangtze River Economic Belt in a better way but also contributes to transforming ecological advantages into advantages of economic and social development and exploring an eco-friendly development model. Therefore, to explore the transition from regional project coordination to regional integrated institutional innovation, to achieve wide consultation, joint contribution, joint management, sharing, and mutual benefits, and to effectively solve the functional orientation conflict between local legislations, it is suggested that localities fully consider the legal system and the actual implementation situations of different regions when promoting legislation for the green transformation of development modes, promote the mutual recognition of technical standards and reinforce the coordination and linkage between region, achieving the organic unity of economic developments, wellbeing of consumers, and sustainable development and exploring a new path for co-construction and sharing across the administrative region, where ecological civilization and economic and social development are mutually reinforcing.

Author: Wan Tunan[1], Tang Wei[2]

---

1   Wan Tunan, a paralegal at Dentons Shanghai, mainly engaged in research on EU policies and legal compliance analysis, WTO dispute resolution mechanism, global climate governance, and comprehensive assessment of green development.

2   Tang Wei, an advisor at Dentons Shanghai, a senior consultant at Shanghai Carbon Neutrality Promotion Center, a member of Carbon Neutrality Expert Committee of Hangzhou Energy Society, and a researcher of the Environmental Resources and Energy Law Research Centre at Fudan University. Ms. Tang is committed to policy research in climate response, resource and environment, and innovative business practices in carbon market, green finance and other fields.

Accelerating the R&D, Promotion, and Application of Advanced Energy-Saving and Carbon Emission Reduction Technologies to Promote Green and High-quality Development

The promotion and application of energy-saving and carbon emission reduction technologies play a key supporting role in fostering the greening and low-carbon transformation of the economy and society, and in promoting high-quality development. China has made considerable efforts to advance the energy-saving and carbon emission reduction technologies and popularize green and low-carbon technologies, but there still exist some problems. These include the weak technology innovation system, an insufficient supply of R&D, difficulties in technology selection and landing, and an incomplete support system for technology promotion. The author proposes a series of countermeasures, with a view to strengthening the technology innovation system, improving the technology supply, building platforms and service systems for promoting energy-saving and carbon-reducing technologies, and improving supporting policies and measures for technology promotion.

The R&D, innovation, promotion, and application of advanced energy-saving and carbon emission reduction technologies is an important approach and tool for improving energy efficiency and reducing carbon emissions, as well as a fundamental guarantee for achieving the goals of "carbon peaking and carbon neutrality" and promoting green and high-quality development. The report of the 20th CPC National Congress stated that "we will accelerate the R&D, promotion, and application of advanced energy-saving and carbon emission reduction technologies", providing direction and guidance to staff in this field.

I. New Opportunities for the R&D, Promotion, and Application of Green and Low-carbon Technologies

Nowadays, green and low-carbon technologies have become an important area in the new round of global competition in science and technology, playing an increasingly important role. General Secretary Xi Jinping stressed during the 36th collective study of the Political Bureau of the CPC Central Committee that "we should pay close attention to green and low-carbon technology innovation, and accelerate the R&D, promotion and application of advanced energy-saving and carbon emission reduction technologies." Scientific and technological innovation is a key link for breakthroughs in green development, which has set higher requirements for green technology innovation and brought unprecedented development opportunities.

First, green development is creating a broad market demand for energy-saving and carbon-reducing advanced technologies. In order to accelerate green development, China has revised a series of laws, regulations, policies, and standards, and introduced the "1+N" policy system for carbon peaking and carbon neutrality, which also strengthened the index constraint such as energy intensity and carbon emission intensity, etc. It is estimated that China will need RMB 56 trillion to achieve carbon peaking by 2030 and RMB 70 trillion to achieve carbon neutrality by 2060.

Second, achieving green and high-quality development will create a huge space for the development of energy-saving and carbon-reducing advanced technologies, which represent an inherent requirement for the optimization and upgrading of the economic structure and an inevitable choice for the cultivation of a new green driving force. Since the reform and opening up, China's energy-saving efforts have achieved remarkable results, but the energy efficiency level is still 1/3 lower than the world average level, and there is a lot of room for improvement. Technology upgrading is not only an important support for the transformation and upgrading of traditional industries but also a key area for the generation of new supply, representing an essential driving force for the establishment of a green and low-carbon circular economic development system.

Third, the "Beautiful China Initiative" has provided sustained impetus for the development of advanced technologies to save energy and reduce carbon emissions. Faced with environmental pollution, low energy efficiency, and other difficulties in the course of economic development, China still needs more efforts to promote ecological civilization construction and meet people's demands for a better ecological environment and a better life. These advanced technologies, which can improve energy efficiency and reduce emissions at the source, are also essential approaches to implementing the "Beautiful China Initiative" and will receive constant impetus from the initiative.

According to the report of the 20th CPC National Congress, "a greening and low-carbon economy and society is crucial to high-quality development". In order to build a model zone of shared prosperity through high-quality development, Zhejiang Province needs to continuously strengthen the positioning of green and low-carbon in its economic transformation and development, accelerate the transformation and upgrading of traditional industries, substantially boost the greening of the economy, and build an industrial structure with high technological content, low resource consumption, and low environmental pollution. The green transformation featured with greening and being low-carbon will reduce resource consumption and pollutant emissions through technological progress and energy conservation, thus creating a high-quality development pattern with efficient use of resources, lower emissions, a clean environment, and ecological security. As a forerunner of socialism with Chinese characteristics and a pioneer of provincial modernization, Zhejiang must continue to embrace the current situation, seize the opportunity and take the lead in a new way to promote the transformation and development of a green and low-carbon economy, clean and low-carbon energy supply, efficient and intelligent energy use and high-quality economic development at the provincial level, so as to create a national and even global highland of green and low-carbon high-quality development.

II. Practices and Approaches in the Promotion of Energy-saving and Carbon Emission Reduction Technologies in China and Zhejiang Province

A. China's Practices in Green Technology Promotion

1. Progressively Improving the Policy Framework for Technology Promotion

First, special support measures have been stipulated in laws and regulations. The *Energy Conservation Law* requires the central government and local governments to allocate special funds to support the R&D, demonstration and promotion of energy-saving technologies, and the construction of key energy-saving projects. Supporting policies such as tax incentives shall be implemented for the production and application of energy-saving technologies and products listed in the national recommended catalogues. China also encourages and supports energy-saving technology renovation and other projects in terms of procurement regulation, credit financing and pricing policies. The *Made in China 2025* initiative has proposed to strengthen the promotion and application of energy-saving and environmental protection technologies, techniques and equipment, and to fully implement clean production. Policy funding support continues to be enforced. For example, the *Guidelines for Green Bond Issuance* has included projects of energy-saving and emission reduction technology transformation, energy-saving and environmental protection industry, and low-carbon industry as its key support categories.

2. Continuously Improved Mechanisms for Technology Promotion and Application

First, catalogues for the promotion of energy-saving technologies cover a wide range of areas and nearly all sectors of the national economy. For example, the *Catalog for Promotion of Key Technologies on National Key Energy Saving and Low-carbon Emission* and the *Green Technologies Promotion Catalogue* issued by the National Development and Reform Commission, the *Recommend Catalogue for National Key Industrial Energy Saving Equipment* and the *"Energy Efficiency Star" Products Catalogue* issued by the Ministry of Industry and Information Technology, the *Reference Catalogue of Green Energy-Saving*

Technology Products for Public Institutions issued by the National Government Offices Administration, the *Announcement on the Promotion and Application of Green Construction Technologies* issued by the Ministry of Housing and Urban-Rural Development, and the *Guidelines for Green Technology in Agriculture* (*2018-2030*) issued by the Ministry of Agriculture and Rural Affairs and so on. These documents have covered nearly all sectors of the national economy. Provinces (autonomous regions and municipalities directly under the central government) have also released their own recommended catalogs related to energy saving and low-carbon. Second, the application cases of energy-saving technologies have made a good model. Typical technology application cases have made good demonstrations and played a leading role, namely the "Top 10 Energy-Saving Technologies and Top 10 Practices of International Energy Efficiency Standard", "Typical Cases of Application of Key Energy-Saving Technologies" of the National Energy Conservation Center, the "National Guide and Cases of Application of Energy-Saving Technologies in Industry", the "Typical Demonstration Projects of Energy-Saving and Carbon Emission Reduction in the Transport Sector", "Typical Cases of Energy-Saving Buildings", the "Top 10 Technologies of Energy-Saving and Carbon Emission Reduction in Agriculture and Rural Areas", etc. Third, the platform for the promotion and application of energy-saving technologies has been continuously improved. National energy-saving centers, industry associations, social organizations, local energy-saving centers, local energy-saving associations, and other promotion and application platforms have been established, forming a situation in which platforms promote, industry experts assist and technology enterprises participate in the promotion and application of technology.

B. The Practice of Promotion of Green Technology in Zhejiang Province

Zhejiang is an important part of the Yangtze River Economic Belt with abundant innovation resources, significant industrial advantages, strong technology R&D strength and active market innovation market entities, and it is a leader in innovative development. Owing to the attempts in exploring market-based mechanisms for promoting energy-saving and carbon-reducing technologies, Zhejiang has achieved remarkable results. In May 2021, according to the *Reply of Letter from the General Office of the National Development and Reform Commission on the Consent to Establish the National Green Technology Trading Center in Zhejiang*, the National Green Technology Trading Center was established with the Entrepreneurship and Innovation Center of the State Grid Zhejiang Electric Power Co., Ltd. as its main body. Focusing on the "dual carbon" goal, the Center provides a matchmaking service between the supply and demand of green technology. A team of green technology specialists and brokers has been set up to provide services such as technology acceptance, public deal and trade authentication for traders. At the same time, an intelligent search system has been jointly developed and built by various parties, and more than 1 million green technology patents have been reserved to help technology brokers to make trading decisions with big data. In more than a year of operation, the Center has facilitated 189 transactions, with the value exceeding 300 million yuan, and leveraged over 10 billion yuan of green industry investment. With green technology trading as the driving force, it guides technological innovation, promotes the transformation of achievements, accelerates the construction of a market-oriented green technology innovation system, and strives to become a comprehensive service platform for market-oriented green technology trading with domestic leadership, international influence and comprehensive openness.

Based in Zhejiang and with a national focus, the National Green Technology Trading Center will conduct technical research on projects listed in the national green technology promotion catalogs such as the energy-saving and environmental protection industry, clean production industry, clean energy industry, ecological environment industry and green upgrading of infrastructure. This will also contribute to China's strengthening of its "blood-making function" in the field of green technology by cultivating its main bodies, namely a group of innovative professionals and leading enterprises. Efforts will be made to promote the green and low-carbon transformation of key industries and fields and to build a market-oriented green technology innovation system. By promoting green technology demonstration, and optimizing its innovation environment and the industrial chain, the Center will also speed up the "bringing in" and "going global" of green technology, grasp the initiative to enhance its competitiveness around the globe, and make a contribution to the cultivation and growth of green industries and help achieve carbon peaking and carbon neutrality.

III. Major Problems in Technology R&D, Promotion and Application

Despite the significant opportunities for the development of energy-saving and carbon-reduction green technologies, it is also important to acknowledge objectively and rationally the challenges in R&D and promotion and application.

A. R&D on Advanced Technologies for Energy Saving and Carbon Reduction Needs to be Strengthened

First, the overall level of energy-saving and carbon reduction technology needs to be improved. The proportion of China's green technology ranking of world leaders, average level, and followers are 10%, 35% and 55% respectively, most of which are followers of the international advanced levels. Furthermore, the commercialization rate of China's technological achievements is still low, and close integration between R&D and promotion and application is urgently needed. The proportion of green and low-carbon technology patents that are applied for by China's research institutes is about 30%, which is higher than the international average, but the proportion of invalidation and abandonment is as high as 60%, and the relevant investment has not resulted in advanced productivity. For example, the provision of basic software for new energy vehicles, high-precision sensors and computer chips relies heavily on foreign suppliers, which is mainly due to the insufficient supply of high-end technology R&D and insufficient integration with applications.

Zhejiang Province has made significant efforts in building major technology innovation platforms and key core technology research in the field of carbon peaking and carbon neutrality science and technology. At present, it has built 5 national key laboratories for clean energy utility, 71 provincial key laboratories for solar energy and energy-saving technology application, 22 provincial new type R&D institutions. Among them, 48 major science and technology projects in renewable energy, energy storage, hydrogen energy, blue carbon, etc. are organized to be implemented. In general, however, there still exist some problems, which include the weak strength of the leading enterprises among the innovation institutions, the lack of independent innovation capacity and the low industrial technology level. Further breakthroughs are needed in key core technologies such as energy storage batteries and liquid hydrogen storage and transportation, and technologies in traditional industries such as efficient energy-saving technologies and carbon capture, utilization and storage (CCUS) still need to be updated.

B. Prominent Difficulties Encountered by both Suppliers and Users

At present, it is difficult for advanced technology suppliers to popularizing their technologies and to get customers, and users also find it difficult to choose and apply appropriate technologies. The reasons are as follows: first, it takes as long as more than 3 years at a low pace to get payback from most energy-saving and carbon reduction technology renovation projects. Many projects are characterized by high investments, low returns and high unpredictable risks, so enterprises are reluctant to use them. Second, there is a lack of risk-sharing mechanisms for the technology application landing. Related parties are in isolated operations with no risk-sharing mechanism for the fulfillment of the social responsibility of energy-saving and carbon reduction, and for the part that cannot generate revenue. Enterprises with high energy consumption, long processes and high safety factors required from industries such as electricity, steel and petrifaction dare not to use these technologies. Third, the lack of fair and objective authoritative evaluation and verification. The new technology needs to be mature through the application with the effect verified by concrete cases, which requires the authorities to make a fair and objective evaluation. But the lack of authoritative evaluation and verification tools has led to widespread difficulties to choose technologies for energy users.

The private sector in Zhejiang's economy is well-developed and there are many small and medium-sized enterprises, but their small size, weak technological strength and lack of professionals make them unable to become the main body of technological innovation. Insufficient strong mechanisms to ensure energy-saving and carbon reduction technological innovation, such as property rights incentives and market incentives, have weakened their technological innovation motivation to a certain extent. Moreover, there also exist some barriers to the commercialization of scientific and technological achievements, such as too many links and a non-corresponding system, so that good energy-saving scientific and technological achievements cannot be effectively commercialized and applied.

C. Inadequate Management Systems Constraining the Development of Advanced Technologies for Energy Efficiency and Carbon Reduction

First, some of the existing laws, regulations and policies are not effectively implemented. China has promulgated several laws and regulations such as the *Energy Conservation Law*, as well as fiscal, tax and financial policies to support the R&D, demonstration, promotion and application of energy-saving technologies, but some of them are not sophisticated or can't be properly implemented, others are weak in mandatory constraints, leading to the inefficient implementation. Second, major difficulties in the bidding system need to be overcome. The bidding system is currently a universal, long-term and fundamentally influential guarantee system for the application of advanced technologies, but some of the key links need to be improved, such as the lack of specific provisions for the "priority" use of new technologies, products and equipment for energy-saving and carbon reduction. Third, insufficient means are there to support technology promotion services. Promotion services are the key bridges to the landing of advanced technologies application, which requires the government, professional institutions and enterprises to work together, perform their respective roles and continuously enrich the means and carriers. Common problems such as inaccurate positioning, isolated operation and simple means still exist, which prevent them from meeting the requirements of development. Fourth, the existing standards cannot better guide the production. China has issued 79 mandatory energy efficiency standards for end-use products and equipment, but only 35% of them have been revised in the past five years, and some of the indicators have fallen behind the actual market situation to some extent. Timely revisions are needed to generate their leading function from action forcing.

Zhejiang Province has carried out successful practices and achieved significant results in the implementation of "Total quantity and intensity target control" for energy consumption, as well as institutional innovation and practical exploration of the management of major energy users. Nevertheless, it is imperative to strengthen the implementation of some energy-saving systems, especially in terms of raising awareness of energy-saving and carbon reduction among energy users and eliminating energy-intensive equipment. In addition, some of the indicators of current energy-saving standards are not science-based and the implementation needs to be strengthened, and the policy atmosphere and environment to support the promotion and application of advanced technologies for energy-saving and carbon reduction needs to be further improved.

IV. Suggestions for In-depth Technology Development and Promotion

The R&D, promotion and application of energy-saving, carbon reduction and other advanced green technologies require efforts of both the supply and demand sides, to uphold problem-oriented and demand-oriented principles and focus on the problems of key links. Based on the practices in Zhejiang, the following suggestions are made.

First, it is necessary to improve the overall level and lead by key technology R&D in the general field. Equipment such as boilers and motors often consume large amounts of energy and have a wide range of applications, and can bring about great driving forces through technological breakthroughs and updates, so we should focus on the further research and development of key technologies in these fields and speed up their application. In addition, joint efforts and investment in the pioneering key common technologies should be intensified, striving to be at the forefront and grasp the initiative. Relying on the existing resource carriers such as major enterprises, universities and research institutions, we should actively build innovation centers, engineering centers and enterprise technology centers, etc., with the goal of breaking through key technologies and forming a R&D service system with its own advantages and complete forms. In the field of fundamental and cutting-edge green and low-carbon technologies, Zhejiang Province has focused on hydrogen energy, energy storage, carbon dioxide capture and other fields, with breakthroughs in green hydrogen production and transmission and storage for offshore wind power, efficient and safe large-scale energy storage, large-scale carbon dioxide capture, ecological carbon sinks and other technologies. As for applied technology research, major projects have been laid out and implemented in an orderly manner by year to accelerate breakthroughs in boilers, motors, pumps, fans, air compressors, low-grade waste heat utilization and other general high-efficiency energy-saving technologies, as well as high-efficiency solar photovoltaic power generation, large-scale low-cost offshore wind power, carbon dioxide capture and mineralization utilization and other key common technologies.

Second, it is necessary to intensify the support of policies and measures for the R&D, promotion and application of advanced technologies. Efforts should be made to speed up the formulation and revision of relevant laws and regulations, and to clarify the quantitative and continuous growing requirements for rigid support to avoid vague descriptions on laws and regulations. Policies on finance and taxation, prices and so on should be exerted more from the perspective of public benefit and faster development, while finance should be mainly market-oriented balanced with public welfare use considered. Governments need to promote the connection between financial capital and energy-saving and carbon reduction technologies, to foster more technologies commercialized. The bidding system is suggested to be improved by focusing on giving priority to the use of advanced technologies in the bidding process. It is important to establish a risk-sharing mechanism for technology application, led by the government and involving both supply and demand sides and finance and insurance, as well as to remove various thresholds and prerequisites that hinder the application of advanced technologies by means of reforms, especially to break unreasonable restrictions on the application of technology by SMEs.

Third, it is necessary to improve the service mechanism of evaluation and testing and technology promotion. It is necessary to establish and improve the evaluation and testing mechanism with multi-level participation of governments, associations and enterprises, especially to strengthen common testing that serves SMEs and reflects public welfare attributes, and to provide supports for technology development. Efforts are required to facilitate the construction of various service platforms such as technology innovation and technology promotion and trading, and to explore models for a government supported, market-oriented and sustainable developed technology promotion services. It is necessary to build technology trading agencies, i.e., to cultivate agencies engaged in testing, evaluation and verification. Industry associations and service platforms at all levels in Zhejiang Province should act as a bridge between governments and enterprises, compile relevant policies and measures recently issued by the central and provincial governments in a timely manner, conduct regular policy training for various enterprises, and build and enrich technology promotion channels and means. The National Green Technology Trading Center is suggested to give full play to its role as a national platform, establish and improve the green and low-carbon technology assessment and trading system, expedite the commercialization and application of technological innovations, and to provide technical support for the green and low-carbon transformation and development of Zhejiang's economy.

Fourth, it is necessary to formulate and revise relevant standards. Standards for energy-saving and carbon reduction technologies should be formulated and revised according to actual conditions and implemented once being mature, and mandatory energy-saving standards for key energy-consuming areas and equipment must be improved to achieve the wider application of advanced technologies. Mandatory energy-saving standards must be thoroughly implemented and inspected with the results fully utilized to enhance energy users' conscientiousness to save energy and reduce carbon emissions. Zhejiang Province shall fully develop the cooperation mechanism of the energy saving and carbon reduction standard, formulate more scientifically sound and reasonable local energy efficiency standards and strengthen implementation, thus creating a space for energy saving potential and promoting the application of energy saving and carbon reduction technologies.

Fifth, it is necessary to strengthen the training of scientific research professionals and reinforce the basic management of energy conservation and carbon reduction. It is recommended that the role of universities, scientific research institutions, industry associations, and enterprises be fully utilized to establish and improve a multi-level cooperation model for training energy-saving and carbon reduction talents, and to cultivate a cross-disciplinary, complex and diversified R&D team who can overcome difficulties by relying on the practice of projects established. We also suggest that enterprises establish rules and regulations, strengthen the training of energy management personnel, and continuously improve the basic management level of energy saving and carbon reduction work. Zhejiang Province has taken the key position of green low-carbon technology innovation. Relying on special support plans for high-level talents, namely the "Kunpeng Program" of the science and technology sector, leading innovation and entrepreneur teams, the "Ten Thousand Talent Program" and the overseas engineer plan, etc., Zhejiang Province will vigorously introduce and cultivate high-end workers and teams from home and abroad, and strive to introduce leading innovation and entrepreneur teams in the field of "carbon peaking and carbon neutrality", so as to provide solid human resources guarantee for the R&D and application of green low-carbon technologies.

Author: Xin Sheng[1]

References

[1] State Council. The "14th Five-Year Plan" comprehensive work program of energy conservation and emission reduction (State Development〔2021〕33).

[2] National Development and Reform Commission, Ministry of Science and Technology. Notice on the implementation plan for further improving the market-oriented green technology innovation system (2023-2025) (NDRC〔2022〕1885).

[3] National Development and Reform Commission, Ministry of Industry and Information Technology, Ministry of Finance and other nine ministries.

---

1 Xin Sheng, senior engineer, director of the Promotion Department of the National Energy Conservation Center, mainly engaged in research and analysis on energy conservation policies, promotion of energy conservation technology, market-oriented mechanisms of energy conservation , and management of key energy-consuming units.

Guidance on the coordination of energy saving and carbon reduction and recycling to accelerate the renewal of key areas of product and equipment (Development and Reform, Environmental Resources〔2023〕178).

[4] National Development and Reform Commission, General Administration of Market Regulation. Notice on further strengthening the update and upgrade of energy-saving standards and the application of implementation (Development and Reform of environmental regulations〔2023〕269).

[5] Guorui Ward (Beijing) Low Carbon Economy Technology Center. China Industrial Energy Efficiency Technology Progress Report 2015[M]. Beijing: China Science and Technology Press.

[6] Hangzhou network, on the "People's Republic of China Energy Conservation Law" and the implementation of Zhejiang Province, the implementation of the report. https://z.hangzhou.com.cn/2022/rddschy/content/content_8291622.html.

[7] Jiang J P, Tong S J, Lin W J. Analysis of the current situation of energy-saving standardization and countermeasures in Zhejiang province[J]. Popular Standardization, 2014, 2: 51-53.

[8] Xin S, Gong P Q. Research on the problems and countermeasures of energy-saving technologies[J]. Journal of Chinese Energy, 2018, 40 (12): 41-44.

Standardization Facilitates Carbon Peaking and Carbon Neutrality Actions in Zhejiang Province

Achieving the goal of "carbon peaking and carbon neutrality" is a major strategic decision in coordinating international and domestic situations under the strong leadership of the CPC Central Committee with Comrade Xi Jinping as the core. Standards are an important part of national quality infrastructure, improving resource efficiency, green and low-carbon development of energy, in-depth adjustment of industrial structure, green transition of production and lifestyle, and comprehensive green transition of economic and social development. Standards are also of great significance for achieving the goal of carbon peaking and carbon neutrality on schedule. This article sorts out the status of local standards in Zhejiang Province, summarizes the opportunities, problems and challenges under the background of "carbon peaking and carbon neutrality". On this basis, targeted standardization construction suggestions are proposed, aiming to support carbon peaking and carbon neutrality actions of Zhejiang Province.

I. Importance of "Carbon Peaking and Carbon Neutrality" Standardization System Construction

From the *United Nations Framework Convention on Climate Change* and the *Kyoto Protocol* in the 1990s to the Paris Agreement in 2015, global climate governance has changed from a "top-down" mandatory reduction of emissions in developed countries to a "bottom-up" approach by countries. The process of global climate governance has been transformed from "top-down" mandatory emission reduction by developed countries to "bottom-up" climate change action targets by countries that are in line with their national strengths. On September 22, 2020, President Xi proposed the "30 · 60" goal, highlighting the China's determination and responsibility in responding to climate change and greenhouse gas emission reduction. Since then, the Communist Party of China Central Committee and the State Council have attached great importance to the goal of "carbon peaking and carbon neutrality" and have deployed various tasks and measures to achieve it.

In the process of promoting the work of addressing climate change and promoting the development of green low-carbon economy, technical standards have become a recognized way to constrain carbon emissions, improve quality and efficiency, and mitigate climate change. It is also an important basis for the transition to green and low-carbon development, R&D, promotion, and application of advanced energy conservation and carbon emission reduction technologies. It also underpins international efforts to promote carbon peaking and carbon neutrality and respond to climate change.

Achieving the goal of "carbon peaking and carbon neutrality" is a broad and profound social change in Zhejiang Province. It is a multi-factor, complex structure and long-term systemic project. It needs to build a full-coverage, multi-dimensional and multi-level standardization system of "carbon peaking and carbon neutrality", serving as essential supplement and support of "carbon peaking and carbon neutrality" work. The operability of "carbon peaking and carbon neutrality" work is strengthened by standard "quantitative" advantage, leading the "carbon peaking and carbon neutrality" work to extend in the directions of concretization and refinement by playing the role of "supplement and refinement", and systematically promoting green transition of economic structure in Zhejiang Province.

II. Current Status of "Carbon Peaking and Carbon Neutrality" Standardization Construction in Zhejiang Province

Since the "12th Five-Year Plan", Zhejiang Province has continued to promote the formulation of "carbon peaking and carbon neutrality" standards as China launched the climate change work. According to statistics, Zhejiang Province has issued 72 "carbon peaking and carbon neutrality" standards, including 20 standards during the "12th Five-Year Plan", 20 standards during the "13th Five-Year Plan", and 32 standards since the beginning of the "14th Five-Year Plan". From the data of past years, the number of standards in 2019 and 2021 is higher than that in other years. Due to the dual control of energy at the end of 2018, 10 standards were issued in 2019; In 2021, the first year of the "carbon peaking and carbon neutrality" goal, Zhejiang Province issued 23 multi-field standards under the influence of a number of policy incentives, the highest amount ever. In 2022, as "carbon peaking and carbon neutrality" work became rational, the number of standards declined to a certain extent,with a total of 9 standards issued.

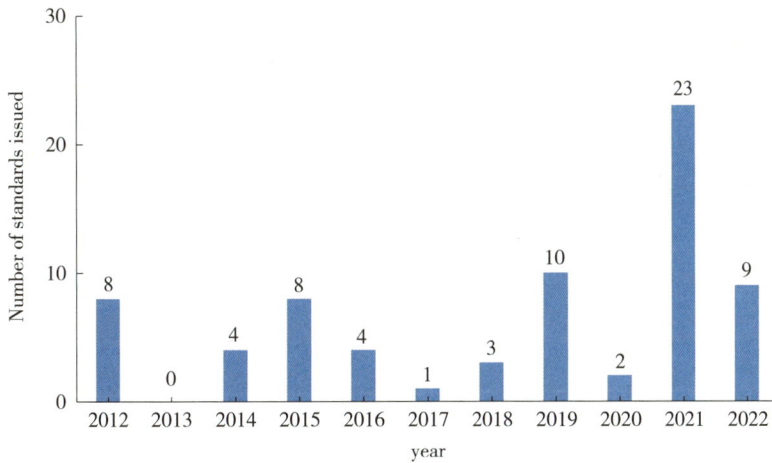

Figure 19-1　Number of "carbon peaking and carbon neutrality"
standards issued in each year from 2012 to 2022

In terms of relevant sectors, the standards cover the "1+6" sectors in Zhejiang Province. Regarding the percentage of each sector, energy accounts for 51%, ranking the first; 17% for residential life, ranking the second; 11% for industry, ranking the third; 8% for construction, ranking the fourth; 7% for comprehensive field, ranking the fifth; transportation and agricultural sectors accounted for a relatively low share of 3%. However, standards in multiple sectors, such as carbon budget, carbon footprint, carbon capture, transportation and storage, are still blank, and further efforts are needed in these fields to carry out research on related standards.

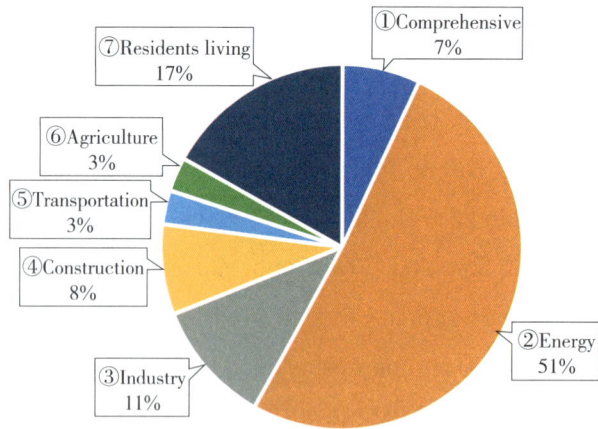

Figure 19-2　Distribution and proportion of local standards of carbon peaking and carbon neutrality in Zhejiang Province

In 2023, Zhejiang Province plans to issue 33 low-carbon standards, including standards in multiple innovative sectors, such as new energy storage, carbon emission accounting system, carbon inclusiveness, and transportation carbon emission accounting in the Yangtze River Delta region, aiming to further improve the "carbon peaking and carbon neutrality" standardization system in Zhejiang Province.

III.New Opportunities and Challenges of "Carbon Peaking and Carbon Neutrality" Standardization System Construction

In recent years, Zhejiang Province has made progress in standardization work, such as energy conservation and carbon emission management, *etc*. However, compared with the urgent requirements for achieving the goal of "carbon peaking and carbon neutrality", the standardization system's extensiveness, coordination, and accuracy remain to be improved. There are still deficiencies in the convergence of standards and policies, the promotion of effective implementation mechanisms of standards, cross-regional mutual recognition of standards, *etc*.

A. The New Opportunities of "Carbon Peaking and Carbon Neutrality" Standardization System Construction under the New Situation

1. The New Problems Brought by "Carbon Peaking and Carbon Neutrality" Proposing New Requirements for Standardization System Construction

Since the goal of "carbon peaking and carbon neutrality" was proposed,

Zhejiang Province has actively carried out and promoted relevant work. However, due to the wide coverage and multiple levels of the "carbon peaking and carbon neutrality" work, new problems may occur during the implementation of each work. The construction of the "carbon peaking and carbon neutrality" standardization system is an extension, refinement and supplement of "1+N+X" policy frame, with strong penetration and wide coverage, which can deepen and consolidate the development of relevant work. To achieve the goal of "carbon peaking and carbon neutrality" as scheduled, Zhejiang Province issued the Implementation Plan of Carbon Peaking and Carbon Neutrality Work Standardization System. It aims to form a "1+6" standardization system covering key sectors and industries by the end of 2024 and put forward the construction requirements, such as consolidating the foundation of common standards,expanding the coverage of standards, etc.

2. Green Development Embracing Bigger Space and Proposing New Requirements for The Improvement of Standards

The green and low-carbon pattern is an intrinsic requirement for high-quality development and the transition from old to new economic engines, which is also the only way for sustainable economic and social development. In this context, the industrial structure and consumption patten of Zhejiang province will undergo significant changes,and enterprises are more willing to transform and upgrade, putting forward new requirements for the construction of a "carbon peaking and carbon neutrality" standardization system. On the one hand, the active transition of traditional industries requires a higher standard threshold. The development of a green economy has boosted the enthusiasm of traditional industries to transform energy conservation and emission reduction. Therefore, the binding force of existing standards is slightly insufficient. It is necessary to improve the identification standards for energy conservation and low-carbon transition for technologies, projects and enterprises, thereby forming strict constraints to promote the transition of industries with high energy consumption and high emission. On the other hand, the development of advantageous enterprises requires innovation and high-quality standards. Due to the continuous influx of green market competitors, in order to maintain and enhance their competitive advantages, advantageous enterprises require advanced and cutting-edge standards to seek greater possibilities and opportunities for emission reduction, further reduce the risks and responsibilities of greenhouse gas emission, and enhance their competitiveness.

3. Persistent R&D and Innovation of Low-carbon Technologies Providing New Scenarios For Standard Application

Low-carbon technology innovation is the core driving force for promoting the realization of the goal of "carbon peaking and carbon neutrality". At present, Zhejiang Province is in the midst of a new round of technological revolution and industrial transition. Innovative development of low-carbon technologies will continue to promote the transition to green and low-carbon development of energy and industry, and provide technological guarantees for achieving the goal of "carbon peaking and carbon neutrality". However, the application of low-carbon technologies needs to be guaranteed by matching standardization system, which can truly transit low-carbon technologies into standardized, large-scale and market-oriented achievements, and realize the leading role of low-carbon technologies in "carbon peaking and carbon neutrality" work. Therefore, the innovation and development of low-carbon technologies can also drive the research and development of new standards, providing new application scenarios for standards.

4. Increasing Market Internationalization Infusing New Impetus For Internationalization of Standards

Achieving the goal of "carbon peaking and carbon neutrality" is one of the major tasks related to high-quality development. Carbon reduction is a global contemporary issue. As a major foreign trade export province in China, Zhejiang Province is more frequently and closely integrated with the international market, and more deeply involved in the competition of the international green market. It is urgent to formulate "carbon peaking and carbon neutrality" standards that are applicable to and even higher than international requirements, contributes the wisdom of Zhejiang Province, provide the Chinese approach, enhance the influence of our country in the formulation of international "carbon peaking and carbon neutrality" standards, strive to express its own interests and demands in international standardization organizations and activities, and vigorously explore the export trading market.

B. New Challenges of "Carbon Peaking and Carbon Neutrality" Standardization System Construction under New Goals

1. Insufficient Extensiveness, Accuracy and Systematization of *"Carbon Peaking and Carbon Neutrality"* Standardization System

At present, Zhejiang Province has issued 72 "carbon peaking and carbon neutrality" standards covering the "1+6" sectors. However, there is still a lack of sub-field, hierarchical, sub-subject standards, the coverage and depth of the current stage is limited. Secondly, the organizations responsible for studying and formulating standards have an insensitive and inaccurate understanding of the requirements of "carbon peaking and carbon neutrality" standardization. It is difficult to play the "hard constraint" role of "carbon peaking and carbon neutrality" standards, such as energy consumption limits and thoroughly implement all aspects of carbon reduction and emission reduction. In addition, the provincial standardization technical committees exist in a "fragmented" situation, the lack of systematic research, the existence of multiple standards, indicator settings, technical requirements are not uniform, the problem of cross and duplication between standards.

2. Insufficient Connection Between "Carbon Peaking and Carbon Neutrality" Standardization System and Policies

Due to the long process of standard formulation, resulting in a poor interface between standards and policies. The formulation of standards needs multiple rounds of communication, coordination and research, with a long cycle. However, policies are dynamically adjusted to development need. If the policies are frequently altered, it will lead to a disconnection between standards and policies and cause inconsistency between standards and policy development. It is difficult to achieve organic integration of standard construction and policy development, affecting the realization of the goal of "carbon peaking and carbon neutrality".

3. Insufficient Effectiveness of "Carbon Peaking and Carbon Neutrality" Standardization System Implementation

Firstly, the goal of "carbon peaking and carbon neutrality" involves a wide range of work and multiple administrative departments, which have different highlights, positions and concerns on the formulation of standards, leading to different requirements for standards and increasing the difficulty in implementing these standards for enterprises. Secondly, the relevant affiliations underperform in interpreting, publicizing, implementing and training these standards, resulting in the failure of enterprises to obtain and understand the information of these standards. Thirdly, market entities lack of active and effective participation and cooperation, leading to multiple problems, such as insufficient attention to the implementation of existing standards, insufficient awareness of standardization, lacking of standards-related professionals, and insufficient disclosure of standard statements of enterprises, which makes it difficult to truly implement these standards. In addition, Zhejiang Province has not established a unified "carbon peaking and carbon neutrality" standardization information service platform. Hence, enterprises and institutions fail to catch up with up-to-date standards and standard requirements at home and abroad in the field of "carbon peaking and carbon neutrality".

4. Insufficient Mutual Recognition of "Carbon Peaking and Carbon Neutrality" Standards Among Regions

New rules for regional interaction and new regional cooperation based on the goal of carbon neutrality are being established. Actively promoting mutual recognition of cross-regional standards has become an important guarantee for successfully achieving the goal of carbon neutrality. However, it is difficult to recognize cross-regional standards due to the barriers between regions and significant differences in technical standards and evaluation criteria. A series of problems exist the in application and promotion of these standards among regions, which hinders cross-regional energy-saving and carbon-reducing management and green product circulation, and limits the development of green low-carbon regional integration.

IV. Suggestions For "Carbon Peaking and Carbon Neutrality" Standardization Work In Zhejiang Province

A. Strengthening the Coordination between Standards and Policies

The standards should adhere to "one goal" and promote "two synergies" in an orderly manner. "One goal" is "to establish the best order and achieve the best benefits", "two synergies" refers to promoting coordinated development of the standard formulation and implementation from top to bottom, and strengthening coordinated cooperation between different standards and policy entities. Strictly adhering to this goal, relevant work should be conducted to study and formulate the standards and establish the system and form a joint force to promote high-quality development through policy formulation and standard planning.

B. Improving *"Carbon Peaking and Carbon Neutrality"* Standardization System

Clarify the "four changes", "four goals" and "seven tasks"[1] of the development of standardization, based on the construction of the "carbon peaking and carbon neutrality" standard innovation highland, a series of standards remain to be urgently formulated according to the principle of "priority for urgent requirement" to resolve the actual requirements of government carbon control, enterprise carbon reduction, and individual low-carbon lifestyle. In addition, the "carbon peaking and carbon neutrality" standardization system should be improved. It is necessary to speed up the improvement of "carbon peaking and carbon neutrality" in the whole chain from basic research, applied technology, and standard formulation to industrial application, innovate standard transition work system, and support the application and transition of innovative carbon technologies. Extensive efforts should be diverted to strengthen the integration of digital technologies, and timely integrate advanced digital technologies, such as artificial intelligence, blockchain, and cloud computing that are applied in "carbon peaking and carbon neutrality" work, into these standards, thereby enhancing the standard level.

C. Strengthening the Implementation and Supervision of Standards

Efforts should be made to promote the establishment of provincial-level expert committees of "carbon peaking and carbon neutrality" standardization, coordinate and promote the smooth implementation of "carbon peaking and carbon neutrality" work, to achieving the goal of "carbon peaking and carbon neutrality" as scheduled to provide important organizational safeguards.. Relevant research should be conducted to build a "carbon peaking and carbon neutrality" standardization technical information public service platform to

---

1   Four transformations, four goals, and seven tasks come from the *National Standardization Outline*.

provide a platform for rapidly understanding the requirements for standard research, timely retrieval of standards, and understanding the status quo of relevant standards at home and abroad. In addition, it is necessary to enhance publicity, organize professional organizations, industry associations and key enterprises to hold standardization exchange and communication meetings in a regular and timely manner, perform standard publicity, technical training, guidance and exchange, and result in transformation and promotion, aiming to promote an in-depth connection between standards and enterprises. Efforts should be made to establish a feedback mechanism for standard implementation information, evaluate the effect of standard implementation, explore the establishment of statistical analysis and reporting systems for standard implementation and introduce a third-party evaluation agency for timely track and feedback. It is necessary to promote the market to strengthen the publicity, implementation and supervision of independent standards, guide public release and promotion of high-quality and original group standards and enterprise standards, accelerate the application of advanced group standards and enterprise "pioneering" standards, encourage groups and enterprises to perform in self-discipline and mutual supervision of standards, and give full play to the market's role of "survival of the fittest".

D. Promoting Mutual Recognition of Cross-Regional Standards

Based on the actual economic development in the region, joint formulation and sharing of "carbon peaking and carbon neutrality" standards should be strengthened. It is necessary to explore a regional standardization joint organization in the Yangtze River Delta, which is responsible for the establishment, release, implementation, evaluation and supervision of unified standards. The organization should coordinate relevant departments, standardization institutes, enterprises and other entities among different regions to hold regular meetings to resolve the problems of standard formulation and application, driving integrated development of "carbon peaking and carbon neutrality" standardization system. It is necessary to establish a coordinated development mechanism for regional low-carbon technology sharing and resource redistribution, further improve cross-regional carbon market mechanism, carbon finance mechanism, carbon asset management policy, financial subsidies, tax exemptions, and scientific and technological innovation support, etc. Efforts should be made to mobilize the willingness and initiate to participate in cross-regional "carbon peaking and carbon neutrality" work, and promote mutual recognition of relevant standards.

Author: Jiang Jianping[1], Zhu Dongfeng[2], Zhang Tianyou[3]

---

1   Jiang Jianping, deputy director of Zhejiang Standardization Research Institute, Senior Engineer, mainly engaged in research on standardization, quality and brand building, and continuous service for green, low-carbon and high-quality development of manufacturing industry. In the past 10 years, he has been responsible for over 15 national and provincial research projects, published 5 monographs, and 67 academic papers, applied for 3 invention patents as the main applicant, won 3 provincial and ministerial awards and 2 deputy ministerial awards, and approved by provincial leaders 10 times. He worked with Tiantong Holding Co., Ltd. to build a new national technical standard innovation base for magnetoelectric and photoelectric information materials. He is a registered expert of ISO/IEC JTC1/SC7/WG7 (system software engineering field) and IEC/TC82/WG9 (photovoltaic field), a national standard technical assessment expert, a member of the Advisory Expert Committee for the construction of "waste-free City" in Zhejiang Province, and a discipline leader of the innovation team for the green, low-carbon and high-quality development of Zhejiang Market Supervision Manufacturing Industry.

2   Zhu Dongfeng, standardization engineer of Zhejiang Standardization Research Institute, mainly engaged in standardization research in fields such as carbon peaking and carbon neutrality, circular economy, etc. He is a member of the second fluorine-containing sub gascommittee of the National Gas Standardization Technical Committee (SACTC/206/SC3), a member of the special working group for carbon peaking in the residential sector in the province, and a deputy secretary general of the Zhejiang Province Ecological Environment Standardization Technical Committee (ZJQS/TC37), among others. He is a member of the second session of the Fluorine Gas sub-standard Committee of the National Gas Standardization Technical Committee (SAC/TC206/SC3), a member of the provincial carbon peak work team in the field of residential life, deputy secretary-general of the Provincial Ecological Environment Standard Technical Committee (ZJQS/TC37), a member of the provincial Biodegradable Materials and Products (ZJQS/ TC85) standard technical committee, and an expert on Zhejiang Standard online storage. He had been responsible for 1 provincial and ministerial science and technology project, 1 department level project, and participated in 4 related topics, 4 national standards, 3 provincial local standards. He is responsible for or involved in more than 50 Zhejiang manufacturing group standards.

3   Zhang Tianyou, a Ph.D. from the Energy and Environment Department of the Zhejiang Provincial Economic Information Center. He has been engaged in work related to addressing climate change for a long time. Since 2017, he has mainly undertaken research on the province's energy consumption dual control system, dual carbon research, as well as the operation service of greenhouse gas inventories and carbon report management. In recent years, he has also participated in the drafting of standards for low-carbon travel and zero carbon public institutions for residents.

A Brief Introduction to Corporate Carbon Asset Management

As China launched its carbon market, carbon asset management is receiving increasing attention. It includes the management of carbon emission allowances and emission reductions, the disposal of carbon assets and financial products, etc. The aim is to promote the sustainable development of enterprises and reduce carbon emissions. This article briefly introduces the concept of carbon assets, focuses on the analysis of key points of corporate carbon asset management, and briefly discusses carbon asset trading and carbon financial services. Finally, taking the case of carbon asset management in Zhejiang Province as an example, the article provides readers with relevant suggestions.

I. The Concept of Carbon Asset and Its Development

With the global consensus on greenhouse gas control and the introduction of China's "30 · 60" goal, more and more enterprises are becoming aware of the importance of carbon assets in their production and operation processes. At present, the trading objects in major international carbon markets are carbon emission allowances and certified emission reductions (CERs). The industry standard for the *Carbon Financial Products* issued by the CSRC on 12 April 2022 has stated that carbon assets are new types of assets generated by the carbon emissions trading mechanism and include those issued by governments and the carbon emission reduction projects which will bring about carbon credit for enterprises.

A. The Concept of Carbon Emission Allowances

Carbon emission allowances represent a mandatory system regulated by government authorities to limit the carbon emissions produced by companies in specific industries. According to the mechanism proposed by the *Kyoto Protocol*, governments were expected to achieve the carbon reduction targets they have committed to within a specified period by allocating their carbon emission rights to enterprises according to the established schedules, and the final carbon emission rights allocated to companies are called carbon emission allowances. One allowance represents one ton of carbon dioxide emissions, measured in tons of carbon dioxide equivalent (tCO_2). There are two types of carbon emission allowance in China, one is from the national carbon market and the other is from the pilot carbon market.

B. The Concept of Carbon Emission Reduction

Project-based emission reductions refer to those generated for a specific emission reduction project against allocated allowances (also known as carbon credit), which, according to their generating mechanisms, is beyond the total quantity control and can be divided into reductions from carbon point trading mechanisms associated with allowance trading and those from other voluntary emission reduction mechanisms. The former is typically represented by Chinese Certified Emissions Reductions (CCER), a voluntary market for emission reductions introduced as a supplement to the Chinese carbon market; while the latter is represented by international voluntary emission reductions, e.g., Verified Carbon Standard (VCS). Carbon points in this type of market can be certified according to different criteria and are generally not subject to compliance obligations, can be purchased by companies that wish to offset their emissions on a voluntary basis.

C. Development of China's Carbon Market

As for the management of carbon emission allowances, the Ministry of Ecology and Environment has formulated allocation plans for allowances based on the *Measures for the Administration of Carbon Emissions Trading (Trial Implementation)* and issued allowances to key emission units included in China's carbon emissions trading market. Allowances are used for transactions, and companies are required to ensure that their accounts have sufficient allowances for compliance clearances during the compliance period based on actual emissions. In the administration of CCERs, China has specifically stipulated diverse voluntary emission reduction methodologies for forestry carbon sinks, renewable energy generation, methane utilization, etc. Through the methodologies, emission reduction projects and the emission reductions they generate are verified and then equated to replace allowances for compliance. Since carbon assets have been given a mandatory compliance nature by the country, they are in rigid demand, i.e., they have an asset value and can reflect a fair price through the carbon market and have properties that are similar to those of intangible assets in the concept of finance and accounting.

II. The Modes of Corporate Carbon Asset Management

In terms of the subjects of carbon asset management, it can be divided into 2 types of modes.

A. Corporate Carbon Asset Management of Enterprises that are Required to Participate in the Emissions Trading System

At present, enterprises that emit up to 26,000 tons of carbon dioxide or consume more than 10,000 tons of standard coal in their production processes in the eight controlled industries of power generation, petrochemicals, chemicals, building materials, iron and steel, non-ferrous metals, paper making, and aviation are included in the national carbon market, forcing them to reduce greenhouse gas emissions through the market-based means of mandatory allowance compliance and national carbon emissions trading. Joining the national carbon market has placed new requests on the efficient carbon management of these companies, especially those that are part of a group. A large number of subsidiary companies and the complex hierarchy of organizations make it difficult to manage carbon emissions and carbon assets.

The key to improving the quality of carbon asset management is to optimize the management of allowances through emission reduction measures. By sorting out the production process and finding out the major emission sources, enterprises should explore the emission reduction potential from energy structure, techniques, equipment, and energy management, such as the use of renewable energy, energy efficiency improvement technology, and efficient energy management system to reduce emissions from the source. In addition, it is also necessary to consider the cost of reducing energy consumption, allowance revenue increase, and investing in energy-saving and emission-reduction transformation costs comprehensively to optimize the quality of allowance management.

B. Corporate Carbon Asset Management of Enterprises that Are Not Required to Participate in the Emissions Trading System

The carbon assets of enterprises that are not required to participate in the carbon trading system are mainly acquired through technological reform and investment in energy-saving and emission-reduction projects. They can use the CCER (China Certified Emission Reductions) methodology research to quantify and certify the greenhouse gas emission reduction effects of renewable energy, forest carbon sinks, methane utilization, and other projects within China, and trade them for profit in the national carbon emissions trading market. For the first type of enterprises mentioned above with a 5% cap on offset allowance, the current need for annual emission reductions from CCER projects is around 150 million tons, thus enterprises that are not required to participate in the trading market can profit from the development of emission reductions.

Their focus of carbon asset management is to identify the reduction potential. Enterprises can analyze various national emission reduction project methodologies from both carbon emission reduction and carbon sink perspectives to clarify the applicable methodologies for the project, develop project design documents, record daily monitoring documents and ledgers, and strengthen communication with third-party verifiers so as to maximize the identification and exploitation of the project's final emission reductions. It is also important to note the difference between theoretical emission reductions and exploitable emission reductions, as there are many projects where emission reductions exist in theory that cannot necessarily be exploited. In addition, enterprises should consider the compliance of the methodology of the theoretical emission reductions and whether the benefits of the emission reductions will cover the development costs.

III. Types of Corporate Carbon Asset Trading

Carbon assets are unique in that they can be used for carbon neutrality offsets by various entities and for compliance payments by emissions from enterprises that are required to participate in the emissions trading system, and can also be realized and bring about revenue. The international market has developed various standardized financial products that are similar to commodities using carbon emission indicators as a trading object. At the same time, the country has also established a unified carbon trading market to ensure that carbon trading is conducted in a healthy and organized manner. Here is a brief overview of the common trading types currently available in the Chinese market.

A. Spot Trading

Carbon spot is a native carbon finance instrument. Carbon spot trading involves the settlement of funds as soon as delivery or transfer occurs, mainly through trading platforms or over-the-counter transactions, etc. Taking the nationwide carbon emission allowance trading markets as an example, there are trading modes available in listing trading by agreement, bulk trading by agreement and one-way bidding.

B. Forward Trading

Carbon forward trading is a non-standardized contract between buyers and sellers to buy or sell a specified number of carbon units (allowances or emission reductions) at a chosen price at a specified time in the future, usually over the counter. Both parties shall determine the price, quantity and delivery time, etc. together, and finally, exercise the contract with physical delivery. Forward trading is not subject to price risk as the price is fixed, but it is subject to default risk due to the weak regulatory structure.

C. Options Trading

A carbon option is a type of carbon financial derivative based on carbon futures, which refers to the right of both trading parties to buy or sell a certain amount of carbon objects at a chosen price at some point in the future. The trading trend of carbon options depends on the buyer's judgment of the price trend of carbon emission rights. It is essentially an option. In the case of CCER options, for example, when the future price is expected to rise, the seller will hedge the opportunity cost of future price increases by purchasing a call option, and if the price is expected to fall, the seller will profit by exercising the call option.

Therefore, like carbon futures, carbon options can help buyers avoid the adverse risks associated with carbon price fluctuations and provide a certain hedging function. Buyers can lock the income level by buying call options or put options respectively. In addition, it is also possible to lock in profits and hedge defined risks by buying and selling a mix of call options and put options with different expiration and strike prices.

D. Exchange Trading

Exchange trading is a unique form for carbon asset trading. As emission reductions can be offset against allowances for compliance, and the value of emission reductions is naturally slightly lower than that of allowances, the market has thus given rise to the business of exchange trading of allowances by CCERs.

Carbon allowances and CCER exchange trading are essentially a kind of forward contractual transaction. Both parties to a transaction will generally agree to trade equal amounts of carbon allowances and certified voluntary emission reduction credits, and the price difference between them within a defined future period. Through the innovative design of carbon allowances/ CCER exchange products and trading business, the two independent trading steps are simplified into a single exchange action to improve trading efficiency, it can also realize forward trading, which is conducive to enterprises and investment institutions to use the products to lock the current market price of carbon assets, reduce future trading costs and better manage their own carbon assets. In particular, large power companies have a large volume of allowances available for CCER offsets, and their cost savings will be more significant when there is a large gap between the market price of allowances and CCERs.

E. Carbon Trading Institutions

Carbon trading institutions are an important part of the carbon market and are the key to securing carbon trading. In order to ensure the healthy and organized development of the carbon trading market, trading institutions should fully understand the various types of risks in the carbon market and anticipate the trends of ups and downs, analyze the policies and rules in terms of admission, trading and financial products, and propose corresponding plans so as to fully play the market-oriented function and promote the smooth and orderly operation of the carbon market. In addition, it is also important to clarify the nature of the carbon emission trading market as a government policy tool, and to promote its healthy development while working with the government to accurately control carbon emissions.

IV. Carbon Financial Services for Enterprises

As carbon assets demonstrate their value as a type of asset, direct investment and financing activities for carbon emission reduction and related financial intermediaries and other service agencies have emerged to help companies revitalize carbon assets, obtain financing for emission reduction projects, reduce financing costs and improve operational efficiency.

A. Carbon Bonds

A carbon bond is a type of green bond, which mainly refers to a bond that uses carbon assets or the proceeds of carbon assets as collateral or source of funding for the repayment of the bond's principal and interest, or uses the funds raised for carbon reduction project activities. There are mainly several types of carbon bonds as follows: first, the projected cash flow is used as additional interest income. The proceeds from CER/CCER transactions are used as part of the funding source for bond interest payments, while the issuance of the bond is still mainly dependent on the credit and operational financial status of the issuing company, and no carbon assets or carbon asset proceeds are used as the debt subject, and the proceeds from carbon credits are only used as variable interest payments. Second, carbon assets are used as collateral for loans. Carbon allowances are administratively allocated by the government and have the nature of property rights, which is the basis for the pledgeability of carbon assets. The willingness of banks to participate in pledging transactions depends crucially on market liquidity, and only when the market is liquid can banks be confident and willing to loan to companies.

Although there are domestic and international precedents for issuing carbon bonds with carbon assets, carbon bond trading is mainly aimed at developing a long-term partnership between the two parties, and there is not much room for specific interest rate concessions, so fewer trading cases can be found in the market. In addition, the issuance of carbon asset bonds as collateral for direct financing is restricted by the size of CCER assets and the duration of carbon allowances, and there are also problems such as limited types of suitable bonds and difficulties in valuation. To solve these problems, a nationwide carbon market needs to be established and gradually unified to expand the market coverage and absorb more enterprises and institutions, thus increasing the trading volume of the carbon market. Futures and options trading should be introduced to effectively hedge the risk of positions and strengthen the price discovery of carbon assets. In this way, there will be more opportunities for enterprises to revitalize carbon assets and inject new vitality into the innovative development of carbon finance.

B. Carbon Fund

Among the many innovative instruments of carbon finance, a carbon fund is an important investment vehicle specifically established for the purpose of trading carbon emission rights or emission reductions. The issuer pools funds from public or private investors for investment activities to generate investment returns and capital gains, the proceeds of which are shared with investors. Carbon funds have introduced a broader source of capitals for tackling climate change and developing a low-carbon economy. As major purchasers of global project-level carbon credits, carbon funds are an important source of financing for the development of emission reduction projects in the initial stages of global carbon market development.

At present, the carbon funds that are currently operated in China are mainly involved in allowance trading and CCER trading in our pilot carbon markets, buying low and selling high according to the market trend so as to trade for margin profits. Most of the early low-carbon funds in China were private equity funds focusing on investing in the equity of green and low-carbon companies, and those investing in the domestic carbon market only emerged gradually after 2014, such as China Clean Development Mechanism Fund, China Green Carbon Fund, Green 1+1 Special Fund, Carbon Neutrality Fund, and Eco-City Development Fund.

V. Cases of carbon assets in Zhejiang Province

First, a cement manufacturing company was established so early that it is known as the cradle of China's cement industry. As a major player in the industry, it is under pressure to reduce its consumption of natural resources and CO_2 emissions. For this reason, the company introduced carbon asset management in 2011 to control its carbon emissions and optimize its operations. As a result, the company has reduced its CO_2 emissions by reducing its consumption of coal and cement and by using waste heat in its production process. At the same time, the company has also promoted energy-saving and environmentally friendly production concepts to meet market demand and improve profitability, while continuously optimizing its production processes.

Second, a large coal-fired power plant, one of the first enterprises that are required to participate in the emissions trading system that entered the national market, had to both secure its power supply in the face of rising coal prices and meet the requirements of the carbon market. In this regard, the power plant realized the pre-issued allowances in the form of carbon allowance forward trading in advance and used the acquired funds for energy-saving renovation, which improved the energy consumption capacity per unit, reduced the emission, and reduced the allowance deficit, forming a perfect closed loop of carbon asset trading-energy-saving technical renovation-reducing emissions-increasing carbon assets-reducing compliance costs.

Third, an IT technology service company has a large carbon footprint from its data center and server operations. To address this problem, the company introduced carbon asset management in 2012 to optimize energy use in its data center and servers, therefore has reduced carbon emissions by improving energy efficiency and saving energy.

Fourth, an online department store with one of the highest sales volumes in China's retail sector has generated significant amount of carbon emissions from its warehousing, transportation and operations. To control its carbon emissions and promote social responsibility, the company introduced carbon asset management in 2013. It has centralized the procurement and sorting of goods, and optimized logistics, transportation and operational efficiency to reduce transportation time and cut carbon emissions. The company has also made use of renewable energy sources such as wind, solar and hydro to generate revenue that benefits the company.

VI. Insights and Suggestions

At present, China's carbon market has been officially opened, but the participants, trading types, trading methods, and regulatory rules still need to be improved and matured, and the research and modes of carbon asset management are also being updated accordingly. Here are some suggestions for enterprises to improve carbon asset management:

A. Upholding the Concept of Low-carbon Development

Companies should always adhere to the goal of low-carbon development, march towards a sustainable development path and continuously reduce their impact on the environment. At the same time, actively developing renewable energy sources as an alternative to traditional energy sources will bring additional benefits to the company while reducing carbon emissions.

B. Developing Carbon Asset Management

Unlike traditional assets, carbon asset is an emerging idea and therefore needs to be managed by consensus within a company and implemented at an institutional level in line with the needs of low-carbon development. Now that we are increasingly aware of carbon emissions, companies should manage their carbon assets in order to optimize their production processes, reduce carbon emissions and generate economic benefits. The value of carbon assets can only be fully reflected through trading, so it is important to ensure a healthy and organized carbon trading process by intelligently designing the trading process and supporting risk control.

C. Using Carbon Trading, Carbon Finance and Other Tools Flexibly

The low-carbon transformation will inevitably bring about corresponding costs due to technological improvement and management investment. Carbon trading and carbon finance tools should be flexibly used to develop appropriate solutions for carbon asset development and trading, so as to minimize costs through market-based means and provide positive impetus. At the same time, enterprises should apply various support policies in a flexible way in the implementation of carbon asset management and strengthen the partnership with other enterprises to share experience and technology.

Author: Huang Hongfei[1], Zhou Liying[2]

1　Huang Hongfei, director of Market Operation Department of Zhejiang Energy Carbon Asset Management Co., Ltd., has engaged in enterprise carbon asset management for a long time. Since 2006, he has been mainly responsible for the low-carbon business within the company such as CDM project development, greenhouse gas inventory preparation, carbon asset management and other Intra-system business. He leads the methodology research, greenhouse gas inventory preparation, low carbon standard declaration and other consulting projects.

2　Zhou Liying, project dirctor of Carbon Market Development Department of Zhejiang Provincial Energe Group Carbon Assets Management Co., Ltd., engages in emission reduction project development, low-carbon consulting, and carbon emission management related work. Undertaking the development of low-carbon products, carbon emissions and asset management within Zhejiang Provincial Energe Group, and participate in consulting projects such as low-carbon standard setting, methodology development, and low-carbon research.

Construction of a Digital Intelligence Governance System to Promote the Realization of the "Dual Carbon" Goals

As a new mode and trend of technology-empowered carbon peaking and carbon neutrality governance in the digital era, digital intelligent governance plays a supporting role in China's realization of the strategic goal of carbon peaking and carbon neutrality (dual carbon goal). By analyzing the main problems facing the current digital governance of carbon peaking and carbon neutrality, this paper systematically introduces the exploration and practice of such a governance of Zhejiang Province as an example, and puts forward relevant countermeasures and suggestions, in order to provide a Zhejiang-style model for the whole country and other regions.

I. Introduction

To Actively promote the modernization of the governance system and capacity for carbon peaking and carbon neutrality, as well as give full play to the key role of digital and intelligent governance in achieving the goal of carbon dioxide peaking and carbon neutrality, is an important measure to implement and fulfill the spirit of the General Secretary's important exposition on carbon dioxide peaking and carbon neutrality. However, due to poor data foundation, weak carbon statistical assessment system, and the lack of digital intelligence governance means, the realization of digital intelligence governance for carbon peaking and carbon neutrality (hereinafter referred to as "dual carbon") still faces great challenges.

Scatter basic data and difficulty in data sharing. Firstly, carbon data collection is difficult and lagging, and carbon data statistics are not comprehensive and timely, which are the main problems facing the high-quality management of carbon data in the whole cycle. Secondly, the sensitivity and closure of carbon data make it difficult to exchange carbon data across businesses, forming data islands. So it is a must to improve data quality and ensure the authenticity, accuracy and comprehensiveness of carbon data, so as to achieve high-quality management and whole-process sharing of carbon data, which is the key foundation for realizing the "dual carbon" digital intelligence governance.

Weak statistical accounting system and insufficient data standardization. At present, the state has not yet established a unified carbon statistical accounting system, and the regional and industrial carbon emission accounting (quick calculation) systems explored by local governments generally have a series of problems such as slow data updating, different accounting calibers, and lagging basic emission factors. It is an important guarantee for promoting "dual carbon" digital intelligence governance to construct a unified and standardized carbon statistical accounting system to achieve accurate accounting, in-depth mining and scientific analysis of basic data.

The lack of governance tools and effective means for specific work. At the government level, the government lacks a strong grasp to monitor and analyze the progress of "dual carbon" work in regions, fields and industries, and thus cannot support the government's scientific decision-making. At the enterprise level, enterprises lack the path guidance for a low-carbon transformation, are not able to clarify the carbon reduction path, and are difficult to achieve intelligent low-carbon management of the producing process to enhance quality and efficiency. At the individual level, there is a lack of platforms to record and quantify individuals' low-carbon behaviors, leading to ineffective guidance for individuals to practice low-carbon life.

Zhejiang Province is featured by the digitalization reform, an important path for helping Zhejiang to achieve the goal of carbon peak and carbon neutrality. Zhejiang Province is actively exploring the construction of a digital intelligence governance system, and so aims to empower the government to accurately control carbon, promote low-carbon transformation of enterprises and advocate low-carbon lives for individuals by building a "dual carbon" digital intelligent management platform.

II. The practice of Zhejiang's carbon peaking and carbon neutrality digital intelligence governance system

A. The foundation of digital intelligence governance

In 2021, Zhejiang took the lead in launching a digital reform in the country, and through the past two years of implementing the digital reform, it has achieved remarkable results and accumulated rich experience. The standard path of digital reform in Zhejiang Province is: (1) through the iteration of the V-model, it gradually sorted out and improved the core business, and formed the lists of requirements, scenarios and reform (referred to as "three checklists"); (2) in line with the three checklists, it built a system architecture with "infrastructure layer, data resource layer, application support layer, and business application layer" as the four horizontals, and "policy system, organizational guarantee system, network security system, and standard and specification system" as the four verticals; (3) the result is a top-level design for digital applications. The standard path and rich experience of digital reform in Zhejiang Province have provided scientific path guidance for the realization of digital intelligence governance ot "dual carbon".

As early as 2014, Zhejiang Province had built the first provincial-level carbon emission management platform in the field of climate change in China, namely the "Zhejiang Climate Change Research and Exchange Platform". Covering the three levels of provinces, cities and country and their key enterprises, the platform has achieved whole-processonline collection, compilation, review, management, analysis and judgment of carbon emission data, and formed a unified basic information database of the province for tackling climate change, laying a solid data foundation for responding to climate change and realizing "dual carbon" digital intelligent governance.

B. Top-level design of digital intelligence governance

1. Establishing a General Idea

To achieve carbon peak and carbon neutrality is an socio-economic systematic change with multiple goals and multiple constraints, so it is necessary to comprehensively handle the four dimensions of economic development, energy security, carbon emissions, and residents' livelihoods.

Based on the balance of the four dimensions and in line with international first-class and common rules, Zhejiang Province systematically analyzes the four core indicators of total energy consumption, total carbon emissions, energy consumption intensity and carbon emission intensity. Taking green and low-carbon transformation in the six major areas of energy, industry, construction, transportation, agriculture and residents' lives as the path, and making full use of the variable of scientific and technological innovations, the province has developed the "4+6+1" work idea. By tracking and monitoring the core indicators, work progress and implementation effects in various fields, we will ensure the realization of carbon peak and carbon neutrality goals across the entire province.

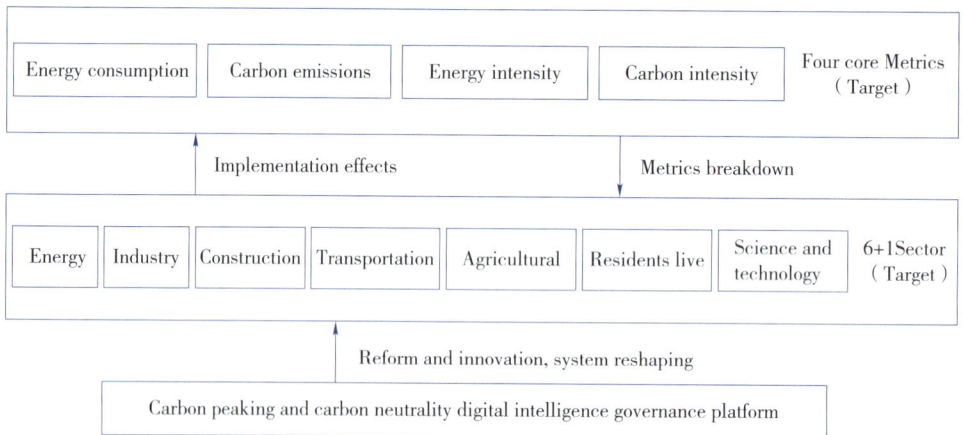

Figure 21-1　Overall idea of carbon peak and carbon neutrality

2. Combing through the three checklists

The government, enterprises and individuals are the three main players in achieving the goal of carbon peak and carbon neutrality. The government serves as the main actor to comprehensively promote the realization of carbon peaking and carbon neutrality goals, and undertakes the design of top-level plans, and the decomposition of task targets. Enterprises are the direct subjects responsible for carbon emission reduction, and implement their emission reduction responsibilities through various methods such as technological improvement, transformation and upgrading. Individuals are the largest carbon emitters in the field of consumption, and are also important subjects responsible for carbon emission reduction. Individuals can minimize their carbon emissions by choosing green and low-carbon lifestyles and consumption ways. Therefore, the key to realize digital intelligent governance is to seek reform breakthroughs with the help of digital means in response to the needs of governments, enterprises and individuals, so as to ultimately help the government accurately control carbon emissions, promote the low-carbon transformation of enterprises, and guide individuals to lead a low-carbon life.

For government governance, it is necessary to focus on solving the problems of what to focus on, how to manage it, and how effective it is. For enterprises, they should focus on solving the problems of why and how they ought to reduce carbon emissions, and what the results of the reduction are. For individuals, they should focus on what behaviors can reduce carbon, how much carbon is reduced, and what the benefits are. Based on the list of requirements, it is needed to design some digital reform scenarios, find breakthroughs in these scenarios, and promote reform breakthroughs, process reengineering and institutional innovation. It can be said that the three lists are the core starting point for the deepening of Zhejiang Province's digital reform.

3. Establishing a data aggregation mechanism

At present, carbon emission data collection faces multiple challenges, such as multiple subjects, scattered data, difficult collection, and high accounting complexity, resulting in difficulties in carbon data aggregation and management. Relying on the integrated intelligent platform of the Provincial Big Data Bureau, Zhejiang Province has established a cross-regional and cross-departmental data aggregation mechanism with the carbon emission data warehouse as the carrier, and frequently collected energy consumption data from various fields, regions and industries in the province, as well as carbon emission accounting data and economic data by region and industry of statistical departments. In this way, multi-source comprehensive data complementarity and aggregation is achieved.

At the same time, a carbon account system is built based on geographic information systems, and the core carbon emission data of enterprises, projects, individuals and other entities are collected into the dual carbon data warehouse, and included into the unified carbon account management, so as to realize the monitoring, query, traceability and comparison of carbon account data, providing an important support for government departments at all levels to promote the "dual carbon" work and build digital application scenarios.

4. Improving the statistical accounting system

Carbon emission statistical accounting is an important foundation for realizing "dual carbon" digital intelligent governance, and also provides a reliable data basis for government decision-making. In 2021, the National Bureau of Statistics listed Zhejiang Province as a pilot area for carbon emission statistical accounting, which undertook the research on carbon emission accounting methods by industry at the provincial level. So far, Zhejiang Province has realized the trial calculation of carbon emissions in six major fields and industrial sub-sectors of the whole society in accordance with the accounting plan. At the same time, the province is actively promoting the statistical accounting of carbon emissions in districted cities, which has laid a solid foundation for Zhejiang Province to build a unified and standardized carbon statistical accounting system, and also provided a reliable and standardized data foundation for the realization of "dual carbon" digital intelligent governance.

C. Construction of the digital intelligence governance platform

1. Helping the government accurately control carbon

The government is not only the main body of action to comprehensively promote the realization of carbon peaking and carbon neutrality goals, but also the main body responsible for implementing such goals. To achieve digital intelligent carbon control, the government should fulfill the crucial tasks to monitor the progress of carbon peaking, supervise key energy use data, and locate various carbon reduction entities.

In order to track and monitor the progress of the "dual carbon" work in sub-regions and sub-fields of the province with high frequency, Zhejiang Province has built a platform for intelligent governance of carbon peaking and carbon neutrality, which has realized dynamic monitoring, comparison, analysis and early warning of regional carbon emissions, total energy consumption, carbon emission intensity, energy consumption intensity and other indicators, and high-frequency monitoring of the completion of major indicators in the field and the progress of major work. It provides scientific support for provincial, municipal and county government departments to dynamically control the process of carbon peaking and carry out real-time early warning for key areas and energy-using objects.

The supervision of energy consumption data of key energy-using units is the key to promoting energy conservation. By building an "energy and carbon digital intelligence platform", Hangzhou municipality has realized the digital intelligence supervision of more than 2,000 key energy-using units in key areas such as industry and transportation in the city. Through the formulation of an accurate energy distribution mechanism, the energy utilization efficiency of key energy-using units in the city has been improved.

The energy conservation review system plays an important role in curbing the blind development of high-energy-consuming, high-emission and low-level projects. The Lin'an District of Hangzhou City has realizedintelligent management of high-carbon projects by building the Tianmu "Lin-carbon" digital intelligence brain, evaluating the energy efficiency of new projects based on the module of "fixed asset investment energy carbon pre-assessment", giving early warning to high-carbon projects, and putting forward rectification suggestions.

In general, Zhejiang Province has built a "dual carbon" digital intelligent management platform to help the government fully grasp the progress of the "dual carbon" work in overall control, critical-path analysis and effectiveness evaluation, improve the government's digital and intelligent governance capabilities, and assist the government to accurately control carbon emissions.

2. Serving enterprises in low-carbon transformation

Enterprises are the mainstay of carbon emission reduction and thus bear important responsibilities in the work of carbon peaking and carbon neutrality. In the process of carbon reduction, however, enterprises face with major challenges, including unfamiliarity with energy use, lack of a thorough investigation of carbon background, and unclear carbon reduction paths.

In order to achieve the independent allocation of enterprise energy budget, Zhejiang Province plans to develop an energy conservation and carbon reduction e-account application. Through the establishment of the "province-city-county-enterprise" energy budget hierarchical management mechanism, the application will support enterprises to query their own energy consumption information, independently measure energy use, and practice energy budget management. In this way, enterprises will be given the ability to independently adjust their production plans and energy use authority, so as to minimize the adverse effects of energy use space restrictions on enterprise production and operation, and fully tap the production potential of enterprises.

In order to accurately serve key fields and key industries, and help them take the lead in achieving carbon peaking and leading enterprises to accurately reduce carbon emissions, Huzhou municipality pioneered the application of "carbon efficiency code". The application innovatively builds a carbon efficiency intelligent benchmarking system to grant industrial enterprises carbon efficiency codes. For enterprises rated as high-carbon ones, the system would carry out energy-saving diagnosis services, formulate carbon reduction plans, and promote the implementation of green technological update projects. Under the joint promotion of relevant provincial departments, a total of 42,000 enterprises in the province have completed the evaluation and coding.

Enterprises need a strong financial support to promote technological innovation, optimize their products and management methods, and achieve carbon reduction and efficiency enhancement. Quzhou municipality has innovatively built a carbon account financial system, which would generate carbon credit reports for enterprises on a monthly basis based on carbon account portraits. After obtaining the authorization of an enterprise, financial institutions can inquire about its carbon credit report and provide corresponding financial service support. At present, the platform has generated carbon credit reports of 3,002 enterprises, and issued more than 53.3 billion yuan of carbon financial loans

In general, Zhejiang Province has built digital platforms such as enterprise energy budget management, carbon efficiency code, and carbon account finance, in order to help enterprises find out their carbon background, and provide financial loans, energy-saving technological transformation and other services for them. With such a method, the province has enhanced the willingness of businesses to reduce their carbon emissions, and promoted their eco-friendly transformation.

3. Guiding individuals to lead a low-carbon life

The area of residents' lives is an important part of the work to achieve carbon peaking, and the carbon emissions generated by individual consumption cannot be ignored. At present, personal carbon emission reduction faces problems such as data fragmentation and difficulty in quantification, and it is of great significance to explore individual participation in carbon emission reduction and form a green lifestyle for the society as a whole in a digital way.

In order to actively guide individuals to practice the concept of a low-carbon life, Zhejiang Province has built the China's first provincial-level "carbon inclusiveness" application, which cooperates with multiple data sources such as Ant Forest, Huge Recycle, and Ele.me to build 20 types of data scenarios to achieve comprehensive coverage of personal low-carbon scenarios. Through the construction of a closed-loop inclusive process of "low-carbon behavior acquisition-emission reduction accounting-carbon point granting-inclusive rights and interests exchange", the concept of green and low-carbon life is popularized to individuals, and their willingness to participate in such a lifestyle is improved.

As a "key little thing" in life, garbage sorting is also the simplest and most effective way for individuals to embrace a low-carbon life. The Yuhang District created the "One-Click Low-carbon Recycling (Huge Recycle)" application, using the "one-stop" collection mode to cultivate users' garbage sorting habits. Through door-to-door recycling, the household garbage put in by residents is paid according to weight as residents' "environmental protection money", which can be exchanged for goods or withdrawn in the online mall. At present, this model has been gradually promoted across Zhejiang Province.

By building a "carbon master" application scenario, Huzhou has developed effective low-carbon behaviors such as photovoltaic rooftop, garbage classification and green travel into emission reduction scenarios. Users can obtain carbon points through personal green behaviors, and redeem their required goods and electronic coupons in the "carbon master" points mall.

In general, Zhejiang Province popularizes the concept of low-carbon life to individuals by building an inclusive mechanism of "low-carbon behavior-accounting for emission reductions-granting points-points exchange rights", and actively guides individuals to practice green consumption and a low-carbon life.

III. Enlightenment and suggestions for digital and intelligent governance of carbon peaking and carbon neutrality

Drawing on the practices and achievements of Zhejiang Province in building a "dual carbon" digital intelligence governance system, this study has developed a good idea and practice route for the construction of a "dual carbon" digital intelligent governance system in other provinces and the whole country.

A. Establishing scientific and effective data aggregation mechanisms

Establishing a scientific and effective data aggregation mechanism and breaking down data silos are the key foundations for realizing digital intelligence governance. In the current "dual carbon" work, there are common problems of scattered basic carbon emission data, poor data quality, and low timeliness of data. Therefore, it is recommended to establish a three-level data aggregation mechanism at the provincial, municipal and county levels under the premise of safety standards, aggregate multi-source complementary data, and improve the accuracy, timeliness and sharing of basic data. At the same time, different databases can be built according to business themes to form a variety of data products to achieve precise carbon emissions, intelligent management and all-round analysis.

B. Studying unified and standardized carbon statistical accounting methods

Establishing a unified and standardized carbon emission statistical accounting system and thoroughly investigating the carbon emission background is an important guarantee for realizing digital intelligent governance. The carbon statistical accounting system involves multiple levels, multiple types of subjects and multiple dimensions, with different boundaries and methods of accounting.

650

Therefore, it is recommended to gradually carry out research on carbon statistical accounting methods and standards for regions, industry enterprises and products in the order of "urgent use first, easy first and difficult later". Such a system lays a credible foundation for the government to formulate policies, monitor and evaluate the progress of work, and provides an important support for enterprises to build carbon emission reduction paths and form low-carbon products.

C. Planning the digital application of multiple entities serving multiple subjects

It is a main path to achieve "dual carbon" digital and intelligent governance to Establish digital applications that serve multiple subjects such as the government, enterprises and individuals. Carbon peaking and carbon neutrality is a multi-dimensional, three-dimensional and systematic project, involving the multiple entities of the government, enterprises and individuals, which requires comprehensive leadership by the government, active initiative by enterprises and active participation of the general public. Therefore, it is recommended to focus on the actual needs of multiple subjects, plan and build demand-oriented digital applications, and support good governance, enterprise services and individual benefits.

Author: The writing group of Zhejiang economic & information centre

New Mission of Green Finance Development in the Context of Carbon Peaking and Carbon Neutrality in Zhejiang Province

In the context of carbon peaking and carbon neutrality, green finance has become an important ripping bar for levering market elements to support low-carbon and high-quality development in Zhejiang Province. The development of green finance requires joint efforts in green financial policies, information disclosure, products services, and other aspects. Zhejiang Province took the green financial reform and innovation experiment as an opportunity. Through several methods such as improving the policy standard system, innovating green financial products and services, and developing green finance digital intelligence tools, Zhejiang Province took the lead in exploring new development ideas and measures centered on carbon efficiency improvement. Finally, it promoted the all-round and multi-field development of green finance in Zhejiang Province.

I. Introduction

Green finance is the blood of the modern economy and the key variable to boosting the economy. And it has a multiplier effect on promoting the development of green low-carbon economy. Since 2017, the State Council has approved green finance reform and innovation experiments in Huzhou, Quzhou, and other places in Zhejiang. In 2019, the National Development and Reform Commission led the compilation of the *Green Industry Guidance Catalogue*. In 2021, the People's Bank of China issued China's first batch of green finance standards, *Guidelines for Environmental Information Disclosure of Financial Institutions* and *Environmental Equity Financing Instruments*, which standardized the environmental information disclosure of financial institutions. Financial resources have been more precisely allocated toward green and low-carbon fields. In April 2022, the People's Bank of China clearly required via the video conference to realize the effective connection between green finance and transformation finance and focus on the integrated development of green finance and inclusive finance.

The proposal of the dual carbon goals further gives a new mission and connotation to green finance, and green finance has become an important foothold for low-carbon and high-quality development in our province. Firstly, it guides the allocation of capital elements in Zhejiang Province. By encouraging green investment and financing and inhibiting high-carbon investment, Green finance guides the flow of funds to the green and low-carbon field, to form financial capital necessary for the development of green and low-carbon industries, which can reduce the cost of capital raising effectively and optimize the allocation of market resources. Secondly, it supports the development of low-carbon industries. On the one hand, green finance can accelerate the transformation and upgrading of traditional industries. On the other hand, green financial instruments such as green bonds and green funds are able to leverage the fund aggregation function of the financial system, to achieve an effective allocation of financial resource elements. Thirdly, it helps deal with climate risks. Our province's brown assets in industries such as the traditional manufacturing industry and fossil energy industry are prone to impact, especially under the dual influence of the current changes in the international trade market and the proposal of China's dual carbon goals. Green finance has a forward-looking view of these environmental and climate risks, thus can reduce the impact on brown assets.

Zhejiang Province has actively promoted the carbon peaking and carbon neutrality progress and has put forward relevant requirements for green finance. Since 2020, Zhejiang Regulatory Bureau of China Banking and Insurance Regulatory Commission has led the issuance of documents such as *Implementation Opinions on Financial Support for the Green Development of Zhejiang's Economy*, *Working Plan for Zhejiang Banking and Insurance Industry to Support High-quality Development and Construction of Common Wealth*

Demonstration Zones (*2022*), *Guidelines on Zhejiang Banking and Insurance Industry Supporting the Pilot Construction of Lishui Climate Investment and Financing* and *Guidelines on Deepening Financial Services for the Whole Clean Energy Industry Chain.* At the same time, Zhejiang Province has made remarkable achievements in green finance. By the end of 2021, the balance of green loans in Zhejiang Province increased by 46.3% year-on-year, 13.3 percentage points higher than the national growth rate; the issuance of green bonds increased by 128.57% year-on-year, and the financing amount increased by 5.63% year-on-year; More than 20 types of green insurance products have been innovated, and various types of green insurance have provided over 500,000 annual services[1].

II. Challenges for the development of green finance in Zhejiang Province

A. The regulatory and policy mechanisms of green finance needs to be improved

With the development of green finance in China up to now, there are still many imperfect policies and regulations related to green finance. Firstly, the lack of legal provisions leads to unclear responsibilities and rights. Regulatory authorities have successively formulated policies and laws to support green credit, but there is a lack of legal provisions defining the rights and obligations of commercial banks in green credit. Most of the green credit policies belong to departmental rules and regulations. Their legislative level is not high enough, and their enforcement and authority are not sufficient. Secondly, there is a lack of supportive government policies and measures. Supporting policies such as green credit risk compensation mechanisms, green credit guarantees, and tax relief have not been fully established. Thirdly, there is a disconnected linkage mechanism between credit allocation and environmental impact assessment information. There are many problems in some enterprises, such as deliberately concealing information and doing image projects in response to environmental protection inspections. Therefore, it is difficult for commercial banks to make accurate judgments on the authenticity of enterprise environmental protection

---

1 Data source: *Green Finance Development Report of Zhejiang Province* (2021).

information. Ultimately, it leads to an increase in the management costs and risks of green credit for commercial banks.

B. Insufficient disclosure of green information by enterprises

At present, there are still some problems in the corporate environmental information disclosure system. Firstly, the entities for mandatory environmental information disclosure are limited. Private enterprises are developed in Zhejiang Province, with small and micro enterprises accounting for over 75% of the total. Most enterprises are not included in the enterprise list of mandatory environmental information disclosure, making it difficult to obtain environmental information from such enterprises. Secondly, disclosure content is incomplete. The indicators disclosed by the enterprise cannot fully reflect the compliance of the enterprise with ecological and environmental laws and regulations and environmental governance, according to relevant laws and regulations. Thirdly, the disclosure form is not standardized and unified. To obtain environmental disclosure information, financial institutions, and others need to adopt various methods to increase acquisition costs. Fourthly, there is a lack of an information authenticity guarantee mechanism. The environmental information of enterprises has strong professionalism. Financial institutions and others lack the ability to distinguish the authenticity of environmental information. In this situation, the authenticity of environmental information disclosed by the enterprise cannot be guaranteed. Therefore, it is difficult for financial institutions to grasp complete, effective, and compliant environmental information of enterprises through corporate environmental information disclosure. Financial institutions are also unable to make accurate risk judgments in credit approval and post-loan management.

C. Green finance products and services urgently need innovation

When developing green finance products in Zhejiang Province, financial institutions are often faced with problems such as imperfect enterprise measurement and evaluation systems and insufficient environmental protection expertise. These problems have affected the targeted launch of various green finance products and services by financial institutions. Firstly, it is difficult to quantitatively evaluate green development in enterprises. When financial institutions analyze the production and operation of enterprises, they always face problems such as a lack of low-carbon-related historical data of enterprises and non-standard data records. Meanwhile, due to the professional limitations of financial institutions, it is difficult to flexibly evaluate the green development of enterprises that cannot meet the ESG indicator system. Secondly, the scope of green finance is limited. Although some documents have proposed that green finance should be linked and integrated with inclusive finance and transitional finance, the main scope of green finance carbon emission reduction support tools is still limited to the industries mentioned in the *Green Industry Guidance Catalog*, and there is a lack of corresponding transitional financial products to support the low-carbon transformation and efficiency improvement of traditional industries and high energy consuming industries in the pillar industries of the national economy. Thirdly, it is difficult to issue green finance loans. Zhejiang Province has a wide range of small and micro enterprises. Therefore, it is difficult to significantly improve the measurement system and statistical accounting system for small and micro enterprises in a short period of time. In addition, the development level of banks varies. They also face issues such as optimizing assets and risk control. Therefore, there is only a few inclusive green finance products for small and micro enterprises in the market.

III. Practice of Green Finance in Zhejiang Province

A. Relevant standard systems of green finance have been formed

Zhejiang Province continues to promote the implementation of green finance industry standards, accelerate the construction of local standard systems, and improve the green finance regulatory evaluation system. At the provincial level, standards such as *Specifications for Micro and Small Enterprise Greenness Assessment*, and *Implementation Specification for Green Building Low Carbon Project Loans* have been successively approved. Provincial group standards such as the *Integrated Service Specification for Credit Investigation of Yangtze River Delta Credit Investigation Chain*, *Evaluation Specification for Green and Low Carbon Project Financing*, and *Management Regulations for Personal*

Carbon Accounts in Banks have been successively approved. *Guidance on Financial Support for Carbon Peaking and Carbon Neutrality*, *Green Bond Endorsed Projects Catalogue* (*2021 Edition*), and *Guidelines on Financial Empowerment of Dual Demonstration Construction for 2021 Credit* have been released successively, promoting the standardization and standardized development of the green finance market. *The Implementation Rules for Green Finance Evaluation of Banking Financial Institutions* (*Legal Persons*) *in Zhejiang Province* was issued, which proposed many requirements such as strengthening environmental information disclosure. At the prefectural and municipal level, Huzhou City has released *Standards for Green Building Project Lenders*, *ESG Evaluation Standards for Banking Customers*, and *Guidelines for Measuring Carbon Emissions from Bank Credit in Huzhou City*. Quzhou City has established local standards for carbon account construction in key areas such as industry, agriculture, construction, road transportation, and energy production. And relevant documents such as *Opinions on Supporting the Development of Green Specialized Institutions in the Banking and Insurance Industry of Quzhou City*.

B. Innovative green finance products and services

Focusing on the dual carbon goals closely, Various regions in Zhejiang Province carry out innovation in products and services such as green credit, green bonds, green insurance, and carbon emission allowance pledge. Finally, a variety of green finance products and services have been formed, including "carbon efficiency loans", "carbon price loans", "low-carbon loans", "carbon accumulation release loans", and "carbon derivative trading loans" that encourage enterprises to reduce carbon emissions and improve efficiency, "carbon sink co-prosperity loans" and "carbon sink collection and storage loans" that encourage ecological environment and carbon sink protection, and "Evergreen Loans" and "Farmers' Photovoltaic Loans" that face fixed subjects such as farmers or small and micro enterprises. Based on regional resource endowments, industrial characteristics, market demand, and other local characteristics, green finance product service practices have also been carried out in various regions.

Huzhou City: Huzhou Branch of the Bank of China innovatively launched the "industrial carbon preferential loan" green finance product in combination with the application of the carbon efficiency code, facilitating the first application of "carbon efficiency code" in the field of bank credit since its launch.

Quzhou City: Quzhou Branch of the Agricultural Bank of China has successfully issued "green carbon reduction loans" to enterprises, which is the first special loan with the "carbon account" as the main reference indicator, helping enterprises achieve carbon sequestration, emission reduction, and green transformation.

Jiaxing City: The Jiashan County Branch of the People's Bank of China guides relevant banks to include local carbon emission allowance trading enterprises, register pledges and release through the CCRC Movables Financing Registration system in Credit Reference Center of the People's Bank of China.

Wenzhou City: The first green finance bond was launched in Yueqing, with an issue scale of 100 million yuan, which is mainly used for the financing needs of green low-carbon projects such as photovoltaic power generation related equipment manufacturing, public bicycles, and smart parking construction.

Jinhua City: In the inter-bank bond market, China's first private enterprise sustainable linked bonds and carbon neutrality bonds were successfully issued. If the linkage target is achieved, it is predicted that it can achieve more than 600,000 tons of carbon dioxide emission reduction by 2023.

Taizhou City: The "Evergreen Loan" small and micro enterprises green credit has been innovatively launched. This loan is based on inclusive finance for small and micro enterprises, reducing the guarantee threshold, achieving customization of green inclusive financial products, differentiated pricing, and normalized effectiveness tracking.

C. Green finance support tools have been developed

Zhejiang Province makes full use of the advantages of digital empowerment to improve the research and development of green finance infrastructure. The Hangzhou Central Branch of the People's Bank of China actively explores the construction of multi-and cross-scenario carbon account finance across the province and develops digital sharing of carbon information and cross-scenario applications. Huzhou City actively promotes the construction of a comprehensive carbon account support platform, with a focus on promoting the carbon account system and developing a digital ESG evaluation system. Quzhou City has developed a credit information platform for green finance services (Qurongtong) to promote the digital development of green finance services for financial institutions through credit information collection, bank-enterprise docking, data analysis, and other functions. Wenzhou vigorously promotes the construction of a carbon credit platform, improves the function of "carbon point + green finance", and provides financially matched carbon reduction preferential services for enterprises according to the results of enterprise credit rating. Taizhou City explores the construction of a multi-and cross-scenario "Weilvda" for carbon account finance in Zhejiang Province and promotes the recognition and entity identification of small and micro enterprises green credit.

In addition, based on the entity of carbon emissions and the current status of industrial development, Zhejiang Province fully utilizes its digital advantages to develop provincial enterprise carbon efficiency data infrastructures and support tools for enterprise carbon efficiency assessment. Relying on the carbon peaking and carbon neutrality smart governance platform of Zhejiang Province, which was set up under the leadership of the Provincial Development and Reform Commission, significant applications such as carbon accounts, carbon finance, and carbon inclusiveness in Zhejiang Province have achieved results. These achievements provide green finance with a carbon efficiency-related data base. At the same time, Zhejiang Province actively carries out the construction of carbon efficiency identification and evaluation tools for enterprises. and helps financial institutions reduce credit-granting risks and innovate green finance products. For example, the Zhejiang Provincial Industrial Carbon Efficiency Code categorizes and tracks the carbon efficiency of enterprises above designated size in the province, the Zhejiang Provincial Economic Information Center has launched a carbon efficiency evaluation model for small and micro enterprises, and the Huzhou Innovative Enterprise Five Color Code and ESG Evaluation Digital System has applied. These explorations provide various supporting tools for financial institutions to promote green finance.

IV. Inspiration from promoting the development of green finance in Zhejiang Province under the carbon peaking and carbon neutrality goals

A. Enterprises enhance the green and low-carbon development capabilities in multiple aspects

Enterprises should fully understand the global carbon neutrality situation and the trend of green transformation. Enterprises are not only the implementation object of green finance but also the demand side of green capital. Under adverse effects such as climate emergencies, energy crisis, and green trade barriers, private enterprises that lack climate response and defense capabilities will face serious challenges. Enterprises should enhance their awareness to the importance, necessity, and urgency of the dual carbon goals, deeply understand the opportunities and challenges that the dual carbon goals may bring to them, and build operational concepts and plans that are in line with the green and low-carbon trend.

Enterprises should actively take green and low-carbon development actions. Enterprises are an important supporting force for China's economic recovery and sustainable development. Enterprises should follow the trend under the guidance of new development concepts, can adjust their business goals and development models based on their actual situation, fully leveraging the advantages of flexible operation and quick decision-making, to seize the new opportunities brought by the dual carbon goals and complete low-carbon transformation within the "window period".

Enterprises should establish and improve carbon emission management systems and working mechanisms. Most private enterprises in Zhejiang Province have not established a specialized system for carbon emission data statistics and management. This current situation not only makes enterprises lack a decision-making basis for low-carbon transformation but also interferes with their green financing. Enterprises should accelerate the establishment of management systems for carbon emission information statistics, accounting, and disclosure. Moreover, enterprises should produce a carbon emission management mechanism covering all manufacturing processes, so as to obtain green finance support and transform "consumptive input" into "profitable output".

B. Financial institutions innovate the green finance services from multiple perspectives

Financial institutions should explore innovative risk assessment standards and quantitative tools. Financial institutions have launched a series of innovative green finance products under dual carbon goals. However, due to the extensive carbon management of some enterprises, the availability and authenticity of data are inadequate, which affects the feasibility and enthusiasm for financial institutions' services. It is suggested that financial institutions should constantly innovate the green finance business model according to the work requirements of dual carbon goals. Financial institutions can use "carbon efficiency" as one of the key indicators for identifying green entities, calculating and evaluating the environmental benefits of enterprises or projects, and fully utilizing technological means to serve a wider user group on the premise that the risks are controllable.

Financial institutions should strengthen the design of green and inclusive financial products that guide high-quality development. Enterprises will generate new financing needs during the low-carbon transformation process. The timely provision of new financial products and services has become a new topic that financial institutions must study. It is recommended that financial institutions innovate inclusive financial service products and channels with "carbon" attributes based on the transformation characteristics of enterprises at different stages under the dual carbon goals, in response to the pain points in their low-carbon transformation, so as to improve financing convenience and further meet the diversified funding needs of enterprises in the process of low-carbon transformation.

Financial institutions should continue to improve green finance capacity building. With the introduction of China's carbon peaking and carbon neutrality policy system, green inclusive finance and transformation finance will play a greater role. It is recommended that financial institutions accelerate the establishment and improvement of the due diligence system and process specifications for corporate environmental information and improve the carbon emission information disclosure mechanism. At the same time, financial institutions should strengthen the training of green finance, cultivate inter-disciplinary talents with professional backgrounds in finance and the environment, and enhance the quality and efficiency of green inclusive financial product innovation paths, risk management, and operational services.

C. Government supports green finance at multiple levels

The government should improve the top-level design of green finance and strengthen supervision. At present, China's green finance system lacks universality and force. The policy correlation and coordination between various departments need to be strengthened. It is recommended that government departments should increase financial support considering the local industrial transformation and the development needs of the green economy, and guide financial institutions to increase the proportion of green and low-carbon business and asset size. In addition, the government should strengthen the supervision of green finance, promote financial institutions and other relevant entities to publicly disclose green information at different levels and steps, and accelerate the construction of a green finance policy system and the mechanism that are compatible with the dual carbon goals.

The government should improve the breadth and depth of green finance through digital means. The government can use digital platforms as a key and systematic measure to promote carbon peaking and carbon neutrality. By strengthening inter-departmental coordination and cooperation, breaking the phenomena of isolated data islands, strengthening green information-sharing mechanisms such as enterprise carbon efficiency, and continuously promoting the construction of enterprise environmental credit systems, the government should provide technological support for building a long-term mechanism of "daring to lend, willing to lend, able to lend, and know to lend", and continuously optimize the financing environment for enterprises. The government should strengthen the application of digital technologies such as big data and the Internet of Things to effectively support financial institutions in continuously tracking the carbon efficiency level of enterprises before, during, and after loaning.

The government should establish a multi-level standard system centered on "carbon efficiency". Let financial institutions and other market entities accurately understand the meaning of "green" is the prerequisite for the standardized development of green finance. Government departments should accelerate the construction of a standard system, with "carbon efficiency" as the core, covering multiple dimensions of industries, enterprises, products, and services, to enable financial institutions to easily identify "green" activities in economic activities, scientifically assess the externality impact of business activities on the environment, and provide a basis for green finance decision-making.

Author: The writing group of Zhejiang economic & information centre

PART FIVE
RESEARCH
MONOGRAPHS

Trend of Carbon Footprint and Carbon Labelling System Development in the Global Transition towards Carbon Neutrality

Driven by the global trend of the transitioning towards green and low-carbon development under the framework of the Paris Agreement, institutions and policies regarding carbon emission reduction and carbon neutrality are gradually improved. Unlike the principle of "Common but Differentiated Responsibilities" under the United Nations Framework Convention on Climate Change, the undifferentiated carbon standard labeling system is being adopted by the developd countries in an increasing number of key industries and applied in key products, and new technical regulations for international trade, new economy and consumption sectors have been introduced over time, which will have a far-reaching impact on the the global supply chain and the growth of the industry. Therefore, it is necessary to prospectively carry out institution-oriented comparative study, explore to establish a carbon footprint assessment technology system that suits China's national conditions, advance the pilot and demonstration programs of carbon labelling for key industries and products, and constantly improve the data platform; it is also essential to formulate relevant standard, rules & regulations and introduce other green public products, cultivate third-party verification, certification and legal service agencies, actively adapt to carbon trade barriers, target a "new arena" for the growth of global carbon-free industry and implement the innovation-driven "carbon emission peaking and carbon neutrality" initiative.

With the implementing of the *Paris Agreement* issued by the United Nations to tackle climate change, a total of 130 countries accounting for about

90% of the global economic output, energy consumption and greenhouse gas emissions have announced in different forms their carbon neutrality goals. In particular, as major economies including China, the United States and the European Union have proposed their carbon neutrality goals, carbon neutrality will gradually become a new rule in such fields as industrial investment, energy market, capital flow and international trade. The carbon trade barrier as a kind of unilateral measure and green technology "decoupling" policy which are implemented or to be implemented by Europe, the United States and the Group of Seven (G7), for instance, Carbon Border Adjustment Mechanism (CBAM), carbon footprint standard of a product in its whole life cycle, "carbon insetting" management of green supply chain, carbon point rating of institutions and list of sensitive entities, will have a profound impact on China and other large developing trade countries.

I. Practices of Carbon Footprint and Carbon Labeling System at Home and Abroad

"Carbon Footprint", a concept derived from "Ecological Footprint", is mainly designed to measure the greenhouse gas emissions associated with human production and consumption activities, which are expressed in carbon dioxide equivalent. Carbon Footprint covers four aspects: carbon footprint of a country, carbon footprint of an individual, carbon footprint of a corporate and carbon footprint of a product. Of which, the carbon footprint of a product is the most widely applied concept to measure the greenhouse gas emissions generated in the whole life cycle of a product. The data from World Economic Forum shows that the carbon footprints of the eight supply chains (electronic products, automobiles, food, architecture, fashion, fast-moving consumer goods, professional services and freight transportation) account for over 50% of the global emissions. Carbon Labelling refers to a measurement of greenhouse gas emitted by a product throughout its whole life cycle (generally refers to the whole process including material, manufacturing, storage, transportation, discarding and recovery), with quantified indexes marked on the product label to inform customers the carbon information of the product. At present, the major international practice of carbon footprint estimate is voluntary, mainly on food and consumer electronics. The carbon labelling markets are well developed in the United Kingdom, Canada and the United States while in France, Germany, Japan and South Korea, the development of the carbon labelling system have been accelerated in recent years.

Although the carbon standard labelling system is being improved internationally, it is generally fragmented in governess and inconsistent in standards. Currently a unified international standard for the accounting and certification of carbon neutrality and emission reduction of a company or a product has yet to be introduced. Relevant certification management is decentralized and fragmented, in particular, the certification on the carbon emission standard (carbon footprint) management of products mainly depends on industry autonomy and enterprise autonomy: industry-leading companies like Apple Inc, IKEA and Volkswagen formulate their own supply chain management standards and carbon management requirements for their suppliers. Meanwhile, some non-governmental organizations and leading companies have jointly set up non-official management systems and launch relevant initiatives to facilitate mutual recognition of carbon emission management standards and satisfy credit endorsement demands of leading companies. There are mainly four technical standards for carbon footprint accounting and certification of products, which are adopted or referred to by non-official organizations established by multinational companies, leading companies and non-governmental organizations.

(1) ISO series standards. Among the current ISO standards, *ISO 14040* (*2009*) and *ISO 14044* (*2006*) are standards relevant to carbon footprint estimate of a product or service; *ISO 14064* (*2006*) is a standard on the measurement of carbon footprints from organizations and enterprises, which regulates and guides the measurement and verification of carbon footprints from organizations and enterprises. *ISO 14065* (*2013*), as a supplement to *ISO 14064*, regulates and guides the GHG validation and verification agencies adopting *ISO 14064* or other relevant standards or regulations; *ISO 14067 Standard* stipulates the specific method of carbon footprint calculation, and is prepared by the International Organization for Standardization (ISO) by referring to *PAS 2050*.

(2) *PAS 2050. PAS 2050: 2011- Publicly Available Specification: Specification*

for the Assessment of the Life Cycle Greenhouse Gas Emissions of Goods and Services is a publicly available specification jointly initiated by Carbon Trust and Department for Environment, Food, and Rural Affairs (DEFRA), and prepared and issued by British Standards Institution (BSI). It is applicable to carbon footprint assessment on multiple types of products and industries, including goods and services, manufacturers, retailers & traders, Business to Business (B2B), Business to Customer (B2C) and international supply chain. *PAS 2050* is to date a widely applied specification for carbon footprints of products.

(3) *IPCC Guidelines for National Greenhouse Gas Inventories.* The Guidelines list countries with anthropogenic emissions of greenhouse gases, which are estimated based on carbon source and carbon sinks. In this sense, the boundary of the research system is the boundary of country, and life cycle analysis method is not followed, but the emission factors and methods of estimating greenhouse gas emissions are applicable to the studies on life cycle assessment.

(4) *WRI/WBSCD Product and Supply Chain Standards.* World Resources Institute (WRI) and World Business Council for Sustainable Development (WBCSD) prepared *A Product Life Cycle Accounting and Reporting Standard* and *A Corporate* (*Scope 3/Supply Chain*) *Accounting and Reporting Standard* (collectively called the *Product and Supply Chain Standards*). The WRI/WBSCD standards change the practice of totally adopting life cycle assessment method in measuring the carbon footprint of a product, allowing and even encouraging the application of input-output analyse method.

On this regard, attention should be paid to the influential management systems and initiatives. In terms of the implementation and supervision of carbon emission reduction and carbon neutrality goals, the enterprises mainly set targets on their own and disclose the relevant information. Currently, a number of non-official institutions engaged in carbon emission reduction certification has been established, in which the Science Based Target Initiative (SBTi) is one of the examples. SBTi offers credit endorsement for enterprises in setting carbon emission reduction goals, and 4,151 global enterprises (including 127 enterprises from Chinese Mainland) have joined SBTi and carry out their carbon emission reduction actions under the guidance of SBTi, of which 1,537 enterprises have made the net zero emissions commitment. Based on the SBTi principle, enterprises making the net zero emissions commitment should realize net zero emissions by 2050 (for power sector, by 2040). The 100% Renewable Electricity (RE100) is a renewable energy initiative launched by the Climate Group in partnership with Climate Disclosure Project (CDP), aimed at getting the world's most influential multinational enterprises including Volkswagen, Apple Inc. and Microsoft to commit to 100% renewable electricity and reach this target in the shortest time possible (by 2050). RE100 member companies are required to disclose data on electricity consumption and progress toward the goal.

The European Union (EU) takes the lead in the establishment of an official product carbon emission reduction standard and management system. EU is now speeding up the formulation of relevant laws and will become the first to propose carbon emission certification management for products entering the EU market (including imported products), which will have an important impact on the import and export trade of related industries. EU is also the first political entity to establish through legislation the carbon trading market covering such industries as power, iron & steel, cement, aluminum, chemical industry, petrochemical industry and aviation, and enterprises of these industries are subject to carbon emission quota arrangement, which is tightened year by year, from the initial free quota to 100% auction of quota. It is expected that all emission quotas will be allocated in a paid way through auction by 2030. Recently, EU has passed successively the new *Batteries Regulation*, the *Carbon Border Adjustment Mechanism* (*CBAM*) and the *Act on Carbon Market Reform*, and amended the *Energy Efficiency Directive* and *Renewable Energy Directive* under the *European Green Deal*. According to the *Battery Regulation*, the battery industrial chain (covering raw material exploitation, procurement, production & processing, battery production and recovery & reuse of waste batteries) should be under the management and control of life cycle carbon footprint quota standard.

In China, the carbon emission statistical accounting standard system is at its initial stage. As a late starter in carbon footprint certification management, China has not proposed requirements for carbon footprint management regarding product market access. However, some Chinese industries have pioneered in the exploration and demonstration on this regard. For instance, the *Regulation for Carbon Labelling Evaluation of Electrical and Electronic Products* and the *LED Street Lighting Product Carbon Labelling* was released in 2018; Carbon Label Industry Innovation Alliance was established in 2019; the *Rules for the Implementation of Voluntary Evaluation of Carbon Labeling of Products Uniformly Implemented by the Industry* (*Interim*) was issued by China Electronics Energy Saving Technology Association in 2021; the *General Guideline for Enterprise Carbon Label Assessment* was released in 2022. China is building a complete, unified and standardized carbon emission statistical accounting system, and is gradually improving the carbon emission statistical accounting system for enterprises. Following the working principle of highlighting the key points and step-by-step advancement, China will focus on carbon footprint certification management of raw materials, semi-products and finished products from key industries, and gradually expand the management scope to products and service-based products from other industries. Based on the improved product carbon emission accounting system, China will explore the way of establishing carbon labelling system, guiding consumers in selection of low-emission products and services, and realizing carbon emission reduction of the whole industrial chain. Many export-oriented enterprises in China, constrained by multinational companies (purchasers) downstream of the supply chain, have to carry out relevant management according to the requirements of purchasers. Meanwhile, with the enforcement of the EU *Battery Regulation*, *CBAM* and the revised *New Energy Law*, Chinese enterprises will face the carbon emission control from the EU, especially for battery industry chain, photovoltaic industry chain, iron & steel, cement, aluminum and other industries.

II. Prominent Problems in the Development of Carbon Footprint and Carbon Labelling System

The first problem is the passive response of enterprise. No official consensus has been reached at home and abroad. In China, there is neither a unified and normative official technical standard nor normative technical guidance on carbon neutrality and carbon emission reduction activities conducted by enterprises, Consequently, it is unknown whether enterprises setting their carbon neutrality and emission reduction goals will acquire international recognition or official recognition inside China. Meanwhile, many export-oriented enterprises have to carry out management on carbon footprints of companies and products pursuant to the requirements of purchasers downstream of the supply chain, but the problem is that the standards for certification and management vary for different export markets and purchasers. As the relevant EU legislation in this field come into force, relevant industries like battery industry chain, photovoltaic industry chain, iron & steel, cement and aluminum should manage carbon emissions and fill in & report relevant data based on the stipulations of the EU laws & regulations. At present, the standard system adopted in European countries is different from the practices of Chinese enterprises, so there will be a high probability that Chinese enterprises have to re-understand and adapt to the corresponding EU standard system even if they have conducted data reporting and management according to the requirements of the Chinese government. The Chinese enterprises have to accept passively as a result of in-consistent standards and a lack of coordination and mutual recognition, as a result, corporate carbon emission management and certification is difficult and costly.

The second problem is institutional influence. For some regions with a developed green energy sector, resource advantages are not necessarily transferred to institutional advantages. The fundamental measures adopted by enterprises carrying out carbon emission reduction and carbon footprint certification are ultimately the same, mainly including: improving energy efficiency, utilizing renewable energy sources, optimizing production process and replacing products or raw materials, of which, the acknowledged emission reduction measure is to increase the proportion of renewable energy utilized. However, as the specific technical standard and accounting method are relevant to the way of identification and avoidance of repeated counting, the practice of an enterprise utilizing renewable energy or procuring green electric electricity may not be recognized internationally.

(1) Different accounting limits may result in overestimating emissions. Taking the CBAM as an example, the European Union currently adopts the accounting system of the EU carbon trading market for incorporated

enterprises. According to this system, the emissions of the carbon contents of imported aluminum products in the EU is accounted based on the production facilities of alumina, pre-cultured anodes, electrolytic aluminum and casting sections included in the EU carbon market. The average emission per ton of aluminum for each section is summed as the benchmark emission. In the future, even if electrolytic aluminum is included in the Chinese carbon market, it is actually only a process stage if the EU standard is adopted, and the carbon emission from aluminum exported from China to the EU will still be calculated based on the total emissions from the above-mentioned four processes. The calculated emissions of aluminium imported from China are actually higher than the figure reported by the Chinese electrolytic aluminium companies to the competent Chinese authorities.

(2) Purchase of green electricity and Green Electricity Certificate by Chinese enterprises may not be recognized internationally. The Chinese green energy market is still under development, so the corresponding policies are not well coordinated. Currently, the Chinese government regularly updates the emission factor for indirect carbon emissions generated when electricity is consumed by enterprises. The reason for updating the emission factor is that the proportion of renewable energy utilized will increase constantly. It is an open question whether electrolytic aluminum manufacturers setting up factories in places with abundant green electricity and procuring green electricity can be fully recognized under the national carbon market accounting system. As China now fails to avoid double counting of emission reduction for the part of emission reduction caused by green electricity, the EU does not recognize the emission reduction effect brought by the purchasing of green electricity and Green Electricity Certificate, and the carbon emission of aluminum is indirectly calculated based on the general electricity consumption.

III. Suggestions on Advancing the Carbon Footprint and Carbon Labelling System

In the future, laws and standards on the management of carbon emission of enterprises and products, market access and supply chain management will have a direct impact on the market competition of enterprises and the industry as a whole, and will also have a significant impact on the industrial competitiveness of national, regional and industrial parks. Therefore, it is necessary to plan in advance and respond positively.

Firstly, an in-depth investigation of export-oriented enterprises should be conducted to determine industries and enterprises which are vulnerable to the international supply chains and carbon footprint management certification of developed countries like those in EU, and identify the main challenges faced by such enterprises.

Secondly, the main international standards and systems of product carbon footprint certification should be further studied and analyzed to find out the key points and should be compared with the Chinese carbon emission accounting system. We should actively participate in the formulation and discussion of the Chinese carbon emission accounting system standard to ensure that the relevant national standard system is compatible and can give full play to the local and industrial advantages.

Thirdly, it is necessary to carry out prospective study, build technical reserves, ad make local and industrial contributions to the subsequent active participation and promotion of mutual recognition of international standards system.

Fourthly, based on the trend of low-carbon management of international supply chain and the new situation of industrial development under the national goal of "carbon peaking and carbon neutrality", it is essential to re-recognize and identify local advantageous industries, adjust and optimize industrial development policies, and cultivate new industrial competitive advantages guided by the "carbon peaking and carbon neutrality" goal.

Author: Chai Qimin[1]

---

1 Chai Qimin, director for strategy and planning in National Center for Climate Change Strategy and International Cooperation (NCSC), guesting professor of Research Center for Contemporary Management in Tsinghua University , and vice chairman and secretary general of Carbon Peaking and Carbon Neutrality Committee in Chinese Society of Environmental Sciences. His main research areas include global climate governance, climate change integrated assessment modeling, energy and environmental economics, etc.

Reflections and Prospects on the System of "Controlling both the Amount and Intensity of Carbon Emissions"

China proposes that the establishment of a total carbon emission control system is one of the priorities of dual carbon targets. This paper provides a literature review on the target assessment and allocation methods of the total carbon emission control system, summarizes the experience and reference of the implementation of relevant international systems, analyzes the relevant systems and policies for controlling carbon emissions that have been implemented at the industry and local levels in China, to propose the suggestions of establishing a "dual control" system for carbon emissions: ① Set the different future scenarios covering economic, social, energy and industry, and adopt a top-down macro calculation, to determine the possible range for achieving the total carbon emissions goals of "peaking before 2030 and achieving stable and moderate decline" and "achieving stable decline by 2035"; ② Make the "region" and "department" as the main responsible subjects, and reasonably use the goal decomposition method; ③ Establish different supporting institutional systems for different emission entities, including local governments, departments, industries, and key enterprises; ④ Establish corresponding guarantee systems and data support systems to ensure the smooth implementation of various policy tools.

I. Introduction

In 2015, China had set the goal of achieving peak carbon emissions by 2030. This goal was modified to "striving to peak carbon emissions before 2030" in 2020, and the *Outline of the 14th Five-Year Plan (2021-2025) for National Economic and Social Development* released in 2021 proposed the goal of "stable and moderate decrease of carbon emissions after carbon peaking by 2030". Since the 11th Five Year Plan, China has implemented energy-saving and emission reduction policies with carbon intensity and energy consumption intensity as binding indicators, and total energy consumption as guiding goals, and relevant goals have been decomposed and assessed by provincial people's governments. Although these measures effectively ensured China's carbon intensity reduction goal of "reducing carbon emissions per unit of GDP by 40%-45% by 2020 compared to 2005" proposed in 2009, they did not effectively control the growth of total carbon emissions (as shown in Figure 24-1). Due to the process of industrialization and urbanization in China, controlling the growth rate of carbon emissions, peaking rapidly, and achieving a decrease before 2030 still poses enormous challenges.

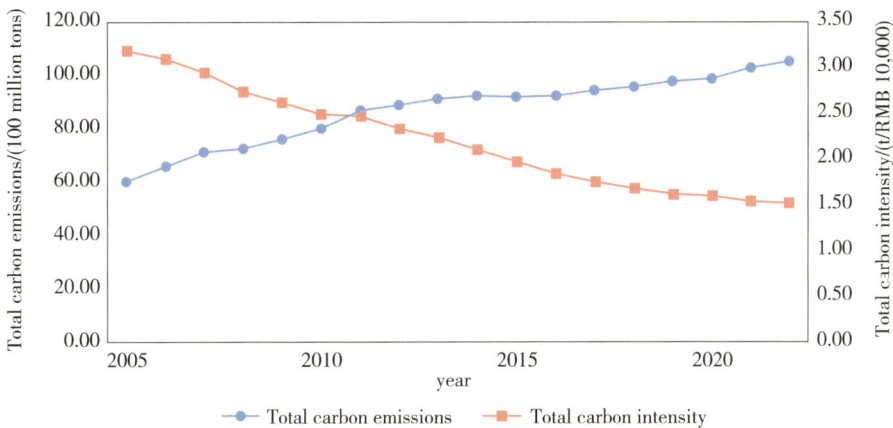

Figure 24-1   Total Carbon Emission and Carbon Intensity of China (2005-2022)

Total carbon emission control refers to setting a total CO_2 emission target for a country, region, or industry over a certain period of time in accordance with relevant laws and regulations, to control the total CO_2 emissions of all emission sources within the targeting amount. China has incorporated the idea of controlling the total carbon emissions into the macro policy documents of carbon peaking and carbon neutrality, and pointed out the overall design of the total carbon emission control system. The *Working Guidance for Carbon Dioxide Peaking and Carbon Neutrality in Full and Faithful Implementation of the New Development Philosophy* issued by the Central Committee of the Communist

Party of China and the State Council emphasized that China will "coordinate and establish a total CO_2 emission control system"; The Central Economic Work Conference of CPC at the end of 2021 mentioned that it is necessary to create conditions to achieve the transformation from "dual control" of energy consumption to "dual control" of carbon emissions and intensity as soon as possible; The *Action Plan for Carbon Dioxide Peaking Before 2030* issued by the State Council proposes to implement collaborative management, decomposition, and assessment of energy consumption and carbon emissions indicators.

However, there is currently no specific policy arrangement on the basic elements and research methods of the total carbon emission control system, and how to transform energy consumption from "dual control" to carbon "dual control". This article proposes a institutional framework and policy recommendations of the total carbon emission control system in line with China's national conditions based on a review of relevant research on the total carbon emission control system, the reference of international institutional experience, and the existing practical experience and challenges in China.

II. Review of Theoretical Methods

A. Target Research Method

Many research institutions and scholars have conducted research on scientifically and reasonably proposing China's current total carbon emissions targets. The report—*China's Low-carbon Development and Transformation Strategy and Path* issued by Tsinghua University proposes that China's CO_2 emissions will enter a peak plateau period around 2025, and the peak CO_2 emissions related to fossil energy consumption will be controlled within 11 billion tons[1]. The Chinese Academy of Engineering's *Carbon Peaking and Carbon Neutrality Strategy and Path for China* pointed out that China's CO_2 emissions are expected to peak around 2027, with the peak controlled at about 12.2 billion tons[2]. Zhang Xiliang et al. [3] proposed that energy related carbon emissions will peak in the middle of the 15th Five Year Plan, with a peak level of less than 10.5 billion tons, then will decrease by about 15% compared with peak by 2035.

According to existing research, the methods for determining the total carbon emission target include three categories: bottom-up, top-down, and mixed methods[4-11]. Based on the research of macroeconomic analysis and policy planning, top-down models are commonly used, with typical representatives including IPAT models, KAYA models, CGE models, system dynamics models, etc. that comprehensively consider population, economy, society, and environment. Bottom-up model paies more attention to the energy, starting from the engineering technology model. Detailed descriptions and simulations are conducted based on the technologies used in energy consumption and production processes, and supply and demand forecasting and environmental impact analysis are mainly carried out based on energy consumption and production methods. The typical representatives are LEAP models, MARKAL models, MESSAGE models, etc. based on various energy technologies. A mixed model that combines top-down and bottom-up approaches to simulate the emission process from energy extraction, transformation, transportation, market to final energy demand. The energy supply capacity, energy prices, demand, and macroeconomic parameters of each department will be predicted through system simulation.

The prediction of emissions from the base year to the target year often uses trend analysis, scenario analysis, KAYA analysis, and other methods, combines with national or regional emission reduction responsibilities and willingness to reduce emissions, comprehensively considers factors such as GDP, population, urbanization rate, industrial structure, energy structure, etc., to ultimately determine future emission targets. The research ideas and methods are shown in Figure 24-2.

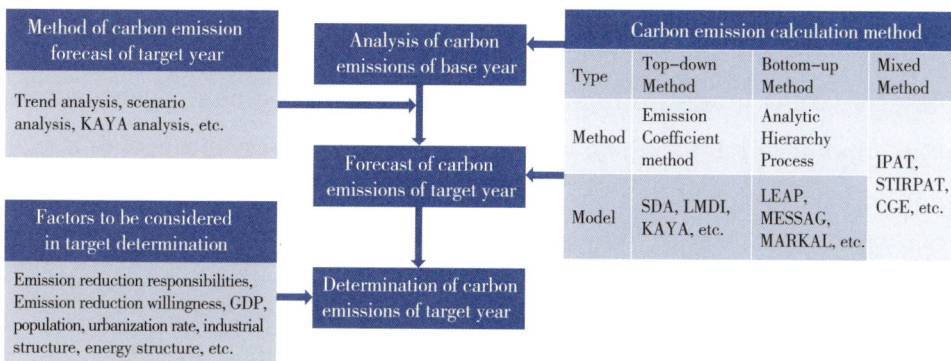

Method of carbon emission forecast of target year		Analysis of carbon emissions of base year	Carbon emission calculation method			
Trend analysis, scenario analysis, KAYA analysis, etc.			Type	Top-down Method	Bottom-up Method	Mixed Method
		Forecast of carbon emissions of target year	Method	Emission Coefficient method	Analytic Hierarchy Process	IPAT, STIRPAT, CGE, etc.
Factors to be considered in target determination			Model	SDA, LMDI, KAYA, etc.	LEAP, MESSAG, MARKAL, etc.	
Emission reduction responsibilities, Emission reduction willingness, GDP, population, urbanization rate, industrial structure, energy structure, etc.		Determination of carbon emissions of target year				

Figure 24-2　Framework of Research on the Total Carbon Emission Control Target

B. Target Allocation Method

The national carbon emissions target needs to be decomposed into responsible and emission entities for implementation. The key of formulating allocation plans is the choise of the principles and methods for allocation. This article summarizes the allocation plans in existing research.

1) Allocation principle. Under the premise of controlling total carbon emissions, fairness and efficiency are the most important principles for carbon emission allocation [12,13]. The principle of fairness generally considers the differences of population amount and development stages between regions[14], and mainly reflected through per capita cumulative carbon emissions, population, GDP, per capita GDP, and carbon emission density, etc[15]. The core of the efficiency principle is to maximize output, which refers to generate more development benefits for the country under the established total carbon emissions target[14], and mainly reflected through energy consumption per unit of GDP, carbon emissions per unit of GDP, carbon productivity, etc[13]. In addition to the principles of fairness and efficiency, some scholars also allocate the total carbon emissions based on the principles of feasibility, ability, responsibility, effectiveness, comprehensiveness, bias, economic index, and emission reduction potential in their research[16-19].

2) Allocation method. The allocation methods can mainly be divided into two categories: indicator system method and model analysis method. The indicator system method can comprehensively consider multiple factors and indicators that affect the total carbon emissions, and the selection of indicators is relatively flexible. It is a widely used provincial total allocation method in domestic policy research. The other method is to build diversified models to allocate the total carbon emissions, including data envelopment analysis (DEA) model, duopoly game model, CGE model, bi-objective programming model (BPM), etc. Some scholars have comprehensively applied existing research methods to develop mixed models, such as comprehensive research, entropy method, k-means method, and shadow price model, etc[12,14-26].

III. International Experiences

After the *Kyoto Protocol* was signed, developed countries are proactive in fulfilling their emission reduction responsibilities and implemented diverse policy measures to achieve the GHG emission reduction goal. Particularly, some countries and regions have adopted the total carbon emission control system. For instance, EU is committed to being a global leader in responding to climate change, setting and reinforcing mid-and-long term climate goals centered on the decrease of total GHG emissions, and working to meet the goals under the EU Emissions Trading System (EU ETS) and Effort Sharing Mechanism. Driven by the total emission control mechanism and laws & regulations regarding renewable energies and efficiency, the GHG emission of EU in 2020 dropped by 31% compared with the figure in 1990, exceeding the target by 20%, showcasing the effectiveness of the total carbon emission control system. The United Kingdom and France have adopted phased carbon budget system to facilitate the realization of the long-term total emission control target. In Germany, the adoption of the *Federal Climate Change Act* enables the quantified allocation of the total emission target among sectors such as energy, industry, buildings, transport and agriculture. Explorations and practices on sub-national total emission control systems have been carried out in California of the USA and Tokyo in Japan. These international systems offer helpful references to China's total carbon emission control work[27].

A. Constantly reinforcing the mid–and–long term target on total GHG control and enhancing its binding force through legislation

In 2008, the EU proposed a legally binding climate target of "a reduction of greenhouse gas emissions by at least 20% compared to 1990, a 20% share of renewable energies in final energy consumption and 20% of savings on the projected EU final energy consumption in 2020" (known as the "20-20-20" Climate Targets) [28]. In 2014, the European Council endorsed the binding target of "at least 40% reduction in economy-wide greenhouse gas emissions by 2030 compared to 1990" as proposed in the *2030 Framework for Energy and Climate*. In 2019, the European Commission released the *European Green Deal*, putting forward a more ambitious EU 2030 Climate Target of "reducing economy-wide and domestically net GHG emissions by at least 55% by 2030", and officially announced the 2050 Climate Neutrality Target. The European Climate Law, adopted in June 2021, enhances the legal binding force of the 2030 Climate Target and 2050 Climate Target[29].

The United Kingdom is a pioneer in responding to climate change through legislation. The UK introduced the *Climate Change Act* (*CCA*) in 2008, the first of its kind in the world. CCA establishes a legally binding target of "net UK carbon account for the year 2050 is at least 80% lower than the 1990 baseline". The target was modified and raised from 80% up to 100% in the revised version of CCA issued in 2019, based on the target adjustment mechanism, indicating that the UK will realize net zero emission in 2050. CCA identifies not only legally binding climate goals, but also carbon budget mechanism, including institutional arrangements on the target adjustment, phased target setting and target implementation progress assessment[30].

B. Allocating the overall goal based on regions and/or sectors, and facilitating emission reduction of main emitters through institutional arrangements

The climate targets of EU are pursued by all Member States collectively[31]. As illustrated in Figure 3, the emission sources (sinks) are divided into three categories: ① large emission sources from power generators, energy-intensive industries, and aviation sector, which are included in EU ETS; ② small emission sources from industrial activities, buildings, transport, agriculture and waste, which are excluded from EU ETS; ③ Land Use, Land Use Change and Forestry (LULUCF) sector. The emission reduction targets are allocated by a "sectors" and "countries" integrating method, and implementation of emission target and allocation plan are jointly supported by EU ETS, Effort Sharing Mechanism and LULUCF Regulation.

EU overall target on total emission control

Overall target

Target of year 2020	Target of year 2030
• at least reduce 20% compared to 1990 • a reduction of 31% achieved	• at least reduce 40% compared to 1990, which has been increased to 55%

Support mechanism & target allocation

EU ETS

Target of year 2020	Target of year 2030
Allocation: annual reduction factor of 1.74%(2013-2020)	A 43% cut in emission compared to 2005 levels, suggested to raise to 61%(not yet passed)

Effort Sharing

Target of year 2020	Target of year 2030
±20% emission cut compared to 2005 levels for EU Member States	0%-40% cut in emissions for EU Member States. An overall 30% cut of emissions by EU compared to 2005 levels, Suggested to raise to 40% (not yet passed)

LULUCF Regulation

Target of year 2030
Increasing the carbon removals from land use, land-use change and forestry to 310 million of tons CO2 equivalent by 2030

Main responsible bodies and relevant emission sources/sinks

Emission installations under EU ETS

• Period 1-3 (2005-2020)	Period 4 (2021-2030)
• Power generators, energy-intensive industries, aviation sector (since 2012), etc.	• Power generators, energy-intensive industries, aviation sector • Road transport, buildings, maritime transport, etc.

EU Member States

• Installations excluded from EU ETS, for instance, small source of emissions from industrial installations, buildings, transportation, agriculture, waste, etc.

EU Member States

• Forest land, corp land, grassland, wetlands, settlements and other lands

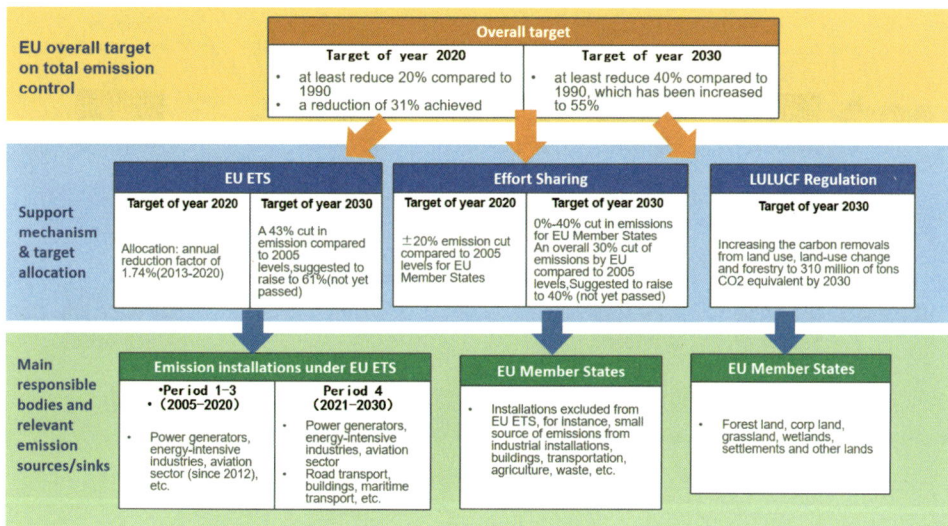

Figure 24-3　Implementation mechanism and target allocation scheme of EU total amount control

C. Implementing a closed-loop management system covering target setting, allocation, implementation and progress assessment

The institutional arrangement under UK Carbon Budget[32] involves target setting, allocation and implementation, target progress assessment and target updating, and identifies different functions of the UK Parliament, the UK government and Climate Change Committee (CCC), as shown in Figure 24-4.

It should be noted that CCC is a third-party organization composed of experts and established by the UK pursuant to the CCA, and its major responsibilities include: ① advising the UK government on carbon budget target; ② assessing the implementation of the carbon budget and reporting to the UK Parliament; ③ offering technical consulting services at the request of state authority. For instance, CCC recommends a net-zero emission target of GHG in the UK by 2050, carbon neutrality in Scotland in 2045 and a 95% cut in GHG emissions in Whales by 2050[33].

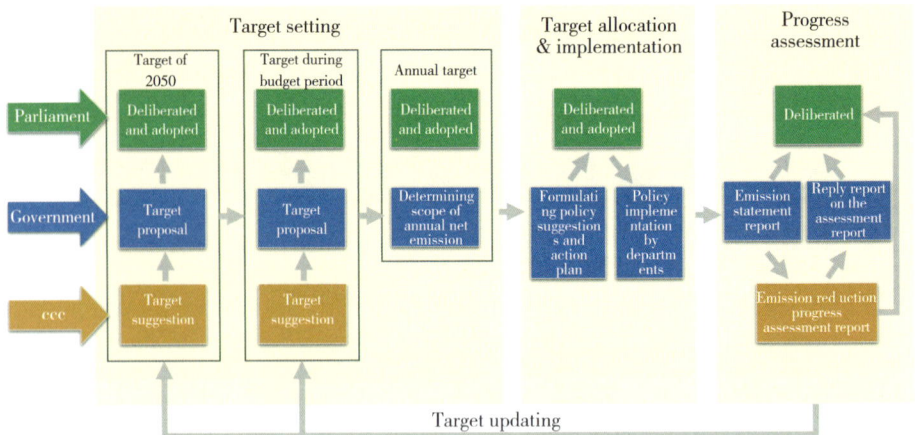

Figure 24-4   Institutional Arrangement under UK Carbon Budget

D. Establishing GHG monitoring, reporting and verification system

One of the difficulties in implementing the total carbon emission is finding a way to acquire authentic carbon emission data based on unified, fair data statistics and calculation method and to correctly assess the carbon emission target progress. The EU has established and improved its greenhouse gas MRV system, and stipulated in the *Regulation on Greenhouse Gas Monitoring and Report* (*2018/2066*) the types of greenhouse gases emitted from different types of installations to be monitored and reported, calculation methods and data quality requirements. The carbon emission reduction effort shared by EU Member States is assessed mainly based on the greenhouse gas inventory. EU Member States should establish and operate a national greenhouse gas inventory system, submit their X-2 year greenhouse gas inventory prior to March 15, coordinate with the EU in the compilation of the overall greenhouse gas inventory, and timely submit it to UNFCCC. Meanwhile, the X-1 year estimate inventory shall also be provided, summarized by the European Commission and released in September of the year.

IV. Practical Experience and Challenges in China

China has implemented policies related to total carbon emission control at the industrial and local levels. At the industrial level, the total emissions from key industries and enterprises are controlled based on the carbon emissions trading system. Starting in 2011, seven provinces and municipalities including Beijing, Shanghai and Hubei were selected to carry out pilot programs on carbon emissions trading. The national carbon market was officially launched in 2017 and the online carbon emissions trading for the power sector was officially launched in 2021.

At the local level, pilot provinces and municipalities of low-carbon emission are encouraged to explore way of controlling the total carbon emission[34]. In 2016, the *13th Five-Year Plan for Economic and Social Development of Beijing* was launched, which identifies the targets of decreasing carbon emission intensity by 20.5% and peaking the total carbon emissions during the 13th Five-Year Plan Period. The binding targets on energy conservation and carbon reduction in Beijing were allocated to districts. Simultaneously, the targets of controlling both the total amount and intensity of energy consumption were allocated to industries and sectors. Besides, the target of controlling both the total amount and intensity of energy consumption and the target of controlling both the total amount and intensity of carbon emissions are allocated respectively to 51 major energy-using entities and 800 major emitters[35]. Shanghai municipal government has set the target of peaking the total and per capita carbon emissions by 2025, and reducing the total carbon emissions by 5% compared to the peaking level by 2035, exploring the way of controlling the total carbon emissions from the aspects of objectives, means, policies, and management[36]. In 2017, Wuhan municipal government launched the *Action Plan for Peak Carbon Emissions in Wuhan* (*2017-2022*), in which, the target of peaking carbon emissions by 2022 is allocated based on two levels (sectors such as industry, buildings, transport, energy, and districts and counties level) and in three steps, responsible entities are identified, the progress will be assessed every two years[37].

The above practices and explorations have provided valuable experience in the establishment of the national total carbon emission control system and served as the basis for the implementation of the system. Problems such as inadequate legal protection, imperfect implementation mechanisms and management means, and unsound data accounting systems are also gradually discovered in this process.

V. Suggestions on the establishment of dual control of carbon emissions system

The transition from the current "dual control" of energy consumption to the total control of carbon emissions needs to combine the needs of carbon peaking, carbon neutrality and high-quality development to establish total control goals, that is, to establish the policy objectives of the system, and to match the corresponding policy tools, so as to incorporate relevant policy objects into implementation. Meanwhile, in order to ensure the implementation effect of the goals and systems, it is also necessary to regularly assess the completion of the goals and the progress of the system implementation, timely update and adjust the decomposition of goals and system design, to form an entire management process for target setting, mechanism design, evaluating and updating.

Based on the above research, with the total carbon control system as the core of the top-level system for double carbon target, the whole process system framework for implementing total carbon emissions control (Figure 24-5) is proposed, which forms a "common but different" regulatory and constraint mechanism for greenhouse gas emissions for different responsibility subjects, and improve the effective use of greenhouse gas emission space as scarce resources. The details are as follows:

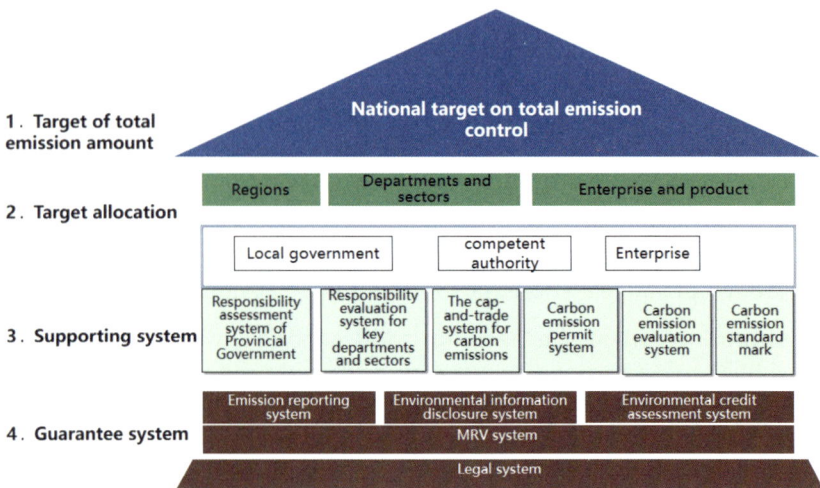

Figure 24-5　Framework of total carbon emission control system

A. Scientifically set the national total carbon emission control targets

According to the demand of the national carbon peaking and carbon neutrality overall goal, research and determine the emission control goals for a period of time in the future (2030, 2035 and other key years), and carry out every five years' periodic decomposition and annual decomposition.

To scientifically set the total amount target, it is necessary to connect the carbon emission target with high-quality development, energy revolution, and other goals at the macroeconomic and social development level. Therefore, it is recommended to adopt a top-down macro measurement method, to determine the possible range for achieving the total carbon emissions of " carbon peaking before 2030 and achieving stable and moderate decline" and "achieving stable decline by 2035" by setting different scenarios for future economic, society, energy development, and industrial structure adjustment. The determination of total carbon emission goals also need to comprehensively consider the changing trends and transformation difficulties of factors such as carbon intensity, energy consumption, energy structure, and environmental protection, to determine scientific and reasonable total amount control goals.

B. Scientifically allocate the total carbon emission target

According to the characteristics and responsibilities of emission sources, relevant entities include the central government, local governments, competent departments, enterprises, and the public. It is necessary to allocate the total amount control goals in a differentiated manner, and set certain emission targets for the main emission entities.

Referring to relevant practices and research at home and abroad, the total carbon emission targets are allocated to four categories: regional decomposition, industry decomposition, combination of regional and industry decomposition without repetition, and dual decomposition and management of regional and industry. Regional decomposition mainly refers to the main responsibility of the people's governments at the provincial, municipal, or subordinate district levels. According to the indicator system method or model construction, the principles of fairness, efficiency, and capacity are comprehensively considered to decompose the subordinate regions. Industry decomposition is aimed at the relevant responsibilities of the regulatory authorities. The determination of emission targets and management measures for sectors such as industry, construction, transportation, and forestry need to consider the emission characteristics and trends of industry, construction, transportation, and other sectors.

C. Establish the implementation mechanism and supportive system

The carbon emission targets promote the implementation of relevant responsible entities through different implementation mechanisms and supporting systems. Referring to domestic and foreign research and practical experience, the focus is on discussing supporting systems applicable to local governments, departments, industries, key enterprises, and other responsible entities.

For local governments, the existing target responsibility system with the provincial government as the main body to implement carbon intensity goals and energy consumption dual control goals will be transformed into an institutional system with the total emission control target responsibility assessment system, and the practical experience of national carbon intensity decline target assessment, energy dual control assessment, and local carbon emission total amount control assessment will be summarized, relevant professionals, capabilities and technical advantages should be built, to accelerate the transition to carbon emission target assessment.

Departments and industries's task is to explore and establish the target responsibility assessment mechanism for key departments and industries, further expand the coverage of carbon emission trading systems, and strengthen the control of emission quotas for key industries.

Key enterprises should explore and establish the greenhouse gas emission licensing system, evaluation system, and standard labeling system, and use the greenhouse gas emission licensing system to promote the formation of a emission rights and property rights system with clear ownership, clear rights and responsibilities, and effective supervision, to promote the low-carbon transformation of production factors; Use the carbon emission evaluation system of major construction projects to strictly control the increment of greenhouse gas emissions caused by major fixed assets investment projects, and promote the low-carbon transformation of major project investment and construction; Improve the carbon emission management standard system and promote low-carbon development of industry, energy, construction, and transportation through measures such as industry emission standards, technical standards, and product standards.

D. Improve the Relevant Guarantee System

To ensure the smooth implementation of various policy tools, it is necessary to establish corresponding guarantee systems and data support systems. Firstly, it is necessary to establish a comprehensive legal and regulatory system for addressing climate change, clarify the legal attributes of carbon emissions and the legal responsibilities and obligations of various entities, to provide a legal basis for the implementation of the system. The second is to further improve the construction of the greenhouse gas MRV system, enhance the authenticity and accuracy of basic data, to ensure the scientificity, comparability, and evaluability of accounting results. The third is to strengthen information disclosure work, which is not only conducive to accept social and public opinion supervision, but also a necessary measure to comply with the international community's requirements for transparency and other related demands. For example, the establishment of a regular bulletin system on greenhouse gas emissions, environmental information disclosure, environmental credit evaluation creates a favorable social environment for controlling total carbon emissions.

Author: Yang Xiu[1], Yang Shanshan[2], Guo Hao[3]

1   Yang Xiu, associate researcher at the Institute of Change Climate and Sustainable Development, Tsinghua University, mainly engaged in in the research fields energy of and climate change.

2   Yang Shanshan, senior engineer the at Tsinghua-Lituo Resources Energy and Sustainability Joint Research Center, mainly engaged in on research climate change policies and greenhouse gas emissions.

3   Guo Hao, assistanter research at the Institute of Climate Change and Sustainable Development, Tsinghua University, mainly engaged research in in the fields of energy and climate change.

References

[1] Chinese Academy of Engineering. A comprehensive report on China's long-term low carbon development strategy and transformation path[J]. *China Population*, *Resources and Environment*, 2020,30(11):1-25.

[2] China Youth OnLine. Chinese Academy of Engineering: China is expected to achieve carbon peaking in 2027 and carbon neutrality by 2060[EB/OL]. https://m.gmw.cn/baijia/2022-04/01/1302876708.html, 2022-04-01/2022-08-12.

[3] Zhang X L, Huang X D, Zhang D, et al. Energy economy transition pathway and policy research under carbon neutral target [J]. *Management World*, 2022,38(1):35-66.

[4] Liu D M, Chen Y, Shi J G. Research on CO_2 emission estimation method for greenhouse gas environmental impact assessment in China[C] // 2012 Proceedings of the Annual Academic Conference of the Chinese Society of Environmental Science (Volume I). *Beijing: China Agricultural University Press*, 2012: 892-896.

[5] KAYA Y. Impact of carbon dioxide emission on GNP growth: interpretation of proposed scenario[R]. *Paris: IPCC Energy and Industry Subgroup*, *Response Strategies Working Group*, 1990.

[6] Zhu Y E, Li L F, He S S, et al. Peak year prediction of Shanxi Province's carbon emissions based on IPAT modeling and scenario analysis[J]. *Resources Science*, 2016, 38(12): 2316-2325

[7] Li Q, Zhuo J X. The Yangtze river economic belt based on STIRPAT model carbon emission peak prediction study[J]. *Journal of Northeast Agricultural University* (*Social Science Edition*), 2017, 15(5): 53-58.

[8] Tang J, Cui W Y, Wen Z J, et al. An empirical dtudy on the peaking of carbon emissions based on the Kaya Model[J]. *Social Science in Shenzhen*, 2022, 5(3): 50-59.

[9] Cheng L J, Wu H M, Fan L, et al. Study on the determination of carbon emission peak and its countermeasures in Zhejiang province[J]. *Journal of Chinese Energy*, 2017, 39(4): 43-47.

[10] Gao X Y. Beijing integrated plan model for renewable energy and policy research[D]. *Beijing University of Technology*, 2011.

[11] Hong J K, Li Y C, Guo S Y. Simulating building carbon emission path with a Rice-Leap model from the perspective of the whole supply chain[J]. *China Environmental Science*, 2022, 42(9): 4389-4398.

[12] Cheng J H. Decomposition of Carbon Cap Targets at Provincial Level in China[J]. *China Population, Resources and Environment*, 2016, 26(1): 23-30.

[13] He Y G, Yan J Q. Initial allocation of regional carbon emission rights in China based on efficiency and equity[J]. *Journal of North China Electric Power University (Social Science Edition)*, 2020(5): 26-32.

[14] Xiong X P, Kang Y B, Feng S B, et al. Study on the regional decomposition method of total carbon emission control target[J]. *Journal of Chinese Energy*, 2015, 37(11): 15-19.

[15] Wang W J, Cheng Z L. Study on the initial carbon quota allocation scheme in China's provincial regions - Based on the perspective of responsibility and target, equity and efficiency[J]. *Journal of Management World*, 2019, 35(3): 81-98.

[16] Tian Y, Lin Z J. Provincial distribution of China's carbon emission rights and assessment of its emission reduction potential under the Paris Agreement[J]. *Journal of Natural Resources*, 2021, 36(4): 921-933.

[17] Fei C W, Qu Z R, Liu R B. Initial allocation of inter-provincial carbon emission rights in China[J]. *Science and Technological Innovation*, 2021(22): 25-27.

[18] Cheng Y L, Gu B H, Tan X C, et al. Allocation of provincial carbon emission allowances under China's 2030 carbon peak target: A dynamic multi-criteria decision analysis method[J]. *Science of The Total Environment*, 2022, 837: 155798.

[19] Zhang H R, Li W. Design of a regional carbon emission reduction allocation mechanism: based on 1.5°C temperature rise target[J]. *Research on Science and Technology Management*, 2020, 40(14): 227-236.

[20] Wu J, Li M, Xu G S, et al. Carbon quota allocation among industries with carbon emission control by using game model[J]. *Journal of Beijing University of Chemical Technology (Natural Science)*, 2020, 47(6): 115-120.

[21] Chai Q M, Fu S, Zheng X Q, et al. Carbon emission cap control target and policy study of selected sectors and industries in China[J]. *China Population*,

Resources and Environment, 2017, 27(12): 1-7.

[22] Du L, Zhang Y. The design of allocation mechanism for China's ttotal carbon emission control trading - based on the experience of EU emissions trading system[J]. *Studies of International Finance*, 2013(7): 51-58.

[23] Xie R L, Zheng Y Q, Su X D. Reflections on the implementation of total carbon emission control system[J]. *China Environmental Protection Industry*, 2020(7): 13-17.

[24] Bian Y, Liu Y. Establish total carbon emission control system[J]. *China Opening Journal*, 2021(5): 14-20.

[25] Tian D Y, Zheng W R, Gao S Y. Accelerating the construction of a long-term mechanism for total carbon emission control[J]. *Environmental Protection*, 2020, 48(12): 55-57.

[26] Wang J N, Cai B F, Cao D, et al. Scenario study on regional allocation of CO_2 emissions allowance in China[J]. *Acta Scientiae Circumstantiae*, 2011, 31(4): 680-685.

[27] Yang S S, Guo H, Yang X, et al. Consideration and prospect of total carbon emission control system under the double carbon target [J]. *Climate Change Research*, 2023, 19(2): 191-202.

[28] Official Journal of the European Union. Effort Sharing Decision[EB/OL]. http://data.europa.eu/eli/dec/2009/406/oj , 2009/2022-07-12.

[29] European Union. European Climate Law [EB/OL]. https://climate.ec.europa. eu/eu-action/european-green-deal/european-climate-law_en. 2021/2022-07-12.

[30] UK Parliament. Climate Change Act 2008 [EB/OL]. https://www.legislation. gov.uk/ukpga/2008/27/contents, 2008/2022-07-12.

[31] Official Journal of the European Union. Effort Sharing Regulation[EB/OL]. http://data.europa.eu/eli/reg/2018/842/oj, 2018/2022-07-12.

[32] Climate Change Committee. The Sixth Carbon Budget The UK's path to Net Zero [R/OL]. https://www.theccc.org.uk/publication/sixth-carbon-budget, 2020/2022-07-12.

[33] Climate Change Committee. 2022 Progress Report to Parliament [R/OL]. https://www.theccc.org.uk/publication/2022-progress-report-to-parliament/ 2022/2022-07-12.

[34] Yang X, Tian D Y, Zhou Z Y, et al. The progress and suggestion of low-carbon provinces and cities in China[J]. *Environmental Protection*, 2018, 46(15): 15-21.

[35] The People's Government of Beijing Municipality. Beijing's 13th Five-Year Plan to Reduce Energy Consumption and Address Climate Change [EB/OL]. http://fgw.beijing.gov.cn/fgwzwgk/zcgk/ghjhwb/wnjh/202204/t20220413_2676116.htm, 2016-08-07.

[36] Shanghai Municipal People's Government. Shanghai Urban Master Plan (2017-2035) [EB/OL]. https://www.shanghai.gov.cn/nw42806/index.html, 2018-01-17.

[37] Wuhan Municipal People's Government. Notice of the Municipal People's Government on the issuance of Wuhan city carbon emissions peaking action plan (2017-2022) (Wu Zheng [2017] No. 36) [EB/OL]. http://fgw.wuhan.gov.cn/zfxxgk/zfxxgk_1/zc/202001/t20200117_1477235.html, 2018-01-04.

Opportunities and Challenges of the Blue Carbon Sink Sector in Zhejiang Province under the Context of Dual Carbon Goals[1]

More and more attention is now paid to ocean, as it is the largest carbon reservoir on Earth and the largest potential carbon neutrality space. Based on the characteristics of different maritime biological systems and spatial differences, this report analyzes the principles and practical significance of ocean carbon sink, with a focus on reviewing the progresses of the domestic and international researches on coastal wetland carbon sink, and identifies the key area of research and priorities of blue carbon sink in Zhejiang Province.

The ocean is a strategic location for high-quality development. The report of the 20th National Congress of the Communist Party of China proposes to develop the marine economy, protect the marine ecological environment, and step up efforts to build China into a strong maritime country. Zhejiang Province is located in the national strategic area for integrated development in the Yangtze River Delta region. At the new development stage of building China into a modern socialist country in all respects, Zhejiang Province is forging ahead with determination towards the goal of Common Prosperity under the Socialism with Chinese Characteristics and modernization of Zhejiang Province while pursuing high-quality development. As the germination site of "Two Mountains Theory", green and low-carbon development and a harmony between humanity

---

1　This chapter is part of the Zhejiang Leading Talents Program: Part of the research results of *Key Technologies and Demonstration Application of Marine "Blue Carbon" Ecosystem Sink Enhancement* (Project No. : 2023C03120) and the Preliminary Research Project of East China Sea Laboratory: *Assessment of Marine Ecosystem Carbon Storage and Blue Carbon Sink Enhancement Potential in Zhoushan Island Group* (project No. : DH2022ZY0006).

and nature have become social consensus in Zhejiang. Zhejiang has a sea area of 44,000 square kilometers. The deployment of the provincial ocean carbon sink work is not only an important part in protection and restoration of marine ecosystems driven by scientific innovation, but also a provincial-level exploration on the implementation of the major strategic deployment of the CPC Central Committee and the State Council concerning carbon peaking and carbon neutrality.

I. Principles and Practical Significance of Ocean Carbon Sink

Advancing ocean carbon sink is an important strategy to effectively respond to climate change. Ocean is the largest carbon sink on the earth, which stores approximately 93% (around 40 trillion tons) of carbon dioxide and can absorbs more than 25% of carbon dioxide emitted into the atmosphere every year[2]. Ocean plays a vital role in reducing atmospheric carbon dioxide, mitigating global warming and supporting biodiversity, and is an important way of "carbon neutrality". Ocean carbon sink (also known as "blue carbon") is a kind of process, which refor to the dissolution of carbon dioxide in the atmosphere by the ocean, and by means of photosynthesis of marine organisms, and then fixed and stored in ocean. It is an important approach to mitigate and adapt to global climate change. Enhancing carbon sink function of the natural ecological system while reducing carbon emissions becomes an inevitable means to realize the goal of carbon neutrality by 2060[19]. *The CPC Central Committee and the State Council on Accelerating the Construction of Ecological Civilization* and the *National Plan for Main Functional Zones of Marine*, introduced comprehensive plans for carbon sink. China advocates to "give full play to the role of ocean carbon sink and develop ocean carbon sink economy".

The consolidating of carbon sinks in the coastal zone is a necessary prerequisite for the achievement of carbon neutrality. Coastal wetlands are located at the ectone of terrestrial and marine ecosystems, and the diversity of the ecological environment contributes to high productivity. Carbon sequestrated of mangrove, salt marsh, and seagrass bed in coastal wetlands, is referred to as "blue carbon" in the coastal zone[7]. The coastal blue carbon ecological system is characterized by a very high rate of carbon sequestration and a long and sustainable sequestration capability. If calculated in carbon burial rate per unit area, the rate of carbon burial in blue carbon system of coastal wetlands is 15 times greater than the carbon sequestration rate of the terrestrial ecosystem and about 50 times greater than the carbon sequestration rate of the marine ecosystem[15]. The blue carbon sink of coastal wetlands is an important ocean-based approach to climate change governance, and a "nature-based solution" [3, 22]. The coastal blue carbon system can effectively address the issue of climate change faced by humans[6] To protect the environment is to protect the productive forces; to improve the environment is to boost the productive forces. Therefore, for coastal blue carbon, the first step is to protect the ecosystem and the carbon sink accumulated and buried in nature for thoustands of years.

Systematic improvement of the coastal wetland blue carbon function is an effective means of achieving the goal of "carbon neutrality" . The biological system of coastal wetlands is highly adaptable and resilient[14, 20]. Human activities can destroy carbon sequestration capacity of such type of blue carbon ecological system, while the function of blue carbon sink can also be enhanced through ecological restoration[5]. Eight Chinese ministries and commissions, including the Ministry of Science and Technology, jointly printed and distributed the *Implementation Plan for Carbon Peaking and Carbon Neutrality under Science and Technology Support* (*2022-2030*), in which, the *Supportive Action on Carbon Peaking and Carbon Neutrality Management Decision* stipulates that "technical innovation should be further promoted to support the development of technical and standard systems for carbon sinks, offering decision support on China's carbon neutrality." Besides carbon sequestration function, coastal wetland also has such biological functions as flood control, erosion control, food supply, habitat provision and water quality improvement. All these biological functions support each other and jointly constitute the overall function of coastal wetland ecological system. Internationally, coastal wetlands worth over US$ 1 billion in terms of biological service function[1], in particularly, it works well in sequestrating carbon dioxide in the atmosphere and removing pollutants, and is called the "Kidney of the Earth". Therefore, the enhancement of carbon sink in coastal ecosystems needs to be achieved within the overall framework of ecosystem restoration and improvement.

II. Progress of the Chinese and International Researches on Carbon Sink in Coastal Wetland

Coastal wetlands are located close to human settlements, but our understanding is still insufficient on the carbon sink distribution pattern, the rate and mechanism of carbon burial of the "blue carbon" ecological system in coastal wetlands[13]. Macreadie et al. summarized ten important problems to be settled in the current blue carbon research[4], and nine of which are relevant to blue carbon function of coastal wetlands, they are: ① In what ways will climate affect the accumulation of carbon in the blue carbon system? ② In what way will human interference affect the accumulation of carbon in the blue carbon system? ③ What are the distribution and spatial-temporal pattern of blue carbon ecosystem? ④ In what way will organic and inorganic carbon cycle processes affect carbon emissions? ⑤ How to estimate the source of carbon in the blue carbon system? ⑥ What are factors affecting the rate of carbon burial in the blue carbon system? ⑦ What is the rate of exchange between the blue carbon system and greenhouse gases in the atmosphere? ⑧ How to reduce uncertainty in blue carbon estimate? ⑨ How to maintain and enhance the blue carbon sequestration function through the implementation of management measures? These scientific problems are not only the focuses of current research, but also the main direction of future research. According to a global research on the simulation and prediction of blue carbon layout in coastal wetlands, the carbon burial capacity of the blue carbon system in coastal wetlands will be elevated constantly by the end of the 21st century[15]. As no nation-wide quantitative analysis and forecast evaluation on the blue carbon function of coastal wetlands has been conducted in China, the blue carbon resources in coastal wetlands are not included in the Chinese carbon sink trading, carbon sequestration and emission reduction system.

Coastal wetland is one of the major organic carbon sequestration areas due to its high primary productivity and favorable condition for organic matter preservation where sediments are of poor air permeability as the surface is often submerged by water[12]. Muddy mudflats occupy a large proportion in the Chinese coastal wetlands, with the area greatly exceeding the total area of mangrove and seagrass bed wetlands, and is characterized by a high burial rate of sediments and carbon sequestration potential. Carbon buried in tidal flat sediments comes from the surrounding salt marsh wetland and mangrove as well as from the sediments of combined carbon component of particle organic carbon and mineral in seawater, which should be included in the coastal wetland blue carbon sink measuring system[22].

Microbial activities will affect the burial efficiency of deposited carbon in coastal wetlands. Organic carbon sequestrated in sediments of coastal wetlands will be degraded due to microbial activity and released into the atmosphere in the form of greenhouse gas, while the remaining organic carbon will finally be settled and sequestrated in the sediment in the form of refractory organic matter for a long time. Therefore, it is of great significance to calculate the sedimentation rate of such organic matters and turnover time in sediments so as to improve the mode of carbon burial in coastal wetlands. The burial rate of deposited organic carbon is subject to several macroscopic factors like salinity, sediment temperature, vegetation type and biomass, land use pattern and redox conditions[16]. In current researches on burial and conversion of organic carbon in coastal wetlands, carbon cycle composition is expressed in total organic carbon, but microcosmic researches on the interaction and coupling process of microorganisms and organic carbon in coastal wetlands are insufficient, leading to insufficient understanding on organic burial mechanism[8, 10]. An important but uncertain problem is the vertical distribution of microbial communities in coastal wetland sediments and their impact factors on organic carbon sequestration efficiency? Is it caused by climate change? it it caused by natural changes?

Jiao Nianzhi, Academician of Chinese Academy of Sciences (2021) pointed out that studying and implementing "negative emission" of ocean is a key approach to carbon neutrality, and proposed the basic ways of "negative emission" and relevant cases (Figure 25-1). Academician Tang Qisheng, Zhang Jihong et al. defined carbon sink fishery as the process of facilitating the absorption of carbon dioxide in water body by aquatic organisms during fishery activities[21, 24], and removing from water body the carbon which has been transferred into bio-products. Although there is no consensus on the magnitude and measurement methods of fishery carbon sinks, optimizing the carbon sink enhancement brought about by green aquaculture through conservation of fisheries and biodiversity should be an important approach.

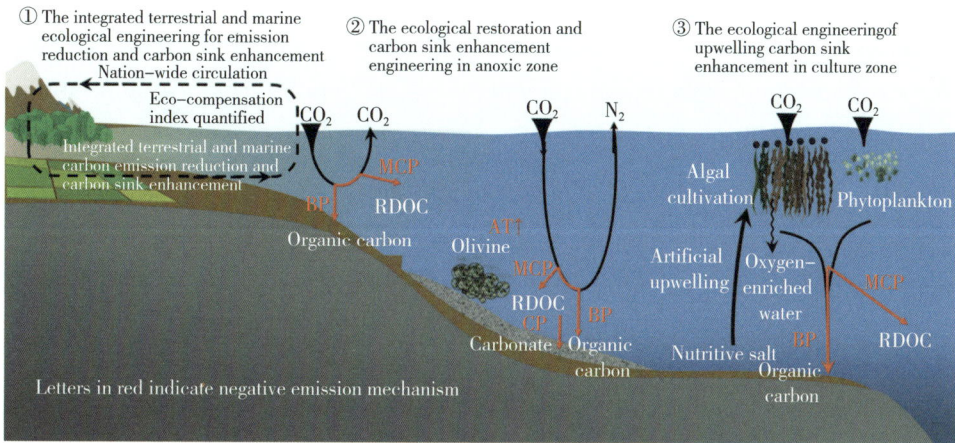

Figure 25-1   Schematic Diagram of the Ecological Engineering of Ocean

Negative Carbon Emission[19]

Note: AT: Alkalinity; BP: Biological Pump; MCP: Microbial Carbon Pump; CP: Carbonate Pump; RDOC: Refractory Dissolved Organic Carbon

Compared with terrestrial green carbon, blue carbon has three advantages: long sequestration period, high capture rate and outstanding ecological environment benefits. In the *Special Report on the Ocean and Cryosphere in a Changing Climate* released by IPCC in 2019, it is stressed that "All biologically-driven carbon fluxes and storage in marine systems that are amenable to management can be considered as blue carbon."The blue carbon function of coastal wetland is featured by a small size and large storage capacity. Muddy mudflat wetland is known as an important "blue carbon" resource which can mitigate global warming for its high primary productivity, low rate of organic decomposition and high burial rate, and is obtaining increasing attention. As mentioned above, muddy mudflat and salt marshes are the main types of coastal wetlands in Zhejiang Province. In view of this feature, the Second Institute of Oceanography of the Ministry of Natural Resources led the study of carbon sink of muddy mudflat in Zhejiang Province, which provides a leading scientific and technological support for the Ministry of Natural Resources to promote the carbon sink function of muddy mudflat nationwide.

The evolution of soil organic carbon sink of coastal muddy tidal flat, as a part of the wetland carbon sink system, is affected by multiple factors, including soil, vegetation and human activities, hydrological & tidal system of marine carbon sink, the sedimentation and burial conditions (Figure 25-2). At the same time, carbon sink of coastal muddy mudflat is also affected by sea level rise caused by climate change, invasion of *Spartina alterniflora*, changes in sediment carbon and nitrogen pools, and other marine carbon sinks from the sea. To achieve of the goal of "carbon neutrality" in China at the earliest date, it is important to strengthen the scientific research on coastal muddy beaches, protect the integrity of the structure and function of the existing wetland ecosystems, stop destructive development of muddy beaches, restore and newly build a coastal wetland ecosystem and enhance the service functions of the blue carbon ecosystem.

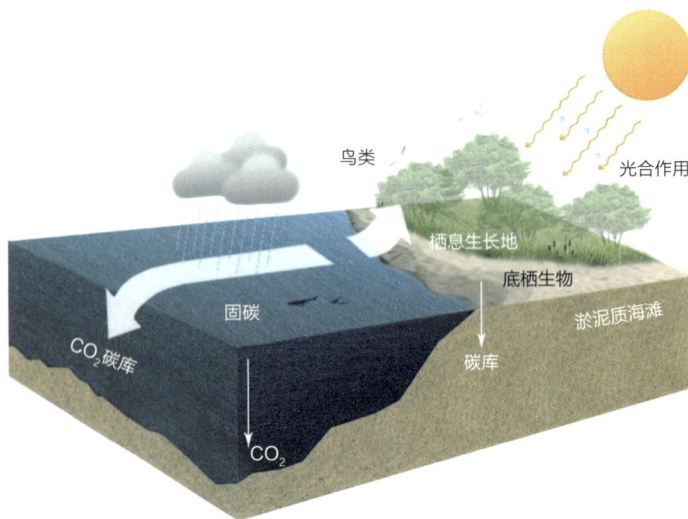

Figure 25-2　Carbon Sink Function of Muddy Beach[23]

III. Opportunities and Challenges of the Blue Carbon Work in Zhejiang Province

The total area of the coastal wetlands in Zhejiang Province is 295.06 square kilometers, of which 217.40 square kilometers are tidal flats, accounting for

73.68%, and 76.60 square kilometers are salt marshes, accounting for 25.96%. Tidal flat and salt marsh are the two major types of the coastal wetlands in Zhejiang, and also the ecosystem to be paid special attention to in the coastal wetland blue carbon study.

While promoting high-quality development and fostering harmony between humanity and nature, the works related to marine carbon sinks in Zhejiang Province should follow the principle of "Adjusting Measures to Local Conditions and Giveing Overall Consideration". The work should be based on understanding the local blue carbon situation of the province, be advanced in the following aspects: establishment and improvement of marine carbon sinks monitoring system, coordinating the promotion of marine ecosystem protection, restoration and elevation of marine carbon sinks capacity, strengthening of integrated development of marine carbon sinks, conducting of basic research on marine carbon sinks, promoting the value realization of marine carbon sinks and construction of blue carbon demonstration site and pilot projects. Considering the maritime, geological and ecological endowments of Zhejiang and according to the ecological civilization requirements of "respecting, adapting to, and protecting nature", the focuses of the blue carbon in the future will include:

A. Attaching Importance to the Impact of Land Based Material Input and Hydro-ecological Process on Carbon Sequestration Capacity of Salt Marshes and Muddy Tidal Flats

Hundreds of millions of tons of sludge or silty sands brought by sea-going rivers are gradually accumulated in the estuaries of coastal zones of a low altitude. Under the combined action of tidal power and water-sediment-salt effect, gentle-slope muddy beaches are formed along the coastal line, especially in bay areas. The sludge and silty sands also bring a large amount of nutrients, providing space and material basis for coastal blue carbon. Muddy beaches are developed from rivers with marine tidal and wave system as the major power. Based on the positions where seawater can reach during tidal process, muddy beaches are divided into five types, namely: ① beaches in supra-tidal zone which are unaffected by tides; ② high tide zones which are submerged by seawater only during spring tides; ③ inter-tidal zones between high tidal mark of neap tide and low tidal mark of neap tide; ④ low tide zones which are above the water only for a short time during the ebb of a spring tide; ⑤ sub-tidal beaches which are always affected by tides (Figure 25-3). The cyclical tidal movements, coupled with the rich organic matters and nutrients migrated from terrestrial rivers, have gradually led to the growth of salt marsh plants on the muddy beaches, and oases by sea have been gradually formed in the process of plant growth, development, and succession.

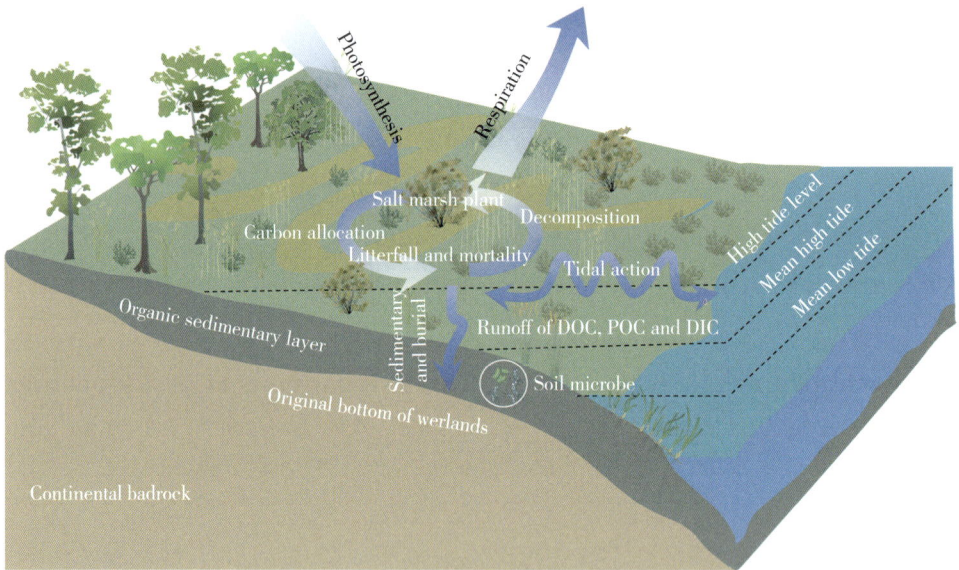

Figure 25-3   Key Processes of Carbon Sequestration in Salt Marsh Wetland under Tidal Action, Including Photosynthesis of Salt Marsh Plants, Phtosynthetic Product Allocation, Carbon Deposit Burial, Mineralization and Decomposition of Soil Carbon, DOC/POC/DIC Losses, etc. [18]

In the coastal wetland ecosystem, if mangroves and seagrass beds are compared to "movie stars", then the open mudflat is a "mass actor". Although the "star" is bright, its area is small and the total carbon sequestration is small. The open mudflat looks desolate, but its area is large and the total carbon sequestration is considerable. Unlike most people's imagination, the open mudflat is actually a highly productive area full of vitality in the marine. On the surface of the open mudflat, abundant and invisible benthic diatoms and other micro organisms grow, and their ability to synthesize organic carbon through photosynthesis is comparable to that of mangrove and salt marsh communities. At the same time, the mudflat also intercepts a large amount of organic matter such as algae from the sea, resulting in a large number of marine organisms such as mud snails, razor clams, and mudskipper thriving here.

But muddy flats are vulnerable to invasive alien species brought by such human activities as irrational sea reclamation and other ocean development activities in the context of global change, and their ecological values might be changed accordingly. Therefore, conducting an integrated hydro-ecological research on salt marshes and muddy tidal flats (covering water, sand, vegetation and sediments) and biogeochemistry are vital to understand coastal wetland in a systematic way.

B. Synergizing Marine Ecological System Protection & Restoration and Carbon Sequestration & Carbon Dioxide Sinks Enhancement

Maintaining and developing ocean blue carbon sinks and steadily enhancing ocean carbon sink capacity are important for the realization of carbon peaking and carbon neutrality in China. In 2021, the *Opinions of the Central Committee of the CPC and the State Council on Carbon Dioxide Peaking and Carbon Neutrality in Full and Faithful Implementation of the New Development Philosophy* and the *Circular of the State Council on Releasing the Action Plan for Carbon Dioxide Peaking Before 2030* were released successively, which stipulated that ocean ecological system protection and restoration shall be advanced comprehensively and carbon sequestration capacity of mangrove forests, sea grass beds and salt marshes shall be enhanced. In the *Construction Plan for Major Coastal Zone Ecological System Protection and Restoration Projects* (*2021-2035*) jointly released by the Ministry of Natural Resources, the National Development and Reform Commission and the National Forestry and Grassland Administration, the work objective of managing & restoring coastal wetlands and enhancing carbon sinks of the coastal zone ecological system was proposed. The Ministry of Ecology and Environment of the People's Republic of China is working on ocean carbon sinks monitoring & assessment and coastal zone carbon flux monitoring, with the aim to explore a new mode for marine ecological protection and restoration which is oriented by enhancing both climate resilience and blue carbon sinks.

During the "14th Five-Year Plan" Period, China will pay more attention on scientific and technological innovation and enhancement of governance capabilities, especially accelerating the filling of fundamental and critical capacity gaps, strengthening capacity building in the field of marine ecological environment, and creating open technological innovation platforms. In terms of marine carbon sinks, the Ministry of Natural Resources, the Ministry of Ecological Environment and other departments will strengthen at coastal regions in the following aspects: monitoring & assessment on ocean adapting to climate change, monitoring & assessment on ocean-atmosphere carbon dioxide exchange flux, monitoring & assessment on carbon reserves in key sea areas, monitoring & early-warning of such marine ecological environment risks as anoxia and acidification, enhancing the resilience of marine ecological system, inclusion of carbon neutrality and indexes for climate change adaption in the protection, restoration and supervision of typical marine ecological systems, including mangrove, seagrass beds, salt marshes and open muddy flats.

The technical researches on the blue carbon sinks enhancement in salt marshes and muddy tidal flats conducted in Zhejiang Province will greatly promote the research & development and application of prospective and disruptive technologies on blue carbon sinks enhancement in coastal zones. The combination of blue carbon and the major ecological protection & restoration projects in coastal zones will synergize ecological protection & restoration and carbon sequestration & carbon sink enhancement. The spatially coordinated industrial layout will be increasingly valued in the process of carbon neutrality.

C. Attaching Importance to the Leading Role of Carbon Sinks Function of Marine Nature Reserves in Realizing the Carbon Neutrality Goal

At the 19th CPC National Congress, the major reform task of "developing a nature reserves system composed mainly of national parks" was put forward, aiming to establish a classified nature reserves system with national parks as the main component, nature reserves as the basis and various natural parks as the supplementary. The report of the 20th CPC National Congress has made further strategic plans for the ecological civilization construction, and has made it clear that the diversity, stability and sustainability of the ecosystem shall be enhanced. Nature reserves are the core carrier of ecological civilization construction and the most diverse, stable and sustainable treasure in the ecological security system of China. Marine nature reserves play an important role in protecting marine biodiversity and enhancing the stability and biomass of marine ecosystem. Efforts in ecological environmental protection & restoration and biodiversity conservation will improve the structure and function of the ecological system of nature reserves, increase carbon sink reserve and total biomass, elevating carbon sinks function. Nature reserves will play a greater role in realizing the goal of carbon neutrality if carbon sinks function can be effectively recognized and give into full play. Through the establishment of nature reserves carbon sink trading mechanism and platform, biodiversity can be well protected and carbon sinks function be elevated. Natural parks like Hangzhou Bay Wetland and Dongtou National Marine Park are important marine nature reserves in Zhejiang Province and also a key blue carbon carrier. In Nanji Islands and Jiushan Islands (the two national marine nature reserves) and island-type marine reserves including Zhongjieshan Islands and Wuzhishan Bird Island, upwelling ecological systems are developed around them. The carbon loading of island upwelling ecological system, storage time, vertical & horizontal carbon flux and other problems are focusing arena in the overall evaluation of the blue carbon potential in the sea island ecological system in Zhejiang and important standpoints for China to make its contribution in global blue carbon management.

D. Promoting the Mechanism for Realizing the Value of Marine Carbon Sinks and Piloting Blue Carbon Demonstration Bases

There are three technical problems to be addressed in the determination, accounting and management of the carbon sinks enhancement capacity of the ocean "blue carbon" ecological system: firstly, multi-dimensional assessment technology for carbon sinks in coastal wetland ecosystem based on multi-temporal and spatial data; secondly, the synergia of nature-based blue carbon sinks capacity reinforcement & improvement and negative engineering emission; thirdly, the technology of building the optimal carbon sinks management mode incorporating policy guidance, space control and industrial collaboration.

The "nature-based solution" focuses on the long-term and sustainable development goal, and provides a new thought in coordinating economic development and ecological protection and in promoting the harmonious coexistence between humanity and nature. The "nature-based solution" covers eight criteria, of which, criteria including scale-based design, biodiversity net growth, ecological system integrity and governess, adaptive management, mainstream and sustainability perform well in international environmental governess. Implementing the "nature-based solution" in the researches on blue carbon sinks in salt marshes and muddy tidal flats in coastal wetlands and relevant engineering practices will facilitate ecological civilization construction and high-quality development.

Based on the two scientific problems of "the characteristics of the blue carbon ecological system in sea area of Zhejiang Province and the key driving factors of carbon sequestration and sink enhancement" and the "scientific principle of synergizing ecological system protection & restoration of offshore wetlands and blue carbon sink enhancement in Zhejiang", and by targeting the bottleneck needs to be settled urgently in the determination, accounting and management of carbon sink enhancement of the "blue carbon" ecological system, the technology of multi-dimensional assessment on the carbon sinks of the ecological systems in coastal wetlands based on multi-source and multi-temporal data should be developed by making breakthrough in difficulties in the cognition of natural science and tackling problems in key technologies, and the technology synergizing the nature-based blue carbon reinforcement & improvement and negative engineering emission should be advanced to achieve the optimum carbon sink management mode which incorporates policy guidance, space control and industrial collaboration, and the nature-based solution for marine ecological system restoration and carbon sinks enhancement system should be adopted to elevate the performance of marine blue carbon ecological system.

Author: Chen Jianfang[1], Zeng Jiangning[2], Jin Haiyan[3],
Yu Peisong[4] , Liu Chenggang[5]

References

[1] Costanza R, Pérez-Maqueo O, Martinez M L, et al. The value of coastal wetlands for hurricane protection[J]. *Ambio*, 2008, 37: 241-248.

[2] Friedlingstein P, O'Sullivan M, Jones M W, et al. Global Carbon Budget 2022, Earth Syst. Sci.Data, 14, 4811–4900,https://doi.org/10.5194/essd-14-4811-2022.

[3] Howard J, Sutton-Grier A, Herr D, et al. Clarifying the role of coastal and marine systems in climate mitigation[J]. *Frontiers in Ecology and the Environment*, 2017, 15: 42-50.

[4] Macreadie P I, Anton A, Raven J A, et al. The future of Blue Carbon science[J]. *Nat Commun*, 2019, 10: 3998.

[5] Macreadie P I, Hughes A R, Kimbro D L. Loss of "blue carbon" from coastal salt marshes following habitat disturbance[J]. *Plos One*, 2013, 8: e69244.

1 Chen Jianfang, researcher at the Second Institute of Oceanography of the Ministry of Natural Resources, director of the State Key Laboratory of Satellite Marine Environmental Dynamics, director of the Key Laboratory of Marine Ecosystem Dynamics of the Ministry of Natural Resources mainly engaged in research areas are marine ecosystem dynamics, monitoring of marine ecological environment, and marine biogeochemistry.

2 Zeng Jiangning, researcher at the Second Institute of Oceanography, Ministry Natural of Resources, Director of Zhejiang Provincial Key Laboratory of Offshore Marine Engineering Environment and Ecological Security, mainly engaged in regional ecology, natural protected areas, and ecological restoration.

3 Jin Haiyan, a researcher of the Second Institute of Oceanography, Ministry of Natural Resources, mainly focuses on marine environmental science and biogeochemistry.

4 Yu Peisong, associate researcher at the Second Institute of Oceanography, Ministry of Natural Resources, mainly focuses on marine carbon chemistry and marine environmental monitoring.

5 Liu Chenggang, associate researcher at the Second Institute of Oceanography, Ministry of Natural Resources, mainly focuses on marine primary productivity.

[6] Macreadie P I, Nielsen D A, Kelleway J J, et al. Can we manage coastal ecosystems to sequester more blue carbon?[J]. *Frontiers in Ecology and the Environment*, 2017, 15: 206-213.

[7] McLeod E, Chmura G L, Bouillon S, et al. A blueprint for blue carbon: toward an improved understanding of the role of vegetated coastal habitats in sequestering CO_2[J]. *Frontiers in Ecology and the Environment*, 2011, 9: 552-560.

[8] Moran M A, Kujawinski E B, Stubbins A, et al. Deciphering ocean carbon in a changing world[J]. *Proc Natl Acad Sci*, 113(12): 3143-3151.

[9] Olsson L, Ye S, Yu X, et al. Factors influencing CO_2 and CH_4 emissions from coastal wetlands in the Lioahe Delta, Northeast China[J]. *Biogeosciences*, 2015, 12: 4965-4977.

[10] Pei L, Ye S, Yuan H, et al. Glomain-related soil protein distributions in the wetlands of the Liaohe Delta, Northeast China: Implications for carbon sequestration and mineral weathering of coastal wetlands[J]. *Limnology and Oceanography*, 65, 979-991.

[11] Raymond P A, Bauer J E. Use of ^{14}C and ^{13}C natural abundances for evaluating riverine, seturaine, and coastal DOC and POC sources and cycling: a review and synthesis[J]. *Organic Geochemistry*, 32: 469-485.

[12] Reddy K R, Delaune R D. Biogeochemistry of Wetlands[M]. *CRC Press*, 2008.

[13] Rogers K, Macreadie P I, Kelleway J J, et al. Blue carbon in coastal landscapes: a spatial framework for assessment of stocks and additionality[J]. *Sustainability Science*, 2018, 14: 453-467.

[14] Wang F, Eagle M, Kroeger K D, et al. Plant biomass and rates of carbon dioxide uptake are enhanced by successful restoration of tidal connectivity in salt marshes[J]. *Science of the Total Environment*, 2021a, 750:141566.

[15] Wang F, Sanders C J, Santos I R. et al. Global blue carbon accumulation in tidal wetlands increases with climate change[J]. *National Science Review*, 2021b, 8(9): 140-150.

[16] Ye S, Laws E A, Yuknis N, et al. Carbon sequestration and its controlling factors in the temperate wetland communities along the Bohai Sea, China[J]. *Marine and Freshwater Research*, 2018, 69: 700-713.

[17] Chen X C, Gao R F, Huang X C, et al. Basic views and technological methods

of salt marsh restoration and its progresses in implementation[J]. Marine Environmental Science, 2016, 35(3): 467-472.

[18] Han G X, Wang F M, Ma J, et al. Blue carbon sink function, formation mechanism and sequestration potential of coastal salt marshes[J]. Chinese Journal of Plant Ecology, 2022, 46(4): 373-382.

[19] Jiao N Z. Developing ocean negative carbon emission technology to support national carbon neutralization[J]. Bulletin of Chinese Academy of Sciences, 2021, 36(2):179-187. DOI: 10.16418/j.issn.11000-13045.20210123001.

[20] Tang J W, Ye S F, Chen X C, et al. Coastal blue carbon: Concept, study method, and the application to ecological restoration[J]. Science China Earth Sciences, 2018, 48(6): 661-665.

[21] Tang Q S, Liu H. Strategy for carbon sink and its amplification in marine fisheries[J]. Strategic Study of CAE, 2016, 18(3): 68-73.

[22] Wang F M, Tang J W, Ye S Y, et al. Blue carbon sink function of Chinese coastal wetlands and carbon neutrality strategy[J]. Bulletin of Chinese Academy of Sciences, 2021, 36(3): 241-251.

[23] Zeng J N, Han G X. Land-sea Zipper—Coastal Wetlands [M]. Beijing: China Forestry Publishing House, 2022.

[24] Zhang J H, Liu J H, Zhang Y Y, et al. Strategic Approach for Mariculture to Practice "Ocean Negative Carbon Emission" [J]. Chinese Academy of Sciences, 2021, 36(3): 252-258.

[25] Zhang Y, Zhao M X, Cui Q, et al. Processes of coastal ecosystem carbon sequestration and approaches for increasing carbon sink[J]. Science China Earth Sciences, 2017, 47: 438-449.

Exploring the Zhejiang Practice Path to Establish a Market Compensation Mechanism for Forestry Carbon Sink Ecological Products

The high-quality development of forestry carbon sink plays a critical role in achieving carbon peak and carbon neutrality strategic goals. Zhejiang, boasting one of the highest forest-coverage rates in China, has a natural advantage and substantial potential for high-quality development of forestry carbon sinks. Drawing from advanced domestic and international practices and experiences and centering on the practical context of Zhejiang, we explore the establishment of a forestry carbon sink trading system in Zhejiang based on the market compensation mechanism of forestry carbon sink ecological products. This approach represents a pragmatic choice for developing ecological civilization in our province and an effective pathway to realize that *"Lucid Waters and Lush Mountains are Invaluable Assets."* It is also a vibrant manifestation of President Xi Jinping's expectations for Zhejiang, encapsulated in his call for *"Endless Pursuit of Practical Achievements, the Search for New Development Narratives, and Demonstrating Leadership Courage in the Vanguard"* while vigorously advancing toward a pioneering zone of shared prosperity through high-quality development.

I. Introduction

On December 12, 2020, President Xi Jinping announced at the Climate Ambition Summit that China aims to peak carbon emissions by 2030, stirves to achieve carbon neutrality by 2060, and intends to "increase the national forest stock volume by 6 billion cubic meters by 2030 compared to 2005" as one of the four national self-initiated action goals to respond to climate change. Achieving peak carbon emissions and carbon neutrality is a major strategic decision made by the CPC Central Committee concerning the sustainable development of the Chinese nation and the construction of the community of human destiny. The report of the 20th CPC National Congress also clearly proposes to actively and steadily advance the efforts toward peaking carbon emissions and achieving carbon neutrality, ensuring the successful achievement of the strategic goal of dual carbon.

As the main body of the terrestrial ecosystem, forests serve as the largest "carbon reservoir" on land and act as a "carbon absorber" in the ecosystem, making them an essential aspect of future carbon sequestration and increase. In March 2022, President Xi Jinping pointed out during a voluntary tree planting event in the capital that forests are not only reservoirs of water, money, and food but should now also be recognized as a reservoir of "carbon sink." According to the IPCC report, it is estimated that forest ecosystems worldwide store about 1.15 trillion tons of carbon, accounting for 57% of terrestrial ecosystems, and their annual absorption accounts for about two-thirds of the total annual carbon sequestration in terrestrial ecosystems. Utilizing the forest carbon sink is the most economical choice to achieve the national carbon neutrality strategic goal, with minimal input, low cost, and high ecological added value. This approach holds great importance in accelerating the achievement of the carbon peak and carbon neutrality goal.

II. Advanced Domestic and International Practices

A. Advanced International Practices in Forestry Carbon Sinks

Forestry carbon sinks play an essential role in responding to climate change, and their importance is gradually recognized by the international community at large. In 1997, the Kyoto Protocol first mentioned the term "carbon sinks," requiring developed country Parties to propose emission reduction targets and measures and to support the increase of carbon sinks through measures such as "afforestation, reforestation and sustainable management of forests." In 2001, the sixth and seventh meetings of the Conference of the

Parties (COP6 and COP7) to the United Nations Framework Convention on Climate Change (UNFCCC) adopted the Bonn Political Agreement and the Marrakesh Accords, respectively. These agreements highlighted the impact of land use, land-use change, and forestry (LULUCF) activities on climate change and allowed developed countries to use the carbon sinks absorbed to offset a portion of the carbon dioxide emissions from industrial activities by carrying out afforestation, reforestation actions. In 2007, the Bali Action Plan included the strategy of reducing greenhouse gas emissions through deforestation and forest degradation (REDD) in developing countries as part of forestry carbon sink projects. In 2009, the Copenhagen Accord stressed the need to encourage action to reduce emissions and increase carbon sinks in developing countries as soon as possible through the establishment of incentive policies and mechanisms, including reducing deforestation, forest degradation, and forest conservation and sustainable forest management. In 2010, the Cancun Agreements clarified that a cap should be set when using accounted-for carbon sinks to offset total industrial and energy emissions. In 2013, the Warsaw Climate Conference clarified that incentives could be provided for developing countries to take REDD + actions, including reducing deforestation, reducing forest degradation, and implementing specific actions for forest conservation, sustainable management of forests, and increasing forest carbon stocks. In 2015, the Paris Climate Conference adopted the Paris Agreement with a separate article on forests, establishing a framework arrangement for a common global response to climate change after 2020, especially introducing a pre-assessment of progress towards the targets proposed by countries, starting in 2018.

In terms of international markets, international carbon credit mechanisms refer to the creation of tradable credits between entities through voluntary mitigation actions. The World Bank report divides carbon credits into three categories based on how they are created and managed: international mechanisms, domestic mechanisms, and independent mechanisms. In 2021, the overall carbon credit market grew by 48%, with the total number of credits increasing from 327 million to 478 million, the largest year-over-year increase since the peak of carbon credit issuance in 2012. Most of the growth in the carbon credit market in 2021 came from the new issuance of independent carbon credit mechanisms. More and more companies are purchasing voluntary emission reductions through independent carbon credit mechanisms, and independent credit issuance grew by 88% to a total of 352 million, accounting for 74% of carbon credit supply that year, while issuance from international and domestic credit mechanisms grew at a slower pace. As the climate change negotiation process continues to advance, the vital role of forestry in responding to climate change is gradually becoming more prominent, and forestry has become the largest sector for carbon credit issuance globally. In terms of the total number of registrations and credits for global carbon credit mechanism projects, the total number of registrations and issuances increased rapidly in 2012 due to the expiration of the first commitment period of the Kyoto Protocol and the financial crisis and oversupply of EU allowances in 2013 led to a decline in the total number of project registrations and issuance under the EU ETS, which subsequently stabilized after 2015. In terms of sub-sectors, forestry carbon offset projects issued the most carbon credits from 2015 to 2019, accounting for about 42% of the total global carbon points, and renewable energy was the second largest source of carbon credit projects, accounting for about 33% of the global carbon credits issued.

B. Exploration of Domestic Forestry Carbon Sink Trading

China actively participates in global climate governance actions and fully values and brings into play the key role of forestry carbon sinks in responding to climate change and low-carbon green development. In June 2007, as a developing country, China took the lead in promulgating the "China National Program to Address Climate Change" and decided to optimize the carbon sink function of forests through afforestation and forest management. In September 2015, the Central Committee of the CPC and the State Council issued the "General Plan for the Reform of Ecological Civilization System," which clearly pointed out the establishment of an effective mechanism to increase carbon sinks. In November 2016, the General Office of the State Council issued the "Opinions on Improving the Collective Forest Rights System," which clearly pointed out that efforts should be made to reconcile the contradiction between ecological protection and the interests of forest farmers and facilitate the incorporation of carbon sinks into the carbon trading market. In 2019, nine departments jointly issued the "Action Plan for the Establishment of a Market-based and Diversified Ecological Protection Compensation Mechanism," emphasizing that voluntary greenhouse gas emission reduction projects in forestry with multiple ecological and social benefits will be prioritized for inclusion in the national carbon emissions trading market, fully harnessing the compensatory role of the carbon market in ecological construction, restoration, and protection. The report of the 20th CPC National Congress clearly proposed to improve the carbon emission statistics and accounting system, improve the carbon emission rights market trading system, enhance the capacity of ecosystem carbon sinks, and actively participate in global governance to respond to climate change.

China is one of the first countries in the world to develop a forestry carbon sink measurement and monitoring system. Since 2003, the State Forestry Administration has organized to strengthen the research of forestry carbon sinks, organize the preparation of carbon sink afforestation series standards and build a forestry carbon sink measurement and monitoring system. In 2004, the pilot forestry carbon sink project was launched, and the Guangxi Pearl River Basin Reforestation Project, registered in 2006, was the first reforestation carbon sink project in the world under the Clean Development Mechanism. In 2010, the *Technical Provisions on Carbon Sink Afforestation* (*Trial Implementation*) and *Carbon Sink Afforestation Inspection and Acceptance Measures* (*Trial Implementation*) were released; in 2011, *Guidelines for Carbon Sink Measurement and Monitoring of Afforestation Projects* were released; in 2012, *the Validation and Verification Guide for Forestry Carbon Sink Projects* (*Trial Implementation*) was released; in 2019, the *National Forestry Carbon Sink Measurement and Monitoring System Construction Work Plan* were formulated, and standards such as the *Technical Specification for Low Carbon Management and Carbon Sink Measurement and Monitoring in Bamboo Forests* and *Technical Specification for the Investigation of Carbon Pools in Forest Ecosystems* were compiled. There are five CCER forestry and grassland carbon sink project methodologies that have been filed with the National Development and Reform Commission, namely, Methodology of Carbon Sink Afforestation Projects, Methodology of Forest Management

Carbon Sequestration Projects, Methodology of Bamboo Afforestation Carbon Sink Project, Methodology of Bamboo Forest Management Carbon Sink Project, and Methodology of Sustainable Grassland Management Greenhouse Gas Emission Reduction Measurement and Monitoring. In addition, the pilot provinces and cities have also developed some local standards, such as the *Technical Specification for Forestry Carbon Sink Project Validation and Terminology* formulated by Beijing, the *Technical Specification for Urban Forest Carbon Sink Survey and Data Collection* formulated by Shanghai, and the *Forestry Carbon Sink Inclusive Methodology of Guangdong Province* formulated by Guangdong Province, etc. The development of forestry carbon sink measurement and monitoring standards and methodology has laid solid technical support for China's forestry carbon sink projects to enter the regional and national carbon trading markets.

At present, China's forestry carbon sink transactions predominantly occur at the project level, and there are four main types of projects: first, the forestry carbon sink projects under the Clean Development Mechanism (CDM) of the *Kyoto Protocol*; second, the forestry carbon sink projects under the China Certified Emission Reduction (CCER) mechanism; third, the provincial voluntary category projects, including the Beijing Forestry Certified Emission Reduction (BCER) project, Fujian Forestry Certified Emission Reduction (FFCER) project and Guangdong PuHui Certified Emission Reduction (PHCER) project, etc.; fourth, other projects, including the Forestry Voluntary Carbon Reduction Standard (Verified Carbon Standard, VCS) project, non-provincial forestry carbon sink projects, Guizhou single-plant carbon sink poverty alleviation project, etc. There are also related carbon sink project businesses carried out by China Greening Foundation and China Green Carbon Foundation.

III. Feasibility of Zhejiang Practice

Zhejiang, characterized by "seven parts mountain, one part water, and two parts farmland," boasts one of the highest rates of forest coverage in the country, with the increase in forest stock per unit area and growth rate leading nationally. According to the latest monitoring results, the province's forest area will be 6,227,200 hectares in 2020, and the forest coverage rate will reach 61.17%. The total carbon stock of forest vegetation is estimated to be 290 million tons, and the forest vegetation will absorb 72.94 million tons of carbon dioxide per year, which has the natural propensity and vast potential for high-quality development of forestry carbon sink.

A. Zhejiang Province has a strong foundation for forestry carbon sink research and technology development

With the support of the Zhejiang Provincial Government and relevant departments, Zhejiang Agriculture and Forestry University has established important platforms for forestry carbon sink research and technology development, such as "State Key Laboratory of Subtropical Forest Cultivation," "State Forestry and Grassland Administration Bamboo Forest Carbon Sink Engineering Technology Research Center" and "Zhejiang Provincial Key Laboratory of Forest Ecosystem Carbon Cycle and Carbon Sequestration and Emission Reduction." These entities have formed a multidisciplinary research group and science and technology innovation team with Zhejiang Agriculture and Forestry University as the main body and Zhejiang Academy of Forestry, Zhejiang Forest Resources Monitoring Center. This consortium has made significant innovations and breakthroughs in forest ecosystem carbon sink measurement and monitoring, sink enhancement and emission reduction technology, carbon sink trading, and policies. They are especially prominent in the field of bamboo forest carbon sink research and corresponding carbon sink project methodology development, establishing themselves at the world's forefront. Their bamboo forest carbon sink research results have won one second prize for national scientific and technological progress and two first prizes for provincial scientific and technological progress. The "Methodology of Bamboo Afforestation Carbon Sink Project" and "Methodology of Bamboo Forest Management Carbon Sink Project" developed under the presidency have passed the record of the National Development and Reform Commission. This recognition helped overcome the technical and institutional bottleneck of bamboo forest carbon sink into China's carbon emission reduction market. Furthermore, the development of the "Methodology of Farmers' Forest Management Carbon Sink Project" has the potential to involve hundreds of millions of forest farmers truly participating in forestry carbon sink projects, thus having solid technical support in forestry carbon sink construction and trading.

B. Zhejiang Province has a strong foundation for the construction of a large platform for forest resources data

Thanks to the efforts of the Zhejiang Forest Resources Monitoring Center, Zhejiang Agriculture and Forestry University, and other units, a resource base database for Zhejiang Province and a unified map of provincial forest lands have been successfully created. This ensures that the forest resources data can be accurately implemented to each hill and plot. Systematic investigations into the carbon stocks and spatial and temporal distribution patterns of five major carbon sinks in forest ecosystems of Zhejiang province have also been carried out. A multi-level linkage monitoring method for forest carbon stocks has been established at provincial, municipal, and county levels to achieve integrated monitoring and inter-year update of forest ecosystem carbon stocks in the province. It has established information systems for the comprehensive management of forestry cadastre and ecological public welfare forest management in the province, which have laid a solid data foundation for forestry carbon sink function assessment, forestry carbon sink project development, and forestry carbon sink trading. At the same time, Zhejiang is home to many world-renowned enterprises, such as Alibaba, with well-developed internet technology and blockchain technology, which can provide technical guarantees for carbon sink trading and help the wide development and promotion of forestry carbon sink trading.

C. Existing Experience in Forestry Carbon Sink Practices

Relying on the technical advantages of Zhejiang Agriculture and Forestry University, Zhejiang Forestry Academy of Sciences, and Zhejiang Forest Resources Monitoring Center in forestry carbon sink measurement and monitoring, carbon sink enhancement and emission reduction technology, and carbon sink trading and policy, the practice of forestry carbon sink development in Zhejiang Province is leading the way nationwide.

(1) The first "carbon sink forestry pilot zone" and the first "bamboo forest carbon sink pilot demonstration zone" in the world were established. In 2010,

Zhejiang Agriculture and Forestry University developed the first county-level carbon sink forestry construction plan, turning Hangzhou Lin'an District into the first "carbon sink forestry experimental area" in China. In 2012, Zhejiang Agriculture and Forestry University, Anji County, and the International Organization for Bamboo and Rattan co-signed an agreement at the Doha Climate Change Conference (COP18), making Anji County the world's first "bamboo forest carbon sink pilot demonstration area." In 2014, based on the Lin'an carbon sink project, the farmers' forest management carbon sink trading system was developed, initiating a new model for farmers to participate in forest management carbon sink projects and sell forest carbon sinks, and in October of the same year, the first 42 farmers in Lin'an District realized forest carbon sink trading.

(2) Establishing a special system of forestry carbon sink fund. After the State Council approved the establishment of the China Green Carbon Fund in July 2010, our province applied for the establishment of the first provincial fund-Zhejiang Carbon Sink Fund; the first municipal fund-Wenzhou Carbon Sink Fund; the first county-level fund special-Zhejiang Carbon Sink Fund Yinzhou special; the first central, provincial and county-level management special-Zhejiang Carbon Sink Fund Beilun special, initially forming a three-level management model of China-Zhejiang–City, and County.

(3) Starting the pilot construction of forestry carbon sink trading. In November 2011, the national forestry carbon sink trading pilot platform was established in East China Forestry Property Rights Exchange in our province. The pilot platform successfully traded 148,000 tons of carbon credits generated from the first batch of carbon sink afforestation projects in China, creating a precedent for carbon sink trading in China's forestry industry. In June 2013, the carbon emission reductions generated from the forest management sink emission reduction project in Yichun City, Heilongjiang Province, were successfully traded through the East China Forestry Property Rights Exchange.

(4) Carrying out forest management carbon sink project development practices. Since 2015, the bamboo forest management project has been developed in Anji, Jingning, Zhuji, Suichang, and Lin'an in Zhejiang Province, involving more than 20,000 bamboo farmers and generating more than 5 million

tons of voluntary certified emission reductions; and more than 20 technical training sessions have been conducted, significantly improving the awareness, ability, and level of forestry technicians and foresters to carry out forestry carbon sink management, and also enabling the project development body to accumulate a wealth of practical experience. In 2016, China Green Carbon Foundation organized and implemented the G20 Hangzhou Summit carbon neutrality project to achieve zero carbon emissions from the summit. In 2021, Kaihua County launched the "Zero Carbon Companion" green financial product and issued the province's first forestry carbon sink value pledge loan of 3 million yuan.

(5) Establishing county-level bamboo forest carbon sink collection and storage trading centers. In December 2021, Anji County's "two mountains" bamboo forest carbon sink storage and trading center was officially launched, using digital reform ideas to build six application scenarios of bamboo forest carbon background, carbon storage, carbon sink, carbon trading, carbon footprint, carbon revenue, etc., realizing complete closed-loop management chain from forest land transfer to unified management, carbon sink storage, platform trading, and revenue feedback, effectively opening up the regional carbon sink trading market. Meanwhile, "bamboo forest carbon sink price index insurance" and "moso bamboo carbon sink surplus value restoration compensation insurance" were introduced to ensure the revenue of carbon sink trading for the platform and village collectives (farmers).

IV. Roadmap of Zhejiang Practice

Zhejiang Province is rich in forestry carbon sink resources, a complete forestry carbon sink science and technology support system, a strong foundation of forest resources data platform construction, rich forestry carbon sink measurement and monitoring and project development practice, while the forestry carbon sink market in Zhejiang Province has great potential and the market prospect is relatively promising. Therefore, Zhejiang Province can take the lead in establishing a regional forestry carbon sink trading center and improve the forestry carbon sink trading system, which can contribute to the enrichment of China's carbon trading market system and create a Zhejiang model for building a market-oriented and diversified ecological protection compensation mechanism, provide a Zhejiang demonstration for vividly practicing green water and green mountains is the silver mountain of gold, and further demonstrate Zhejiang's responsibility in addressing global climate change and carbon peak and carbon neutrality strategic goals.

A. Enhancing the capacity of forestry carbon sink in Zhejiang Province

Focusing on the expansion and enhancement of forest quality is essential for effective carbon sequestration. Increasing the quantity, improving the quality, and optimizing the structure of forests are valid strategies for enhancing forest carbon sinks. Efforts should continue to promote the new million acres of national greening action and constantly increase the area of forest cover. Initiatives should also be started to improve the quality of ten million acres of forest precisely, and pilots for the ecological restoration of degraded bamboo forests should be organized. These actions will help maintain and enhance the quality of bamboo forests, thereby boosting their function as carbon sinks.

In the context of protecting forest health, it's essential to focus on reducing emissions from forests. Forest fires, pests and diseases, and illegal expropriation of forest land will increase emissions from forests. It is necessary to protect forest resources strictly, strengthen the management of forest land use, enhance the construction of forest disaster prevention and control systems, strengthen the capacity of forest fire prevention and suppression, and continuously promote the integrated prevention and control of pine wood nematode to provide a solid foundation for safeguarding forest health.

Focusing on the rational utilization of forest resources, we should give more attention to carbon sequestration in bamboo and wood products. As forest trees grow and mature, their carbon sequestration capacity will gradually decline after reaching its peak. In order to maintain and improve the carbon sequestration efficiency of forest land, forest resource conservation and harvesting, and utilization need to be given equal importance. It is necessary to continuously improve the processing of bamboo and wood products to promote product carbon transfer and improve the carbon sequestration function of bamboo and wood products.

Focusing on innovation in forestry carbon sink technologies, we should work on providing sound scientific and technological support. Taking the common and key technology demand for forest carbon sink development as the guide, we will deeply promote the research of forest ecosystem sink enhancement and emission reduction technology and strive to make new breakthroughs in the selection and breeding of high carbon fixation tree species, forest quality and sink enhancement, forest protection, and sink promotion, and key technology of bamboo and wood products carbon fixation. It is crucial to perfect and promote the establishment of systems for measuring and monitoring forest carbon sinks and for calculating the carbon footprint and carbon labels of bamboo and wood products. This will lay a solid foundation for enhancing carbon sink capacity, precise monitoring of carbon sinks, and effective carbon sink trading.

Focusing on pioneering demonstrations of forestry carbon sequestration, we should work on building successful pilot projects. Concentrating on four main areas—afforestation, quality improvement, carbon sequestration in bamboo and wood products, and innovation in mechanisms—we should carry out pilot projects for forestry carbon sequestration throughout the province. We should effectively play the role of carbon sequestration in forest and wetland ecosystems, strengthen ecological protection and restoration, and enhance carbon sink increment in ecosystems. We should explore the application demonstration of "carbon labels" for bamboo and wood carbon sequestration products and guide social entities to purchase bamboo and wood products and obtain "carbon credits" for the products. Additionally, we should explore regional carbon sink trading mainly for forest carbon sinks, guide the whole society to participate in the construction of forestry carbon sinks, and help to achieve the goal of carbon neutrality.

B. Establishment of forestry carbon sink trading system in Zhejiang Province

(1) Target Setting. The primary goal is to establish a forestry carbon sink trading center in Zhejiang Province and improve the construction of the forestry carbon sink trading system in Zhejiang Province. There are three main aspects in terms of target setting: Firstly, we provide forestry carbon sink products

for key emission units' quota offset trading, non-key emission units' carbon neutrality trading, low "zero" carbon pilot demonstration projects, "zero carbon" agencies, conferences and activities, etc., open up the forestry carbon sink channel of "two mountains" transformation, give full play to the role of forestry carbon sink trading platform, and gradually realize other ecological forestry products trading. Secondly, focusing on the city and county carbon peak carbon neutrality action plans and goals to provide municipal and county forestry carbon sink horizontal trading services, we plan to build a total balance trading mechanism between economically developed areas and forestry carbon sink-rich areas, to provide a supportive mechanism for the leapfrog development of mountainous areas and the province's ladder peak, and to promote the realization of the provincial carbon neutrality strategic goals. Thirdly, we will align with the international and domestic carbon emission trading markets, unify the development of forestry carbon sink project methodology and project cultivation, and provide financial, legal, policy, and intermediary services for forestry carbon sink trading, with a focus on serving Zhejiang, but also radiating to the whole country, and strive to become an effective supplement to the national unified carbon emission trading market.

(2) Key Tasks. Firstly, formulating administrative methods is crucial. With regard to regional forestry carbon sink trading, the development of administrative methods is required. Initial efforts will include low "zero" carbon pilot demonstration projects, "zero carbon" bodies, conferences, and activities in the scope of forestry carbon sink trading. The gradual establishment of a trading mechanism connecting net carbon discharges and net carbon sink increases between municipalities and counties is also aimed. This will stimulate mountain governments' enthusiasm for developing forestry carbon sinks. Drawing on the national carbon emissions trading management mechanism, there are plans to develop a quota management and trading mechanism for key emission units in Zhejiang Province (annual emissions below 26,000 tons of CO_2 equivalent, the specific range will be determined according to the province's conditions). The ratio of forestry carbon sink offsets to carbon emission rights quotas is also proposed to be increased appropriately. Secondly, the construction of a trading platform is vital. The East China Forestry Property Rights Exchange, established

in Hangzhou in December 2010, is the only province-wide forest rights trading platform in our province. It's mainly engaged in forest rights trading, forestry carbon sink trading, and trading of logs and other bulk forest products. Considering the current policy from relevant state ministries against approving new local carbon market trading organizations for pilot provinces, it is proposed to rely initially on the East China Forestry Property Rights Exchange (one of the exchanges approved by the State Council's inter-ministerial joint meeting of trading venues) for the carbon sink trading pilot platform, establishing the province-wide forestry carbon sink trading center.

Thirdly, the development of a trading mechanism is essential. Based on different carbon sink trading objectives, such as forestry emission reduction carbon, neutral carbon, and international standard forestry carbon, it is crucial to develop forestry carbon sink trading methodologies and rapid measurement and monitoring methods that match the province's conditions. Key areas such as trading targets, measurement and verification standards, and trading prices will be refined and improved according to the content of forestry carbon sink trading. Experiences from provinces like Guangdong and Fujian will be used as references to standardize processes such as project design, third-party auditing, compliance auditing, implementation supervision, certification, registration, and issuance. Fourthly, the establishment of a regulatory mechanism is required. Adhering to a government-led, market-operated, and cooperative model, the plan is to enhance the forestry carbon sink trading regulatory mechanism. The Provincial Development and Reform Commission, the Provincial Department of Ecology and Environment, and the Provincial Forestry Bureau will take on responsibilities in accordance with their roles. This includes setting up the carbon peak and carbon neutrality target system, managing carbon emission rights quotas, developing forestry carbon sink projects, and certifying them. This group will also study and formulate rules for Zhejiang Province's forestry carbon sink market trading. To strengthen the use of big data, there are plans to construct a data platform for forestry carbon sink trading in Zhejiang Province, providing open services for various entities, including forestry carbon sink demanders, suppliers, and intermediary service providers.

(3) Construction Content. Firstly, it's necessary to implement the structure

for the operation of the trading center. Led by the Lishui Municipal People's Government, the East China Forestry Property Rights Exchange will be restructured, promoting it as the primary operational structure for the forestry carbon sink trading center. This process includes establishing a comprehensive forestry carbon sink trading platform comprised of industry regulatory departments, research institutions, trading organizations, financial institutions, and key emission reduction enterprises. The goal is to create a forestry carbon sink trading center rooted in Zhejiang, influencing the Yangtze River Delta and serving as a model for the entire nation. Secondly, the establishment of a routine operation mechanism for the trading center is required. This would involve the formulation of a working model for the forestry carbon sink trading center, which consists of the forestry carbon sink demand side, supply side, and guarantee institutions. The realization of the value of forestry carbon sink products necessitates multi-department collaboration. The Provincial Development and Reform Commission will be responsible for setting the path for realizing the value of ecological products, establishing a regional forestry carbon sink trading platform, and formulating related management rules. The Provincial Department of Ecology and Environment will study and develop regional carbon emission rights offset methods. The Provincial Forestry Bureau will organize the application and implementation of forestry carbon sink projects, with the Provincial Department of Natural Resources overseeing the strengthening of territorial spatial planning control and assigning ecological carbon sink values to land value assessments. The Provincial Forestry Department will undertake the task of enhancing the capacity for the forestry carbon sink, aiming to form a multi-sectoral, coordinated mechanism for the operation of the forestry carbon sink trading center, with various measures being implemented concurrently. Thirdly, the enhancement of the trading center's technological support is vital. Depending on Zhejiang Agricultural and Forestry University, Zhejiang Forestry Research Institute, and the Zhejiang Forest Resources Monitoring Center, efforts will continue to strengthen the forestry carbon sink measurement and monitoring system. Furthermore, the research and development of methodologies for forestry carbon sink trading projects will be deepened, aiming to establish the provincial standard for forestry carbon sink trading in Zhejiang.

Drawing on the province's advantage in digital reform, there should be plans to accelerate the establishment of digitalized application scenarios for forestry carbon sinks, with the goal of effectively reducing the development and trading costs of forestry carbon sinks and supporting the daily operation of Zhejiang Forestry Carbon Sink Trading Center

V. Outlook and Policy Recommendations

A. Innovation in Forestry Carbon Sink Trading Product

Accelerating the establishment of the forestry carbon sink trading market. The forestry carbon sink can be divided into two categories: "CCER carbon sink," which is used to offset the national carbon emission quota, and "neutral carbon sink," which is used to offset the non-mandatory emission reduction. While actively promoting the trading of carbon sinks related to mandatory national emissions reductions, it's essential to strongly foster the establishment of a "Neutral carbon sink" trading mechanism. In the context of regional "Neutral carbon sink" trading, we will develop regulations for forestry carbon sink trading and be the first to include low "zero" carbon pilot projects, "zero carbon" offices, meetings, and activities in the scope of regional "Neutral carbon sink" trading. We will gradually establish a trading mechanism linking net carbon emissions with net increases in carbon sinks at the city and county levels to inspire enthusiasm for building forestry carbon sinks among mountainous governments.

Actively reinvigorate existing forestry carbon sink products. Efforts should be made to translate the outcomes of afforestation and forest management into national carbon emission offset trading products. Likewise, the achievements of land greening and forest conservation should be transformed into regional forestry carbon sink trading products. This push to realize forestry carbon sink trading will aid in enabling prosperity among mountain forest farmers.

B. financial Support in Forestry Carbon Sink Trading

Expanding the green financial channel. Based on the existing forestry right collateral, mountain forest management right collateral, green financial bonds, etc., we are actively promoting models such as forestry carbon sink collateral loans and forestry carbon sink options collateral loans. These serve to widen the financing channels for forest quality enhancement, mountain forest nurturing projects, and others, thereby aiding the development of forestry carbon sink projects and carbon trading.

Innovating forestry carbon sink insurance. We are establishing innovative financial insurance products tailored for forestry carbon sinks, enhancing forestry's resilience against risks. This ensures that the ecological benefits of forests and their role in reducing carbon emissions are maintained. It also provides protection from potential economic losses from carbon reduction, which may occur due to natural disasters or accidents throughout the growth of the forests.

Establishing a new carbon sink financial model. We are actively promoting innovative approaches such as the Anji bamboo forest carbon sink "Two Mountains" bank storage and Kaihua "Zero Carbon Companion" forestry carbon sink collateral loans. Through these, we are constructing a new "Forest Insurance + Carbon Sink Loan" green financial model throughout the province. This helps to realize the benefits of forestry carbon sinks early, ensuring that the farmers truly receive substantial returns from forestry carbon sinks. We are promoting the involvement of social capital and other entities in the development of forestry carbon sinks. We also actively encourage and guide the investment from social capital and all sectors of society in forestry carbon sink initiatives, providing practical pathways for corporations, communities, and individuals to reduce their carbon emissions voluntarily.

C. Supporting Policy Measures for Forestry Carbon Sink Trading

Initiating pilot explorations. We are selecting mountain counties with a strong potential for developing forestry carbon sinks as pilot sites. With the integration of the high-quality development "one county, one strategy" in the 26 mountain counties, along with other related policies such as low-carbon pilot counties, we provide support for forestry carbon sink offset mechanisms. We urge industries with high energy consumption and carbon emissions to allocate a certain proportion of forestry carbon sinks based on their total carbon emissions, prioritizing the purchase of forestry carbon sink quotas from the 26 mountain counties and forestry carbon sink pilot counties.

Strengthening performance assessment and incentives. We are fully implementing the "Chief Forester" system, incorporating the development of forestry carbon sinks into the system's evaluation. Forestry carbon sinks are included in the ecological protection compensation scope. We are establishing a green development fiscal reward mechanism that links with the ecological product value of forestry carbon sinks, tying forest vegetation carbon storage with financial transfer payments. We are also exploring the use of mandatory carbon emission reduction targets to encourage forestry carbon sink trading. Regions or businesses that have not met their carbon reduction goals can purchase forestry carbon sinks in equivalent or differentiated quotas to offset their emissions.

Bolstering legislative guarantees. We are actively advocating for the early adoption and trial of forestry carbon sink trading regulations. The related rules, systems, and responsibilities associated with forestry carbon sink trading are integrated into the "Zhejiang Province Green Low-carbon Transformation Promotion Regulations." This ensures effective safeguards for the smooth operation of forestry carbon sink trading.

Author: Zhou Guomo[1], Li Chong[2], Gu Lei[3]

1 Zhou Guomo , doctoral supervisor, Special Expert of Zhejiang Province, Professor at Zhejiang Agriculture and Forestry University, and Leader of Key Scientific and Technological Innovation Team of Zhejiang Province "Forestry Carbon Sequestration and Measurement Innovation Team".

2 Li Chong, master's degree supervisor, associate professor at Zhejiang Agriculture and Forestry University, and Core Member of Key Scientific and Technological Innovation Team of Zhejiang Province "Forestry Carbon Sequestration and Measurement Innovation Team".

3 Gu Lei, master's degree supervisor, associate professor at Zhejiang Agriculture and Forestry University, Core Member of Key Scientific and Technological Innovation Team of Zhejiang Province "Forestry Carbon Sequestration and Measurement Innovation Team", and Chairman of Hangzhou Yiheng Carbon Technology Co.